A026509962

D1826388

William Bernard Ullathorne 1806–1889:

A Different Kind of Monk

*'... whenever they come to a true sense of things,
they will find deliverance from sin a much
greater blessing than deliverance from
affliction ...'*
Daniel Defoe, *The Life and Strange, Surprising
Adventures of Robinson Crusoe of York,
Mariner* (1719)

William Bernard Ullathorne 1806–1889:

A Different Kind of Monk

Judith Champ

GRACEWING

First published in 2006

Gracewing
2 Southern Avenue, Leominster
Herefordshire HR6 0QF

ISBN 0 85244 654 3

Typeset by
Action Publishing Technology Ltd, Gloucester, GL1 5SR
Printed by
Biddles Ltd, King's Lynn PE30 4LS

Contents

List of Illustrations

Items 1 and 2 reproduced with permission from North Yorkshire County Council from the unnetie digital archive www.northyorks.gov.uk/unnetie

Items 6 and 14 reproduced with permission from Downside Abbey.

Items 8, 9, 10 and 11 reproduced with permission from the National Library of Australia.

All other items photographed by the author.

Acknowledgements

I am very happy to acknowledge the generous help I have received with this project from numerous archivists and librarians. In particular, thanks are due for permission to use material from Birmingham Archdiocesan Archives, Cardiff Archdiocesan Archives, Southwark Archdiocesan Archives, the Archives of the Archbishop of Westminster, of the Dioceses of Clifton, Leeds, Middlesbrough and Dublin, and for the use of material from the Archdiocese of Sydney and New South Wales State Archives obtained by Dr Paul Collins. I am also grateful to many other institutions and religious orders for the use of archival material, especially Downside, Ampleforth, Colwich and Stanbrook Abbeys, the Birmingham Oratory, the archives of the Society of Jesus at Farm St, the Sisters of Mercy at Handsworth, the Dominican Sisters of St Catherine of Siena at Stone, the Sisters of Charity of St Paul at Selly Park, Oscott College, Ushaw College, the Venerable English College, Rome, the Congregation of Propaganda Fide and the Australian Sisters of Charity. Material from libraries at the University of Birmingham, National Library of Wales (Papers of the Archdiocese of Cardiff), Birmingham Central Library and Scarborough Library has proved invaluable, and I am happy to acknowledge its use. In all of these places, the generous assistance of archivists and librarians (past and present) has been unstinting, and I am enormously grateful to them all, especially those prepared to deal with my enquiries at long distance.

For illustrations, I gratefully acknowledge the assistance of the National Library of Australia and North Yorkshire County Council Digital Imaging Project, along with permission to photograph items from Downside Abbey, Olton Friary, St Chad's Cathedral, St Dominic's Convent, Stone, Archbishop's House, Birmingham and the Trustees of Oscott College.

There are many individuals who have encouraged and

supported this work over the years, not least my previous colleagues at King's College, London and present colleagues at St Mary's College Oscott, and fellow historians around the country and further afield. These include especially Dom Aidan Bellenger and Philip Jebb of Downside Abbey, Abbot Geoffrey Scott and Dom Alban Hood of Douai Abbey, Dom Terence Richardson and Anselm Cramer of Ampleforth Abbey, Dame Margaret Truran of Stanbrook Abbey and Sr Benedict Rowell of Colwich Abbey. I am grateful to friends among the membership of the Catholic Record Society, especially Professor V. A. McClelland, Fr Tom Rock and Dr Marie Rowlands for their interest and encouragement. One individual has played a greater part than any other in providing huge amounts of Australian material and local insight, happily sharing my convictions about Ullathorne over a bottle or two of red wine, and cajoling me into finishing this book – Dr Paul Collins of Canberra, to whom I am grateful for all that and more.

Finally, I am happy to record my warm appreciation of the care, dedication and expertise of all at Gracewing Publishing and Action Publishing Technology, without whom Ullathorne would never have seen the light of day.

Introduction

This study of the life of William Bernard Ullathorne, monk of Downside and first Bishop of Birmingham, has had a long gestation, having begun as a suggestion by Bishop Joseph Cleary, Auxiliary Bishop of Birmingham, as long ago as 1981. Ullathorne was one of Cleary's heroes and he had known Fr Joseph Parker, the secretary who cared for the old bishop in his last years, and who worked in the Archdiocese of Birmingham until 1935, so his sense of Ullathorne was almost first hand. The benign shadow which Ullathorne cast over the Archdiocese as its first and longest serving bishop has been immense, and the oral tradition of stories and legends about him continues to be strong. Many are the tales of him dropping his aitches (he never lost his Yorkshire accent), some of which are recorded in the following pages. Others will be readily supplied by the clergy of the Archdiocese of Birmingham. Ullathorne was more than a caricature and more than a conventional diocesan bishop, and a modern biography is long overdue. He left a partial autobiography, which is obviously a starting point for any biographer, but he never took up his pen to complete the work which ends in 1850. A collection of his letters was edited by Mother Francis Raphael Drane OP in 1892, and in the last years of his life, both a celebratory number of *The Oscotian* magazine (1886) and a collection of samples of his writings were published (*Characteristics of the Writings of Archbishop Ullathorne*, ed. M. Glancey, 1889). These offer something of a contemporary assessment of Ullathorne, and reflect the huge respect and affection in which he was held after forty years as Bishop of Birmingham.

Dom Cuthbert Butler, like Ullathorne himself, a monk of Downside, immersed himself in his confrère's life and writings in the 1920s and produced both a two-volume *Life* in 1926, and an important study of the Vatican Council in 1930 based on Ullathorne's letters. It was long thought that Butler had said the last word on Ullathorne, but many of his judgements are ripe for reassessment and there are aspects of the life to which he gave scant attention. In the intervening generations, scholarly and popular biographies of Ullathorne's great contemporaries, Wiseman, Manning and Newman have abounded, and he has receded somewhat into the shadows shed by them. The achievements and problems of the revival of English Catholic life in the nineteenth century have been discussed from many different angles, but from whatever direction it has been approached, Ullathorne is never far from centre stage.

Much attention has been given in studies of the nineteenth-century Catholic episcopate to the controversies, disputes and arguments which preoccupied the first generations of the restored hierarchy of bishops after 1850. It is all too easy to gain an impression of a disunited gaggle of disparate and competing characters, all bent on their own aggrandisement within the Church. However, there is another context within which the controversies can be interpreted, that of the attempt to reproduce a form of episcopal government and church organisation which met the needs of a religious minority in the circumstances of religious fragmentation and pluralism in Victorian England, and of an embattled Catholic Church in a hostile Europe. The bishops appointed after 1850 were developing a style, a theology and a spirituality of European Ultramontanism for the Catholic Church in England, and it has rarely been examined closely.

The public career and influence of William Bernard Ulllathorne has been recounted and acknowledged to some extent, partly in his own autobiography, and partly in the words of others. What is less clear is what lies behind the public clerical persona of the man whose attitudes and ideas so shaped the direction of English Catholicism into the twentieth century. The shape which he gave to English Catholicism is still not lost, though radically altered in recent years. While some may wish that it was already consigned to history, there is no denying that the Church which Ullathorne influenced has borne fruit. It cannot be abandoned, willingly or unwillingly, without some appreciation of the part it has played in the re-emergence of Catholic identity in English life.

Ullathorne's role in the emergence and shaping of modern English Catholicism was based partly on his wide theological reading, partly on his unique practical pastoral experience and partly on his clear vision of the Church. His basic theology was learned in his monastic training at Downside, but it was augmented throughout his life by his own careful and systematic reading and consideration of the Church's teaching. The fruits of his study in his own copious writings were never intended as theological explorations but as pastoral tools for the use of clergy and laity. His writings lean heavily on his deep knowledge of the Church Fathers, but he also engaged with the life and works of saints including his own patrons Benedict, Gregory the Great, Bernard of Clairvaux, Catherine of Siena and more contemporary figures such as John Vianney.

Of his eighty-three years, Ullathorne spent forty-three years as a bishop, forty of them in Birmingham, so his ideal of the Church is that seen mainly through episcopal eyes. The English recusant tradition of vicars apostolic had little to offer to the new generation in instructing them in episcopal duties and responsibilities. The restored hierarchy was designed not only to regularise church government in England but to return the local Church to the orbit of the universal Church around Rome. Therefore it was vital to recover the established traditions of the Church, based largely on the teachings of the Council of Trent as expounded by the post Enlightenment popes, especially Pius IX. Thus in 1846, when the possibility of appointment to the vacant Western Vicariate was hovering over his head, Ullathorne recalled, 'My reflections and the conversations I had with Dr Pagani, who combined Italian with English experiences, led me to consider the English Vicariates and the actual condition of things in England as but provisional and transitional.'[1]

This conviction became deeply rooted in Ullathorne, and his certainty that the 'provisional and transitional' arrangements had to be eradicated came to dominate his thinking on the role of the episcopate. His concept of how this was to be achieved was through discipline and order, exercised by the bishops through the clergy; proper ecclesiastical government became

[1.] *Autobiography*, p. 276.

his preoccupation, as he made clear at his first Diocesan Synod in Birmingham in 1853: 'And now what does this hierarchy mean? ... It means the restoration of that discipline by which the saints awakened and directed the energies of pastoral solicitude ... It means the regulation of ecclesiastical government by subordination of authorities, under the influence of that unity which is the secret of all strength. It means subjection to precise rules both for bishops and their clergy, and obedience for those who govern in the Church, as well as those who are governed.'[2] This is an important statement: order and obedience were important, for himself as much as anyone else, and they were not an end in themselves, but a means of awakening pastoral energies. Ullathorne was not an organisation man simply in order to keep people in line and subservient – the organisation was to serve the mission, to harness resources and co-ordinate activities which would build the Church of the future.

Ullathorne became imbued with the Ultramontane ideology current in the Church after the French Revolution, but he was no extremist. The law of the Church, as expressed by the Magisterium, was his watchword. There is no doubt that Ullathorne had a streak of legalism in his character, believing that the law of the Church was what bound it together in unity, but this was tempered by his innate humanity and pastoral common sense. An example of this was his often outspoken critical attitude towards his fellow bishops. In 1855 he reprimanded Wiseman over his conduct of the bishops' meetings, and expressed his conviction that business would be better dealt with if the bishops 'sat in their canonical order, delivered their sentiments on each subject in order and voted in order'.[3] His advice evidently fell on deaf ears, as years later he was still complaining to his friend Bishop Grant in Southwark that the bishops were 'altogether a slovenly set' who conducted their business in a 'desultory' fashion.[4] The point was that, without order, the affairs of the bishops, and therefore the mission of the Church, was being inhibited.

[2.] *Discourse delivered a the conclusion of the first Diocesan Synod of Birmingham* (1853).
[3.] AAW 79/3, Ullathorne to Wiseman, 8 February 1855.
[4.] SAA, Ullathorne to Grant, 19 August 1868.

His qualities as a diocesan bishop were immense, and have been recognised. 'He handed on to his successor his diocese of Birmingham, second to none in organisation, equipment, vigorous life, corporate spirit, and above all, in its devoted body of clergy'.[5] Yet that is not the whole story. Ullathorne circumnavigated the world twice and was the most widely travelled of any Victorian cleric: this gave him an unparalleled breadth of perception of the natural and human world. His name is scarcely mentioned as a penal reformer, yet few other priests saw as much of the effects of transportation and accompanied so many convicted criminals on their journey to the gallows. His experience was direct and vivid and he brought it to bear on circumstances in the home country. While he was much less well known as a national political figure than some of his contemporaries, Ullathorne weighed in fiercely when politics threatened to obstruct the work of the Catholic Church, whether it was in the sphere of education, government policy towards the Papal States and the new Italy, the problem of Ireland or the preservation of the integrity of convent life.

Like so many public figures in Victorian England, he was a prolific writer of letters to an astonishing range of correspondents, not only other clerics. He was also more than ready to use the modern technology of cheap printing to communicate his thoughts and views, and published dozens of speeches, sermons and tracts, as well as three longer theological works, between his controversial years in Australia as a young man and his old age. Few of his writings are read today, and his rather formal, heavy style does not commend attention. Yet his briefer writings and the unpublished letters display a brisker, more forthright and dynamic style. The voice of these is energetic, humorous and passionate, with a deep and instinctive faith. Bishop Hedley's sermon at Ullathorne's funeral was entitled, 'A Spiritual Man', which is perhaps surprising, given the typical view of Ullathorne as a bluff, forthright, occasionally pompous Yorkshireman who delighted in putting others right. Hedley's assessment is closer to the truth. Ullathorne has been generally misread: he was drawn to a profound conversion of

---

[5.] Alexander Austin, 'Archbishop Ullathorne' in D. H. Farmer, *Benedict's Disciples* (1980), p. 324.

heart, to monasticism, to the Australian mission and to the revival of Catholicism in England by a romantic vision of God's work in the world. However, his romance was tempered by a pragmatism and an appreciation of human nature gleaned from his extraordinary life and career. Ullathorne knew the heart and mind of people, women as well as men, and brought this to bear constantly in his approach to the issues he faced. His nature was proud and impatient, and he spent eighty years curbing these instincts, much of which fed into the writing, on and off for many years, of *The Endowments of Man* (1880), *The Groundwork of Christian Virtues* (1882) and *Christian Patience* (1886). This made him a humane and sympathetic leader, religious superior and friend, and a far more interesting and complex person than we have hitherto appreciated.

Ullathorne's three priorities when he became a bishop in 1846 were the restoration of the hierarchy, the creation of diocesan seminaries and the institution of cathedral chapters. He achieved all of these over forty years in Birmingham, and so, in recognition of his achievement and of those who followed in his footsteps, this book has a triple dedication:

- to the Metropolitan Chapter of St Chad's Cathedral who have so generously supported its publication
- to the seminary of St Mary's College, Oscott where most of it has been written, with the patient forbearance of colleagues and students
- to Ullathorne's episcopal successors in Birmingham, particularly to Archbishop Vincent Nichols, for his sustained interest and encouragement.

Chapter 1

Northern Lights 1806–1830

On a chill Sunday morning late in 1822, an undersized, clumsy youth from the crew of an English cargo ship, the *Ann's Resolution* blinked nervously and pulled off his hat as he stumbled into a small wooden church. He was many miles from his Yorkshire home, in a Baltic seaport. Nudged from behind by the ship's first mate who had taken him there, the boy was surprised into an experience of religious faith which was to change his life. The wooden church was on the outskirts of the strategic medieval seaport of Memel, which, having frequently changed hands, was in the possession of the city of Koenigsberg and was a melting pot of ethnic and religious groups from Russia, Prussia, Sweden and Austria. It was later renamed Klaipeda and placed in modern day Lithuania, in the 'land of crosses'; Klaipeda's modern church was mined by the Nazis, rebuilt, and confiscated by the Communists in the post-1945 period, before the collapse of the Soviet empire.[1]

In 1822, the small Catholic church, a barn-like construction, stood well outside the bustling port, and by the time the two shipmates arrived, the Mass had started. The devotion of the local people struck the fourteen-year-old cabin boy to his core, and he recalled the experience in detail even forty years later. 'The moment I entered I was struck by the simple fervour of the scene; it threw me into a cold shiver, my heart was turned

[1.] Michael Bourdeaux, *Land of Crosses: the struggle for religious freedom in Lithuania 1939–78* (1979), pp. 184–8.

inwards upon myself, I saw the claims of God upon me, and felt a deep reproach within my soul.'[2] This moment of revelation and conversion of heart was the turning point in his adolescence, and it marked the direction of his adult life. The boy was William Ullathorne, the difficult eldest son of William Ullathorne senior, a prosperous Yorkshire tradesman, and his wife Hannah. Though his parents had met and married in London, they settled in William's home ground of Pocklington in East Yorkshire, where William junior was born on 7 May 1806. Pocklington, twelve miles east of York, was already well established as a small market town with a population of about fifteen hundred and a prosperous middle class, with whom William's father was on good terms.[3] Among their neighbours were the first generations of the Sotheby's, who founded the international auction house[4] and Joseph Terry, who became a famous confectioner in York.[5] Catholic recusants were numerous in all parts of Yorkshire, rooted in farming and gentry families, and in the Ullathornes' part of the county it revolved around the patronage of the Constable family of Everingham Park, who had 'twisted like eels' to avoid confiscation and sequestration of land.[6] The Constables were among a group of Yorkshire Catholic landed gentry (including the Fairfaxes, Langdales and Stapletons) who, despite their recusancy, became ennobled during the seventeenth century and who, often through intermarriage, became rich and powerful enough to discriminate in favour of poor Catholic tenants and to maintain both a domestic chaplain and a tenant missioner to serve the local area.[7] By the time the Ullathornes

2. *Autobiography*, p. 34.

3. Ibid., p. 7.

4. Frank Herrmann, 'Sotheby family (*per.* 1778–1861)', *Oxford Dictionary of National Biography*, Oxford University Press, 2004 [http://www.oxforddnb.com/view/article/64165, accessed 12 Sept 2005].

5. T. A. B. Corley, 'Terry, Joseph (1793–1850)', *Oxford Dictionary of National Biography*, Oxford University Press, 2004 [http://www.oxforddnb.com/view/article/39052, accessed 12 Sept 2005].

6. Barbara English, *The Great Landowners of East Yorkshire 1530–1910* (1990), p. 83.

7. John Bossy, *The English Catholic Community 1570–1850* (1975), pp. 84, 178, 260.

were living in Pocklington, Everingham (only four and a half miles away) was a fashionable Georgian mansion with a classical chapel, built by William Constable-Maxwell, 10th Lord Herries, the heir to the property through his Haggerston ancestor who had married the heiress of the Constables of Everingham.[8] The Constables had strong recusant roots, Sir Robert Constable having been accused of being a ring leader of the so-called Pilgrimage of Grace, a rising of traditional Catholics against Henry VIII in 1536–7.[9] In the 1660s, four hundred recusants from the surrounding area were presented at the Sessions at Pocklington,[10] and a century later eighty-five recusants were listed at Everingham in 1767.[11]

William's father, a clever, humorous man with a good head for business, dealt in drapery, wines and spirits and grocery in Pocklington. Born a Catholic, William senior was rooted in the tradition of Yorkshire Catholic recusancy; his great grandfather John had begun the drapery business and probably become a Catholic on marrying Mary Binks in 1749. She connected the family to Sir Thomas More[12] who had gone to the scaffold in defiance of Henry VIII's reforms, and to the Catholic Watertons of Walton Hall, near Wakefield. Family tradition also linked the Ullathornes with the Jacobite Rising of 1745, though the evidence hardly supports this.[13] John and Mary's second son, also John, settled around Everingham, possibly as a tenant farmer of the Constable family, and married a local Catholic girl, Mary Robinson. It was their son William (1780–1829) and his wife Hannah, who became highly respected members of the local community in Pocklington, who 'did half the business of the town'.[14] The cabin boy was their first child.

[8.] Mark Bence-Jones, *The Catholic Families* (1992), p. 192.
[9.] R. W. Hoyle, *The Pilgrimage of Grace and the Politics of the 1530s* (2001), pp. 406–9.
[10.] CRS *Records Series* volume 4 (1907), pp. 267–8.
[11.] CRS *Records Series* volume 7 (1909), pp. 257–9.
[12.] More was revered in the family and among English Catholics as a martyr, but not canonised as a saint by the Church until 1935.
[13.] B. L. Kentish, *The Chronicles of an Ancient Yorkshire Family* (private pub. 1963), pp. 70–76.
[14.] *Autobiography*, p. 3.

The tiny chapel at Pocklington was provided by the Constable family in 1807 and Miss Constable would occasionally attend Mass there. It was mentioned in the 1851 Census as having space for around a hundred people, with an average attendance of seventy to eighty, and, by then was served by a priest from Everingham.[15] Despite the elegant Georgian chapel at Everingham, recusancy had taken its toll on the Constables, and their landed fortunes were in decline by then.[16] Nevertheless, they and other local gentry helped to provide for a new church in Pocklington, built in 1863.[17]

The Pocklington mission appears to date from around 1790, when a French émigré priest, Francis Peter Foucher, arrived there.[18] At some point before 1798, he moved to Hull, where he built the chapel.[19] French priests had fled the revolutionary violence from the mid-1790s in fear of their lives, and had been received in thousands in England.[20] Most had returned home after the end of the worst atrocities, but a small percentage settled in England, learnt sufficient English and fulfilled a much needed ministry among the scattered Catholic population. Foucher was probably succeeded by Abbé Fidele, who stayed for a long time, certainly into the 1830s, when (presumably as an old man) he was making financial provision to secure the future of the Pocklington chapel and a resident priest. He anxiously encouraged the Vicar Apostolic of the Northern District to make use of Pocklington's 'healthy air' for convalescent priests or to view it as a small enough mission to prepare junior clergy for larger responsibilities.[21]

Young William recalled the presence of the Abbé Fidele, but the definitive study of French émigré priests finds no trace of

---

15. John Wolffe, ed., *Borthwick Texts and Calendars No 25*, Yorkshire Returns of the 1851 Religious Census, vol. 1, Introduction, City of York and East Riding, p. 29, no. 177.
16. English, p. 30.
17. Middlesbrough Diocesan Archives, typescript notes on Pocklington mission by Fr Dominic Minskip.
18. Ibid.
19. D. A. Bellenger, *The French Exiled Clergy in the British Isles after 1789*, (1986), pp. 185, 268.
20. Bellenger, pp. 67–82.
21. Minskip notes on Pocklington.

him in the records.[22] He remains something of an enigma, as he cannot be clearly identified; perhaps the name by which the good people of Pocklington knew him was in place of an unpronounceable French name, and he was to them, 'the faithful abbé'. Certainly his grasp of English did not appear to be great, as young William recalled him as having only four printed sermons, so that as soon as he read the first line, the congregation could say the rest by heart.[23] Although William makes no mention of early contact with English monks in his autobiography, the mission at Everingham was manned by Benedictine missioners at times between 1721 and 1831, and John Edmund Hadley, a monk of St Gregory's Douai, was serving Pocklington (on a pension of £40 provided by Lord Stourton) between 1803 and his death there in March 1807.[24] It is, therefore, highly likely that William was baptised by an English Benedictine monk from the original home of what would become his own monastic community at Downside.

Their Catholicism did not apparently inhibit the Ullathornes' life in Pocklington, either commercially or socially. A large family followed the birth of William: Owen in 1807, James in 1808, Charles in 1810, Lucy in 1812, Bernard in 1814, Francis in 1816, Rebecca in 1818, Christopher in 1819 and the last child Hannah in 1821, who died aged less than three months in the same year.[25] Only Christopher would outlive William, and none of their other siblings lived beyond middle age.[26] The growing family were cared for by a ferocious Methodist nurse, who did not hide her contempt for priests and Catholic trumpery, and the elder children received their first education at the hands of the daughter of an Anglican clergyman. William and Owen were sent to nearby Burnby to school as weekly boarders in a non-Catholic school, where they were specifically excluded by their parents' wishes from classes in the Protestant Catechism. However, as William recalled, 'by

---

[22.] Bellenger, p. 267.
[23.] *Autobiography*, p. 6.
[24.] Birt, p. 126; Athanasius Allanson, *Biographies of English Benedictines* (Ampleforth, 1999), p. 281.
[25.] Kentish, pp. 78–9.
[26.] Stone G/ULL/VII/35 Family list, no date.

sitting in the school over our books whilst it was said, we knew every word of it by memory'.[27]

Young William was a clumsy and unattractive child, more so in comparison with his 'quick and agile'[28] younger brother, and was obviously the butt of much teasing, perhaps even bullying, as a child. Like many children who feel excluded from the easy companionship of their fellows, William retreated into a private world. He had a vivid imagination, and a strong streak of romanticism in his nature manifested itself early. Visits with his father to York Minster, which loomed in the misty distance across the Wolds from Pocklington, created in him a vivid and curious sense of mystery. The cycle of growth and decay in the natural world around him also captured his imagination as 'something inexplicable'.[29] However, what really populated the inner world of young William were the story books to which a family friend introduced him. The world of the *Arabian Nights* and *Gulliver's Travels* became an eagerly sought substitute for boyish pranks and games. Nothing, however, seized William's imagination like *Robinson Crusoe*. His father perhaps came to rue the day when he put Daniel Defoe's classic tale of seafaring adventure into his eldest son's hands, especially when, soon after, he moved his family to the coastal town of Scarborough.

The combination of Defoe's tale of sea adventures, which William 'never tired of reading and of talking of it to everyone who chose to draw me out',[30] and his first view of the sea at the age of nine or ten was a potent mix. William senior's business flourished and he became one of the leading tradesmen in the fashionable seaside resort, playing a major part in breaking a price fixing agreement among traders, which kept retail prices artificially high.[31] The business, listed in trade directories variously as, 'Grocer and Tea Dealer, Linen Draper and Spirit and Wine Merchants' and as 'Hatters, Linen and Woollen Drapers and Wine and Spirit Merchants' was based at 65 Newborough

---

27. *Autobiography*, p. 9.
28. Ibid., p. 7.
29. Ibid., p. 6.
30. Ibid., p. 7.
31. Ibid., p. 12.

St.[32] It flourished sufficiently to allow him to secure an education for his two eldest boys at a well known local Protestant school run by Mr Hornsey, a man of some eminence in the world of English grammar. Two younger brothers also went to another school run by an Anglican clergyman. This might suggest that the family's Catholic practice and the catechising of the boys was being treated somewhat casually, and there certainly were many gaps in their Catholic upbringing. Yet this was more due to circumstance than any lack of interest on the part of their parents. Assuming that the larger town of Scarborough (with a population of eight thousand) would be at least as well served for Catholic worship as Pocklington, the Ullathornes were somewhat dismayed to find that Fr George Haydock and Fr John Woodcock, the local Catholic missioners, visited only once every six weeks. French émigré priests had bolstered numbers in some areas and seminaries at Ushaw College near Durham, Oscott College near Birmingham and St Edmund's Ware were beginning to produce a trickle of English-trained clergy to augment those from the surviving continental colleges founded in the sixteenth century, but priests were still thin on the ground in England. George Haydock, who travelled from the mission further up the coast at Whitby to minister in Scarborough, had a considerable reputation as a biblical scholar, having published a new English edition of the Bible, based on the eighteenth-century translations of Richard Challoner. He became a major, and controversial, figure in northern Catholicism, but between 1816 and 1822 was the hard pressed missioner for Whitby, Scarborough and Egton Bridge.[33] John Woodcock, a Lancashire man trained at the English College in Douai, before the French Revolution, found himself across the Pennines working with Haydock in Egton Bridge as well as Scarborough.

Although Fr William Coghlan had lived in the town and built the chapel, there would be no resident priest again until 1828. However, the Ullathornes were obviously very much at the centre of the Catholic life at Scarborough; William senior took it

---

[32.] Information provided by Scarborough Library and Information Centre.
[33.] Gillow, vol. III, pp. 211–21.

in turns with another local man to lead the communal prayers on the Sundays when no Mass was available for the congregation. When either of the priests did visit Scarborough, they normally dined with the family. This 'hand-to-mouth' religious upbringing was not untypical of recusant England, when priests were few and far between and provision of chapels largely dependent on gentry patronage, but by the 1810s it was unusual to find a town like Scarborough so ill-served. Scarborough had developed as a port and health resort since the early eighteenth century and was famous for its beach and spa and its healthy environment. It was an affluent town, with elegant cliff top walks and Georgian terraces of houses. The building of Catholic chapels had been licensed since 1791. Catholics in Scarborough had met in a variety of locations until 1809, when a substantial chapel (large enough to seat four hundred people) was built in Auborough St, so this property, now used as the Catholic school, was the chapel which William and his family knew.[34] The Catholic congregation may have amounted to around forty people.[35] By 1878 this had grown to over a thousand, especially in the summer months, and a new Gothic church had been built to replace the classical pillastered chapel.[36]

In between clergy visits, Mr Ullathorne and his colleague Mr Pexton (a former student for the priesthood at Ushaw College) based the devotional and catechetical programme in Scarborough on the prayers of Richard Challoner, especially the *Garden of the Soul*, and on the published sermons of James Archer. Described as, 'the most enchanting preacher in England',[37] Archer was a pot-boy in the London pub where Challoner preached illicit sermons among the beer tankards, and was himself later ordained. His sermons were published in numerous editions, and according to his contemporary, Charles Butler, 'To almost every library and to many a Protestant toilet Mr Archer's sermons have found their way.'[38] He was not to all Catholic tastes. During the time when the Catholics of

34. Dominic Minskip, *A History of St Peter's Mission, Scarborough (1783 to the present)* copy provided by Middlesbrough Diocesan Archives.
35. Minskip, *Scarborough*, p. 7.
36. Ibid., pp. 8–9.
37. Anstruther, vol. 4 (1977), p. 11.
38. Ibid.

Scarborough were being treated to readings from Archer's words, they were banned in the Midland District by the Vicar Apostolic John Milner, who regarded them as too liberal. Thus young William's Catholic upbringing was essentially that of recusant England, steeped in the ascetic and domestic piety which sustained Catholic life and practice between the late sixteenth century and the nineteenth century. It was not a faith nurtured in regular public worship and communal devotions, but in the intimate setting of the family, with prayers led by his own father and religious conversation around the dinner table. This was a rapidly disappearing world, to be replaced within a generation by energetic fund raising, building of churches, convents and schools, and the ordering of mission life along quasi-parochial lines in accord with church law. The gauche schoolboy who seemed to live in a world of his own daydreams, and who had been baptised but received no other sacraments of the Church, did not at the time appear to be a likely protagonist in this revolution in Catholic life.

William's father, in despair at his son's dreaminess and lack of concentration, removed him from school in 1818, when he was only twelve, in the hope that a taste of reality working in the family business would wake his ideas up, and enable him to resume his education in a better frame of mind. Like many another desperate parental sanction, it did not work. William began work in the family business, but continued in his free time to explore the horizons of his mind through the contents of the circulating libraries in Scarborough. He read voraciously, mostly travel and adventures, gazed out at the sea and perhaps thought of stories his mother had told him of meeting Sir Joseph Banks, the President of the Royal Society who travelled with Cook to the Antipodes and of her cousin, the explorer John Franklin, who had circumnavigated Australia, served in the Napoleonic wars and in 1818, commanded an Arctic expedition.[39] William's head was full of ideas of seeing the world, and he pestered his parents to let him go to sea.

39. B. A. Riffenburgh, 'Franklin, Sir John (1786–1847)', *Oxford Dictionary of National Biography*, Oxford University Press, 2004 [http://www.oxforddnb.com/view/article/10090, accessed 12 Sept 2005].

For a long time they held out against the idea, but eventually realised that the best way to get it out of his system was to let him go and experience the hardships of the merchant navy. Scarborough was established as a port with a royal charter by the thirteenth century, but it was in its heyday between the late eighteenth and late nineteenth centuries. When the Ullathornes moved there, the Outer Pier was newly built (1800) and the lighthouse newly constructed (1806) and the young 'seastruck' William was no doubt fascinated by watching the new harbour dredging scheme which had just begun, to deepen and widen the access for shipping. His father's trade depended on imports of wine, spirits and textiles, so there was doubtless plenty of excuse for the boy to loiter around the harbour and ships. There was no shortage of ships in Scarborough harbour, as many as fifteen new ones being launched each year from the eleven shipyards active in the early part of the nineteenth century.

In a last desperate attempt to protect their wayward thirteen-year-old, the Ullathornes secured him a job on board a new ship owned by George and William Stephens, William Harrison and Samuel Bielby, who were friends of the family.[40] The *Leghorn* was launched on 21 July 1819, with a hand-picked crew, including Captain Wrangham,[41] whose wife (unusually) always sailed with him. The final precaution was to ensure that one of Mr Ullathorne's mature employees, 'having taken a fancy to the sea'[42] was also employed on the *Leghorn*. She was a 74 foot brig, weighing 160 tons, built in Scarborough by George Woodhouse Porritt, and William was on her maiden voyage on 21 July 1819.[43] By the time William went to sea on the *Leghorn*, she was one of over a hundred Scarborough ships insured at the local office, and he was one of at least a thousand seamen on the muster roll.[44] His parents' anxiety was not,

---

40. Information supplied by Scarborough Library and Information Centre.
41. Information supplied by Scarborough Library and Information Centre. Ullathorne misremembers the name as Wrougham.
42. *Autobiography*, p. 14.
43. Collins thesis, p. 24.
44. '*Scarborough Records*': *notes and records compiled by Sydney Foord* (unpublished 1970, pp. 30–3). Copy provided by Scarborough Library.

however, assuaged by William's last dealings with Fr George Haydock. The priest also failed in his attempts to dissuade William from going to sea, and in a sulk, the boy failed to keep an appointment with him to receive the sacraments of Confirmation and Holy Communion before sailing.[45] The disgruntled adolescent went off to an uncertain and perilous future, ill disposed to the religion of his birth and stubbornly resisting all the sound advice of the adults around him. His mother, however, ensured that in the bottom of his sea trunk was packed a copy of the familiar Challoner prayers of the *Garden of the Soul* – just in case.

William's autobiography is rich in memories of his seafaring career, which lasted three years and clearly had a great influence on him. His contact with all manner of men on board ship, where he could not avoid the coarseness and drunkenness which was the common lot of early nineteenth-century merchantmen, gave him a much broader perspective on life than his comfortable, sheltered Yorkshire home. He was not a natural sailor and was inevitably teased, and occasionally taunted for his Catholicism, and quickly nicknamed 'Lumpy' for his awkward and clumsy demeanour. Bullying was only kept at bay by William regaling his fellow crewmen with recollected stories of derring-do from his constant reading of adventure stories.

The *Leghorn* gave William his first experience of drunkenness – not in himself but others – when the ship docked in Gibraltar and the men were allowed ashore to buy cheap rum. The excitement of viewing the strategic rock of which he had read so many heroic stories was somewhat marred by finding himself almost the only sober man left on board the vessel: 'the men lay sprawling, half on deck, half on the forecastle'.[46] His experience of the power of drink to destroy human dignity and a passionate determination to draw men and women away from their addiction became a lifelong campaign, the seeds of which had been sown in Mediterranean ports. The personal difficulties he encountered and the miseries of harsh weather, terrible food and rough companions did little to dampen

---

[45.] *Autobiography*, p. 14.
[46.] Ibid., p. 17.

William's romantic notions of travel and the sea. The first voyage on the *Leghorn* did not cure him, as his parents had hoped.

The romance of the Mediterranean set his spirits alight. Quarantined on board the *Leghorn* for three weeks in Livorno because of yellow fever, he passed the idle days in fascinated amusement at the music boats which would gather around the ship to entertain the crew with snatches of Rossini in return for coins tossed into the boats. He was enraptured.[47] The name of his ship, the *Leghorn* was also the English name given to the Italian port of Livorno, which was largely built by an English expatriate marine engineer, Robert Dudley, in the early seventeenth century. It contained an English cemetery, full of the remains of eighteenth-century Grand Tourists, including the novelist Tobias Smollett. Both Byron and Shelley were in Livorno at the same time as the *Leghorn* was lying idle in the bay, but William's youthful romantic spirit was more stirred by the poetry of the natural world than of contemporary writers.

Although he was fascinated by the warm south, it was the stark beauty of the cold northern seas which captured his imagination most. On a second voyage out of Hull, the *Leghorn* was bound for St Petersburg. 'The summer skies of the Baltic enchanted me even more than those of the Mediterranean ... Perhaps the most beautiful scene that I ever saw in creation was a sunrise in the Baltic, the summer nights in that climate were to me enchanting. The sun went down with a large glowing disc, and in a couple of hours was up again, so that one could read a good print at midnight.'[48] Elsinore reminded him of Hamlet; no self-respecting English teenager could see Copenhagen without recalling the victories of Admiral Nelson, and St Petersburg itself was full of exotic grandeur. For the first time, William found himself moved by the grandeur of the natural world, and there was little likelihood of his imaginative fantasies being disappointed by reality. At least for the time being, he was prepared to endure the rigours of seaborne life for the sights and sounds which it enabled him to experience.

[47.] Ibid., p. 19.
[48.] Ibid., p. 22.

There was also another factor, of which William only slowly became aware, which was his own stubborn pride. He was not prepared to admit that he had had enough or could not cope. That same characteristic pride was to be a challenge to his better nature throughout his life.

After a winter on shore studying navigation with a retired sea captain, William set sail again as an apprentice on the *Ann's Resolution*, a ship similar in size to the *Leghorn*, (77 feet and 157 tons) but still, to William's disappointment, a merchant ship. 'I wanted to go on an Arctic discovery ship, or somewhere where I could have more adventure and see a greater variety of the world. But my father wished to sicken me of the sea.'[49] The ship, built in 1815 by George Dale Smith, another local ship-builder, was owned by Catholic friends of his parents, a Mr and Mrs Craythorne, whose nephew (also a Catholic, educated at the Jesuit college of Stonyhurst) was to be first mate. The first master of the *Ann's Resolution* was also a Craythorne family member, Robert, but on William's voyages, she was probably under the command of Stephen Hart.[50] On the *Ann's Resolution* William came across, for the first time, the natural religious sense of people whose common currency was not formal Christianity but often crudity, foul language and promiscuity: 'With all their licentiousness, genuine seamen have in the main warm, childlike and generous hearts ... and some few were even devout men.'[51] He learnt not to judge by appearances or first impressions, and it was a lesson which stood him in good stead.

It was the owner's nephew, the ship's first mate, Mr Craythorne, who, on their second Baltic voyage, decided it was time to take William in hand. William's autobiography occasionally referred to encounters with Spanish monks, or observances of Orthodox religion in Russia, but on no other

---

49. Ibid., p. 29. His mother's cousin, Sir John Franklin, returned a hero in September 1822, from a three-year Arctic exploration. After a spell as Governor of Van Diemen's Land between 1837 and 1844, he ended his life in the Arctic in 1845, lost with another exploration ship.
50. Information provided by Scarborough Library and Information Centre.
51. *Autobiography*, p. 29.

occasion did he specifically state that he had the opportunity or inclination to practise his Catholic faith. He did not suggest any particular desire in his own mind, when the ship was docked in Memel, but simply stated that, 'One Sunday morning in that harbour, Mr Craythorne, the mate, said to me, 'William, let us go to Mass.'[52] The experience at Memel was life changing; though brought up in a Catholic home and familiar with the prayers and teachings of Catholicism, Memel was his first serious religious experience. It brought about a genuine conversion of heart, which nevertheless was still that of a romantic and proud hearted youth. Initially, it was his imagination as much as his heart which had been touched.

William managed to speak of this profound experience to his companion, and quickly devoured the limited religious reading matter that Mr Craythorne's locker afforded. He recorded this as Gobinet's *Instruction of Youth*, and an English translation of Marsollier's *Life of St Jane de Chantal*. Charles Gobinet was a seventeenth-century Doctor of the Sorbonne and Rector of the College Du Plessis for forty-three years. Renowned throughout France as a preacher and teacher, his *Instruction of Youth in Christian Piety* was a best seller and a classic for a century and a half. An English edition was published in 1783, and a sequel in 1809.[53]

There was much in Gobinet to stiffen the sinews of a young boy newly charged with religious fervour and idealism, including chapters headed: 'That salvation generally depends on the time of youth', 'Examples of those who have corrected the vices of their youth, but with very great difficulty' and, even more uncomfortably: 'Of the intractableness of young people'. Gobinet also gave William his first introduction to the words of St Bernard of Clairvaux, whose name he later took in religion, and his first opportunity to explore the virtue of humility, which would occupy much of his thinking and reading, until at the end of his life he expressed all that he had learned in a book on the subject entitled *The Groundwork of Christian Virtues*. Gobinet described humility in his sixty-third chapter, as, 'that which gives perfection to all others, and which is necessary to

52. Ibid., p. 34.
53. Oscott College Recusant Library Catalogue, vol. II, p. 76.

their preservation and increase'.[54] There are echoes of this sixty years later in *The Groundwork of Christian Virtues*: 'Although humility is the receptive virtue, every Christian virtue increases humility in proportion to its right and due cultivation.'[55] The work by Marsollier was actually *The Life of St Francis de Sales, Bishop and Prince of Geneva, Founder of the Order of the Visitation*, which was translated into English by W. H. Coombes in 1812.[56] This combined biography of St Francis de Sales and St Jane Frances de Chantal had a profound and long lasting effect on William. Not only did it, 'introduce me to a new world of which I had hitherto known nothing. A life filled with the sense of God, and devoted to God, was what I had never realised,'[57] but as he later recalled, 'imprinted on my then fervid mind two perfect ideals, like two immovable seals: the ideal of a bishop in the image of St Francis de Sales, and the ideal of a nun in the image of St Jane Frances'.[58]

The story of friendship and collaboration between St Francis and St Jane Chantal was to echo deeply in his own life and his friendship and collaboration with Margaret Hallahan. Sixty years later, he remembered the effect of reading Marsollier and how he, 'caught the first idea of conventual life as a complete and perfect notion'. He had no idea at that point just how directly he would become involved in the development of convents in England, but insisted that all his, 'subsequent notions of religious life for women have been but the fillings up in detail of that early vision invested with no better surroundings than a crew of rough sailors'.[59] The story of the young Francis de Sales disagreeing with his parents' wishes and finding himself confronting the fragility of human life on board a storm-tossed ship echoed in William's own

54. C. Gobinet, *The Instruction of Christian Youth in Christian Piety* (seventh edition 1809), p. 187.
55. *The Groundwork of Christian Virtues* (1882), p. 224.
56. Coombes was a Douai-trained priest of the Western District, who, according to Anstruther, vol. IV, p. 70, 'went to Shepton Mallet for a fortnight and stayed nearly forty years'. He retired to Downside in 1849, where he died in 1850.
57. *Autobiography*, p. 34.
58. *Letters*, p. 527.
59. *Letters*, pp. 370–1 [28 December 1877].

experience.[60] St Francis de Sales, 'who could never endure that the suggestions of human prudence should have too much influence when the cause of God was concerned',[61] gave William a role model for a different kind of adventure.

With exactly the same single-mindedness with which he had forced his parents to let him go to sea, William announced that he wished to leave the sea and return home. Losing no time at all, his relieved father brought him back to Scarborough and the family business. He resumed the study of his catechism with the young priest by then resident in Scarborough, Fr John Woodcock, but that did not last long. However, the Memel experience was clearly more than a passing fancy, and William's new-found devotion to his faith was striking deep roots. Through a chance encounter with a business contact of his father, who had a son in the noviciate of the Benedictine monastery at Downside, he learnt something of monastic life. His father's friend was trying to encourage William's fourteen-year-old brother James, who had a fine voice, to try his vocation in the monastic choir. James was not drawn to what he heard of monastic life but, with typical directness and romantic ardour, William made it clear that he would like to go to Downside. William Ullathorne senior was perhaps readier to indulge this new passion of his wayward eldest son that he had been his seafaring, maybe hoping that, if nothing else, the monastery might imbue him with a little stability and complete his education. Without delay he wrote to the Prior of Downside, Fr Luke Barber, and the matter was settled. At the beginning of February 1823, William arrived at Downside, near Bath, aged almost seventeen, but having seen, heard and experienced more than most men twice his age.

William's first view of Downside, in the village of Stratton on the Fosse near Bath, was nothing like the splendid range of buildings which can be seen today. The community of St Gregory's Monastery, founded in Douai in 1605, had been driven out of France by the French Revolution in 1794 and after twenty years living at Acton Burnell in Shropshire under

60. M de Marsollier, *St Francis of Sales, Bishop and Prince of Geneva*, translated by W. H. Coombes (1812), vol. 1, pp. 62–5.
61. Ibid., vol. I, p. 139.

the protection of the Smythe family, they finally settled at Downside in 1814. Downside was still in its early stages of development when William arrived, and it was geared towards the maintenance and expansion of missions as much as to the life of the cloister. It was a small, cramped set of buildings, with half-built premises combining monastery and school, in which William's arrival made twenty pupils. He arrived there unlettered except for his prodigious and uncritical reading habits, spiritually unformed, and with no idea at all of what a monastic vocation might entail. In fact, it is highly unlikely that he had ever met a monk before arriving at Downside.

What is now known as The Old House was the original monastic building, an eighteenth-century house with earlier origins. Within William's first months there, the new chapel adjoining the house was completed, and probably about the same time, the main entrance was moved from the east side of the house to its present southern aspect. A solid, squarely built house, it spread over five floors, including attics and cellars. The novices lived in the attic, with scarcely room in which to stand up.[62] William's first director and a key influence on his monastic formation, was John Bede Polding, eventually to become the first Bishop of Sydney. The poverty of William's religious training is indicated by the fact that Polding, having heard his general confession, held him back from receiving his first Holy Communion until Christmas 1823: only two weeks later, he entered the monastery as a postulant, along with four companions. To the intense relief of his parents, their difficult eldest son seemed to have found his vocation, and he was readily forgiven for the years of anxiety which he had given them. The Ullathornes remained a close family.

William embarked on the second great romantic adventure of his life with gusto and his customary bookish approach. It did not take his school fellows long to nickname him 'Old Plato' for his studious habits. His school education, crammed into ten months, consisted mainly of classics and history, which became his favoured reading matter. Although by his late teens William had grown in stature, and according to early sketches of him

62. John Lambert, 'Round About Downside' in *Downside Review*, vol. VIII (1889), pp. 168–97.

(which may have flattered) he had developed a more elegant and less 'lumpy' figure, still he was ill-disposed to sporting activities. His free time was more likely to be spent with his nose in a book, his early favourites being Richard Challoner's *Lives of the Desert Fathers* and Alban Butler's *Lives of the Saints.* These classics of eighteenth-century English hagiography rooted in William a love of the history and tradition of the Church. Richard Challoner was the dominant figure of eighteenth-century Catholicism, being Vicar Apostolic of the London District (1740–81) and a prolific author of books designed to augment and support the pastoral work of the clergy and the domestic devotions of the laity. The most famous of these was *The Garden of the Soul*, which was meat and drink to families like the Ullathornes and was used by William senior when he led the congregational prayers in Scarborough. After its publication in 1740 it went through thirty-four editions before 1824 and hundreds more afterwards, and became a sort of generic Catholic prayer book. Challoner's popular devotional works were accompanied by studies of English Reformation martyrs, early British saints, the Desert Fathers and individual saints' lives to instil in English Catholics a sense of history and continuity in their faith. Alban Butler was a Douai-trained secular priest, whose literary career was mainly preoccupied with hagiographical and biographical works, of which the *Lives of the fathers, martyrs and other saints, compiled from the original monuments and other authentic records; illustrated with the remarks of judicious modern critics and historians,* (published in 1759) and usually known as the *Lives of the Saints* was the most substantial.[63]

The English Benedictine Congregation, newly re-established on native soil, was more concerned with missionary and educational activities in the difficult conditions of early nineteenth-century England than with the perfection of cloistered monastic life. Catholic life in England in the years just before the Catholic Emancipation Act of 1829 was in a state of flux. Numbers were increasing, in part due to waves of migrants from Catholic

63. J. A. Hilton, 'Butler, Alban (1709–1773)', *Oxford Dictionary of National Biography*, Oxford University Press, 2004 [http://www. oxforddnb.com/view/article/4177, accessed 26 Sept 2005].

Europe overrun by Revolutionary and Napoleonic forces and in part to increasing poverty in Ireland; the political atmosphere surrounding Catholicism was heating up as Daniel O'Connell's campaign for political freedom in Ireland dominated popular and parliamentary debates; centres of Catholic life were springing up in newly affluent towns as the first wave of industrialisation brought 'new money' into the Catholic congregations. Yet institutional life and buildings were still lacking, with churches and chapels limited in number and quality, schools still thin on the ground and religious orders forced to flee Europe still seeking permanent and settled homes. Thus the task of English monks would lie as much outside the monastery as within, establishing the missions which were the lifeblood of English Catholicism. In fact, it was in the missions that the vitality of the English Benedictine Congregation lay.

Aged just under nineteen, little more than two years after his arrival at Downside, the young William began his noviciate as a monk and became Brother William Bernard Ullathorne on Easter Tuesday, 9 April 1825. Even within the monastery it was still regarded as unsafe to wear the monastic habit which had not been seen in England since the time of Henry VIII. The monks simply wore a black tail coat, and within the monastery a soutane, college gown and cap. The young novice was still conscious of his physical awkwardness and embarrassed by it; although he was no longer the heavy, clumsy schoolboy, Ullathorne had a muscular weakness in his right side and a lisp. To try and cure both afflictions he would stand for hours on one leg leaning at his study window with a book, and would make himself walk uphill declaiming texts aloud with his mouth full of pebbles to strengthen his leg and improve his pronunciation at the same time.

His boyish, almost fragile looks, which he retained well into adulthood, were something of a trial to him, and it seemed that even as he entered his twenties, he was still trying to grow into his body. He had difficulties establishing himself with older priests, and even Pope Gregory XVI, in 1837, took one look at him (aged thirty-one) and exclaimed, 'Quel giovane!' (What a youth!)[64] Solitary habits and a degree of self-induced isolation

[64.] *Autobiography*, p. 144.

were formed early. It was well known that he continued to study at night in the attic novice dormitory, by the light of a candle screened under an old hat, as on one occasion, his illicit reading of the Fathers probably saved monastic lives and property. His dimmed candle enabled him to spot a small fire beginning in the roof caused by smouldering embers which had been left by plumbers melting lead to seal the joints.[65]

The Rule of St Benedict, the basis of all monastic life, was compiled in the mid-sixth century as 'a little rule for beginners' and based on earlier monastic rules, but became the dominant one in western Christianity. Benedict, therefore, had long been called the 'father' of monasticism. William learnt the Rule by heart while he was washing in his attic room, by propping it up on the washstand, and his love of it was deep and abiding.[66] His most developed reflection on the Rule was an address on the Feast of all Benedictine Saints, published in 1875, by which time he had been a professed member of the Order for fifty years.[67] Cuthbert Butler described it as the clearest and truest short exposition of the spirit of Benedictinism.[68] In his 1875 text, Ullathorne drew a likeness between the monastic orders and the prophets of the Old Testament as lovers of solitude, humble of heart, austere in self-denial, undoubted in courage, strict enforcers of the Divine Will, rebukers of the sensuous world, and proof that God never abandons his people.[69] Even after fifty years, he had not lost his romantic belief that monasticism was 'the grandest expression the world has seen of that elevation of soul to which men may ascend through the power of grace'.[70] Genuine monks, he wrote, 'belong to the grand poetry of life'. The spirit of St Benedict he described as one of 'luminous discretion', a spirit of largeness and freedom, which was powerful because rooted in the solid centre of stability. This powerful blend of stability and freedom of spirit was a lifelong inspiration to him.[71]

[65] 'Round About Downside' in *Downside Review*, vol. VIII (1889), pp. 182–3.
[66] Lambert, p. 180.
[67] *Sermon on All Monks*, 13 November 1875.
[68] Butler, *Life*, II, p. 213.
[69] *Sermon on All Monks* (1875).
[70] Ibid.
[71] Ibid.

Curiously, William's early spiritual training did not reflect a particularly strong monastic tradition, but more the spirit of English Counter-Reformation recusancy and the French tradition absorbed by the Downside community in its time in Douai. A few books which Ullathorne himself recalled as formative included Gobinet's *Instruction of Youth*, which he had first encountered on board ship after his Memel experience. Challoner's *Think Well O'nt* was in a similar tradition of practical spirituality grounded in everyday life. It emphasised ascetic discipline and well-schooled virtue rather than the higher flights of contemplative prayer. It did however (along with the same author's *Lives of the Desert Fathers*) bring Ullathorne into his first and formative contact with the early monastic tradition of the Desert Fathers. In the same English recusant tradition, but with the mystical approach more suited to monasticism, was the work of the seventeenth-century English monk, Augustine Baker, which he does not specifically mention as being used at Downside, but which he used in spiritual direction and in his own private reading all his life.

The main text book for his noviciate was Rodriguez' *Practice of Religious Perfection and of the Christian Virtues*, 'to which our master added instructions drawn from the Rule of St Benedict'.[72] This was another Counter-Reformation classic by a Spanish Jesuit, much used in the English refugee seminaries, and further evidence that monastic education was more rooted in the practical needs of the Counter-Reformation recusant world, and that it had drifted somewhat from its monastic roots. *The Practice of Religious Perfection* shaped Ullathorne's lifelong devotion to Scripture and the Desert Fathers, on both of which he drew heavily in his own writings. It was during his monastic education that the shape of William's intellectual life was set, in so far as he grew into a habit of self-directed reading in theological and spiritual subjects. As well as Challoner and Butler, his autobiography mentions *The Spiritual Combat*[73] This

---

[72.] *Autobiography*, p. 40. When Downside later had cause to appeal to Rome, the use of Rodriguez was regarded by the Congregation of *Propaganda Fide* as reassuring evidence of orthodoxy. (*Autobiography*, p. 47).

[73.] Misidentified by Madigan as St Ignatius' Spiritual Exercises.

was a set of spiritual conferences based on meditations on the crucified Christ by Lorenzo Scupoli, a Theatine priest, who was for a time under suspicion by the Inquisition.[74] *The Spiritual Combat* helped William with his youthful inner battles, and he continued to regard it as 'the best book ever penned for help in laying solidly the foundations of an interior life'.[75] Forty years later, preaching at the funeral of a Catholic public figure in Birmingham, he noted with approval the deceased man's reliance on this same little book, insisting that, 'whatever knowledge I have myself acquired for the conducting of souls, I gained from that book'.[76] Philosophical and theological training followed in the noviciate, his main philosophical textbooks being Isaac Watts' *Logic: or the Right Use of Reason* (1725) and a textbook produced at the Paris convent of Port Royal, the main centre of Jansenism, alongside the eighteenth-century Scottish philosophers including Hume, Blair and Campbell. Philosophy appealed to Ullathorne's mental taste, 'for few things have ever fascinated me more than the analysis of mental operations and the study of the mental and moral faculties'.[77]

William's romantic nature, removed from the glamour of the high seas, sought fresh outlets. The writings of the Desert Fathers, the earliest hermit monks, 'became to me what *Robinson Crusoe* had been to my earlier years – a grand, romantic spiritual idea, to be somehow realised and acted upon',[78] and nurtured in William a romantic ideal of religious life. This, and his reading of the French Abbot Armand Jean de Rancé (1620–1700) put into William's head the notion of a vocation to the more enclosed and rigorous Cistercian life. De Rancé had established an austere reformed Cistercian house at La Trappe in Normandy, and William had taken the religious name of Bernard (of Clairvaux), one of the greatest Cistercian reformers of the medieval monastic world. This notion, just as seafaring had done, grew into an obsessive determination. His novice master and prior were wise in their

---

[74.] Collins thesis, p. 40.
[75.] *Autobiography*, p. 37.
[76.] *A Discourse preached at the Funeral of Mr Councillor Maher* (1862), p. 11.
[77.] *Autobiography*, p. 44.
[78.] Ibid., p. 40.

handling of the still headstrong youth, and warned him that if he went to La Trappe and failed (which they were convinced he would) he would probably lose his monastic vocation altogether. They persuaded him to continue to his monastic profession at Downside, and if after two years he was still of the same mind, then they would release him to La Trappe. No more was heard of the idea, but it is revealing of William's character. The strong streak of imagination and romance which had taken him to sea was still evident, and for him the life of a monk was the ultimate grand vision. Equally powerful in his character was the element with which he struggled all his life – what he once described as 'my damnable pride'.

As novice master Bede Polding had a profound effect on the young monk who, 'found in him all my soul needed',[79] including another grand romantic adventure. Allanson described Polding in complimentary terms as an 'able and estimable father', a faithful and regular monk, a beloved and respected confessor and a zealous missioner.[80] There were to be other opinions. Born in Liverpool and educated at Downside's first home at Acton Burnell, Polding was professed as a monk in 1812 and ordained priest at Downside in 1819. He was a tall, energetic figure, commanding in appearance and full of vitality.[81] It is little wonder that the awkward, limping Ullathorne was drawn to him. He grew very fond of Polding and attached to him, although he could see Polding's faults as a novice master. 'Dr Polding himself was not a very deep or persistent thinker',[82] but he steeped the young novices in Scripture, spiritual classics and the Rule of St Benedict. After half a century as a professed monk, Ullathorne reflected on his formation at Polding's hands, calling him his 'vigilant prefect and well-trusted spiritual guide'. He recalled Polding's first talk to the novices in which he advocated docility in the hands of their masters, and warned of the dangers of pride: it was significant

[79.] Ibid., p. 36.
[80.] P. Athanasius Allanson, OSB, *A History of the English Benedictine Congregation 1619–1856* (1860), vol. III, p. 33.
[81.] Frances O'Donoghue, *The Bishop of Botany Bay: the Life of John Bede Polding* (Australia, 1982), p. 4.
[82.] *Autobiography*, p. 44.

that he recalled that warning above all. From 1826 Polding was sub prior of Downside and secretary to the President of the Benedictine Congregation, so was at the heart of all English Benedictine developments.

The English Congregation was committed to missionary activity which would flow from solid monastic foundations. The English black monks were bred as missionaries, often living isolated and unsettled lives in the circumstances of recusant England. Therefore it was uncommon, but not irrational, that Polding developed a passionate interest in the pastoral needs of distant lands where few priests were to be found. Fired by childhood imaginings, Polding became obsessed with stories of Botany Bay and the spiritual desolation of the convict colonies there: so much so, that his companions dubbed him, 'the bishop of Botany Bay'.[83] He shared this passionate commitment with his younger companions and charges at Downside, and not surprisingly, Ullathorne was one of the keenest to share Polding's vision of a Benedictine mission in the remote and largely unknown land of Australia.

The other main formative influence on Ullathorne was Thomas Joseph Brown, who taught him theology and became his good friend and mentor. Years later, when both men were bishops, Brown still occasionally addressed him as 'My dear Barney'.[84] Brown was an excellent teacher, unlike Polding, and a gifted theologian, described as 'articulate, combative, relentless'.[85] Through French contacts, Brown had imbibed Gallican ideas which he conveyed strongly to the novices. French Gallicanism was a school of thought which sought to diminish the direct influence of Rome over the French Church in favour of a Catholicism more wedded to political and ecclesiastical realities as perceived from Paris. A form of English Gallicanism had taken root in the late eighteenth century, though nothing like as thoroughgoing as the French version which strongly

[83.] O'Donoghue, p. 11.

[84.] AAW St Edmunds Papers 58, Thomas Brown to Ullathorne, 10 February 1849.

[85.] David Daniel Rees, 'Brown, Thomas (1798–1880)', *Oxford Dictionary of National Biography*, Oxford University Press, 2004 [http://www.oxforddnb.com/view/article/3657, accessed 12 Sept 2005].

maintained an ecclesiastical position of independence from Rome.

Brown was not alone in England in the 1820s in thinking that Rome was best kept at a safe distance, in order to win government and public support for complete political freedom for Catholics. In 1812, three out of four Vicars Apostolic had been prepared to vote in favour of a proposal that the British government have a veto on the appointment by Rome of English Catholic bishops. Brown was horrified to find Ullathorne one day reading Joseph de Maistre's work *Du Pape* (1819), which was written by a reformed revolutionary to contradict Gallicanism. It became the classic text of nineteenth-century pro-papal Ultramontanism. Ullathorne was a curious reader, and Brown need not have worried about the influence of De Maistre. Neither Gallicanism nor the extreme papalism of De Maistre appealed to Ullathorne, and his own position became that of a moderate Ultramontane.

The possibly Jansenist philosophical influences and Gallican ecclesiology in Ullathorne's formation were counterbalanced by the use of the works of Alphonsus Liguori in moral theology and by the generous breadth of the Downside formation, which, as well as continental Counter-Reformation ideas, included elements of the monastic tradition. Apart from his formal teaching, Ullathorne was left much to his own devices. A solitary reader with an opaque way of expressing himself, he admitted that 'I was more or less a puzzle to superiors as well as to brethren.'[86] However, he continued happily enough at Downside and in October 1828 received the sacrament of confirmation and received the minor clerical orders and sub-diaconate within a few days, all at the hands of Bishop Thomas Weld, a widower and member of the aristocratic Dorset land owning family of Lulworth Castle. After his wife's death, Weld trained for the priesthood and was ordained in 1821. He was made bishop with a view to an appointment in Canada, which he never took up, and was named cardinal in 1829. He was the first English cardinal to be nominated in a hundred and fifty years and it was a signal of approval from Rome of the achievement of Catholic Emancipation. That year Weld moved to Rome with his

[86.] *Autobiography*, p. 45.

daughter and son-in-law Hugh, 7th Lord Clifford.[87]

It is indicative of the conditions of Catholic life in the 1820s that Weld was only the second bishop Ullathorne had ever seen in his life, and that several liturgical ceremonies requiring the participation of a bishop therefore took place on the same visit. Bishops were rare creatures in England at the time. Four Vicars Apostolic governed the Catholic community, the country being divided into geographical segments. Downside fell within the Western District, then under the control of Bishop Peter Collingridge, a Franciscan. In March 1829, just before the passage of the Catholic Emancipation Act for which he had campaigned, Collingridge died, leaving his coadjutor, Peter Baines, to succeed him. Baines was a Benedictine monk of Ampleforth, whose impact on Ullathorne's career would be significant. He had spent three years convalescence in Rome, which, it has been suggested, gave him delusions of grandeur. Nicholas Wiseman, then Rector of the English College in Rome, recalled Baines in astringent terms which may have been influenced more by later events than experience of the 1820s. 'When he undertook great and magnificent works, he would stand alone: assent to his plans was a condition of being near him: anyone that did not agree, or that ventured to suggest deliberation, or provoke discussion, was easily put aside: he isolated himself with his own genius: he had no counsellor but himself.'[88] Baines embarked on a bitter conflict with his own Order over ambitious plans for his college of Prior Park, near Bath which he bought in 1829 for £20,000.[89] Baines wanted Prior Park to become a grand and important centre of learning, and tried to persuade Rome that the English Benedictine houses were ill-disciplined and not even legal in church law, and that they should close so that the monks of Ampleforth could staff his new enterprise. Within a year, Baines was educating forty boys (soon to double) in his Western District college and seminary.[90] The story of the wran-

[87.] Judith Champ, *The English Pilgrimage to Rome: a dwelling for the soul* (2000), pp. 158–60.
[88.] Nicholas Wiseman, *Recollections of the Last Four Popes and of Rome in their Times*, (1858) p. 205.
[89.] Harding thesis, pp. 22–4.
[90.] O'Donoghue, p. 10.

gling and financial disaster which embroiled Prior Park and Ullathorne is a long and bitter one.

In its first phase, it had an accidental effect on the young Ullathorne. The Chapter of the Benedictines met at Downside and rejected Baines' plan, but sufficient men (including the superior of Ampleforth) followed Baines, leading to the break-up of the northern monastery. The young monks at Downside had been curious but silent observers of the Chapter, but when Baines placed Downside under interdict and appeals were sent to Rome, all members of the community were asked to add their signatures to papers in defence of Downside. The cause was explained to them, and of course the young members of the community loyally signed the petitions, but for Ullathorne it marked a loss of innocence and an early, unwelcome introduction to ecclesiastical politics, 'a lesson stored up'.[91] The effect of the dispute within the Order and the fragmentation of Ampleforth was even more concrete and immediate. Ullathorne and another young monk were sent to Ampleforth to help the new prior restore the community there.

En route to Ampleforth, Ullathorne and his companion, Michael Placid Sinnott, with Luke Barber as chaperone, broke their journey at Abbot's Salford, the home of the community of Benedictine nuns which eventually settled at Stanbrook. Many years later, he recalled his amazement at this visit, the first he had ever made in his life to a convent. It was an inauspicious start for the man who was to become the greatest friend and supporter of convents in the Victorian Church. The three monks were lodged and treated as members of the community and spent much of the day walking the grounds with the nuns (enclosure was virtually unknown). They were then invited into the community room, given rum punch and invited to sing for the entertainment of the nuns! That was not the worst of the horrors:

> ... what struck me as most strange was that we were awak-
> ened in the morning by a sister coming into the room and
> lighting a candle close by our beds. All was meant in the

91. *Autobiography*, p. 49.

most kind and sisterly way, but it completely destroyed my ideal of a community of Benedictine religious.[92]

Another romantic myth was exploded. Experiences like this are a reminder of just how undeveloped English Benedictine life was by 1830. While at Abbot's Salford, Barber sung a high Mass in the convent chapel with the young monks as deacon and subdeacon because, extraordinarily, the community had never seen one.[93] Barber himself soon afterwards became chaplain at Abbot's Salford and moved with the nuns to Stanbrook, where he remained until his death in 1850.[94]

In the midst of all the disputes and trials involving his monastic home, Ullathorne faced his own personal trials, including his first bereavement. In November 1829, his beloved father died at the age of forty-nine, leaving his entire estate to his wife Hannah, and entrusting the two sons Owen and James as trustees. William senior at least had the reassurance of knowing that his eldest son was (at last) settled in life, as his will (made two months before his death) initially excluded him, as being 'amply provided for'.[95] This was not a vindictive act but a sensible provision for the rest of his family, since the common ownership of property to which monks are vowed would have meant that any bequest to William was effectively a donation to Downside. However, paternal affection (or perhaps unease about his son's future, if he had heard anything of the Benedictine difficulties from nearby Ampleforth) got the better of him, and he gave his wife discretion to give their eldest son £50–100 from the estate after his death.[96] Father and son had been close, despite the boy's headstrong behaviour, and his recollections of childhood are coloured with warmth and affection. It is not clear whether Ullathorne reached his father before he died, but, 'he received the last sacraments surrounded by his family' and as a result, one of his

---

[92.] Stanbrook 47, Ullathorne to Abbess Gregson, 2 August 1878.
[93.] Ibid.
[94.] Birt, *Pioneers*, vol. 1, p. 149.
[95.] Borthwick Institute of Historical Research, Last will and Testament of William Ullathorne of Scarborough, 10 September 1829 (quoted in Collins thesis).
[96.] Collins thesis, p. 56.

father's assistants who was present was so moved that, having been secretary of the local Orange Lodge, he became a Catholic.[97] His mother and brothers kept the family business going in Scarborough until 1847, by which time Owen had moved to Liverpool where he continued the business alone until his death in 1850.[98]

Family sadness was not the only trial, making his first return to his native Yorkshire an unhappy one. Early in 1830 Ullathorne found himself a reluctant and unpopular Prefect of Discipline in the school at Ampleforth. It was his first experience of exercising authority rather than being subject to it and it revealed (even in his own mature recollection) characteristics which did him little credit. He was judgemental about what he found at Ampleforth, stringent in the exercise of discipline (including flogging a boy) and critical in the letters he wrote back to Downside. His first impressions, conveyed unprompted to the President of the Congregation, John Birdsall, with all the arrogance of youth, verged almost on gossip.

> At our first arrival in company with Fr Prior who came over to York to meet us, we found the house in great disorder and everything in a state of disorganisation and Mr Towers in great difficulty and anxiety of mind. In the monastery and the school everything, or nearly so, was utterly neglected except where he himself was bodily present. Choir was almost deserted in the morning, Holy Communion forborne and it was a common thing to see a snuffbox handed to each other in chapel and to see religious men with their heads together, talking, smiling and remarking during a sermon or catechising, and the boys under their eyes of course following their example.[99]

Birdsall, himself a stern man, was not impressed at the self-righteous tone of the letters he received from the young monk.[100]

[97.] *Autobiography*, p. 54.
[98.] Kentish, pp. 78–9.
[99.] DA Birdsall Collection, Ullathorne to Birdsall, 14 May 1831.
[100.] Collins thesis, p. 58.

Ullathorne wrote to Birdsall again a couple of months later, assuring him that he now, 'possessed both the hearts of the lads and the goodwill of the community', but that he was anxious for the safety of the house if Fr Edward Clifford returned to Ampleforth, 'of whose principles, or more truly his want of principles, we all know too much'.[101] In his dealings with this fellow monk, Ullathorne revealed a trait which was frequently evident later in life, of showing initial hostility and mistrust towards someone on first encounter, which was only overcome through a confrontation, leading to reconciliation, genuine friendship and appreciation. He was inclined to act on first impressions, which were, of course, not always right, but at least he had the grace to realise this. In his autobiography Ullathorne records the inevitable clash over (in his view) Clifford's excessive familiarity with the schoolboys. It resulted in a public showdown, tears and a final reconciliation.[102] This was typical of his quickness to judge and readiness to react with a pomposity which would earn him enemies, coupled with a warmth and readiness to forgive and be forgiven which would seal his closest friendships.

On Ember Saturday (24 September) 1831 Ullathorne was ordained priest by Bishop Painswick of the Northern District at Ushaw College near Durham.[103] En route to the College for his ordination he met two of the seminary professors, Richard Gillow and John Walker, who from 1835 was the resident priest at Scarborough and became a family friend. Ordination was, of course, a momentous event in the young man's life, sealing his future course. In Ullathorne's case, it marked not only a transition from youth to adulthood, but a deeply felt recognition that he was not only to live a monastic life for his own personal and spiritual fulfilment, but that he had given his life in the service of God's people and was therefore committed to sacrifice his own delights for the good of others.[104]

The sulky boy who had given his parents such grief was beginning to grow up. On a practical note, ordination meant that he could be removed from his unpalatable and unpopular

[101.] DA Birdsall Collection, Ullathorne to Birdsall, 22 July 1831.
[102.] *Autobiography*, p. 52.
[103.] BAA B73 Ordination certificate, 24 September 1831.
[104.] *Autobiography*, p. 54.

duties in the school at Ampleforth and gain his first taste of life as a monk-missioner in the nearby villages of Craik and Easingwold. Ironically, the cause of his northern sojourn, Bishop Peter Baines had also begun his preaching career in Easingwold a few years earlier, and Ullathorne was intrigued to find there a copy of Archer's Sermons (familiar from his youth) with Baines' own annotations.[105] He was also, in exploring the lanes and farms of Easingwold, Oswaldkirk and Ampleforth, unwittingly treading on ancient Ullathorne ecclesiastical territory, as his great great great grandfather had been the vicar of Ampleforth village in the late seventeenth century.[106]

To his immense relief, Ullathorne was rapidly sent back to Downside by Birdsall, who was clearly unimpressed with the young monk; relations between the two men were never warm or open. However, Ullathorne's time back in his own monastery was to be limited. Edward Bede Slater had gone to Rome on behalf of the English Benedictines in 1817 to try and secure the return of Lamspring Abbey in Westphalia after the end of the Napoleonic wars. He found himself instead appointed bishop *in partibus infidelium* and given the vicariate of the Cape of Good Hope, in the hope that he would take English Benedictine missioners with him.[107] William Poynter, Vicar Apostolic of the London District had long been involved in negotiation with Rome to secure the appointment of Catholic bishops in the burgeoning British colonies, and Slater's appointment was the result.[108] The astonishing range of Slater's post covered half of the southern hemisphere – Mauritius, Madagascar, South Africa, Australia and the islands of the Pacific including New Zealand and a considerable part of British India.[109]

Slater's base was changed from the Cape to the island of Mauritius, which the French had relinquished to British control in 1810, but which ecclesiastically still looked to Paris. Rome withdrew that French jurisdiction in 1819 and Slater

[105]. Ibid.
[106]. Kentish, pp. 65–7.
[107]. Birt, *Pioneers*, vol. I, p. 9.
[108]. Collins thesis, p. 81.
[109]. *Autobiography*, p. 56.

hastily returned to England to raise funds and recruit helpers. Two monks accompanied Slater to Mauritius and he found two Irish priests, Frs Philip Connolly and John Joseph Therry to volunteer for Australasia. Slater, dismissed by Birt as 'a vain, impulsive man, whose elevation to the episcopate was not justified by any really inherent gifts suitable to one in his high station'[110] soon ran into difficulties, getting into debt, quarrelling with his clergy, with the colonial government and with the lay leaders, and being scolded by Rome. By 1828, one of his priests was in Rome requesting the bishop's removal from the vicariate.

The business inevitably dragged on until Slater was finally withdrawn and William Placid Morris, a Downside monk, agreed to replace him at the beginning of 1832. Not surprisingly, this was not an easy post to fill; Polding himself turned it down for fear of the intense heat[111] and Morris tried to decline it, only agreeing at Birdsall's urging.[112] Once having agreed to go, Morris was keen, not only to have a colony of monks working in Mauritius, but to send a group of monk-missioners to Australia. He sounded out Birdsall, writing that he had been 'led to hope that Mr Ullathorne ... might wish to labour in the other hemisphere if he could be spared from this'. The President of the Congregation did not answer directly, but word seemed to get round that Ullathorne's antipodean appointment was on the cards.[113]

Two possibilities lay ahead of him in England: either Ullathorne would find himself teaching in the school, for which his scholarly tastes might seem to fit him, or he would be sent to one of the Downside missions. His brief taste of school mastering had settled his feelings towards that, and his missionary instincts were beginning to stir. Downside (to its credit) had done little to squash Ullathorne's desire to follow a grand romantic ideal and Polding, to whom he was devoted, had shared with him his passion for the missionary needs of Australia. There was still, of course, within the missionary monk, the little boy who loved the sea and yearned for adventure.

[110.] Birt, *Pioneers*, vol. I, p. 57.
[111.] *Autobiography*, p. 56.
[112.] Birt, *Pioneers*, vol. I, p. 72.
[113.] Collins thesis, p. 60.

Things seemed to move rapidly. Polding mentioned Ullathorne's name directly to Bishop Morris, who wrote to Ullathorne. Inspired by Polding's table talk, his response was typical. 'I replied that I had about a hundred reasons against going to Mauritius, and almost as many for going to Australia'.[114] His Ampleforth interlude and attempts to justify himself had not done Ullathorne's reputation any good within the English Benedictine Congregation, but Polding was obviously keen for him to go to Australia. Brown expressed the view that he was certain that he would not give trouble on the mission, although he was much less enamoured of the idea. Although Birdsall was keen on missioners going overseas and had no particular desire to keep Ullathorne in England, he seemed to throw matters into confusion late in the day over whether Ullathorne had final permission to go.[115]

By the end of August 1832, Ullathorne had visited his mother and brothers and sisters in Scarborough for what he believed to be the last time, and was ready to sail for New South Wales. His mother had given him his father's legacy, which he spent in collecting the library which would sustain him on the long voyage and beyond. He was conscious in himself of a 'fondness for reading pursued to excess'[116] and, aware that the remote colonies might not furnish much material, he set out to compile a library of about five hundred books. Ullathorne's personal book collection later formed the core of the collection which went to St Patrick's College, Manly in New South Wales. It consisted not only of standard theological works, but of literary and spiritual classics in any language he could manage; this reading material consumed on board ship fed his wide-ranging appetite and enriched his theological learning along traditional Catholic lines. It also began to nourish his reputation as a self-educated man.

He was ready to leave for the Australian colony when interventions from beyond the English Benedictines changed the basis of his appointment, so that he would no longer go simply a mission priest. The two priests, Connolly and Therry, who

114. *Autobiography*, p. 57.
115. Collins thesis, p. 66.
116. *Autobiography*, p. 58.

had gone to Australia in 1820, were at loggerheads and had split up to work separately in New South Wales and Van Diemen's Land. The Governor, Sir Richard Bourke, had requested the British government that 'some Catholic ecclesiastic should be sent out invested with the authority to manage the affairs of that Church'.[117] Bourke's predecessor, Governor Darling, had sacked Therry from the post of official chaplain in 1825, and disputes in the colony raged around Therry, who was described by Collins as, 'impetuous and almost impossible to deal with'.[118] Therry's successor as official chaplain, Daniel Power, soon succumbed to the hardships of colonial life and died in 1830, and his successor, Christopher Dowling was effectively driven out by Therry's clique of supporters.[119]

Morris proposed to the government that the youthful and inexperienced Ullathorne be sent to New South Wales with authority as vicar general to resolve the situation – was it this proposal which caused Birdsall to hesitate? Ullathorne was twenty-six years old, with no experience of exercising authority except the disastrous interlude at Ampleforth, which he had justified with self-righteousness. Ullathorne, as a courtesy, consulted Birdsall as President General on this new arrangement:

> As Dr Morris obtained from you, Very Reverend Father, some time since, your permission for me to accompany his lordship as a missionary to New South Wales, I did not think it necessary to write to you on the subject. An arrangement has since been made and proposed to me to which I think it is proper I should obtain your concurrence.[120]

Birdsall responded with a rigid silence, apparently viewing any further contact between them as unnecessary, even duplicitous. Ullathorne was used to Birdsall's harshness, but was wounded by Polding's failure to point out to the President General that

---

117. *Ibid.*, p. 59.
118. Collins thesis, p. 98.
119. Ibid., p. 99.
120. DA H468, Ullathorne to Birdsall, 31 August 1832.

the young monk was only trying to act properly in seeking Birdsall's agreement to take up this very different appointment. Ullathorne wrote again desperately, pointing out that he was acting on Polding's advice in approaching the President General.[121]

Polding's failure to intervene, amounting to cruelty, left Ullathorne feeling abandoned and enduring, 'anguish of soul' and, 'trying perplexity'. This was his first, but by no means his last taste of Polding's weakness. He had no illusions about what lay ahead of him, as he assured Birdsall, '... my heart yearns for the religious suffering of the colony of New South Wales. I do not think the situation one of honour, but of labour, of trial, of unceasing labour.'[122] Even recalling events thirty years later he felt the complete loneliness of being more or less written off by his English Benedictine superiors as he began his 'solitary way across the ocean'.[123] To sail for Australia in the early 1830s was a hazardous venture and a massive personal commitment, from which it was not expected that many would return, even if they survived the hardships of the journey and colonial life in the remote and alien land of which few people knew anything. No time limit was put on Ullathorne's placement as missioner or vicar general, so he was effectively being exiled.

Morris' recommendation to the government was accepted by the Colonial Office and Ullathorne was appointed vicar general on a government salary of £200 per annum, with £150 towards his travel costs.[124] This was an extraordinary situation for an English Catholic priest who had grown up in the atmosphere of recusancy where priests were just about tolerated and Catholics had only just received the full political rights accorded by the Catholic Emancipation Act of 1829. Catholicism in England had no political relationship with the government, yet Ullathorne was going to Australia, effectively as a civil servant. He received his letter of appointment and faculties as vicar general on 7 September 1832, and sailed from London for Australia on the 331 tonne *Sir Thomas Munro* on 16

121. DA H469, Ullathorne to Birdsall, 5 September 1832.
122. Ibid.
123. *Autobiography*, p. 60.
124. Collins thesis, p. 63.

September 1832.[125] The cabin boy now had a cabin of his own, but the prospect ahead of him was both more exciting and more terifying than anything he had experienced in the Mediterranean or the Baltic – and that was just the journey.

[125.] The *Sir Thomas Munro* was more than twice the size of the largest ship he had been on previously, the *Leghorn*.

Chapter 2

Chaplain to the Ends of the Earth 1830–1842

Ullathorne spent the next decade of his life in Australia, or crossing the oceans on business related to the Church in Australia. From the age of twenty-six he was placed in an exposed public position in a distant land of which few English people had any notion. He went out to Australia as a callow and inexperienced youth with a pompous style and a somewhat judgemental turn of mind, and returned a mature man of remarkable humanity and insight into human affairs as well as religious matters. Australia made Ullathorne the man he became, and built the foundations of his character.

The story of his time in Australia and his contribution to the building of the Australian Catholic Church has been told, not only in his own autobiography and his account of *The Catholic Mission in Australasia* published in 1837, and in Benedictine texts such as Butler's *Life and Times of Bishop Ullathorne 1806–1889* and Birt's *Benedictine Pioneers in Australia*, but in the growing modern historiography of Australian religious history. The most detailed account of his role in the emergence of the institutions of Catholicism in Australia can be found in Paul Collins' 1989 Doctoral thesis.[1] Collins suggests that, until relatively recently, Ullathorne's contribution to the creation of the Australian Catholic Church has been underplayed, and

---

[1.] Paul Collins, *William Bernard Ullathorne and the Foundation of Australian Catholicism 1815–40*, Ph.D., Australian National University (1989).

suggests that this is related to factional interests in the early historiography of Catholic Australia, to the brevity of his time there, and to his emphasis on order and organisation, rather than the more colourful heroics of missionary endeavour.[2] Collins' thesis has done much to redress the balance, but there is no doubt that Ullathorne's position in relation to the history of Australian Catholicism is an ambiguous one.

The voyage on board the *Sir Thomas Munro* was very different from Ullathorne's last sea crossing ten years earlier; he was no longer a cabin boy, but a monk and a priest charged with an overwhelming task. He never lost his love of the sea and treated the long voyages of the next decade of his life as prolonged spiritual retreats devoted to prayer and study: his only regret was the impossibility of celebrating Mass on board, but otherwise, 'I was always inclined to regret when the voyages came to an end'.[3] In his days with the merchant navy, he had never 'crossed the line' and sailed the vast southern oceans, and here again, as in his younger days, the beauty of the natural world enriched his spirit. The grandeur of endless ocean and sky and the limitless stars spoke vividly to him of God's, 'never ceasing action in the created universe'.[4] The southern oceans, with their vast and terrifying power, were a different prospect to anything else Ullathorne (or indeed, anyone sailing from the British Isles) had encountered. 'Out in these vast seas humankind is bluntly reminded of its fragility in the face of the brute force of the natural world'.[5]

What he recalls of his dealings with people on board the *Sir Thomas Munro* is revealing of his character, especially aspects which would bring him into difficulties as a young man dealing with experienced colonials. He was very aware of his position and dignity, in a way which seems exaggerated to the modern mind, but which was perhaps less striking in the 1830s when distinctions of social status, and the particular distinctiveness of 'the cloth' were universally respected. Even allowing for the

---

2. Collins thesis, pp. 402–4.
3. *Autobiography*, p 62.
4. Ibid.
5. Paul Collins, *Hell's Gates: The Terrible Journey of Alexander Pierce* (2002), p. 13.

social mores of the time, Ullathorne could be pompous and patronising. He scarcely spoke to the crew, though he convinced himself that they sensed his innate sympathy for them as a fellow sailor, and 'always showed me particular respect'.[6] He kept himself apart from the general group of people travelling, but was sympathetic and kindly to 'a very quiet Methodist minister with his wife and family on board'.[7] Much of his time was spent in study, particularly of Canon Law, of which he was largely ignorant, and which would be vital to the exercise of authority in the name of the Church. The particular role and responsibilities of vicar general weighed heavily on the twenty-six-year old, knowing that his bishop would be four thousand miles away in Mauritius, Rome would be half a world away and therefore he would have to act, 'almost as if the complete authority of the Church were concentrated in my office'.[8] His sense of his office and the authority which it vested in him was to be a trial both to him and some of those he was charged to govern.

The journey was broken at Cape Town, where Ullathorne happily received the hospitality of an Ampleforth monk, Fr Clement Rishton, who was feeling the psychological effects of prolonged isolation and was later recalled to England, 'with the loss of his mind'.[9] This lesson on the effects of a solitary life was not lost on the young Ullathorne. In the Cape he also made his first personal encounters with non-European people in the entrepot colony. Individual contact with non-European races was still rare for Englishmen in the 1830s, unless they were traders or colonial servants, and Ullathorne was fascinated by the variety of peoples. His youthful travels had already brought him into contact with more foreigners than most Englishmen of his age and generation. Though clearly a man of his time, Ullathorne did not adopt the typically colonial view of native peoples as inferior, and was relaxed in the house of

---

6. *Autobiography*, p. 62.
7. Ibid., p. 63. Some forty or so passengers are listed as far as Hobart, including The Revd Mr and Mrs Martin. Only about twenty or so went on to Sydney.
   www.list.jaunay.com/ausnzpassengers
8. Ibid.
9. Ibid., p. 64.

the priest's friend who was a West Indian dealer in exotic animals for European zoological gardens, and had 'lions, tigers, ostriches and other wild animals ready in iron cages for shipment'.[10]

On leaving Cape Town, the *Sir Thomas Munro* entered the Roaring Forties, the power of which drove all shipping rapidly in the dominant east-west direction towards the next landfall, thousands of miles south-west. Enormous seas, with waves up to ninety feet high, were common and rough weather arose suddenly and violently, driving shipping at remarkable speed towards the unknown continent of Australia – or in many cases, to the bottom of the icy seas.[11]

The second stop was made at Van Diemen's Land, after the *Sir Thomas Munro* had skirted the western and southern coast of Australia and sailed up the Bass Straits within sight of the coasts of both Australia and Van Diemen's Land.[12] An island roughly the size of Scotland lying one hundred and forty miles south-east of the southern tip of Australia, Van Diemen's Land had been discovered and named by the Dutch explorer Abel Janszoon Tasman in 1642.[13] In 1820, Van Diemen's Land had a population of 4,901, of whom 2,666 were convicts: by 1826 this had rocketed to 11,700 men and 3,300 women.[14] It did not fall under Ullathorne's jurisdiction, being under the care of Fr Philip Connolly. Putting in first at the harbour of Circular Head (the headquarters of the Van Diemen's Land Company, now Stanley), at the beginning of 1833, Ullathorne set foot for the first time on antipodean soil, and experienced both its beauty and its harshness. He later regretted the fact that his brother's widow had destroyed the many descriptive letters he had written to his brother Owen recounting the 'sweet odoured shrubs, and scentless flowers, the rich plumaged birds, and the sponges and shells which covered the shore' of the Antipodes.[15] This is to be regretted by historians too, as he was, at all times, a keen and curious observer of nature, and

10. Ibid.
11. Collins, *Hell's Gates*, pp. 14–5.
12. *Autobiography*, p. 65.
13. Collins, *Hell's Gates*, p. 33.
14. Ibid., p. 33, p. 55.
15. *Autobiography*, p. 66.

the descriptions which do survive in his writings are vivid and immediate.

The settlement at Circular Head was almost completely populated by convicts, with only a government manager and superintendents. Soon after landing, he met the only Catholic family in the town (Mr and Mrs Curr, who managed the Van Diemen's Land Company, and to whom he carried letters from Mr Curr's brother, Joseph, a priest in Manchester). He baptised three of their children, Fr Connolly, the only resident priest on Van Diemen's Land, being on the other side of the huge island. Hobart Town (the capital founded from Sydney in 1803), where Fr Connolly was resident, was even more of a shock to Ullathorne, when he landed there on 30 January. The most southerly human settlement in the world, it was only just evolving from a prison camp into a town, with four or five hundred houses (some substantial and stone-built) and twenty public houses, but scarcely any paved roads.[16]

Connolly was away visiting Launceston when Ullathorne's ship docked at Hobart, and he found himself bombarded with complaints about Connolly's severe treatment of the people, and appalled by the shabby, neglected and filthy state of the chapel. He was reduced to mending the altar steps and cleaning the silver used on the altar before he could even celebrate Mass there. Having 'the complete authority of the Church concentrated in my office' did not carry him far in the reality of the Australian mission, where a man like Fr Connolly could languish for years without sight of a brother priest. Connolly returned while Ullathorne was there and responded graciously enough to his presence, and in Ullathorne's words, they 'parted friends'.[17] Not many weeks passed though, before Connolly was writing in furious terms to Morris of his surprise at Ullathorne's appointment to New South Wales. He had nothing against Ullathorne, but believed that he should have been consulted and even perhaps given the job himself.[18] Disgruntled he might have been, but he was also prescient in remarking that the appointment of a young English vicar

[16.] Collins, *Hell's Gates*, pp. 50–1.
[17.] *Autobiography*, p. 68.
[18.] DA Morris Papers, Connolly to Morris, 16 August 1833.

general to a predominantly Irish mission would prove a mistake: Ullathorne himself came to much the same conclusion in the years to come.

The *Sir Thomas Munro*, one of ninety-five ships to arrive that year, docked at Sydney harbour on 18 February 1833, after a journey of 152 days. Ullathorne entered a world unlike anything he had experienced before, dependent on shipping, migration, trade and the strange business of transportation for its very existence: 'early colonial Sydney was not a cultivated town'.[19] The first ever census of population in Australian history, in 1828, recorded a total in New South Wales of 36,598, comprised of 20,930 free and 15,668 convicts. Men greatly outnumbered women in New South Wales by 27,611 to 8,987.[20] Between 1820 and 1837, the tonnage of shipping leaving New South Wales and Van Diemen's Land increased from 1,291 to 18,846, and the tonnage of imports increased even more rapidly from 2,823 to 47,240.[21] Sydney was the centre of the rapidly growing colony of New South Wales and its adminstrative hub. The year of Ullathorne's arrival, 1833, was the peak of the transportation system, with 51,200 people arriving (more than in the previous two decades). Of these, 6,779 were prisoners.[22]

Ullathorne, having planned his tactics carefully, walked straight from the harbour to the priest's house, unannounced. He knew that first impressions on both sides would count for much, and, having heard stories of the current situation, was determined to assert his authority quickly and firmly. Resident in the house were Fr John McEncroe, Mrs Dwyer the housekeeper and her two daughters, and Fr John Joseph Therry who arrived during dinner. That first evening meal in Sydney was extremely awkward. Both the housekeeper and Therry made Ullathorne uncomfortable by their patronising remarks about his youthful appearance, though he quickly realised that he could turn this to his advantage by retaining an element of surprise when he made his first move. Therry was certainly

19. Robert Hughes, *The Fatal Shore: a History of the Transportation of Convicts to Australia 1787–1868* (1988), p. 338.
20. C. M. H. Clark, *A History of Australia* (1968), vol. II, p. 153.
21. http://setis.library.usyd.edu.au.
22. Hughes, p. 162.

surprised when Ullathorne produced the documents appointing him vicar general and giving him jurisdiction over the
whole colony. He had the wit to react gracefully and with due
respect, but Therry and his clique reassured themselves
privately that the youth could easily be dispatched to some
remote settlement and not trouble them again. Within twenty-
four hours, Ullathorne had disabused Therry of the notion
that the new boy was a pushover. When the experienced old
hand began to try and explain about the factions which split
the community, he was stopped in his tracks:

> Fr Therry, listen to me. There were two parties yester-
> day; there are none today. They arose from the
> unfortunate want of some person endowed with ecclesi-
> astical authority, which is now at an end. For the present,
> in New South Wales, I represent the Church, and those
> who gather not with me, scatter. So now there is an end
> of parties.[23]

Round one definitely went to Ullathorne.

As the young vicar general began to take control of his new
and strange territory, his organisational gifts emerged and his
hatred of disorder became clear. He had to deal not only with
the difficulty of asserting his authority in the management of
the Catholic mission, but also to forge an appropriate understanding and working relationship with the colonial
government. Central to both activities was the web of relationships into which he now stepped, where his office would
be less useful than his personal qualities. If he could not
untangle the knots within the web, no amount of ecclesiastical
paperwork would enable him to exercise leadership in the
colony. The most difficult and intractable knot was that
surrounding the management of the clergy, especially where
Therry was concerned, who had been in the colony for thirteen years.

The British colonies, in terms of any Catholic administration,
fell under the authority of the Vicar Apostolic of the London
District. From 1812 until his death in 1827, this was William

---

23. *Autobiography*, p. 71.

Poynter, who was the first vicar apostolic to try and seriously confront the problems of Catholics in the colonies.[24] His negotiations with Rome and Whitehall throughout 1817 and 1818 eventually resulted in the appointment of Edward Bede Slater as Vicar Apostolic in Mauritius in 1818.[25] In the meantime, unbeknown to Poynter, the maverick Fr Jeremiah O'Flynn used his own personal Irish/Australian contacts and simply preempted what the bishop was trying delicately to negotiate. O'Flynn was born in County Kerry, but somehow came to enter the Cistercian Abbey at Lulworth in Dorset, from where it was planned that he would be part of a group establishing a mission in Canada. However he abandoned his Cistercian confrères in the West Indies en route, and embarked on a complicated and controversial career, which led to him being appointed to Botany Bay directly from Rome, without reference to Poynter. The London Vicar Apostolic's jurisdiction over Catholic matters in all British colonies was an impossible task in itself, hampered by interference from Rome in the case of O'Flynn. It seems that the Colonial Office of the British Government had no difficulty in allowing Catholic priests to go to New South Wales, but O'Flynn fitted none of their criteria. Poynter also knew his background and was not prepared to act as his sponsor to the Colonial Secretary, Bathurst, and was carefully diplomatic in his conversation with him. The result was that O'Flynn was turned down by the Colonial Office, but he sailed anyway on the *Duke of Wellington*, arriving in Sydney on November 1817, the first priest to step onto Australian soil.[26] He, and others who followed, had no structure or organisation within which to operate in New South Wales, and simply acted as wandering missioners as best they could. It was that lack of organisation which Ullathorne eventually had to remedy; in this lay his real skill, but it led to conflict and frustration. O'Flynn has taken on mythical status in the history and legend of Australian Catholicism as the Irish hero of a Catholic community bullied by British colonialism, and that heroic

---

24. Collins thesis, p. 80.
25. See Chapter 1.
26. Paul Collins, 'Jeremiah O'Flynn: Persecuted Hero or Vagus?' in *Australasian Catholic Record*, January and April 1986.

status had already begun to take root when Ullathorne arrived.[27]

The colonial government, well aware of the high proportion of Irish migrants and convicts, was not averse to Catholic priests operating in the colony, but Governor Macquarrie was trying to establish and maintain a fragile social order and his own position was far from confident. He was suspicious of O'Flynn, as he was of other wandering preachers without proper ecclesiastical or civil authority, and he ordered O'Flynn to quit the colony. Ullathorne, in his pamphlet on *The Catholic Mission in Australasia* (1837) described O'Flynn in glowing terms as, 'a man of meek demeanour, who speedily won the deep love of his people'[28] and who became a victim of the governor's jealousy. This reinforced the popular heroic legend. Maquarrie's motivation was not, as Ullathorne and Birt would have it, 'petty jealousy'[29] nor was it anti-Irish bigotry, but rather unease, 'because he had arrived in an unauthorised way, and because the governor foresaw trouble arising from his presence in the colony'.[30]

There was a core of staunch Catholics who supported O'Flynn and mourned his departure, and the manner of it. They even hid O'Flynn until after the *Duke of Wellington* had sailed on its return journey in January 1818. He was eventually deported in May 1818, leaving behind a devoted following, though the deep Catholic faith among the early settlers and convicts has been another persistent and powerful Australian Catholic myth. Tradition has it that, after his departure, the devout little flock would gather to pray in a Catholic household in Sydney where the priest had placed the Blessed Sacrament. St Mary's Cathedral was eventually built on the site of this house. The public interest generated by the O'Flynn affair in England as well as Australia encouraged renewed determination by Poynter and Rome to get some properly organised provision. The result was Slater's unhappy appointment to Mauritius, and Philip Connolly and John Joseph Therry's

27. Ibid.
28. *The Catholic Mission in Australasia*, p. 8.
29. Birt, vol. 1, p. 117.
30. Collins thesis, p. 84.

arrival (with episcopal authority) in Sydney in May 1820, followed rapidly by their falling out.

Connolly almost immediately set out for Van Diemen's Land, while Therry settled in Sydney and began to build a church. For the next thirteen years Therry dominated Catholic life in the colony. He was zealous and energetic but, 'impetuous and almost impossible to deal with',[31] as Maquarrie's successor found. Governor Darling eventually sacked him as official Catholic chaplain to the colony in 1828, but Therry's power base was strong. His successor in the post, Christopher Dowling, was rapidly driven into effective exile beyond Sydney and his fellow priest John McEncroe, who also arrived in 1832, was weakened in influence by the rapid onset of alcoholism.

Against this backdrop of a dozen years of haphazard if energetic ministry by a succession of priests, the most dominant of whom was Therry, Ullathorne knew that his task was to bring a measure of order and improve relations with the government. Ullathorne's relationship with Therry was inevitably touchy as their personalities were diametrically opposed. Therry was an energetic, volatile, unpredictable and restless man, who readily responded to the needs of people around him and was rewarded with their warm affection. The new vicar general was awkward with people, bookish, orderly in his manner and anxiously conscious of his new authority. Therry had laid few firm foundations for long term development of the colonial Church, which by this time had an estimated sixteen or eighteen thousand Catholics, some five thousand of them in Sydney.[32] Ullathorne's direct, even pugnacious approach seemed (surprisingly) to work with Therry, but, as Collins suggests, 'he shrewdly perceived the ambiguity of Therry's attitude to authority: "I am convinced that he has always been disposed to submit to ecclesiastical authority ... (but) it has been his misfortune that his warm temperament has been under no control of authority".'[33]

The first battleground was the building project for the church in Sydney, for which Therry had obtained land and

31. Ibid., p. 98.
32. Ibid., 126.
33. Ibid., 129.

begun raising funds as soon as he arrived. However, when Ullathorne got there Therry was in a long running dispute with the colonial government over exactly how much land had been granted, the fund-raising was chaotic and the project had no prospect of completion. Thus, all the problems inherent in the colonial Church were focused in one disordered scheme. In his first letter to Bishop Morris in Mauritius two months after his arrival, Ullathorne described what he had found in language of crisis and impending doom. 'A few days more would have brought the Catholics, divided in sentiment, into angry conflict with each other and with the government.'[34] Therry was claiming more land than the government had allocated; he not only refused to agree to the results of a government survey, but threatened the surveyors with physical violence if they put down any boundary markers. The Attorney General (a prominent Catholic) was in turn promising legal action, and Governor Bourke (so unwell that he had to meet Ullathorne in his bedroom) pleaded with him to come up with 'anything reasonable, for the sake of peace'.[35]

The impasse was resolved by Ullathorne's proposal of a new set of trustees, three clerical and three lay, elected by the congregation, to negotiate with the government and see through the whole building project. Speed was essential to avoid getting bogged down in the arguments, and on the third Sunday after his arrival, he preached a 'strong and somewhat vehement'[36] sermon on unity and then called the congregation to meet for the purposes of electing three trustees. No one was allowed to speak and voice their grievances, Ullathorne insisting that a line be drawn under past troubles and divisions. The three names which emerged were those of the Solicitor General Plunkett, Commissioner Roger Therry of the Court of Requests and Mr Murphy, a respected and respectable Emancipist.[37] The three clerical trustees were, of course, Therry, McEncroe and himself. He then expressed a willingness to hear any comments from the floor, which consisted

34. DA Morris Papers, i39 Ullathorne to Morris, 17 April 1833.
35. *Autobiography*, p. 78.
36. DA Morris Papers, i39 Ullathorne to Morris, 17 April 1833.
37. *Autobiography*, p. 79.

mostly of expressions of relief and gratitude that a fresh start had been made.

It was a triumph for Ullathorne. He had resolved the most contentious issue among the Catholics in Sydney, established his own authority and salvaged the good will of the government towards the Catholic Church – and all within his first month. The land issue was settled, with the government allocation for the church agreed and a plot being provided elsewhere in Sydney for a seminary. The building blocks for the future of the Church institutions in Australia were literally and metaphorically laid. 'By Christmas night (1833) the great church was completed.'[38] Begun in 1821, this church, dedicated to St Mary, eventually became the first cathedral in Australia and the mother church of the new nation. It was extended in 1851 to designs by Augustus Welby Pugin, but destroyed by fire in 1865. Polding laid the foundation stone of the present cathedral in 1868.

No proper accounts of the Therry building fund existed, and the best estimate that Ullathorne could achieve was that £6,000 had been raised and spent on the incomplete church and house. Government contributions were made towards its completion over the next couple of years, once the disagreements were resolved. There was never any suggestion that Therry had been misappropriating funds, but there had been a 'great deal of mismanagement somewhere of the money collected for the Sydney church'.[39] Ullathorne was horrified to find that he had made use of professional fundraisers who had pocketed a percentage. The only solution was to insist that henceforth, all fund-raising was to be under Ullathorne's control.[40] The proper financial control of the building project was one aspect (and an important one) of the gradual shift in the balance of power between himself and Therry. The Australian experience sowed in Ullathorne's mind a firm belief that true religious and social freedom flowed from order, and true religious unity from clear structures of authority. His experience of *laissez faire* missionary enterprise and the

---

38. *Autobiography*, p. 94.
39. DA Morris Papers, i74 Ullathorne to Morris, 10 July 1833.
40. Collins thesis, pp. 137–8.

anarchy of Therry and Connolly's time convinced him that his task was to organise and establish structures, which as soon as possible would be crowned with a resident bishop.

As Ullathorne reported to Morris, Therry initially had required 'some management', regarding the newcomer's ideas as 'absurd' or 'folly'. His second tactic of 'insinuation' was even less successful, but within a couple of months Ullathorne believed that Therry was, 'sincerely with me'.[41] He may have been overgenerous in his estimation of wholehearted support from Therry, who remained unresponsive to Ullathorne's determination to remove Mrs Dwyer and her daughters from the house. His early hostility to the female sitting tenants in the Sydney clergy house, who were Therry's closest confidantes, was not misplaced. Not only was their presence a cause of scandal but their close alliance with Therry, to whom they carried every bit of gossip, was a source of discord between the clergy.[42] Mrs Dwyer had arrived with her late husband Michael, the last of the Irish rebels deported in 1806.[43] He died in 1825, so by the time of Ullathorne's arrival, his widow and daughters were well established in residence, and refused to be shifted until Therry was moved to Campelltown in 1835. The women who found themselves in Australia as the wives of settlers, freed men and civil servants were a tough breed. The upheaval from home and family, the strange and inhospitable conditions and the shortage of female company created a resilience and independence in colonial women. The women he encountered in the colonies taught the inexperienced Ullathorne a good deal about the strengths and capacities of women.

Although Ullathorne came to appreciate Therry's pastoral energy and rapport with the poorest Irish part of the mission, he treated him warily, realising that Therry found it difficult, 'after so long of having full sway, to have to account to another person'.[44] In a letter of almost excessive deference (especially for Ullathorne) he assured Therry of his goodwill, of his refusal to listen to accusations against him and his determination to

---

[41.] DA Morris Papers, i39 Ullathorne to Morris, 17 April 1833.
[42.] DA i74, Ullathorne to Morris, 10 July 1833.
[43.] Collins thesis, pp. 130–1.
[44.] DA i74, Ullathorne to Morris, 10 July 1833.

check any 'inclination to prejudice against you'. The praise of Therry's qualities and Ullathorne's willingness to listen to any 'complaint and remonstrance' offered by Therry are almost out of character, but Ullathorne was determined to give Therry no cause for complaint, in order to win his co-operation.[45]

Ullathorne got off on good terms with the civic officials responsible for the running of the colony and he looked to them as allies in his programme to bring order within the Catholic community. The colonial government had specifically asked for ecclesiastical authority to be brought to bear within the Catholic community, so Ullathorne was pushing at an open door. His early and cordial approaches to Governor Bourke, which led to a speedy resolution of the church land difficulty, got him off to a good start. He wanted structures in place which would enable Catholicism to grow and flourish in Australia and which would facilitate good relations with civil authorities. Catholics in Australia, for all the hardship and lack of priests and churches, enjoyed a political and religious freedom denied them in Ireland and scarcely achieved in England. It was a costly freedom and therefore not to be jeopardised by antagonising the government. Ullathorne wanted to achieve co-operation and a freedom of action within the law of the Church and of the land. Expenses were substantial and his income limited; Governor Bourke did his best to help, sympathising with Ullathorne's appeal for more money when he was travelling two hundred and fifty miles in a week. The Governor applied for an increase for him, but in the meantime 'fudged' it by advising him that he was entitled to a higher rate when travelling 'as vicar general'. 'By vicar general I mean the general superintendence of the Catholic clergy and establishment throughout the colony'.[46] Bourke was a remarkable man, who though not a Catholic himself, was a staunch supporter of Ullathorne. Newly arrived himself less than a year before Ullathorne, he was 'endowed by nature with a rare gift of beauty of manner, he had acquired by discipline, training and experience that other great asset to men in high places, the gift

---

45. SAA Ullathorne File 28, Ullathorne to Therry, 2 October 1833.
46. NSWSA 4/2175.2, Ullathorne to Colonial Secretary, 9 December 1833.

of a presence which both set people at their ease and encouraged them to give of their best'.[47] This he certainly did with the young priest, nearly thirty years his junior.

A petition drawn up in 1832 by Roger Therry, the leading Catholic layman in the colony, for public money to support church maintenance, caused a huge public furore. Provision of space for Catholic worship, and the costs involved, were major headaches for Ullathorne. By the summer of 1835 he was pleading for government money to make provision in Parramatta (where the Catholics had to meet in the gaol), Windsor (which had the shell of a building needing £300 of government subsidy to complete) and Illawara (where a stone and wooden building had been started).[48] Education was, of course, a major headache in establishing a stable and thriving society in the colony and Ullathorne moved quickly to organise Catholic schools in Sydney and Maitland, with government support. There was scope and support in other towns such as Appin, Campbelltown, Parramatta and Windsor, but teachers were at a premium, and Ullathorne became heavily involved in the education campaigns and debates of the 1830s. At times, it seemed, the government did not believe the reports which spoke of the high level of attendance at Catholic schools in Parramatta and in Windsor, where the teachers were too poorly paid to be able to rent large enough schoolrooms, and Ullathorne pleaded for money to educate seventy children.[49]

Ullathorne got involved in a public dispute about school provision in 1834 with the publication of a pamphlet *On the Use and Abuse of Holy Scripture*. This was a direct response to the plan to form a branch of the British and Foreign School Society in the colony, which was a Nonconformist supported body founded in England in 1808, and now receiving British government grants to support its work. Its purpose was the promotion of non-denominational, scriptural teaching in schools. His pamphlet was a sledgehammer treatment of Protestant teaching on Scripture, mocking the idea of 'sola scriptura' and concluding in no fewer than fifteen points why it

[47.] Clark, p. 84.
[48.] NSWSA 4/2270,1 Ullathorne to Colonial Secretary, 1 May 1835.
[49.] NSWSA 4/2224,1 Ullathorne to Colonial Secretary, 24 February 1834, 11 March 1834.

was untenable. These included the assertion that the logic of Protestantism was that no one could be saved unless he could read![50] This was countered by a trenchant defence of Catholic teaching on Scripture and its Divine commission to interpret and teach the law, emphasising the unity of the Church and the Catholic's dependence, 'not on his own frailty, but on the voice of millions uttering united testimony'.[51] Ullathorne was gaining something of a public reputation in the colony, and not always to his own advantage.

In 1836 legislation was passed which gave government funding for the maintenance of churches, and in the same year Governor Bourke and the Catholic Solicitor General John Plunkett attempted to introduce a system of general education.[52] It was immediately seen by non-Catholics as a scheme to benefit the children of Irish Catholic convicts, which Bourke's opponents regarded as the responsibility of the British government, not the colony. A torrent of anti-Catholic abuse poured from the press on an unprecedented scale. In the end, Bourke left the colony the following year and it was thirteen years before Plunkett would chair the first Board of National Education.[53] Nevertheless, the Irish born Plunkett, a friend and supporter of Daniel O'Connell in 1830, was one of Ullathorne's staunchest allies. In 1836, following his appointment as Attorney General, he got the Church Act passed, which effectively disestablished the Anglican Church in Australia and thereby gave equality to the Catholics and Presbyterians.[54] Ullathorne also formed an alliance, and a lifelong friendship, with Sir Roger Therry, another Irish-born lawyer who had a spectacularly successful career in Ireland, but less so in Australia. He did however, under the patronage of Governor Bourke, become Crown Grants Commissioner in 1833 and

[50.] *On the Use and Abuse of Sacred Scripture* (1834), pp. 41–4.
[51.] Ibid., p. 68.
[52.] J. N. Moloney, *John Hubert Plunkett in New South Wales 1832–69*, Ph.D. thesis, Australian National University (1971), p. 34.
[53.] Moloney thesis, p 36.
[54.] F. J. West, 'Plunkett, John Hubert (1802–1869)', *Oxford Dictionary of National Biography*, Oxford University Press, 2004 [http://www.oxforddnb.com/view/article/22417, accessed 12 Sept 2005].

acting Attorney General in 1839, succeeding Plunkett.[55]

Ullathorne became a public and controversial figure in Australia as he got himself increasingly enmeshed in social and political issues. Some of these were domestic Australian matters, material to the future of the Church there, and Collins has discussed them fully. The two issues which dominated his thinking and shaped his future priorities were his involvement in the treatment of criminals, and the scourge of alcohol. His commitment to both causes lasted well beyond his Australian career and, in relation to them, it is possible to explore his emerging human empathy and wisdom and his keen social conscience. An overemphasis on Ullathorne as the framer of institutions has led to the neglect of these aspects of his character.

The management of criminals, apart from the horrific prisons into which the transported convicts were herded, depended largely on the process of 'assignment', by which the entire colony was treated as a gigantic prison from which escape was impossible, and convicts were assigned to work for settlers. Guidelines existed by the time Ullathorne arrived, put in place by Governor Darling, but he had left the colony before effective supervision was put in place.[56] Demand for assigned convict workers always exceeded supply and there were constant disputes between settlers (especially landowners) and the local powers of government. Throughout the 1830s over 60% of male convicts were assigned. Female convicts were much in demand as household servants and shorter in supply, as well as being more subject to the kind of abuse that Ullathorne recorded. 'The poor Irish girls, through being assigned to wicked masters, were not infrequently exposed to great perils, especially in lone and country places.'[57] Convicts and their masters frequently complained about each others' behaviour, which could result in floggings on the one hand or

[55] J. M. Bennett, 'Therry, Sir Roger (1800–1874)', *Oxford Dictionary of National Biography*, Oxford University Press, 2004 [http://www.oxforddnb.com/view/article/27173, accessed 12 Sept 2005].

[56] S. G. Foster, 'Convict Assignment in New South Wales in the 1830s', *Push* No 15, April 1983, pp. 35–80.

[57] *Autobiography*, p. 86.

removal of servants on the other, but this depended on the conscience and powers of entry of local magistrates. Despite further reforms of the system in 1838, assignment was one of the targets which the abolitionists had in their sights. Ullathorne was not wholly ill-disposed towards assignment in principle at least, as he believed that it offered the possibility of reform of life, as long as convicts were removed from the evil company of the hardened and brutalised among them. However, he saw enough of it in action to doubt its practical effectiveness.

Ullathorne travelled a good deal around the settlements of New South Wales, but the single location which had the most powerful effect on him, and seared itself into his memory, was Norfolk Island. He visited Norfolk Island twice, although in his autobiographical account he conflates the two visits into one. His first visit followed a prison riot in January 1834 which had resulted in thirty-one men being condemned to death, and he was there from September to October of that year, accompanied by a Church of England chaplain, Henry Stiles.[58] His second visit was in December 1835. Ullathorne described Norfolk Island himself as, 'about a thousand miles from Sydney. It is small, only about twenty-one miles in circumference; of volcanic origin, and one of the most beautiful spots in the universe'.[59] This tiny speck in the vast southern Pacific Ocean was chosen as the place of ultimate and final punishment for recalcitrant convicts. In 1788 it had been settled by the First Fleet to prevent the French taking it and as a source of pine and flax for ship repairs, though Norfolk pine proved useless for shipbuilding. Gradually its agriculture developed and it provided other resources for Sydney, including wheat and vegetables, while offering a usefully remote spot to dump difficult criminals and officers. However, by 1814, Norfolk Island was deserted, as agriculture had expanded around Sydney, and the remote territory no longer served a useful purpose.[60]

[58.] Ullathorne mistakenly recalls his name as Short in his autobiography. See Collins thesis, p. 252.
[59.] *Autobiography*, p. 113.
[60.] Norfolk Island website – www.pitcairns.org

In 1824, as the New South Wales convict colonies grew in size and complexity, the British government ordered the Governor, Sir Thomas Brisbane, to open up Norfolk Island again as an island prison. It was intended that Norfolk Island's remote inaccessibility would be made to serve as a place of extreme punishment for the most recalcitrant and violent convicts. This dramatically beautiful island became, for the next twenty years, an indescribable hell-hole of human degradation. The breathtaking beauty of Norfolk Island was described by Ullathorne in great detail: he was struck by the 'curious wild shrubs, wild flowers and wild grapery', by the 'intricacy of dark foliage, interluminated with chequers of sunlight, until beyond it opens a receding vista to the blue sea' and the whole verdant, pure and varied environment he found there.[61] He was profoundly struck by the contrast between the pure clear air of the dramatically beautiful surroundings, 'beauty like the shadow of the countenance of the Creator'[62] and the depravity of its unwilling residents. Norfolk Island was a modern Gomorrah, where 'the human heart seemed inverted, and the very conscience reversed'.[63] The only occupants were the military guard, the officials and the convicts. No ship other than a government vessel was permitted to approach the narrow bar in the coral reef which was the only access to the island.[64] The only buildings, when Ullathorne visited, were the prison, barracks and offices, and the governor's mansion. The military barracks and prison and ancillary offices were built around an incongruously elegant Georgian quadrangle, with the governor's house a little further removed, planned to be easily defensible against attack and protected by cannon, with the windows barred.[65] The prison was completed in 1835, containing a central three-storey building accommodating nine hundred and seventy-three prisoners, (although Ullathorne speaks of there being two thousand prisoners when he visited)[66] who slept in rows of hammocks, or in some cases

[61.] *The Catholic Mission in Australasia*, pp. 36–7.
[62.] Ibid., p. 39.
[63.] Ibid., p. 40.
[64.] *Autobiography*, p. 113.
[65.] Ibid., p. 118.
[66.] Ibid., p. 119.

individual wooden cubicles.[67] Until Ullathorne's visit in 1834, no Christian clergyman had ever set foot on Norfolk Island.

Ullathorne and the Reverend Mr Stiles went at the request of the governor, as the condemned men tried after the prison riot were to be executed on Norfolk Island rather than risk further insurrection on board ship. This was an unusual decision, provoked by unique circumstances. So desperate were the convicts of Norfolk Island, that they were murdering each other in the hope of being taken to Sydney for trial; escape was then a remote chance and execution a more likely, and only marginally less welcome, outcome. By imposing trial and execution on Norfolk Island, it was hoped that further insurrection would be discouraged. The remaining prisoners would also witness the executions, rather than seeing their heroes sailing off into the sunset, hopelessly optimistic about the possibility of living to fight another day. Having some sense of what his purpose was there, Ullathorne used his shipping experience to be the first to make the hazardous jump from the ship onto the rocky outcrop which was necessary to avoid the ship being holed. Always conscious of his place in history, Ullathorne was determined to be the first Christian clergyman ashore, but his purpose was not self-aggrandisement. While Mr Stiles and the others were conducted to Government House, Ullathorne insisted on being taken at once to the prison, with a list of the condemned men and those to be reprieved.

He was given five days to prepare those who were to die (three of whom were Catholics, but a further four placed themselves in his care). Mr Stiles therefore had four requiring his ministry. Though both men were totally inexperienced in such work, Ullathorne seems to have adapted more quickly and set the pattern. He spent twelve hours a day with the condemned men, preparing them for death, inculcating a spirit of penitence in them and receiving last messages to be passed on to parents, brothers and sisters. He encouraged them to gather all their thoughts and prayers into one simple phrase, 'Into Thy hands I commend my spirit; Lord Jesus receive my soul', and to think and say nothing else while on the scaffold. He and the thousand convicts brought out to witness the executions

[67.] www.pitcairns.org

were much impressed by the way in which 'they all repeated the prayer I had taught them, aloud in a kind of chorus together, until the ropes stopped their voices for ever'.[68]

Ullathorne also undertook to speak to those who had been reprieved from death by the courts, each of whom 'wept bitterly'[69] at the prospect of continued endurance of the hopeless, violent, dehumanising conditions of Norfolk Island. Ullathorne's experiences there in 1834 and again in 1835 made him into a convinced abolitionist in the political debate about transportation under way in both Britain and Australia, and shaped his attitude to the exercise of corporal punishment. Apart from imbuing Ullathorne with a convinced abolitionist viewpoint, Norfolk Island also affected him profoundly as a sensitive human being. After the executions he continued to spend long days in the stinking holes of cells offering spiritual care to the remaining convicts, most of whom had not seen a clergyman since they boarded the convict ship in England or Ireland, often several years before. His psychological and physical well-being was preserved by the actions of the wife of Major Anderson, the governor of Norfolk Island, who had the determination and Christian devotion to follow her husband into public service in the most extraordinary of circumstances. Mrs Anderson had no illusions about the horrors and the physical and emotional exhaustion which Ullathorne endured during his two visits to the penal colony, and she did her best to alleviate his anguish of mind and body. On his return from the prison and the scaffold where he had been in the midst of unspeakable human degradation and violence, she would take him for a gentle ride before dinner around the most exquisite parts of the breathtakingly beautiful island. It was an act of remarkable perception, to appreciate that he needed to get the stench of blood out of his nostrils and the images of death out of his brain in order to be able to return afresh the next day.

These evening conversations were perhaps his first real social contact with a woman to whom he was not related and he absorbed an important lesson about dealing with women. She told him the story of how the Protestant clergyman who had

---

[68.] *Autobiography*, p. 121.
[69.] Ibid., p. 118.

travelled to Norfolk Island with Ullathorne, had criticised her manner, accusing her, in looking after her husband's guests with courtesy and grace, of affectation. 'But I turned to him,' she told Ullathorne, 'and said, "Mr Short, there is some mistake. I am not Mrs Short".'[70] Ullathorne began to learn from women like Mrs Anderson to respect the dignity and integrity of the female sex, and to value the particular gifts of women who were not always 'the weaker sex'.

Despite the best efforts of Mrs Anderson, the effect of his time on Norfolk Island was to provoke in Ullathorne a kind of nervous collapse from physical and emotional exhaustion. It began with a fever, from which he quickly rallied, but once on board ship back to Sydney, his task completed in so far as it could be, he collapsed into a coma for a week.[71] Once recovered, Ullathorne began to commit himself clearly and publicly to the cause of penal reform, which remained a lifelong commitment, even after the ending of transportation. His developing interest in the purpose and methods of imprisonment took public form later in life as a bishop, when in 1866 he published a substantial pamphlet, *On the Management of Criminals*, in the light of a new Prison Act passed in the previous year.

In 1840, civil authority over Norfolk Island was transferred to Van Diemen's Land. Governor John Franklin appointed Alexander Maconochie, well known in England as a penal reformer, as superintendent of Norfolk Island.[72] He attempted to introduce reforms, but was sacked after four years. Ullathorne admired his principles and applauded his attempted reforms. Maconochie served a brief period as governor of the new Birmingham prison from 1849–51, just as Ullathorne was beginning his life as bishop in Birmingham.[73] When the newly appointed Bishop of Hobart, Ullathorne's friend Robert Willson, paid his first visit to Norfolk Island in

[70] Ibid., pp. 123–4.
[71] Ibid., p. 124.
[72] M. F. G. Selby, 'Maconochie, Sir Alexander (1787–1860)', Rev Felix Driver, *Oxford Dictionary of National Biography*, Oxford University Press, 2004 [http://www.oxforddnb.com/view/article/37725, accessed 12 Sept 2005].
[73] Ibid.

1846, he was appalled by what he found there. Little had apparently changed. Later in the same year he took to London all the evidence of barbarity and torture that he had witnessed there, but a whitewash government report followed and nothing was done. Only after Willson made two further visits and bombarded the government with further evidence of cruelty and depravity and pleaded for action was something done, and the last prisoners were removed from Norfolk Island in 1855.[74]

In 1835, circumstances changed dramatically for Ullathorne in the shape of Bede Polding, his old novice master from Downside, who arrived in Sydney in September of that year with three other priests and four church students. To Ullathorne's immense relief, Polding had really been appointed 'bishop of Botany Bay' and Vicar Apostolic of New South Wales: the onerous burden of ecclesiastical responsibility for the colony was lifted from his shoulders. Or was it? The initial government proposal was that Polding would take responsibility for New South Wales and Ullathorne be removed to Van Diemen's Land.[75] It was Polding who had inspired Ullathorne with a missionary zeal for the Antipodes, although he had never worked outside Downside himself. This lack of experience showed in his governance of New South Wales and in his hopes for creating a large scale monastic mission in the colony with Sydney as an abbey-diocese. The appointment of a vicar apostolic for New South Wales was a remarkable advance for the youthful Australian Church, and a recognition of the importance of it as a mission and not just a gaol. However, it was soon evident, to Ullathorne and to others, that Polding was utterly dependent on him. He was still left to handle all dealings with the civil authorities, so there was little relief for him in being taken out of the front line.[76] It did not take Ullathorne long to realise that he would have to guide his old mentor strongly and carefully. Even as the bishop landed with his new recruits, Ullathorne insisted, before they

[74.] Typescript, J. H. Cullen, *The Catholic Story of Norfolk Island* (Copy loaned by Paul Collins).
[75.] *Historical Records of Australia* Series 2 vol. XVII, Earl of Aberdeen to Sir Richard Bourke, 20 February 1835.
[76.] *Autobiography*, p. 130.

had left the harbour, that one of them, 'a perpetual failure', was sent straight home again on the same ship.[77]

The growth of the Catholic mission in New South Wales during the 1830s was, in Ullathorne's own words, 'almost miraculous',[78] but expansion required personnel to maintain and continue it. Not only were the number of attenders at Mass at St Mary's in Sydney expanding, but a new scheme which he and Polding instituted for dealing with newly arrived Catholic convicts was bearing fruit. Each Catholic transportee was taken directly from the ship to a secluded place, where they were put through a type of retreat for ten days by the priests. The emphasis was on bringing them to a recognition of their position, inculcating a spirit of repentance and determination to serve their sentence peaceably and reform their lives. Only three out of fourteen hundred Catholic convicts who went through the retreat found their way into prison for further crimes committed in the colony, whereas previously it had been crowded with newcomers. In 1836, twenty-six Catholics had been executed for further crimes committed while under sentence: this had dropped to one in the first half of 1837.[79]

Polding, finally fulfilling his own long held dream of serving in Australia, hoped that more English Benedictine missioners would be forthcoming. He nurtured a belief that Australia would become a completely Benedictine mission under the care of the English monks. On 1 May 1836 Polding told Birdsall that he had decided to send Ullathorne to England to select much needed recruits for the mission. Nevertheless, Polding was clearly anxious about his departure. 'How I shall manage without him, I scarcely know ... He is most careful to me. His intelligence, aptitude for business and zeal render him a most valuable coadjutor.'[80] He wrote to Birdsall, 'If any of your confrères are willing to join me I am sure no objection will be raised on your part, but they must be of the right sort – zealous laborious missioners.'[81] Polding's optimism was sadly misplaced.

[77.] Ibid., p 129.
[78.] DA, Ullathorne to Brown, 10 January 1838 (Birt I, p. 193).
[79.] Ibid.
[80.] DA J142, Polding to Birdsall, 1 May 1836.
[81.] DA J168, Polding to Birdsall, 7 June 1836.

Ullathorne left Australia in June 1836, headed for England, and did not return until the last day of 1838. His journey back to England began with a second trip to Van Diemen's Land accompanying Polding, where he was used as the bishop's instrument in suspending the unfortunate Connolly. He then took ship via New Zealand, Cape Horn and South America before crossing the Atlantic. It was far from being a prosperous voyage, being led by an incompetent ship's captain who was too busy having an affair with one of the passengers to pay due attention on the bridge. He took the ship into danger of icebergs (by sailing too far south) and of starvation, due to his inability to find his way to Rio de Janiero and was nearly subject to a mutiny. The company on board ship was little to Ullathorne's liking, and he spent much of the time reading and writing or trying to feed an indigenous South American bird he had been given in Rio. Unfortunately, no one on board had any idea what a 'Great Crested Screamer' ate, and so it died. This was hardly surprising, as the Horned Screamer or Southern Screamer comes from a family of ducks and geese which flourish in the swampy backwaters, vegetation-choked lagoons and lakes of wetlands. Apart from Ullathorne breaking up a fight between two other passengers, 'nothing particular occurred during the rest of the voyage', but it made him one of a very small number of Victorian Englishmen to have circum-navigated the world.[82] This dull voyage was the start of what he called 'the two most eventful years of my life'.[83]

Two things became very clear to him during his absence from Australia. He became increasingly convinced that the connections between the English Benedictines and those in Australia could not continue as a permanent arrangement, and that the idea that Australia was an English Benedictine mission, as Polding dreamed, had no future. Distance, as much as anything else made it hopelessly impractical:

On the proposed connection between our body in England and in Australia, on mature deliberation it appears to me, as also to Mr Barber, impossible to have a

[82.] *Autobiography*, pp. 137–41.
[83.] Ibid., p. 142.

practical connection of government between the two countries considering that the space of twelve months must be allowed for any mutual communication. Reverse the case, put yourself in our position. Suppose the source of authority to be in Australia and England a province, you will at once, without my expanding the circumstances of the case, see the difficulty of anything like a practical exercising of authority, even in cases of appeal and how much it must enfeeble, and weaken the confidence of local authority.[84]

He was also clear that an episcopal hierarchy would be needed very soon to enable the local exercise of authority and leadership to be placed on a proper footing. A solitary bishop, with the limited authority of a vicar apostolic, was no good. His lack of confidence in Polding was also already evident, though he veiled his unease in pompous generalities, '... a filiation with its own internal structure of government, the bishop provincial with due checks is the only flexible, prudential plan. Its value to Australia would be unquestionable and the sacrifice would be all on your side, but this would not be much greater than has already been made, and the very essence of religion is sacrifice'.[85] Nevertheless, Polding's ambition for the Australian mission held sway. In January 1838 (during Ullathorne's absence), a rescript came through from Rome placing the Australian mission under the direct control of the English Benedictines for as long as Polding and his successors were members of the English Benedictine Congregation.[86]

Soon after arriving in England, Ullathorne was summoned to Rome to give some account of the progress of Catholicism in Australia. This was the first of ten visits to the Eternal City which he would make over the next thirty years or so, on business connected with the Church in Australia or England. The invitation to Rome came from Cardinal Thomas Weld, who, as bishop, had presented Ullathorne to the subdiaconate at Downside in 1828. He was now resident in Rome, with his

84. DA J357, Ullathorne to Brown, 27 February 1837.
85. Ibid.
86. DA Ullathorne Papers 756, Collier to Ullathorne, 13 January 1838.

daughter and son-in-law (Lord Clifford) at the centre of an influential circle of English expatriates.[87] En route to Rome, Ullathorne fell into the company of Prosper Guéranger, the Frenchman who went on to restore Benedictine life in France through his monastery of Solesmes, which also influenced reformed monasticism in England and further afield. They travelled part of the way to Rome in each other's company, and lived together in the monastery of San Callisto, while Guéranger obtained formal approval for his new foundation and Ullathorne encountered the cardinals of the Roman curia and the pope himself. At the end of his life, when Solesmes was influencing reforms at Stanbrook, he still recalled Guéranger with affection, and with some pride:

> I was the first professed monk, he told me, he had ever seen. I therefore claim some interest in the monks and nuns of Solesmes, who are his children, and I shall be obliged if you will tell the abbess and community that I claim an interest in them and their prayers, as I also claim some right to thank them for their tender and sisterly care of the Abbess of Stanbrook.[88]

The two men were almost the same age, and obviously got on well. They talked of church history and of the writings of the Fathers as they travelled, and Guéranger educated the Englishman in European art as they visited Genoa, Pisa, Florence and Siena on their way to the Eternal City. These Renaissance treasuries must have been a revelation to Ullathorne, who had not before had the opportunity to experience art other than glimpses of medieval architecture in York as a boy. Few of the ports he had seen on his travels had offered much in the way of aesthetic stimulus. Beauty had, so far, only been encountered through Divine creation in the natural world rather than human. Ullathorne's artistic education continued in Rome as he encountered its treasury of museums, galleries and churches. Keeping in mind the needs

---

[87.] Judith Champ, *The English Pilgrimage to Rome: a dwelling for the soul* (2000), pp. 158–60.
[88.] Stanbrook 88, Ullathorne to Abbess, 29 September 1885.

of Australia, he collected a lot of cheap reproductions of religious art to decorate the simple churches and chapels in the colony. He particularly mentioned that he was pleased to get a picture of a black saint (he does not say who), 'having an eye to the Aborigines'.[89]

Ullathorne was an unusual Victorian Englishman in his sympathy and understanding for other races, particularly the Australian native peoples. They were rapidly being decimated by white settlers who either murdered them for sport or introduced habits and diseases to which they had no natural resistance. 'The decay of fringe dwelling blacks on the edge of white urban culture ... was inexorable and all-pervasive, to sympathetic onlookers it seemed a plague, and to racist ones a bestial joke.'[90] Typical colonial accounts of 'the blacks' included sensational press stories of violent attacks on white servants and livestock, such as that in the *Sydney Morning Herald* of 21 May 1838, in which 300 aborigines were alleged to have coordinated a 'desperate outrage'.[91] One of the popular stories illustrative of attitudes to the native Australians was of a runaway convict, George Clark, who disguised himself as an aboriginal native to evade recapture and lived a 'degenerate' life until the police caught up with him.[92] Ullathorne appreciated quickly that, 'we were the intruders upon their dominions, not they upon ours' and was in no doubt about the effects of this: 'Whenever the white man came, the tribe was ruined by the communication of his vices and by drink.'[93] Even more surprisingly, when government policy was to convert them to Christianity, he took the trouble to gain some understanding of the Aboriginal understanding of religion, which did not involve a concept of God, but a transmigration of souls and, 'great fears of a malignant spirit'.[94] He understood that generations of tribal religion and culture would not be eradicated, and that contact with European culture was as likely to corrupt as to convert them. Ullathorne displayed a remarkable

[89.] *Autobiography*, p. 150.
[90.] Hughes, p. 274.
[91.] http//setis.library.usyd.au
[92.] Ibid.
[93.] *Autobiography*, p. 81.
[94.] Ibid.

sensitivity to the native peoples and to the land which was being wrenched from them, wistfully recalling the tradition that the first gift from Captain Cook's party accepted by the Botany Bay tribe had been 'the axe which was destined to clear their woods and to make way for the white man'.[95]

Ullathorne came to love Rome, but his first encounter was disheartening. He had scarcely caught a glimpse of the pope at the Holy Saturday ceremonies, when he was bundled out of the Sistine Chapel by a Swiss Guard for not wearing his habit – which, of course, he did not even possess! This was followed swiftly by his first meeting with Cardinal Luigi Fransoni (Prefect of *Propaganda Fide*) and Pope Gregory XVI, both of whom greeted him with the same remark – 'Quel giovane!' (What a youth!)[96] After these dampening indignities, Ullathorne decided to keep his head down and work on his report, which eventually was received with keen interest and approval, and won round the Roman authorities to the serious young monk. 'You will know how much the Holy See was pleased with Dr Ullathorne's account of the Australian mission. At first they thought him a very young man, but by degrees they began to see his merits, gave him the title of DD and parted with him with many expressions of esteem.'[97]

Rome in the 1830s was being reclaimed by English pilgrims and tourists in the wake of the end of the Napoleonic Wars and the Catholic Emancipation Act of 1829. The Papal States, which straddled the peninsula from Rome, north east to just south of Venice, were still in considerable turmoil. The revolutionary ideas which had taken root during the Napoleonic period of occupation were stirring movements towards democracy, independence from papal rule and unification of the diverse and fragmented Italian states. Despite the unrest throughout the Italian peninsula, many of the key figures in the English Catholic revival found their way to Rome during that decade, including Ambrose Phillips de Lisle, John Henry Newman, George Ignatius Spencer, the 16th Earl of Shrewsbury and his family, and of course, the Weld / Clifford

[95] Ibid., p. 82.
[96] Ibid., p. 144.
[97] Ampleforth, H. Collins (Subiaco) to T. Fisher (Liverpool), 31 August 1837.

family.[98] Thomas Walsh, who Ullathorne would eventually succeed as Vicar Apostolic in the Midlands, was among a group of bishops from Britain staying in the English College, who treated the young English monk with 'great kindness'. They and the monks of S Callisto and the Roman curial officials did their best to make Ullathorne feel at home, and his time in Rome between Holy Week and the feast of Corpus Christi, was clearly one of 'tranquillity' for him, which restored his energies. He even recalled how, wearing his monastic habit for the first time forced him to walk more slowly than usual and therefore to think more slowly too.[99]

One of the key figures in Rome was Nicholas Wiseman, then rector of the English College, and when Ullathorne met him for the first time, he had recently returned from a visit to England filled with the possibilities of revived Catholic life. However, Ullathorne's main recollection of Wiseman was from after the sudden death of Cardinal Weld. At the funeral in S Marcello al Corso, he was hissed by the Romans for preaching for too long, when they wanted to hear more of the Mozart Requiem which was being sung by the choir.[100] Ullathorne's attention though, was still focused, not on the English Catholic revival, but on the needs of the fragile Australian Church. Having completed his business in Rome, he made his way back to England overland, visiting abbeys at Perugia, Florence and Bologna on the way.

His main focus now had to be on recruiting priests to go back to Australia with him, and he publicised this by publishing his pamphlet, *The Catholic Mission in Australasia* and giving public lectures on the subject wherever he could. Raising funds proved easier than raising manpower in England, but Ireland was more profitable. Archbishop Murray of Dublin and Bishop Kinsella of Ossory were enthusiastic, as was the president of the main Irish seminary at Maynooth. He was able to recruit a priest and five seminarians from Ossory, as well as Frs Geoghan and Coffey, all of whom accompanied him back to Australia, or followed soon after. His other acquisition in

---

[98.] Judith Champ, *The English Pilgrimage to Rome*, pp. 137–67.
[99.] *Autobiography*, p. 151.
[100.] Ibid., p 46.

Dublin was the twelve volume first edition set of Luther's works, which the Irishmen teased him about, but which he insisted would accompany him back to Australia, where they still form a rare and valuable part of the library of St Patrick's College, Manly.[101]

The greatest and most far-reaching success of the visit to Ireland was his contact with Mary Aikenhead, foundress of the Sisters of Charity. For a man whose intimate contact with women had been limited to his long-suffering and devout mother and his younger sisters, Ullathorne developed a ready sympathy for and understanding of the position of women in the convict colony. He met many examples of domestic violence, one of his earliest household visits being to tend a woman who 'lay near to death' having been savagely beaten by her husband.[102] Such cases were not unusual, for as Ullathorne soon realised, convict women would embark on any semblance of marriage to gain their freedom. Freed convict men were given the opportunity to 'choose' a wife from among those who volunteered themselves at the female factory at Parramatta. Ullathorne saw no real harm in this arrangement, which could offer the prospect of a stable home life for both partners, as long as the couple settled at a safe distance from public houses.

Ullathorne was one of many men with experience of Australia who colluded in the derogatory and often unjust descriptions of women convicts. His view has been very much the accepted one, until challenged by historians in recent years, who have concluded, rather, that, 'convict women were small time sneak thieves and robbers whose human capital compared favourably with workers left behind in Ireland and England: many convict women were literate, numerate, skilled and semi-skilled workers in their most productive and repro-ductive years'.[103] The hostile and negative judgements on the women by contemporary men can be associated with class, language and morality. The Australian penal code criminalised working-class behaviour, which in other situations would have

[101.] Ibid., pp. 159–60.
[102.] Ibid., p. 86.
[103.] Deborah Oxley, 'Representing Convict Women' in Ian Duffield and James Bradley (eds), *Representing Convicts: new perspectives on convict forced labour migration* (1997), p. 88.

gone unremarked. Even the Board of Management of the Female Factory at Parramatta noted how quickly female servants were sent back, 'for awkwardness or misbehaviour which, in free servants, would be noticed by a gentle reproof'.[104] It seems that these women were often condemned for swearing, smoking, answering back, speaking Irish and for the immorality which was endemic in a male-dominated colony.

Women, Ullathorne observed, were even more likely than men to go wild on their release, especially under the influence of alcohol, and become 'the wildest and most scandalous of reprobates'.[105] Like his fellow Victorians, he clearly thought of women as weaker than men and more capable of foolishness. He regarded the female convicts as, 'far more difficult of reformation than the man'[106] yet less blameworthy than the men, since they were placed under constant pressure. The convict ships were effectively floating brothels, where young girls were corrupted by older women and both on assignments and in the female factory at Parramatta, sexual depravity, violence and abuse were rampant, so that at times the military were brought in to restore order.[107] There were few women around, and drunkenness, promiscuity and bigamy were major problems in dealing with the female convicts.

Ullathorne gave no indication in his letters or autobiography of when he came to realise that a solution to some of these perceived difficulties might be met by religious sisters, nor did he hint at the radicalism of his plan. By 1837, active uncloistered religious sisters were beginning to emerge onto the Irish and (to a lesser extent) English scene. In Dublin, Ullathorne met two of the leading women in this new phenomenon, Catherine McAuley, foundress of the Sisters of Mercy, and Mary Aikenhead, foundress of the Sisters of Charity. In a quite matter-of-fact way he recalled not being over impressed with the formality of the Sisters of Mercy, but quickly arranged with Mary Aikenhead, 'a filiation of five sisters to accompany me to

---

[104.] Quoted in Oxley, p. 91.
[105.] *Autobiography*, p. 90.
[106.] *The Catholic Mission in Australasia*, p. 26.
[107.] Ibid., p. 28.

Sydney'.[108] The five Sisters of Charity from Dublin who returned with Ullathorne to Australia were the first women religious to set foot there, but Ullathorne seemed (at least on the surface) to be oblivious to what he was asking of them and the novelty of what he was proposing, at a time when female religious were still a rarity even in the streets of Dublin and London. Nevertheless, the plan came to fruition, as he told Brown the following year: 'I have five excellent Sisters of Charity busily preparing to sail with me'.[109]

They became very important, not only in the foundations of Australian Catholic life, but in Ullathorne's own life, and fifty years later, he took great delight in celebrating a, 'singular jubilee with the Sisters of Charity with the breadth of the world between us'.[110] By then, the five sisters had become, 'more than a hundred and ten sisters, have a large hospital in Sydney of a hundred and fifty beds and then in Parramatta, in the very house in which I placed them, an orphanage, a young ladies college, and teach three thousand children besides, and are about to establish another hospital in Melbourne, towards which one lady has offered £10,000'.[111]

It was evident to Ullathorne that the Australian mission was becoming increasingly Irish, and that the future of Catholic Australia lay in the hands of the Irish. He already knew that a high proportion of convicts were from Ireland, and discovered why, when he visited there for himself. At first hand he witnessed the strains of Irish Catholic life under British rule, and the poverty of tenant farmers scraping a living from the land. The poorest Irishmen thought that, by committing a petty crime or two, which would earn them transportation, they could gain free passage to a new life and an escape from rural poverty. It was only someone with Ullathorne's direct experience who could remove this 'monstrous delusion', and to do so, he was asked by the Irish Secretary to spell out the reality. In his pamphlet, *The Horrors of Transportation Briefly Unfolded to the People*, he tried to show the difference between

[108.] *Autobiography*, p. 161.
[109.] DA Birt Collection, Ullathorne to Brown, 21 June 1838.
[110.] DA Birt Collection, Ullathorne to ?, 14 January 1889.
[111.] Ibid.

emigration and transportation in a way which 'applied to the popular mind stingingly'.[112] The Irish church leaders he met were aware of this problem, and of the need for Irish clergy in the convict colony. They had already contemplated a distinctive seminary or extension to Maynooth to supply priests for Australia, and there was even talk of bringing the Church in Australia under the care of the Irish hierarchy.[113]

Thus, Ullathorne, who had left Australia believing he was recruiting personnel for a predominantly English Benedictine operation, was brought firmly to the view that this was not the case. There was a distinct reluctance to release further monastic manpower to go abroad, and even Ullathorne's friend Brown had urged Birdsall not to send any more men abroad.[114] Birdsall, who had been President General since 1826, and from whom Ullathorne had parted coolly in 1832, died in 1837, but this made no difference to the English Benedictine attitude: they had more than enough missions to man in England. The refusal of the English Benedictines to release any more monks to Australia, combined with his Irish experience, made him realise that any idea of 'Benedictinising the colony', which he had thought 'both feasible and desirable', was dead. Before he had even returned to Australia, he began to see that, because of this, his own long-term future might lie elsewhere.[115] While irritated by Birdsall's refusal to release any more men, he was realistic about the future.

> It is a subject to me of very deep regret. This failure will have much to do with my own future destiny. With all this failure in England, the colony will become, of course, an Irish mission, and perhaps ought to be so. I shall most likely leave the mission myself in the course of three years, for under the circumstances I should probably be an obstacle to the mission's advancement and shall content myself with forwarding it in England. I speak this

---

[112.] DA K85, Ullathorne to Brown, 2 August 1838.
[113.] Ibid.
[114.] Alban Hood, '"Stirring up the pool": Bishop Thomas Joseph Brown, OSB and the dispute between the hierarchy and the Benedictines' in *Recusant History* vol. 25 (2000), p. 316.
[115.] DA K85, Ullathorne to Brown, 2 August 1838.

after serious deliberation and have advised with (sic) more than one wise head on the subject. To do anything Benedictine in the colony is now out of the question, and I see not amongst stronger reasons of utility to the Church, why I should secularise myself.[116]

During his recruitment visits to England and Ireland, Ullathorne had, unwittingly, become something of a public figure, especially for his publicly expressed views on the perils of the transportation system. The eminent Catholic priest and historian, Dr John Lingard, had, without Ullathorne's knowledge, placed a copy of his *Catholic Mission in Australasia* in the hands of an MP of his acquaintance. The result was a summons to give evidence to the parliamentary committee being convened to consider the future of transportation:

I have received a letter from Mr Molesworth, chairman of the committee of enquiry into the efficiency etc. of transportation, putting a series of questions and asking whether I should object to be summoned to give evidence. Now I have read the report already published – about a thousand pages folio, the horrors brought forward by the parties examined with all of whom I am acquainted, completely throw my statements into the shadow, yet as to their general accuracy I can attest.[117]

The Molesworth Committee sat during the course of 1837–8 and played some part (though perhaps not the decisive part) in the ending of transportation to New South Wales.[118] Ullathorne was not a lone voice in the 1830s crying against the system of transportation. English missionaries and Australian colonists shared his views in growing numbers. All opponents were agreed that the system of assigning convicts as servants and workers in the colony was the most damaging aspect of the

116. DA K77, Ullathorne to Heptonstall, 11 July 1838.
117. DA K2, Ullathorne to Brown, 10 January 1838.
118. John Ritchie, 'Towards Ending an Unclean Thing: the Molesworth committee and the Abolition of Transportation to New South Wales 1837–40' in *Australian Historical Studies* vol. 17 (1976) pp. 144–64.

system as it affected human dignity and the possibilities of penal reform. However, the landowners and businessmen beginning to build the economic foundations of a new country depended on assigned labour. Whatever the inherent difficulties, assignment was widely believed to be vital. Too many commercial interests were involved to make reform straightforward.

The committee established in 1837 was chaired by the twenty-six-year-old William Molesworth, who had proposed its formation in the House of Commons, one of a string of radical political moves during his political career. Molesworth himself was a wealthy Cornish heir to a baronetcy, and MP for East Cornwall. A self-proclaimed radical, he entertained a fantasy of political revolution, leading inevitably to disillusion. This did not, however, destroy his early interest in the British colonies and their reform, and in 1833 he joined the committee of the South Australian Association. This made him a natural choice to chair the committee on the transportation question.[119] Australia and transportation was not his only sphere of interest – Canada and New Zealand also came within his view, and he was ferocious about his colleagues' conduct of colonial government, which he described in March 1838 as, 'government by the misinformed with responsibility to the ignorant'.[120]

Not only his youth and his outspoken radicalism made Molesworth an extraordinary figure, but he was obviously something of a dandy, greeting an astonished Ullathorne for the first time in a silk flowered dressing gown![121] The young clergyman was not the only one to find Molesworth unlikely. His fellow radical, Richard Cobden described him as 'a youthful, florid-looking man of foppish and conceited air'.[122] The

---

[119.] Peter Burroughs, 'Molesworth, Sir William, eighth baronet (1810–1855)', *Oxford Dictionary of National Biography*, Oxford University Press, 2004 [http://www.oxforddnb.com/view/article /18902, accessed 12 Sept 2005].

[120.] Ibid.

[121.] *Autobiography*, p. 163.

[122.] Peter Burroughs, 'Molesworth, Sir William, eighth baronet (1810–1855)', *Oxford Dictionary of National Biography*, Oxford University Press, 2004 [http://www.oxforddnb.com/view/article /18902, accessed 12 Sept 2005].

committee naturally included a cross-section of political and social opinion and had sufficient 'big guns' to give it credibility, including Lord John Russell, the Home Secretary, Sir George Grey, Under Secretary for War and the Colonies, Viscount Howicke, Secretary at War and Sir Robert Peel, Leader of the Opposition.[123]

Between April 1837 and August 1838 the Molesworth Committee met thirty-eight times and examined twenty-three witnesses, one of them being Ullathorne.[124] The evidence he gave to the Molesworth Committee was based on the text of his two pamphlets, *The Catholic Mission to Australasia* and *The Horrors of Transportation*, both published in England and Ireland in 1837. The taking of evidence, framing of questions, choice of witness and the final report was manufactured to produce Molesworth's desired result, and Ullathorne was not the only one who was put under personal pressure by the chairman to give the 'right' sort of evidence.[125] Certainly some of the questions put to Ullathorne were leading, for instance, 'Are the less hardened convicts, do you think, liable to ill-treatment and outrage and ridicule from their more hardened associates?'

It is clear that Ullathorne was already beginning to develop his philosophy of prison reform (drawing on his Australian experience) which he would give voice to in his pamphlet of 1866, *On the Management of Criminals*.

> I see clearly that they have not yet got hold of the right thread of ideas – viz. the effect of the system upon the minds and feelings of the prisoner and the specific result in his moral habit, nor have they got anything satisfactory about Norfolk Island. I believe my being examined would be of very great advantage as well to our cause as to the giving corrected views of the workings of transportation.[126]

[123.] Ritchie, p. 147.
[124.] Ibid., p. 149.
[125.] *Autobiography*, p. 163, 'When we came to a very embarrassing point, I told him I was doubtful whether I ought to speak on it. He pulled up his head, gave me a menacing look, and said, "Do you know how grave would be the consequence of your refusing?"'.
[126.] DA K2, Ullathorne to Brown, 10 January 1838.

Ullathorne gave detailed evidence on 8 and 12 February, which ran to twenty-two closely printed pages, answering questions on the ships, processing of convicts on arrival, the assignment system, further criminality including sexual deviance, Norfolk Island and finally on his general view of the transportation system. He stated categorically his conviction that, 'hitherto it has utterly failed as a means of reformation'.[127] Not only did the system fail in its effect on the prisoners for the most part, but also as a deterrent, which meant that he was busy in Ireland trying to convince men of the horrors facing transportees and dissuade poor deluded Irishmen from thinking it a free passage to a new life.

The conclusion was that the system had failed as a means of reforming convicts and as a deterrent, and had debased the residents of the colonies. The conclusions seem to have been written in advance of the evidence. 'The collection, the presentation and the interpretation of the evidence was unfair; the conclusions presented in the report amounted to an unprincipled indictment'.[128] It was not the dramatic turning point in the campaign for abolition which Ullathorne portrays, but rather part of a developing programme of penal reform under the Whig government. Lord John Russell had already introduced proposals for penal reform into Parliament before Molesworth even began sitting.[129] 'The abolition of regular transportation to New South Wales in 1840 was one example of administrative gradualism. There was less of a revolutionary change in the system than an evolutionary redirection'.[130]

However, Ullathorne's involvement in the Molesworth Committee, his outspoken evidence and public lectures on the subject, and the final heavily weighted report which degraded the whole of New South Wales, portraying it as 'the moral quagmire of the Empire'.[131] was disastrous for his own future in Australia. He had publicly taken up a moral position on

[127.] Minutes of Evidence taken before the Select Committee on Transportation, House of Commons Parliamentary Papers vol. 22 (1837–8), pp. 14–37.
[128.] Ritchie, p. 149.
[129.] Ibid., p. 159.
[130.] Ibid., p. 164.
[131.] Ibid., p. 150.

transportation and its effects which would travel ahead of him in the press back to Australia, and make enemies among wealthy settlers to greet his return. For Ullathorne, Molesworth was his first direct experience of the workings of government and Parliament and he overestimated its significance and his own role. It was a more valuable experience for a young priest than it was for Parliament. The most absorbing part of the whole experience was not giving evidence to a rigged committee, but passing many of his winter evenings in London sitting in the Strangers' Gallery of the House of Commons listening to the business of Parliament and 'studying men and things' often accompanied by Daniel O'Connell or Richard Shiel.[132] In later years he turned this experience to good effect in his dealings with government over penal reform, convent inspection and education questions.

The voyage back to Australia, accompanied by two priests and the Sisters of Charity was, unusually, one when he was glad to see the anchor dropped. 'I had more anxieties on the voyage out than I ever had in my life.'[133] Called upon to intervene in disputes and even fights between passengers and members of the crew, and preoccupied with protecting the dignity and privacy of the Sisters of Charity under his care, he arrived at Sydney on the last day of 1838 ill-prepared for what was to face him, and in poor health. Within weeks, he was on sick leave. 'Dr Ullathorne is very poorly in health. It is however hoped that a little rest from all his clerical duties may bring him round. The bishop has therefore *prohibited* him to exercise his functions unless in extraordinary emergencies.'[134] His relationship with the wider community of the colony deteriorated rapidly and despite Polding's care for his health, he found the difficulties with his bishop gone from bad to worse. The last two years in Australia were markedly different from those which had preceded his European trip, and the strain quickly told on his physical and psychological health. Tired out from travelling England and Ireland, as well as visiting Rome, and a

---

[132]. *Autobiography*, p. 164.
[133]. DA K275, Ullathorne to Brown, 18 October 1839.
[134]. MDMC Box 34 Murphy Papers, Francis Murphy to John Fitzpatrick, 19 February 1839.

trying voyage back to Australia, his confidence in what he was doing drained away and he felt increasingly isolated and ill at ease.

His only consolation was the immediate success of the sisters with the female convicts, especially in the Female Factory at Parramatta, where they made huge improvements in a short time, though he omits to mention that there was a riot there in May 1839.[135] The Female Factories acted, 'not only as prisons, but also as workhouses, as well as labour and marriage bureaux', so there was plenty for the sisters to do. He lived at Parramatta in order to support the sisters, and travelled weekly to Sydney to deal with matters with Polding.

> The nuns are doing wonders at the factory. Cursing has almost ceased among the Catholic prisoners. These good ladies have divided them into three classes which are attended three times every day. They also attend the hospitals in Parramatta and have converted the only two Protestants whom they found in one of the wards. [136]

Typically, he had taken control, and despite a few irritations, he had

> had it all my own way from the beginning. It is a community of saints. I have had almost to recast the greater part of them, there is something radically wrong in Mrs Aikenhead's management, but she has most valuable subjects ... We have two novices. I believe the prayers of the convent have brought things about more than anything else.[137]

Once again, he may have overstated his case. In fact, Governor Darling had reformed the Female Factories in the

---

[135.] Joy Damousi, '"What punishment will be sufficient for these rebellious hussies?" Headshaving and Convict women in the Female Factories 1820s to 1840s' in Ian Duffield and James Bradley (eds), *Representing Convicts: new perspectives on convict forced labour migration* (1997) p. 204.

[136.] MDMC Box 34 Murphy Papers, Francis Murphy to John Fitzpatrick, 19 February 1839.

[137.] DA K275, Ullathorne to Brown, 18 October 1839.

1820s into three classes, the first being the recently arrived or the destitute, the second being those who had been returned from assignment for bad behaviour or who had progressed from the third class, which was the penitentiary, enduring hard labour every morning.[138] Nevertheless, the impact of the kindly, dignified, courteous and well-motivated nuns on the women enduring humiliating punishments such as head-shaving and wearing punishment uniforms must have been extraordinary.[139] Ullathorne formed a close bond with the sisters, appointing himself (understandably) as their protector, even escorting them between the convent and the Female Factory, particularly after they had a startling encounter on the road with a transvestite.[140] Collins suggests that he became somewhat over involved in the working of the convent and had to be warned to back off a little.[141] He also hints that his close friendship with one of the sisters might have added to the psychological and emotional pressures which drove him to leave Australia for good.[142]

He was soon desperate to leave Australia, for a combination of reasons. Polding's failure of leadership was one key element, the other was the savage treatment accorded him in the Australian press over his outspoken views on transportation. Thirdly, there developed obvious antagonism between him and two of the priests he had recruited, Murphy and Lovat, who lived with Polding in Sydney, while Ullathorne was removed to Parramatta.[143] He had, as he put it himself, 'deeply wounded both freemen and emancipists in two ways, had touched them in two most sensitive points, in their pride and in their pockets'.[144] *The Australian*, within days of his return, reported his evidence to the Molesworth Committee in scathing terms, accusing him of violating justice and truth. 'For whatever purpose he offended principles that we desire to uphold – he offended us as the representative of a large body

[138]. Damousi, p. 206.
[139]. Ibid., p. 207.
[140]. *Autobiography*, p. 181.
[141]. Collins thesis, pp. 341–2.
[142]. Ibid., pp. 357–8.
[143]. Ibid., pp. 345–54.
[144]. *Autobiography*, p. 176.

of our fellow colonists – he must have offended his own conscience – and he has offended God'.[145] Undaunted, Ullathorne knocked on the door of *The Australian* and demanded an apology – characteristically, not for himself but for Polding who, he believed, had been insulted in the article.

He got his apology but the anti-Catholic tone of *The Australian* did not abate, provoking him into establishing a rival Catholic newspaper, the *Australasian Chronicle*, which appeared on 2 August 1839.[146] Its first number defended the need for a Catholic paper in light of the warning in one of the other Sydney papers against dealing with Catholic tradesmen or servants, on the grounds that they would rob their neighbours with impunity.[147] It seems that the old tribal enmities towards Catholicism had been translated into the new world from the old, and the attitudes typical of Victorian England were to be found alive and well in Her Majesty's colonies. Ullathorne used his pen vigorously to counter prejudice in the columns of the *Australasian Chronicle* and elsewhere; it prepared him for what he would encounter on his return to England, though he would never again find himself quite so much the personal target as in New South Wales. The culmination was a public meeting at which he defended himself from 'being selected as the mark by which to attack the Catholic community ... I have been accused of various uncharitable and bigoted acts perpetrated in the course of my Christian ministry'.[148] These public conflicts gained him the unpleasant nickname of the 'Very Reverend Agitator General' and he bore the brunt of opposition towards the ending of transportation, without feeling support from either his bishop or the other lay and clerical leaders in the colony.[149]

Increasingly convinced that the English Benedictine future in Australia was limited, and facing frequent criticism with little support or encouragement, he began to long to return to Downside. The circumstances of his last years in Australia were

---

145. *The Australian*, 15 January 1839.
146. B. J. McGrath, 'Catholic Journalism in New South Wales to 1850' in *Journal of the Australian Catholic History Society* 1/3 1964, p. 28.
147. *The Australasian Chronicle*, vol. 1 No. 1 Friday 2 August 1839.
148. *The Australian*, 6 August 1839.
149. *Autobiography*, p. 194.

singularly trying, especially in having to virtually control his old novice master and now bishop, Polding. This sat awkwardly with Ullathorne and he found it a strain, fighting his own propensity for asserting authority while wanting to see canonical order established. His situation drove him almost to despair:

> What would I give to live the simplicity of obedience in St Gregory's. No one but who has experienced it, knows the pain of the evil effect on self of being obliged to govern and almost command your own superior, and he a bishop. God help me, my dear friend, what a confidential letter I have written to you; pray for me, counsel me.[150]

A combination of public and personal stress, combined with his growing conviction that the future of the Australian mission lay in Irish secular hands rather than English Benedictine ones persuaded him that his time there was coming to an end. The last straw was the prospect of an episcopal appointment. As plans for expanding the leadership of the Australian mission were put in place, including the appointment of an auxiliary bishop for Van Diemen's Land, it was obvious that Ullathorne would be a candidate for this post. This might have seemed a solution to everyone's problems, removing Ullathorne from under his enemies' noses, separating him from the clergy who clearly resented him and giving him relative freedom from Polding. There was only one problem. Ullathorne was determined to flee before it became a reality which tied him to Polding and to Australia for ever.

He was all set to leave in the autumn of 1839, even having his passage booked, when Polding won him round with a promise of better organisation and appropriate management of the other clergy and of finance. He was also given control of the small seminary he had founded.[151] However, even as he confided to Brown what had happened, he knew that his

---

[150.] DA K275, Ullathorne to Brown, 18 October 1839.
[151.] K. T. Livingstone, *The Emergence of an Australian Catholic Priesthood 1835–1915* (1977), p. 11.

enemies ('the bigots') had not disappeared, and he agreed to stay only 'for the present'.

> Entre Nous, my dear confrère, I have had much to suffer from the bishop's weaknesses. I have twice entreated permission to give up the vicar generalship, and twice resolved to return to my order. I had nearly completed my arrangements last week and had actually taken my cabin ... Dr P's penchant for the mission makes him neglect business, the government correspondence is in a scandalous state, the duties towards the clergy and general business, done or put off or abandoned according to impulse ... His eyes are at length open, he confesses it is only such a trial as I have put him to would have done it. He wrote me letter upon letter in most yearning language and could not understand why I should leave him ... He admits he has not treated me well and that I am justified in my intention of leaving him, confesses he has not firmness enough to govern the Church, that if I go, all things must be confused, that there is none to succeed me whom the clergy will look up to, and surrenders the management of all affairs into my hands. I have insisted as a basis of all arrangements, a statement of accounts and that he live by himself separate from the clergy in whose hands he has put himself, that all may have equal access to him, that he will conceal nothing from me in which the Church is interested. That when a thing is once deliberated upon and decided, it should be committed to execution and not changed by the first flitting whim or nearest influence. On these terms with the public invitation of the bishop and clergy I consent to remain for the present. There will be much congratulation in the Church and much sorrow among the bigots at the news of my remaining ...[152]

He found it easier to resign once things were on a slightly better footing and relations with Polding had improved, rather than leaving in a huff or seeming to run away. He seized the

---

[152.] DA K275, Ullathorne to Brown, 18 October 1839.

opportunity of the 'present promising and prosperous state of things to fulfil my intention of retiring' and managed to convinced Polding that it was for the best.

> The bishop, after a struggle with himself, has at length come into my wish, says it is arranged by providence for the greater ultimate service of the mission, as he trusts I shall be allowed to have an eye to the general interests of the colonies etc. etc. ... I am coming away from a contemplated coadjutorship held out here, and I know of nothing that could induce me to go there (Van Diemen's Land). I write this of course in confidence.[153]

Ullathorne's mind was made up, not (as has been suggested) because of 'ambitious tendencies',[154] but from despair, mental strain and poor health, and in December 1839 he formally resigned from government service.[155]

Ullathorne might have convinced himself that Polding was reconciled to losing him, but in a last ditch attempt to hold on to him, Polding sent Ullathorne to Adelaide, perhaps hoping a change of scene might act upon his health and spirits, and persuade him to retract the resignation he had already submitted. His concern for Ullathorne was genuine enough, but his despair was for his own situation without his most effective aide at his side – not seeming to realise that he himself was part of the problem.

> My Vicar General has informed me of his mind to leave this country ... Thus I am disconcerted. I know not what I shall do. Poor Ullathorne's health is indeed sadly shattered and his spirits have become affected. The savage calumnies heaped upon him by our wretched press have alienated his mind from the country and he imagines, I am sure groundlessly, that there is existing against him a general prejudice ... since his return, his services in the cause of religion have been beyond all praise.[156]

153. DA K289, Ullathorne to Brown, 4 December 1839.
154. Livingstone, *Australian Catholic Priesthood*, p. 12.
155. SCA H412/5 Ullathorne to Colonial Secretary, 2 December 1839.
156. DA K354, Heptonstall quoting Polding, March 1840.

The settlement which Ullathorne visited in Adelaide was only four years old and he celebrated the first ever Mass there. Mr and Mrs Phillips, a Catholic couple who had been among the first arrivals in 1836, had sustained the basics of Catholic life among the small number of Catholics and welcomed Ullathorne warmly. Rather than restoring his enthusiasm for the Australian mission, Adelaide confirmed Ullathorne in his determination to leave. When he returned to Sydney on 9 July, despite rumours that he was to remain, and the Australian territory was to be divided between himself in Adelaide and Polding in Sydney, his mind was made up. His health and spirits were broken and his enthusiasm for the Australian mission disintegrated, and it is evident that his situation in 1840 would now be described as 'burnout'.

Nevertheless, Downside continued to think that Ullathorne's future lay in Adelaide. Brown himself was recommended for one of the new vicariates created in 1840 in a reorganisation of the English Church, and hoped to help his friend escape Adelaide by securing an English nomination instead, or at least, to get him appointed prior of Downside in his own place. He was disappointed that his plot was foiled.[157] However, Brown was gracious enough to feel that Polding's need was greater:

> Thank God, you are now resolved what to do, and are, I doubt not, decided in conformity with His holy will! I should have been glad on our account, to have welcomed your return to St Gregory's, but I feel much for Dr Polding, who must have suffered cruelly by your departure, and for the interest of our holy religion which cannot as yet forego your support. On our account, as I said, I should have been delighted to see you return, for we were on the point of needing you greatly, or rather we still do.[158]

In the end, evidently feeling that things were closing in on him, Ullathorne made a swift and largely unannounced departure

---

[157.] DA Birt Collection, Brown to Ullathorne, 7 July 1840.
[158.] Ibid.

from Australia, taking the opportunity of Polding's decision to go to Europe himself in order to recruit further manpower. Polding's other task was to go to Rome and petition for bishops to be appointed to Hobart (Van Diemen's Land) and Adelaide. The question of a bishopric in either place for Ullathorne was still not fully removed from Polding's mind, and Ullathorne, 'having a sort of half-understanding about the bishopric'[159] plainly did not trust Polding to act in his interests where this was concerned when he got to Rome. In the end it was agreed that both men would travel to Europe together; Ullathorne had refused an arrangement suggested for managing affairs in Polding's absence and simply insisted that either he accompany him to Europe or he would resign as vicar general.

Butler perpetuated the notion implied by Ullathorne, that only Polding and Ullathorne knew that it was the latter's final departure from Australia.[160] This is highly unlikely, as thousands walked from the cathedral to the boat to see him and Polding board the ship, with huge festivities and parting gifts for both bishop and vicar general. It was well known that Ullathorne had submitted his formal resignation to the bishop and the government five months before, and that his health and spirits would not survive much longer under the stress of managing Polding and the public animosity constantly launched at him. Few in the crowd at the dockside could have expected to see the careworn figure of the Very Reverend Agitator General back on Australian soil.

His concern for the Sisters of Charity had been the only pull in the opposite direction, as he began to plan his escape from Australia. Although he was officially the one who was offering guidance and protection, it was also true that they had sustained and encouraged him, and he clearly felt that he was deserting his 'dear convent of Sisters of Charity'. 'It is the sense of the desolation of the convent without a soul to know or understand them which tugged most desperately at my heart and conscience strings, or I believe I should not now be here.'[161]

Ullathorne's strong bond with the nuns had kept him in

---

159. *Autobiography*, p. 207.
160. Butler, *Life*, I, p. 85.
161. DA K275, Ullathorne to Brown, 18 October 1839.

Australia beyond his own inclination or wishes, but they knew what was afoot as Polding and Ullathorne boarded the *Orion* on 16 November 1840. He said Mass for them one last time on the morning of his departure as they wept quietly, and they all travelled from Parramatta to Sydney to see him off, 'feeling that the one person who thoroughly understood them, who had looked to their interests and had guided them, was leaving them, most probably for ever'.[162] After his departure, the letters of his friend among the Sisters of Charity, Mary de Sales O'Brien give an indication of the deep personal attachment between them. In between all the friendly chatter about events and people in New South Wales, she wrote, 'I will not dwell on what we felt at parting from you. We cannot even now speak of that morning without shedding women's tears. You say "When shall we forget all but God" – I must tell you that I think the feelings I have in your regard come from God.'[163]

Another eventful journey around the world followed, with a lengthy stop in New Zealand and in Chile. The plan had been to cross South America by land, but civil wars in Brazil and Argentina made this inadvisable, and so the last leg of the journey, around Cape Horn and across the Atlantic, was made in a French whaling vessel. It was during this journey that Ullathorne sketched the scheme of a hierarchy for Australia, for which Polding gained approval in Rome at the end of 1841. The hierarchy plan was his parting gift to Polding, in order to help him overcome his organisational inadequacy and inability to manage Australian affairs. A hierarchy of bishops with canonical authority would at least solve some of those difficulties, would free Ullathorne from any moral obligations and would be a clear recognition that Australia was not just a Benedictine mission. In all three respects, Polding saw things differently; none of the problems were wholly solved and all came back to haunt Ullathorne sooner or later.

Ullathorne finally landed in England, in June 1841, but soon left for an extensive tour of Ireland to recruit more volunteers from Maynooth for Australia, suggesting that he was as good as his word, in trying to help the mission from a distance. He

---

[162.] *Autobiography*, p. 208.
[163.] DA Box 756, M de Sales O'Brien to Ullathorne, 7 January 1841.

continued to resist attempts to tie him to Australia, especially under the title of Bishop of Hobart. His more general concerns about the role of Benedictines in Australia (and therefore his own future role) were exacerbated by his extreme reluctance to work closely with Therry in Tasmania. Polding finally recognised that the game was up and released him from obedience. Ullathorne settled affairs with the government and returned to Downside. In his autobiography, Ullathorne was honest enough to admit that he found this difficult, 'flat and unexciting',[164] and found settling to a life of monastic obedience very hard after exercising independent authority for so long in Australia. He was not to be long in the monastery, nor long before Polding tried to persuade him across the seas again with the offer of a mitre.

Ullathorne had come to realise and acknowledge what many of those around him, as yet had not. Australia was no longer, in Catholic terms, an English mission, still less an English Benedictine one. It was a national Church in its own right, needful of its own hierarchy and local organisation, independent of vicars apostolic in London or Mauritius. The fundamental reason for this (apart from practicalities of distance) was that Australia was no longer a prison camp or a settlement, but a growing country, making its own way in the world. It was no longer morally defensible to transport criminals there and the settlers, traders and administrators had to recognise that Australia had a future which was different from its past. Ullathorne saw a new world emerging, which had to forge a new relationship with the old world and the old Church; it would be forged in gold in the next generation.

This perception of the need for a healthy local Church to have orderly structures stayed with Ullathorne all his life and shaped his conduct as a bishop. It is too easy, however, to gain from the emphasis on law and structures in existing historical discussions of Ullathorne a sense that he was overly preoccupied with them. Two things need to be borne in mind: firstly, for him structures were a means to an end, not an end in themselves and secondly, the religious culture within which English Catholic history was first written has overly emphasised the

---

[164.] *Autobiography*, p. 240.

triumph of the institution in telling the story of Victorian revival. Cuthbert Butler, in the 1920s, was working out of a framework of restored institutional life in which the hierarchical order was heavily emphasised. The creation of ecclesiastical order was, to him, the great achievement of the Victorians.

Within the framework he established in Australia, Ullathorne learnt and cultivated a deep understanding of human nature and a sensitivity to the difficulties which people faced in life. Australia provided him with a unique training in the human psyche, which stood him in good stead. Few people in this world encountered the sheer physical suffering, the degradation and injustice and the utter hopelessness which he found within the convict colonies of Australia. The world of a Victorian churchman was a staid and sheltered one, but Ullathorne returned to England with his memory crowded with experiences too vivid and shocking to be shared with anyone. His accounts of convict life in the autobiography and in his pamphlet on Australasia clearly revealed only the tip of the iceberg. In terms of the biography of a man who spent most of his life in positions of leadership in England, three key themes emerge from Ullathorne's career in the Antipodes which shaped his future approach to life: the absolute certainty that true religious and social freedom could only be achieved within a framework of order and authority; the capacity he developed for understanding human nature and dealing with men and women; the social conscience which was shaped by his dealings with convicts and alcoholics.

The young, optimistic monk, full of dreams, who had set sail a decade earlier on the *Sir Thomas Munro*, and been teased by everyone from the presbytery housekeeper to the pope himself about his youthful appearance, had grown up in a hard school. He had learnt a great deal about the ways of the world and the highs and lows of human nature. He had struggled painfully with a difficult working relationship with Polding, to whom he had been devoted as novice master at Downside, and formed his own judgements on the men and women around him. The air of pomposity which had been his unconscious guard against patronage by older men had grown into a single-minded confidence in his own ability to lead and govern. Australia, as it has for generations of settlers, turned the boy into the man.

Chapter 3

'The Happiest and Most Fruitful Years' 1842–1846

Ullathorne had returned to his monastery, and for a time began teaching in the school at Downside, while his health recovered. It was unlikely that this would last long, and he was evidently unsettled, and did not entirely rule out the possibility of a return to Australia, as long as he could be assured that a mitre would not settle on his head. Even a year later, he was willing to return as a subject of his friend Robert Willson, newly appointed Bishop of Hobart.[1] Not surprisingly, he jumped at the chance of going to Coventry to take on the Downside mission there, although he knew nothing of Warwickshire and the growing industrial towns of the Midlands. The England to which Ullathorne had returned after nearly ten years absence, was entering what became known as the 'hungry forties'. It was markedly different in religious, social and political terms from that which he had left in 1832, as a result of social legislation and population changes. Just before his departure, the 'great' Reform Act of 1832 had reshaped popular politics, streamlining Parliament and widening the franchise. More importantly, it had helped to create a mood for reform. Whig governments in the 1830s had introduced far-reaching social legislation, including the Poor Law Reform of 1834 and the Factory Acts. Migration into the cities had taken on epidemic proportions, including thousands of Catholic Irish, and living conditions were deteriorating in the overcrowded urban centres.

[1.] Butler, *Life*, I, p. 121.

In religious terms, Protestant Nonconformity, and in particular Methodism, was growing rapidly and becoming more organised and institutionalised under the leadership of Jabez Bunting. Other Protestant churches and sects were making inroads into the burgeoning towns and cities. The Church of England was in the midst of its greatest upheaval since the Reformation, which would have profound implications, not only for the Established Church, but for the Catholic Church as well. For the Catholics, the period after Catholic Emancipation in 1829 was one of massive growth in numbers, largely due to the tide of Irish migration flowing into England, fleeing agricultural disaster and starvation. It reached its peak in the great potato famine of 1847–8, but was already well under way at the start of the decade.

In the wake of the Catholic Emancipation Act of 1829 which had given Catholics full civil and political liberty, Catholic life in the 1830s had taken on a more public shape with a stronger sense of identity and organisation. Ullathorne, by chance, had been in England in 1838 to attend the opening of the new college of St Mary's, Oscott, the school and seminary built by Bishop Thomas Walsh to be the showplace of English Catholicism and the launching pad for a hoped for revival. The Birmingham cathedral of St Chad (also designed by A. W. Pugin) had opened in 1841. In 1840, the four Vicars Apostolic had managed to convince Rome that growing numbers of Catholics merited the doubling of their number to eight, and pressure was growing for the institution of a full hierarchy. Numbers of Catholics had increased, largely through the growing influx of Irish migrants, and the increasing economic wealth generated by industrialisation was affecting the Catholic congregations as much as any other group in society. Churches, chapels, charities and religious houses – the physical surroundings of Catholic life – were returning to the English landscape.

The impact of Catholic Emancipation on constitutional affairs was as dramatic as its effect on Catholic life. The combined impact of this Act, plus an earlier one applicable to Protestant Nonconformists and the Reform Act of 1832 was to change the nature of Parliament. It was no longer the closed shop of a self-selected coterie of members of the Church of

England, but potentially at least, a body more representative of the variety of people of Britain and Ireland. The seeds of modern democracy and constitutional monarchy were being sown in the 1830s, and religious pluralism (not merely tolerance) was a reality. The reliance of the Church of England on the capacity of Parliament to look after its affairs was becoming shaky, and voices of complaint were being raised in the intellectual and ecclesiastical heartland of Oxford. The sermon preached on the occasion of the opening of the Oxford Assize Court in 1833 by John Keble was a flashpoint, and triggered what became known as the Oxford Movement among clerics attached to the university. For a time, the apparent threats to the establishment, including the religious tests for university membership at Oxford, brought the older tradition of high churchmanship into alliance with the newer Oxford Tractarians (so called from their campaign of publishing tracts for the clergy). The early tracts struck a conservative chord among the clergy, but the Tractarian agenda was more radical than their tastes.[2]

This new and complex movement would have ramifications through the rest of the nineteenth century and beyond, for the Church of England and the Catholic Church in England. The result of the intellectual and spiritual struggle to reclaim Catholicity and authority within the Church of England, while retaining the constitutional role of the Established Church, led to anguish for some of those involved. Splits between more radical and conservative camps ensued. The final outcome for some of the leading Oxford men, including most famously, John Henry Newman, was conversion to Rome. The converts of the second half of the nineteenth century made a striking impact on the emergent Catholic community in terms of status, dynamism, intellectual power and financial muscle. In 1842, much of this lay ahead, and would be a dominant factor in Ullathorne's life. Newman at this point was still a member of the Church of England, grappling with his own deepest intellectual and spiritual convictions and the Church authorities. During Ullathorne's time in Coventry, the Oxford Movement entered its crucial phase, following the publication of

[2.] Peter Nockles, *The Oxford Movement in Context* (1994), pp. 274–9.

Newman's Tract 90 in 1841. In this he examined some of the Thirty Nine Articles of faith of the Church of England in the light of Catholic doctrine, to see how far (if at all) they could be reconciled. 'Too many hostages to fortune were being given to the movement's enemies,'[3] and a furore broke around Newman's head. 'Newman's Anglican world crashed around him.'[4] It led to his retirement with a group of supporters to Littlemore, near Oxford and ultimately to his final reception into the Catholic Church in November 1845.

While scarcely anything to compare with New South Wales in its social problems and lack of Catholic presence, Coventry was exactly what Ullathorne needed to get his teeth into. It had been a Benedictine mission since 1803, and after a series of weak and ineffective or ailing priests in charge of the mission, it was in a very dispirited condition and many of the Catholics had abandoned the Church. Those left were often troublesome and argumentative. There was a small chapel and house built in 1807, both of which were in a poor state of repair when Ullathorne arrived in November 1841. He jokingly offered his friend Brown the hospitality of 'a vacant cell and just room for a second person at a very small table in the parlour'. Most of the congregation were tradespeople, and, according to Barber, 'there is not a gentleman in the entire place'.[5] The architect, Charles Hansom, was the only Catholic in Coventry who kept servants. The city, whose medieval prosperity had long since faded, was dominated in the first half of the nineteenth century by the ribbon trade, meeting the demands of fashionable society, until French imports caused its collapse in the 1860s. Among the largest employers was the Quaker family of John and Joseph Cash, who were well known locally as philanthropists and benevolent employers.[6]

His first impressions, conveyed to Brown are positive and couched in light-hearted and even comic tones.

[3] Nockles, p. 279.

[4] Ibid., p. 294.

[5] Ampleforth, Copy of letter, Ullathorne to Brown, 30 November 1841.

[6] Adrian Room, 'Cash, John (1822–1880)', *Oxford Dictionary of National Biography*, Oxford University Press, 2004 [http://www.oxforddnb.com/view/article/38982, accessed 14 Sept 2005].

Only think of a man being sent to Coventry. Why, Falstaff refused to march through the place, much less to stay in it!' I am now in full occupation and very happy in the midst of it. I gave a lecture last night, Monday, which I intend continuing to do, to a full chapel. There is a good deal of religion amongst the poor people. For want of an efficient pastor they have been involved in dissensions and have fallen off some deal, but I trust to see things soon return to order ... a considerable portion of the congregation are converts ... I think conversion will progress ... A priest here has very full occupation and must make himself a thorough fixture in the town ... I am surprised to find with what facility and pleasure I have begun to plead, and trust I shall never have any other than my present duties and those of a similar character.[7]

Ullathorne had found a niche where he had the freedom to run the mission as he saw fit, and where he could see the effects of his work.

The success of his Monday evening lectures gave him the incentive to publish some of the sermons he had preached in Australia. He had gone into print on several occasions on *The Catholic Mission in Australasia* (the first ever attempt to chronicle the history of the penal colony), *Observations on the Use and Abuse of Sacred Scripture* (as part of his campaign to resist Protestant control of religious education in Australia) and *The Horrors of Transportation* (to try and persuade poor Irishmen that transportation was not a cheap form of emigration). His most famous sermon, *The Drunkard*, was widely and regularly reprinted in England and Ireland, including an edition of 20,000 sponsored by the great Irish temperance campaigner Fr Theobald Mathew. Ullathorne met Fr Mathew in Cork on his final return journey to England in 1841. By then the Capuchin friar had created a mass movement in Ireland, with thousands of people taking the pledge of total and lifelong abstinence from alcohol, and temperance societies were estab-

7. Ampleforth, Copy of letter, Ullathorne to Brown, 30 November 1841.

lished all over Ireland.[8] Ullathorne saw the Irish temperance movement at its height and was much impressed, as it resonated with his own efforts in Australia.[9]

In 1842 he decided to publish a volume of sermons, edited with a substantial preface on the responsibilities of the preacher, aimed at stimulating missionary outreach in England.[10] After only a year back in the less heated atmosphere of English Catholicism he was already impatient to see more vigorous and energetic missionary activity and determined to do something about it. He expected his book to be controversial, gleefully telling Brown that 'the general preface will bite some people'[11] and the content was based on homilies preached, as he put it, 'at the two extremities of the globe'.[12] He recalled preaching them in the old court house in Sydney, the guard room at Parramatta gaol, barns, public houses and makeshift chapels in Van Diemen's Land and Norfolk Island.

The biting General Preface was an extended and heartfelt plea for inspirational preaching to reach the hearts and minds of the English people, Catholic and non-Catholic. Its tone suggests that he was not impressed with what he had seen and heard since his return to England.

> When will these preachers of the Cross come forth? Those crucified men, the intrepid heroes of the Divine Word. When will they come forth as of old? Those men of prayer – those men of penance, deeply wounded with the dishonour of the Divine name amongst men – those ardent lovers of God – those patient sufferers impassioned of the Cross. When shall we see them in the midst of us? Moved with sorrow and compassion for a people who, like sheep, lie about without pastors; who, always seeking and never finding, fill the air with their anxious questionings.[13]

8. Colm Kerrigan, 'Mathew, Theobald (1790–1856)', *Oxford Dictionary of National Biography*, Oxford University Press, 2004 [http://www.oxforddnb.com/view/article/18328, accessed 14 Sept 2005].
9. Butler, *Life*, I, p. 129.
10. W. B. Ullathorne, *Sermons with Prefaces* (1842).
11. DA Birt Collection, Ullathorne to Brown, 7 January 1842.
12. *Sermons*, p. 63.
13. Ibid., p. 58.

He was convinced that much could be achieved by powerful preaching by 'men of divinely kindled hearts' who would 'meet the spirit of the time and the wants of this nation'.[14] Like the best of Ullathorne's many publications, these sermons were an adjunct to his pastoral and missionary work, and his constant effort to draw the best out of people.

The subjects of the sermons were varied, and topics included 'The Evil Tongue', 'The Penitent' and 'The Sinner's Delay', as well as the most famous one, 'The Drunkard'. This had been first preached in Sydney and in many other parts of the missionary territory in the first months of Ullathorne's residence, when he realised the powerful effects of alcohol on the social fabric of colonial life and on the capacity of the individual to reform his or her life. Alcohol and its attendant social evils was one of Ullathorne's lifelong concerns. He himself never drank, and scarcely even touched tea or coffee. The sermon is a hard hitting discourse on the harsh reality of drunkenness and its degrading effect on the human person.

> The drunkard is a self-made wretch, who has depraved and gratified the depraved cravings of the throat of his body, until he has sunk his soul so far that it is lost in his flesh, and has sunk his very flesh beyond comparison lower than that of the creatures who serve him: a self-degraded creature, whose degradation is made manifest to every one but himself; a self-made miserable being, who, whilst he is insensible to his own misery, afflicts everyone else with misery around or belonging to him.[15]

Ullathorne spared nothing in his portrayal of the slippery slope on which the habitual drinker finds himself, while the silent judgement of God awaits, and the social imbiber becomes the hopeless addict. The solution he recommended lay in an early determination of self-control, restraint and limitation which was never to be broken. If broken, the advice was to 'renew your resolution – strengthen it with prayer; observe the

14. Ibid., p. 61.
15. Ibid., p. 114.

occasion of your past fall, and remove it.'[16] The best protection of all from the destructive vice of drunkenness was to seek the advice and support of a spiritual director who would help the victim to fight his or her destructive tendencies.

The effects of drink on Victorian behaviour and on social and economic trends was noted with concern by many social observers, and alcohol consumption rose to an all-time peak in 1875.[17] It was a cause taken up by Evangelical and Non-conformist Christians, who focused on the social effects of drink on family life and on the limits it placed on self-improvement. Those committed to tackling the social evils consequent upon drink had an uphill battle; pubs were, 'amazingly plentiful' and, 'where homes were least homely, work most uncertain or disagreeable, people least able or willing to save, pubs and other drinking places naturally became social centres'.[18] Various societies and organisations sprang up, with considerable success, to wean people away from consumption of alcohol, nearly all based on solemn pledges to abstain and on the provision of alternative social venues such as music halls and 'coffee palaces'.[19] Few general accounts of the Victorian Christian temperance movement discuss the Catholic contribution, except an occasional mention of Fr Theobald Mathew and Cardinal Manning's later involvement. The authoritative account of Victorian temperance asserts that Mathew was 'a lone figure, with influence mainly in Ireland' and that there were only one or two other identified Catholics among the temperance movement leadership. In fact, it was suggested that elements of the mainly Evangelical temperance movement were specifically anti-Irish and anti-Catholic.[20] Ullathorne did not merit a single mention.

Ullathorne's approach was somewhat different to the 'self-improvement' model of Evangelical Christianity which emphasised corporate activity and parliamentary pressure for

16. Ibid., p. 125.
17. Geoffrey Best, *Mid-Victorian Britain 1851–75* (1972), p. 218.
18. Ibid., p. 220.
19. David Edwards, *Christian England (vol. 3) from the eighteenth century to the First World War* (1984), pp. 243–5.
20. Brian Harrison, *Drink and the Victorians: the temperance question in England 1815–72* (1971), p. 165.

controls on alcohol. His concern was less for the economic damage and the social impoverishment than for the sheer human degradation involved. Ullathorne joined no organisation and took no public pledge. To him, this was a personal concern of the individual, to do with the care of one's soul, and he continued to keep up the pressure within the framework of a personal moral campaign. Drunkenness was a problem among the poorest Irish in England, as in Australia, and the Catholic clergy quickly picked this up. Temperance societies did emerge, especially among the Irish population, but were often disassociated from the national movements.[21] Fr Mathew travelled over from Ireland and campaigned with some success in the northern English cities in 1843, administering the pledge in Gaelic, but was hounded out by London publicans.[22] Mathew was part of the movement in the first half of the century emphasising moral persuasion to try and encourage abstinence, but which, by the 1850s had been superseded by the pressure for government action to control access to alcohol.[23] The only other English Catholic leader strongly associated with temperance pressure groups was Cardinal Manning, who threw his support behind the UK Alliance in 1867 and took the pledge himself.[24]

For a time, Ullathorne's sister Rebecca lived with him at Coventry, in the hope that she could help him in the house and mission, but this proved an unsatisfactory arrangement. Ullathorne tactfully described her in his autobiography as 'a good deal of an invalid'[25] but private letters to his friend Brown indicate that she suffered from some sort of a religious mania, enduring unusual ecstatic experiences, including temporary stigmata which appeared only on Fridays and which ceased as suddenly as they started. This may well have fed his desire at this time to visit the Austrian ecstatic Marie Moerl, who was attracting much attention. However, even with her improved health, his sister planned to leave for

---

[21.] Harrison, p. 168.
[22.] Edward Norman, *The English Catholic Church in the Nineteenth Century* (1984), p. 199.
[23.] Harrison, p. 210.
[24.] David Newsome, *The Convert Cardinals* (1993), p. 335.
[25.] *Autobiography*, p. 242.

Dublin.[26] In the event, she married, but died young in 1846. The Coventry mission had a small school and a schoolmaster, Mr Walsh, and Ullathorne was able to obtain the assistance of Fr Clarkson (John Athanasius Clarkson OSB, an Ampleforth monk, ordained in 1840).[27] With the help of his own mother for a while on the domestic front, and that of Mrs Louisa Amherst, a wealthy Catholic living in nearby Kenilworth, Ullathorne was able to get the mission onto a decent footing before long.

From the time of his return to England, having declined to return to Australia as Bishop of Hobart, Ullathorne was inevitably the subject of clerical speculation in respect of episcopal appointments.[28] There is no doubt that he knew he could do the job of bishop if called upon, and the self-confidence in his manner, which had earned him enemies in Australia, persuaded some that he was itching for a mitre. Some of the gossip said that the 'Bishop of Coventry' would be 'pleased with his mitre and ring'. Although, while at Coventry, he resisted all idea of episcopal preferment, he could not help his mind turning over ideas,

> at present my mind is completely pervaded with the idea that, were I a missionary bishop, I should be impelled to stir about a good deal, and when resident, to be where there was a large population to be acted upon by a mission which I should endeavour to make a model for the rest and where I might train missionary instruments of various kinds amidst scenes of actual labour. I do not now speak of a seminary when I say this. I trust you will pardon my presumption . . .[29]

This reveals an image of Ullathorne as a man, in certain

[26.] Stone G/ULL/III T893/1, Ullathorne to Mrs Amherst Septuagesima Sunday 1842 (Typescript copy).

[27.] C. Fitzgerald Lombard, *English and Welsh Clergy 1801–1914* (1993), p. 129.

[28.] Farm St Foreign Correspondence 1776–1859 No. 388, 15 Aug 1843.

[29.] Ampleforth, Copy of letter, Ullathorne to Brown, SS Placidus and Socinius, 1843.

respects, beyond his time in developing a vision of the episcopate, and offers an insight into his thinking and the style of
bishop he eventually became. Although often credited with
establishing order and authority in the English hierarchy,
mission was his ultimate purpose and vision.

Despite the gossip, Ullathorne's oft-repeated denials of episcopal ambition do have a ring of truth, partly because they are
so frequent and vehement, and partly because, later in life, he
made more than one attempt to resign his bishopric. He had
no illusions, as he commented to his friend Brown of the troubles of bishops, including Polding. 'Who would exchange the
quiet I experience, plodding among my poor Coventry people,
for all these cares and heartburnings?'[30] The following year he
wrote again, rejoicing in the fact that he was to be 'left to enjoy
my happy freedom at Coventry and feel free at the thought'.[31]

Having refused Hobart, Ullathorne found that his name had
been put forward in Rome by Polding for Adelaide. Clearly
depressed at this prospect, he went with a heavy heart to
Loughborough in Leicestershire and made an eight-day retreat
with Fr Giovanni Battista Pagani, the provincial superior of the
Institute of Charity (Rosminians) in England. The Rosminians,
along with the Passionists and Redemptorists were among the
Italian missionary orders which began to take root in England
in the 1840s, and had remarkable success in evangelising the
growing industrial towns.[32] Ullathorne knew something of
them, having explored the possibility of Rosminians going to
Australia in 1837.[33] This retreat, under Pagani's direction,
convinced Ullathorne to have nothing to do with Adelaide, or
any future episcopal appointment. He was convinced that
Polding's plan (which differed from Ullathorne's own original
proposals) to cut out Adelaide as one of three distinct vicariates, but leave it dependent on the remote authority of Polding
as Archbishop of Sydney was doomed to failure. His sources
told him that there were no more than two thousand Catholics
in the Adelaide area, all in a state of extreme poverty, the

[30.] Cardiff, Ullathorne to Brown, 1st Sunday in Lent 1842.
[31.] Ampleforth, Copy of letter Ullathorne to Brown, SS Placidus and
    Socinius, 1843.
[32.] Norman, pp. 224–5.
[33.] *Autobiography*, pp. 151–4.

remaining population consisting of violent and brutal cattle drovers and aborigines. Not only was the organisation proposed a disaster in Ullathorne's view, but he resented Polding's lack of personal consideration in apparently having forgotten how Ullathorne's constitution suffered in the extreme heat of southern Australia.[34] Polding continued to urge his acceptance, and the strain clearly began to affect Ullathorne's health, playing on his digestion and causing headaches and depression.

Desperate, Ullathorne set out for Rome himself to petition *Propaganda Fide* for release from the proposed appointment. He went with a heavy heart, dubious about Polding's capacity for straight dealing. After he had extracted a promise from him not to put his name forward before leaving Australia, he was fearful of getting 'entangled in this sad affair' and being forced into 'a state of life for which I feel not a single attraction of any kind'.[35] It was on this occasion in Rome that he met Fr Thomas Grant, who would become a friend and confidante until his death in 1870 as Bishop of Southwark during the Vatican Council. In 1842 he was secretary to Cardinal Charles Acton, who was a close papal advisor on matters concerning England.[36] With Grant's skilful knowledge and experience of the Roman curia, Ullathorne had an invaluable ally.

He achieved his purpose, and again escaped a return to Australia with a mitre in his luggage. Preparing with a light step to travel back to England, he was asked by a Roman acquaintance to accompany an elderly Scottish lady on the journey home. He readily agreed, as she shared his interest in visiting the Austrian ecstatic, Maria Moerl and another similar case in Sansovino, also receiving a good deal of attention at the time. Their journey took them from Rome via Assisi, Cortona and Perugia and on to Sansovino. Ullathorne devoted a disproportionate number of pages of his autobiography to his investigation of this case and his questioning of local clerics about the girl's behaviour. This was more than morbid

---

[34.] Ampleforth, Copy of letter, Ullathorne to Brown, Feast of the Ascension 1842.

[35.] Cardiff, Ullathorne to Brown, 8 May, 1842.

[36.] Michael Clifton, *The Quiet Negotiator : Bishop Grant of Southwark* (1993), p. 18.

curiosity, as he was troubled by his own sister's similar experiences. Sceptical about what he had heard, Ullathorne attended Mass in the ecstatic's presence and witnessed her remarkable levitations at key moments in the liturgy. He spoke privately with her, and somewhat severely warned her of the dangers to her soul inherent in her practices; his anxiety was evident even in his own much later account, where he only obliquely refers to asking her, 'spiritual questions bearing on my own habits and surroundings'.[37] This is surely a reference to his own sister's sufferings, and the young Italian girl became one of the very few to whom he confided this. When his sister's troubling ecstatic experiences came to an abrupt end, his own close interest in the Italian case waned; as he remarked, 'I never thought of making any further enquiry respecting her subsequent history'.

Still in the company of Mrs Hutchinson, his Scottish companion, Ullathorne journeyed on to Florence, Bologna and Mantua but at Mollia Gonsaraga, the good lady was stopped from crossing the border. Chaos ensued over passports and visas, and only the intervention of the British Ambassador in Florence resolved what was evidently a case of mistaken identity. On his advice, they took ship from Livorno to Genoa, where they picked up a steamer for Marseilles, which coincidentally had among its passengers Bishop Polding and Fr (later Abbot) Gregory en route back from Rome to England. Ullathorne does not record what must have been rather uncomfortable conversations on board ship for both parties. The affair of the border crossing was still not finished, and provoked a minor diplomatic incident. The travellers wrote an account of their treatment at the hands of the Mantua border guards, which Mrs Hutchinson's brother, a Scottish Law Lord, sent to Lord Aberdeen, the Foreign Secretary. He took the matter up with no less a figure than Prince Metternich himself, and obtained an ample apology and the removal of all British names from the list of persons forbidden entry to Austria.[38] Mrs Hutchinson herself, who had been an Irvingite, became a Catholic and later founded the Edinburgh house of the Sisters of Mercy.[39]

[37.] *Autobiography*, p. 248.
[38.] Ibid., p. 253.
[39.] College Irlandais Paris, Ullathorne to Kathleen O'Meara, 2 January 1887.

Returning to Coventry after his Italian adventure, safe in the knowledge (as he thought) that episcopal appointments were off the agenda, Ullathorne settled to building up the mission in his growing but poor industrial city. He was delighted to find that surprising progress had been made in his absence by the woman who was to become his greatest ally and closest friend, Margaret Hallahan. She was only a little older than him, the daughter of Londoners who had fallen on hard times. The only child of London Irish Catholic parents, Margaret was brought up in the 'Irish ghetto' of St Giles. Although there were Catholic mission schools there, she was educated in Somers Town in a school established by a French émigré, Abbé Carron, but the death of both her parents within months of each other from consumption in 1813 left her destitute and orphaned at the age of nine.[40] She was then placed in service and spent several years with the French émigré family of Madame Caulier. Although Madame Caulier was fond of Margaret and contemplated adopting her, she treated the child with a severity which induced timidity, and even provoked her to run away on one occasion. However, Margaret stayed under Madame Caulier's protection on and off until the age of twenty, when she was placed in the service of an elderly doctor for whom she cared until his death. His married daughter, Mrs Thompson, kept Margaret on as a companion and children's nanny for twenty years, fifteen of which she spent living with this family in Belgium. While with the Thompsons in Kent, she first met Mary Louisa Amherst who was the daughter of relatives holidaying nearby, and around this time began to feel the first stirrings of a vocation to religious life. The Amherst family, who eventually built a church in Kenilworth, near their home, were closely involved with the Catholic community in Coventry, and in the Midlands.

Margaret's instincts and Catholic piety were greatly enhanced by the decision of the Thompsons to move to Bruges in 1829,[41]

[40.] Several details of Margaret Hallahan's early life as described in her biography of 1869 have been corrected by later research. See Stephen H. Hancock, 'From Hagiography to History: a Critical Re-examination of the first forty years of "the Life" of Mother Margaret Hallahan and of its manuscript sources' in *Recusant History* vol. 23 (1997), pp. 341–71.

[41.] Not 1826 as in Drane, *Life*: See Hancock, p. 357.

when at the age of twenty-three, Margaret, despite her fears of the change, went with them. The environment of Catholic Bruges encouraged her aspirations to religious life and she entered the English Convent of Augustinians in the city, but soon found that it was not for her. She returned to the Thompsons swiftly, to her life of hidden service and increasing domestic responsibility as they were forced by straightened circumstances to reduce their household. In addition, she gained a considerable reputation around Bruges for her private acts of charity to the poor. The atmosphere of Catholic Bruges certainly influenced her.

> The contrast between the bare, impoverished mission chapels Margaret Hallahan used to attend in England, and the Gothic splendour and baroque magnificence of the Flemish churches she worshipped in at Bruges, certainly gave her the impression that the Church of the catacombs she had left behind in Southwark and St Giles could become the militant renascent Church she saw emerging in Bruges following the stormy years of the French occupation and the Belgian revolution.[42]

Through the local priest, Abbé Capron, and Abbé Bruno Versavel (who was her spiritual director), Margaret was introduced to the writings and spirit of St Dominic and in particular to St Catherine of Siena. Like Margaret, Catherine was a laywoman drawn to the charism of St Dominic at an early age, who dedicated her life to the service of God. Born in the mid-fourteenth century, Catherine was part of a Europe devastated by the Black Death and of a Church riven by faction and division. The most famous achievement of her short and intense life was to persuade Gregory XI to return the papacy from Avignon to Rome. However, what appealed to Margaret in her reading of Catherine's letters and mystical dialogues was an extraordinary combination of an intense contemplative inner life with an active apostolate among the poor and needy of her own society.[43] This devotion to the Dominican Order, and to St

---

[42.] Hancock, p. 359.
[43.] Mary O'Driscoll OP, *Catherine of Siena* (Strasbourg, 1994), pp. 8–9.

Catherine in particular, shaped Margaret's spiritual life and in 1835 she was professed as a Dominican Tertiary (a member of the religious family of St Dominic without solemn vows, but Margaret chose to make a personal solemn vow of lifelong chastity). This was her time of real spiritual formation and pastoral development, though a serious illness came close to taking her life prematurely and left her weak and unable to return to work.

Indirectly, this led to her return to England and her arrival in Coventry. Attempts to form a small residential community of Tertiaries in Bruges met with difficulties, and influential clergy, including her own confessor, put a damper on the project. Abbé Versavel placed her under obedience to accept an invitation to return to England. Mary Louisa Amherst, the daughter of Francis Fortescue Turville of Bosworth Hall, was linked to the Thompson family by marriage and both families were part of a close-knit Catholic Anglo-Indian network.[44] She was the mother of Francis Kerril Amherst, who was a schoolboy at Old and New Oscott, who eventually went on to ordination and appointment as Bishop of Northampton in 1858. After leaving school, he trained as an engineer, partly in Bruges (1839–41) where he lodged with the Thompsons.[45] Mrs Amherst had heard from her son of 'Peggy' and her role in the Thompson household and the local community, and urged Margaret Hallahan to return to England, where there was so much work to be done.[46] The Amherst family home was in Kenilworth, Warwickshire, and she took a close interest in the nearby Coventry mission. Her husband, who died in 1835, was buried in Coventry and later reinterred in the church built by Ullathorne. Eventually, husband and wife were reunited in a tomb in the church built by their own efforts in Kenilworth.[47] It was she who approached Ullathorne with the proposal that Margaret Hallahan would be an asset in building up the spirit of Catholics in Coventry. Convinced by Mrs Amherst's warm recommendation, Ullathorne agreed to Margaret's appointment to Coventry. He assured Mrs Amherst that her arrival

[44.] Hancock n. 108, p. 370.
[45.] Mary Francis Roskell, *Memoirs of Francis Kerril Amherst* (nd), p. 134.
[46.] Roskell, p. 134.
[47.] Roskell, pp. 121–2.

would be providential, and that she would be 'an instrument destined to do much in this town'.[48] His mind went back to Parramatta and the immediate and beneficial impact which the Sisters of Charity had made among the women. The proposed episcopal appointment to Adelaide was a hitch, but Ullathorne assured Mrs Amherst that his intention was to remain in Coventry, and the scheme went ahead.

On 30 April 1842, Margaret landed in England, and made her way to Mrs Amherst's home in Kenilworth and thence to Coventry. There she met Ullathorne for the first time. Her first impressions are not recorded, but his are quoted in her biography:

> I shall never forget my first meeting with her, in the little house I then occupied at Coventry. She was then in her vigour, well-proportioned, very erect, and having an impression of dignity and simplicity combined, yet with a spiritual softness pervading features that indicated her remarkable powers of mind and heart. It seized me with a sense of surprise as well as gratification. I at once felt that Mrs Amherst's promise that I should find her a valuable co-operator in my mission was far more than realised.[49]

Margaret moved into the cramped, damp and crumbling house, sharing the kitchen with a bad-tempered housekeeper, and within a fortnight found herself alone in her new post, as Ullathorne left for Rome to plead his cause against the appointment to Adelaide.

He was, inevitably, away for some months, occupied with his adventures with Mrs Hutchinson in Italy, but on his return was amazed and heartened to find that Margaret had already gathered a hundred local girls into a school, made contact with all the sick and impoverished people in the area, and begun to gather around her a group of co-workers. To his great credit, there is never in any of his accounts of life at Coventry a whiff of jealousy, or of Ullathorne wishing to limit or control the

---

48. Stone, G/ULL/IIII T893/1, Ullathorne to Mrs Amherst, Septuagesima Sunday 1842 (typescript copy).
49. Drane, *Life*, pp. 53–4.

ministry which Margaret exercised. His experience of working with the Sisters of Charity in Parramatta had convinced him of the authenticity and value of religious women who were not bound by the cloister. Ullathorne played a unique role in advancing several of these enterprises started by women, although he never planned one himself. He was content to encourage where he saw female endeavours which were authentically of God and of the Church. He had learned in Australia of the value of the Sisters of Charity in reaching areas of society in which priests could do very little. This, however, was very different from the Sisters of Charity. Margaret was a Dominican tertiary, but not a vowed religious, and had no religious community around her. The greatest achievement of his early years back in England was to enable the foundation of Margaret Hallahan's congregation of Dominican Sisters under the patronage of St Catherine of Siena.

Margaret was strongly committed to the Dominican Order, but wanted to introduce to the English mission the concept she had encountered in Belgium of unenclosed Third Order Dominican women actively involved in pastoral work. The precedents were not good: in the seventeenth century Mary Ward had found herself scoffed at, opposed, and finally subject to papal imprisonment for such a notion.[50] Her Institute had still not received any ecclesiastical recognition, and all the English communities of religious women who had returned to native soil after the French Revolution were monastic and enclosed. Bishop Walsh, Vicar Apostolic of the Central District, tried to get Margaret Hallahan to join the Sisters of Mercy, failing to appreciate that she had already taken vows as a Dominican.[51] Ullathorne must at least have appreciated the significance of religious vows, but as a Benedictine missionary priest in Coventry he had no authority and could offer only encouragement and support.

The European style of life of Dominican Tertiaries had been interpreted in a number of ways, but was unknown in England. On her fund-raising visit to Belgium in February 1844, she also

---

[50] Henriette Peters, *Mary Ward: a World in Contemplation* (1991) (trans. Helen Butterworth, 1994), pp. 611–2.
[51] Drane, *Life*, p 87.

collected as much supporting evidence and material about the practice of Dominican Tertiaries as she could. Even before she had chance to place this before the Provincial of the English Dominican Friars, he took the view that his authority, together with that of Ullathorne's superior (the Prior of Downside) and that of Bishop Walsh, was sufficient for the tiny Dominican Institute to be founded by Sr Margaret under Ullathorne's direct oversight.[52] Once established in Coventry, with the permission of the Provincial Superior of the Dominican Order in England, Fr Henry Whiteside, Margaret placed herself and her institute under Ullathorne's personal direction.[53]

This was an unusual arrangement, given that he was simply the mission priest and a monk of an entirely different religious order, subject to his own monastic discipline. She worked alongside Ullathorne in the mission, running the girls' school and establishing contacts among the factory girls of Coventry, and although not a professed religious in the accepted sense, 'even the Protestants of Coventry seem to have understood that the plainly dressed priest's housekeeper had something of the nun about her'.[54] She began to gather around her a group of women prepared to devote themselves to the work of the Church in Coventry, joining her in collecting funds to build the new church and helping with the gatherings of young factory women or visiting the poor.

As a monk he was well aware of the ancient monastic tradition of cloistered women, but he and all the other Catholic clergy in the British Isles were only just being familiarised with the vocation and ministry of women religious who moved outside the cloister. Religious or conventual life for women in England had been destroyed at the Reformation, and female convents had disappeared from the landscape. Women wishing to pursue religious life were forced to go abroad, and convents of English nuns sprang up in European towns and cities. Throughout Flanders and France in the seventeenth and eighteenth centuries, there were convents of English women living under Franciscan, Benedictine, Augustinian, Carmelite,

---

52. Ibid., pp. 93–4.
53. Ibid., pp. 58–9.
54. Ibid., p. 64.

Bridgettine and Ursuline rules. Douai, Brussels, Louvain, St Omer, Liège, Paris and Cambrai were as important as refuges for recusant women as they were for men training for the priesthood. They were important centres for the preservation and development of Catholic spirituality, and most houses ran schools to provide Catholic education for the daughters of wealthier families. From the schools came many of their recruits, and there were an estimated forty refugee English convents sustaining female religious life in the seventeenth century.

At the end of the eighteenth century, as the French Revolution destroyed refugee Catholic institutions across Europe, the nuns fled to England, often with only what they stood up in. They were taken into the houses of gentry Catholics and given bases from which to re-establish themselves. Their own severe financial situation and the increasing demand for female educational provision among Catholics ensured that several of the contemplative houses continued to run schools on their return to England.[55] Slowly and painfully, female religious life re-established itself on English soil in the early years of the nineteenth century. Still there was no thought of an active, uncloistered apostolate being available for women until the likes of Catherine McAuley, Mary Aikenhead, Elizabeth Prout and Margaret Hallahan emerged on the scene.

Margaret Hallahan herself was one of a remarkable generation of women who revolutionised religious life for women in England and Ireland, and who, in many cases, encountered the same resistance which Mary Ward had met two hundred years before. In Ullathorne's absence, Margaret had already begun to make an impact on the society around her in Coventry and to gather loyal supporters and allies. She continued to work and live under the rule of life of the Dominican Tertiaries, although (with Dominican permission) Ullathorne became her spiritual director. The ill-natured housekeeper was dismissed and oversight of the household placed in Margaret's hands, with a maidservant to assist.

The great spiritual partnership and friendship of both lives had taken root. They shared a common purpose during the

---

55. Champ thesis, pp. 200–1.

years in Coventry, but their friendship deepened and lasted until Margaret's death in 1868. All accounts of her speak of her great warmth of personality, amongst the conventional compliments paid to her piety, devotion, hard work etc. Ullathorne noticed quickly the influence she exercised among young women in the town, and pondered on the source of it. He came to the conclusion that 'it lay not only in that great, warm, loving soul of hers, that was always going to God, but also in her faith in other souls, in what they are, in what they have latent in them, and in what they are capable of'.[56] It was a capacity which also enabled her to understand and appreciate Ullathorne's soul, and to support his changing ministry over many years. Ullathorne had seen for himself what women could achieve in pastoral outreach to other women, and had no reason to doubt their powers of organisation and strength of purpose, as well as their faith and sense of vocation. He shared Margaret's conviction that, even in the most depraved human soul, there was the possibility of good.

While she was clearly fulfilled and busy in the work at Coventry, Margaret still hankered after full religious life, and aspired to joining a convent of Dominican nuns at Atherstone in Warwickshire. Yet the idea of some sort of foundation in Coventry was already in mind; Ullathorne had scarcely met Margaret Hallahan in the spring of 1842 when he began to dream of her missionary work forming, 'the germ of a [religious] institute'.[57] As Ullathorne got to grips with the problems and possibilities of Coventry, free from the shadow of episcopal appointments in the southern hemisphere, his work with Margaret Hallahan began to bear fruit. She was drawing women into her work with the school and the sick, and the embryonic religious institute of which he had dreamed looked like becoming reality. By the end of 1843, he was convinced of the benefit of establishing a Third Order Dominican convent under the direction of Sister Margaret (as she was universally known). He wrote to the Provincial superior of the Dominicans and was ready to help her to begin as soon as he had his concurrence.

56. Drane, *Life*, p 64.
57. Cardiff, Ullathorne to Brown, 8 May 1842.

I am ready to commence with four excellent persons, all
thorough workers, with good sound sense and solid devotion. Sr Margaret is invaluable. The quantity of good
works and of charities that pass through her hands is
almost inexplicable; the manner she is spiritualizing this
congregation is admirable [sic]; and all this amidst a good
deal of personal suffering.[58]

Until the middle years of the nineteenth century, religious life
for women meant the enclosure of contemplative orders. The
battle to achieve acceptance for communities of women bound
by vows, but committed to active apostolic work in the Church,
was a long and hard one. The women religious of the nineteenth century were a startling new presence, and the frisson
created in Victorian minds by the sight of women in distinctive
religious habits was considerable. By 1829 there were an estimated twenty convents in England, and after Catholic
Emancipation the number began to increase rapidly.[59] A
variety of new orders and congregations sprang up alongside
the traditional enclosed orders, designed to meet the changing
needs of Catholic life. Many of these new active religious
orders were French or Irish in origin, but were ideally suited to
the changing needs of English Catholicism. Some were devoted
wholly to education and others to a mixed apostolate of charitable work, catechesis and education. This reflected not only
the new-found Catholic freedoms of the nineteenth century,
but a public assertion of female Catholic enterprise. Each of the
new female orders and congregations owed its origin to the
vision and drive of an individual woman; there was no grand
scheme, but a variety of small scale endeavours, some of which
grew into enormous multinational operations to rival any
commercial corporation. They offered scope for Catholic
women to commit themselves full time to a serious life of
prayer and devotion and to engage in active charitable and
educational work with respectability, while not being married.
For the next century and beyond, these orders became an inte-
gral and vital part of Catholic parish life and the reinvention of

[58.] Ampleforth, Copy of letter, Ullathorne to Brown, 30 January 1844.
[59.] Champ thesis, p. 201, n. 220.

English Catholicism, and they absorbed much of the devastating human impact of the industrial revolution in English society.

On 28 March 1844, Margaret and three companions took up residence in the parish house, with few resources and little income beyond the generosity of benefactors including the enclosed Dominican nuns at Atherstone, Mrs Amherst who had brought Margaret to Coventry, and of course Ullathorne himself. Though he could ill afford it, he bought them one of the first texts in their community library, the writings of St Catherine of Siena, to whom the community was dedicated. Neither the letters of St Catherine nor her *Dialogue* were available in English at that time, so this was presumably a French edition which Margaret could read or a Latin one which Ullathorne could translate for them. Knowledge of Catherine's life and writings must therefore have been very limited for the tiny English Dominican congregation, as the first English biography was not produced until 1887, when Margaret Hallahan's second successor, Francis Raphael Drane wrote an authoritative and scholarly work.

The Dominican Congregation of St Catherine of Siena was launched under the patronage of this medieval mystic, who though canonised as a saint within a century of her death, had not then received the public reverence and acclaim which led to her being proclaimed co-patron of Italy, co-patron of Europe and a Doctor of the Church in the twentieth century. Catherine's passionate and profound love of God, which manifested itself in mystical writings and visions combined with her immense practical desire to serve people in need commended itself to Margaret, so that her new congregation would be classified neither as contemplative nor apostolic, but a hybrid. The Congregation of St Catherine of Siena, inspired both by its foundress and patron, would do as Catherine had been instructed by God – walk on two feet.

Catherine of Siena walked firmly and joyfully on the two feet of love of God and love of neighbour, of contemplation and action. Whenever she encountered people who were reluctant to leave the consolation of a quiet prayer-life, when it was God's will that they should serve those in need, she was quick to urge them not to be afraid to do so.[60]

This would be Margaret Hallahan's inspiration and model for her own life and that of her community. It was the nearest female equivalent to Ullathorne's ideal of the monk-missioner living in a religious community and serving the needs of the people in the surrounding area.

In June 1844 the three new members were formally clothed as novices by Ullathorne. The rule of the Third Order, drawn up for those living outside a religious community, required adaptation for the use of a new religious institute which aspired to conventual life, and Margaret, with Ullathorne's aid, began the preparation of provisional regulations. Other laywomen continued to support their work and to assist the sisters in the school and with sick visiting, but the reaction of their neighbours was not always so positive and they were subject to ridicule and worse.[61]

Until this point, Ullathorne had made few friendships outside the monastery, and keeping contact with Australia was difficult and laborious. While at Coventry, he found the friend-ship of Margaret Hallahan and others who would be a part of his life for years to come. Among these was Ambrose Phillips de Lisle and his wife Laura. She was the sister of Lord Clifford, Cardinal Weld's son-in-law whom he had met in Rome. Phillips de Lisle was a key figure in the extraordinary outpouring of energy and resources into the revival of Catholicism in the 1840s and beyond. A convert, he was a close friend of the men of the Oxford Movement in the Church of England and of the sixteenth Earl of Shrewsbury. Giovanni Pagani, to whom Ullathorne had gone for his retreat before leaving for Rome, cared for the mission at Loughborough in Leicestershire, maintained by de Lisle. It was through Pagani that de Lisle came into contact with Ullathorne, who paid the first of many visits to the de Lisle home at Grace Dieu on 18 January 1843, to take part in the blessing of a Calvary in the grounds, the first to be created in England since the Reformation. It was an

---

60. O'Driscoll, p. 25.
61. Drane, *Life*, p. 109.

elaborate affair lasting all day with a variety of liturgical celebrations, Ullathorne preaching at both the High Mass in the
morning and Vespers in the evening.[62] As he was a relatively
unknown missioner in a poor urban district some distance
away, this was obviously a personal invitation rather than an
official one, and a compliment to his growing reputation as a
preacher.

This visit enabled Ullathorne to begin to understand something of what was going on in the Church of England, since De
Lisle was in close contact with the leaders of the Oxford
Movement, and later correspondence enabled De Lisle to share
this with Ullathorne.[63] Preaching on the Cross of Christ in
Christian history on this occasion, he saw the revival of interest
in the Cross in England as a sign of promise for the future.
Ullathorne had quickly picked up on the dynamic optimism
which characterised Catholic life in the 1840s, when all things
seemed possible: these were 'days which are replete with
mystery, and full of the expectation of things to come'.[64]
Ullathorne's optimism was not only for the Catholic Church in
England but also for his own settled part in it; the memory of
the stresses of Australia was fading, and seeing progress in
Coventry, Ullathorne was looking forward to the future with
equanimity and confidence.

Ullathorne reported confidently to Brown that the Oxford
Movement men, by early 1843, had

> been so far enlightened as to see and acknowledge that
> the whole fault and blame of the schism rests with
> England ... However, they argue that it is right to stay
> where they are, in the hope of bringing the whole Church
> back into communion ... Newman now begins to hope
> that reunion may take place in his own days. The feelings

[62.] M. Pawley, *Faith and Family: The Life and Circle of Ambrose Phillips de
Lisle* (1993), p. 151.

[63.] AAW St Edmund's Papers, Ambrose Phillips de Lisle to Ullathorne,
5 July 1843. De Lisle addresses Ullathorne as 'my dear Father', a
form of clerical address little used at the time. Ullathorne continued
the older practice all his life of addressing secular clergy as Mr x.

[64.] *The Blessing of the Calvary on Grace Dieu Rocks* – a sermon (1843),
p. 16.

towards Catholicism in this district are becoming very remarkable, and the numbers of people received into the Church is extraordinary. We have our share. But in other places where the Italians Fr Dominic, Gentili etc. are preaching in the streets and villages, it is much more remarkable.[65]

At this point, Ullathorne's grasp of the Tractarian issues was simplistic in the extreme, and never became very nuanced or sophisticated. He certainly did not appreciate the complexity of Newman's relationship with the episcopate of the Church of England after 1841, or the ways in which this might shape his anxious response to bishops once he was an ordained Catholic.

Nicholas Wiseman, previously rector of the English College, Rome, was, from 1840, coadjutor bishop to Thomas Walsh in the Central District and equally ebullient about the progress and direction of the Oxford Movement. He had written scathingly about Anglican claims to antiquity and Catholicity in the *Dublin Review* of 1839, and was anxious to see Tractarians fully acknowledge the doctrine of the Catholic Church. He, like Ullathorne, had been impatient with what he saw in England after a period abroad, and saw the Oxford Movement as the key to the revival of Catholicism. In contact with some of the early Oxford movement converts themselves, he shared a dissatisfaction with the rate of progress, but, 'Wiseman was premature in his judgement, relying upon reports from unduly optimistic Catholics, like Phillips and Spencer, as well as devotees of Newman within the Anglican communion who tended to race ahead of their leader and whose ardour he in fact tried to subdue.'[66]

In August 1841, Wiseman responded sympathetically to Newman's Tract 90 in the *Dublin Review* and in a public *Letter On Catholic Unity*. He made light of difficulties in the way of reunion between Catholicism and the Church of England and encouraged hopes that they might be overcome, urging,

[65.] Ampleforth copy of letter, Ullathorne to Brown, Feast of St Marcellus 1843.
[66.] R. J. Schiefen, *Nicholas Wiseman and the Transformation of English Catholicism* (Shepherdstown, 1984), p. 118.

'trustfulness in the sincerity of others, and in the goodness of
their motives, hopefulness in the result of our endeavours ...
unwearied kindness and charity ... zeal that abates not in
warmth'.[67] De Lisle hoped for a form of unity in which
Anglicans could retain their own rite and tradition, and spoke
optimistically of the relaxation of the laws of celibacy and
certain aspects of canon law.[68] He acted as a go-between for
Wiseman with his Anglican contacts, but it was clear that in
their zealous idealism, de Lisle and perhaps Wiseman did not
fully appreciate the gulf which, despite the Oxford Movement,
still stood between Rome and the Church of England. By the
end of the decade, Ullathorne had cause to regret Wiseman's
early enthusiasm for Anglican converts, and was accused of
being 'anti-convert'; this was certainly not true, but it was one
of several sources of irritation between the two men.

It was no surprise in this more optimistic atmosphere of
Catholic revival, that one of Ullathorne's early ambitions in
Coventry was to build a decent church. Like many urban miss-
sioners of his generation, Ullathorne had inherited a mean and
shabby structure, too small for a growing congregation. The
mission had been in Benedictine hands since 1803, and Fr
John Dawber had opened a small church in 1807, which was
now a tumbledown wreck. Ullathorne's vision, shaped by his
Australian experience of monk missioners living in isolation,
was to rebuild the church and create a missionary priory in
Coventry from where a small group of monks could eventually
serve the wider neighbourhood. After travelling the great open
spaces of New South Wales, the distances between towns and
villages in England must have seemed negligable, and a roving
mission from a stable urban base the ideal solution. Ullathorne
insisted that solitary Benedictine missioners (the pattern in
English recusant society, and in Australia) was essentially a
temporary arrangement to meet particular needs. For monks
to live alone was unsatisfactory, a short-term emergency
arrangement which should be brought to an end. He insisted
on this throughout his life, but even in his early days in
Coventry, when he had no authority to alter things, he

[67.] Wilfrid Ward, *The Life and Times of Cardinal Wiseman* (1897), I,
p. 405.
[68.] Pawley, p. 178.

reflected upon the missionary role of the English Benedictine congregation, and saw that circumstances were changing from those which had made missionary constitutions necessary. New religious orders were coming into England and demonstrating the possibility of community life, yet those whose ancient tradition and purpose was one of common life were still living as isolated missioners. This was bad for the individual monks and bad for the future of English monasticism, since few people had any chance to experience what the reality of Benedictine life was in its full monastic form.

> This led me to reflect that, if on the mission, and especially in important towns, we could only live in community, and with as much community life as the circumstances of a mission would allow of, we should not only ourselves have the kind of life which is natural and proper to us, but that the spirit of our Holy Order would become understood, and fit and generous minds would be drawn towards us and towards our state of life, and our parent monasteries would thus become supplied with a proportionate supply of men and means.[69]

This idea took shape early in planning the development of the Coventry property, as he wrote to Downside,

> I beg leave respectfully to commend to your kind zeal and patronage the proposed Church of the Holy Sacrament of Coventry. *Magnum opus et arduam* ... It is planned with a view to a priory which I hope we shall live to see attached, small of course, to each of our churches in large towns. Thus we may return to our Holy Apostolate even on the mission, and what a force would it not give us. In writing to the Prior of Coventry, I have expressed my hope of seeing him preside at the opening of this church over a full choir of *habited* missionary monks.[70]

Missionary priories were dear to his heart, and given the time

---

69. Ampleforth 246/46, Ullathorne to President General, 20 July 1874.
70. DA L230, Ullathorne to Prior Peter Wilson, 15 February 1843.

and scope it is not unlikely that his energy and drive would have made them happen.

> What ample work would there be here for a small community of say, six monks, priests and choir monks, or let them be lay brothers, though that would not meet my views. I shall require a person for music, then two school-masters, then another priest, besides one for Kenilworth. It would take very little more than our present resources to do all this with the right spirit. Why seek for Brothers of Christian Doctrine, or pay schoolmasters when we could have monks to keep choir, observe discipline and do all this much better?[71]

In Ullathorne's view, these urban priories could achieve great things in towns like Coventry, Liverpool and Bath where there was already a Benedictine presence.

Augustus Welby Pugin (the architect of St Chad's and Oscott) was at the height of his powers, working on projects all over the Midlands, but Ullathorne did not apparently contemplate choosing him as architect for Coventry. Instead he secured the services of Charles Hansom, a young Catholic architect and town surveyor of Coventry. Cost was almost certainly the reason, rather than any distaste for Gothic design. He could not risk Pugin's notorious extravagance in the poor conditions of Coventry, and he thereby gained something of a reputation for cheapness.[72] However, Charles Hansom was obviously not to be disregarded as an architect, as Pugin himself recommended Charles Hansom's practice (and specifically not that of his more famous brother, Joseph) as a good place to send a pupil architect to learn the business.[73] Hansom gained a considerable reputation, and in the 1850s he undertook work at Downside on the school buildings.

Ullathorne himself was becoming increasingly interested in

[71.] Ampleforth, Copy of letter, Ullathorne to Brown, January 30 1844.
[72.] Pugin commented to John Hardman on an acquaintance who was 'going to Coventry where Dr Ullathorne got his candles at half price' rather than using Hardman's Birmingham factory. Margaret Belcher, *The Collected Letters of A. W. N. Pugin* (2003), II, p. 435.
[73.] Ibid., p. 392.

Gothic architecture, and as Hansom's knowledge of it was limited, he took him off to Belgium and France and on to the magnificent cathedral of Cologne to educate his taste and stimulate his ideas.[74] They visited Bruges, Ghent, St Trond, Leau, Louvain, Aix-la-Chapelle, Liège and Cologne, picking up ideas and images of pre-Reformation art and architecture. Stopping at Antwerp, Ullathorne was particularly struck by the Seven Sacraments painting in the museum there, which he described in great detail, but attributed wrongly to Van Eyck rather than Rogier Van de Wieden. He was clearly enjoying a taste of northern European art, and relishing the task ahead of him, telling the Prior of Downside cheerfully that, 'every priest must be an architect now'.[75]

Margaret Hallahan organised fundraising locally for the new church and was the means of a large donation from an English friend resident in Bruges, Charles Eyre. Ullathorne went on begging tours around the country and work began on the site in May 1843. The church was to be dedicated to St Osburg, an eleventh-century abbess of Coventry, whose shrine was a popular place of pilgrimage, and whose feast was celebrated locally on 30 March.[76] By early 1844 the church was well under way, with the spire over fifty feet tall, and was 'universally admired'.[77] Some of the money came from the sale of the remarkable library which Ullathorne had personally collected and left in Sydney, including the rare first edition of Luther and Melancthon in nineteen half-calf volumes, which he bought in Dublin in 1837.[78] Anxious that the collection (of which he knew the intellectual value) should remain in Australia where the need was great, he offered them to Polding in return for £150 to buy a set of the Church Fathers.[79] The valuation Polding obtained was only £140, and Ullathorne was furious that Polding did not get him a better price, but this was

---

74. *Autobiography*, p. 261.
75. Norbert Birt, 'Archbishop Ullathorne on Church Furniture and Decoration' in *Downside Review* vol. XXVIII (1909), pp. 108–13.
76. D. H. Farmer, *The Oxford Dictionary of Saints* (1987 ed.), p. 326.
77. Ampleforth, Copy of letter, Ullathorne to Brown, 30 January 1844.
78. *Autobiography*, pp. 159–60.
79. John Fletcher, 'The Library of St Patrick's College, Manly' in *Australian Catholic History* 54/2 (1977), pp. 169–81.

only one source of irritation with his former ally, whose, 'stomach for power' had soured relations between the two old friends.[80]

The fundraising for St Osburg's was the subject of the first of many angry disputes between Ullathorne and Wiseman, often involving money, which blighted co-operation between the two of them. Increasing demands for funds for church building in growing industrial missions had stimulated Bishops Walsh and Wiseman to launch regular collections throughout the Central District from 1843 for their newly founded Mission Fund. Money from this fund was made available to enable or enhance local building schemes, especially in poorer areas, where fund raising was laborious and slow. However, Ullathorne's scheme at Coventry was for a Benedictine mission, and part of the problem which arose between him and Wiseman seemed to centre on whether or not missions run by the religious orders fell within the remit of the Mission Fund. The row exploded in the summer of 1844, by which time Ullathorne's new church dedicated to St Osburg was well under way, and the flashpoint was the collections undertaken by Fr Clarkson (Ullathorne's assistant) outside Coventry itself. Wiseman hauled Clarkson in and told him off for exceeding his brief, and wrote a harsh reprimand to Ullathorne, insisting that Bishop Walsh had specifically mentioned the needs of Coventry and its 'miserable chapel' in his pastoral letter of 25 March 1843 and had promised £200 immediately and 'a fair share' of forthcoming Mission Fund collections.[81]

Wiseman was heavy-handed in his criticism.

But you prefer taking your chance by a collection of your own, or acting so as to produce further irritation in your flock against the Bishop, whose intentions, if allowed to be carried into effect, would, I am sure, have ended without the humiliation, harassing anxiety and expense of a collection (not to speak of loss of time so valuable to a priest, especially of this person) all that could have been put together by your proposed plans ... That harm has already

80. DA L271, Ullathorne to Heptonstall, 22 December 1843.
81. DA (unnumbered), Wiseman to Ullathorne, Ember Saturday 1844.

been done to the Bishop's plan I feel certain, that religion has gained on any other side in compensation I have no ground to hope. Had the simple course been followed cheerfully and at once, of ascertaining clearly his wishes (if any grounds for doubt existed) and acting upon them, all would have been gainers. As it is, I fear all shall suffer.[82]

Ullathorne was furious at this attack on his freedom of action (and that of his Order) which he regarded as undermining the, 'future existence of regular missions'. In equally strong and uncompromising tones he insisted to Wiseman that he had 'not the least intention of questioning the canonical right involved in any bit of jurisdiction exercised by the bishop', but, was incredulous that 'Your Lordship expressly forbids all collecting of the alms of the faithful for church building, private as well as public.'[83] Ullathorne had taken the view (shared by most of the clergy) that the pastoral letter setting up the Mission Fund had not forbidden private collections undertaken by individual missioners, especially where the religious orders were involved, who might have access to benefactors outside the immediate locality. Ullathorne had not seen off the likes of John Joseph Therry to be treated in this fashion once back in his own country and running a Downside mission. Wiseman was perhaps a tougher prospect than Polding, but Ullathorne was undaunted and responded with a blunderbuss when Wiseman (through his secretary) turned his coat a year later, asserting that no promises of money for Coventry had been made and the fund was empty anyway.[84]

Ullathorne reminded Wiseman in no uncertain terms that, when he had reprimanded Clarkson in the previous year for taking unauthorised collections, he had promised £100 from each collection for the Missionary Fund until the church was completed. This promise was repeated to the architect Charles Hansom (reluctant to be drawn in to the row), when he showed Wiseman the plans when visiting Hinckley, and also by Walsh himself to Ullathorne in Coventry early in the previous year. In his usual relentless fashion, Ullathorne piled on the

82. Ibid.
83. DA (unnumbered), Ullathorne to Wiseman, (draft) 10 March 1844.
84. DA (unnumbered), Wiseman to Ullathorne, 2 June 1844.

evidence of broken promises about money for Coventry, and even hinted at repercussions:

> I beg to add that the promises I have cited are publicly known in Coventry and that my object in making this known was to exalt the Bishop's kindness in our regard ... Your Lordship must allow me to add in conclusion that whatever embarrassment I am cast into by reason of your Lordship's reply arises out of the confidence with which I have built upon the word of the episcopal promise.[85]

No further money was forthcoming from the Mission Fund, but there must have been some smoothing of ruffled feathers, as Wiseman presided at the opening of the church in September 1845. Years later, though, the question of the financing of St Osburg's still rankled, and it stands as an example of Ullathorne's prodigious memory and tendency to bear a grudge if he felt that the truth had been denied. As bishop, over a decade later, he came across a reference to his having run up a debt of £4,500 in building the Coventry church. Furious, he set out for the benefit of the unfortunate, and no doubt mystified, annalist of the EBC, Fr Peter Athanasius Allanson, the facts of the financial record:

> The wretched little chapel there, I found in a most dilapidated state, and not above a hundred people, if so many, attended it. The congregation so increased that the place would not hold them. I spent all the little money I had left upon it from my stipend in Australia:

The sale of my library there	£200
From Bishop Walsh	£200
From Dr Wiseman	£100
One donation	£700
Collected from the people £100 per an	£300
Collected by going about	£500
Another donation	£150
	£2150

85.   DA (unnumbered), Ullathorne to Wiseman, 11 June 1844.

The stained glass was made by donations, the chancel and the house with money provided by the Provincial, and other donations provided the rest. Ullathorne suggested that the misinformation passed on to Allanson stemmed from the jealousy and bitterness of Ullathorne's predecessor, who at the opening of the church, had done nothing but carp and criticise.[86] By the time Ullathorne was removed from Coventry in April 1846, he had left no debt on the church, which was a remarkable achievement, due largely to his and Margaret Hallahan's energetic fund raising.[87]

The consecration of the church of St Osburg in September 1845 was a symbolic moment for Ullathorne; his hope of a choir of habited monks was not realised, but he himself donned his monastic habit in public for the first time in England. He had, of course, first had the opportunity to obtain and wear the habit on his visit to Rome in 1837, but had not worn it since. His appearance in it in Coventry caused raised eyebrows and even hostility, not only among non-Catholics, but among his fellow monks who were not yet used even to wearing the habit within the monastery. Clerical dress was still largely unknown (and remained technically illegal until 1926), and Ullathorne's practice of wearing his habit around the house and church was distinctly unusual. By this time, the bishops of the Central District and the people of Coventry certainly knew that Ullathorne meant business and was not diffident when it came to getting his own way. He may not have read the situation well, and not realised that critics would see it as another example of Ullathorne drawing attention to himself.

Throughout 1843–4 Ullathorne was widely spoken of as a possible successor to Baines in the Western District, or it was hinted that Brown would be translated from Wales to the Western District and Ullathorne would go to Wales.[88] One of Ullathorne's Roman friends, a Carmelite Archbishop, Francis

---

[86.] DA N456, Ullathorne to Allanson, 5 December 1856.

[87.] Ampleforth 262/36, Fr Jenkins to Abbot President (Rome), 15 April 1846.

[88.] Farm St Foreign Correspondence 1776–1859 388, Anon. to Fr Glover SJ in Rome '... you can state authoritatively that Ullathorne will go there [Western District] or any place else in England. You saw his letter to that effect.'

Joseph Nicholson was sure that, before long, Ullathorne would be one of the much needed regular clergy among the vicars apostolic, on which he believed 'the *real* conversion of England' would depend. He warned him that, for the sake of the Church in England, he would do nothing to extricate him, but would put him 'into the net'.[89] W. H. Coombs, a secular priest of the Western District, who had unwittingly played a significant part in Ullathorne's spiritual formation by translating Marsollier's *Life of St Francis de Sales*, tried to influence his career further by writing to Cardinal Acton, the English agent in Rome, within days of the death of Bishop Peter Baines in the Western District:

> The regulars, and principally the Benedictines, have always had the government of the Western District, since the establishment of the present form of the hierarchy in the days of James II ... Among the Benedictines of the present time, one character stands prominently conspicuous, and in my judgement fully qualified to succeed the late Dr Baines. I allude to Dr Ullathorne, whose merits are fully known at Rome. The vigour and energy of manhood, his piety, talents, zeal, his writings and his apostolic labours in Australia, all speak in his favour, and seem to designate the man, whom providence has selected for the work in question.[90]

His achievements in Coventry in creating a new kind of missionary model were beginning to be recognised locally and the value of his work was being appreciated by others, including his fellow monk missioners. It was not only Ullathorne himself who feared the shadow of an Australian mitre, but his fellow missioners feared to lose him.

> I should exceedingly regret if any arrangement respecting New Holland or any colonial appointment should induce you to quit England or to abandon your present scene where your zeal is probably as usefully employed as

[89.] AAW St Edmunds Papers, Nicholson to Ullathorne, 9 May 1843.
[90.] DA L252, W. H. Coombs to Cardinal Acton, 22 August 1843.

it could be in any other quarter. The mere good done at Coventry is but a small proportion – the example – the school to learn missionary zeal, where such examples are so few, will be more general in its effects, and more lasting in its consequences, than the simple good performed by one zealous missionary and I look upon Coventry as a school of that description, and where I hope many will learn how to employ their talents usefully.[91]

In the event, Brown stayed put and the choice for the Western District fell on Baggs, rector of the English College in Rome and a secular priest. This was interpreted as something of a rap on the knuckles for the squabbling Benedictines, not least by Ullathorne: 'The regulars have had a salutary humiliation. We must make ourselves worthy to be called to great works. We must exhibit the regular spirit on our missions and then their value will be felt in the right quarter.'[92] As far as he was concerned, it was an immense relief and left him feeling like a released prisoner,[93] but he was still not free from the importunate requests of Polding and Willson (now Bishop of Hobart) in Australia. Willson begged Downside to send him back to the Antipodes and continue the work he had begun there:

But Oh! my dear friend, do prevail on my little apostle Dr Ullathorne to come to this land. *He is made for this peculiar mission* – do for mercy's sake ask his superiors (if he agrees to it), which God may grant, that they will allow it. Remember we have *all* the convicts now, and from all the colonies, including the double and treble dyed men from NSW. Mr Therry has ruined religion here for years. Do not blush – we have *no schools*! no church of our own – no charities – no Sisters of Mercy, nor Brothers of Christian Doctrine, nor guilds nor societies for Propagation of the Faith, nor Catholic Inst. – but debt, strife, misery with the renowned Dr Therry.[94]

[91.] DA (unnumbered), William Dunstan Scott (Little Malvern) to Ullathorne, 28 March 1845.

[92.] AAW St Edmunds Papers, Ullathorne to Wiseman, 1 January 1844.

[93.] Cardiff, Ullathorne to Brown, January 10 1844.

[94.] DA i410, Willson to Prior Heptonstall, 8 August 1845.

That kind of desperate pleading could not be lightly ignored, but his mind was made up. In 1845 Ullathorne was offered the Diocese of Perth (the third see in Australia for which he was nominated) and he swiftly declined on the grounds that his health was not up to it.[95]

His gloom at the prospect was deepened by the thought of leaving Coventry, which was 'just beginning to develop itself' and where he could already see the possibilities of what could be achieved by his 'very valuable aid' Margaret Hallahan.[96] The work of the continental religious Orders, especially the Rosminians and Passionists, began to meet some of the need Ullathorne identified in the preface to his published sermons of 1842 for preaching which would 'meet the spirit of the time and the wants of this nation'.[97] He got Fr Gentili, a Rosminian, to preach his second large-scale mission at Coventry in May 1845. This was a deliberate and well planned protest on Ullathorne's part at the annual events surrounding the procession of 'Lady Godiva' through the streets of Coventry. The re-enactment of the naked protest by a medieval Lady of the Manor at her husband's harsh treatment of the tenants had become an excuse for ribaldry and coarse behaviour. Ullathorne was determined to draw the Catholics away from participation in the Lady Godiva procession and to offer a counter-attraction to the rest of the city. Gentili and Margaret Hallahan provided the solution in reviving, as part of the mission, another medieval procession, that of the Virgin Mary. A statue, surrounded with flowers, garlands and lights was placed on a bier and carried through the streets of Coventry, for the first time since the Reformation.[98]

Two things are clear about Ullathorne's years in Coventry: firstly, he was enormously happy and fulfilled there, feeling that he was setting in motion missionary projects which had the potential to bear fruit, and secondly that he was absolutely clear about not returning to Australia. He got over his misgivings about leaving the Sisters of Charity and abandoning

---

95. BAA B859/865, *Propaganda Fide* to Ullathorne, 22 March 1845, Ullathorne to *Propaganda Fide*, 9 April 1845.
96. Cardiff, Ullathorne to Brown, 8 May 1842.
97. *Sermons*, p. 61.
98. Butler, *Life*, I, p. 132.

Polding, and rejected the offer of Perth with much greater speed and equanimity than he had turned down Hobart or Adelaide. There was no personal appeal to Rome, but simply a letter of refusal. Ullathorne knew that his own future lay in England and he hoped that it would be in the developing mission of Coventry, alongside Margaret Hallahan. His health and spirits recovered at Coventry, as well as his sense of purpose.

He was not averse to becoming something of a public figure, prepared to publish trenchant sermons and to take on injustice at the hands of bishops. The self-confidence which had taken a battering in the last couple of years in Australia began to flow back, and he knew what he could achieve. Did he, as contemporaries suspected, want to be a bishop? He was certainly not averse to exercising leadership and had plenty of ideas about the direction the Church in England should be taking, but there was still a strong pull towards a more solitary and recollected life, in keeping with a monk-missioner. He also relished the direct contact with people in his mission work, and the fulfilment which came from that. The combined impact of Ullathorne and Margaret Hallahan's small religious community on the people of Coventry was huge and both became revered figures among the industrial workers in the ribbon factories. He became as fond of Coventry and its people as they of him. Twenty years later, he was delighted, when on an episcopal visitation to his old home, not only to be remembered by the people, but mobbed by them in the sacristy after Mass, 'all wanting some little word to take home and live upon'.[99]

[99.] AAW Ullathorne Correspondence, Ullathorne to Manning, 23 May 1865.

Chapter 4

The Reluctant Bishop 1846–1850

By 1846, Rome was well acquainted with Ullathorne's unwillingness to accept episcopal positions in Australia, and was
reluctantly reconciled to this. England was another matter.
Baggs, who had succeeded Baines, had not lived long, and by
1846 the Western District, with its tradition of Benedictine
bishops, was again vacant. The English Curial Cardinal Acton
won Ullathorne's compliance by sheer cunning.

> If honour and riches had gathered around the mitre now
> hanging over your Lordship's head, then perhaps you
> still might have found out some motives to allege, or flies
> of excuses for rejecting the offer, but in the present
> circumstances, [of the Western District] My Lord, it is
> pain, trouble and labour which is offered you and there-
> fore I trust that through love for Christ and His Church
> you will immediately accept the burden.[1]

He had caught Ullathorne exactly right, and left him no
choice. 'After reading the letter before the Most Holy
Sacrament, I bent down in submission. Not a part of my heart
would permit me to resist the Will of Almighty God and of the
Holy See. Today's post conveys my acceptance.'[2]

He wrote to an old school friend who sent congratulations on

[1.] DA L461, Ullathorne to Brown, 28 April 1846.
[2.] Ibid.

his appointment, recalling their schooldays with affection, 'my dear old schoolfellow ... I wonder if I should recognise you ...' He invited him to his consecration, begging his prayers, 'for the presence of God in this monk', and reiterated his reluctance to take up the dignity of a bishop. 'I feel all the kindness of your thus recollecting me and following me with your true hearted sympathy. Indeed, my dear friend, there is nothing less desirable to flesh and blood than an English mitre under any circumstances in this age. And my experience as the vicar general of two bishops always taught me the emotion of compassion rather than that of envy in their regard'.[3] He never had cause to alter that view.

His appointment as Vicar Apostolic of the Western District was acclaimed by the Prior of Downside, Luke Barber, writing to a fellow Benedictine in the Western District. 'A worthy child of Christ is your new Bishop Elect – Dr Ullathorne, who is with me accompanied by his credentials. Alleluia, alleluia, alleluia'.[4] Not everyone in the Western District was so enthusiastic. Thomas Brindle, who had acted as vicar capitular in the interregnum after the deaths of three previous bishops, who had been regarded by many (including himself) as the obvious choice.[5] The stage was, therefore, set for the conflict which was not long in coming.

Ullathorne was consecrated as bishop in the church of St Osburg, which he had built at Coventry, on 21 July 1846 – the same day that Pius IX was crowned as Pope in St Peter's. He pointedly insisted on the use of vestments of the 'old and ample form' which were borrowed from Oscott College. This was to put down a very clear marker: Baines had made a big issue over the style of vestments and had complained to Rome of the spread of the 'old and ample' Gothic style used by Bishop Walsh in the Central District. Ullathorne was not obsessed with vestments, but this was a signal to the Western District that change was ahead.[6]

[3.] Colwich, Ullathorne to Thomas Taunton esq. of London, 12 May 1846. His sister was later prioress of Colwich.
[4.] DA L460, Barber to Prior Wilson, 28 April 1846.
[5.] John Cashman, 'Old Prior Park – the Final Years 1843–1856' in *Recusant History* vol. 23 (1996), p. 80.
[6.] CDA Letters vol. 1838–49 No. 499, Ullathorne to Brindle, 14 June 1846.

Newman and his former Oxford colleagues, newly received into the Catholic Church and now settled at Old Oscott (which he renamed Maryvale) attended the consecration. This was Newman's first appearance at a large scale Catholic occasion and his first meeting with Ullathorne, who, within a few years would be a dominant influence in his life. His first impressions are not recorded. Ullathorne parted tearfully from the people of Coventry, who presented him with a gift of a chalice which he used at the altar for forty years. What he described as 'the happiest and most fruitful years of my life',[7] came to an abrupt end.

After an overnight stay in Bath at the Benedictine mission, he proceeded next morning to Prior Park College, overlooking Bath, which had been the residence of both his predecessors, Baines and Baggs. Another sign of change was not long in coming, as he made clear his intention to live in the largest city of the District, Bristol. The new bishop lost no time in moving the episcopal quarters out of Prior Park and into rented accommodation in King's Square in the centre of Bristol. Luigi Gentili commented in his reports sent to Propaganda in late 1847 and early 1848 that Ullathorne, 'lives like a poor man and is content with very little'.[8] This continued to be his style of life to the end of his days; he chose to live as a bishop in monastic simplicity with few possessions apart from his books.

The move to Bristol was a reflection of his missionary priorities, his distaste for the grandeur of Prior Park and his awareness of its troubled history. He was conscious of the need to focus his attention on the main centres of population and develop what a modern bishop might call a missionary strategy, gathering around him an effective set of priests and encouraging religious communities. As a Benedictine whose monastic home lay in the heart of the District, he had to establish quickly and clearly a sense of leadership of the secular clergy of the area.[9] Only a week after his consecration, he was asserting his new authority by announcing a whole series of clergy moves between missions.[10]

---

[7] *Autobiography*, p. 278.

[8] Quoted in Richard J. Schiefen, *Nicholas Wiseman and the Transformation of English Catholicism* (1984), p. 149.

[9] *Autobiography*, p. 222.

[10] CDA Letters vol. 1838–49 No. 505, Ullathorne to Brindle, 29 July 1846.

While trying to be even-handed with the diocesan and religious clergy as bishop of the District, Ullathorne remained passionate in his devotion to Downside and the Benedictines. In May 1848, as he was about to leave for Rome to negotiate the possible restoration of the hierarchy, he vehemently expressed his 'true and hearty love for the order to which I owe not only my education but whatever good I have been able in the hands of God to accomplish', insisting that any apparent severity in his manner sprang only from his zeal for the good of the Order and Downside.[11]

Ullathorne's short time as Vicar Apostolic of the Western District was dominated by the problems of Prior Park, which had clearly contributed to the early death of his predecessor. Butler gave a limited account of a controversy he regarded as having 'no abiding value',[12] but it does reveal something of Ullathorne cutting his teeth in the exercise of authority as a bishop. Prior Park had been purchased in 1829 for £22,000 by Peter Baines, the Benedictine Vicar Apostolic whose disputes with Downside had formed a controversial backdrop to Ullathorne's own early monastic career. In 1836 a disastrous fire had destroyed the mansion, and inadequate insurance cover meant that an estimated repair bill of £15,000 was nowhere near covered. In addition, Baines had already lavished £50,000 (much of it on loan) on refurbishments, now ruined.[13] The whole District was embroiled in the disputes and the antagonism surrounding Prior Park, and numerous lay people were well out of pocket as a result of Baines' extravagance. Even the college servants had invested their wages in it. Ullathorne's Downside connection did not help in sorting out the factions, because the main supporters of Prior Park were former Benedictines of Ampleforth who had left to help Baines establish his new college, and of course, Baines had been party to an almighty row with Downside which had gone as far as Rome.

It did not take Ullathorne long to get to grips with Prior Park, as he had heard enough of its difficulties in advance of

---

[11.] DA M87, Ullathorne to President General, 9 May 1848.
[12.] Butler, *Life*, I, p. 140.
[13.] Harding thesis, p. 24.

his arrival. Even in Cardinal Acton's letter announcing his appointment, he had warned him, in veiled terms, that Prior Park, 'in which the secular clergy are so much interested', would be a delicate problem requiring prudent action.[14] It seems obvious that the choice of Ullathorne for the Western District was driven by this 'delicate problem', and the need for a tough approach. Little over a week after his episcopal consecration he mentioned Prior Park to Wiseman. He feared putting the possessions of religious orders in danger as a result of the forthcoming Parliamentary Bill on charities, but admitted ruefully that, if it had already been in place, 'Prior Park would not be in the condition it now is in', because it would have brought things to a head by enforcing the payment of interest owing on loans.[15] Not only did Ullathorne find financial mismanagement but extravagance and worldliness which meant that 'Prior Park was stamped all over, inside and out, with a secular tone'.[16] In his dealings with Prior Park, Ullathorne clearly expressed a certain distaste for its grandiose style, which made him disinclined to try and resolve its financial problems in a way which secured its future. It was obvious from the start that he would shed few tears if it was forced into closure.

The president of Prior Park was none other than Dr Thomas Brindle, who had been considered by some (including himself) as a candidate for the episcopal appointment and his disappointment was compounded by his traditional alliance with the Baines camp. There had been animosity between Baines and Walsh of the Central District, not only over the use of Gothic vestments, but more seriously over the deployment in the Western District of a priest, Thomas McDonnell, a thorn in the flesh of both Walsh and Wiseman in Birmingham, who had found a new home in the Western District.[17] Dr Brindle was an ally of Baines in supporting McDonnell, who would raise his

[14]. BAA B940, Cardinal Acton to Ullathorne, 16 April 1846.
[15]. CDA Letters vol. 1838–49, No. 495, Ullathorne to Wiseman, 1 July 1846.
[16]. *Autobiography*, p. 226.
[17]. Judith Champ, 'Priesthood and Politics in the Nineteenth Century: the turbulent career of Thomas McDonnell' in *Recusant History* vol. 18 (1987) pp. 289–303.

head again in Ullathorne's time, causing further irritation and embarrassment.[18] Ullathorne was stepping into a complex web of clerical gossip, vanities and sensitivities not unlike that which he had found in Sydney. This time, his approach was a little more circumspect, a result of greater maturity and self awareness.

Unlike Sydney, where he had felt the need to act quickly, he bided his time over Prior Park, and no doubt listened to what he could glean from others. By not rushing into Prior Park, he also gave an indication that it would not be his dominant preoccupation. The problems of the college could wait till he was good and ready. Ullathorne's first visit to Prior Park, which took place a full month after his arrival in the District, was coloured by the bizarre treatment he received at Brindle's hands, who lived in splendid isolation in a veritable palace. Despite the new bishop's arrival, Brindle made no attempt to alter his regular pattern of celebrating Mass alone, breakfasting and then spending most of the day mixing in fashionable society in nearby Bath. Ullathorne spent only a few nights there, otherwise travelling around the District, 'dropping down here and there, and hearing all I could learn of the state of things'.[19]

Though still only forty, Ullathorne had behind him the experience of Australia, and his early success there had been based upon swift and decisive action and forthright speech. The old Antipodean spirit came upon him again, and before the summer was out, he had assessed the situation and was tackling Brindle head on. His mind was soon preoccupied with the severe financial state of the college, which had virtually bankrupted the District, its poor spirit and its ineffective management. Drastic change was needed, and (other than closure) there were only two possibilities. Ullathorne was willing to relieve the trustees of the financial problems if he had total control, and could run it as a carefully managed ecclesiastical operation, or he offered them an ultimatum that they could continue it as an independent school but not a seminary, without any financial involvement on the part of the

---

[18.] See Chapter 5.
[19.] *Autobiography*, p. 288.

Western District.[20] In other words, if it had any ecclesiastical role as a college, the bishop had to be in charge, which meant setting policy and governing personnel as much as it did financial control.

Ullathorne had a heavy literary style in which he was fond of piling up repetitions, and his letter to Brindle setting out the options is a model of its kind.

> Now, my dear Mr Brindle, it is time we looked at the truth of the case. If a superior does not meet the difficulties of his position, if he does not concentrate his mind upon them, put his energies into them and pervade them with his personal presence and superintendence, if he does not bring forth in some clear, definite and comprehensive shape all needful information, if he does not give precise and definite answers and directions, if instead of this his time is much consumed in minor and subordinate occupations, if his time is mainly divided between his private apartments, the reading rooms and society, if this is felt by everyone, what must be the result?

He made it clear that he expected Brindle to pull himself together and take proper control of the college, and highlighted three urgent areas requiring attention. The first was to sort out the financial mess and extricate Prior Park's accounts from those of the District; secondly he expected staff changes to bring about greater co-operation; thirdly he expected the new arrangements to be actually carried into effect.[21] Prior Park could survive as a diocesan seminary and possibly also as a school, but firm and immediate action was needed.

Throughout the autumn months of 1846 little was achieved in the overdue reform of Prior Park, and relations between Ullathorne and Brindle deteriorated. It did not take long before there was a complete breakdown in confidence between the two men, Ullathorne accusing Brindle of reneging on his promise to co-operate fully and warning him in his familiar,

---

20. Cashman, p. 81.
21. CDA Letters vol. 1838–49 No. 508A, Ullathorne to Brindle, 29 August 1846.

somewhat pompous tones that he no longer trusted him. 'You cannot be surprised, dear sir, if henceforth the commonest prudence dictates to me the utmost reserve and caution in any communications I may have with you.'[22] This was only the first of three letters exchanged in a single day, which culminated in Ullathorne sacking Brindle from his post as vicar general (the bishop's closest advisor) in the District. There was no literary elaboration, not even any episcopal pomposity, but a curt and angry note spelling out sheer frustration: after thanking him for 'such services as you have rendered', he ended briskly and brutally. 'Having no more occasion for your services in that capacity, as I have previously given notice, you will have the goodness to consider the powers of vicar general ceasing on receipt of this letter.'[23]

Little progress was made in reforming the management and direction of the college's academic life. Several convert clergymen from the Church of England had found posts there, and they, Collins, Neve and Northcote only clung on to their posts in the hope that the bishop would be taking direct control. Their frustration grew, and they looked increasingly to Ullathorne for help. For the first time in his career, Ullathorne came into close contact with a number of Anglican converts. These included James Spencer Northcote and Edgar Edmund Estcourt, both of whom would eventually accompany him to Birmingham and play key roles in the diocese and seminary, as well as becoming close personal friends. One of the best known anecdotes about Ullathorne is of an argument, late in his life, with Henry Edward Manning which ended abruptly when the Bishop of Birmingham reminded the convert Cardinal Archbishop of Westminster, in his blunt Yorkshire fashion, that he had been 'already teaching the catechism with a mitre on my 'ead when you were still an 'eretic!' This has been taken as evidence, not only of antagonism to Manning, but to convert clergymen in general; in both respects it is a false assumption. Ullathorne's attitude to the Anglican converts of his generation was described more temperately by Wilfred Ward (son of

22. CDA Letters vol. 1838–49 No. 518, Ullathorne to Brindle, 22 September 1846.
23. Ibid.

another famous ex-Anglican) as moderate, occupying a 'middle position' between the old traditional Catholics and the newer converts, while 'he deplored and resisted what he took as the exaggerations and indiscretions of people whose inexperience was as great as their zeal'.[24] Ward's more nuanced view is nearer the truth. Ullathorne's trust and appreciation of men of the ilk of Estcourt and Northcote was deep and lasting.

The last straw at Prior Park was when he took the then unusual step of making a formal visitation of the college; he exploded with rage when Brindle suggested that, as it was raining, the Blessed Sacrament might be brought over from the chapel to him, rather than the Bishop getting wet paying a visit![25] This and other bizarre behaviour convinced Ullathorne that he had to have recourse to Rome in order to resolve the Prior Park crisis, and he set out at the end of January 1847, only six months into his episcopate. He would have gone even sooner, but was delayed by exceptional winter floods in Rome. Brindle still did not have the measure of the man he was dealing with, and tried to drag him back by means of a letter in the hands of a messenger sent to overtake the Bishop. This was to no avail: Ullathorne had the ear of Cardinal Fransoni (the Prefect) and Mgr Barnabo (the Secretary) at *Propaganda Fide*, whose respect he had gained on his visits to Rome concerning Australia. A commission was set up to investigate Prior Park consisting of Bishops Griffiths and Sharples and an ally of Brindle, Dr Cox, the President of St Edmund's College, Old Hall Green. Naturally, Brindle insisted that the college had, 'refused the bishop nothing that he has called for',[26] but his protestations fell on deaf ears. The commission reported quickly on the failure to follow the Bishop's directions and on the disastrous financial state, with debts piled up to £60,000. Some unsuccessful attempt was made to realise the capital tied up in works of art, but with little success.

The other English bishops were also engaged in Rome over larger matters concerning their own position and authority.

24. Wilfred Ward, *Life and Times of Cardinal Wiseman* (1897), II, pp. 153–4.
25. *Autobiography*, p. 292.
26. Brindle to Acton quoted in Cashman, p. 82.

Bishops Sharples and Wiseman were dispatched to Rome just after Easter 1847 by the other vicars apostolic, who had agreed to begin negotiations towards bringing about the restoration of the hierarchy in England. They carried the report on Prior Park with them to *Propaganda Fide*, but no further action was immediately forthcoming. Ullathorne asked disaffected staff members to stay on until matters were finally settled, which he seemed optimistic would come about in the summer.[27] That hope was misplaced and the Prior Park saga continued to run on. When the discussions began in 1847 about a possible restoration of the hierarchy, Ullathorne was drawn into a scheme for dividing his Western District into two new dioceses, Devon and Cornwall to be hived off into a diocese based in Plymouth. He had some unease on financial grounds, but felt that the new Plymouth diocese should go ahead as long as he was not moved there, in case it was interpreted by his enemies in the Western District as, 'a censure of disapproval of my conduct in my transactions with Prior Park, Bristol and Clifton'.[28] He was not convinced, in reality, that the college's problems could ever be solved. 'From £15,000 to £20,000 would be required to make Prior Park at all at ease and would still leave it with an immense burden ... and in a few years we should be in a position quite as bad as before. This all thinking men of the District understand'.[29] Rather than *Propaganda Fide* wishing to remove him to a new district or diocese, the Roman congregation was at pains to stop Ullathorne resigning from the Western District in sheer desperation.[30] The Prior Park fiasco not only reinforced Ullathorne's own determination that proper management and financial acumen in all ecclesiastical matters was vital, but fixed in his mind a determination that each bishop (even as a vicar apostolic) had to be master in his own diocese or district and, 'independence of all but the Holy See was essential to success'.[31] Had he stayed in the

[27] CDA Letters vol. 1838–49 No. 562, Ullathorne to Brindle, 8 August 1847.
[28] CDA Letters vol. 1838–49 No. 582, Ullathorne to Wiseman, 22 November 1847.
[29] BAA B1057, Ullathorne to Polding, 5 September 1847.
[30] BAA B1062, Propaganda to Ullathorne, dissuading him from resigning, 28 September 1847.
[31] *Autobiography*, p 291.

Western District, it is more than likely that Prior Park would have been closed and sold off by Ullathorne. One thing to which he was developing a clear aversion was financial indebtedness, and he would take extreme measures to eradicate it. He was, after all, the son of a small tradesman whose business had flourished by good management and just dealing, and he had been brought up in a fair but careful financial environment.

The counterbalance to the stress and difficulty induced by Prior Park was the hope and generosity of the small religious community founded by Margaret Hallahan with Ullathorne's active involvement. When he was appointed to the Western District in April 1846, the future of the little community of Dominican Sisters looked fragile. Ullathorne and Sr Margaret were clear that they could not continue with the arrangement at Coventry once he had left. The dilemma was whether she should place the sisters under the direction of their own Dominican Order, or go with Ullathorne to the Western District, where 'they could have a better opportunity of realising those objects which Sr Margaret and myself alone understand and which it would be difficult for another person who has nothing to do with their formation to enter into so far as to realise'.[32]

The Dominican friars naturally wanted them to move from Coventry to Leicester, near to them, but Margaret's instinct was that they they would stand a better chance of survival if they stuck with Ullathorne and went to the Western District. The local convents rallied to their aid, the Dominicans at Atherstone offering them temporary accommodation and Mother Mary Clare Knight, the prioress of the Benedictines at Colwich, near Stafford, urged her wealthy brother with estates in Somerset to help them. However, in the long term, his generous financial support was less vital than the lifelong friendship forged between the Benedictine and Dominican superioresses: Margaret now had the support of an experienced religious superior, of whom there were few around in the 1840s, and close ties developed between the two communities.

[32.] Ampleforth, Copy of letter, Ullathorne to Brown, 29 May 1846.

Butler gave scant attention to the transfer of Margaret Hallahan and her companions to the Western District, or to their role in the District.[33] Yet the move was important, not only for the little religious community, but for the local Church in Bristol. In July 1846 they left Coventry and passed an anxious few months divided between hospitable convents and the new bishop's rented house in Bristol. Eventually, they settled in their own rented house in Bristol, reliant on the generosity of others, including the Franciscan nuns in Taunton. They began work among the poor and sick of the area, while developing the conventual life of the sisters. In Rome trying to sort out the frustrating business of Prior Park in early 1847, Ullathorne also made time to secure the agreement of the Master General of the Dominicans to his own appointment as canonical superior to all houses of the English Third Order of St Dominic.[34] This was an unusual arrangement, based on the unique personal involvement of the Benedictine bishop in the foundation of the new religious congregation, and secured his long-term relationship with it. Determined that Bristol would be the centre of the District, Ullathorne bought the unfinished shell of a large church in Clifton, on the edge of Bristol; the project had been abandoned when the money ran out and the bank had reclaimed the property. It lay derelict for years until, in late 1847, Ullathorne bought it for £3000, with a view to constructing a potential cathedral and a convent for the sisters. The Dominican sisters used a gift from the generous Mr Knight towards £1000 to purchase their share, and Ullathorne found the rest to buy the wreck of a church. Without the selfless aid of the sisters, nothing could have been done and the site would have continued to crumble and been converted to secular purposes.

He was warned that to complete the original architectural scheme of the Clifton church would now cost £10,000 and in any case, the walls were insecure. It seemed madness to take it on, but Ullathorne contacted his old friend, Charles Hansom, the architect of St Osburg's church in Coventry and told him to

---

[33.] Butler, *Life* I, p. 147.
[34.] Drane, *Life*, pp. 144–6.

'put his architectural reputation into his pocket, and simply follow my directions'.[35] For friendship's sake, the architect agreed and followed the bishop's instructions to build what was, in effect, an upside down ship's hull. Ullathorne's seafaring experience was not wasted! For £2000 he got himself a cathedral, which remained in regular use until the 1970s and still stands. The preparation of the cathedral and the adjoining convent continued through the early months of 1848, while Ullathorne was again absent in Rome. As far as Ullathorne was concerned, it was the generosity of the sisters which made the acquisition and completion of the cathedral possible.[36] This collaboration and mutual trust set the seal on the relationship between Ullathorne and Mother Margaret Hallahan and her new community, which would last to the end of his life.

Ullathorne later recalled in his own account of the English hierarchy how, on the very day of his episcopal consecration (21 June 1846) he was struck by the need for England to have its own hierarchy and how he found ready agreement among the other vicars apostolic. Conversations had already started before Ullathorne's appointment, so he cannot claim all the credit. The hoped for hierarchy would bring about the most significant change in English ecclesiastical government since the Reformation. There was a long and controversial background to this issue reaching back to 1585 when the last bishop of Mary Tudor's Catholic hierarchy, Thomas Goldwell, died in Rome. Throughout the seventeenth century attempts were made to establish a viable administration in the political conditions of penal times, and disputes over jurisdiction damaged the Catholic community.[37]

In the reign of the Catholic king, James II, John Leyburn was appointed Vicar Apostolic in September 1685. His post and those of the three additional vicars apostolic appointed in 1688, served the community until 1840, when the number was doubled to eight. They were direct papal appointees consecrated as bishops of defunct sees often from the ancient lands

[35.] *Autobiography*, p. 301.
[36.] Stone, G/ULL/III/130, Ullathorne to Editor of *Weekly Register*, 12 February 1856.
[37.] John Bossy, *The English Catholic Community 1570–1850* (1975), pp. 11–74.

of the Middle East and Byzantium, each being given jurisdiction over a sector of England, but with no administrative
structure. Residence and support for much of the eighteenth
century was provided by their families. Business with Rome
was conducted with *Propaganda Fide*, which handled all business to do with missionary territories, through a resident
English agent. The desire for local bishops who would have
closer ties with the congregations and clergy which they served,
rather than direct papal appointees, was keenly felt, and
disputes over appointments to missions, particularly where
religious orders or lay patrons were involved, formed a regular
and painful feature of a vicar apostolic's life.

The issue of church government and the rights and powers
of bishops and clergy arose anew in the 1790s, when liberal lay
and clerical leaders among the Catholics led the campaign for
removal of the penal laws. Joseph Berington, the mission priest
at Oscott, and the lawyer, Charles Butler argued for the
restoration of bishops in ordinary in the face of opposition
from John Milner, an Ultramontane before his time, whose
advocacy of papal authority was powerful.[38] The liberals
argued that bishops with clear canonical authority, who had
been elected by the clergy of the local chapter, would be the
acceptable face of Catholicism to a nervous English establishment, rather than 'vicars' appointed by Rome. This liberal
standpoint continued to find a voice into the nineteenth
century, especially the argument for local clergy participation
in the election of bishops.

John Lingard, the historian, and Daniel Rock, the liturgical
writer and chaplain to the Earl of Shrewsbury at Alton Towers,
launched a campaign for a restored hierarchy, insisting on full
canonical rights for the clergy, including a voice in episcopal
nominations. In 1842 Rock addressed a circular letter to his
fellow clergy.

Long had a yearning for such a measure been growing in
the minds of several among the secular clergy of this land;
but for a combination of reasons none of them would

[38.] John Milner, *Pastoral Letter to the Clergy of the Midland District*
(1803).

venture on the first step in this direction. For myself it had been the darling of my younger days of missionary duty ... It was agreed then that I should, at the next yearly meeting of the Midland clergy, begin to moot this point about the hierarchy. We met at Sedgley Park and at my suggestion a petition to His Holiness for the restoration of our long lost hierarchy was adopted and a committee of our elder clergy was chosen to draw it up and forward it to Rome.[39]

Rock was a priest of the Midland District, and his Vicar Apostolic, Thomas Walsh, while lukewarm about the idea, did not oppose the move. Wiseman opposed any group which had its roots in clerical dissatisfaction, though he was certainly not antagonistic to the idea of a restored hierarchy.[40] As a result of Rock's campaign the Adelphi Club was formed to work to secure clerical rights beginning in 1843 with twenty-six members attending monthly meetings, and growing to a hundred and twenty.

Pressure was, therefore, growing on the English vicars apostolic to move, and the first discussion of a petition to Rome among the bishops had taken place at the spring 1845 meeting of the vicars apostolic, before Ullathorne's consecration as bishop. At the first meeting he attended, in 1847, it was agreed to dispatch Bishops Wiseman and Sharples to Rome to counteract hostile rumours and clergy campaigns like Rock's, and to raise the question of a hierarchy.[41] Plans began to take shape for the possible new dioceses but in the event, the negotiations fizzled out. Wiseman was forced to return early to England and Sharples became ill and died, so although the petition to restore the hierarchy was readily welcomed in Rome, nothing happened at that stage.

In May 1848, Ullathorne was sent to Rome by his fellow vicars apostolic to press for the filling of the vacant vicariates and to revive the hierarchy scheme. Already recognised as the one among them who had more experience of dealing with the

---

[39.] K. O'Meara, *Thomas Grant* (1874), pp. 66–7.
[40.] Schiefen, p. 139.
[41.] *Restoration of the Hierarchy* (1871), pp. 21–3.

Roman curia than anyone else but Wiseman, and as the architect of the Australian hierarchy, he was given authority to open
formal negotiations. He was also to intervene with the Pope in
support of a memorial drawn up by English and Irish bishops
declaring that British diplomacy was operating to the detri-
ment of Catholicism, particularly in Ireland, and that Lord
Minto, the well-received British representative to the Holy See
and father-in-law of the Prime Minister Lord John Russell, was
one of the prime culprits.[42] The bishops were faced with the
raised political temperature resulting from their increasingly
public role in relation to the English political and religious
Establishment, Ireland and the Italian Risorgimento.

This was Ullathorne's second visit to Rome during the early,
turbulent days of Pius IX's papacy, who was as new and inexperienced a bishop as Ullathorne himself. The first two years had
been painful for the new Pope. He inherited a complex political
and religious situation in the Papal States, where, since the time
of Napoleon, liberal democratic ideas had taken root, and
demands for a unified Italy under secular rule, but with papal
support, were becoming louder. At a personal, emotional level,
Pius IX had a certain sympathy with the cause of Italian nationalism, but felt deeply his responsibility to maintain the Papal States
as the fiefdom of the popes, and pass on to his successor the
'Patrimony of Peter'. His reign began with conciliatory gestures,
freeing political prisoners and embarking on moderate administrative reforms, but this was a false dawn for liberalism.

Austrian sabre rattling in opposition to Italian unification
scared the Pope, and as Europe collapsed into the 'year of
revolutions' of 1848, Pius IX drew back from giving any
impression of liberalism. He refused to go to war with Austria
along with Piedmont and those favouring Italian unification,
and despite the introduction of a Council of Deputies and a
two-house parliament in the Papal States, his liberal credentials
were wearing thin. Agitation was becoming widespread and
political assassinations became commonplace.[43] Wiseman, well

42. Donal Kerr, 'England, Ireland and Rome 1847–8' in *Studies in
    Church History* vol. 25 'The Churches, Ireland and the Irish'
    (1989), p. 259.
43. H. Jedin, *History of the Church* vol. 8 'The Church in the Age of
    Liberalism' (1981), pp. 57–67.

known around Rome, encouraged the embattled Pius IX and the Curia to believe that England would stand alongside the beleaguered papal government. He saw this as a means of normalising relations between England and Rome and advancing the cause of the hierarchy. This was unlikely, as England had given shelter to the exiled prophet of Italian nationalism, Giuseppe Mazzini, and the majority of English opinion favoured the spread of democratic ideas in Europe. Indeed, one author has suggested that the liberation of Italy from papal rule became an obsession of English Protestants in the middle years of the nineteenth century, 'its greatest crusade since the campaign against slavery'.[44]

It was as a result of Wiseman's approach to the British government on behalf of the Pope that Minto was dispatched to Rome to reopen diplomatic relations.[45] The British government's interests would be served by getting papal support in banning the involvement of Irish Catholic clergy in politics. 'Minto's mission was to persuade the Pope in his hour of need, to agree to a concordat or to exchange diplomats with a view to gaining control over the Church either by paying the clergy or nominating the bishops.[46] Support for this from some Tory, anti-Irish English Catholics including the Earl of Shrewsbury,[47] was part of a scheme to push Wiseman's candidacy as leader of the new hierarchy. This created a sense among many Catholics that Wiseman was closer to the British government than was healthy. 'Too often the public perception was that he sided with the more conservative element, which tended to be hostile to Ireland, and thus Wiseman himself earned the reputation of being opposed to the Irish.'[48]

Ullathorne showed no interest in political or diplomatic ques-

[44.] John Pemble, *The Mediterranean Passion: Victorians and Edwardians in the South* (1987), p. 10.

[45.] Kerr, pp. 260–1.

[46.] Ibid., p. 266.

[47.] Ullathorne strongly disapproved of this interference: 'Lord Shrewsbury's letters to the Irish prelates are considered a very strong instance of lay interference and are fraught with mischief.' AAW R79/3 Ullathorne to Wiseman, 10 April 1848.

[48.] Oliver Rafferty, Nicholas Wiseman, 'Ecclesiastical Politics and Anglo-Irish relations in the mid-nineteenth century' in *Recusant History* vol. 21 (1993), p. 386.

tions, but wanted to see a measure of independent self-government, under canon law, for the Catholics of England, and to see an end of the stream of appeals to Rome. He was no advocate of Daniel Rock's clergy campaign which had limited support. The Earl of Shrewsbury reprimanded Rock, and while supporting the hierarchy and canonical status of clergy, he ridiculed the idea of their participation in nomination of bishops.[49] Rock was not the only one causing irritation. Ullathorne was furious to find when he went to Rome in 1848 to begin the hierarchy negotiations, that one of the most notorious priests of his Western District, Thomas McDonnell (who had left the Central District after savage disagreements with Walsh and Wiseman) was in Rome complaining about his treatment by the Central District bishops. He was also deputed to present the petition signed by Rock, in the name of the clergy of England, 'begging that the bishops be not made titular till the rights of the clergy be settled, lest their last case be worse than their first'.[50]

McDonnell had been the missioner at St Peter's Church in the centre of Birmingham in the late 1820s and 1830s and was a vocal friend and ally of Daniel O'Connell and the Irish Catholic Emancipation movement. He was a well-known public and political figure on the Birmingham scene, and a contentious one. The building of St Chad's Cathedral, completed in 1841, set the seal on his deteriorating relations with Walsh and Wiseman. He furiously opposed the scheme, on the basis that St Peter's was the mother church of the city, and should have been the chosen site. Having barricaded himself in the clergy house for months, he organised the St Peter's Church fete to coincide with the Cathedral opening, and later in the day disrupted the celebration dinner in the Birmingham Town Hall. This was the last straw, and McDonnell was thrown out of the District. Baines, who had clashed with Walsh over his support for Pugin and all things Gothic, took pleasure in giving McDonnell refuge in the Western District. Mc Donnell's brother, James, was his close confidante and financial adviser.[51]

[49] Schiefen, p. 157.
[50] AAW St Edmunds Papers, Ullathorne to Wiseman, 3 June 1848.
[51] Champ, *Recusant History*, pp. 289–303.

He was no less political in his activities in the Western District and far from straightforward in his behaviour. Having received Ullathorne's permission to go to Rome in 1848, 'simply as an act of piety and for a little recreation',[52] he embarked on a vitriolic campaign of vilification against Walsh (accused of injustice) and Wiseman (accused of heresy). This was exactly the kind of behaviour which convinced Ullathorne of the need for proper ecclesiastical government in England. The extent of his irritation, and the impact of McDonnell's campaign, is indicated by the fact that Ullathorne devoted several pages of his autobiographical account of the hierarchy negotiations to this troublesome priest.[53] McDonnell's actions in Rome were defused by Ullathorne, 'entering into a full explanation of Mr McDonnell's past conduct and principles'.[54] He met McDonnell on his arrival in Rome and demanded in no uncertain terms the retraction of offensive letters which he had sent to Ullathorne just before travelling.

The tendency of those letters is to dissolve the moral bounds which hold a subject to his superior. I therefore have concluded, as I stated to you in my letter of 2 March, that the spirit of those letters being such as no bishop can conscientiously with what he owes to his office, approve of in anyone subject to his authority. They were to be considered as a proof of your intention of not returning to the ministry in the Western District ... you have misstated my conversations, acts and motives, you have charged me with injustice, you have addressed me and you continue to address me in a carping and captious spirit ... It becomes my duty to remind you that you are not by your ordination a subject of the Western District but that you were received to employment in it, at a time when you had become alien to your own District.[55]

McDonnell backed down hastily; Ullathorne was a different

---

52. *Autobiography*, pp. 319–20.
53. Ibid., passim pp. 319–43.
54. Leeds Diocesan Archives No. 1763, Wiseman to Briggs, 29 June 1848.
55. BAA B1144, Ullathorne to McDonnell, 28 May 1848.

opponent from the mild-mannered Walsh. He asked the Bishop to regard the letters as never having been written; his letters were graciously returned and an amicable settlement reached, with Ullathorne assuring McDonnell that the tone of his retraction had given him 'much consolation' and that the whole business was forgotten, and promising to do all he could to protect the rights of the clergy under the new hierarchy.[56] Ullathorne's sheer humanity and belief in the innate goodness of people shines through this exchange, but McDonnell's aggression was not soothed so easily. He went straight home and wrote to *Propaganda Fide* and to the mystified Pope, urging them not to grant the new hierarchy until the English missionary priests had received the full rights of parish priests. This would give them rights to a parish in perpetuity, which could not be rescinded by a bishop.

The cardinal prefect of *Propaganda Fide* was not impressed and Ullathorne was embarrassed, but they both had bigger issues to concern them. In Ullathorne's case, he was anxious to secure the hierarchy, and Fransoni and the other Roman cardinals, while willing to do all they could for the English, were looking out on a city collapsing towards anarchy and revolution in the summer of 1848. McDonnell eventually left for England with his tail between his legs and by the end of June, Ullathorne had got the prize within his grasp. By then, Wiseman was able to tell the other bishops that Rome and Ullathorne were optimistic that the matter was straightforward and a bull establishing the hierarchy would be published speedily, with the new bishops being left to deal with the division of dioceses, clergy privileges and institutional organisation.[57]

Ullathorne, however, was unhappy about Wiseman's dealings, accusing him of lack of communication on diplomatic affairs, and of being less than open in relation to lay interference in ecclesiastical matters on his own behalf, when he was all too ready to criticise others.

56. BAA B1170, Ullathorne to McDonnell, nd (July 1848).
57. Leeds Diocesan Archives Briggs, Papers No. 1763, Wiseman to Briggs, 29 June 1848.

On the subject of lay interference, your Lordship must now allow me to speak very plainly or we shall never come to the point. The most glaring cases have been ascribed to your Lordship's friends, to those over whom you have been supposed to have sufficient influence to have been able to guide them. A bishop wrote to me and I believe to others, that members of the aristocracy with Lord Shrewsbury at their head had petitioned Rome to place a particular bishop in the archiepiscopal see of Westminster. I know nothing further of this matter, or whether the petition was ever sent, but it was complained of to me as of a fact of strong lay interference with the bishops, they themselves being unconsulted ... Thus whilst your lordship lays open the supposed errors of other bishops, others consider these facts as mere reactions upon the acts and omissions of your lordship. Without putting the case in some point of view like this, I do not see how your lordship can catch the full bearing of the whole of this case of misunderstanding.[58]

Wiseman had already written furiously to him about interventions by the editor of *The Tablet* in matters which he regarded as private episcopal business, and Ullathorne had replied warmly that 'expressions of indignation at the lay dictation exercised in ecclesiastical affairs is [sic] very strong on all sides ... I do not wish the memorial to go to Rome. I do not wish a further proof to be given of our dissensions, especially in our own body'.[59]

Ullathorne's unease about Wiseman's role behind the scenes was shared in Rome. The lack of confidence in Rome in dealing with Wiseman was brought home by the fact that the Curia insisted on secrecy and on dealing with Ullathorne alone, and he therefore exercised considerable influence over the outcome, including the decision that

the new districts will not at once be severed from the present districts but will be constituted and put under

58. AAW R79/3, Ullathorne to Wiseman, 10 April 1848.
59. BAA B1132, Wiseman to Ullathorne, 13 April 1848.

> administration of their present bishops until it is found
> expedient to give them to their own bishops. So that
> certain bishops will be bishop of such a diocese and
> administrator of such another. I need scarcely add that I
> have throughout, as my documents and minutes of audi-
> ences will show, contended for the views which the
> bishops hold in common.[60]

The Pope, he commented in the same letter, 'is very anxious to
see our affairs brought to a conclusion'.

Ullathorne himself took much of the responsibility for the
framework of the hierarchy, the titles to be given to the episcopal sees and even made recommendations for the men to fill
the posts created.

> I stated with reference to London, that London could be
> taken as the title of the Archiepiscopal see as it was only a
> bishopric with the Protestants. I thus suggested London
> or Westminster. For the see on the south of the Thames I
> suggested the title of Southwark ... Dr Walsh was
> disposed to write to Dr Grant suggesting Westminster and
> Southwark as the two titles.

Rome was determined that Thomas Walsh, as the most senior
of the vicars apostolic, should lead the new hierarchy from
London, aided by Wiseman as coadjutor. Questions about
diocesan boundaries and appointments were largely settled
when word came that Bishop Walsh was gravely ill and not
expected to survive. The Roman cardinals, however, were
decided: 'whether living or dead, he shall be the first
Archbishop of Westminster'.[61] This meant that Birmingham
would need a new appointment, and it was decided that
Ullathorne should move there. The new Diocese of
Birmingham would be almost as big as the old Central District
and was potentially a larger and more complex diocese than
the new Clifton Diocese which would replace the Western
District. This close involvement in detail and personnel was to
bring criticism on Ullathorne's head.

60. AAW, Ullathorne to Wiseman, from Rome, 4 July 1848.
61. *Autobiography*, p. 342.

Butler was cool in his assessment of Ullathorne's handling of the problem, suggesting that his unconcealed (and by implication, unjustified) animosity to the Western District was part of the reason for his removal to the Central District.[62] Some of the clergy of the Western District were convinced that Ullathorne had asked for the move, in order to be rid of Prior Park.[63] This is unlikely. It had taken Ullathorne long enough to reconcile himself to the mitre, so he was hardly ready to seek a further upheaval after such a short time, and was certainly not a man to run away from a challenge.[64] He was aware of the gossip. When the hierarchy was under final negotiation in the summer of 1848, he was also sensitive to the notion that the other bishops might think he had used his position in Rome to escape the stranglehold of Prior Park by getting a different see in the new hierarchy. He insisted that his appointment to Birmingham was for 'reasons too favourable to myself, and which have not the slightest relation to the affairs at Prior Park, a fact which I take the liberty to record here, in a letter to your Right Rev Sir, lest the contrary should happen perchance to be asserted elsewhere'.[65]

He was also acutely aware of his position as a Benedictine in relation to the secular clergy, and felt himself in a cleft stick on the matter.

> It is curious that in the past, some, or one at least, seemed at our meeting to have looked upon me as working for a particular interest, for that of the regulars, the regulars themselves and my own order in particular have more than once taken alarm at what they equally erroneously, conceived to be my too strong secular tendencies. I have, I trust, no party tendencies of any kind, but as a bishop I am the superior of the secular clergy. It is my duty, I conceive, to identify myself with them. And that they have

---

62. Butler, *Life* I, p. 144.
63. Cashman, p. 83.
64. One of Brindle's henchmen had soon put the word around on Ullathorne's arrival that they had killed two bishops and were likely to kill a third. *Autobiography*, p. 290.
65. BAA B1166, Draft of an unfinished letter from Ullathorne to *Propaganda Fide*, 29 July 1848.

no other superior to look to, like the regulars might have continually before them, in remembrance of my originally being of another class from themselves. The previous visit to Rome, I asked and obtained permission to wear purple, that I might externally as well as internally identify myself with those who had no one else to look to.[66]

He was, therefore, aware that he might meet accusations of favouritism if he suggested a fellow Benedictine to replace him, and warmly recommended the Franciscan, Francis Hendren for the Western District.

You will easily understand why I did not recommend a Benedictine. Instead therefore of being charged with working for the order with which I have no longer any material interests, though I must always have those of affection and gratitude, I might have been allowed the credit I think, in the delicate position in which I was placed, of having expressly avoided my order in the recommendations.[67]

Ullathorne was, nevertheless, accused of using undue influence to secure Hendren's appointment to the Western District.

Although Hendren was appointed to the Western District in 1848, Brown of Wales was given special responsibility for Prior Park as Episcopal Visitor; Ullathorne was not keen on this arrangement and insisted on corresponding only with Hendren on any matters concerning Prior Park and declined to offer any monetary support from the financially stretched Central District.[68] Ullathorne and Hendren shared the view that the Western District (and later the Diocese of Clifton) would be better off without Prior Park, but it broke the health of another two bishops (Hendren and Burgess) before it was closed in 1856. Ten years later it was bought again by Bishop Clifford and finally closed as a seminary twenty-five years later.

[66.] AAW R79/3, Ullathorne to Wiseman, 12 August 1848.
[67.] Ibid.
[68.] Cashman, p. 86.

By late July 1848, the Pope had approved everything for the English hierarchy and Ullathorne was invited to a papal audience a day or two later. After his return from Rome, Ullathorne set out before his fellow bishops the results of his negotiations, to everyone's satisfaction. The formal appointments of Walsh to London, of two new vicars apostolic for the north and the west, and his own to the Central District arrived on 28 July 1848. Poor old Thomas Walsh, having spent all his life at Oscott or as Vicar Apostolic in the Midlands, was forced to spend the last months of his life in exile in London, and in August 1848, Ullathorne left the Western District to move to Birmingham. All was in place for the new hierarchy and the creation of English dioceses in communion with the pope for the first time in three hundred years.

However, the optimistic prospects were to be darkened as Rome collapsed towards revolution. Pius IX's refusal to go to war against Austria in April, despite his gestures towards a more inclusive constitution for the Papal States, left the liberals, who had looked to him for support, disillusioned. Popular protests forced him into appointing the radical Mamiani as interior minister, but he lost his nerve when disorderly troops streamed back into Rome after the Austrian defeat of the Piedmontese in July. His response was to replace Mamiani with a hard liner, Count Pellegrino de Rossi, who was stabbed to death on the steps of his office in November. A week later, Pius IX fled the besieged Quirinal Palace under cover of darkness and in disguise, and sought refuge in Gaeta in the Kingdom of Naples. All papal business ground to a halt, which, as far as the English vicars apostolic were concerned, left the job inconveniently half done, with the preliminary moves made, but no restored hierarchy in place.

Ullathorne moved as soon as possible to Birmingham, which may have added to suspicions that he could not wait to be out of the Western District: the first envelope addressed to him in Birmingham is dated 1 August 1848.[69] His faculties arrived the next day,[70] quickly followed by a rescript agreeing to

---

[69.] BAA B1171, Empty envelope addressed to Ullathorne at Birmingham, 1 August 1848.
[70.] BAA B1172, *Propaganda Fide* to Ullathorne, 2 August 1848.

Ullathorne's request to place the Central District under the patronage of the Immaculate Conception.[71] This title given to the Virgin Mary was not yet defined as an article of faith until 1854, but was an ancient devotion with strong English roots, in which Ullathorne took an active interest.[72] After the definition in 1854, the patronage of the Virgin Mary under that title would be extended to all of the original 1850 episcopal sees, which thenceforward celebrated their major diocesan feast day simultaneously on 8 December, the feast of the Immaculate Conception and date of the definition. Ullathorne stole a march on the others, personally requesting Pius IX when he was in Rome for 'the especial protection and patronage of Mary preserved immaculate from the stain of our origin', and announcing it to his new vicariate in November 1848.[73] Speaking through Grant, by then rector of the English College, and agent for the bishops in Rome, the Curia assured Ullathorne in early 1849 that the only thing holding up the promulgation of the hierarchy was 'the existing political difficulties of the Holy See'.[74] Nothing could be furthered until April 1850, when, with the help of French troops, Pius IX was restored to Rome.

Ullathorne had been a bishop for little more than two years when he left for Birmingham and in that space of time had made two trips to Rome, each lasting around three months (firstly on Prior Park business and secondly on the hierarchy). Therefore his time in the Western District allowed him to achieve little, bogged down as he was with financial and administrative nightmares, mostly surrounding the ill-starred college. Ullathorne was determined to draw a line under his unhappy time in the Western District and refused to be drawn into any matter concerning the Western District, especially Prior Park, and responded sharply when Wiseman accused him of colluding with his successor in the Western District, Hendren, to ensure the closure of Prior Park.[75] He was distinctly chilly with Wiseman's apparent attempt to draw him into correspondence

---

71. BAA B1173, Bishop F. J. Nicholson to Ullathorne. 4 August 1848.
72. See Chapter 5.
73. Pastoral Letter, 22 November 1848.
74. Cardiff, Ullathorne to Brown, 1 February 1849.
75. AAW St Edmunds Papers Series 7 (1836–67), Ullathorne to Wiseman, Christmas Day 1848.

on the subject: 'It is my fixed decision to keep myself aloof from Prior Park affairs, and from all interference in any way with my former district.'[76] Nevertheless, there is no doubt of Ullathorne's immense relief at being freed from the trials of the Western District: 'for the first time in my agitated life I found myself placed in a peaceful jurisdiction, over a united clergy conspicuous for their devotion to the episcopal authority'.[77] His Downside affiliation did not carry the weight which it inevitably did in the Western District, and there were those in the Midlands who knew his mettle from his Coventry days. It had perhaps slipped his mind that his old bête noire, Thomas McDonnell, had begun his career a mile from Bishop's House in Birmingham, and it did not take him long to discover that his new posting had complex difficulties of its own. He quickly found himself so submerged in work and in sorting out the tangles left by Walsh and Wiseman, that he hardly had time to recite the Divine Office.[78]

He had, of course, left behind in Clifton his dear friend Mother Margaret, but she continued to have his interests at heart, sending someone recommended to look after the bishop, with careful directions about the care of his health from his Bristol doctor. The rigours of the Western District and Rome had taken their toll, and she was already anxious that he was 'looking very ill' and should take the medicine prescribed.[79] This is the first real inkling that, although Ullathorne lived to a great age and was energetically involved in a wide range of activities, travelling his diocese and to Rome on frequent occasions, his health was never robust. Within a year, Ullathorne was feeling the strain of caring for his new District and sorting out its parlous financial state, while still awaiting the completion of his work on the new hierarchy, and had retreated to the family home at Scarborough for a time to recover his physical and mental well-being.

One thing which had hit him very clearly, and perhaps added to his depression, was that he would never again live the

76. AAW St Edmunds Papers Series 7 (1836–67), Ullathorne to Wiseman, 5 February 1849.
77. *Autobiography*, p. 358.
78. Cardiff, Ullathorne to Brown, 25 September 1848.
79. BAA B1247, Margaret Hallahan to Estcourt, nd September 1848.

life of a monk, and he obviously regretted that deeply, 'I have always loved my order and have always had faith in Downside ... there is no more thorough Gregorian outside or within the walls of Downside than myself, and I can no more repay what I owe to it than I can what I owe to my mother'.[80] In the summer of 1850, he was forced to miss the General Chapter of the English Benedictine Congregation (EBC), and knew that, as a bishop, he would never sit in one. Regretting his absence, he described himself as a 'grateful and attached member of the congregation'. He declared that he had derived from the Order of St Benedict 'whatever of a good spirit may have supported and directed me in a life of uninterrupted labours'. The 'tranquil stability of conventual observance and remembrance ... have given me substantial support amidst the ever shifting changes of my life'. It was that essentially monastic combination of high principle, humility and gentleness for which Ullathorne strove, and in part, at least, achieved. He also wanted to see the Benedictines play a bigger a role in the revival of Catholic life in England.

> I know well that this religious expansion of the congregation would serve the best interests of the Church in England in very important ways ... It is a deep conviction in my mind ... that the spirit of St Benedict is as well fitted for the exigencies of the Church in modern days as it was for those of the Middle Ages, for it is a spirit at once generous, practical and accommodating to circumstances.[81]

Many of the apparent contradictions in Ullathorne can only be resolved if the monk within the bishop is revealed, but in the rough and tumble of church life, this rarely happened. Glimpses appear every now and then, such as when he mourned the death of Luke Barber, Prior of Downside when Ullathorne entered, and for years the president general of the EBC, who ended his days at Stanbrook. '... in no man's judgement did I ever put so much fraternal confidence. He is a particular loss to me ... he formed an especial link with the

---

80. DA M119, Ullathorne to Mr Davis, 17 December 1848.
81. BAA B1941, Ullathorne to General Chapter, 15 July 1850.

order'.[82] Barber's death not only severed another link with his old monastic community. Recalling him a few years later, it is evident the extent to which Barber was his model and ideal of ecclesiastical authority.

> All his views were high, and all his feelings strong on the side of the high principles of government, yet in the exercise of authority ... there was a striking contrast between the high tone of his principles and the gentleness and considerateness of his practice ... Fr Barber had little of that jealousy so common to men in authority. He had no jealousy because he had no ambition. He had that habitual humility which is the distinguishing trait of a truly religious man.[83]

If Ullathorne ever strove to imitate any man, it was perhaps Luke Barber, but his relationship with his monastic confrères was often regarded ambiguously and he was forced to defend himself as a true son of St Benedict.

The strange, cobbled-together cathedral in Clifton remained as his monument and the Dominican sisters struggled to complete their convent and to work in the missions of Bristol, including the establishment of an orphanage and attending the sick and dying impoverished women of the area in their own homes. Such was their tender care for the dignity of these poor women with no other means, that they tended their bodies after death and prepared them for burial.[84] The community grew slowly, but was gradually gaining the confidence of the local people. Ullathorne's departure was a real blow, especially to Margaret Hallahan, just as the tiny religious community was getting on its feet under his protection. 'Her correspondence bears traces of deep mental disquietude, and of that sense of fear and isolation with which her soul was so often beset.'[85] The fragile little enterprise was not helped by Margaret's weak

---

[82.] Stanbrook 1, Ullathorne to Abbess Gregson from the convent at Clifton, 31 December 1850.

[83.] Ullathorne obituary in *Downside Review* vol. VIII (1889), p. 74.

[84.] Stone G/ULL/III/130, Ullathorne to Editor of the *Weekly Register*, 12 February 1856.

[85.] Drane, *Life*, p. 161.

health and refusal to take proper care and medical treatment until ordered to by Ullathorne.[86] Not surprisingly, she was keen to establish a house in the Central District which would also be a noviciate, under Ullathorne's direct influence and care.

In moving to the Central District, Ullathorne returned to relatively familiar territory, since Coventry lay within the District, but he was taking on episcopal responsibility in a very different situation from the Western District which he had so briefly and unhappily led. The Central District consisted of the four traditional counties of Staffordshire, Warwickshire, Worcestershire and Oxfordshire, which would become the Diocese of Birmingham in 1850 when the restoration of the hierarchy was completed. He did not have the same difficulties over accommodation as in the Western District, as Walsh had engaged Augustus Welby Pugin to build the cathedral of St Chad and its adjoining house as early as 1841: it was the first Catholic cathedral to be built in England since the Reformation, and Pugin's work and inspiration was visible in ecclesiastical buildings all over the Midlands. However, this project, and Walsh's other ambitious schemes had left the District in dire financial straights. Ullathorne, like his predecessor, came to rely heavily on the extraordinary financial generosity of the Earl of Shrewsbury in building and maintaining the churches and chapels of his new diocese, until his death in 1852. Despite their differences over the policy needed towards Rome, the Earl welcomed Ullathorne warmly, and lost no time in inviting him to his spectacular home, Alton Towers in north Staffordshire, 'whenever it may suit your convenience to favour us with a visit'.[87]

The Midland counties were geographically, economically and ecclesiastically a world away from the Western District. Birmingham and the surrounding Black Country, Wolverhampton and Coventry were all heavily industrialised by the 1840s and had spread rapidly and absorbed massive population growth, a substantial proportion of which was provided by poor Catholic Irish migrants. The industrial West Midlands was far more Catholic in its religious makeup than

---

[86.] Drane, *Life*, pp. 164–5.
[87.] BAA B1197, Earl of Shrewsbury to Ullathorne, 26 August 1848.

the West Country, and the impact of Irish migration had added to it. The most recent study based on the 1851 religious census reiterates the truism that Catholicism was generally stronger north of a line from the Wash to the Bristol Channel.[88] The West Midlands was one of its areas of strength, with pockets in central and south Staffordshire and high church attendance figures in Birmingham and Wolver-hampton.[89] However, the counties of the Central District also contained significant survivals of gentry recusancy in its rural areas, such as the Stonors, Berkeleys, Staffords and Dormers, and key figures, including the Earl of Shrewsbury and Ambrose Phillips de Lisle were major benefactors to the local church. By the time Ullathorne arrived in 1848 there were seventy-three missions in the four counties in addition to the magnificent Pugin cathedral and college at Oscott, Sedgley Park school, founded in the eighteenth century by Richard Challoner, and a handful of convents.

The city in which Ullathorne found himself living for the rest of his life was unlike anything he had experienced before. Birmingham was one of the fastest growing industrial centres of Victorian England, priding itself on being the 'city of a thou-sand trades', of which the most famous and prosperous involved brass, guns and jewellery. It also suffering the conse-quences of rapid population growth in insanitary conditions, poor housing, inadequate water supplies and extreme poverty. Provision for working-class education in Birmingham was poor in the mid-nineteenth century, with school accommodation for less than one in ten children, well below that of many other neighbouring towns or the national average.[90] Yet conditions in Birmingham were never quite as bad as some other indus-trial centres, and by the end of the century it was described by an American observer as 'the best governed city in the world'.[91]

Birmingham was also the home of well-known Christian philanthropists including the Cadbury family, Joseph Sturge

[88] K. D. M. Snell and P. S. Ell, *Rival Jerusalems: the Geography of Victorian Religion* (2000), p. 175.

[89] Ibid., p. 178.

[90] Eric Hopkins, *The Rise of the Manufacturing Town: Birmingham and the Industrial Revolution* (1989), p. 160.

[91] Victor Skipp, *The Making of Victorian Birmingham* (1983), pp. 8–9.

and Josiah Mason, whose college was the foundation of Birmingham University, and they had their counterparts among the Catholics, including John Hardman senior (1737–1844) and junior (1811–1867). Father and son were head of a remarkable Birmingham family of manufacturers who were closely linked to Pugin and the revival of Gothic design. Both contributed generously to St Chad's Cathedral and many associated charities.[92] So too did families such as the Hendrens (the family of Francis, who became Bishop of Clifton and of Nottingham), the Clarksons (also in the metal trades), and the Powells, who were booksellers and printers and also vestment makers.[93]

Birmingham had a strong tradition of Protestant Dissent and flourishing Evangelicalism, and the impetus for the formation of the Evangelical Alliance, the powerful umbrella body of Protestant sects and churches, came from a speech made at the Congregational Union in 1842 by John Angell James, a leading and well-known independent minister in Birmingham.[94] The Protestant Association, which mobilised anti-Catholic sentiment, formed nearly fifty branches between 1836 and 1844, and Birmingham's was a vigorous one, set up in 1847. During its first year of existence, it held seven public lectures, collected a library of fifty volumes and gathered a membership of between sixty and seventy.[95] The activities of the Protestant Association were boosted by the locally notorious 'Bible burning' incident, when an infuriated Catholic priest, Fr William Molloy from St Chad's, found that the British and Foreign Bible Society had been distributing tracts and copies of the New Testament among local Catholic families. This was not unusual, but was vexatious to the Catholic clergy, and Molloy lost his temper and took a copy of the Protestant New Testament which had been given to a Catholic child, and flung it into the fire.[96] Protestant hysteria and anti-Catholic press coverage followed, but, as usual, was something of a storm in a

[92] Brian Doolan, *The Pugins and the Hardmans* (2004), passim.
[93] Champ thesis, pp. 62–8.
[94] John Wolffe, *The Protestant Crusade in Great Britain 1829–60* (1991), p. 137.
[95] Ibid., p. 157.
[96] Champ thesis, p. 249.

teacup. Chapels of various sects and groups proliferated throughout the city and the buildings often changed hands. In fact, one, in Moor St, built by the Congregationalists in 1846, was sold to the Catholic community in 1862.

The religious census of 1851 showed that church accommodation existed for only 13.3% of the population of Birmingham (232,841) – well below Horace Mann's estimate in the Census Report of 58% of the population who might be expected attend places of worship. In fact, only 36% of Birmingham's population attended church on Census Sunday, well below the Leeds and Liverpool average of 45–47% and the national average of 50%.[97] It was also well below Wolverhampton's 53% and Worcester's 66%.[98] A little under half those counted in the Birmingham census were chapel goers, of which Methodism in its various forms accounted for about a third, followed by Baptists, Congregationalists, Unitarians, Quakers and Presbyterians.[99] The Birmingham Church Building Society, founded in 1836, built five new Anglican churches and a further nine were added by 1865. Ten more were added in the late 1860s, and the Established Church remained numerically strong and influential.[100] The Catholic churches in the city were surprisingly few. Apart from St Chad's Cathedral, there was St Peter's, the mother church where McDonnell had caused such a furore, and the beginnings of Newman's Oratory in the disused gin distillery near the market area. Beyond that, missions lay in the villages which would soon be absorbed into the suburbs of the sprawling city.

It did not take Ullathorne long to discover that the administration of the District he had inherited was chaotic and the financial state parlous. The best thing to happen to Ullathorne in Bristol was the friendship he made with Edgar Edmund Estcourt, who accompanied him to Birmingham and remained as his financial secretary (later Diocesan Chancellor) and close advisor until Estcourt's death in 1884. His experience in Australia and his brief attempt to create order in the Western District had imbued

[97.] Skipp, p. 116.
[98.] Hopkins, p. 139.
[99.] Skipp, p. 117.
[100.] Ibid., p. 114.

Ullathorne with an implacable determination that order and financial stringency were the only means of securing a stable future for the Church in its move away from the provisional and temporary world of penal times. It was Estcourt's astute and careful financial control which ultimately enabled the security of the District and later Diocese to be established.

In his first pastoral letter in the Central District, issued in November 1848, Ullathorne set out the two headings under which he saw his episcopate being governed – the development of the seminary at Oscott, 'the very fountain of the future prosperity of the District', and the 'temporalities' of the District – in other words, money. These he described as being the 'two heads of church government ... the foundation of order and confidence'.[101] This letter emphasised the need for sound temporal administration, and in all but name, implied a contrast between the old regime and the new in the Central District, and thereby, a public rebuke.

> We are sensible that this administration, to be just and prudent, requires a systematic method, and asks an uninterrupted attention, and especially so in these times; that each resource may be kept secure; that each particular fund may be applied to its destined purpose; that the intentions of religious benefactors may be observed with a religious exactness; that nothing may be alienated from its original purpose, in accordance with those fixed and certain laws which the Church lays down for our guidance, and without the observance of which we are always in peril of her just censures, and incurring the risk of our immortal soul.[102]

This was precisely not what had happened under Walsh and Wiseman's direction, and the after effects would prey on Ullathorne's mind for years to come.

Walsh's management of the financial affairs of the District had been haphazard and Wiseman's conduct of Oscott less than judicious. Before and after Walsh's death in 1848,

[101.] Pastoral Letter, 16 November 1848.
[102.] Ibid.

Ullathorne pursued Wiseman relentlessly over money which he believed was owed to the District and Diocese as a result of Walsh and Wiseman's management.[103] Wiseman had been nominally president of Oscott during the 1840s, but the day-to-day running had been in the hands of Henry Logan. Within a month of his arrival in Birmingham, Ullathorne insisted that Logan provide him with a list of students and their pensions, the number of professorial and domestic staff and their wages, the credit and interest to be paid, and the annual running costs of the college and its farm. He quickly began to discover some of the difficulties and to make detailed investigations, which ruffled Wiseman's feathers. Ullathorne had to reassure Wiseman that his financial management was not being called into question – although this was exactly what he was doing, and the issue of finance became one of the major irritants between the two bishops. This soured relations between Birmingham and Westminster for years.[104]

The first matter which Ullathorne felt he had to raise with Wiseman was the paucity of record keeping which he had inherited, making it impossible to know exactly how the District stood. Ullathorne had clashed with Wiseman before over money, in the case of the fundraising for St Osburg's Coventry, and having just escaped from the financial morass which threatened to engulf the Western District, was in no mood to tiptoe around the issue.

> With reference to the investigation of the accounts, any remark which came from me could only refer to my habitual idea of not unnecessarily in any way exposing the administration of the temporalities. I never had any notion about anything having been wrong either in Your Lordship's management or Dr Walsh's, but there is a good deal that is obscure for want of clear statements and clear accounts ... In fact we have not found a clearly kept account book in the District. It is however satisfactory to know that, the more we investigate, the more satisfactorily Dr Walsh's dispositions come out, quite independently of

---

[103.] See Chapters 5 and 6.
[104.] Schiefen, pp. 128–31.

any statements of his own. At first they looked alarming enough. We have now a full report of the general disposition of the District funds ready drawn up, with plans for future arrangements for the first meeting of the council ... Your lordship will distinctly understand that I do not for a moment doubt of the rectitude of your administration but explanations of appropriations become essential for business purposes and it is wholly on that ground that I ask the confirmation of this item about which no-one who has had the accounts can inform me.[105]

Wiseman, while president of Oscott, had borrowed money which he had spent on the college, and for which he therefore regarded it as liable. Rumours circulated that he had used the funds for private purposes, which he denied, insisting that, on the contrary, he had used his own money to pay college debts. He, therefore, claimed that he was due to be reimbursed and that the suddenness of his departure had prevented accounts being tidied up before he left.[106] These financial irritants between Ullathorne and Wiseman were not easily smoothed over. Ullathorne's frustration at the fog of rumour and confusion made him short-tempered and pompous. For his part, Wiseman took an aggrieved and high-handed tone, refusing Ullathorne's attempt to establish a committee to look into the financial position between Wiseman and his former District. 'Allow me to say that it is a novel proceeding, to constitute a committee of priests in one district to pronounce on the claims of a bishop in another.'[107] Schiefen's view is that this problem and the similar one over London District funds with Grant of Southwark were exacerbated by Wiseman's typical approach to problems: 'a single step towards reaching a solution was followed, more than once, by long periods of inaction and apparent indifference'.[108]

Wiseman attempted a more emollient approach with Ullathorne in the new year, hoping that things had blown over,

---

[105.] AAW R79/3, Ullathorne to Wiseman, 30 November 1848.
[106.] Schiefen, p. 231.
[107.] BAA B1445, Wiseman to Ullathorne, 30 January 1849.
[108.] Schiefen, p. 232.

and that 'there will be no more trouble between us'.[109] This was not the case, because Ullathorne was like a dog with a bone when he got hold of a problem, especially where money was concerned. By the late summer of 1849, Ullathorne was suggesting again that he and Wiseman needed to put the complicated disagreements over the financial affairs of the District to independent arbitration. 'I propose to write to your lordship in a few days on that very unpleasant subject, the financial affairs which remain unsettled between us. I wish to propose an arbitration for their final settlement.'[110] Wiseman, no doubt wishing it would just go away, coolly agreed that he too was, 'most anxious to have a final settlement'.[111]

Ullathorne assured Wiseman that all he intended was a 'friendly arbitration' undertaken by a couple of their fellow bishops, certainly not involving the kind of expense incurred in a similar arbitration in earlier years between Bishops Walsh and Griffiths, which he regarded as 'simply a scandal'.[112] Financial difficulties and the limitation these put on his ability to run Oscott and provide the much-needed priests for the District were his major concerns, and he pressed Wiseman on this.

> We are living at present from hand to mouth at Oscott. Although we have made considerable reforms in management and saving of expenditure our deficit is still very great, and I shall be compelled to give up one half of the year's collections for its support, although that will put us into immense difficulties in the District.[113]

He was faced with a circle which would not be squared for many a year – the need for good quality clergy in order to staff the seminary which would form the priests so desperately needed on the missions. His instincts told him that the seminary needed home-grown priests on the staff to imbue students with the spirit of the district and diocese; importing clergy from else-

---

109. BAA B1466, Wiseman to Ullathorne, 12 February 1849.
110. AAW R79/3, Ullathorne to Wiseman, 30 August 1849.
111. AAW Molloy Collection, Wiseman to Ullathorne, 1 September 1849.
112. AAW 79/3 , Ullathorne to Wiseman, 4 September 1849.
113. AA W R 79/3, Ullathorne to Wiseman, 28 September 1849.

where to staff the college would not work. 'I have but one real difficulty, want of priests, want of priests . . . I am fully aware of many of our deficiencies. I am most anxious about a body of regular professors at Oscott, but they must grow out of our own people. A homogeneous body will work best together.'[114]

He was not going to be trapped into another Prior Park situation, and looked around for a trustworthy figurehead to fulfil Wiseman's presidential role at Oscott, not having much faith in Logan. The obvious choice was Henry Weedall, who had laboured alongside Walsh to create the new college, and had been the last president of the old college and first president of the new in 1838. He was cruelly ousted in 1840 to make way for Wiseman, and Ullathorne wanted him back.

> I have decided after much consideration and enquiry on placing Dr Weedall at Oscott. I perceive that this step is essential. The temporalities of the college are in an unsatisfactory state and the ecclesiastical spirit has confessedly sunk down. Nothing else will satisfy either myself or the clergy.[115]

Weedall, he believed, was the man who could restore the confidence of the clergy in Oscott, but it was not that easy, and Ullathorne was impatient. 'The difficulty is to get Dr Weedall to stir fast enough. Had it been my affair I should have been in Oscott in an hour after my appointment, but this I find a common mistake, the not seeing the value of time in certain circumstances.'[116] Also, it was clear that Weedall's delicate health and poor eyesight made it impossible for him to exercise day-to-day responsibility in the college.

Logan was too closely associated with the old regime, and after first appearing to take it 'in very good spirit', took offence at being asked for a full account of his superintendence, circulating Ullathorne's request for information to other bishops and lay friends.[117] The bishop, remembering his dealings with Dr

---

114. AA W R79/3 2, Ullathorne to Wiseman, 22 November 1848.
115. AAW R79/3, Ullathorne to Wiseman, 4 October 1848.
116. Ibid.
117. Ibid.

Brindle, acted swiftly: Logan was removed. Weedall could not cope with the job, so John Moore, whom Ullathorne had hoped to see as first Bishop of Birmingham instead of himself, was appointed president.[118] Oscott had been one of Ullathorne's stated priorities in November 1848, and within a year he had changed the management and made strenuous efforts to get the finances back on track, but this was only the beginning. Convalescing in Ramsgate the following year, Weedall confirmed Ullathorne's sense that the clergy had little confidence in Oscott, and that there had been 'too much of splash and dash at the expense of its sober ecclesiastical character'.[119]

These words from a man after his own heart reinforced in Ullathorne a determination to press ahead with reforms in the life of the college, including greater separation between lay and clerical education. When Thomas Walsh built the new Oscott College in 1838, his vision was twofold: that it would become a launching pad for the great revival of English Catholicism for which he longed, and that it would eventually become 'a purely ecclesiastical seminary' without the need for fees from lay students to sustain it.[120] He blamed himself for allowing the clergy to override him on the seminary question, and instead of converting the existing college to exclusive seminary use, he built a grand and expensive college which would not be maintained without lay students' fees for at least another fifty years. Walsh's desire to see Oscott become 'a purely ecclesiastical seminary of pious, talented and efficient missionaries'[121] was pursued energetically by his successor.

Ullathorne, however keen, was less optimistic than Walsh had been about converting Oscott to purely seminary use, because all the expenses would then fall on him, and he was determined first to untangle the financial, administrative and educational chaos left by Walsh and Wiseman. He consulted the Earl of Shrewsbury, whose money had been poured into Oscott as well as many other Midland schemes, and they agreed that relatively simple alterations could enable to two

[118.] *Autobiography*, p. 325.
[119.] BAA B1681, Weedall to Ullathorne, 18 September 1849.
[120.] Ushaw, Walsh to Shrewsbury, No. 73 (later dated 1847).
[121.] Ibid.

institutions (school and seminary) to exist separately under the same roof, as long as the church students remained at Sedgley Park school for their philosophy studies (the early part of formation for priesthood).[122] However, Ullathorne was already wondering if that was adequate and toyed with the idea of a house of philosophical studies attached to the new church at Erdington, only a couple of miles from Oscott, with the theology students in a part of Oscott under separate management and direction from the school.[123]

Walsh's, and later, Ullathorne's desire to separate clerical and lay education reflected the direction which Catholic and non-Catholic ecclesiastical thinking was taking more generally. The Church of England and Nonconformists were moving deliberately in the direction of specialist professional clerical training in newly established theological colleges, and the 'clerical profession' became a distinctive feature of Victorian England.[124] The increasing emphasis within Ultramontane Catholicism on the separate, sacramental and distinctive nature of clerical life demanded the exclusion of lay influence in education and training. To be ready for the challenges ahead, priests needed to be withdrawn from the world and its priorities, and formed as specialists for the task ahead. Ullathorne shared a common desire to extend to England the full teaching of the Council of Trent, which, with a restored hierarchy would make England fully a part of the universal Church again. This was a key part of Ullathorne's programme for the Church in England. The arrangements which had sustained English Catholicism during the recusant period, while heroic, were essentially temporary expedients for emergency circumstances, and he set out his three priorities for a fully Tridentine Church in England: the restoration of the hierarchy, the re-establishment of cathedral chapters and the creation of Tridentine ecclesiastical seminaries.[125] Preoccupied though he often seemed with structures and organisation, the point was always that they were a means to an end. The renewal of

---

[122.] BAA B1872, Shrewsbury to Ullathorne, 23 March 1850.
[123.] *Letters*, p. 8.
[124.] See A. Haig, *The Victorian Clergy* (1984), passim.
[125.] Pastoral Letter, 16 November 1848.

English Catholicism in unity with the universal Church required, in his view, more than missionary fervour, but sound foundations. It is possible in this, as in so much else, to see the influence of monasticism on Ullathorne's approach.

However, though he believed that foundations for the future could only be laid with just, prudent and systematic administration, he was determined not to become so preoccupied with financial administration as to neglect the spiritual aspects of government. With this in view he immediately set up permanent councils of clergy and appointed Henry Weedall as vicar general. This was an astute, as well as a humane move. Weedall had worked alongside Thomas Walsh all his adult life as vice rector and then rector of Oscott, supporting him wholeheartedly in the rash project to build the new college. In 1840, he had been nominated for one of the new northern vicariates and struck with terror at the prospect, set off for Rome to argue for his incapacity (including poor eyesight) for the post. Having successfully pleaded his cause with Gregory XVI, he returned, relieved, to his beloved Oscott, only to find that Wiseman had been appointed rector in his absence. This led to a period in the wilderness for the unhappy Weedall, only brought to an end by Ullathorne.[126] Weedall had formed most of the priests in the Central District over his long career at Oscott, and few men knew the local Church as he did or was so respected by the clergy. Despite Weedall's poor health, Ullathorne could not have made a better move at the start of his career in Birmingham in the eyes of the local clergy.

It was clear from Ullathorne's immediate attention to Oscott that the priesthood would take centre stage, and the devotion of this Benedictine bishop to the training, support and encouragement of the secular clergy became legendary. The need he had voiced in the Western District to 'identify myself with them' shaped his whole life as a bishop. His first public opportunity to give voice to this was at the funeral of Fr William Richmond at Brewood in Staffordshire in November 1848. He had only been Bishop in the Central District for a few months when he was called upon to preach the eulogy on one of its

---

[126.] Judith Champ, *A Temple of Living Stones: the Chapel of St Mary's College, Oscott* (2002), pp. 64–6.

great figures in the heart of traditionally Catholic Staffordshire. He had to speak about the much loved pastor and nephew of another revered priest, Robert Richmond, and he made it clear that it was men like the Richmond uncle and nephew who were his model of devoted and solid pastoral priests. William Richmond had been born to Protestant parents, but under the influence of his priest uncle, Robert, from the age of eleven, he was brought up a Catholic. Robert was one of the first handful of priests ordained from Oscott, part of the new beginning made by the native seminaries forged out of the flight from the French Revolution, and was for a time on the college staff. He built the Pugin church at Brewood, near Chillington, which had been the residence of successive vicars apostolic in the Midland District. Robert died suddenly within days of opening the church and was succeeded by his nephew William.[127] Thus Ullathorne found himself enmeshed almost at once into the historical roots of his new District, and recognised from his own recusant upbringing the faithful witness of the generation of priests now passing.

The tone of tender affection and appreciation for his clergy, which would characterise the next forty years, shone clearly in his sermon in celebration of a priest he scarcely knew, but of whom he quickly found the measure. William Richmond clearly fulfilled Ullathorne's ideal of the pastoral priest, and he spoke movingly of Richmond's fervent devotion and zeal, of his love for justice and care for the poor, his nurture of younger clergy and candidates for seminary and his active encouragement of retreats for the clergy. 'He was a priest from head to foot. Interiorly and exteriorly he breathed the spirit of the priest. and his greatest praise amounts to this – that he was nothing but a priest.'[128] This became his ideal and his model in the way in which he inspired, begged, cajoled and masterminded the creation of a diocese, 'second to none ... above all, in its devoted body of clergy'.[129]

The claims and counter-claims between Ullathorne and

[127.] Gillow, vol. V, p. 417.
[128.] *Funeral Oration for William Richmond*, 16 November 1848.
[129.] Alexander Austin, 'Archbishop Ullathorne' in D. H. Farmer, *Benedict's Disciples* (1980), p. 324.

Wiseman rumbled on for years, and Ullathorne was perpetually anxious about the shortage of money and the management of Oscott. However, the early years in Birmingham were not only dogged by financial impecunity, but by complicated dealings with personnel in his new diocese. These reveal something of the development in Ullathorne, both as a bishop and as a mature man. One of the unique features of the diocese Ullathorne inherited was the presence, not only of the city of Oxford within its boundaries, which had been at the eye of the storm in the Church of England, but of the most famous (even notorious) of those who had converted to Catholicism as a result.

John Henry Newman, after a period of residence in Rome, had been ordained in the Catholic Church in 1847. Since then, he had been resident near Birmingham in the disused college premises of Old Oscott, which he renamed Maryvale, and later in a city centre church, as he developed the first ever English Oratory under the rule of St Philip Neri. Ullathorne was faced with the delicacy of establishing a proper relationship with Newman as a controversial public figure, and understanding the nature of the newly formed Oratory. The ensuing crisis was the start of his difficult, but ultimately affectionate and respectful friendship with Newman. It revealed Ullathorne's qualities of judgement and his weaknesses, which stemmed from his tendency to act quickly and assert authority strongly and at times outspokenly. It also revealed something of his dealings with religious orders and congregations beyond his own experience; he was not an uncritical admirer of the new movements stirring in the Church which are traditionally associated with the dynamics of the Catholic revival.

In personality, Newman and Ullathorne could not have been more different. Newman, uncertain of his future as a Catholic priest, was the former Oxford don, intellectually rigorous, with a sharp wit and a highly developed conscience. Ullathorne, the monk, was largely self-educated theologically, a straightforward Yorkshireman, humorous rather than witty, a natural leader, solidly rooted in the Church. Newman's faith was nuanced and thoroughly grounded in academic theology. Ullathorne's was profound and instinctive. Their backgrounds could not have been more different: while Newman was a Fellow of Oriel College, striving to refine the theology of the

Church of England, Ullathorne had been working almost single-handed to rescue the souls of the world's most degraded Englishmen, the convict prisoners of New South Wales. They had met briefly, when Newman and his companions were invited to Ullathorne's consecration as bishop in July 1846, only months after Newman's reception into the Church, and also in Rome while Newman was preparing for ordination and Ullathorne was dealing with Prior Park matters in early 1847. Estcourt, himself an Oxford friend of Newman, travelling with Ullathorne, was the link, and although there was no inkling at this time of Ullathorne going to Birmingham, they did have conversations about the planned Oratory.[130] Theirs was the most unlikely of partnerships, yet it grew over forty years to be a powerful and influential one in the English Catholic Church. In Newman, Ullathorne had to cope with a recent convert untutored in English Catholic practice, who became the superior of a religious congregation unfamiliar in England, while Ullathorne himself was trying to evolve and establish his own sense of episcopal authority in changing circumstances.

Newman was in contact with Ullathorne as soon as his appointment was made public, to assure him that the notion that the Oratorians intended to leave Maryvale was mistaken. They had been given the old Oscott College premises as a temporary home, but were content there until Oratories could be established in the cities. St Philip Neri had specifically intended that the Oratory should be a city-based form of communal and missionary life. London looked promising, as property was available, but though they were ready and willing, no property in Birmingham was yet provided. What Newman did want to be rid of, at least temporarily, was the large property of St Wilfrid's, near Alton Towers, and hoped the new bishop might have a use for it.[131] They seem to have got off on a reasonable footing, with cordial relations quickly established. Ullathorne did not want St Wilfrid's, which was in danger of becoming a financial millstone to the Oratorians, but he was keen to have them established in the centre of Birmingham, and

[130.] L&D XII, p. 48, 21 February 1847.
[131.] L&D XII, pp. 254–5, 21 August 1848.

had some ideas about how to make this happen.[132] By late September the move from Maryvale to Deritend, in one of the poorest quarters of Birmingham, was planned, with some Oratorians going temporarily to St Wilfrid's.

However, the first clash was also brewing, and the Oratorian Frederick Faber's, *Lives of the Saints* was the provocation.[133] The series of hagiographical essays, 'translated from foreign sources, which exuded exactly the sort of extravagant and credulous piety which English Catholics found distasteful and Protestants merely ridiculous'[134] drew Ullathorne into the fray. The *Lives* were intended to 'raise the spiritual temperature of English Catholicism, by giving prominence to those revivalist, ascetic and contemplative emphases' which some of the converts felt were lacking.[135] The temperature was certainly raised, but not quite in the way hoped, when the convert editor of *Dolman's Magazine* published a damning review. Newman, as Faber's religious superior, felt he had to ally himself with the author, and sought Ullathorne's advice as to the best course of action. Ullathorne consulted with other bishops and religious superiors and took the view that the *Lives* were wholly unsuited to the English temperament, and advised ending publication forthwith. Newman was dismayed by this reaction. What he had wanted was advice on the best way of counteracting the accusations of idolatry made by the hostile reviewer: here was Ullathorne appearing almost to agree with the critic. Newman irritated Ullathorne by taking on himself, as superior of the Oratory, the responsibility of cancelling publication of the *Lives*. His obedience to the bishop left him no choice, but he was determined to protect Faber.[136] Writing to Faber (in a letter copied to Ullathorne and published in *The Tablet*) Newman insisted that 'no-one can assail your name without striking at mine'.[137] What really annoyed Newman was that Ullathorne and the other bishops appeared to want the *Lives* stopped, 'before they have made

132. L&D XII, p. 264, 19 September 1848.
133. L&D XII, Appendix 6, pp. 402–4.
134. David Newsome, *The Convert Cardinals* (1993), p. 201.
135. Sheridan Gilley, *Newman and His Age* (1990), p. 256.
136. L&D XII, p. 278, 4 October 1848.
137. L&D XII, p. 316, 30 October 1848.

Price [the reviewer] eat his words publicly'.[138]

It became clear that Newman and Ullathorne took diametrically opposite views of the value and tone of the *Lives*, and would never agree. Correspondence between them in late October and early November became chilly. Ullathorne took the opportunity whenever he could to instruct Newman very carefully and precisely on his lack of experience and understanding of English Catholicism.[139] He sent tart and formal replies to Newman's enquiries about the use of Oratorian novices in catechising local people, revealing in the process his lack of understanding of the Oratorian constitutions.[140] This issue would arise again a month or two later. Ullathorne was clearly agitated and feared losing complete control of Newman and the Oratory. The hostility between them stemmed fundamentally from a clash of jurisdictions rather than any personal animosity. The bishop was not convinced of the real spiritual submission of the Oratorian converts, who 'should not have everything their own way', and Newman resented Ullathorne's apparent lack of appreciation of his position as religious superior of the Oratory. The atmosphere was not helped by a hard-hitting letter of Ullathorne's in *The Tablet*, which was intended as a response to criticism of the standards of Catholic education in colleges such as Downside, but which ended up as a broadside aimed at 'those who are but as children amongst us, forgetting their pupillage, have undertaken to rebuke, censure and condemn the acts of the English Church, and the sentiments of her members, which they seem unwilling to understand'.[141] Nevertheless, Newman refused to be thrown off course, and was mildly amused by Ullathorne's long and impassioned letter expressing severe anxiety and warning him of the dangers of sensitiveness and intellectual pride.[142] He believed the bishop to be 'a kind-hearted man' who wished to get on with the Oratory, but, 'just as gentlemen make acquaintance with bowing and civil speeches, so the way to be good

---

138. L&D XII, p. 304, 22 October 1848.
139. L&D XII, pp. 317–9, 31 October 1848; pp. 320–2, 3 November 1848.
140. L&D XII, p. 328, 9/11 November 1848.
141. *The Tablet*, 8 December 1848. Reprinted in *Downside Review* vol. VII (1888), p. 7.
142. L&D XII, pp. 352–3, 29 November 1848.

friends with him is to begin with a boxing bout'.[143] This was a perceptive assessment, and there were several instances throughout life when Ullathorne launched a hostile broadside at a new acquaintance, only to find later that they had the basis of a firm friendship. Fierce disagreements were never a barrier to friendship with Ullathorne; in fact, they were almost an expectation.

An apology by the hostile reviewer of the *Lives* finally solved the public issue and the series resumed on more restrained lines. Ullathorne was prepared to settle for this, though he was never very impressed with Faber's writings, commenting privately to his friend Thomas Brown several years later in relation to Faber's best known works, *Growth in Holiness* and *All for Jesus* that 'a want of a thorough theological course and of theological caution is apparent throughout his writings'.[144] Relations between Newman and Ullathorne were still sensitive, and the more of Newman's emollient letters Ullathorne received, the more irritated he became. He was worried by his own inability to handle Newman:

> I have done my best to get into Mr Newman's heart, but though we manage very well in conversation, in correspondence he is curt, trenchant and somewhat polemical in spirit ... What all the world sees in them (the Oratorians) is a spirit of isolation from the Catholic body and much ignorance of our spirit. A critical spirit with regard to us, a tone like that of a party. Mr Newman after all the kind, familiar confidence shown him both by other bishops and myself, stands stiffly on his own opinions. I think the little rubs we have had, have had the effect of bringing things together and awakening more consideration.[145]

Misunderstanding continued between Newman and Ullathorne over questions of jurisdiction, and one of Newman's friends, John Moore Capes, convert founder of *The Rambler*, was convinced that 'he does not in the least recognise

---

143. L&D XII, p. 337, 19 November 1848.
144. Ampleforth, Copy of letter Ullathorne to Brown, 10 August 1855.
145. AAW R79/3, Ullathorne to Wiseman, 22 November 1848.

you as the head of a religious order, with duties towards your members'.[146] The further dispute mainly centred on the closure of the Oratorian mission of St Wilfrid's in Staffordshire. Newman suspected that Ullathorne was less ready than he to reach agreement,[147] but it was rather that Ullathorne was still troubled over their proper relationship. He was enthusiastic about the Oratory and keen to keep it alive in the diocese, but equally anxious to secure proper ecclesiastical submission from its members. Co-operation with the familiar and traditional religious orders was one thing, but as Newman himself realised, ' ... such co-operation implies a basis and cannot take place, till his Lordship knows what we are and how we are to co-operate'.[148]

The Oratorian rule said nothing about the role of the bishop, and Ullathorne himself was still uncertain how to deal with them, insisting to Newman that his probing letters were provoked only by a wish 'simply to understand the precise relations which canonically exist between the English Oratory and the Vicar Apostolic'.[149] He consulted Grant in Rome, but the situation there was vague; Barnabo himself, at *Propaganda Fide*, could only suggest consulting the Roman Oratory as to their normal practice.[150] The issue of jurisdiction came to a head when the Oratory proposed to leave St Wilfrid's to set up an Oratory in London. St Philip Neri's model was always designed to be an urban foundation, and Newman had only ever regarded St Wilfrid's as a temporary home in the remote north Staffordshire countryside. However, the bishop took the view that, having taken on the Staffordshire mission, it was the responsibility of the Oratorians to continue to provide mission clergy for St Wilfrid's. In his view, this was a legitimate expectation which he would have had in the case of any other religious order. He could not afford to lose the services of the Oratorians. The problem was that missionary activity of this kind, separated from an established Oratory, was not part of

146. L&D XII, p. 358, 30 November 1848.
147. L&D XII, p. 365, 6 December 1848.
148. L&D XII, p. 380, 20 December 1848.
149. L&D XII, pp. 369–70, 10 December 1848.
150. AAW St Edmund's Papers 54, Grant to Ullathorne, 18 January 1849.

the Oratorian rule of life. Newman was fearful, though, that the angry bishop could oblige them to do it.[151]

As in the controversy over the *Lives*, Faber's immaturity and lack of judgement were contributory factors. He continued to treat St Wilfrid's, not as ecclesiastical property, but as his private property which he could therefore close up as he wished.[152] Ullathorne refused any negotiation with Faber, impatient with his interpretation of the means of holding property: civil law meant that, at the time, Catholic property had to be vested in the hands of an individual person. He insisted on dealing with Newman, recognising at last his position as the canonical superior. The St Wilfrid's crisis became a turning point for Newman and Ullathorne: crucially, Newman took the bishop's side and told Faber he was wrong and could 'have no conscience in the matter'.[153] He and Ullathorne agreed to get a dispensation from Rome to continue St Wilfrid's as an Oratorian mission (not a fully constituted Oratory). This was an important moment in his relationship with Newman. Newman agreed with Ullathorne that St Wilfrid's was plainly church property, and it was the responsibility of the Oratory to staff it. He told Faber bluntly that the only difference between himself and the bishop was Faber's own claim to be able to close the Staffordshire premises unilaterally.[154] A measure of understanding between Newman and Ullathorne began to emerge as Newman reprimanded Faber for describing Ullathorne as 'the little man', and began to speak more warmly of the bishop, who, he said, may be little, but in the eyes of the Church was a tall man.[155]

When the dispensation to continue St Wilfrid's as an Oratorian mission was refused, both Newman and Ullathorne were dismayed. It was a sharp lesson for the bishop in trying to waive the rules of a religious congregation – he had regarded it as a matter of course.[156] More significantly, the rescript from Rome made clear the proper relationship between the Oratory

151. L&D XIII, p. 73, 4 March 1849.
152. L&D XIII, pp. 143–4, 11 May 1849.
153. L&D XIII, p. 149, 15 May 1849.
154. L&D XIII, p. 146, 13 May 1849.
155. L&D XIII, p. 145, 12 May 1849.
156. L&D XIII, p. 306, 24 November 1849.

and the bishop, and settled once and for all the open questions of jurisdiction. Every Oratory was to be independent of each other and under the direct supervision of the diocesan bishop in whose territory it lay. Thus a major difficulty was finally settled, but it still left Ullathorne with the problem of sustaining the Staffordshire mission and over the next few years he desperately tried to get both the Benedictines and Jesuits to take it on, before it became a Passionist mission and eventually diocesan property.[157] Faber's departure for the London Oratory also helped to remove irritation, and it was Butler's view that animosity between Newman and Ullathorne came to an end in 1849.[158] It was not quite as simple as that, and the evolution of a deep and complex friendship took many years, which were not without their difficulties. However, gestures were made on both sides. Newman credited their mutual friend Margaret Hallahan with removing Ullathorne's mistrust and enabling the growth of a real friendship, for which she earned his lifelong gratitude.[159]

In 1850, Newman, in a gesture of solidarity, drew much of the fire on himself by preaching a sermon entitled *Christ Upon the Waters* in St Chad's during the local Papal Aggression furore, and in the following year Ullathorne willingly chaired a public meeting which acclaimed Newman's support of Catholicism in the ill-fated Achilli case. This, despite the fact that Ullathorne had misgivings about whether Newman should have gone to court. Confidence between them grew and was marked in 1852 by Ullathorne's encouragement of Newman to preach at the first Provincial Synod of the English and Welsh bishops, held at Oscott. The sermon, *The Second Spring*, was one of his most famous. In it Newman spoke reverently and proudly of restored episcopal authority and (in a clear reference to Ullathorne) of 'St Benedict speaking to us by the voice of bishop and priest'.[160] It marked a high point in Newman's early Catholic career, and was a sign of new confidence between Ullathorne and himself.

---

[157] Farm St (Residence of St Mary) 118 Ullathorne to SJ Provincial Superior, 4 December 1855.
[158] Butler, *Life*, I, p. 162.
[159] L&D XII, p, 358, note.
[160] J. H. Newman, *The Second Spring* (1852).

Ullathorne's first contact with the superior of a female religious institute arose soon after his arrival in the Central District, and was just as complex and problematic as his dealings with the Oratory. It was very unlike his dealings with Mother Margaret, or even with the great Irish foundresses he had met in Dublin. In October 1846 Cornelia Connolly, an American convert, the wife of an episcopalian minister who had received permission to separate from his wife so that he could become a priest, arrived in Derby with three companions to establish a missionary community there. She had become determined not only to enter religious life, but to establish her own religious institute dedicated to the Holy Child Jesus, and was sponsored by Wiseman while he was coadjutor to Bishop Walsh. The foundation flourished in its early life, quickly increasing to seven and establishing a night school for working girls and a boarding school. Wiseman was delighted, but their early success was blighted by financial difficulties.

The Derby mission was under the care of Thomas Sing, and when the convent was built, he mortgaged it and counted on the community to pay the interest. Cornelia Connolly understood that the property was going to be transferred to Wiseman under an agreement between him and Sing, and that he was enthusiastic about their presence.[161] Thomas Sing was no fool, and was an experienced missioner by the time Cornelia Connolly arrived. Educated at Sedgley Park and Oscott, he was ordained in 1834. Only two years later he was sent to Derby, where he built a fine Pugin church, always known by the antique spelling of 'St Marie's'. Further financial liability for the convent was not part of his plan, but he was keen to encourage their educational ideas. Later he was a key figure in forming the Catholic Poor Schools Committee in 1851 and became a canon of the new diocese of Nottingham a year later.[162] However, his relationship with Wiseman and with Ullathorne over the Derby convent was tetchy to say the least.

Frustrated that no money was forthcoming from Wiseman or Connolly, Sing complained bitterly to Bishop Walsh. His anger and jealousy had also been roused by the arrival of a young

[161.] Radegund Flaxman, *A Woman Styled Bold* (1991), p. 119.
[162.] Gillow, vol. V, p. 509.

Italian chaplain at the convent, Samuel Asperti, who, though zealous and well-meaning, alienated Sing and the other local clergy by interfering in mission affairs. Asperti was a friend of Pierce Connolly, and his appointment was engineered by him as a way of trying to regain control of Cornelia's life. In 1848, Walsh was already a sick man, his more energetic coadjutor Wiseman had gone ahead of him to London, and nothing was resolved. The property transfer to Wiseman never materialised, nor did much in the way of substantial help from him, who now had other concerns in London. This was yet another instance of Wiseman's financial vagueness and unreliability, and the unfinished business and consequent problems which he left Ullathorne to pick up.

Ullathorne, while in Rome negotiating the hierarchy, had been asked for a view on the constitutions of Cornelia Connolly's new foundation, bizarrely, drawn up by her estranged husband. This suggests that his knowledge of female religious orders had already registered with the Roman Curia. His comments are as revealing as they are damning, showing the tone of his policy towards the new women's religious institutes. He was critical of an attempt to link it with the Visitation Order founded by St Francis de Sales, as there was not much evidence of the saint's particular charism in the constitution, but most cuttingly, he drew the Holy See's attention to the fact of its foundation by converts and, 'neophytes in religion'. They lacked any 'person experienced in religion and in religious rules to guide their steps'. He referred to similar difficulties in other orders,

> including the Sisters of Mercy, whose constitutions are almost as scanty and limited in their details as those of the congregation of the Holy Child Jesus, from which has arisen both defective formation of the religious character and the greatest difficulty in the government of many of the houses; all attempts to remedy this state of things having hitherto proved failures ... the key to the difficulties of the proposed constitutions of the Congregation of the Holy Child Jesus is that unlimited power is given over the entire proposed congregation in the hands of one superioress who is constituted in reality, though not in name, General, with unlimited authority.

Anxious not to become embroiled in what he could see was an impossible situation, he assured the Holy See that,

> In attaching these remarks the undersigned most earnestly disclaims all feelings respecting this infant institute, of the persons comprising it he has no personal knowledge, but being invited to give an opinion, and having had some little experience of religious women, having superintended the founding of two distinct communities for the active life, he could not close the eyes of his conscience to the evils which have arisen from rules hastily formed before experience.[163]

Having given his opinion, as asked, Ullathorne returned to England and packed his bags to move from Bristol to Birmingham. When Ullathorne arrived in the Central District in the late summer of 1848, he had temporary administrative responsibility for the Eastern District so found himself unwittingly drawn closely into the Derby convent affair. Sing's anger, by this time, was focused less on the financial issues and more on the power wielded by Cornelia Connolly as superior.[164] Ullathorne was so concerned that he wasted little time in visiting and went to Derby to see for himself on 17 September.[165] His notes on the visit suggest that relations between Connolly and Sing had deteriorated to such an extent that they could not continue to work together. One of Connolly's sympathetic biographers suggested that Ullathorne accepted the view that, 'Sing had made it impossible for them to continue with him',[166] but Ullathorne's own words to Wiseman a few weeks later gave a rather different impression. He was less than impressed with what he had seen at the Derby convent, describing it as, 'experimental'. Knowing that when the hierarchy was eventually re-established, Derby would fall within the Diocese of Nottingham, he was reluctant to take on the formation and guidance of the community at such a

163. BAA B1148, Ullathorne to *Propaganda Fide*, 9 June 1848.
164. Flaxman, p. 121.
165. BAA B1248, Notes in Ullathorne's hand on sisters at Derby, nd September 1848.
166. Flaxman, p. 122.

distance himself, and was not optimistic about its future, unless 'a solid minded and discreet director' could be found. Unless absolutely forced to, Ullathorne wanted nothing to do with the case.[167]

This view may well have been influenced by the strange, and probably psychologically disturbed actions of Cornelia Connolly's estranged husband (now ordained as a Catholic priest) who tried to portray himself as the founder of the congregation and Wiseman as a malign influence. Ullathorne had condemned the rules drawn up by Pierce Connolly[168] (in this regard he was sympathetic to Cornelia), but on the financial question, he bluntly told Wiseman that the problems he had inherited at Oscott and in the District (largely of Wiseman's making) made it impossible for him to help, and he proposed that Mr Sing should be paid off and the property be conveyed to the sisters. The last thing he wanted was to 'put myself into the case'.[169] On the deterioration of relations between the convent and the local clergy, he was in no doubt that the mistrust which had soured things was, 'more deeply seated in the mind of the superioress than on the other side'. Ullathorne's conclusion was that it was impossible for the convent to be settled financially and spiritually in Derby in the future, and the best course would be for them to move elsewhere, preferably under Wiseman's jurisdiction. Clearly unimpressed with the whole set-up at Derby, he breathed a veiled threat that if they did remain and looked to him for guidance and supervision, the sisters themselves might find they were not so keen, as he would 'require some very decisive regulations which might not at first prove palatable'.[170] By the end of the year, Cornelia Connolly and her companions had decamped from Derby to St Leonard's in Sussex, with Fr Sing continuing to chase them for the money he believed owed to him. Ullathorne's relief was intense.

[167.] BAA B1385, Ullathorne to Bagshawe, 3 January 1849.
[168.] AAW R79/3, Ullathorne to Wiseman, 30 October 1848. 'There is one fact of some importance regarding the Rule. When in Rome I was required to give an opinion upon it and I felt obliged to point out several things contrary to the general spirit of the canons.'
[169.] Ushaw OS/M 12, Ullathorne to Bagshawe, 1 July 1849.
[170.] AAW R79/3, Ullathorne to Wiseman, 27 October 1848.

It was short-lived though, as he was dragged into the notorious case of Connolly v Connolly in which Cornelia's husband abandoned both his priesthood and his Catholicism and tried to reclaim his wife by all possible means, including recourse to the courts. As the sisters prepared to leave Derby, Pierce Connolly wrote a series of letters to Ullathorne, claiming that Wiseman and Asperti had come between him and his wife and asking him, in furious terms, to intervene.[171] Ullathorne's response was that he would do his best to explain Pierce Connolly's position to Wiseman, but he no longer exercised any jurisdiction himself over Cornelia Connolly. He urged Connolly to do nothing without taking advice and not to depend on his own judgement in his present frame of mind, and to be careful of his own reputation and that of his former wife.[172] Pierce Connolly clearly became very agitated and tried to lay down conditions, including forbidding contact between her and Wiseman. 'He has since written to me that nothing shall prevent him from bringing back Mrs C under his protection ... I do not of course approve of Mr C's desire of re-establishing communication with Mrs C.' Ullathorne conceded that the case was 'complicated' and he clearly wanted as little to do with it as possible.[173] Connolly promptly threw his lot in with a rabidly anti-Catholic lawyer, Henry Drummond, and began legal proceedings. It is more than coincidence that in 1851, Drummond was the author of a proposed Parliamentary Bill aimed at government control of convents.

Ullathorne's attitude to Cornelia Connolly is revealing; his enthusiasm for women's religious life was undoubted but not uncritical. Although he had been, and would continue to be, a warm supporter of Mother Margaret Hallahan and other religious institutes of women, he was cautious and careful in his encouragement of new convents. Ullathorne insisted on exercising appropriate and canonical episcopal duty and authority in respect of convents, and the adherence to proper processes

---

171. Flaxman, p. 138.
172. AA W R79/3, Ullathorne to Wiseman, 6 December 1848.
173. AAW R79/3, Ullathorne to Wiseman, 28 December 1848. Several other letters to Wiseman at the same time suggest his anxiety to know that the matter is settled.

were not mere pedantry but protections which he saw as necessary for everyone's sake. The rigorous application of canon law
was not so much a restriction as a measure of the respect and
dignity with which he treated women religious. He regarded
them as a serious and significant element in the Church's life,
to be protected and governed by its legal processes just as
much as the clergy. This would become evident in later years as
convents came under popular suspicion and prurient attack.
Despite Cornelia Connolly's departure with her community to
the other end of the country, Ullathorne continued (as Bishop
Grant's friend and confidante) to be drawn back into the
disputes which dogged her foundation in Sussex. Problems
arose again concerning convent property in 1852–3, and
Cornelia Connolly's early warm relationship with Wiseman
turned sour when he came to regard her as insubordinate to
episcopal authority. In 1860 Ullathorne was appointed by
Rome to arbitrate in a long-running property dispute;
Cornelia Connolly was anxious, knowing as well as anybody
that he was not favourably disposed towards her and her institute. She was probably right to be uneasy, but his innate sense
of justice was offended more by her rash statements than his
own prejudice.[174] In the course of his judgement he spoke
forthrightly of the 'well-known determination, self-will, imperi-
ousness and often insolent manner of the present superioress.
It is not necessary to insist on the peculiarities of her character,
for they are known all the world over'.[175]

His opinion, conveyed to Rome, was that she was the cause
of the trouble, and it seems that Ullathorne never had cause to
revise that view. It is nonsense to suggest, as Cornelia
Connolly's earlier biographer does, that Ullathorne was 'preju-
diced' against her partly because of his hostility to anything
involving Wiseman and converts;[176] in fact he came to agree
with Wiseman that her unresponsiveness to episcopal authority
was the nub of the problem. The contrast with Mother
Margaret Hallahan's collaborative labour with Ullathorne to

[174.] Mother Marie Therese, *Cornelia Connolly, a study in fidelity* (1963),
     p. 187.
[175.] Flaxman, pp. 271–2.
[176.] Mother Marie Therese, pp. 310–11.

achieve approval for the constitutions for her order is in marked contrast. Writing confidentially from the Vatican Council in 1870 to Hallahan's successor, he commented critically and 'raised objections' to aspects of Connolly's rule, still under consideration in Rome.[177] The strange business of Pierce Connolly's interference in the constitutions of the institute in 1848 cast a long shadow, and it was not until 1882, after Cornelia Connolly's death, that the Society of the Holy Child Jesus received Roman approval for its constitution. Ullathorne apparently wrote in support, but making the point that the death of the foundress had changed the picture.[178] The struggle for women's religious life to flourish was much harder if it was undertaken without episcopal support, guidance and encouragement. Ullathorne clearly learned a good deal from his involvement with the strange and complicated case of Cornelia Connolly and her religious congregation. It sealed in his mind the need for care and attention in the compiling of constitutions and the advice of canon lawyers; it made him even more insistent on appropriate checks and balances where the authority of a religious superior was concerned, and, inevitably, it made him yet more scrupulous in ensuring the financial security of any convent with which he had dealings.

If the Coventry years were the happiest of Ullathorne's life, it is almost certain that the two years which followed his reluctant appointment to the Western District were among the unhappiest. The transition to episcopal authority was one for which he thought Australia had prepared him, but he found that personal frustrations and difficulties could be just as intractable in England. His strong exercise of episcopal authority and readiness to take the Prior Park case to Rome are indicative of characteristics which would earn him enmity as someone all too ready to assert himself and stand on his dignity as a bishop. However, his experience and determination obviously also gained him respect, persuading his colleagues that this young and relatively inexperienced bishop was the person to negotiate the most fundamental change to church government in England in nearly three hundred years. The success of

---

[177.] Stone G/ULL/III63, Ullathorne to Poole, 1 January 1870.
[178.] *Mother Marie Therese*, p. 251.

his task in handling the hierarchy negotiations brought him into the spotlight on the national and international Catholic stage; his influence had been extraordinary, especially after *Propaganda Fide* refused any communication with England except through him. A further two years, during which the hierarchy hung in abeyance during the pope's exile from Rome, were enough to see him making a successful fresh start in the Central District.

By the spring of 1850, Ullathorne was feeling more optimistic about the progress being made, though still concerned about finance. 'I am happy to say we are all pulling on very peaceably and in good will and heart together, and doing my best to settle our financial difficulties which will require much care and attention for some time to come'.[179] In the summer, after the pope's return to Rome, the matter of the English hierarchy was expedited, and rumours began to fly that Wiseman was to be appointed cardinal. Catholic Emancipation in 1829 had been marked by the creation of Thomas Weld as cardinal; perhaps the restored hierarchy would produce a similar compliment to English Catholicism? Wiseman himself feared the rumours, and tried to set things in order before setting out for Rome.[180] An appointment as cardinal, it was assumed, would mean his return to residence in Rome and curtail his succession to Walsh in the new Archiepiscopal see of Westminster. What might this mean for Ullathorne?

The gossip reached fever pitch, even among Ullathorne's close allies.

> I believe it is true that Dr Wiseman will be made cardinal and leave England soon. It is reported that Dr Ullathorne will be translated to London. We have not heard anything on authority [*sic*] ourselves but I think it not unlikely. I hope not, as I do not wish to move again so soon and would not fancy living in London.[181]

Even John Lingard, who rarely left his country fastness in

[179.] Cardiff, Ullathorne to Brown, 20 March 1850.
[180.] AAW Molloy Collection, Wiseman to Ullathorne, nd 1850.
[181.] BAA B1945, Estcourt to Harley, 17 July 1850.

Hornby, told a mutual friend that, if Wiseman acted in a way hostile to the government, he would 'not be surprised if the archiepiscopal mitre were to find itself on the temples of Dr Ullathorne'.[182] Ullathorne got wind of this and of the possibility that it might mean yet another move for him, to Westminster.

> I will not conceal from Your Lordship a certain uneasiness which I feel on account of the positive manner in which it is asserted that there is an idea of transferring me once more. It has unsettled the clergy and convents in this District. I should attach no importance to it were it not asserted so very confidently.

He was desperate to know if there is any truth in the rumour and sick with apprehension lest it be true.[183]

In the event, Wiseman was elevated to the rank of cardinal, but as Archbishop of Westminster, so he was not removed to Rome. Ullathorne's relief was intense, as it meant that he was now settled in Birmingham for the foreseeable future. The final announcement of the hierarchy in September 1850 and Wiseman's letter, *From Out of the Flaminian Gate*, provoked a furore, and public meetings voicing anger at the 'Papal Aggression' were held in Birmingham, as elsewhere in the country.[184] The first meeting in Birmingham was actually instigated by the Catholics themselves, as a result of the excitement, and hosted by Ullathorne at Bishop's House in November of 1850. An address of congratulation was presented to Ullathorne, proposed by Newman and seconded by John Hardman junior, offering the 'united congratulations' of the clergy and laity, on the new hierarchy, and lamenting the 'moral persecution now raised against the religious liberties of the Catholics of England'. Despite the fervent hope expressed that Birmingham 'would not now be induced to join in the outcry with which our rights and liberties are at present

---

[182.] M. Haile and E. Bonney, *Life and Letters of John Lingard 1771–1851* (1911), pp. 354–5.
[183.] AAW R79/3, Ullathorne to Wiseman, 16 July 1850.
[184.] The following account is taken from Champ thesis, pp. 250–4.

assailed',[185] a public meeting was called at the Town Hall three weeks later.

Like many which took place up and down the country, it was noisy, overcrowded, heated and long. People were shouted down or stopped from speaking, and six hours of haranguing preceded the vote on an address to the Queen. This address described the Pope as arrogant and his action as an 'insult to Your Majesty, a violation of the spirit of the constitution under which we live and an audacious attack on our civil and religious liberties'. A counter proposal begged for non-interference by the government and for the royal sanction to 'such measures as may be proposed for securing liberty'.[186] A considerable number of surprising allies were ranged on the Catholic side, including several Anglican clergymen, the Free Churchman George Edmonds, the MPs Joseph Scholefield and George Frederick Muntz and the Quaker Chartist leader Joseph Sturge. Even John Angell James, the leading independent Evangelical and one of the instigators of the meeting, insisted on 'no popery and no intolerance'. George Edmonds struggled to get a hearing, but pleaded with the heated crowd to decide 'whether the mere change of name or title gave the Bishop of Birmingham any more power or authority over them than he had as Dr Ullathorne'. Joseph Sturge finally turned the meeting by his oratory, accusing those who were 'ostensibly the ministers of peace (of) exciting one class against another on a question of a purely religious character'. He implored his fellow citizens 'not to seek the correction of erroneous opinions by reference to the law or the executive, but by the exercise of charity and forbearance'. Both the tabled addresses to the Queen were argued down, and even a more moderate version opposing the 'Papal Aggression' was defeated.[187]

The outcry which arose, provoked by Wiseman's letter, and the political crisis which had surrounded events, were treated by Ullathorne as side-shows, especially once local opinion had shown itself more in favour of peace and tolerance than

---

185. BPL 250938 *Report of a Meeting of Catholics*, November 1850.
186. BPL 34971 *Report of a Meeting on 'The Catholic Question'*, December 1850.
187. AAW R79/3, Ullathorne to Wiseman, 11 December 1850.

conflict. For him the public benefit of the restored hierarchy was that the power of the papacy had been exercised for all to see, and the British government, 'both divided and conflicting in its views and perplexed by the act of its leader', (a reference to Lord John Russell's equivocal position) would learn to treat it with more caution and respect in the future.[188] The fire unleashed around Wiseman's head, stoked by the Prime Minister himself, at least proved to all that Wiseman was not in the pocket of the government. This, in Ullathorne's view, would strengthen relations between the Irish and English Churches, damaged by Wiseman and Minto's attempt to use the papacy to control the troublesome Irish clergy.[189]

Ullathorne assured Rome that the public furore was not provoked by the restoration of the hierarchy itself, but by 'a combination of accidents, among the chief of which was the unfortunate publication of a pastoral written in Rome in entire unconsciousness of what was passing in England, and published by a young and inexperienced vicar general who himself told me that he did it amidst perplexity as to what he ought to do'.[190] It would have the virtue of drawing together the old and new elements of the Church and carry weight with the men of the Oxford Movement making decisions about whether to remain in the Church of England or not. Overall, he expressed satisfaction with the course of events, believing that, 'however unfortunate have been those accidents to which I alluded, the establishment of the hierarchy is worth all the trouble we have been or might be put to'.[191] He declared himself 'morally certain' that but for the 'strange acts of publishing the Apostolic letter' there would have been no serious trouble, but even had he foreseen the furore, 'I would yet have said – establish the hierarchy.'[192] This somewhat contradicts the impression which the Earl of Shrewsbury had

---

[188.] *Propaganda Fide*, Ullathorne to Fransoni, 2 December 1850. The reference is to Prime Minister Lord John Russell's disingenuous claim to know nothing of the planned hierarchy, despite Minto's presence in Rome and his careful reporting of events.

[189.] *Propaganda Fide*, Ullathorne to Fransoni, 2 December 1850.

[190.] *Propaganda Fide*, Ullathorne to Fransoni, 29 March 1851.

[191.] Ibid.

[192.] Cardiff, Ullathorne to Brown, 20 March 1851.

gained, that Ullathorne agreed with him that 'the time and *manner*' of the hierarchy had been a mistake. 'The hierarchy per se could never have been a bad thing; we should have had it long, long ago: or not quite so soon perhaps. But the *manner* has done, and will I fear still do us a world of mischief.'[193]

Ullathorne was, in reality, much more sanguine about the future than Shrewsbury. The new order meant primarily the assertion, for the first time since the Reformation, of proper episcopal government for English Catholics and the new bishops were certainly put to trouble to make it work. Its development after 1850 was a painful process, dogged by conflicts between bishops, negotiations with government and continued occasional outbreaks of hostility in society. However, in Ullathorne's view if matters were conducted according to canon law and Tradition, they could not go far wrong. In that sense he was a radical figure in the new hierarchy, wanting to see substantial change in methods of operation, but change shaped by pastoral experience. The great difference in canonical status between a vicar apostolic and a bishop in ordinary was the bishop's right and duty to set up a chapter and councils of clergy with responsibilities and duties permitted and controlled by church law. Thus much of the administrative burden which previously fell on vicars apostolic could legitimately be shifted onto diocesan bodies, leaving the bishop free to take a larger vision of matters. Ullathorne had a sense of this larger vision, that the restored hierarchy was more than an administrative or even canonical readjustment, more than an assertion of Catholic identity and organisation, but a recreation of true episcopal leadership.

In the midst of a Church becoming increasingly centralised and authoritarian, and a public and political establishment in England preoccupied with perceived encroachments on existing sources of power and authority, Ullathorne was not concerned with the exercise of autocratic power, but with the burdens, responsibilities and duties of office. He rarely used the words power or authority in describing the office of bishop, but saw the episcopate chiefly in terms of service and co-operation with clergy and laity for the building up of the Church.

[193.] BAA B2202, Earl of Shrewsbury to Ullathorne, 6 June 1851.

The authority a bishop exercised, he believed, was only that of Christ. 'His motive must be one and simple and repose on God. He must do nothing of himself for his force is drawn from heaven.'[194]

He was clear that the new hierarchy was a genuine restoration of what had existed before the Reformation, not an institution of novelty. In a pastoral letter commemorating the twenty-fifth anniversary of the hierarchy in 1875, he would define it as,

> that sacred order of Church government which belongs to the ordinary constitution of the Church, and which has come down from apostolic times ... What the great Pope St Gregory did in the year 596, that Pius IX did anew in the year 1850.[195]

It meant, to him, that the Church in England was brought back into full unity in the Church of the saints.

> It means an episcopacy and a clergy imbued with the deep wisdom of the Sovereign Pontiffs, of the Fathers of the Councils. It means the regulation of ecclesiastical government by subordination of authorities, under the influence of that unity which is the secret of all strength. It means subjection to precise rules both for bishops and for their clergy and obedience for those who govern as well as for those who are governed.[196]

The restoration in Ullathorne's opinion was not a carte blanche for the English bishops either to take a free hand or to carry on as before; he warned his diocesan synod that the Church would be watching and would expect to see fruit borne. For this reason he warned against any temptation to rest on the laurels of the achievement of the restored hierarchy.

[194.] *The Office of Bishop* (1850), p. 18.
[195.] Pastoral Letter, 13 September 1875.
[196.] *Discourse* (1853), pp. 3–4.

For we are not as they who have a certain work traced out, with exact limits, which done, their work is over ... we are missioners ... The missioner is one who has as much work before him as by the utmost stretching of his strength he can accomplish.[197]

In his tract on *The Office of Bishop*, issued in 1850 to mark the new hierarchy, Ullathorne spelled out his own understanding of the pastoral tasks of the bishop by which he was to fulfil his duty to God and the Church. The order of priorities is revealing. Ullathorne himself commonly made such an issue of order and the restoration of canonical government, and historians' discussion of the purpose and effects of the restored hierarchy are so often couched in terms of organisation and administration that it comes of something of a surprise to hear Ullathorne's statement. He insisted (along with the Council of Trent) that to give priority to preaching was a 'principal duty' of a bishop. The bishop was primarily a teacher, but that was not the whole picture. Pastoral care of the people in his charge was paramount, and it was the bishop's task to have solicitude for all the churches, 'to know the spiritual state of pastor and people; in what they fail and in what they abound and in what they require at our hands'.[198] This involved him in visiting, confirming, exercising justice, healing division, giving fatherly counsel and putting down division. The tenderness of Ullathorne's pastoral concern for his flock shines through the legalism of his language.

The bishop's second priority had to be providing for the succession of the priesthood, without which the pastoral priorities could not be met. To Ullathorne, it was a task 'of whose importance no man can form an overestimate'. The selection, training, financial support and pastoral placement of clergy was a major episcopal responsibility. Beyond these two primary functions lay the tasks of co-ordination with religious orders, oversight of female communities, support of schools, foundation of new missions, raising and administering of financial support, mediating and judging in private cases, dealing with

---

197. *Discourse* (1853), p. 5.
198. *The Office of Bishop*, p. 13.

the continual flow of correspondence and having care for the poor. Finally the bishop must have consideration for his own soul and his own spiritual life and must be aware of the need for refreshment in solitude with God.

He took to heart a phrase of St Gregory Nazienzen, who fled his country in the hope of escaping episcopal office, and remarked that, 'No wise man has joy in being created a bishop, if he considers the perils and sufferings set before him'.[199] Time and time again over the years he reiterated that sentiment to friends who were appointed to episcopal responsibilities, and there is no doubt that Ullathorne felt deeply the immense weight placed on a bishop, particularly his responsibility for the souls of others. His outpourings of distaste for the episcopal office did not stem from any false modesty, but were genuine expressions of reluctance to take up and hold an office of such magnitude. He entered into the task with a tough-minded enthusiasm for what was needed, but he remained a reluctant bishop to the end of his days, constantly aware of the sheer size of the task.

What was the task he had taken on? Perhaps a little more than the elderly and weary Bishop Walsh had promised him, 'writing letters and hearing grievances'.[200] Although he would certainly have agreed with Walsh, his more considered view was that the role of the bishop was

> to guide and perfect the priesthood, to rule and sanctify the religious communities, to provide for the spiritual wants of the faithful people, to bring conversion to sinners – light to those who stray in the ways of error, and to defend, uphold and advance the Church of God.[201]

Amidst all this, there was still the care of his own soul to consider. His view of episcopal responsibility was direct, specific and immediate and his career for the following forty years reflected his adherence to those priorities in a singular way.

[199.] *The Office of Bishop*, p. 4.
[200.] *Autobiography*, p. 278.
[201.] *The Office of Bishop*, p. 4.

In describing the office of bishop he quoted St Gregory the Great, his Downside patron, as describing it as a burden which the shoulders of angels might fear to receive, and meditated upon stories of bishops in the early Church dragged reluctantly to office while reflecting that the reluctant have often distinguished the office.[202] Was this a touch of pride, recalling his own long expressed reluctance, or a means of bolstering his own confidence for the future? He faced with fear and trepidation the care of thousands of souls and stood in no doubt that their ultimate responsibility lay in the hands of the bishop; while fearing the task he was not prepared to minimise it. The more a bishop knew of the responsibilities he bore, the more it should alarm him, and for Ullathorne there never was anything but a sense of the burden of office.

202. Ibid.

Chapter 5

Building a Diocese 1851–1856

When Ullathorne went to Birmingham, he was still only forty-two, and recovering from bruising experiences in the recent past, but he had also been given an extraordinary level of trust and influence in negotiating the hierarchy on behalf of his fellow bishops. Ullathorne was still a reluctant bishop, hopeful for the future with the new hierarchy, but still blighted by the ongoing problems of Prior Park which continued to haunt him, the inherited financial difficulties in Birmingham and the constant bombardment of criticism which went to Rome over the heads of the vicars apostolic. He was convinced of the desperate need for order and regularity which the hierarchy would bring. 'The vicars apostolic might devise expedients, but they had no canonical force or authority.'[1] The hierarchy did not (as he had hoped) put an end to the Roman tittle-tattle. In 1851 an accusation went to Rome that Ullathorne had exercised undue influence over Bishop Hendren (his successor in the Western District and by then Bishop of Nottingham) over Prior Park. He was angry and embarrassed at the accusation, and seriously contemplated (not for the last time) offering his resignation, but was dissuaded by others.[2] This was the sort of thing which got on Ullathorne's nerves, and created moods of depression. The idea of resignation clearly did not go away, nor the sense of gloom, as months later he was still begging

[1] *Restoration of the Hierarchy* (1871), p. 3.
[2] AAW R79/3, Ullathorne to Hendren (copy), 19 July 1851.

Wiseman to give him any hope that the Holy See would allow him to resign.[3]

By early 1851, the furore over the restoration of the Catholic hierarchy was dying down and the real work of recreating a diocesan organisation, which had not existed in England since the time of Mary Tudor, began in earnest. Ullathorne had set out his priorities in his first pastoral letter to the district in 1848 and in his lecture on *The Office of Bishop* in 1850. He was not facing these tasks, which he had set out so clearly, in good shape; his health was not good and the stresses of recent years had clearly taken their toll. An attack of a type of dysentery had left him weak and exhausted and scarcely able to write. 'I have not been myself for some time past … I have much more to do, and more places to go and on indispensable duty than I can get through, and my weak and poor stomach is a great check on my energies.'[4] The early 1850s were dominated by the rapid expansion in the number of missions in the diocese and the need for continued energetic fund raising. The rate at which land was bought and building projects undertaken across the industrial and rural parts of the diocese was remarkable, and Ullathorne did not mince his words about the financial pressure which this created for him and everyone else. His first pastoral letters after the restoration of the hierarchy recorded church building in progress in Wolverhampton, Coughton and Studley, Stratford, Stourbridge, Brierley Hill, West Bromwich, Leamington, Rugeley, Coventry, Burton upon Trent and Wood Lane, and at the new Birmingham Oratory. The Rosminians were building at Rugby, the Dominican sisters at Longton and Stone, the Sisters of St Paul and the Poor Clares were also involved in projects. Maryvale was being converted to an orphanage and hospital for aged and infirm women, to be run by the Sisters of Mercy.[5] Yet, despite all this activity, Ullathorne proclaimed a spiritual famine, characterised by a desperate shortage of priests and churches in many parts of the diocese, including the city of Birmingham itself, leaving thousands of Catholics unprovided for.

[3.] AAW 130/1, Ullathorne to Wiseman, 21 April 1852.
[4.] Stanbrook 3, Ullathorne to Abbess Gregson, 20 January 1851.
[5.] Pastoral Letters, 2 April /23 November 1851.

In his pastoral letter in the spring of 1850 Ullathorne had quoted the Council of Trent at length on the duty of a bishop to provide well-trained clergy, and of the laity to support him in this. He wanted the clergy to stand in right relationship to the laity, as the professional specialists who would lead the Church forward. He wanted

> a body of clergy, clean of heart and illuminated of God; wise in sacred knowledge and devoted to souls; skilled as divine physicians in the world's maladies, but showing no share of that world's spirit in their lives: such a clergy, with diversity of gifts but of one spirit, and that the spirit which was in Christ, the spirit of the saints, is the firm foundation, the secure support and crown of a district or diocese.

He ended with a serious plea to the people of the District to take the financial situation to heart, appealing to each person to make it 'his own personal concern ... if each one will do but his own individual part in the Apostleship of the Church to poor lost souls, and the regeneration of his country unto God ... then we should see the Church flourishing among us indeed'.[6] Paying for the upkeep of the clergy was also a problem: he reckoned that in a poor mission, a second priest might have to be satisfied with £30 per annum and a senior priest with £35–40.[7]

For this purpose, soon after the hierarchy was in place, he set up the Ecclesiastical Education Fund, emphasising to the people of the diocese the desperate need for priests. 'Hence the first duty of a bishop is to train up a body of clergy sufficient for the entire extent of his pastoral charge. And there exists a corresponding duty on the part of the clergy, the communities and the people to furnish him with the means to realise his great work.' After recounting the suffering and difficulty of penal times and the exertion it had taken to reach the current situation, he spelt out the present reality, which was, 'that we have no funds with which to educate our clergy. A

6. Pastoral Letter, 23 April 1850.
7. Cardiff, Ullathorne to Brown, 9 August 1853.

noble college indeed we have; we have also an excellent preparatory school at Sedgley Park; but we have no funds to maintain our church students, except the little that can be raised from the labour of teaching the laity'.[8] To meet this need he established a scheme to create an ongoing fund to be comprised of £5 a year from the bishop himself, £1 a year from each priest, and from all families, 'above the labouring class' 1d a week. Those of labouring families were asked to contribute 1d a month, and collecting boxes would be placed in all churches. Another capital fund would be collected from larger donations to provide income from interest only.

The importance which Ullathorne placed on the need to train more priests is clear from his direction that this collection should be given preference over all other charitable collections. 'For all the works of mercy and charity, corporal and spiritual, are shut up in this work, as the future plant is contained in the seed.' He was also, as ever, practical and realistic: to make sure that money was not wasted on candidates with no sign of a vocation to the priesthood, the bishop would receive a half-yearly report on each student. The pastoral letter ended with an impassioned plea to the clergy and people of the diocese for their help in this. 'Shall we have more difficulty in giving our money than our fathers had in giving their blood? Not so, beloved brethren, not so. For we are the children of saints and martyrs, and God has appointed us a great work to do.' There was a passion and determination, and a sense of destiny in the language of this pastoral; it is hard to be unmoved by the intensity of his insistence that the provision and training of sufficient priests for the growing missions was the root of the revival of Catholicism.

In July 1852 the first synod of the newly restored hierarchy took place, hosted by Ullathorne at Oscott, fulfilling Walsh's vision of it as a platform for the revival of English Catholicism. The 1852 synod (the first of three during the 1850s to be held at Oscott) was a momentous occasion, largely ceremonial and cele-bratory, usually remembered more for the 'Second Spring' sermon preached by John Henry Newman than for any signifi-cant legislative acts. It was more a display of unity than an

8. Pastoral Letter, 15 November 1850.

important series of debates. Newman's sermon had most of the clergy in tears, and the emotional power of his evocative words reflected that of the occasion.[9] Wiseman, as Cardinal Archbishop of Westminster, presided over a gathering of ten bishops; two (George Brown of Liverpool and Francis Hendren of Nottingham) did not attend due to illness. Some of the male religious orders were represented and theologians from the colleges along with Newman and Manning (only ordained as a Catholic priest little over a year earlier in June 1851). Henry Weedall represented the Birmingham Chapter. The matters discussed were largely uncontentious, and the already vexed question of ecclesiastical education and the maintenance of the existing colleges by the new dioceses was shelved, much to Ullathorne's irritation. Oscott had belonged to the old Midland District, subdivided in 1840 into the Central and Eastern Districts. The Central District in 1850 was divided between the new Diocese of Birmingham, and those of Shrewsbury and Nottingham. The Eastern District became the Diocese of Northampton and part of Nottingham. Division of property was a ticklish issue, but the real dispute centred on Oscott where (although the college was located in Birmingham) the three other bishops sent students and claimed a legitimate interest in the college.[10] Bishop James Brown of Shrewsbury took a particular interest in Oscott, having been a staff member there in the 1830s, and was deeply disappointed that his share of the funds amounted to little over £560, and his input in the running of the college was clearly not required.[11] The *Epitome Decretorum*, drawn up by Wiseman for the synod, contained anodyne directions for the standard of teaching, formation and administration of the colleges. Ullathorne thought these inadequate, but they were approved, unity maintained and the problem shelved.[19]

9. Butler, *Life*, I, p. 197.
10. Much of this discussion has been published in an earlier form in my essay, 'The Crown of the Diocesan Structure: W. B. Ullathorne and the foundation of the seminary' in Judith Champ (ed.), *Oscott College 1838–1988* (1988), pp. 93–105.
11. Peter Phillips, 'Or else we shall be bound hand and foot: Bishop James Brown of Shrewsbury and the Oversight of Seminaries' in *Recusant History* vol. 25 (2000), p. 240.
12. R. J. Schiefen, *Nicholas Wiseman and the Transformation of English Catholicism* (1984), p. 209.

The only thing Ullathorne did insist on ensuring, was that the synod of 1852 laid down a system of missionary rectorships under which to organise the clergy. This was, he believed, vital to eradicate the disputations and appeals by clergy over the heads of vicars apostolic to Rome so common in the pre-1850 Church in England. Embarrassed by his dealings with Thomas McDonnell in Rome before the final promulgation of the hierarchy, Ullathorne was anxious to move things on, and if necessary to establish rules and regulations for his own District if there was any further hold up.[13] It was a clear example of his conviction that legal clarity made for pastoral effectiveness.

> It was the intention of the bishops, when they projected the plan of the missionary rectorships to reserve to the bishops the exclusive power of subdividing the territory attached to a rectorial church and of establishing new missions without leaving any power in the rector to intervene as a *parochus* might. And it was felt to be the only condition on which rectorships or quasi-parochial rights could be judiciously constituted in a missionary country … The decree is perfectly clear in giving the power exclusively to the bishop, after taking the light of his chapter by consulting them.[14]

His insistence on this reflected the fact that disputes within the new dioceses were still commonplace, and appeals to Rome not infrequent. Discussing the difficulties which Bishop George Brown encountered with his new chapter (the first to be put in place after 1850), Peter Doyle has made the point that, whatever different groups hoped for from the new hierarchy, it required 'a regularisation of diocesan business and the establishment of proper structures so that episcopal authority would be acceptable to all'.[15] Ullathorne knew this instinctively.

The synod also attempted to tackle the thorny problem of episcopal authority over missions run by religious, including

[13.] Cardiff, Ullathorne to Brown, 27 March 1850.
[14.] Leeds Diocesan Archives, Ullathorne to Briggs, 17 May 1858.
[15.] Peter Doyle, 'A Tangled Skein of Confusion: the Administration of George Hilary Brown, Bishop of Liverpool 1850–56' in *Recusant History* vol. 25 (2000), p. 301.

Ullathorne's own Benedictines. It stated that bishops were free to make visitations to missionary and public churches, faculties were granted by the bishop only and superiors were urged to consult him before moving clergy, religious were encouraged to live according to their own rule as far as possible, and no new religious missions were to be built without express permission of the bishop.[16] These regulations proved far from satisfactory, and the issue of episcopal authority in relation to religious orders continued to be an irritant for many years.

However, all was not strain and difficulty, and the presence of women religious whom he could trust was a great comfort and support to Ullathorne. He was anxious to fulfil his promise to help secure premises within the diocese for Mother Margaret and the Third Order Dominicans. Founded by Hallahan and Ullathorne in Coventry and uprooted together to the Western District in 1846, this new Dominican family required space for a noviciate. In Clifton, on the outskirts of Bristol, they had established a convent alongside the shell of a church which became the cathedral, where they began their apostolate, 'amidst workmen and bricks and mortar'.[17] During this time Margaret Hallahan began work on establishing constitutions for her new community, the number of sisters grew and their reputation was such that requests arrived from all over the country, asking them to establish houses.[18] Mother Margaret's mind was set on establishing a noviciate house, preferably in the Midlands, close to her old friend and protector. The first attempt was made at Longton, a mining town in north Staffordshire. Mother Margaret set out for Longton in late October 1850. The hierarchy was now in place and Ullathorne securely established as Bishop of Birmingham, and therefore responsible for the whole of Staffordshire. The local people told her that Longton was 'the fag end of the Potteries', but she herself thought it was 'the fag end of the world'.[19]

16. Alban Hood, 'Stirring up the pool: Thomas Joseph Brown OSB and the Dispute between the Hierarchy and the English Benedictines' in *Recusant History* vol. 25 (2000), p. 319.

17. Stone G/ULL/III, Ullathorne to Editor of *Weekly Register*, 12 February 1856.

18. Drane, *Life*, p. 175.

19. Ibid., p. 198.

However, a small community was duly established, and Margaret returned to Clifton in time for the consecration of the new convent chapel there at Christmas. By this point, she had fifteen professed sisters, two novices and six postulants.[20]

A visit to England by the Master General of the Dominicans in spring 1851 gave added impetus to Margaret's desire to establish a noviciate within the Diocese of Birmingham, but at the same time she realised that Longton was hopelessly inadequate for such a purpose. The problem was finally solved by one of their Staffordshire patrons, James Beech, whose own daughter had joined the community, and he provided land in the nearby town of Stone.[21] The Passionists, led by Dominic Barberi, had established themselves at the nearby Aston Hall, and a small Pugin chapel had been built in Stone to provide for the Catholic townspeople. Building of the new convent, to house the noviciate, was begun in August 1852. The great partnership between Ullathorne and Margaret Hallahan had been reforged in Staffordshire, and the new convent and church became his second home, and his final resting place. He continued to defend them stoutly, insisting that the congregation founded by Margaret Hallahan was not some new, 'fly by night', but a full part of the ancient Order founded by St Dominic himself, who gave both men and women the black and white habit, 'to distinguish them and to be a sign of innocence and humility'.[22]

No sooner had the furore over the restoration of the hierarchy died down and the Ecclesiastical Titles Act been passed to pacify Protestant opinion, than another spark of anti-Catholic prejudice leapt into flames, which would scorch the habits of the nuns. Newman went to court (in Ullathorne's view, illadvisedly) against the Italian former priest Giacinto Achilli, whom he had accused of promiscuity. Achilli sought restitution for libel and the case became the Victorian version of a tabloid tale. A jury, which according to the leading Protestant statesman Lord Shaftesbury, was biased, found against Newman, but, as John Wolffe commented, 'whatever the truth of the

---

[20.] Ibid., p. 203.
[21.] Ibid., p. 235.
[22.] Stone G/ULL/III /128, Ullathorne to unnamed priest, (nd *c*.1848).

matter, the Roman Catholic Church was the loser'.[23] The Achilli case served only to stoke the fires of anti-Catholicism in its most prurient guise, feeding the commonplace view in Victorian society that Catholics were in some way 'dubious' in relation to sex, and that mandatory vows of celibacy and chastity for priests and nuns were a screen for unsavoury behaviour.

The ideal of marital fidelity and family unity, exemplified by what, under Queen Victoria, came to be called 'the Royal Family' was a main plank of the strength of Evangelical religion. A celibate clergy and the increasing numbers of houses of chaste single women contradicted this from the Catholic world view. Virtually all Christian writers in the nineteenth century were agreed that the only proper realm for a woman was the home, and 'the Victorians' excessive adulation of domesticity, combined with their elevation of the moral view of men's work, was at the heart of much of their distinctive frame of mind'.[24] As the number of convents increased, so did the attention which Protestantism gave to them, since they posed a direct challenge to the universal view that marriage, home and family constituted the religious vocation of women.[25] A Parliamentary campaign was launched to institute government inspection of convents, in particular to ensure that women were not being held against their will. This was the stuff of popular novels. The campaign originated in Edinburgh in the second half of 1851.[26] The Achilli case fuelled it, as did another notorious case alleging mistreatment of a child by nuns in Norwood, and the Talbot case in which a member of the family was alleged to have been imprisoned by the Franciscan nuns in Taunton. This case involved Ullathorne's friend and successor in the Western District (by now the Diocese of Clifton), Francis Hendren. It was taken up by *The Times* and by *Punch*, which lampooned

---

[23.] John Wolffe, *The Protestant Crusade in Great Britain 1829–60* (1991), p. 125.
[24.] Frances Knight, 'Male and Female he created them: men, women and the question of gender', in John Wolffe (ed.), *Religion in Victorian Britain vol 5 Culture and Empire* (Open University 1997), p. 27.
[25.] Ibid., p. 28.
[26.] Wolffe, *Protestant Crusade*, p. 269.

Hendren mercilessly.[27] Pierce Connolly, the estranged husband of Cornelia Connolly and a bitter enemy of Ullathorne, threw his lot in with a rabidly anti-Catholic lawyer, Henry Drummond, when he began legal proceedings to get his wife back, and in 1851, Drummond was the author of a proposed Parliamentary Bill aimed at government inspection and control of convents. The promoter of the Parliamentary Bill was Henry Charles Lacy, who urged the extension to convents of the legislation governing the inspection of lunatic asylums.[28] In the same year, to add fuel to the fire, Pierce Connolly published his account of the case between him and his wife.

Ullathorne responded to the Bill's publication by issuing a defence of convents against the proposed inspections, claiming a right to speak based on the fact that, at one time or another, he had been the ecclesiastical superior of at least half the convents in the country. In his *Plea for the Rights and Liberties of Religious Women*, Ullathorne cleverly took on the opposition on its own terms, and even in his title, used the language of those who styled themselves as defenders of English liberal traditions. His detailed knowledge of church law and established practice in relation to convents came into its own. He set out in detail the clear canonical regulation for the establishment of convents and for the admission of members to a community, but his killer blow was even more deft. Having set out the process of postulancy and noviciate, of the detailed and frequent questioning of the individual and consultation of family and friends and of the aspiring nun's community before vows were entered into, he posed the following question. Was this long process of testing and enquiry anything to compare with the 'lottery or the bondage which a lady subjects herself to in entering the married state?' Marriage had no such long period of probation and had 'infinitely smaller checks and reserves against the despotism of authority'. The bond between a sister and her community was lifelong as in marriage, and

---

[27.] Maurice Whitehead, 'Educational Turmoil and Ecclesiastical Strife: the Episcopal Career of Joseph William Hendren 1848–53' in *Recusant History* vol. 25 (2000), pp. 270–3.

[28.] Walter L. Arnstein, *Protestant versus Catholic in Mid-Victorian England: Mr Newdegate and the Nuns* (1982), pp. 62–3.

almost certainly, Ullathorne asserted, made with much greater care and consideration. If Parliament claimed the right to enter a convent and examine the sisters individually, then presumably it could also enter other dwellings and examine wives separately from their husbands. After all, as he commented mischievously, 'it only requires the extension of a principle to another class of cases'.[29] This, of course, destroyed the 'defence of the family' argument on the part of the Protestant agitators.

He further mocked the proposed legislation in the light of the perennial allegations of unsuitable levels of intimacy between clergy and religious women. This was strictly controlled by the rules of convent enclosure, which forbade any man, even the bishop, from entering the enclosure, 'without a weighty and absolute reason'. Yet the inspection legislation designed to 'protect' these women, 'actually proposed that these gentlemen shall have the power to search for and enter the most retired chambers of a lady's residence at any time from dawn till dusk'.[30] This hit right at the essence of what was known increasingly in Victorian Christian parlance as 'Christian manliness', which sought to act the noble and protective gentleman in the face of threats to feminine dignity and delicacy. Ullathorne's righteous anger shone through, even in the polite language of a public document, and he railed against the 'injustice' by which the 'pure fame, the unsullied honour and good repute of their countrywomen were assaulted' by speakers in the nation's Parliament. 'The age of chivalry is indeed gone'.[31] Such fierce public opposition was uncomfortable for the government, following close on the heels of the fiasco of the Ecclesiastical Titles Act, especially when they were trying to pacify Catholic Ireland. The Peelite group, led by former Home Secretary, Sir James Graham, forced Russell's government into killing the legislation. The stay was only temporary, though, and the convent question continued to twitch into life periodically for years.

On 10 May 1853 Thomas Chambers moved a resolution in

[29.] *A Plea for the Rights and Liberties of Religious Women* (1851), p. 10.
[30.] Ibid., p. 20.
[31.] Ibid., p. 23.

Parliament in another attempt to get legislative power for government inspection of convents, but the Parliamentary campaign was effectively shelved again by an unenthusiastic administration. An attempt in February 1854 to get a select committee on convent inspection was frustrated only by Catholic parliamentarians harnessing a measure of growing public repugnance towards the measure. Ullathorne again went into print, both in a public letter published as a pamphlet, *A letter addressed to Lord Edward Howard on the proposed committee of Enquiry into Religious Communities* (1854) in which he surveyed the development of convent life in England since the Revolution, mainly among the active orders, in order to refute the charge of increasing numbers of enclosed nuns. Lord Edward Howard was the only Catholic elected by a British (non-Irish) parliamentary constituency until 1865, and sat for the Norfolk family pocket borough of Arundel.[32]

Describing the current attack on religious communities, Ullathorne was vitriolic in his condemnation of their Evangelical opponents.

> Whatever is most Catholic, they hold in greatest fear, and whatever they fear, that they greatly hate; and their hatred they in vain strive to disguise ... putting on a mask of zeal for the good of the very communities, which they at every opportunity assail, have laid their cunning snares against them ... There is one unpardonable crime in England, and that is to hold the Catholic faith. And, above all, it is accounted criminal to bind yourself by vows to God, and to follow the evangelical counsels of Our Lord ... The communities are already placed under the suspicion of criminality. A large portion of the public are but too ready to join in the suspicion. No proof has been alleged. The public prejudice, stirred up and kept alive by men who deal in it for their daily bread, is assumed to be proof enough.[33]

[32.] J. A. Stack, 'Catholic Members of Parliament who represented British Constituencies, 1829–85: a prosopographical analysis' in *Recusant History* vol. 24 (1999), p. 350.

[33.] Pastoral Letter, 22 March 1854.

The issue was finally quietly dropped in Parliament, but not before the Catholic bishops had taken legal advice about the lines of evidence being pursued and, at Ullathorne's urging, had set up a committee of laymen to handle matters.[34] Ullathorne had begun preparing material for a public defence of convent life through this committee, but to his immense relief it proved unnecessary. What was at stake was the dignity and privacy of the nuns, and he, with his customary tact where the convents were concerned, returned the material submitted to him by Stanbrook unopened. 'I therefore return your documentation with thanks and unopened. For I only intended to open it in case I should need it.'[35] He was paternal, but never patronising, and always respectful where the religious orders of women were concerned.

However, the dignity of the nuns could always be assailed in the press, where they were regarded as fair game. Stories could always be concocted or elaborated to put the worst possible gloss on convent activities, and Ullathorne's name was dragged through the mud in a notorious case involving Colwich in 1856.[36] It was alleged that Catherine Selby, one of the community, had climbed a tree in order to escape, and the matter was subjected to enquiry by the Warwickshire MP Charles Newdegate and the Protestant Alliance, who would return to the convent question several times. Ullathorne's own letters in the Colwich archives reveal that she was emotionally unstable, making him uneasy about her insistent wish to enter a more rigorous convent. She had taken matters into her own hands in an extreme form, determined to 'escape' in order to present herself at a more ascetic religious house. Ullathorne's response was one of kindness and considerable common sense.

The Sisters of Mercy, founded in Dublin by Catherine McAuley in 1827, and devoted to a range of educational and charitable work, were the first to make a real impact on the English scene. Thomas McDonnell, the notorious missioner at St Peter's in Birmingham, had tried to steal a march on Wiseman in 1840 and attract the Sisters of Mercy to his mission

---

[34] BAA B3130, Ullathorne to unnamed bishops, 3 April 1854.
[35] Stanbrook 8, Ullathorne to Abbess Gregson, 29 April 1854.
[36] Arnstein, p. 65.

through his great friend Daniel O'Connell, who was also a close friend of Mother Catherine.[37] In the end his plan was thwarted and Wiseman established the convent under his own jurisdiction. As well as meeting Mary Aikenhead in Dublin in 1837, who responded readily to his request for sisters to return to Australia with him, Ullathorne also met Catherine McAuley. He was less impressed with her community, where he sensed 'something much too formal, a defect of freedom in their tone and bearing'.[38] However, by the time Ullathorne arrived in Birmingham, Catherine McAuley had died but her flourishing Order was already established in the city, and he had good reason to revise his youthful judgement on them.

In April 1840, a group of Birmingham women left home to join the Dublin noviciate of the Sisters of Mercy. These included Juliana, the daughter of John Hardman, Pugin's close collaborator in all his building and design projects and the leading member of the city's Catholic community. The Hardmans were a Lancashire Catholic family who moved to Birmingham in the late eighteenth century and became one of the first generation of wealthy Catholic industrialists in the city. John Hardman senior gave the land for the Handsworth Convent of Mercy and met most of the building and furnishing costs, totalling £5,335.[39] Wiseman took an active interest, and visited the novices in Dublin several times. He and Walsh were to go to Dublin to receive the vows of the new sisters, but were prevented by other business; it was agreed not to delay the profession, as it was feared that John Hardman was dying, and all were anxious that he should see his daughter back in Birmingham as a professed Sister of Mercy.

The Birmingham sisters returned in August 1841, led by their new superior, Mother Juliana Hardman, and accompanied by Catherine McAuley herself, now close to death. They moved into the Pugin designed convent opposite Hardman's own home. The entire house (built for twenty sisters) fulfilled Pugin's image of a medieval convent, to the extent that no cloth was used anywhere and he designed rush chairs and solid

---

[37.] Champ thesis, p. 202.
[38.] *Autobiography*, p. 161.
[39.] Brian Doolan, *The Pugins and the Hardmans* (2004), p. 19.

oak tables. Almost at once Birmingham began its own noviciate, one of the first entrants being Lucy Powell, daughter of
another influential local family linked by marriage and business connections to Pugin and Hardman. Before long, the
sisters were totally immersed in the development of Catholic
life in Birmingham. A House of Mercy for destitute girls was
opened in 1844 and a year later the sisters began a girls' school
attached to the cathedral mission, as well as instruction classes
for children and adults. Mrs Hardman moved the orphanage
she had founded to the House of Mercy (known locally as
'Hardman's Hospital') and in 1845, after her husband's death,
she moved into the convent until her own death in 1872.
Juliana's sister, Mary, also became a Sister of Mercy and for
some years ran the orphanage at Maryvale, also founded by
their father.[40]

Further Mercy convents were founded around the Midlands
from Birmingham, including Nottingham in 1844,
Leamington in 1847, Derby and Wolverhampton in 1849, and
the sisters were among the first to make use of government
grants to begin training Catholics for public examinations as
school teachers. The convents quickly became crucial instruments of charity and education within the Catholic community
and further afield. When Mother Juliana Hardman appealed
for the building of a separate church alongside the convent
because their chapel was overflowing at Mass times, it was clear
that the sisters were the only link with the Church for many of
the poor of inner city Birmingham who, 'if they are neglected
much longer will entirely fall away from the practice of their
religion'.[41]

Finance of missions, support of convents and maintenance of
buildings and personnel was a major source of anxiety and the
death of John Talbot, 16th Earl of Shrewsbury, in 1852
provoked a long running and major crisis. In the midst of it,
another (unrelated) financial problem which Ullathorne faced
came to a very public head in 1853, when he and Dr John
Moore, the President of Oscott, found themselves incarcerated
in Warwick Gaol for debt. The situation was brought about by

[40.] Ibid.
[41.] Champ thesis, p. 205, n. 238.

a mishap based on an earlier legacy, but it was a vivid illustration of the difficulties ensuing from haphazard management. Under Ullathorne's predecessor, an Oxfordshire benefactor of the Catholic mission, Charles Mostyn, had left some shares jointly to the bishop and president of Oscott for the benefit of the mission of Radford. Years later, the Monmouthshire and Glamorganshire Banking company (in which the shares were held) went bankrupt. As shareholders, the bishop and president (in the years before limited liability) were called upon to meet their liability, amounting to £4,800. The Bishop's solicitors insisted to the bank that neither Ullathorne nor Moore had any private property on which to draw, and were dependent on 'the trifling incomes of which they are in receipt [which] depend altogether upon their continuance in those offices in virtue of which alone the shares were transferred into their names as trustees for a public charity'.[42] Ullathorne's income amounted to £196. 10s. 00d a year and he was already paying interest on a £1,000 loan taken out to meet the bank's demands. A formal request to the bankers' solicitors to use their personal discretion and cease proceedings, given the circumstances, was met with an officious and offensive reply, asserting that the two churchmen should not have become shareholders if they could not meet their obligations.[43] There is more than a whiff of anti-Catholic sentiment about the whole affair, and a certain relish in dragging a Catholic bishop's name through the debtors' court.

They had no means of raising the amount themselves, and refused to ask the hard-pressed Catholic community to pay their debt. Ullathorne insisted that Estcourt, as diocesan chancellor, make it clear that, 'he has no other resources, is not a householder and has no means or intention of raising any more money'. He was ready to take the consequences and not bothered about any effect on public opinion, 'for that my character and the explanation I can give will carry me through all'.[44] A final warning came from the bank in autumn 1852,[45]

[42] BAA B2473, Harting Bros to Bank, 19 May 1852.
[43] BAA B2474,Thomas Nicholson on behalf of Bank to Ullathorne and Moore, 21 May 1852.
[44] BAA B2485, Ullathorne to Estcourt, 4 June 1852.
[45] BAA B2588, Harting and Co to Ullathorne, 23 October 1852.

which was studiously ignored, and so Ullathorne and Moore found themselves imprisoned. Ullathorne treated the whole thing as a bit of a joke, assuring George Talbot, the English agent in Rome that 'this is no great affair', and that, rather than fuelling anti-Catholic sentiment, it had elicited much sympathy for their plight from Protestants as well as Catholics. All were agreed that 'no disgrace will attach'.[46]

He took huge delight in telling his friends that

> we are not worse accommodated than a Carthusian monk, our cells are quite as good as those of a convent and we said Mass in one of them this morning. We have a ward to ourselves, and all the attention and civilities that our position admits of. We are quite happy and rather enjoy our quiet, except that it is interrupted by the visits of our friends from Leamington Spa. When I said we were not worse than Carthusians, I ought to have added that they don't have their diets from a hotel.[47]

He reminded another of his friends how he had 'long been in the habit of saying I should like a few months in gaol, but then I hoped for solitude and silence'. His brief experience of Warwick Gaol seems to have been more a time of sociability and, as he acknowledged himself, very little in the way of suffering.[48]

Joking apart, Ullathorne sent a copy of his public letter issued to the diocese to explain the situation to Rome and offered the Pope his resignation: this public embarrassment gave Ullathorne just the lever he needed to try and persuade the Holy See to let him relinquish his charge. The disinclination Ullathorne had shown to take on the role of bishop in 1846 had not diminished with the years of experience and growing stature and public respect. Thoughts of retirement were never far away from his mind, but were usually disregarded by others. The letter from prison was met with a papal

---

46. VEC Talbot Papers, Ullathorne to Talbot, 29 April 1853.
47. Stanbrook VI, Ullathorne to Abbess Gregson from Warwick Gaol, 24 April 1853.
48. Selly Park, Ullathorne to Genevieve Dupuis, 27 April 1853.

blessing by return of post, and in December of the same year Wiseman, in Rome on business, studiously ignored Ullathorne's heartfelt plea.

> I wish with all my heart you could get them at Rome to let me retire from office. I sometimes think that, like some of the old men, I shall bolt clean away. Your Eminence may be assured that you shall have my prayers to the end of my life, if you can do anything for me in that way.[49]

The distaste which Ullathorne had for the life of a bishop stands in marked contrast to his reputation at the time as someone who rather relished the status and exercise of power and who had rather a high opinion of himself, which has passed into the common currency of Catholic historiography.

Relaxation did not come easily to Ullathorne and his main escape route was often to spend a few days at one of the convents. Even that had complications which gave him anxiety: 'I do not see why I should not recreate a little now and then in a quiet conventual way, though the world is out of joint. The only question is whether a bishop really can recreate in his own diocese'.[50] Writing from his prison cell, rather than a monastic cell, which unexpectedly provided him with the space for a brief retreat, he mused,

> I find that in a gaol, like a convent, everything helps recollection. Indeed it is the world without that takes us from attention to God within. If we will only look away from our own subjective existence, and look straight towards our Lord, who is always with us, even when we are not with him, we shall find all places alike, for God is our true place. The real bane of our life is that love, the inward living on our own personal feelings, always and at all times searching the agreeable and shunning the disagreeable ones, sifting them in the service of self-love, coiling ourselves up in our cherished sentiments and sensations, as the snail coils up his poor viscera within his shell, never fairly

49. AAW 130/1, Ullathorne to Wiseman in Rome, 20 December 1853.
50. Stanbrook 6, Ullathorne to Abbess Gregson, 17 December 1853.

throwing ourselves out openly and faithfully to our Lord. How can He operate on such material kept closed within the sensitive coil of nature by such a will?[51]

Within a matter of days a public letter announced their release from prison and the end of Ullathorne's enforced retreat, after the Court of Rolls had thrown the case out completely. A party of friends conducted Ullathorne and Moore back to Birmingham, where a *Te Deum* was sung in thanksgiving in St Chad's. Ullathorne's relief was enormous, as the threat from the bank had been hanging over his head for two years, so that he was now able to 'breathe anew'.[52] However, the financial pressures were not so easily removed, and writing to his friend Brown in 1856 he talked of the parlous financial state of the diocese and again mentioned his temptation to run away.[53] The problems of the diocese, more in the temporal than the spiritual sphere, were made more difficult by the loss of the 16th Earl of Shrewsbury, the greatest benefactor of the Church in the Midlands, who had died in 1852.

The Shrewsbury will case, one of 'extraordinary complexity'[54] rumbled on for some years and prevented much needed financial stability from being established quickly. There was evident confusion in November 1852 when 'the good earl' died, leaving his financial affairs in a state of disarray. Ullathorne expected a legacy to the diocese of £25,000 which had been mentioned in letters, but was apparently not set down in the will.[55] Family complications added to the confusion, with Shrewsbury's heir, Earl Bertram, going to court to get an additional executor appointed alongside his mother.

---

[51]. Stanbrook VI, Ullathorne to Abbess Gregson Warwick Gaol, 3 May 1853. A note attached to this letter by Cuthbert Hedley OSB, Bishop of Newport and Menevia , dated 1889, the year in which he preached at Ullathorne's funeral and quoted the letter, described it as, 'a very early exposition of his interior life expressed in his peculiar language'.

[52]. VEC Talbot Papers, Ullathorne to Talbot, 7 May 1853.

[53]. Cardiff, Ullathorne to Brown, 15 September 1856.

[54]. Margaret Pawley, *Faith and Family: the Life and Circle of Ambrose Phillips de Lisle* (1993), p. 271.

[55]. BAA B2629, Estcourt to Ullathorne, 27 November 1852.

Ambrose Phillips de Lisle, who became an executor, thought that there had been a falling out between Ullathorne and the late earl over one of the bishop's letters to the press about the hierarchy. They had disagreed to some extent, but that would scarcely have been cause to provoke the earl to change his will.[56] There was talk of a 'secret paper' attached to the will, which never came to light, but as executor, Ambrose Phillips de Lisle insisted that he could only act on the legally attested will. The problem seems to have centred on a moral rather than legal responsibility, and it caused something of a rift between Ullathorne and his old friend de Lisle, whose conscience, he felt was, 'wrongly instructed'.[57]

By 1854 the matter was still not concluded, and Ullathorne's consequent financial anxieties remained extreme. It is not surprising that he continued to blame Walsh and Wiseman for the chaos inherited, and to plead with the young earl to honour his late uncle's commitments.

> Of course I do not defend the circumstances which led to the crisis described above. Of course Dr Walsh had fallen into a course of proceeding contrary to the canons of the Church. But those at present charged with the administration of these dioceses are not responsible for those acts, and he who is responsible has gone to his account, and deeply as the thought of these things weighed upon his mind in his last days, yet when he died, he supposed that for the heaviest part of them he had made restitution ... We are about to make an application to the executors to make up to us for not having possession of the properties assured to us. Our hopes of being saved from the ruin described, depend then on your Lordship ... It is not an increase in our funds or the undertaking of new works for which we are looking, but the maintenance of our present position, the standing or falling of many old established missions, and the hope of averting a grievous scandal.[58]

[56.] BAA B2633, Estcourt to Ullathorne, 29 November 1852.
[57.] Pawley, p. 273.
[58.] BAA B3254, Copy in Estcourt's hand of letter from Ullathorne to Earl Bertram, (nd 1854?).

His hopes of 'being saved from the ruin described' were dashed, when Earl Bertram followed his uncle to the grave within two years. The impact on the diocese was disastrous.

Earl John paid £1,000 a year during his life and promised to leave a capital equal to that sum at his death. This was intended to cover alienations of missionary property made in the time of my predecessor, which were owing throughout the extent of the old Midland District. He first left me £50,000, then altered it to £25,000, and finally changed this arrangement and left me £20,000 in railway debentures. But these it had been more than once decided in law belonged to the estate, so I got nothing. He left me some leases in lieu of which Earl Bertram gave £500 a year, which I divided with the three other bishops,[59] to pay the interest on alienated property. The other bishops and I met to arrange the division of the fund, and we found that nothing remained but this £500 from Earl Bertram, and as we had just heard of his death, even this was gone. He has left me £10,000, if I can get it, in part from his personalia, but no estate; and in addition to other difficulties all the Shrewsbury missions are now thrown on my hands without one penny of endowment.[60]

In the end, as Ullathorne acknowledged, the liabilities on the Shrewsbury estate outweighed the legacies in any case, but the effect on Ullathorne and the diocese was the same – the Shrewsbury tap had been turned off. The title passed out of Catholic hands and lengthy dynastic and financial battles were fought out between rival claimants to titles, property and even the furnishings of Alton Towers.[61] He clearly found these financial strains depressing, reflecting at this time that, 'one floor has broken away from under the feet after another, ever since I came to this indebted and involved diocese'. Yet in the same letter, he acknowledged that his personality was such that the worse things

---

59. Nottingham, Shrewsbury and Northampton dioceses also had claims.
60. *Letters*, pp. 79–80 [15 September 1856].
61. Pawley, pp. 274–6.

got, the more it galvanised his energies.[62] Financial pressures convinced him to raise again the unsettled issues between Wiseman and the Diocese of Birmingham. 'I refer of course to the sums of money placed in Your Eminence's hands by the Rev Dr Haigh[63] for the use and benefits of this diocese, and to the surplus due to the common fund'. Tact and delicacy, he says, have prevented him from raising it before, hoping that Wiseman himself would be forthcoming, but circumstances forced him into action. It was also for him an impulse driven by duty and conscience to settle the affairs of the diocese, as a matter of justice as well as urgency. He asked Wiseman for his suggestions, with the somewhat menacing hint that, 'the expression of my desire [is] that this question may be settled without any reference being made to the Sovereign Pontiff'.[64] This veiled threat did not go down well with Wiseman.

The loss of contact with Downside and monastic life, which Ullathorne regretted, was somewhat alleviated by the presence of the Benedictine Priory of Colwich, a few miles from Mother Margaret's convent at Stone, which would be one of Ullathorne's favourite spots, where, as well as giving retreats and visitations, he often made his own retreat. It was one of four houses of enclosed Benedictine nuns in the Diocese of Birmingham all being reincarnations of houses which had survived abroad during the times of Catholic persecution in England, and been forced to flee at the time of the French Revolution. The arrival of the Colwich community in the Midlands was the result of another conflict with an unsympathetic bishop, which reinforced Ullathorne's determination to do things properly.

The Benedictine nuns in Paris, founded in 1651 as an offshoot of the house in Cambrai, survived for a century and a half in peace, but the nuns found themselves at the eye of the French Revolutionary storm in the early 1790s. The monastic house was regularly searched, the nuns terrorised and finally imprisoned in terrible conditions. In 1795 they were released

---

[62.] Handsworth, 21 August 1856.

[63.] An Oxford convert, who when ordained, built a new church at Erdington. See Chapter 9.

[64.] AAW Molloy Collection, Ullathorne to Wiseman (copy), 18 May 1853.

and able to flee to England where they found friends among the English Catholic community. The nuns settled first in Marnhull in Dorset, where they remained for twelve years before moving to Cannington in Somerset, under the patronage of Lord Clifford of Chudleigh. Lord Clifford's agent was a member of the Knight family who helped them settle at Cannington, and one of whom entered the convent and became its superior in due course.

Mary Clare Knight, as superior of Cannington, fell foul of Bishop Baines at the same time as the row with Downside at which Ullathorne had been an onlooker during his noviciate. The Bishop of Paris, Cardinal de Retz, had insisted that the English convent was placed under direct episcopal jurisdiction, and so it remained, outside the English Benedictine Congregation. The problems began in 1830, when Baines appointed Thomas Burgess to the mission at Cannington, and complaints about the running of the convent began to flow from Burgess to the bishop. In particular, he resented Mother Mary Clare's insistence on her control over visits by him to individual nuns, and he removed the nuns' trusted confessor, a French secular priest. Irritation continued to develop when she refused to invest the convent capital in mortgages on property owned by the bishop; Baines was furious and responded in a highhanded tone: 'henceforth you will not be troubled with much advice from me. You will therefore be pleased to consider the following regulations as coming not from a counsellor who throws away his advice, but from a superior who expects to be obeyed'.[65] Relations continued to deteriorate, despite Mary Clare Knight's efforts, and Baines and Burgess became convinced that she had far too much independence and authority within the convent, and that the constitutions gave too little power to the bishop.

The climax was a public humiliation by Baines of the Superior in front of the whole community. In despair, she wrote to Cardinal Thomas Weld, an old friend and benefactor whose family were the main Catholic landowners in Dorset. He took soundings in Rome, including from Cardinal Odescalchi (a

[65.] Robert Eaton, *The Benedictines of Colwich 1829–1929* (1929), qu. p. 144.

personal friend of many of the English Catholics including Weld, Wiseman and Baines himself), and the opinion received was that the bishop was in the wrong as far as authority over the convent was concerned. Both Baines and Burgess were furious at her for bypassing them and taking the problem to Rome. A bitter stalemate continued; Burgess was removed but an even more hostile chaplain put in his place, and Mary Clare Knight was driven to seek help from Fr W. H. Coombs, confessor to the Visitation nuns at Shepton Mallet, who told Baines in no uncertain terms: 'I deem the grounds on which you stand to be untenable', and pleaded with him to put things right.[66] The only effect of the letter was to place Coombs in what Baines regarded as the enemy camp. Mary Clare Knight was driven again to seek the help of Cardinal Weld and in July 1833 the convent was taken under papal protection with Weld appointed as protector and the old chaplain reinstated. The only permanent solution was to move out of the Western District, and the community and its supporters began to search for a property, casting eyes in the direction of the Midland District under Bishop Walsh, who had a certain sympathy with their difficulties with Baines. Walsh recommended them to the property at Colwich, which had been on the market for ten years and was therefore going cheaply. Mary Clare Knight visited the site and met Bishop Walsh there and all were delighted at the prospect; they took possession on St Benedict's day, 21 March 1835, and moved in during the summer of 1836.

Ullathorne was already disposed to be sympathetic to Colwich before he arrived in the Midlands, knowing something of the qualities and difficulties of convents in the Western District.[67] One of the first letters he wrote on his arrival in Birmingham was a tender greeting to Mary Clare Knight and her community.

> I will frankly tell you that no sooner had the voice of God, through his vicar on earth, fixed on my feeble person to bear the great office in the Central District, which St

[66.] Eaton, qu. p. 175.
[67.] The difficulties of Colwich are succinctly told by Sr Benedict Rowell OSB in *Absent Brethren: The Monastery of Our Lady of Good Hope and the EBC* (EBC History Symposium 2000).

Denys says, is that of perfecting souls, than I felt I already had a resting place for my weary feet at St Benedict's Priory. A spot where I could imbibe peace when I wanted it, where I could find repose when I needed it, where I could draw strength when most pressed with the burdens of church government, and where I could obtain the prayers I needed in those difficulties with which the providence of God besets the path of a bishop for his protection.[68]

Ullathorne spent many happy hours at Colwich. He was a frequent guide and advisor to all in the community, and Mary Clare Knight was Mother Margaret Hallahan's closest friend beyond her own community. She often spent a few days at Colwich to restore her strength and spirits, and with the bishop's permission was able to enter the monastic enclosure. A second house of perpetual adoration was set up at Atherstone in a house previously occupied by Dominicans.

It took Ullathorne until the end of 1853 and his first diocesan synod to get the mechanics of the diocese in place, which was a source of immense relief to him.

You will be delighted to know that I have appointed the administration of temporalities. The vicar general is getting into his proper work and I am doing all I can to disentangle myself from daily details, so as finally to set myself free for missionary and spiritual work. By the time the synod is over I shall be quite free, and more in the position of one of the old bishops, with a regular administration of affairs conducted more under me than through me. For this I have been working ever since I had the sacred mitre on my head, but it has cost all these years to bring it round.[69]

Significantly his vision of restored episcopate was that of a pre-Reformation model, rather that a nineteenth-century Ultramontane one. Indeed he was determined opponent of

[68]. Colwich, Ullathorne to Prioress, 20 August 1848.
[69]. *Letters*, p. 44.

fashion in all things, but especially in matters of church government. 'A bishop ought to see through our Lord's eyes, and should be free from the spirit of the age in which he lives, which is but the passing fashion of the passing world.'[70]

His pastoral letter for Lent 1853 returned to an already familiar theme, and was typical of his passionate and forthright appeals for money:

> Are you in real earnest in your love? You hope so. But if you would be sure, you must ask yourself what you do for the Church of God and for souls. What sacrifices do you make for her great cause? Is your heart silent? Is it souls then, or money? Is it the Church or yourself that you love? Give, and have faith in God. The world, if you trust it, will not carry you to God. But if you trust in God, He will carry you through the world.[71]

Only two years later he was furious that the Church Education Fund collection had dropped from a little over £369 in 1853 to only £277 in 1855. 'It is a plain proof, dearly beloved, that indifference has taken the place of zeal in a number of persons, who have ceased to take an interest in supporting the education of the clergy.' He castigated the people fiercely for letting it slip, so that he could not meet more than a third of the needs; he could only afford to maintain thirty church students in school and college where there should be a hundred, and he was only ordaining two a year instead of the five or six needed. If it came to a choice, the Church Education Fund must take priority. 'The question we all have to decide is, whether the Catholic Faith is to be continued and to thrive in this part of England, or whether it is slowly to perish through a dearth of priests.' He even went so far as to repeat the words from his April 1850 pastoral letter setting up the fund, and commended the action of one priest who had increased his collections by having this printed in large type above the collection box.

---

70. *Letters*, p. 46.
71. Pastoral Letter, 28 February 1853.

IT MUST EVER BE BORNE IN MIND THAT OF ALL
GENERAL COLLECTIONS, THAT FOR CHURCH
EDUCATION STANDS FIRST IN THE ORDER OF
CHARITY AND NECESSITY. WHERE PERSONS,
THEREFORE, CANNOT GIVE TO ALL, THEY
SHOULD GIVE TO THIS. FOR ALL THE WORKS OF
MERCY AND CHARITY, CORPORAL AND SPIRI-
TUAL, ARE SHUT UP IN THIS WORK, AS THE
FUTURE PLANT IS CONTAINED IN THE SEED.[72]

One thing which remained to be tackled afresh, now that
Ullathorne found himself somewhat freer of day-to-day administration, was the conduct and leadership of Oscott. He told
John Moore, the president, that, while he appreciated what he
had done, 'to put Oscott on a sound footing', he now was even
more convinced that what Oscott needed was the return of its
founder Henry Weedall,

> in order to bring back the full affection of the clergy to it,
> and to secure the obtaining of those means which have
> now become essential for its security. It is generally justly
> felt, and I am sure you are one of those who feel this, that
> Dr Weedall holds peculiar influences arising out of his
> particular merits, and that through those influences he
> could bring back both the heart of the clergy and such
> temporal aids as present emergencies may require, and
> that the more effective men of the diocese might devote
> themselves to Oscott under his leading in a way that they
> would not necessarily do under any other, however meri-
> torious, they being of his own forming.

He had spoken to Weedall and could see that, 'with such co-
operation as he could command, he might do something to
right the finances and to re-establish the confidence of the
clergy'.[73] Though in poor health and with failing eyesight,
Weedall was persuaded to return to his beloved college and
oversee its restoration. Ullathorne described him publicly as

[72.] Pastoral Letter, 10 March 1855.
[73.] BAA B2886, Ullathorne to Moore, 28 September 1853.

'the father of the college', and even as the father of the clergy and the bishops, who was both loved and venerated by all.[74] He continued his long service of Oscott which extended for a full fifty-five years, until his death in 1859, taking on the role of an *eminence grise* in his later years.

The question of dividing funds between the new dioceses remained ticklish and Ullathorne attempted to reach a fair agreement with the Bishops of Shrewsbury, Nottingham and Northampton over the common fund for the training of students at Oscott. The interested bishops met in 1853 and reached an agreement similar to that in operation at Ushaw, based on the relative interest of each bishop in the college. Shrewsbury was all but excluded, since geographically only a small portion of the old Midland District was now in that diocese, and the bishop had vested interests in both Ushaw and Prior Park.[75] Ullathorne was determined to reach an amicable agreement and wrote to Bishop Brown of Shrewsbury in that spirit, that he wanted to continue in 'friendship and brotherhood'. 'You shall not quarrel with me if I can help it, and I will not write a word in retaliation.'[76] He also told Brown that the issue was 'not about the appropriation of funds but about making Oscott the regularly constituted seminary of the three dioceses'.[77] In other words, he wanted to get the structure right for the future, rather than worry too much about money claimed from the past.

Ullathorne was asked by the other two bishops to draw up a discussion document of the general principles and issues based on the practical arrangements which were to apply at Oscott, Ushaw and Old Hall Green. Brown of Shrewsbury was bitter at being excluded, but Ullathorne insisted that, 'though you have a certain interest in Oscott on account of the claims of Shropshire, yet owing to the position of the diocese, Oscott cannot be your diocesan seminary'.[78] This agreement eventually formed the basis of the synod decrees of 1859,[79] but Brown

---

[74.] Address to Dr Weedall, 11 June 1854, published in *The Oscotian*, Ullathorne Number (1886), p. 73.

[75.] D. Milburn, *A History of Ushaw College* (1964), pp. 206–7.

[76.] BAA B2995, Ullathorne to Brown of Shrewsbury, 3 October 1853.

[77.] Ibid.

[78.] Ibid.

[79.] BAA B3915, Notes by Ullathorne at Wiseman's request, nd., 1859.

continued to nag away at the issue, not satisfied with Ullathorne's attitude or the decrees of the later synod.

The second provincial synod of 1855 paid as little attention to the college question as the first had done, despite a directive from *Propaganda Fide* to Wiseman that the synod should legislate on the issue. Perhaps it was hoped to reach amicable arrangements between the bishops concerned without formal decrees, but in any case, Cardinal Fransoni's letter arrived too late to incorporate a debate in the synod schedule. So many disputes were flaring up that it might also have been deemed unwise to air them in formal session. The only relevant decree from the 1855 synod was one which established that all religious buildings were to be considered as belonging to the place where they were located, unless it had been made clear that they belonged to a particular religious order. While this related particularly to mission property, it clearly had implications for the college dispute.[80] Under the terms of the synod decree, Oscott belonged to Birmingham, and Shrewsbury, Nottingham and Northampton could not lodge any further claims.

However, following the 1855 synod, a committee was set up under the chairmanship of Bishop Grant of Southwark, which forced the issue into the open, and at least produced a clear statement of the conflicting views. The bishops had two models before them, that of the Council of Trent which demanded, where possible, individual diocesan seminaries under the sole control of the local bishop, and that of the English colleges abroad, over which no English bishop had sole jurisdiction, but to which all contributed support. All these colleges, and those on native soil, including Oscott, had an *ad hoc* history of jurisdiction and finance. The theoretical question was whether or not they could properly be regarded as Tridentine seminaries, especially as Oscott, Ushaw and Old Hall Green combined seminary training and lay education. If so, they ought to be the sole responsibility of the bishop in whose diocese each of them lay. In practice, a number of bishops sent students to each of the colleges and thereby helped to maintain them. It was widely believed among clergy and laity that it was unrealistic for each new English diocese to support a seminary, and some

---

[80.] Schiefen, p. 242.

tried and failed. Like so many other internecine disputes among the bishops, it ended by going to Rome.

Ullathorne was in danger, in the early 1850s, of becoming completely overwhelmed with financial and administrative problems. His sense of the weighty burden of office often depressed him, and his health was rarely strong. This gave him good enough reason to take a real break in 1854, and he took the opportunity to visit the shrine of La Salette in the French Alps, where, in 1846, a reported apparition of the Virgin Mary had taken place. The story of La Salette told how two young cowherds claimed that on 19 September 1846, they had seen a very tall woman sitting on a rock and weeping profusely. She was crowned with white, red and blue roses and a diadem of stars and under a golden apron shone a starry gown studded with pearls and her whole figure was covered in coloured roses out of which shone a sort of flame that burned like incense and mixed with radiant light surrounding her. There was a long tradition of apparitions in the area, and this one, bearing a message about the social and religious ills of the time, soon took hold of the popular imagination. Up to sixty thousand pilgrims a day began to gather on the site, and Louis Veuillot, a leading Ultramontane journalist, cautiously promoted it in *L'Univers*. There was little support from the French clergy, but in May 1848 the Bishop of Grenoble allowed the establishment of an Archconfraternity of prayer dedicated to Notre Dame de La Salette. Signs of Roman support followed and the foundation stone of a basilica was laid and a new congregation of Missionaries of Our Lady of La Salette was established in 1851.[81] Ullathorne took himself there in 1854, visiting the great Carthusian monastery of La Grand Chartreuse and the home of John Vianney, the famous Curé of Ars, en route.

His description of the journey to the remote Alpine shrine is another reminder of Ullathorne's powers of observation and recall, his love of nature and his capacity to appreciate the glory of God's creation.

[81.] Nicholas Perry and Loreto Echeverria, *Under the Heel of Mary* (1988), pp. 102–6.

At St Laurent du Pont mules are in requisition and at a
mile beyond, the huge mountains begin to close upon the
stream of the Guiers Mort, and the ascent begins in
earnest. We reach the point of the old timber-built iron
forge, well known to artists, the single-span bridge and
the aged gateway. The steep and whitened precipices go
up into the clouds, whilst their bases and ravines are full
of the most diversified foliage. The winding torrent, by
which we ascend, rushes down its rocky bed, broken still
more by great boulders agitated and covered with foam.
The silver pines rise like dark giants, and go feathering
up in places to the very summits ... The mountains at
length receded on both sides, though reaching up to still
greater altitudes, whilst our way lay through dense forest
of pines and beeches, mingling together the lightest with
the darkest green, until at length, in the midst of an
island of bright green meadow, the vast monastery of the
Grand Chartreuse appeared.[82]

There was no official seal of approval from the Holy See, but
Ullathorne was confident that 'the number and extent of spiritual favours which the Sovereign Pontiff has accorded to the
sanctuary of La Salette' were sufficient in themselves to inspire
confidence.[83] Ullathorne wrote an approving account of the
visions and the detailed investigations himself. 'And who that
studies God's ways sees not how, as error thickens, and the
devil gains power, his adversary, THE WOMAN, extends her
power more and more within the Church'.[84] He also took
himself to the tiny village of Ars, about eighteen miles from
Lyons, to meet the humble, uneducated parish priest, already
regarded by many who met him as a living saint. This
encounter made a striking impression. John Vianney lived a
life of extreme asceticism and constant dedication to the people
of his parish and to the thousands of pilgrims who flocked to
hear his words and to visit this remarkable confessor.
Ullathorne was mesmerised.

82. *The Holy Mountain of La Salette*, pp 8–9.
83. Ibid., p. 125.
84. Ibid., p. 89.

He spoke of God, so good, so amiable, so loving, and his hands, his shoulders, his very person, seemed to gather on his heart. It was impossible not to feel that God alone was there, and was drawing the whole man to that seat of His repose. Then there was a word about being in the heart of Jesus, and in that word one felt that he was *there*.[85]

He received the bishop with 'the disengaged self-abandonment and simple politeness of a saint',[86] and the record of his dealings with the visionaries of La Salette was proof enough for Ullathorne. He remained a solid advocate of La Salette as a place of genuine apparition, and believed that his own involvement in the controversy surrounding it would eventually 'rebound to the honour of Our Lady and the Apparition and will tend to steady the Catholics of this country'.[87]

However the vision of La Salette remained controversial and he was driven to defend it in the pages of *The Edinburgh Review* and *The Rambler*, and to publish the letters as a pamphlet four years later.[88] Large numbers of English pilgrims followed in Ullathorne's footsteps, including at least one of his own priests, Francis Amherst (later Bishop of Northampton) in 1856, who described it as a, 'happy place, where primitive Christianity seems to have taken up its abode'.[89] His friend and colleague as president of Oscott, James Spencer Northcote, devoted a large section of his study of the Marian shrines of Europe to La Salette, and while acknowledging that controversy surrounded it, defended it staunchly, insisting that Ullathorne's 'valuable work' had solidly refuted the doubts expressed.[90] However, by the 1860s it was already being overshadowed by Lourdes, where the Marian apparitions took place in 1858 and which became the most popular Catholic pilgrim destination in

---

85. Ibid., p. 130.
86. Ibid., pp. 131–2.
87. Selly Park, Ullathorne to Genevieve Dupuis, 31 October 1857.
88. *Letters on La Salette in reply to articles in the Edinburgh Review and Rambler* (1858).
89. Mary Francis Roskell, *Memoirs of Francis Kerrill Amherst* (nd.), p. 200.
90. J. S. Northcote, *Celebrated Sanctuaries of the Madonna* (1868), p. 222.

Europe within a generation.[91] La Salette waned in popularity, and has been written off sceptically by some twentieth-century writers.[92] Nevertheless, it still remains a popular place of pilgrimage in modern times.

Ullathorne's interest in Marian devotion went further than La Salette, and when the Immaculate Conception of the Blessed Virgin Mary was finally defined as an article of faith in 1854, Ullathorne embarked on his first extended piece of writing. He had, of course, pressed Rome in 1848 for the Central District to be placed under the patronage of the Immaculate Conception of Mary, so this was not a new-found devotion for him. His exposition of the doctrine was his first attempt to deepen the faith of the laity and awaken them to the richness of Catholic tradition which he had absorbed by long periods of private study.[93] It set him on a course of pastoral writing which lasted until the very end of his days – some of it with more success than others. *The Immaculate Conception* was a model of its kind.

The pastoral value of Ullathorne's writing was emphasised by Newman:

> I am rejoiced to find that you contemplate a work on the Immaculate Conception – it will, I am sure, do extensive good. Not only Catholics but a number of enquiring Protestants need and ask information about the subject – and any thing which came from your Lordship would be received with great respect and read with interest. I hope you will write it so far popularly that all classes may read it. Your sketch of chapters seems exceedingly good.[94]

[91.] See Ruth Harris, *Lourdes: Body and Spirit in the Secular Age* (1999) passim.

[92.] Donald Flanagan dismissed it as a place of 'turbid uncertainty' in Alberic Stacpoole (ed.), *Mary's Place in Christian Dialogue* (1982), p. 7.

[93.] Some of the material in this section was originally published in an article by the author 'Dogma as Pastoral Necessity: Archbishop Ullathorne and the Definition of the Immaculate Conception of Mary' in *The Month*, August/September 1987.

[94.] L&D XVI, pp. 280–1, 19 October 1854.

Ullathorne's book, published in January 1855, only a month after the promulgation of the definition by Pius IX, had obvious pastoral roots and sprang from his own experience. 'I never preach on that subject without seeing how much it [his book] is wanted, from the remarks that are made. It will not be an original but a popular book.'[95] It was urgent enough in his mind to be compiled in the midst of his first diocesan visitation, and he even declined to go to Rome for the celebrations to mark the definition itself in order to work on the book.

Ullathorne's treatment of the subject reflected his own personal priorities, as he described the definition of the dogma by Pius IX as a triumph for episcopal authority and popular devotion over the mental gymnastics of theologians. Still delighting in the renewed position of the bishops in England and Wales and wanting his audience to remember this, he relished the process leading to the definition which saw 'bishops capsizing the theologians. The bishops are all authority and the theologians are all reason'.[96] He placed great emphasis on the significance of the popular devotion surrounding the Immaculate Conception over many centuries. Ullathorne's own theological reading and reflection never strayed into the speculative, and he had little patience for it.

> It is curious that so long as the Immaculate Conception was believed, received and preached with a simple unreasoning faith, as it always was in the east, there was no difficulty about it. The moment reason touched it, it became obscured and darkened and the language of divines got perplexed. And it has taken six centuries to get back from reasoning to faith, and for the wisdom of man to get back to the foolishness of faith.[97]

In other words – once the theologians got their hands on it, things began to go wrong! It is not surprising that he found Newman difficult to fathom at times.

The strength of popular devotion to the Immaculate

95. *Letters*, p. 58, 22 September 1854.
96. *Letters*, p. 59, 6 November 1854.
97. *Letters*, p. 60, Christmas Eve 1854.

Conception was, for Ullathorne, almost the overriding authority in favour of the definition, and he was at pains to restore
that devotion in his own time. His praise of the 'universal
conviction of pious Catholics' reflected his own instinctive faith
and his well-tuned pastoral awareness. Although Newman was
the one who would write famously and influentially about the
religious sense of the laity, Ullathorne knew it in his bones and
valued it as the touchstone of faith. 'It is the devout who have
the surest instinct in discerning the mysteries of which the
Holy Spirit breathes the grace through the Church, and who
with as sure a tact reject what is alien from her teaching.'[98]
Ullathorne preferred to trust the instinct of the devout faithful
formed by sound pastoral leadership than the speculation of
theologians, and his role in trying to recreate this in his own
time has scarcely been noticed.

The particular context of England in the first years of its
restored hierarchy was clearly significant for Ullathorne, and
his emphasis on the importance of the devotion to the
Immaculate Conception in medieval England was another
symbol of hidden continuity. He made the point strongly that
'it was from England that this festival took its most remarkable
rise and diffusion in the western Church'.[99] He recounted the
story of the vision of Abbot Helsinus of Ramsey, an envoy of
William the Conqueror caught in a storm at sea in 1070. An
angel gave him safe passage in return for a promise to celebrate the feast of the Immaculate Conception. The image of a
seafaring monk clearly had a certain personal appeal for
Ullathorne. The feast was established by Anselm in the
Province of Canterbury and the English Benedictines and
Franciscans played a major part in promoting it.[100]
Controversy raged between the Franciscans and Dominicans
over whether (in Thomas Aquinas' view) the Immaculate
Conception was incompatible with universal redemption for all
humanity, or (in Duns Scotus' view) it was the supreme act of
Christ's redemption, the most perfect act of mediation.

98. *The Immaculate Conception* (1855), pp. 166–7.
99. Ibid., p. 161.
100. H. F. Davis, 'The Defence of the Immaculate Conception: a
national heritage', *Clergy Review*, vol. 21 (1941), pp. 213–20.

Eventually Duns Scotus' interpretation prevailed, that redemption by exemption in the unique case of Mary revealed Christ's redeeming power in full.

By Ullathorne's time, a revival of the traditional devotional practices and prayers associated with the Immaculate Conception was well under way and had provoked renewed interest in defining it as an article of faith. The petition 'Queen conceived without original sin' was added to the popular Litany of Loreto in 1839,[101] and in England John Milner, one of Ullathorne's predecessors in the Midland District had approved a translation of the Little Office of the Immaculate Conception of the Blessed Virgin Mary as early as 1822.[102] The Archconfraternity of the Holy and Immaculate Heart of Mary, founded in Paris in 1836 following the Marian apparitions in Rue de Bac and given papal approval in 1838, quickly spread to England. In 1846 a branch of this sodality was founded in Birmingham and when Ullathorne arrived there it had nearly three hundred lay and clerical members (including Frederick Faber). Popular and papal attention had been drawn afresh to both the theology and the devotion; perhaps as Newman said, 'it required the break-up of the religious establishment, it required the French Revolution, to bring the Church into such a state that the question could be considered on its own merits'.[103] Petitions for a definition increased and Perrone's treatise of 1847 finally settled the remnants of the theological debate and formed the basis of the papal bull *Ineffabilis Deus* issued in 1854. Ullathorne's book quickly became something of a classic in its time and was quoted approvingly by Newman in his later treatise *On Consulting the Faithful in Matters of Doctrine*.[104]

The clarity of Ullathorne's account of the historical and theological development of the doctrine was remarkable. When Newman spoke of the faithful as 'one of the witnesses to the fact of the tradition of revealed doctrine',[105] he was forced to

---

[101.] *Immaculate Conception*, p. 176.
[102.] F. C. Husenbeth, *Life of Bishop John Milner* (1852), p. 566.
[103.] L&D XIX, p. 365, 15 June 1860.
[104.] J. H. Newman, *On Consulting the Faithful in Matters of Doctrine* (1961 edn), p. 63.
[105.] Ibid.

explain himself, yet Ullathorne's chapter entitled 'The Voice of the Liturgy and the Voice of the Faithful' expressed a less sophisticated but clear sense of the development of doctrine and the unity of laity, priests, bishops and Pope in the Church. In dealing with the very specific topic of the Immaculate Conception, Ullathorne expressed, more clearly than in most of his other publications, the achievement of a pastoral bishop coming to terms with the issues and ideas of his time. The contemporary relevance of the definition was to him, 'a sure sign that a renewed vigour is animating her [the Church] and strengthening her interior life'.[106] He interpreted this as having very specific contemporary pastoral implications. It was a blow against that brand of Evangelical Protestantism which denied baptismal regeneration and encouraged 'a religionism self-righteous and self-sufficient'.[107]

The rejection of regeneration by baptism, he argued, 'leads on to the rejection of original sin, a doctrine which is already sapped and undermined in almost all sects of Protestantism. And that doctrine is the foundation which underlies the whole structure of Christianity'.[108] The 'growing evil' of rationalism which advocated the perfectibility of mankind was now faced with Mary as, 'the highest example of human perfection and of created happiness'.[109] The possibility of human perfectibility and self improvement, which was such a popular concept in the nineteenth century, was anathema to Ullathorne's view of the world. He believed that contemporary values based on human reason were wholly undermined by contemplation of the Immaculate Conception, which is the 'mystery of God's strength in weakness, of His height in humility, of His glory in purity'.[110] In the light of that mystery, the 'self-help' values of Victorian England and the Calvinist emphases of Protestantism stood nowhere. For Ullathorne, the definition of the Immaculate Conception was a sign to his generation that its religion, its values and its society were false. 'Our pride sinks

106. *Immaculate Conception*, p. 203.
107. Ibid., p. 204.
108. Ibid., pp. 205–6.
109. Ibid., p. 211.
110. Ibid., p. 211.

down rebuked, our false ambition stands reproved, our sensuous strength betrays the weakness of its origin and our confidence in the perfection of our nature is discovered to be that broken reed of which we had so often heard in vain'.[111] The humility of Mary and the proclamation of her perfection stood as a challenge to the rest of humanity, 'the one bright star, which, in the universal night of human conceptions, makes the darkness still more visible'.[112]

By late 1854, refreshed from his pilgrimage in the Alps, he was not only immersed in his writing on the Immaculate Conception and on La Salette, but on the process of formal visitation around the diocese, prior to making his first *ad limina* report to Rome. He spent two years travelling the diocese, and 'in each place gave the people free access to him as well as the clergy'.[113] He visited all the missions and schools and examined the children on their catechism, and in only two missions did he report finding any discontent among people or clergy. By late 1855 he was coming to the end of the punishing round of journeys which took him from the Potteries to the Thames, and was encouraged by what he found.

> We take this opportunity of expressing to you all, dearly beloved, how much consolation we have received in the course of our pastoral labours. With scarcely an exception, have we witnessed the peace, unity and order of the congregations ... God has given us ample consolation for the trials that surround us, of which indeed, some are spiritual, but those which are of the most pressing kind are of a temporal nature.[114]

The 1851 Census had recorded a population of 1,407,510 in the four counties which comprised the Diocese of Birmingham (Oxfordshire, Warwickshire, Worcestershire and Staffordshire), of which 68,000 were recorded as Catholics, though this is generally understood to be an underestimate, and Ullathorne

[111.] Ibid., pp. 211–2.
[112.] Lenten Indult 1855.
[113.] Stone G/ULL/V/2.1, Status Animarum of the Birmingham Diocese 1856.
[114.] Pastoral Letter, 15 November 1855.

thought the true total was more like 75–80,000. In his *ad limina* report he recorded that the number of parochial missions was eighty-five, of which fourteen were attached to private dwellings and four to convents; they were served by a hundred and thirty-one priests of whom a hundred and seventeen were on missions and of whom seventy-eight were seculars, nine English Benedictines, three Dominicans, nine Oratorians, seven Passionists and thirteen Rosminians. Ullathorne rejoiced in the 'union and peace and the spirit of brotherhood which reigns among the clergy of the diocese', and also that, 'what has been said of the clergy may be said also of the spirit of the laity'.

In describing his residence, the Pugin house adjoining St Chad's Cathedral, he indicated that 'the table of the bishop is open daily to all the clergy who come to visit him, and his house is as a home for them'. As regards the cathedral, 'It is the constant wish and effort of the bishop to make his cathedral a model of the mission spirit as well as of rubrical propriety.' Though not a rigorist in terms of Gothic design, it was clearly his preference ever since his building of St Osburg's in Coventry. He rarely commented in matters of decoration or of vestments, but in a letter to Stanbrook he gave a clue that his opinions were mainstream but characteristically definite.

> The form of Gothic vestments is not to be disturbed. It is not to be so broad as to cover the elbow, but to be kept an inch or two clear of it. It is not to be cut to a point at the bottom. The pallium form of cross, used in one or two places, is not to be adopted. In short, the form generally used in this diocese, and especially at St Chad's, is permitted by the sovereign Pontiff.[115]

Ever the pragmatist, he declared robustly that, 'For my part, *au fond*, I care very little for gothicism or any other fancy, so long as souls are saved and sanctified.'[116]

He was a Goth in so far as Church music went, assuring Rome that plainchant was used exclusively by the cathedral choir, which contained 'some of the most respectable laymen of

[115.] Stanbrook 8, Ullathorne to Abbess Gregson, 29 April 1854.
[116.] *Letters*, p. 64 nd.

the city'. In this he had definite views too, insisting that singing in the diocese should be 'grave in character' and that, apart from St Chad's, non-Catholics did not sing in church choirs. However, he did not succeed in excluding females from parish choirs, which, he acknowledged, would be difficult to do without stopping all singing. The cathedral choir was founded in 1855 by John Hardman, with the express purpose (supported by the bishop) of expanding and developing the use of plainchant in the cathedral liturgy. It would, believed Ullathorne, have a beneficial effect on the cathedral liturgy and further afield.[117] Celebrating the silver jubilee of the choir in 1880, he congratulated it on being 'a school to the diocese of what is best'.[118] He emphasised, as only a monk could, the fundamental difference between the ancient chant and modern polyphony.

> I will simply say that modern music is addressed to the human imagination and that the song of the Church is addressed to God; that the object of modern music is entertainment and that the object of Church music is prayer; that modern music breathes the spirit of the world and that the song of the Church breathes the spirit of God; that the song of the Church brings the soul to inward recollection and that modern music draws the soul out to the senses.[119]

A decade after the choir's foundation, he could confidently assert that the clergy knew that there were two things he hated: 'flash singing in churches, and advertising church exhibitions in newspapers, and therefore we have not much of either'.[120]

The establishment of the cathedral chapter was one of his priorities in regularising the life of the local church, and by 1855 it was securely in place. Its membership consisted of the

---

[117.] BAA B2333, Ullathorne to Hardman, Formby and Lambert, 5 December 1851.
[118.] *Church Music: a discourse given in St Chad's Cathedral on the half jubilee of its choir* (1880), p. 25.
[119.] *Church Music*, p. 16.
[120.] AAW Ullathorne Correspondence, Ullathorne to Manning, 13 November 1868.

Rev. Provost, Henry Weedall (President of Oscott), John Dunne of Cresswell, James Jones of Cheadle, Ralph Bagnall (Vice-President of Oscott), Henry Richmond (Procurator of Oscott), James Jeffries from Leamington, George Morgan (Professor of Theology at Oscott), John Moore (Chaplain to the Sisters of Mercy in Birmingham), George Jeffries the vicar general who lived at the cathedral and Thomas Flanagan from Hanley Swan in Worcestershire. They were all described in the *ad limina* report as 'men of prudence who have grown up in the diocese'.

Naturally, the *ad limina* report detailed the state of Oscott, reminding the Holy See that technically the English colleges could not be described as seminaries, since they combined lay and clerical education. There were nine priests on the Oscott staff, nineteen students in theology (of whom eight were deacons); eleven students were for Birmingham, two for Northampton, one for Shrewsbury, and three for Clifton. The students in humanity and philosophy totalled one hundred and sixteen, of whom sixteen were aspirants to priesthood. His overall comment revealed his mind on the running and management of Oscott and his real hopes for priestly training. 'It is much to be regretted that in this magnificent building, built with ecclesiastical funds, the ecclesiastical students should be so few, and the lay element should so much preponderate', but he had no choice, having inherited a debt on the college of £14,000. Although he had instituted the Ecclesiastical Education Fund, this did not pay for more than a quarter of the number of students required, and he was very dependent on importing clergy from Ireland. Through Weedall's efforts since 1853 the debt had been reduced to £10,000, and he nursed hopes that when it was eradicated, the clerical side of the college could predominate. He expressed his unhappiness with the present system, believing it was not healthy for the clerical students, who had too much contact with the school and were looked down on by their aristocratic confrères, nor was it conducive to recruitment to the priesthood. 'It is the opinion of the bishop that if ever the lay colleges in England can be made separate from the seminaries, yet placed under the management of ecclesiastics, a greater number of the higher classes will be attracted to the Church.'

Sedgley Park, the preparatory school founded by Challoner outside Wolverhampton in the early 1760s, had a hundred and forty boys in it, but 'one of the most important elements in the English mission is the education of the poor'. It was a constant battle to keep Catholic children out of Protestant schools, and in virtually every mission there was at least one school. The diocese maintained a hundred and ten schools, eleven of them in the city of Birmingham, educating 2,068 children. The number of children in school in the whole diocese was 9,190, but because of social and economic conditions they often left school aged seven or eight to work in factories, and were so exhausted by long working hours that nothing could be done to supplement their education out of hours. The only remedy was Sunday Schools, which were conducted by the clergy in all missions.

While grudgingly acknowledging financial help from the state, he was apprehensive that government influence in education would increase and, that consequently, the Church would lose control. This was a perennial fear of Ullathorne's and he was keen to keep government at arm's length. The social evils of industrial cities and the effect these had on Catholic families was already becoming clear to Ullathorne, whose diocese embraced huge swathes of manufacturing and industrial development. He was conscious that increasing migration to the towns and cities and also, in large numbers, to the colonies was reducing the population of some rural areas and weakening the Catholic missions. In these areas there was also evidence of wives being left behind temporarily and without means, or even abandoned completely. Just as he had done in Australia, Ullathorne identified the abiding and most damaging social problem among the poor as drunkenness, especially, though not exclusively, among men. It was 'the main source of all their crimes, as well as their destitution'. This opinion was reinforced by experience, in places like the Black Country town of Wednesbury, where the missioner found it impossible to collect funds for the mission, because 'the Irish here spend hundreds annually in fines for being drunk and disorderly.'[121]

[121.] BAA B2455, Fr Montgomery to Ullathorne, 24 April 1852.

In the final section of his report, Ullathorne commented on some of the 'more pressing wants and difficulties' of the diocese. Unsurprisingly, he devoted much of this to the inherited financial and administrative mess which inhibited his governance and the management of the diocese. This had caused him frustration and embarrassment, and so tried his spirit that he had half a mind to 'cast himself at the feet of the Sovereign Pontiff and to implore him leave to retire from his see', but acknowledged that this would be pusillanimous on his part.[122] In fact, the *ad limina* visit was the highlight of the first decade of his episcopate, despite the 'pressing wants and difficulties.' His pride in the achievements of his diocese was matched only by his deep and genuine affection for the people under his care. On his return from Rome, he wrote warmly in a pastoral letter that, 'A bishop at Rome seems to carry the flock of his diocese represented in his person and their best aspirations in his single heart. He prays for them more earnestly, he thinks of them more constantly, he speaks for their spiritual good, he seems to be nothing without them, and everything for them.[123]

Having finally completed his first visitation of the diocese ready for the *ad limina* visit by the end of 1855, Ullathorne returned again to the vexed question of the financial division of assets consequent on setting up of the diocese, and Wiseman's involvement. His extended visits to all the missions of the diocese and the compilation of the report for Rome highlighted again the financial stress under which most of the clergy and laity were placed, and made him determined to raise the matter again. His tone was polite and deferential, masking a deep sense of frustration, but, realising that aggression would get him nowhere, he tried a calm and reasonable approach.

Amongst the elements of these temporalities, one item is the unsettled account between the diocese and Your Eminence. I have delayed from time to time the renewal

[122.] All the above information is gleaned from Stone G/ULL/V/2.1 Status Animarum of the Diocese of Birmingham 1856.
[123.] Pastoral Letter, 19 November 1856.

of that subject, naturally a perplexing and painful one to
both parties, from a sense of delicacy, suggested by those
various incidents which from time to time have arisen,
and which I thought at the time were proper reasons for
my not inconveniencing Your Eminence by adding
anything to your occupations and solicitudes, all absorbing as they often must have been. And if I now introduce
the subject once more, I do so certainly in a most respectful spirit and with the view of submitting the question to
Your Eminence, and to ask whether you would entertain
any objection to the whole subject being arranged
through the medium of an arbitration, to be constituted
either of one or more of the bishops upon whom we
might agree to confide in.[124]

By February of the following year, Wiseman had not replied
and Ullathorne tried again. He spelt out the specific claim
which he believed the Diocese of Birmingham to have on
Wiseman – £360 trust money belonging to endowments, which
he had chosen not to mention in his report to Rome on the
state of the Diocese, but to leave to Wiseman's conscience. He
reminded Wiseman of the 'pitiful' state in which he found
himself, with four dioceses having claims on the old Midland
District funds (Nottingham, Northampton and Shrewsbury, as
well as Birmingham) and about two-thirds of the funds having
disappeared. The complexity and fragility of their relationship
was revealed in Ullathorne's acknowledgement that Wiseman
might have gained an impression that Ullathorne was hostile
towards him, but Ullathorne insisted that he was often the
Cardinal's only defender against his critics.[125]

Wiseman's response to this letter was swift and furious,
written on the same day as Ullathorne's own, which he says he
received, 'with great regret and pain'. He rejected any suggestion of arbitration and really pushed the blame onto the late
Bishop Walsh, telling Ullathorne that he should have taken it
up with him at the time: the suggestion is, at the least, disingenuous, given that Walsh was a dying man when Ullathorne

---

[124.] AAW R79/3, Ullathorne to Wiseman, 30 December 1855.
[125.] AAW R79/3, Ullathorne to Wiseman, 8 February 1856.

succeeded and within months of his removal to London was indeed dead. Ullathorne's attempt to keep the peace was trampled on by Wiseman's insistence that the matter was a grave and public one, 'a criminal charge' which he insisted must be taken to the ultimate court of appeal. Wiseman talked angrily of going to Rome himself, where 'the Holy Father will not deny me this justice'.[126] This attitude, as Schiefen suggested, was pretty much par for the course with Wiseman.[127] Within days Ullathorne had determined to go to Rome himself to try and settle the financial disputes over the Central District funds once and for all.[128]

The year 1856 began with Ullathorne's visit to Rome to present his first *ad limina* report on the diocese, and he took the opportunity to break his journey at the shrine of St Benedict at Subiaco, about fifty miles east from Rome, above the River Aniene. The ancient monastery of Subiaco was built over the 'Sacro Speco', the holy cave, in which St Benedict lived as a hermit for three years around the year 500. It was here that he built the first of a series of twelve monasteries in the area, and one of only two which survive. To any Benedictine, a pilgrimage to this remote and beautiful hillside shrine offers the most immediate and evocative sense of St Benedict himself and the origins of western monasticism.

Ullathorne was deeply moved by his visit, and wrote a series of articles which were published as a booklet along with a new translation of Gregory the Great's life of Benedict, taken from the *Dialogues*. There is a poignant sense of longing in Ullathorne's description of the shrine:

> Here then it was that in his youth, St Benedict dwelt in solitude with God; clad in skins like the Baptist, and unknown to all save one poor monk, on whom he depended for a share of his pittance of food, he passed the sweet time of youth; here he was compensated for the sacrifice of human learning and became the disciple of inspired wisdom; here his Creator and Redeemer grew

126. Ibid.
127. Schiefen, p. 248.
128. AAS Ullathorne Papers, Ullathorne to Grant, 13 February 1856.

while the creature diminished in his soul; here he inter-
changed the delights and trials of contemplation with the
study of the Holy Scriptures, as his rule so abundantly
demonstrates; here by the operation of the Holy Spirit
and the continuous oblation of his will, he grew by the
purity of his prayer to that unity, peace and lightsome-
ness of soul, so to behold the greatness of his Creator as to
be able to comprehend that the whole world with all its
creatures, was in comparison, but as a mote which plays in
one beam of the sun.[129]

Here again, in the fifty-year-old bishop is the romantic youth
who found his life's inspiration in the life and rule of St
Benedict and his monks. He also took delight in investigating
another romance, that St Bede's body had been secretly buried
at Subiaco. The legend was that he had been brought to Genoa
by Durham monks, and that there was a two hundred-year-old
cult of Bede in the Italian city. Though sceptical about it, he
thought that, as growing numbers of English visitors were
going to Subiaco and he was writing on it, he should try to
clarify the situation.[130] He came to the conclusion that, 'the
relics of Venerable Bede never left England; and that the
relics, formerly at Genoa and now at Subiaco, are those of St
Bede the younger.'[131]

After his return from Subiaco, he continued to drive himself
and the diocese hard, insisting on greater efforts to meet the
missionary needs of the Midlands. Few years passed without
reference in a pastoral letter to the need for generosity and
self-sacrifice to meet the needs of church building and especially the training of priests, and he made the point frequently
that it was no good leaving it to others. 'Let no one think that
others will make up what he himself may fail in doing. Let no
one imagine that this is not his own personal concern.'[132] He
reported regularly to the diocese on mission projects started,

[129.] *A Pilgrimage to the Proto-monastery of Subiaco and the Holy Grotto of St Benedict* (1856), pp. 40–1.
[130.] AAS Ullathorne Papers, Ullathorne to Grant, 14 January 1856 and Ushaw UL3, Ullathorne to Walker 29 May 1856.
[131.] *Pilgrimage to Subiaco*, p. 31.
[132.] Pastoral Letter, 18 March 1857.

completed or under way. Advent 1857 was typical, with reports of building schemes from end to end of the diocese, at Coughton, Walsall, Willenhall, Tunstall, Hanley, Kidderminster, Aston, Stafford, Smethwick and Banbury.[133] The financial row with Wiseman was not forgotten, but to save Wiseman's feelings and avoid Roman involvement, Ullathorne dropped the matter, and claimed that the 'pecuniary questions' between Wiseman and the old Central District had 'remained in abeyance ever since the year 1849'. In November, however, Estcourt sent a statement of claims on the part of the diocese of Birmingham to Wiseman accompanying a chilly and polite letter from Ullathorne, assuring Wiseman that, 'I have no other feeling or desire than to satisfy my own conscience' and if Wiseman was satisfied with the proposed plan of an independent referee, he would be 'contented with the award of any bishop your eminence might think well to accept as a medium of reference'.[134] Nothing seems to have been resolved and Ullathorne finally gave up, but, 'he had not heard the last of it'.[135]

During his first decade in Birmingham, as vicar apostolic and bishop, Ullathorne began to shape the diocese, its seminary, schools and institutions to carry forward the revival in Catholic life now well under way. This was happening in all the new dioceses, with varying degrees of success and frustration, but a unique element in Birmingham was the heroic extent to which its bishop enabled and encouraged women to be a part of the revival. Religious orders of women dedicated to pastoral work in missions, schools, hospitals and the community burgeoned in the 1850s, and in Birmingham, Ullathorne was a powerful advocate of these women. The notion of women being consecrated to a particular religious task and setting themselves apart from the normal expectations of society mirrored that of the creation of a distinctive clerical caste among men, in both Catholic and non-Catholic life. Religious sisterhoods also appeared within the Church of England, but were never as numerous as in the Catholic Church. This was

---

[133.] Pastoral Letter, 17 November 1857.
[134.] AAW 79/3, Ullathorne to Wiseman, 10 November 1856.
[135.] Schiefen, p. 248.

nothing short of a revolution in Catholic life and in English society, and has only in recent years begun to receive the attention it deserves from historians of the period.[136]

The valuable work among the sick and poor by the sisters of all congregations and orders helped to eradicate some, though not all hostility to religious life. The stories of Catholic nuns, including the Sisters of Mercy,[137] nursing in the Crimea have now become better known.[138] Florence Nightingale herself verbally lashed her fellow Protestant women for remaining, 'idle cowards' while Catholic women laboured so zealously.[139] However, not all Protestants (or indeed Catholics) were so convinced by the sight of convent veils. In 1856 Ullathorne was forced to write a long and indignant letter to the *Weekly Register* in defence of the Dominican sisters who had been accused of taking it upon themselves, 'to direct missions, and even to guide priests in the performance of their duties. And the ridiculous story has reached its climax by the addition, that in part of my own diocese, they have gone about and preached to the people'. The local clergy were indignant on the nuns' behalf at this tittle-tattle, and insisted with Ullathorne that in the places where the nuns lived, 'there is and could be no mission of any kind for the people but for the nuns' church'.[140] He was convinced of the value of nuns in missions, not only because they often helped to make provision for church premises which otherwise would not exist, or because of their caring and generous work among the people, but because 'many souls are raised to a higher and more peculiar sanctity, or they are influenced towards God, by joining in the devotions to be found in the churches of religious orders'.[141]

In 1856, he was able to report to Rome with enthusiasm, that the female religious houses in the diocese were flourishing.

[136.] See, for example, the work of Susan O'Brien, Edna Hamer and Marie McClelland.

[137.] See Evelyn Bolster, *The Sisters of Mercy in the Crimean War* (1964).

[138.] Ruth Gilpin Wells, *A Woman of her Time and Ours: Mary Magdalen Taylor SMG* (1988), pp. 33–59.

[139.] Champ thesis, p. 205 n. 239.

[140.] Stone, G/ULL/III/130 Ullathorne to Editor of *Weekly Register*, 12 February 1856.

[141.] Ibid.

There were by then eighteen houses in all, of which six housed contemplative nuns (Benedictines in four, and one each of Poor Clares and enclosed Dominicans). The other fourteen contained women devoted to an active apostolate in the missions and schools in which they lived, and represented the Third Order Dominicans, the Sisters of Charity of St Paul and the Sisters of Mercy. In 1850 there had been only seven, and by the end of Ullathorne's life there were thirty-six convents.[142] All but the two exempt Benedictine houses were under Ullathorne's direct jurisdiction, and he was particularly sensitive in his dealings with them. He believed, from his reading about the Early Church, that a bishop had a special responsibility for nuns, but, as in so many other areas of life, he was at pains to ensure that it was exercised within appropriate structures and the laws of the Church. Commiserating with Abbess Gregson of the exempt house at Stanbrook with her problems, he offered assistance in the most delicate and tactful way – another instance of the side of Ullathorne not covered by the common description of him as a 'bluff, blunt Yorkshireman'.

> If at any time, not as bishop but as a friend I can be of the least use to you, I beg of you, my dear sister in Christ, to have no doubt or hesitation in applying to me. I have every confidence in you, and I feel all a brother's interest in the community and you need have no apprehension of my treading on your immunities. I like everyone to tell me when they think I do too much or too little.[143]

His tact, discretion and understanding in his dealings with female religious houses was extraordinary, and reveals a hidden aspect of his personality. What is also remarkable is that he was probably unique in this among the bishops. Women religious were a new and largely alien phenomenon to Victorian clergymen, and few had any appreciation of their vocation to serve God's people in the missions and schools. He was conscious that, although the Sisters of Charity had made a massive impact on New South Wales in their first couple of

---

142. *The Oscotian*, Ullathorne Number (1886), p. 57.
143. Stanbrook 3, Ullathorne to Abbess Gregson, 20 January 1851.

years, 'they had never been thoroughly sympathised with except by myself', and it was only the thought of that which had made him hesitate to leave Australia.[144]

Not all the new Catholic bishops were by any means sympathetic to women religious; it came to Ullathorne's attention that Burgess of Clifton was proving difficult, and he told Talbot, the Roman agent, bluntly that he sympathised with the nuns, because 'the convents have no confidence in him'.[145] In other situations, episcopal support was only forthcoming when religious were prepared to fulfil the needs identified by the bishop, as the Sisters of the Cross and Passion did for Bishop Turner of Salford in the 1850s.[146] Other bishops presided over the growth of convents within their dioceses, including Hogarth in Hexham,[147] Hendren in Clifton and Nottingham and George Brown of Liverpool.[148] None, however, became such an advocate of the ministry of nuns in the local Church and its surrounding society, nor did they take such a personal interest in them as communities and as individuals. Ullathorne did not take a utilitarian view of women religious, nor did he expect to receive absolute obedience to his will, as was commonplace.[149] His growing understanding and appreciation of the consecrated women religious brought out a strong humanity and humility in Ullathorne which was rarely seen in other situations. Gradually, he also came to recognise that he received back from the convents in full measure all that he gave. He was humble enough to admit to Mother Margaret and the Dominicans at Stone that 'there was a time when I should have been too proud to have admitted, even to myself,

---

[144.] *Autobiography*, p. 208.

[145.] VEC Talbot Papers, Ullathorne to Talbot, 14 August 1853.

[146.] Susan O'Brien, 'Lay Sisters and Good Mothers: working class women in English convents 1840–1910' in *Studies in Church History* vol. 27, Women in the Church (1990).

[147.] Sheridan Gilley, 'The Legacy of William Hogarth 1786–1866' in *Recusant History* vol. 25 (2000), p. 258.

[148.] Peter Doyle, 'A Tangled Skein of Confusion: the administration of George Hilary Brown, Bishop of Liverpool 1850–56' in *Recusant History* vol. 25 (2000), p. 301.

[149.] Susan O'Brien, 'Lay Sisters and Good Mothers: working class women in English convents 1840–1910' in *Studies in Church History* vol. 27, Women in the Church (1990).

that there was any good worth noting in all your charity towards me'.[150]

The unusual circumstances which gave rise to the development of women's religious life meant that it was often surrounded by controversy, as much within the Catholic community as beyond. Few English people, even Catholics, understood much about nuns, and the clergy were often more guilty than most of acting wrong headedly or misguidedly. The newly formed religious institutes needed, in Ullathorne's view, careful organisation and planning in order to ensure that they were properly integrated into the life and tradition of the Church. Maverick houses and casual disregard of rules were damaging both to the women involved and their reputation, and to the mission of the Church. His disapproval of informal and uncanonical practices within the Institute of Charity, which had a convent at Loughborough, a small house at Newport and one at Manchester, was an illustration of his determination that things must be done properly.

> I have to state that they have not yet been approved by the Holy See, but that Dr Walsh allowed of their exemption. The consequence is that I know scarcely anything of them or of their affairs. I have called occasionally and seen the community together in a formal manner. And in consequence of five or six sisters having been hastily professed without either my knowledge or the knowledge of their friends, who were mostly persons of family and property, and professed before the time specified in their rules, by a special dispensation from their general superior, I have signified that, henceforth, I shall require the canonical notice a full fortnight before any profession and shall declare invalid any profession not previously signified to me.[151]

As the great defender of the integrity and dignity of female religious, he became conscious that public scrutiny meant that they had to be scrupulously careful in the internal and outward

[150] *Letters*, p. 45, 21 June 1853.
[151] AAW R79/3, Ullathorne to Wiseman, 20 February 1851.

workings of their convents. Close co-operation with local clergy, bishops and the authority of Rome was vital in order to ensure that the religious institutes of women were understood to be fully part of the Church with their own rules and constitutions accepted in the same way and with the same force as those of the traditional men's orders. His training and experience as a Benedictine was valuable in this and he was able to judge situations with care and balance. A convent or religious institute which did not have the full support of the priests and bishops was destined for failure, and anything which did not have the full protection of the Church institutions was vulnerable to attack from a hostile public and from authoritarian clergy. His paternal pride in the achievements of the religious communities was evident in his report to Rome, when he rejoiced that 'there is not a single religious in the diocese who causes any uneasiness to the bishop'.[152]

Ullathorne was never guilty of the mistaken emphasis associated with the Victorian mindset, that the Church consisted only of bishops, priests and religious, and the duty of the laity was merely to 'pay and pray'. Although he constantly appealed to the generosity of the diocese, he emphasised that churches without priests to minister in them were useless. He was also anxious to remind people that

> the Church of Christ consists in her ordained clergy, and in her faithful people, and in their living and life-gaining work; and not in the walls and ornaments of material temples ... Pride in the material condition and the outward display of the Church smothers the inward spirit of her life. And when that pride has mounted high, and broadly spread, then the God of Heaven has only one resource left. He leaves those temples to their desolation, and takes refuge in a few faithful hearts, and His sacramental abode within their humble dwellings ... It is one thing to build up churches for the living God, in the spirit of worship; another to build up temples to our own pride, in the spirit of vanity.[153]

[152.] Stone G/ULL/V/2.1, Status Animarum of the Diocese of Birmingham 1856.
[153.] Pastoral Letter, 30 March 1859.

The close of his first decade in Birmingham found him still anxious, driven, not by pride or vanity, but by his own determination, to continue to build up the people and missions of his diocese. Never content to sit on the laurels of what had been achieved, he was constantly looking to the next task.

Chapter 6

Resignation? 1859–1865

Ullathorne's visit to Subiaco in the early months of 1856 clearly had a consoling and healing effect on his health and spirits, and strengthened his resolve to set his face towards the future. He wrote to Genevieve Dupuis, superioress of the Sisters of St Paul, at a time when she was feeling the heat, both physically and metaphorically,

> Believe me dear Reverend Mother, our fault, our great fault is, that we do not at this present instant give our hearts to God, but waste away its force in repining on what we fancy we have or have not been. Let us neither trouble our heads about what we are, or what we feel, or with what we fear, but let us simply love God now and at this moment, and do our duty now and at this moment, and all will be well, and we shall not lose our time, or waste our powers, or leave the grace of God uncultivated.[1]

Ullathorne's own health was still fragile, due to overwork, and his loss of energy and spirits is revealed in his Lent pastoral letter of 1857. It began, as usual, with the dispensations from fasting and abstinence in certain conditions for the coming penitential season, which he rather grumpily asserted were necessary because, 'the infirmities of our fallen nature have

[1.] Selly Park, Ullathorne to Genevieve Dupuis, 23 May 1856.

increased'. He was surely speaking more personally, however, when he wrote that,

> We are a careworn, nervous, languid, excitable race. We are careworn because, loving this world excessively, as Our Lord foretold, the cares of the world choke up in us the seeds of grace. We are nervous because we indulge in every kind of stimulating enjoyment which the inventions of a mere human civilisation, and the spread of commerce over the world can bring within our reach; and because we are so keenly alive to every man's opinion, whether it be true or false, just or unjust ... We are excitable, both from feebleness of the nerves, made weak by luxury, and from the inflammable pride of the soul. And these passions, like wood and coal when kindled, act one upon the other and increase the fire.[2]

He began, about this time, to suffer from fits of dizziness. 'When I was in the pulpit yesterday the church seemed to rock about and everybody to be turning round, and I was obliged to come down.'[3] A short break in Scarborough and a brief pilgrimage to St Winifred's Well in north Wales did nothing to alleviate his symptoms, and he was advised to take a period of complete rest, so in June he set off with Fr Joseph Souter for a tour of the Swiss Alps.[4] The highlight was a visit to the ancient monastery of Einsiedeln, which he described as 'the greatest and noblest monastery I have ever seen'.[5] Its buildings spread over eighteen acres and housed eighty-five choir monks as well as lay brothers and a college of a hundred students. He was much taken with the surrounding area and the lives of the Swiss Catholics, who, he asserted, 'have all the good qualities of the English and Irish combined; all the faith and fervour of the Irish, and all the care, foresight and economy of the English of the old stamp'.[6] He returned to England at the end of July, but on his return plunged back into work too quickly and was

[2] Pastoral Letter, 16 February 1857.
[3] *Letters*, p. 84 [9 March 1857].
[4] Butler, *Life*, I, p. 183.
[5] *Letters*, p. 86 [June 1857].
[6] *Letters*, pp. 86–7 [June 1857].

forced to take a more prolonged period of convalescence, retiring for some months to Little Malvern, the home of the Beringtons and a Downside mission.

Ullathorne's devotion and dedication to monastic life was always a significant part of his life, and he followed the ups and downs of the English Benedictine Congregation with intense interest. By the late 1850s he was happier with what he observed than for many years.

> The first thing which I mark in the congregation is that spirit of unity and fraternity, which began with the close of the conflicts for its existence with Bishop Baines, and which has gone on perfecting more and more, and which the common noviciate for all the congregation, now, I understand in course of preparation, will, I trust, tend greatly to consolidate. The disunity following the removal of the priories from continental Europe had purged providentially the congregation and brought it into greater unity. The next thing which I observe with great satisfaction is the gradual amelioration of discipline and the higher cultivation of the Benedictine spirit, which last is especially giving conspicuous signs at the present moment.

He has observed 'a tendency in the priories to cultivate the ascetic spirit according to Benedictine traditions', and noted with satisfaction the cordial spirit of missioners in co-operating with bishops and secular clergy, which in Birmingham is 'proverbial'.[7]

This 'proverbial' co-operation was not always the case, and Ullathorne gained something of a name with other religious orders for being 'difficult' over missionary placements in the diocese. Ullathorne's reputation, often ill-founded, went before him and he was constantly thwarted by rumours and allegations of how difficult he was to deal with. Ullathorne had natural Benedictine instincts, and had been consciously determined to nurture the secular clergy, but his dealings with the Jesuits over

---

[7.] Ampleforth 263/209, Ullathorne to President General Burchall, 18 October 1858.

missions in Birmingham and Oxford (as well as his early run-in with the Oratorians over St Wilfrid's) serve to illustrate his attitude to non-diocesan clergy. In 1858 the idea was raised of the Jesuits taking over St Anne's in Birmingham, the original city centre home of the Oratorians until the building of their new church in Hagley Road. Ullathorne offered St Anne's to the Jesuits, having received assurance that the Society would be interested, and was irritated when the offer was finally declined by the Provincial.[8] He made excuses, asserting that the two men who had offered the assurances were not empowered to do so, but Ullathorne was perhaps less sensitive to others' jurisdictional authority than to his own, and his impatience was evident. 'It will be a relief to me and will enable me to see my own way if I can have a definite answer at your earliest convenience.'[9] The Jesuit who was sent to assess the Birmingham situation was in no doubt as to the difficulties inherent there:

> Judging from what I know of the bishop, who certainly has said very hard things of us as missionaries, though I am also aware that His Lordship does at times use very different language, I should think it very unwise to place ourselves in a disadvantageous position on our very entrance to Birmingham. Position may easily be forgotten and the bishop's mind, in consequence of being worked on, be poisoned against us, if it should chance that we do no more than the missioner has previously done.[10]

There was a measure of mistrust on both sides, although Ullathorne was not fundamentally opposed to the Jesuits. Indeed, in the same year he hoped that they might take on the Oxford mission which would benefit from 'the services of that Society which of all others in the Church I should myself be disposed to consider the most fitted for it'.[11] It did not happen

---

[8.] Farm St Letters of Bishops and Cardinals (1840–91)132, Provincial to Ullathorne, (nd.) July 1858; 140, Provincial to Ullathorne 16 July 1858; 138 Provincial to Ullathorne, 15 July 1858.

[9.] Farm St,138 Provincial to Ullathorne, 15 July 1858.

[10.] Farm St Letters of Bishops and Cardinals (1840–91)116 (nd.).

[11.] Farm St 149, Ullathorne to Provincial, 1 November 1858.

in 1858, and when the question arose again in 1871, Ullathorne was not prepared to be messed about, or 'to make a mere convenience of the clergy of the diocese, to place and remove them on the change of mind of any religious body'.[12] Although he regretted the lack of male religious to teach in schools, he was not overwhelmingly welcoming to religious priests in missions. The whole issue of relations between bishops and religious orders involved in missions was a contentious one, with a long and troubled history, which would finally come to a head in the late 1870s, when Ullathorne made very clear his view that, for all his affection for his own order, right was on the side of the bishops.

The one congregation of clerics which he had come to admire increasingly was the Oratory. The early difficulties between Ullathorne and Newman were now safely behind them, and as Newman became increasingly involved in issues of national and international importance such as the foundation of the Catholic University in Dublin, he relied more and more on Ullathorne. He took Newman's part where necessary, mediated for him and interpreted his work to those who (like his earlier self) failed to understand him. This new quality in their relationship was sealed by the *Rambler* crisis of 1859. Since its foundation in 1848, *The Rambler* had been the mouthpiece of liberal Catholicism and had a reputation for outspoken radicalism, which irritated the bishops. The liberal Catholics attempted to reconcile the Church to progress, liberalism and modern civilisation by addressing the 'new orthodoxies of science and democracy, liberalism and nationalism, industrialism and socialism',[13] just at a time when the papacy and the English bishops were most resistant to such ideas. Ullathorne himself became drawn into controversy with *The Rambler* in 1857, when he replied sharply to an article on schools' inspection by J. M. Capes, the founder and for thirteen years editor of the journal.[14]

[12] Farm St 198, Ullathorne to Provincial, 3 February 1871.
[13] Dermot Quinn, *Patronage and Piety: the Politics of English Roman Catholicism 1850–1900* (1993), p. 6.
[14] AAW Molloy Collection, Capes to Ullathorne, 6 April 1857.

In 1858, it came under the management of John Acton and Richard Simpson, who stood publicly for the European liberal tradition and responded to the same impulses as Newman in encouraging an educated laity. It was less to Ullathorne's taste, in its open criticism of bishops; he described the spirit against the episcopacy in *The Rambler* as 'quite revolting' and 'subversive'.[15] Ullathorne was keen to see some official censure, but instead was deputed by his fellow bishops to ask Newman to intervene and use his influence in *The Rambler*, as it became more outspoken. Simpson's editorial tone was the nub of the problem, and Ullathorne prevailed upon Newman to tell Simpson that 'nothing will satisfy us [the bishops] but his retiring from *The Rambler*, and to advise him to do so'.[16] The situation was made worse by *The Rambler's* support of government policy towards the Papal States, especially during the General Election of 1859, when Acton was vocal in support of Palmerston,[17] while the policy of the bishops was trenchantly pro-papal (as expressed by Ullathorne at a public meeting in Birmingham Town Hall). Only Simpson's immediate retirement would prevent the bishops publicly criticising *The Rambler* in a forthcoming pastoral letter.[18] Newman was reluctantly prevailed upon to take up the editorship himself in order to prevent direct episcopal censure and probable closure. He was caught between his friendship for Simpson and his loyalty to the bishops, especially Ullathorne.[19] In his very first issue Newman 'stuck fast in the mud',[20] when he asserted the rights of the laity to be consulted in the preparation of a dogmatic definition, such as that of the Immaculate Conception in 1854.

It only slowly dawned on the bishops that a liberal journal with Newman's name attached would be even more dangerous than before. This created a storm, which Ullathorne, sharing the unease expressed by the other bishops, did his best to quell. After about six months of irritation it came to a head when Newman declared that he wished he had never taken the job

---

[15.] AAS Ullathorne Papers, Ullathorne to Grant, 5 February 1859.
[16.] AAW R79/3, Ullathorne to Wiseman, 16 February 1859.
[17.] Quinn, pp. 10–11.
[18.] AAS Ullathorne Papers, Ullathorne to Grant, 16 February 1859.
[19.] Sheridan Gilley, *Newman and His Age* (1990), p. 302.
[20.] Ibid., p. 303.

on. Ullathorne grabbed at the chance to suggest that, in that case, why didn't he resign?[21] Newman took the option to resign, when he saw that Ullathorne was discomfited by the incident, and that he clearly wished him, though did not order him, to do so. The *Rambler* crisis was the clearest illustration of the delicacy and complexity of Newman and Ullathorne's relationship. 'I must not convey a wrong impression. Our bishop expressed his *wish*; it was not an act of *authority*.'[22] After their early difficulties, Newman had become attuned to Ullathorne, and took the decision to resign as soon as he sensed the unease expressed by Ullathorne, declaring, 'I never have resisted, nor can resist, the voice of a lawful superior, speaking in his own province. I should have been in an utterly false position, if I had continued a work ... of which my bishop disapproved.'[23] Ullathorne had learnt to be more tactful in his approach than over the *Lives* or St Wilfrid's, and the matter was settled in conversation between the two men with respect for each other and 'no sort of unpleasantness'.[24] It did however generate one of the most oft-repeated anecdotes of the exchanges between Newman and Ullathorne, when the bishop, listening to Newman discoursing on the need for an educated laity, burst out in exasperation, 'Who are the laity?' To which came the quiet reply, 'Well, the Church would look foolish without them'.[25]

Newman was further criticised for additional writings on consulting the faithful, and Ullathorne was not fully in sympathy, though he declined Newman's request that he appoint a theological censor for *The Rambler*.[26] Newman (writing anonymously) developed an assertion made in earlier published lectures that, 'in all times the laity have been the measure of the Catholic spirit'.[27] This exacerbated the row and led to Newman being delated to Rome by Bishop Thomas Brown of

[21.] L&D XIX, p. 144, 24 May 1859.
[22.] L&D XIX, pp. 148–51, 29 May 1859.
[23.] L&D XIX, p. 150, 29 May 1859.
[24.] Ibid.
[25.] L&D XIX, p. 141, 22 May 1859.
[26.] J. Altholz, *The Liberal Catholic Movement in England* (1962), pp. 102–3.
[27.] David Newsome, *The Convert Cardinals* (1993), p. 221–2.

Newport. Brown was one of Ullathorne's oldest friends and a fellow Benedictine from Downside, yet there is no evidence of any exchange of correspondence on the matter, and it seems that Brown did not consult Ullathorne and 'acted with characteristic precipitation'.[28] Both Wiseman and Ullathorne were in Rome at the time, and Ullathorne called on Wiseman to make a vigorous defence of Newman, reducing him to tears by reminding him of past occasions when Newman had resented his failure to come forward on his behalf.[29] *The Rambler*, relaunched as the *Home and Foreign Review* in 1862, continued to be antagonistic to the bishops and vice versa, as all engaged in a dialogue of the deaf.[30] The matter of Newman's delation dragged on for years in Rome, causing him great distress. In this, he came to depend totally on Ullathorne's defence. Ullathorne did what he could to 'remove erroneous impressions about Dr Newman in Rome and even spoke to the Holy Father'. He pleaded with Talbot to put pressure on Barnabo and anyone else with influence.[31] Wiseman (already in poor health and preoccupied with other issues) and Manning did nothing, despite promises given to Ullathorne. Only Ullathorne laboured on Newman's behalf to present his case to *Propaganda Fide* and obtain a formal rescript.[32] The shadow of this hung over Newman for most of the 1860s. In England, the publication of Newman's *Apologia Pro Vita Sua* in 1864 contributed greatly to his rehabilitation. Ullathorne took the opportunity to write a long personal tribute to Newman, in which he virtually apologised for his early treatment of Newman, which was published as a postscript in later editions. He remarked that in ecclesiastical duty, Newman had been ever ready to go 'even beyond the slightest intimation of my wish or desires', and spoke of his feelings of respect, confidence

---

[28.] David Daniel Rees, 'Brown, Thomas (1798–1880)', *Oxford Dictionary of National Biography*, Oxford University Press, 2004 [http://www.oxforddnb.com/view/article/3657, accessed 14 Sept 2005].

[29.] Newsome, p. 223.

[30.] Quinn, p. 11.

[31.] VEC Talbot Papers, Ullathorne to Talbot, 28 October 1862.

[32.] Newsome, p. 224 is inaccurate in implying that Ullathorne did nothing.

and affection towards him, describing their friendship as 'one of the singular blessings which God has given me among the cares of the episcopal office'.[33]

Questions of ecclesiastical discipline arose again, in a very different, but horribly familiar context. His experience and knowledge of the English Benedictine Congregation extended, of course, to its mission in Australia, and he was consulted frequently throughout the 1850s on Australian affairs, both by the local bishops and by Rome, being 'the only person in Europe with practical experience of administering the Australian Church'.[34] Despite the difficulties surrounding his departure, Ullathorne had still something of the aura of a legendary figure in Australia. In 1851, Edward Hargreaves had found his famous 'grain of gold' and Australia was transformed within a few years. The following year, New South Wales yielded 850,000 ounces of gold, one of which found its way to Ullathorne.

The first native-born priest in the colony, Fr Daniel Vincent Maurus O'Connell OSB was ordained in 1851 by Polding. In October that year, he and Polding had visited the gold fields around Bathurst, with the notion of building a church to serve the gold diggers and appointing O'Connell. This never happened, but O'Connell went on to be Dean of Sydney Cathedral.[35] He marked his ordination by sending Ullathorne his first sample of Australian gold. In doing so, he expressed 'the greatest pleasure in making this small offering of the richest produce of the land, in order to testify my gratitude to one who has done so much for the country at large, and for myself individually in being one of the instruments in the hands of God of bringing me to the religious state'.[36] It is not recorded what Ullathorne did with his gold nugget. What perhaps pleased him even more was that the gold rush of the 1850s was a major factor in finally ending transportation.

In late 1859 Ullathorne found shadows from the past coming

[33.] *Letters*, p. 141, 1 June 1864.
[34.] Collins thesis, pp. 379–84.
[35.] John O'Brien, T. J. Linane and F. A. Mecham (eds), *The Men of '38 and other pioneer priests*, Kilmore, Victoria (1975), pp. 143–4.
[36.] BAA B2466, Fr Daniel O'Connell, St Mary's College, Lyndhurst to Ullathorne, 6 May 1852.

back to haunt him, when he was consulted by the Holy See on matters in Australia surrounding his old friend and superior, Polding. For a time, he faced the very real prospect of setting sail again for the Antipodes as Papal Legate with authority to investigate matters. The prospect appalled him at every possible level: after two years of poor health a journey across the southern ocean was hardly conducive to recovery; revisiting the places and people which he had put behind him nearly twenty years previously was not inviting, and last but not least, being asked to adjudicate on difficulties stemming from the governance of Polding would have been his worst nightmare. No wonder he described it as 'a diet of thistles'.[37]

The stress in Australia flowed from Polding's governance and his dependence on his vicar general and fellow monk Henry Gregory, who was increasingly unpopular among clergy and laity alike. Polding's Benedictine dream for Australia had withered and died; in fact it had been finally killed off by Roman intervention, but Polding was still widely believed to favour his own order in Sydney. This was compounded by the ineffectiveness of his administration, as Ullathorne had so bitterly experienced in the late 1830s.[38] Lay people and clergy were losing patience, and 'many people were not prepared to exonerate Polding completely'.[39] McEncroe, who was regarded by Ullathorne as one of the finest priests in Australia, and was an old friend from the 1830s, travelled to Europe with Bishop Gould of Melbourne in early 1859 and they made their way to Birmingham to consult Ullathorne before going to Rome to *Propaganda Fide*.

Ullathorne was determined to offer advice in this instance which would remove the need for him to visit Sydney, and wrote to his old friend Barnabo, the long serving Secretary and now Cardinal Prefect of *Propaganda Fide*, listing his reasons for not going to Australia: it would foster intrigue; it would be difficult for him to approach Polding, given their past history; it would humiliate Polding unnecessarily; the influence of the vicar general (Gregory) would in any case cancel out any advice

[37.] *Letters*, p. 102 (nd.) [December 1859].
[38.] John Hosie, 1859, 'Year of Crisis in the Australian Catholic Church', in *Journal of Religious History* vol. 7 (1973), pp. 342–61.
[39.] Hosie, p. 353.

Ullathorne could give; lastly, he insisted that he was far too busy in his own diocese. He was clear in his mind that the removal of Gregory was the only solution and he felt that Polding would agree to this in order to relieve the difficulties of the situation.[40]

It was certainly true that he had plenty of work in his own diocese; apart from the routine business, Henry Weedall, the venerable president of Oscott had died in 1859, leaving a crucial vacancy to be filled, and the bishops were to gather again for their third provincial synod, with the vexed college question on the table. A measure of agreement had been reached between Birmingham, Nottingham and Northampton at their annual meeting in 1858, but the major issues of status and jurisdiction hung on until the synod of the following year. Ullathorne wanted a thoroughgoing debate on the whole seminary question, based on documents from the Council of Trent. Instead, he got a compromise, based on practice at Oscott and Ushaw, whereby a board of bishops was responsible for major decisions. Ullathorne voted with the majority, presumably in order to reach a measure of accord between the bishops, but later regretted it. He became more and more convinced that one individual bishop had to have direct authority over the seminary in his territory. The continual nagging he endured from Bishop Brown of Shrewsbury was certainly a factor in his change of attitude, but even more significant was the immediate issue of the presidency of Oscott.[41]

After Henry Weedall died, and the position of president fell vacant, Ullathorne appointed George Morgan, who had been vice-president briefly in the 1840s and professor of theology since 1851. This proved to be disastrous and, within months, Ullathorne was forced to remove him. The irrational tone of Morgan's correspondence, and Ullathorne's statement that, 'his head was too weak for that difficult and complicated office' suggests some form of mental breakdown.[42] Before he had

40. Frances O'Donoghue, *The Bishop of Botany Bay: the life of John Bede Polding* (1982), pp. 117–8.
41. Judith Champ, 'The Crown of the Diocesan Structure: W. B. Ullathorne and the foundation of the seminary' in Judith Champ (ed.) *Oscott College 1838–1988* (1988), pp. 98–101.
42. Ibid., p. 100.

settled the question of the Oscott presidency, he was forced to act on the Australian problem.

Ullathorne was called to Rome in December 1859 to advise *Propaganda Fide* on the Australian crisis, determined that he would not have to travel any further.[43] It was Ullathorne's own recognition of the impossibility of Australia being run as a monastic mission which had set his own course back to England in the late 1830s. He was no more convinced of Polding's policy now. His appraisal to *Propaganda Fide* of the Australian situation was hard-hitting and outspoken: 'the difficulties of its ecclesiastical government are neither few nor small'.[44] He went on to recount how, at one time, Polding was 'the most popular man in New South Wales' and widely venerated, but the difficulties stemmed from his desire to act more as a missionary than a bishop and to delegate to a young and inexperienced vicar general (Dr Gregory). This was exactly what Ullathorne had discovered when he was Polding's vicar general himself. Gregory proved to be stronger willed than the bishop, and most Australian observers were agreed that the problems began from Gregory's 'ill-directed, inopportune activity'. Ullathorne was savage in his criticism of Gregory's 'haughty' attitude, describing him as 'a nuisance'.[45] One the other hand, he did not shrink from giving his old friend and mentor his share of the blame. Polding was over sensitive, fearful of public opinion and had no business sense. He was unjust in his unfavourable comparisons of the secular clergy with his own Benedictines, particularly in the accusations levelled at Therry of hoarding vast wealth, but Ullathorne's most savage words were kept to describe Polding's injustice to his beloved Sisters of Charity. Polding claimed to have brought them to Australia and paid the cost – in fact it was, of course, Ullathorne himself who had done that, and obtained charitable support for them. After he left the colony (as he had feared) both Polding and Gregory had treated the nuns badly.

McEncroe, for all his good qualities, had got himself into some radical and outspoken company and had linked up with

---

[43.] Butler, *Life*, I, p. 184.
[44.] *Propaganda Fide*, (see Collins thesis, p. 387).
[45.] Ibid.

them to complain about Polding to the Holy See, floating the idea of Ullathorne being asked to visit Australia as Papal Delegate. He was foolish enough to write to George Talbot, the English agent in Rome, telling him that Ullathorne had agreed and thought it a good idea, when nothing could have been further from the truth.[46] The report became very personal on another point, regarding a list drawn up by Polding of priests who had left the colony for one reason or another, most of whom were described as 'drunkards, incontinent or adulterers'. Ullathorne was not impressed to find his own name at the top of a list of 'persons without reputation' and with the misleading explanation that he had left because the climate did not suit his health.

Furious at this, Ullathorne then set out the clearest and most outspoken explanation he ever gave in a written document, of his reasons for leaving Australia and refusal to return as a bishop.

> When I returned to Australia [in 1838], I was much harassed and persecuted because I had damaged the interests of the wealthy [by speaking out against transportation to the Molesworth Committee]; and I had yet to carry on a land dispute with a certain judge called Barton who had done great harm to the Catholics, and who was afterwards recalled by the government. Moreover, I had to deal with all unpleasant business and coercive measures, and while the Archbishop [Polding] supported me in secret, before the public he did not not show me any co-operation or help. This was what ruined my health; even more, I acquired a fear of being his suffragen bishop: because in short he could never treat those who had been his novices or disciples otherwise than if they were still novices or scholars. Moreover I knew that the great fear that he had of public opinion would lead him to abandon others in difficulties, at the same time that he would want to be followed in everything. This is only a sketch of a story too long to tell further.[47]

46. Ibid.
47. Ibid.

This extraordinary outpouring of long repressed bitterness and frustration sits oddly in a formal report to the Holy See on a situation in which he was not involved, and is out of character for Ullathorne, although he knew that it would be his old friend Barnabo who would read it. It is as if, by 1859, after more than twenty years as a bishop in his own right, he felt the freedom to speak out and hang the consequences, and was determined that (at least where it counted most) people should know once and for all that he had not run away from Australia lightly. By speaking so freely he meant no disrespect to the Holy See, but rather a feeling that he had nothing to lose and had an opportunity to do some good for the Church in Australia for which he felt such loyalty and affection.

His final advice was that to send a Papal Delegate to Australia would make matters worse. It would appear to meet the demands of the Archbishop's opponents, undermine the Australian Catholic Church in the eyes of the colonial government and would give credibility to factions and parties interfering in Church matters and appealing to Rome over the head of the local bishop. In addition, it would undermine Polding and embarrass the other bishops, while playing into McEncroe's hands. For Ullathorne himself to fulfil such a role would be embarrassing for all concerned, would humiliate Polding and probably lead to his resignation. It would not resolve the issues anyway, since Polding was incapable of making 'a full explanation of any difficult business whatsoever'. In the end *Propaganda Fide* followed Ullathorne's clear guidance that Gregory was at the root of the problem, and that a resolution of the difficulties between Polding and the discontented secular clergy was only possible if he was removed.[48]

This whole incident is revealing of hidden aspects of Ullathorne's character. He still harboured a deep sense of grievance over his treatment in the last months in Australia, for which he largely blamed Polding, yet his affection for his old teacher and brother monk was genuine, as was his determination not to undermine his authority as a bishop. Often accused by contemporaries and historians of arrogance, in this instance Ullathorne knew that he could easily stride back into Australia,

48. Ibid.

armed with papal authority and two decades of episcopal experience and his unrivalled knowledge of the situation, bang some heads together, put Polding right on a few things and leave swiftly, brushing the dust from his shoes. He would have emerged with an enhanced reputation, and Polding would have paid for his inadequacies. He chose not to, which indicates a greater sensitivity to other people and personal humility than he is often credited with. Inevitably, though, his advice did get Gregory sacked and recalled to England, leaving Polding aggrieved and bitter. However, Rome was grateful, and Ullathorne sat close to the papal throne among the assisting bishops in St Peter's on Christmas morning 1859.[49]

The following year, Ullathorne was able to focus again on domestic matters, and appointed James Spencer Northcote to be President of Oscott, which was to usher in something of a golden age for the college, although the initial reaction was mixed. There were those who felt that his former Anglicanism, his youth (less than forty) and his inexperience (five years ordained) were against him. Northcote was educated at Corpus Christi, Oxford, where he formed a lifelong friendship with Newman. After graduation in 1841 he married and was ordained in the Church of England. He worked as a curate in Ilfracombe, Devon, where he became close friends with the other leading Tractarian, Edward Pusey. In 1845 his wife and three sisters converted to Catholicism and he was not long in following. After a brief period teaching at Prior Park, he moved to Rome in 1847 and spent three years there, during which time he wrote a series of articles for *The Rambler* on the new developments in the archaeological study of the catacombs. He went on to publish the most authoritative account of the catacombs in English, in 1854.[50] Ullathorne had known him since the difficulties both had endured at Prior Park and appreciated his gifts of intellect and leadership. Like many of the Anglican converts of the day, Northcote endured family trials and difficulties. His ordination as a Catholic priest was, of course, only made possible by the death of his wife, Susannah, in June 1853,

49. Butler, *Life*, I, p. 184.
50. Judith Champ, *The English Pilgrimage to Rome: a dwelling for the soul* (2000), pp. 171–4.

and all but one of the six children to whom she had given birth died in childhood. Little more than a year after her death, he was ordained by Ullathorne at St Dominic's Stone, where his eldest daughter, Mary Cecilia was later professed as a nun alongside Ullathorne's niece, Philomena. As president of Oscott, he had to endure the death of his young son Edward who was a pupil in the school.

On his appointment Northcote immediately wrote the bishop a detailed account of the changes he wished to make at Oscott, on which he had been working for months. Much of what he achieved at Oscott was influenced by his friendship with Thomas Arnold of Rugby, also a Corpus man, whose educational model shaped Northcote's thinking. One of the key features on which they were agreed was the replacement of juvenile student teachers with adult teachers. He recommended an immediate rise in fees, regarding the present forty guineas charged by Oscott as 'a ludicrous price for such a house as this and such an education as we profess to give'. As he hoped to improve things further it would cost more. He was unhappy about the amount of school teaching expected of the church students and the extent of their association with the younger boys in the school, so proposed with immediate effect to reduce their teaching by half and gradually to eradicate it altogether. Association with the smaller boys would be stopped and more of their time given to theological education (at present only one hour a day). To improve the spirit and behaviour of church students he wanted to institute shared meals with professors, as they had never stopped behaving like schoolboys – and the same could be said of the professors too![51] Further regulations were amended or drawn up in the next few years to secure the proper behaviour and training of the clerical students. An episcopal visitation in 1864 resulted in rules that all priests and divines should be in choir in time for meditation; clergy and students in theology required special permission to leave during the vacation; other regulations concerning domestic detail were also drawn up. All of these reforms were evidence of the close supervision of Oscott life

[51.] BAA B3957, Letter with attached notes from Northcote to Ullathorne, 7 July 1860.

undertaken by Ullathorne and Northcote, and the desperate need for a fresh approach.[52] Despite this, Ullathorne became increasingly convinced that seminary education had to be separated from the school.

Northcote's conversion to Catholicism had caused a bitter rift between him and his father, which, according to his obituarist in *The Oscotian* lasted for twenty-eight years and was not healed until the father was close to death.[53] However, that may be somewhat exaggerated, as a letter from Ullathorne to the Rector of the English College in Rome revealed. Soon after Northcote had taken over at Oscott, Ullathorne asked for Dr English's help in obtaining for him an honorary Roman doctorate. Not only was this a mark of appreciation for the man who 'has truly saved that college and has taken from my heart a heavy anxiety of twelve years duration', but he hoped that it might help reconciliation with his father who had always hoped to see him awarded a doctorate. The father had apparently begun to speak of his son again lately, 'since he sees that his character and talents are appreciated'.[54] This little act of thoughtfulness on Ullathorne's part, at a time when he was under considerable strain himself, is indicative of his true nature and further contradicts suggestions that he was antagonistic to converts.

Ullathorne's appreciation of Northcote was considerable, even though they came to differ over questions related to higher education for Catholics, and in 1870 it was Northcote who accompanied Ullathorne at part of the Vatican Council. His judgement in appointing Northcote to Oscott was absolutely right, despite the scepticism of others, and his impact on the college over seventeen years was a positive one. It made even more startling and disturbing the relatively rapid decline in the college's fortunes in the following decade or so after Northcote's retirement in 1877. That Northcote was not appointed a bishop is surprising, and can only be put down to the fact that it was a breakdown in health which caused him to resign. In the event he lived to minister actively in the Potteries for another thirty years, outliving most of his fellow Oxford converts.

[52.] BAA B 4280, Regulations resulting from visitation, 5 July 1864.
[53.] *The Oscotian* 1907, p. 127.
[54.] VEC, Ullathorne to English, 9 December 1860.

Rome loomed large on the horizon of the English bishops in the late 1850s and 1860s both in terms of ecclesiastical relationships and their growing assertion of Catholic identity, and in relation to Anglo-Italian political relationships which affected Catholics in England. The first two decades of the new hierarchy and the internecine struggles within it were played out against a background of massively shifting political realities. The march of Italian nationalism and the success of the *Risorgimento* supported by the British political establishment inevitably coloured Catholic dealings with government, especially in relation to Ireland. Rising Ultramontanism within the Church was reflected in much closer exercise of supervision and authority by the Holy See, and the English bishops, keen to stake their position within the universal Church, were ready to embrace the demands of political, ecclesiastical and emotional loyalty to Rome. Political and military affairs were coming to a head in the Papal States, with Pius IX increasingly embattled by Italian nationalists who were gaining more and more territory and political credibility.

Political pressure on the Papal States built up during the 1850s, as the dream of a united and democratic Italy began to take more concrete shape. In 1859 war broke out across the Italian peninsula, with several provinces demanding annexation to Piedmont, the centre of nationalist hopes. The 'Roman Question' became not only a political issue, but the great emotional prop of the Ultramontane Church. The defence of Rome was the symbol of pro-papal Ultramontane feeling, enhanced by Pius IX's refusal to negotiate with Victor Emmanuel. As King of Piedmont, he was proclaimed King of the new Italy in 1860. Before leaving for Rome to deal with the Australian affair in late 1859, Ullathorne issued a trenchant pastoral letter in response to the political storm gathering around the pope's head.

> Shall the sovereign Pontiff, the representative of Christ, the veritable head of Christianity, be hurled from his temporal throne, or shall he retain that position of freedom and independence which he has held for more than a thousand years?

Ullathorne took the same general line as the pope himself, that this was not a matter concerning only Italy or even the papacy, but the very existence of the Church itself. 'All the enemies of the Church ... a motley array of powers, who, with brain and tongue, with the sword and the pen, are aiming at the Catholic Church of Christ in her central position, and in the independent standing of her Supreme Ruler'.[55]

He followed it up the following year, fresh from Rome himself, just before the proclamation of the Kingdom of Italy, by delivering a speech in defence of the Papal States at a public meeting in Birmingham Town Hall attended by some 8,000 people. After a survey of papal history from Constantine to Napoleon to explain the necessity of the temporal power in defending the independence of the papacy, he went into some detail on the developments of the previous quarter of a century. Attacking the half-hearted support of the French, and setting out 'the expansive system of liberal reform which the Pope has granted', he rejected the moves of the King of Piedmont to usurp the papal throne. His passionate conclusion was that this was another example in Christian history of popes suffering ignominy at the hands of kings and emperors, but being embraced by the loyal Catholic populace. 'Wherever the sun searches the habitation of man with his rays, the Catholic people of every tribe and tongue and colour are stirring for the Pope.'[56] This went down well in Rome. Talbot was complimentary, but the loss of the Papal States was, in Ullathorne's mind, a gloomy foreshadowing of the crumbling of civilisation itself.

My devotedness to the Holy Father, both his sacred office and his person, renders any work of that kind a labour of love, which is no labour. The utter abandonment of all principle, even of such principle as was left to this country by the deeds of 1688, by our public men, is a grievous omen for the future of this country. Everything floats loosely in the wake of our newspapers. The subtle cunning of Palmerston, and the wretched radicalism of Lord John, have brought the government of this country

[55.] Pastoral Letter, 15 November 1859.
[56.] *Speech on the Question of the Pontifical States*, 14 February 1860.

to a condition such as it has never known before. Unfortunately we have not ourselves a single man of mark in the House.[57]

Domestic matters were also tense. The 1859 synod had brought back to the fore all the difficulties between Wiseman and the other bishops. Ullathorne had a long history of frustration and irritation with Wiseman over what he regarded as his predecessor's poor administration and financial sloppiness in the Central District, which had left him with such intractable difficulties. Money was not the only source of irritation, nor was Ullathorne the only bishop to find Wiseman infuriating. Grant, who had been appointed to the Diocese of Southwark in 1851, had encountered similar problems over the division of old London District funds between the new dioceses.

Both Grant and Thomas Brown (and presumably others) shared a long-running disquiet over the way Wiseman managed the business of the hierarchy. Writing in 1854, Brown had complained to Ullathorne: 'I am very dissatisfied with the way in which our business meetings have been conducted of late, as you must be and the other bishops who have any regard for their position.' His main complaint was that the accepted practices of giving a month's notice of agenda items and of the bishops speaking in order of seniority were not being maintained, so that 'the cardinal and those few to whom he may make his mind known come prepared – before the others'. He also told Ullathorne, in confidence, that Pius IX himself had told Grant to come and make his case about the money in person, but Brown suggested that someone should go with him (perhaps, he hinted, Ullathorne) because of his excessive humility.[58]

Ullathorne had made the point strongly to Wiseman himself about the meetings some months later, telling him that he had 'a deep conviction' that 'it would contribute much both to the good result of our deliberations and to the content of the bishops, if they sat in their canonical order, delivered their sentiments on each subject in order and voted in order'. He

---

[57] VEC Talbot Papers, Ullathorne to Talbot, 15 August 1860.
[58] AAW Molloy Collection, Brown to Ullathorne, 8 May 1854.

also insisted that proper discussion was impossible without advance notice of subjects.[59] The issue was not really about the efficient and effective running of meetings, but about Wiseman operating like a primate with supreme authority over the other bishops, rather than *primus inter pares*. This was a long-running sore in the hierarchy, never resolved in Wiseman's time, and led to incidents like the occasion when Ullathorne castigated Charles Langdale (Secretary of the Catholic Poor Schools committee) for appointing a Poor Schools Inspector without consulting 'more than one of the thirteen prelates who constitute the English episcopacy, and in any of whose dioceses Mr Morrell may be appointed to inspect'. He knew full well (as Langdale protested) that Wiseman had approved the appointment.[60]

If the financial irritation between Ullathorne and Wiseman was at least shelved, the more general issues between the Cardinal and the other bishops about Wiseman's style of leadership were not. They came to a head over the question of the Catholic Charities Act. The possibility of conflict or inconsistency between Canon Law and Civil Law in the matter of the trusts under which Church property in England was governed, was a long-running one. Until the Roman Catholic Charities Act of 1860, Catholic trusts had no legal standing under English law. The Act required the registration of all Catholic charitable and religious trusts under the law, which Wiseman opposed on the grounds that it placed the Church under legal penalty again and put Catholic property in jeopardy. Most of the other bishops took the opposite view, that it would give them protection under the civil law, and they began to register their trusts.[61] The trusts debate between the bishops became entangled with the prolonged discontent with Wiseman's management of affairs, and this affected its treatment in Rome. Butler told the story in some detail, quoting relevant letters in full,[62] but he treated it as a partisan dispute, in which Manning, as Wiseman's agent in Rome was acting with 'a

[59.] AAW Molloy Collection, Ullathorne to Wiseman, 8 February 1855.
[60.] AAW Molloy Collection, Ullathorne to Langdale, 8 March 1857.
[61.] Butler, *Life*, I, pp. 217–8.
[62.] Ibid., pp. 217–55.

certain intellectual fanaticism' on Wiseman's behalf, and in collaboration with 'a small group of familiars', all Ultramontanes to a man.[63]

Ullathorne had largely given up in his old disputes with Wiseman over money which he believed was still owed to Birmingham. However, in 1860, Wiseman himself attempted to revive the argument and link it to another financial dispute over pensions for lay students at Oscott. In a counterclaim Wiseman reckoned that fees he owed for a number of lay students he had sponsored should be set off against amounts he claimed were still owing to him from the college.[64] The particular case involved the young Count Randolfo Gabrielli, who was Wiseman's nephew, and the college president, Northcote, who threatened to remove him from the college on account of his unpaid debts, allegedly due from Wiseman.[65] Further angry letters were exchanged. Ullathorne was clearly furious and opposed to any link being made between the old arguments and the matter of Count Gabrielli's Oscott fees.[66] Estcourt, as diocesan chancellor, insisted that if the old disputes were to be reopened it must be in a formal way through *Propaganda Fide*: the bishop was clearly tired of the ancient arguments and lack of any possible resolution between him and Wiseman.[67] The end result was further dissatisfaction and irritation between the two bishops, as well as the ignominious removal of the young aristocrat from Oscott.[68]

Ullathorne's relationship with Wiseman over the course of more than twenty years was turbulent, and while Ullathorne respected his position as Cardinal Archbishop, there were many aspects of Wiseman which did not impress him, especially his management of episcopal affairs and of finance. He remained discreet during Wiseman's lifetime, but fifteen years after his death, wrote this devastating assessment to Kathleen O'Meara, who was planning a biography of the late cardinal (never written).

[63.] Ibid., p. 227.
[64.] Ushaw OS/M32, Estcourt to Searle, 30 December 1860.
[65.] Ushaw OS/M34, Northcote to Searle, 4 March 1861.
[66.] Ushaw OS/M44, Estcourt to Searle, 11 April 1861.
[67.] Ushaw OS/M45, Estcourt to Searle, 8 June 1861.
[68.] Ushaw OS/M42, Wiseman to Northcote, 22 March 1861.

If there was success there were also many failures in his career, owing to an utter deficiency of steady, straightforward business habits, and a peculiarly sensitive temperament. He was in many respects a child; indeed I have long noticed that this is the character of men of genius, they carry the child through the life of the man, with its intuitions and its susceptibilities ...[69]

It was perhaps predictable that Ullathorne was deputed by the other bishops to go to Rome in 1861 to try and get a definite ruling from *Propaganda Fide* not only on the permissibility of acting within the English law on the matter of trusts, but on Wiseman's assertion of primatial jurisdiction over the other bishops. This was a task he did not relish. 'I have no liking for such a commission and would escape it if I could, but I cannot in honesty deny the necessity of someone going.'[70] He was very irritated and was pinning hope on Barnabo being able to place all the difficulties before the pope personally. Barnabo appreciated the difficulties but, 'is not master in his own'.[71] However, Ullathorne was determined that the bishops had to act in order to clarify their dealings with Wiseman. 'If we do not, things will get worse instead of better and we shall get into inextricable difficulties.'[72]

He discovered in Rome that the Cardinal [Barnabo] and *Propaganda Fide*, 'also find the Cardinal [Wiseman] a real difficulty', and were not impressed by his refusal to pay Grant what was owed to the Diocese of Southwark. Ullathorne was not one commonly to deal in gossip and was familiar enough with the hothouse of Roman tittle-tattle to take it for what it was worth, so it was perhaps a sign of his irritation and frustration with Wiseman that he (rather spitefully) told Grant that he had heard that the pope himself 'believes Cardinal Wiseman is in the wrong and the bishops in the right'.[73] Manning's report to Wiseman on

---

[69.] College Irlandais Paris, Ullathorne to Kathleen O'Meara, 5 October 1879.

[70.] AAS Ullathorne Papers, Ullathorne to Grant, 12 September 1861.

[71.] AAS Ullathorne Papers, Ullathorne to Grant, 4 April 1862.

[72.] AAS Ullathorne Papers, Ullathorne to Grant, 12 September 1861.

[73.] AAS Ullathorne Papers, Ullathorne to Grant [from English College, Rome], 26 November 1861.

his audience with the Pope completely contradicted this rumour, telling him that 'in the merits of the pending questions your Eminence was beyond all doubts in the right'.[74]

Ullathorne found himself in Rome no fewer than four times between 1856 and 1862. In 1856 he went to present the *ad limina* report; at the end of 1859 he was there on Australian affairs and went twice in 1862, firstly on the Wiseman v bishops row, and secondly for the canonisation of the Japanese Martyrs. Retirement was never very far from Ullathorne's mind, and this was probably well known in Rome. Early in 1859 he had asked Northcote (on a visit to Rome) to act as an emissary for him in this; Northcote sensibly made an excuse for not raising the matter with Barnabo, suggesting that he was notoriously indiscreet, 'keeps nobodies' secrets and talks about things assuming they are public knowledge'.[75] In Rome for Christmas of 1859, Ullathorne was appointed an Assistant at the Pontifical Throne, as a mark of personal esteem, in recognition of his services to the Church and perhaps as a token of encouragement to continue.

> To His Holiness for this addition to all his paternal and affectionate kindnesses to myself, I feel more grateful than I can express, and the less I am worthy of his attention, the more grateful I must feel. The grave tests and afflictions to which so good a Pontiff has been and is subject, is a constant source of affliction and distress to the good Catholics of this country.[76]

It was during his first visit in 1862, probably the most difficult time he ever spent in the Eternal City, that he had his 'accident in St Peter's'. This was his own description of an extraordinary occurrence at a crowded public ceremony in the vast basilica. Ullathorne's longing to be relieved of his episcopal office became so strong that he became determined to do something concrete about it. Presuming that he would probably not be in Rome again for some time, he

---

[74.] Quoted in Schiefen, p. 311.
[75.] AAW St Edmund's Papers 82, Northcote to Ullathorne, 21 May 1859.
[76.] VEC Talbot Papers, Ullathorne to Talbot, 26 September 1859.

put a solemn petition before the Pope, showing how my laborious life had acted upon my constitution, and petitioning to be released and to be let return to the conventual life. I got no sign of reply for a fortnight. Mgr Talbot came twice to me and begged me to withdraw it. I begged that no one would stand between me and the Pope. But on the Feast of the Purification [Candlemas – 2 February], the Pope officiating in St Peter's, after the procession, after all the dignitaries, clerical and lay, had received their candles, after the Pope had chanted the solemn blessing of the Mass and was reseated on the throne, he had me called before him. I went up and knelt down, and he said, 'Monsignor, in the name of St Peter, I tell you from this holy chair of truth, that your demission cannot be accepted. Stand to your place. Persevere unto death. You have yet many things to do.' What could I do, but bend, kiss his ring and retire. Preaching two days after in the old church of St Agatha on her feast, there were three cardinals present. Cardinal Barnabo told me the Pope had first commissioned him to convey the answer, but had decided afterwards to take this most unusual and unprecedented course. Sitting next to Cardinal Antonelli at dinner, he said as well, 'The Pope has told me what he said to you, and you must find it far more tranquillising than if he had answered you in private.' Such was my accident in St Peter's.[77]

This serious attempt at resignation was evidently also known by Wiseman and Manning (Wiseman even believed that he was the cause of it), and soon by everyone else in Rome. Butler linked it specifically with the business in hand, and interpreted it as a political act of a frustrated man, which 'whatever the motive' had the effect of getting the bishops' side of the argument heard, 'with final victory on a number of the counts'.[78] As far as he was concerned, Ullathorne's desire to resign was the ultimate reaction to Wiseman and Manning's machinations over the trusts question, and he suggested that it tipped the

[77] BAA B4115, Ullathorne to his brother, 11 May 1862.
[78] Butler, *Life*, I, p. 236.

balance in the bishops' favour.[79] It has even been suggested that the attempt to resign was a ploy, deliberately aimed at winning the case against Wiseman and Manning.[80] This is to overplay the significance of what was happening in Rome, and is based on a view of party factions led by Wiseman and Manning on the one hand, and Ullathorne on the other. It is largely based on Herbert Vaughan's malicious comments from Rome in late February, cruelly nicknaming Ullathorne (or repeating it), 'Mgr Ego Solus'.[81] Above all things, Ullathorne did his best throughout his career to avoid factionalism between the bishops. There is a huge body of evidence that Ullathorne's priority in all things was the unity of the Church, and specifically of the English bishops, whether it be over colleges, liberal theological views expressed in the press, higher education or the Vatican Council.

His health was not robust, and during the previous few years he had been forced to take prolonged periods of convalescence: poor health was not sufficient excuse. At the same time he was burdened with the knowledge of Newman's delation to Rome in late 1859 by his old friend Thomas Brown, which still rumbled on unresolved, and he was mourning the death of his mother in September 1860. In her will she left her house, 3 Crown Terrace on the South Cliff at Scarborough, to the bishop; the rest of a substantial estate, including another house (possibly 30 Queen St)[82] and cash bequests were divided between James, Bernard and Christopher – the only other survivors of the Ullathorne children, the latter two of whom had moved across the Pennines to Liverpool.[83] James continued to live in Scarborough at 1, Mount Pleasant.[84] On the death of their family friend, and resident priest in Scarborough, Canon John Walker in 1873, Ullathorne

79. Ibid., I, p. 232.
80. Robert Gray, *Cardinal Manning: a biography* (1985), pp. 186–7.
81. Butler, *Life*, I, p. 236.
82. She is listed at this address in an 1858 trade directory according to information provided by Scarborough Library and Information Centre.
83. Stone G/ULL/VII/33, Hannah Ullathorne's will.
84. Information provided by Scarborough Library and Information Centre.

reported to the canon's nephew that, 'My dear mother once told me that the only thing that kept her at Scarboro the latter years of her life was her old friend and pastor Canon Walker and her desire to be of use to him.'[85] She would otherwise perhaps have moved to the Midlands, and as agreed with his mother and Margaret Hallahan, Ullathorne buried her in the church at Stone on 19 September. There is almost no recorded evidence of his grief, except the phrase, 'She deserved a worthier son than I am.'[86] Otherwise his sorrow was deeply buried and he spoke matter of factly of his loss even to close friends.[87]

After fifteen trying years as a bishop, it would not be surprising if he felt he had reached the end of his tether. He was not one for grand public gestures, and, of course, did not seek the very public response from the pope to his petition. After a number of intimations of resignation from as early as 1848, by using the opportunity of being in Rome to write formally to Pius IX in this fashion, he made it clear that this was no half-hearted notion brought on by periodic pressure of work or personal difficulties, but a deeply felt need to reclaim his monastic silence and recover health in mind and body. He and Pius IX had been ordained bishop of their respective sees on the same day in 1846, and there was a close bond of friendship and confidence between them, borne out by Ullathorne's very public defence of his policies and person the previous year. The pope's reaction was an extraordinary public exercise of papal authority, a curious combination of a telling off and a vote of confidence, and a clear message to Ullathorne that he wanted to hear no more of it. It was a turning point. The Pope's words restored his inner energy and 'brought [him] clear light'.[88] As at other difficult moments in his life, Ullathorne recognised that the prayers and support of his beloved nuns would get him through and save him from 'deserved failure', when he feared that his 'conscious indiscre-

---

85. Ushaw UL 25 Ullathorne to Walker, 9 July 1873.
86. In a letter of 20 September 1860, quoted in *The Oscotian* Ullathorne Number (1886), p. 144.
87. Selly Park, Ullathorne to Genevieve Dupuis, 26 September 1860.
88. *Letters*, p. 115 [6 February 1862].

tions and failings' would get him into more trouble.[89] Despite periodic bouts of poor health and depression, Ullathorne did not mention retirement again until he was eighty-three years old and paralysed by a stroke.

On his return from Rome, Wiseman wrote Ullathorne an emollient letter, hoping that 'any sentiments to which differences of judgement may have given rise, may be considered, and will in fact, be at an end, and that the course of episcopal joint action will be resumed harmoniously as it used to be before late divergence of views came in to disturb it'.[90] Ullathorne was less hopeful and a conversation with Manning had only served to confirm his view that 'it would take a little time to heal the wounds that have been opened in our hierarchy'.[91]

Pius IX was not always so kindly disposed or so patient towards the English bishops, whose endless disputes exasperated him. It was during the visit of summer 1862, in honour of the Japanese Martyrs, to which the English hierarchy had been virtually summoned, that the Pope took the opportunity to vent his irritation with the quarrelsome English bishops. He effectively banged their heads together, telling them to 'take the highest and largest mountain in the Alps and put it over all past questions and dissensions without any tunnel through to get at them'.[92] At that point the decision of *Propaganda Fide* on the trust issue had not been made public, and relations between the bishops were still rocky owing to the unresolved colleges question and the more general resentment of Wiseman's way of operating. When the decision on the specific point of registering trusts arrived, it took the view expressed by the episcopate, that where necessary to protect property, individual bishops should register under the law.[93]

This was a pragmatic solution which, in one sense, suited Ullathorne, but he was never keen on too close a relationship with civil law and government. State interference, above all, should be discouraged in Ullathorne's view. 'Religion, Trusts,

---

[89.] Selly Park, Ullathorne to Genevieve Dupuis, 10 May 1862.
[90.] AAW Molloy Collection, Wiseman to Ullathorne, 3 March 1862.
[91.] AAW R79/3, Ullathorne to Wiseman, 7 March 1862.
[92.] Quoted in Schiefen, p. 312.
[93.] Butler, *Life*, I, p. 252.

Education and what next? We shall simply encourage by admitting the principle of universal investigation into all our religious and domestic affairs'.[94] Equally threatening in his mind was state legislation such as that allowing for civil marriage and divorce, which provoked a stern warning. This was a stepping stone to a dangerous future, 'when anti-Christian doctrines become mingled with the civil law and inspire the practice of the civil courts, they become diffused throughout society, they animate the public press, and work their way into the mind through a thousand influences'.[95] He continued to be insistent that government should be kept at arm's length, and when the possibility of another religious census in 1861 was mooted, Ullathorne was adamantly opposed, insisting that the Catholics should join with the Dissenters in blocking another attack on civil and religious liberty. Ullathorne was well aware that political and religious liberalism was having an increasingly powerful influence in society. The one element of constancy in an inconstant world was the Church itself, but he warned Catholics that 'the world is ever angry with the Church because she will not change as the world changes'.[96] His understanding of religious liberty was quite different from that of *The Rambler* or of Gladstone.

In the wake of the party factions which had emerged in the Church of England following the Oxford Movement and defections to Rome, the established Church had also thrown up liberal voices of influence, particularly in the area of biblical studies. Ullathorne's extraordinary breadth of reading encompassed the writings of Protestant liberals, including the authors of *Essays and Reviews*, published in 1860, which had to be challenged. This collection of liberal theological essays by a group including Benjamin Jowett, Frederick Temple and Baden Powell, was aimed at generating 'free and honest discussion of biblical questions'.[97] It caused mayhem within the Church of England and disgusted Ullathorne. It was, he said gloomily, 'a sign of the times ... The intervention of God in the universe, the possibility of miracles, the veracity of Scripture, the resur-

[94.] AAS Ullathorne Papers Ullathorne to Grant, 30 May 1857.
[95.] Pastoral Letter, 30 January 1858.
[96.] Pastoral Letter, 4 March 1861.
[97.] Owen Chadwick, *The Victorian Church* (1970), II, p. 75.

rection of the dead, the divinity of Christ, the action of providence are all crudely but boldly denied, and the sacraments are
declared to be but copies of pagan magic ... yet this book *Essays
and Reviews* has not awakened public notice, or brought out a
single sign from the authorities of the establishment'.[98] He was
too quick off the mark, because *Essays and Reviews* did awaken
public notice and opprobrium in the Church of England, but
obviously Ullathorne had read it very soon after publication.
By early 1861, the bishops of the Church of England forcibly
expressed their disapproval, declaring that the holding of such
views was incompatible with subscribing to the articles of the
Church of England.[99] Prosecution through the courts was
attempted, and finally in 1864 both houses of Convocation
condemned it. This did not prevent Ullathorne being sceptical
in the extreme about liberal Protestantism, and describing
Anglicanism as 'a communion which has not unity whether of
faith or principles ... if St Paul were among us he would hear a
civil tribunal deciding with the force of law that the doctrine of
eternal punishment need not of necessity be taught'.[100]

Despite his frequent distaste for the content, he maintained
an interest in the theological writings of non-Catholics and the
issues raised by the emerging liberal Protestant interpretation
of Scripture, and the impact of the contemporary science and
religion debate. Darwin's *Origin of Species* had been published
in 1859, raising a storm of controversy and making the science
and religion debate even sharper than it had been since scientific geology had begun to emerge in the 1830s. Ullathorne was
fearful, as were all Catholic churchmen, of the effects of
modern scientific scholarship on traditional understanding of
the origins of mankind and the creation of the world. He
remained sceptical that the 'new science' could disprove the
accepted theory of creation as derived from a literal interpretation of Scripture.

I think with Simpson so far, that if you grant such a
theory of man's origin, you open the floodgates to a flood

[98.] VEC Talbot Papers, Ullathorne to Talbot, 15 August 1860.
[99.] Chadwick, p. 79.
[100.] Pastoral Letter, 2 March 1864.

of consequences that will sweep away the landmarks of both Scripture and Tradition. The theory concerning man rests on the theory of the uncounted acts required for certain geological formations, and I do not consider that theory as yet rests on proved facts. Everything is running one way for the moment, but there are signs of a turn, and the other side of the question has not yet been fairly examined ... Suppose we had given up the deluge on the theories of half a century past, when water was not found to cover the earth, where should we be now, that it is determined that water has been the agent to a far greater extent than the Mosaic deluge can explain, and where the atmospheric waters are appealed to as more than enough to drown the Himalayas and the Andes. Depend upon it, the whole question is in its infancy and is for the present all running on one side. No-one seems to think of the difference between the growth of youth and of maturity.[101]

He was certainly right that 'the whole question was in its infancy' but he was obviously well read in the current science and religion debates. He kept up to date on the issues, and discussed with some assurance the effects of water and heat on geology, having heard the eminent geologist, Sir William Hamilton in 1837, speaking of mathematical laws involved in the gradual recession of heat from the earth's surface.

I do not think the science of the subject is in that developed and certain condition, or that it has so exhausted the facts within its scope, as to justify us throwing overboard, on its account, the tradition of all humanity, as well as that of the Church, as to the comparatively recent origin of man. But even then, I do not think we are bound to the chronology commonly received. It will be difficult to reconcile the ape theory with any substantial right to oppose Colenso's views on the authority of the Pentateuch. It will be equally difficult to hold our ground against either materialism or against pantheism, if we

[101.] Ampleforth, Copy of letter, Ullathorne to Brown, 28 May 1863.

allow these new broached theories to have greater authority than universal tradition, and the unbroken catena of
interpretation. I have thrown up these rough and rudi-
mentary remarks, simply to show that it comes natural to
me to mistrust, and doubt if we need be so much afraid of
the so-called science of the hour, as to abandon the letter
of the Scriptural and Patristic account of the origin of
man, as formed corporally by God himself from the dust
of the earth.[102]

He was clearly absorbed with the implications of the new
science, and was not prepared either to reject it entirely or to
insist utterly on the traditional chronology of creation. Taking
up the science debate again only a week later, he asserted that
he 'by no means accept[ed] the *Rambler*'s reading of Galileo's
case',[103] and before the end of the year had issued a trenchant
pastoral letter warning of the dangers. 'The ceaseless deluge of
new books reveals the thoughts of many hearts. And how many
of those hearts are a prey to the return of the old pagan spirit,
which the Son of God became incarnate to destroy.'[104]
Ullathorne would never go against the traditional teaching of
the Church on creation as understood in his own day, but
could see that it was facing challenges from the new learning.
Victorian Christianity was functioning in a complex and radically changed context, not least due to the frequent and bloody
conflicts within the established Church itself. These could not
fail to affect the Catholic community and its leadership.

In 1845 and again in 1850–1, at the height of the Oxford
Movement, hopes had been raised in some circles of mass
conversions from the Church of England in the wake of
Newman and Manning. It was widely held (with some justifica-
tion) that Ullathorne thought that Wiseman and Walsh had
made far too much of the Church of England converts, and
that they needed a restraining hand. Wiseman had shared the
dissatisfaction of some of the converts with the rate of Catholic
revival in the 1840s, but Ullathorne was more cautious and had

102. Ibid.
103. Ampleforth, Copy of letter, Ullathorne to Brown, 7 June 1863.
104. Pastoral Letter, 19 November 1863.

a more pragmatic view of what might be achieved. He hoped that one benefit which might accrue to the Catholic Church in England from the Papal Aggression furore of late 1850 was that 'it has pressed the new and old elements of the Church in England more closely together and will impress in a salutary way the importance of adding caution to zeal upon our converts'.[105] More bluntly, he had confided to Brown that, 'It is time that the neophytes should not have everything their own way.'[106]

One of those encouraged by Wiseman's sanguine view of the future possibilities for reunion was Ambrose Phillips, a convert himself from the 1820s who medievalised his name to Ambrose Phillips de Lisle. He was one of the arch gothicisers of his generation and a close ally and friend of Augustus Welby Pugin, and wanted nothing less than the conversion of England and a complete restoration of English monasticism in his own lifetime. He built a Cistercian monastery on land near his Leicestershire home, Mount St Bernard's, where Ullathorne had preached at public ceremonies in 1843. Ullathorne remained a close friend of the family all his life, although he had little patience for the excesses of his friend, who pinned all hopes for the Catholic revival on the Oxford Movement.[107] In fairness, Ullathorne himself was not beyond pinning hopes on the actions of converts. In March 1851 he wrote delightedly to *Propaganda Fide*, not only that Edward Pusey (the mainstay of the Tractarian-influenced high churchmen in the Church of England) had failed to prevent the conversion of two Anglican clergymen whom he had just received, but reported with some glee the following exchange between Pusey and the two would-be converts: 'When they asked him where now was the true Church in England, they assure me he answered that it consisted in the new hierarchy and in the orthodox portion of the Anglican Bishops.' Ullathorne dismissed the last part of Pusey's statement as 'absurd' but, 'the admission regarding the hierarchy I consider

---

[105.] *Propaganda Fide*, Ullathorne to Fransoni, 2 December 1850.
[106.] L&D XII, p. 365, 6 December 1848.
[107.] E. S. Purcell, *Life and Letters of Ambrose Phillips de Lisle* (1900), II, p. 214.

of sufficient importance to communicate to your Eminence.'[108] To Ullathorne, such incidents illustrated the importance to England of the new hierarchy, but it is also the best possible illustration of English Catholic episcopal attitudes to the Oxford Movement. Tractarianism was useful in bringing Anglicans (especially clergymen) to the threshold of Rome, but any notion that there was anything Catholic in the Church of England was 'absurd'. In this respect Ullathorne was far more representative and influential than Wiseman.

Ullathorne's friend from Leicestershire, Ambrose Phillips de Lisle, was among those who maintained close contact with Anglican Oxford men. One of them was an Oxford graduate and an early alumnus of Cuddesdon Theological College, Frederick George Lee, who founded a periodical entitled *The Union*, devoted to advocating corporate reunion between Rome and Canterbury, to which Phillips de Lisle was a regular contributor. The journal encouraged moves towards corporate reunion, not individual conversion, and therein lay its difficulty.[109] Phillips de Lisle told both Wiseman and Cardinal Barnabo that the 'reunionists' were on the brink of a breakthrough, assuring a bemused Barnabo that two thousand Anglican clergymen and ten bishops supported them.[110]

Wiseman warned Barnabo of the dangers in what Phillips de Lisle and Lee were proposing, in talking of reunion of three 'branches' of the one Church.[111] Barnabo cooled quickly, especially when Wiseman spelt out the true extent of Anglican support for the notion, but Phillips de Lisle, Lee and Bishop Forbes of Brechin were not deterred from forming the Association for Promoting the Unity of Christendom in September 1857, with thirty-four initial members. It was widely regarded as harmless and ineffectual. No Catholic bishop joined, nor did any senior Anglican cleric and the older generation of the Oxford Movement were conspicuous by their absence. While it advocated no policy but prayer, it worried

[108.] *Propaganda Fide*, Ullathorne to Fransoni, 29 March 1851.
[109.] M. and B. Pawley, *Rome and Canterbury Through Four Centuries* (1975), p. 187.
[110.] Butler, *Life*, I, p. 337.
[111.] Wilfred Ward, *Life and Times of Cardinal Wiseman* (1897), pp. 480–5.

no-one and indeed Pius IX gave his blessing to one of the Anglican secretaries of the association who visited Rome to plead its cause.[112]

The difficulties began to arise, not so much from the APUC itself but from the material published in *The Union*. It was never intended to be the official organ of the association but under Lee's editorship was inevitably regarded as such. Its policy was described even by Lee's eulogistic biographer as 'uncompromising'.[113] Many leading Anglican high churchmen were unable to stomach it; Benson of Cowley withdrew his subscription, Liddon would not touch it and even J. M. Neale and Bishop Forbes of Brechin (a founder of APUC) feared its tone. Lee was unwise in his choice of correspondents, many of them being disaffected Anglicans or Catholics and even Forbes was provoked to describe one article as 'mischievous trash'.[114] *The Union* was replaced in 1862 by *The Union Review*, which at best has been described as 'lacking in taste and discretion'.[115] It became hostile to English Catholicism, offering a platform to disgruntled Catholics and thus causing distress to Phillips de Lisle. Increasingly it espoused the 'branch theory' of reunion in its articles and thus gave several causes for unease among the English Catholic hierarchy.[116] The last straw was a series of articles by a recent convert E. S. Ffoulkes, who eventually returned to the Church of England, under the title, *Experiences of a 'vert*.[117]

Ullathorne expressed the bishops' unease with the *Review* in a letter to the Archbishop of Dublin.

> Our annoyance in England at this moment is with the *Union Review*, the organ of the APUC. A certain number of laymen and even of priests have blindly formed this association and the *Review* itself has been opened for the contributions of discontented converts who are doing mischief by pouring out their conceits and their misconceptions of the Catholic spirit before that class of

[112.] M. and B. Pawley, pp. 191–2.
[113.] H. R. T. Brandreth, *Dr Lee of Lambeth* (1951), p. 90.
[114.] Ibid., p. 93.
[115.] M. and B. Pawley, p. 192.
[116.] Butler, *Life*, I, pp. 345–6.
[117.] Brandreth, p. 98.

Protestants who are nearest to the Church.[118]

The matter of the APUC and the *Union Review* was taken up by the bishops at their Low Week meeting of 1864 and the matter was referred to Rome.

The early historians of the ecumenical movement perpetuated the idea that, at this point, Wiseman's poor health gave Manning and the 'arch-Ultramontanes' chance to influence the hierarchy and prevail on Wiseman to change his opinion from the sympathetic and conciliatory tone he had used in his *Letter on Catholic Unity* in 1841. 'Cardinal Wiseman had been friendly to the project, but by 1864 had virtually become incapable of directing affairs, and more and more had passed into the unyielding hands of Dr Manning, a former Anglican but now a bitter enemy of the Church of England.'[119] This view was adopted from Wiseman's first biographer Wilfred Ward who asserted that Wiseman's original sympathy for the movement was overshadowed by 'the vigorous and resolute line of policy adopted by Manning and W. G. Ward'.[120] Butler agreed: 'Manning was looked on as the prime mover ... there is no direct evidence of his action at this time, but the charge was probably well founded.'[121] Ward quoted a letter from Lee to himself in which W. G. Ward, Manning and Ullathorne were blamed for taking the lead and overriding Wiseman.[122] However, Lee's assessment is undermined by his continued reliance on Wiseman's gentle words in favour of corporate reunion in 1841, while ignoring his much stronger statement of 1857. The Unionists had placed too much reliance on Wiseman's early sympathetic attitude, and in private correspondence he may have led them further than he intended and thus left problems for other bishops.[123] Schiefen

118. Dublin Archdiocesan Archives, Ullathorne to Archbishop of Dublin, 16 May 1864.
119. R. Rouse and S. C. Neill, *A History of the Ecumenical Movement 1517–1948* (1954), p. 279.
120. Ward, *Life*, II, p. 475.
121. Butler, *Life*, I, p. 349.
122. Ward, *Life*, II, p. 490.
123. VEC Talbot Papers, Ullathorne to Talbot, 17 December 1865, 'On consulting Dr Manning I was confirmed in my apprehension that though the late cardinal most certainly accepted the first decree, yet he might probably be committed by some earlier correspondence so far as to make it inexpedient to provoke retaliation by

argued strongly that, 'it is difficult to see where Wiseman had changed his basic approach ... His receptiveness to non-Catholics and his friendly relations with them had never led him to view their religious convictions with favour, except where these indicated an acceptance of Catholic doctrine or practice that, he supposed, would dispose them for eventual conversion.'[124]

It was, in fact, Wiseman himself who proposed placing the reunion question before the Holy See.[125] In the light of Wiseman's ill-health it was Ullathorne, as the most senior bishop, who handled the matter. Ullathorne and Rome took it seriously when he set out the Unionists' espousal of the branch theory, the use of the *Review* as a refuge for disaffected Catholics and the tendency to discourage individual conversions.[126] Barnabo immediately placed the matter before the Holy Office, as the affair touched on matters of doctrine; any ruling from that source carried greater gravity and authority. Ullathorne asked for guidance specifically on Catholic membership of APUC and Catholic priests offering Mass for its intention. In September 1864 the reply came back unequivocally.

> The fundamental principle on which it rests is of such a nature as utterly to subvert the Divine constitution of the Church ... That the faithful of Christ and even ecclesiastics should pray for Christian unity under the direction of heretics, and what is worse, according to an intention thoroughly defiled and infected with heresy, is a thing by no means to be tolerated ... The Catholic Church is therefore one by a unity conspicuous and perfect, embracing the whole earth and all nations ... Catholics, by belonging to this association, are the occasion of spiritual ruin to Catholics as well as to non-Catholics.[127]

publishing his letters to Phillips de Lisle or some other person, which were certainly not very decided in their tone on the subject of the condemnation.'

[124.] Schiefen, p. 334.
[125.] Butler, *Life*, I, p. 346.
[126.] M. and B. Pawley, p. 193.
[127.] *Letter on the Association for Promoting the Unity of Christendom* (1864) pp. 47–9.

The members of APUC were stunned, and at once set about drafting an appeal to Rome. Phillips de Lisle resigned his membership under obedience, but also under protest. Ullathorne lost no time in issuing his detailed letter on the subject to his own clergy, and a briefer Advent pastoral letter to the diocese, in which he accused the APUC of looking for a 'spurious unity'.[128] He referred only briefly to the mischief created by the *Union Review*, although this had brought the matter to a head, but dealt at length with the APUC's advocacy of the branch theory of the universal Church, which contradicted Catholic teaching on the visible unity of the Church, and rebutted the APUC claims of Catholic support. Lee and the leaders of the APUC believed they had been misrepresented at Rome,[129] and with that in mind, Lee visited Ullathorne on the very day of the publication of his pamphlet in November 1864. 'There was no question of repudiating the branch theory or claiming misunderstanding. Indeed he [Lee] volunteered the statement that my explanation of the idea of the Union as being a sort of confederation of three churches with the Pope as court of appeal in certain defined cases, was a direct representation of their plans.'[130] Thus Ullathorne had no fear of the outcome of the appeal, but did fear the continued mischief of Lee and the *Review*. 'It is their policy to represent the Catholics as being devoid of union as much as themselves, and to deter Anglicans in every way from entering the Church. Mr Lee's own principles are of a purely negative order.'[131] Ullathorne was keen to see a quick and decisive statement by the English Catholic bishops as an active expression of unity with the Holy See. In some agitation, he warned his friend Thomas Brown that his name and Wiseman's were being bandied about as regretting the condemnation by Rome.[132]

In February 1865, Wiseman died, though not before Phillips de Lisle had prevailed upon him for a deathbed interview about the Unionist appeal to Rome. It was the supposedly hostile

[128.] Pastoral Letter, 16 November 1864.
[129.] Brandreth, pp. 100–1.
[130.] VEC Talbot Papers, Ullathorne to Talbot, 24 November 1864.
[131.] Ibid.
[132.] Ampleforth, copy of letter Ullathorne to Brown, 12 November 1864.

Manning who carried the pointless APUC appeal to Rome, which argued that while it espoused the branch theory, there was no obligation on any Catholic member to do so.[133] When the inevitable response arrived, Ullathorne was almost gleeful, 'I have already got the reply of the Holy Office to the one hundred and eighty-nine appellants and was very much pleased with it. Nothing but the plainest terms will ever disabuse these men of the notion that their correspondence with Rome is not actual communion with the Holy See.'[134] His irritation with the APUC men continued, who he believed were (despite the condemnation) still doing 'great mischief' among Catholics.[135]

By the end of 1865, the most substantial and enduring piece of Anglican writing to come out of the whole sorry affair, Edward Pusey's *Eirenicon*, had already sold eight thousand copies.[136] Ullathorne was biding his time before writing further, but Newman was already at work on his *Letter to Dr Pusey*. Newman told Ullathorne that 'for the the first time he has some hope of him' (ie of Pusey's conversion to Rome).[137] Ullathorne's *Second Letter*, published in spring 1866, responded both to the APUC appeal and Pusey's *Eirenicon* and consisted of a lengthy exposition of Catholic teaching on the visible unity of the Church. He sent a copy to Pusey, who denied any involvement in the APUC and its plans, but insisted that he would continue to pray for organic union between Rome and Canterbury.[138] Any lingering hope that Ullathorne was more liberal than Manning, Talbot or Ward disappeared in the light of a letter written just after his second publication on the matter, in which he vented his spleen on 'the detestable heresy of the Church put forth by Dr Pusey in the *Eirenicon* ... I am disgusted at the way some Catholic writers have praised this book and have thought it high time to expose its abominable eclecticism and universalism'.[139] Butler rather prissily

[133.] Butler, *Life*, I, p. 348.
[134.] VEC Talbot Papers, Ullathorne to Talbot, 17 December 1865.
[135.] AAW Ullathorne Correspondence, Ullathorne to Manning, 23 June 1865.
[136.] VEC Talbot Papers, Ullathorne to Talbot, 17 December 1865.
[137.] Ibid.
[138.] DA Box 756, Pusey to Ullathorne, 12 April 1866.
[139.] VEC Talbot Papers, Ullathorne to Talbot, 19 March 1866.

expressed himself as 'pained' by Ullathorne's description to Manning of the *Eirenicon* as 'a vile Jansenistic document' and passed quickly on to compliment Ullathorne on his 'solid, careful, learned ... telling defence of the visibility of the Church and its visible unity as proclaimed in the Holy Office documents'.[140] Ullathorne's reputation for vigorous and intemperate language was not undeserved.

There is no doubt that the unity of the Church was Ullathorne's prime concern, and he was not persuaded by talk of organic union. In this he was at one with the other bishops, who were united and clear where they stood on Catholic understanding of the Church. No Catholic bishop would oppose prayer for the reunion of Christendom, but neither would he agree that Rome was one of three branches of an invisibly united Catholic Church. There were many issues which divided the English hierarchy, but this was not one of them. Ullathorne made it clear that to talk of factions in this connection was misleading. 'It is unfair and ungenerous to speak of doctrines as Ultramontane or as held by Ultramontanes which are universally held in the Catholic and Roman communion; thus leaving the effect of an insinuation that they are the doctrines of some party among us.'[141]

Ullathorne was becoming the acknowledged expert, not only on the workings of the Roman curial machinery, but on the organisation and canonical standing of convents. No sooner had he returned from his 'Australia' visit to Rome, than he was asked, in 1860, to arbitrate in the long-running property dispute over the convent of the Holy Child Jesus in Mayfield, Sussex. His enquiry lasted a year and was almost complete when he received a letter from Emily Bowes, a former member of the community, blackening Cornelia Connolly's name. He wrote personally to Thomas Grant, Bishop of Southwark, in whose territory the convent lay, 'Mrs C is a strange production, a woman who requires to be held with a strong hand. Rose water will not do with her.' Fearful of further trouble, he washed his hands of the matter and referred the whole matter

---

[140.] Butler, *Life*, I, p. 355.
[141.] *Second Letter*, p. 36.

to *Propaganda Fide* in a twenty-nine page report.[142] This was the clearest possible evidence that his support and encouragement of female religious was not uncritical or sentimental, but neither was he vindictive, and in 1881 the Sisters of the Holy Child Jesus opened a convent in Birmingham near the Oratory in order to teach in the parish schools.[143]

During the later 1850s the work of the nuns in the diocese began to make a real impact. The number of houses grew rapidly, and the commitment of the women religious to the educational and social needs of the community was legendary, so questions of constitutions, in order to give the foundations legal status and internal regulation became more significant. These required the co-operation and approval of Rome, and would determine the shape and conduct of the next generations of nuns, as well as giving them an independent and clear identity, free of undue interference from clergy or lay patrons. Margaret Hallahan went to Rome in autumn 1858, accompanied by Imelda Poole (later her successor as superior of the Order) and James Spencer Northcote, who, of course, knew Rome well. The purpose of the visit was to obtain formal approval for her Congregation's constitutions, and thereby secure its permanence and its membership of the Dominican Order.[144] Ullathorne's continued poor health prevented him from accompanying the party, but he commended them to the care of Mgr George Talbot, the influential Englishman in the Roman Curia, who handled all English business.[145] Talbot found the little party suitable accommodation and steered them through the complexities of Vatican bureaucracy.[146] Although the little party spent a good deal of time visiting the churches and holy places of Rome, especially those associated with St Dominic and St Catherine, the process through *Propaganda Fide* was tedious.[147] They left for England after Christmas without the matter of the constitutions finally

142. Michael Clifton, *The Quiet Negotiator: Bishop Grant of Southwark* (1993), p. 45.
143. L&D XXIX, p. 404, 1 August 1881.
144. Drane, *Life*, p. 416.
145. VEC Talbot Papers, Ullathorne to Talbot, 12 October 1858.
146. Drane, *Life*, pp. 419–21.
147. Ibid., pp. 421–7.

concluded, but the documentation followed soon after, which approved the creation of the Congregation of St Catherine of Siena, with Margaret Hallahan as Prioress Provincial, under the direction of the Master General of the Dominicans, who delegated his authority personally to Ullathorne for life.[148]

Ullathorne's understanding of the fragility of female religious life and the urgent need for properly drawn up constitutions was exemplified in his treatment of the Sisters of Charity of St Paul, founded in England by Genevieve Dupuis in 1847. Although the mother house was in his diocese, the sisters came under the government of the bishop of each diocese in which they operated. He was concerned that this left them exposed in conflicts with priests who did not understand religious life, and with 'no ecclesiastical authority or advice to have recourse to this side of Rome itself'. 'When the sisters are in other houses', explained Ullathorne, 'I never interfere, they are under the jurisdiction of the Diocesan. But when they return to the mother house, or are recalled, they then come under the jurisdiction of Birmingham.'[149]

By 1861 the English foundation had twenty-six houses in England, seven of them in the Diocese of Birmingham, as well as the mother house in Banbury, and had applied to Rome for approval of the constitutions. The application failed, but Ullathorne took advice from his old friend Barnabo at *Propaganda Fide* and counselled caution, suggesting an application only for the approval of the Congregation, while he returned to England and helped them formulate the Rule more carefully. The matter dragged on until finally in March 1864 the Congregation was approved, 'bearing in mind the commendation of the Bishop of Birmingham, and persuaded that this new society is likely to produce much good in the Church'.[150]

Interestingly, the two points on which Rome expressed unease and which Ullathorne took seriously, related to the relationship between the local bishop and the jurisdiction of the superioress, and is indicative of the care he took in all cases to ensure proper independence but also appropriate support

---

148. Ibid., p. 440.
149. Mgr Hudson, *Mother Genevieve Dupuis* (1929), p. 218.
150. Ibid., qu. p. 211.

for the superior. Carefully guiding Mother Dupuis through the detailed critique of the constitutions given by Rome, he expressed real concern that the constitutions as framed would leave the superior at the mercy of clergy who, 'from ignorance of what religious life requires, cause affliction and distress to the sisters and imperil the establishments'.[151] He had seen plenty of examples of this, and was still conscious of the unhappy foundation of Cornelia Connolly's Holy Child convent and the disputes with Fr Sing in Derby. At the same time he was sternly urging Mother Juliana Hardman, the superior of the Sisters of Mercy at Handsworth, not to commit herself to decisions made by a majority of superioresses, and even warned her that he would not sanction anything which undermined her independence.[152] Always conscious of the autonomy of each convent and the superior's independence from the bishop, on another occasion he reminded her briskly that when the majority of the community had voted against an individual's profession, 'it requires no further authority to intimate to her that her religious life has ceased, and all that has then to be done is to report the fact to the bishop'.[153] Revealingly, Ullathorne betrayed his personal opinion, that religious life was preferable to marriage for women, condemning any notion of temporary vows. If a women left religious life after a period in temporary vows, he was convinced that the contrast they would feel between religious life and married life, 'would make the lives of most of them wretched'.[154] This was an echo of his forthright suggestion in the early 1850s that the freedom of religious life was infinitely preferable to the lottery and bondage which women entered into in the marriage market.

On Mother Dupuis' return from Rome in 1864 with the papal approval of her constitutions, she found that Ullathorne had acquired property in Selly Park near Birmingham to be the new mother house. This would fulfil his ambition that the sisters be based in the city itself, at the heart of the diocese. He had

[151.] Selly Park, Ullathorne to Genevieve Dupuis, 26 March 1864.
[152.] Handsworth, 27 February 1864.
[153.] Handsworth, 8 December 1865.
[154.] Selly Park, Ullathorne to Genevieve Dupuis, 14 February 1864.

Scarborough from Plantation Hill (1822). (North Yorkshire County Council)

Scarborough Harbour in the early nineteenth century. (North Yorkshire County Council)

Ullathorne's mother, Hannah.
(Archbishop's House, Birmingham)

Ullathorne's father, William.
(Archbishop's House, Birmingham)

Ullathorne as a young man, before entering the monastery at
Downside. (Archbishop's House, Birmingham)

The monastic buildings at Downside, showing the original church and the 'Old House'.
(Downside Abbey)

Ship in full sail passing Sydney Heads
(Joseph Fowles 1810–1878). (National Library of Australia)

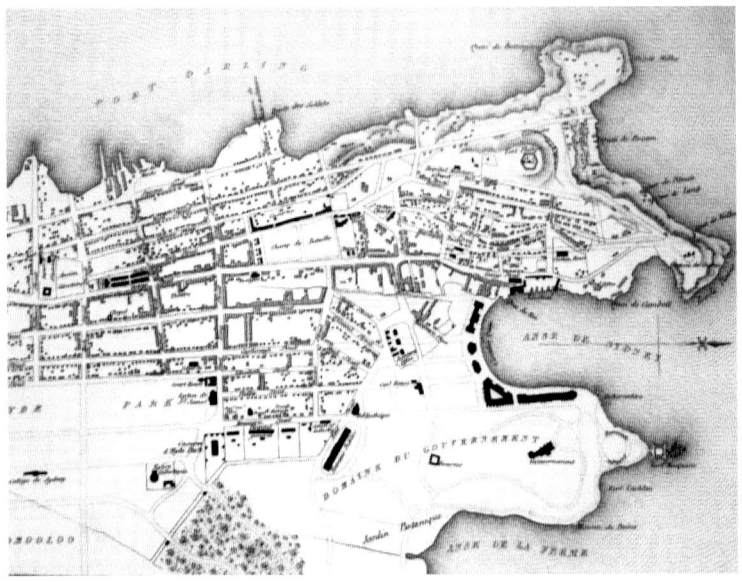

Plan de la ville de Sydney (Paris: Gide 1841).
(National Library of Australia)

Norfolk Island: the convict system (1847).
(National Library of Australia)

Catholic Chapel, Hyde Park (Robert Russell 1808–1900). Built
during Ullathorne's time in Australia, this became St Mary's
Cathedral. (National Library of Australia)

Ullathorne portrayed by Fidanza of Rome (1842).
(Oscott College)

The face of a longcase clock showing the church of St Osburg,
Coventry. (Archbishop's House, Birmingham)

Ullathorne as a newly consecrated bishop in the late 1840s.
(Oscott College)

The head of Ullathorne's crozier, with an ivory carving of the
Virgin and Child in the centre. (St Chad's Cathedral,
Birmingham)

Ullathorne's pectoral cross: a medieval cross worn by the last
Abbot of Croyland before the dissolution of the monasteries.
(Oscott College)

Portrait of Ullathorne in 1852 by Richard Burchett.
(Downside Abbey)

Detail of a window in St Dominic's Church at Stone,
commemorating Mother Margaret Hallahan OP.
(St Dominic's Convent, Stone)

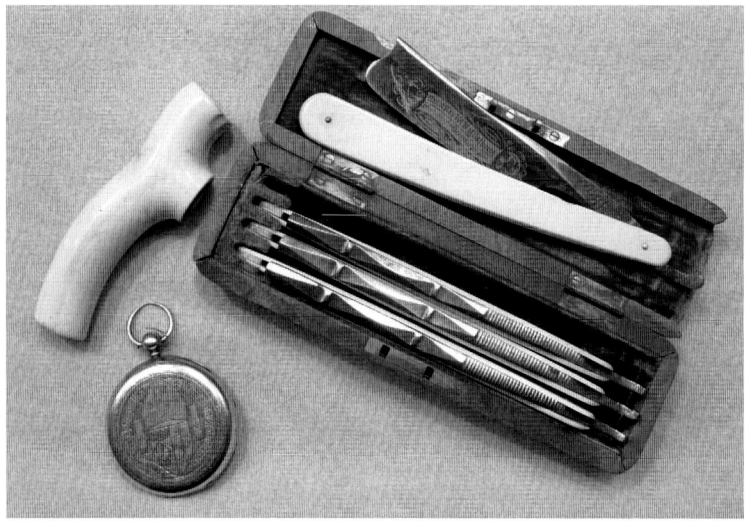

Personal items belonging to Ullathorne: his pocket watch,
razors and the ivory head of his walking stick. (Oscott College)

Bishop's House, Birmingham, designed by A. W. Pugin
in 1841. (*Dublin Review* vol. XII February 1842)

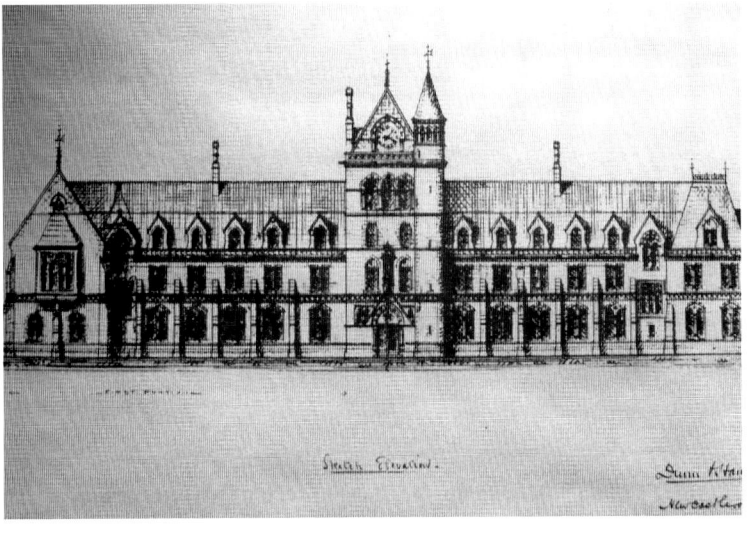

Edward Hansom's design for the seminary at Olton, of which
only the section to the left of the main entrance was built
(1871). (Olton Friary)

Ullathorne's passport, showing his last foreign journey on 19 November 1869, to attend the first Vatican Council.
(Oscott College)

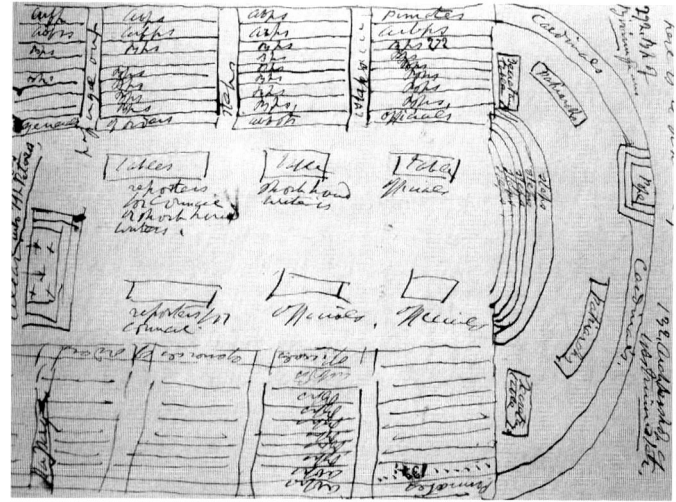

Ullathorne's own sketch of the seating arrangements at the Vatican Council, with his own seat number (272) and that of the Archbishop of Westminster (134) noted in the corner.
(Colwich Abbey Archives)

Photograph of the missing portrait by John Pettie (1871)
which was exhibited at the Royal Academy and the Paris
International Exhibition, but may have been sold in the 1890s
to an unknown owner. (Oscott College)

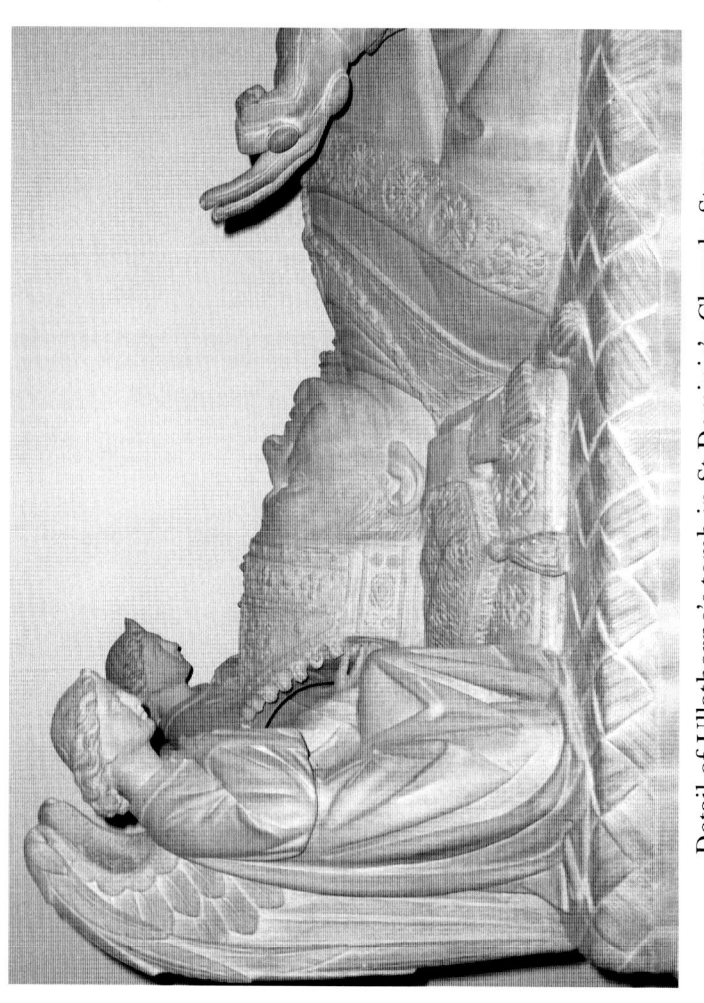

Detail of Ullathorne's tomb in St Dominic's Church, Stone.
(St Dominic's Convent, Stone)

considered the possibility of land close to Oscott's Holdford Farm, but in the end the financial deal available at Selly Park was better, so sentiment did not get in the way.[155] In September, the move to Birmingham was completed. Ullathorne preached at the opening of the temporary chapel on 29 September and showed his appreciation and human kindness by appointing Fr Tandy (their original friend and protector in Banbury) as chaplain, and leaving him with the nuns till his death in 1886. Selly Park, as Ullathorne predicted in his homily, became the heart of the enterprise which spread all over the country and eventually to many parts of the world, but which always had a special place and role in the Diocese of Birmingham. Speculating what Selly Park might be in ten or even in fifty years time, he warned that it would be what those sitting in front of him would make it, by being 'fervent, exact, faithful to your Rule' or alternatively, 'negligent and careless' in which case they would 'frustrate the work of God in this place'.[156]

Selly Park was not the only convent building project he was overseeing in the early 1860s, for Stone and Stanbrook were also putting down deep roots in the Midland soil. The 'new' hierarchy was now in its second decade and Catholicism was rapidly becoming a settled (if not always welcome) part of the landscape of England and Wales, not only metaphorically but literally too. Ullathorne celebrated this in his Advent pastoral letter of 1860, in which he commended

> the great co-operation of all people, priests and bishop in rebuilding the Church. We have succeeded to the inheritance delivered to the saints, we have entered upon the field of their labours, which the God who has rewarded their exertions has delivered up to ours. To rebuild the temples that have fallen from the Church, to restore the sacrifice where its oblation had long ceased, to revive the word of God, where the sound of its truth had been extinguished, to gather the lost sheep into the one fold of the good Shepherd; is it possible to to imagine any work more glorious? As the work of re-creation is more difficult

155. Ibid.
156. Selly Park, Homily, 29 September 1864.

than the work of first creation, so is it a more difficult work than our Fathers had in planting the Church upon our soil, for us to raise it anew from the ashes ... It is like the work of raising up the dead, a work which advances by miracles of grace. Slowly, and one by one, the sheep are brought into the fold. Essentially is the English mission, in its very nature, a laborious mission, demanding for its success the most steady faith and constant perseverance, and an endurance undaunted by the number of disappointments encountered, or by the slowness of the success secured.[157]

The building of Catholic churches and institutions went on at a remarkable pace and the convents were among the most striking and unusual, provoking curiosity and hostility. Their substantial presence in town and country, however, indicated that female religious life had a presence and an identity which was permanent, and Ullathorne encouraged building for the long term wherever possible. His interest in the convents was not only spiritual but practical and he often actively oversaw the building projects. In the summer of 1862, the new church at Stone 'requires attention from time to time. I shall probably be there again next week as the chancel is just at the critical point when it requires careful superintendence'.[158] His practical turn of mind was always brought to bear, at times with unwitting hilarity, as in the solemn advice he gave to Stanbrook a decade later about their new conventual buildings, to be wary of flat roofs, prefer slates rather than tiles and to by mindful of the positioning of drains, gas connections and the drafts of chimneys, where 'the best architects often fail'.[159]

It was not only convents which were expanding and building, but parochial missions too, which depended on the continued financial support of the laity. Following the unhappy confusion over the Earl of Shrewsbury's will, Ullathorne's preference was for general appeals and hard cash rather than endowments by wealthy individuals which might or

---

[157.] Pastoral Letter, 21 November 1860.
[158.] Colwich, Ullathorne to Prioress, 4 August 1862.
[159.] Stanbrook 37, Ullathorne to Abbess, 13 September 1876.

might not appear or might be discontinued without notice. He had learnt the virtue of patience in governing the diocese and building on secure foundations. 'A real ruler, wise and far-seeing, of course checks the impetuosity of the impatient and lets short-sighted remarks go by and sustains the work on its own principles, until at last everybody discovers in the result that wisdom has been at work.' The greatest fallacy in government was to 'kill the goose instead of waiting till the eggs are mature; it is to draw the bread from the oven before it is duly baked; it is to meddle with and choke the fountain, instead of being contented with the stream it can normally give forth.'[160] In other words, patient, steady consolidation was the way forward in building up God's Church. His policy was clearly beginning to bear fruit, as Estcourt was able to give him reassuring news of the financial position by 1863, suggesting that they could even congratulate themselves on the current position. Although there was still a large debt on the diocesan account of £7,440, the capital fund had increased from £6,000 to £11,000. There was though, further evidence of Ullathorne's own frugality of life, in that he had only £76. 4s. 9d in his personal account, despite an income of £700, most of which went on episcopal or diocesan expenses, including the visits to Rome.[161]

Reflecting on Benedictine matters and on leadership and authority, believing patience to be an essential quality, which he was learning himself with difficulty, he mused that monasticism was best calculated to form strong, patient and solid characters.

> Such solid characters, freed from restless fancies and heated anticipations of future employment, are precisely those who are most fitted to undertake any future works, however arduous or delicate, that may be committed to them.

Surely thinking of his twenty-six-year-old self in Australia, he said,

160. Ampleforth 244/186, Ullathorne to President General, 23 October 1863.
161. BAA B4212 Estcourt to Ullathorne, 3 September 1863.

Hence when the Church has had great and new works to accomplish, it has often passed over those ahead in career, and presumptively the most experienced, and has sought out the fittest men from among those who had done nothing except in their stable conventual life, to accumulate light and discipline themselves into patience and self control, and then sent them to missionarize a new country ... The most perfect monk is he who thinks of nothing but making himself a perfect monk. And this most perfect monk will turn up the most perfect missioner, by the confession of all men, when ever the voice of authority calls him to it.[162]

This is an indication, not that Ullathorne thought himself 'the perfect missioner', but that, at last, he had finally become reconciled to the task of being a bishop, called by 'the voice of authority'.

His patient, steady consolidation was producing the fruits for which he hoped, giving him cause for contentment. By the end of 1865, fifteen years after the restoration of the hierarchy, Ullathorne did allow himself a little pride and recorded publicly that there were twice as many chapels than in 1843 when Walsh and Wiseman had first started regular collections for the Mission Fund. In 1843 there had been eighty-eight priests in the four counties of the present diocese; now there were a hundred and forty-two, serving ninety-six missions instead of sixty-eight. The number of schools had more than doubled from thirty-nine to eighty-five, and while Handsworth had been the only convent of active nuns in 1843, there were now twenty-one similar houses.[163] He also had another very personal reason to be content by the end of 1865.

[162.] Ampleforth 244/186, Ullathorne to President General, 23 October 1863.
[163.] Pastoral Letter, 22 November 1865.

Chapter 7

Public Affairs and Private Griefs
1865–1870

As Wiseman's health deteriorated through 1864, there was inevitably speculation about who would succeed him at Westminster. There was talk of a new coadjutor (perhaps even Ullathorne), and wild suggestions that George Errington, who had been removed as coadjutor after a furious row with Wiseman,[1] could claim the succession, though he clearly, 'never entertained the notion'.[2] The moment Wiseman died in February 1865, the plotting and whispering in England and Rome began in earnest. Ullathorne evidently agreed with the view expressed by Dr Neve, rector of the English College in Rome, that what the English bishops needed was 'a dignified ecclesiastic, neither connected with the courts nor president of the college, but free and independent, to represent the English episcopacy. This I have always thought'.[3] It was, of course, not impossible that Ullathorne, the longest serving of the bishops and still less than sixty years old, would be nominated himself.

In 1850 the appointment of Wiseman had allegedly taken place with the compliance of the British government, although his letter *From out of the Flaminian Gate* had given rise to misgivings in political circles. His dealings with the government had never been comfortable, and it was often Thomas Grant of

[1.] For the Errington problem, see Schiefen, pp. 298–302.
[2.] Ampleforth, Copy of letter Ullathorne to Brown, 26 February 1864.
[3.] Ibid.

Southwark who handled tricky negotiations on behalf of the hierarchy.[4] By 1865 political conditions had changed dramatically, both in terms of Anglo-papal relations and in domestic dealings between the administration and the Catholic Church. This meant that government interest in the appointment of Wiseman's successor was considerable, and Odo Russell, the nephew of Lord John Russell (now Foreign Secretary, previously Prime Minister during the Papal Aggression controversy) had been dispatched to Rome as a special envoy in the late 1850s to report on papal affairs to Whitehall.

The Foreign Secretary told his nephew as soon as Wiseman had died that the government were 'rather uneasy here about the succession to Cardinal Wiseman. A very pompous announcement of a successor might raise a flame here, and be detrimental not only to our design of doing full justice to the Roman Catholic Church, but to the Roman Catholic Church itself'.[5] A repetition of 1850 would not be helpful to anyone concerned. Government policy was influenced, not only by its wish to have a malleable spokesman for the Catholics, but by its support for the Italian nationalist cause, and its unwillingness therefore to have vocal opposition from the leader of the English Catholics. Ullathorne had already made his attitude to government policy clear in a published speech on the Pontifical States in 1860, in which he spoke scathingly of 'the British Lion' and the Emperor Napoleon colluding in 'a plan for separating a third of the Pope's dominions from their lawful sovereign'.[6]

The government's preference, not surprisingly, was for Thomas Grant, Bishop of Southwark, to 'quietly extend his spiritual influence over London' and there was no enthusiasm for Ullathorne who was regarded as 'a very injudicious man, capable of putting forward claims which would rouse resistance and indignation in every part of England'.[7] Odo Russell did as

---

[4.] Michael Clifton, *The Quiet Negotiator: Thomas Grant of Southwark* (1993), Chapters 6–8.

[5.] Noel Blakiston (ed.), *The Roman Question: extracts from the despatches of Odo Russell from Rome 1858–70* (1962), p. 308.

[6.] *A Speech on the Question of the Pontifical States* (1860), pp. 17–18.

[7.] Blakiston, *The Roman Question*, p. 308 Grant was a familiar figure to government ministers, due to his responsibilities for obtaining support for military and prison chaplaincy.

he was bid and had a quiet word with Papal Secretary of State, Cardinal Giacomo Antonelli, conveying Her Majesty's Government's view of Ullathorne's unsuitability, but he reported back that among the expatriates in Rome, 'Dr Ullathorne appears to have the largest number of adherents among his countrymen'.[8]

As well as a national appointment, the Archbishop of Westminster was also a diocesan bishop, with local responsibilities. The Westminster Chapter would naturally be consulted on their view about the succession, and John Morris, who had been Wiseman's secretary, and a canon of the chapter, was busy machinating and gossiping about the prospects. Morris was an Eton and Cambridge educated convert, who had been ordained in Rome in 1849. After a period as vice rector of the English College in Rome, he had hoped to join the Jesuits, but in 1861, Wiseman took him on as private secretary, where his influence was considerable. He did eventually become a Jesuit and a major figure in their scholarly institutions, before retiring to be postulator for the cause of the canonisation of the English Martyrs.[9]

Morris too, in 1865, knew that Ullathorne must be in the running, and was both hostile and dismissive about the possibility, declaring it 'extremely unlikely that Dr Ullathorne will be mentioned. I shall be surprised if he gets a single vote'.[10] Morris's snobbish and gossipy letters to the unpredictable George Talbot, the English agent in Rome, were full of venom towards Ullathorne and reveal something of the negative reputation which he had gained in certain clerical circles.

> I hear that Dr Ullathorne declares that he will not accept if it is offered to him, and I confess that I hope that it may not be him the Holy See will send. He is an excellent bishop and I have a very great respect for him ... but he seems to me to have all the faults of a self educated man. I may be quite misinformed but I have the impression that he carries centralisation to as great an extreme as the

[8.] Ibid., p. 309.
[9.] Gillow, vol. V, pp. 122–30.
[10.] VEC Talbot Papers, Morris to Talbot, 4 March 1865.

cardinal set the opposite policy. For instance, I have heard that it is said that (say) a convent of nuns shall first be humiliated and knocked into submission, and then encouraged into reformation after his own fashion. I should be very sorry to see our clergy or our religious put through this discipline ... Dr Ullathorne again carries his idea of episcopal power and position very far, and in this respect ... I mean he is a singular contrast to the Cardinal. In his great love of secrecy, he has much in common with Dr Clifford ... in Dr Ullathorne it always seems to me to spring from a painfully exaggerated sense of dignity. Of Bishop Clifford ... better far to have him ... than have Dr Ullathorne dropping his h's in London.[11]

According to Morris's gossip, the only thing worse than Ullathorne dropping his h's in London was the possibility of Archbishop Errington returning to the scene of his devastating rift with Wiseman. The clergy, he reckoned,

have a great dread of Dr Ullathorne, but that they would have a much greater dread of Dr E ... For the others, I think I am getting to like the thought of Dr Ullathorne more and Dr Clifford less ... Dr U's principles are better than these, though he did make a wonderful, unconscious mistake about Oxford.[12]

It is perhaps not surprising that Ullathorne's own comment to Manning was that what Westminster needed was, 'a man who, sound in principles, will combine a firm with a conciliatory spirit'.[13]

Despite Morris's dismissal of Ullathorne's suitability for Westminster, Barnabo, his oldest friend in Rome and now Cardinal Prefect of *Propaganda Fide*, was very keen to see him appointed. Although Ullathorne's name may have been much talked of (not surprisingly, given his seniority and public

[11.] VEC Talbot Papers, Morris to Talbot, 18 March 1865.
[12.] VEC Talbot Papers, Morris to Talbot, 1 April 1865 (For the Oxford business see pp. 308–16).
[13.] AAW Ullathorne Correspondence, Ullathorne to Manning, 1 April 1865.

standing) and had support in Rome, he was not, it seems, a serious contender in the minds of the Westminster Chapter or the other bishops. He was too outspoken and too insistent that government be kept at a distance, and the possibility of a monk Archbishop of Westminster seemed remote at that point in Catholic history. It is possible that his determined attempt to resign only three years earlier may also have put him out of the running in other people's minds. The appointment in the end was a surprise one, determined by the Pope's anger at the way in which the English hierarchy handled the matter. Ullathorne's own recollection of what he called the 'curious history' of the succession was set out to his old friend Thomas Brown many years later, long after the dust had settled.

He recalled that three names (Errington, Grant and Clifford) were presented by the Westminster Chapter to the bishops. The bishops sent them to Rome as the 'terna' exactly as presented by the Chapter, since they felt it would be inappropriate and invidious for them to pass judgement or comment on fellow bishops. The fly in the ointment was that, unknown to the other bishops, the diffident Grant had induced Clifford to join him in writing a letter to Rome renouncing any possible appointment for either of them. The Pope, not understanding or appreciating the delicacy of the bishops' reasons for not giving an opinion on the names offered, combined with the Grant/Clifford letter putting themselves out of contention, thought he was being set up. This provoked him to set aside the terna, 'being very indignant and thinking it was a scheme to force the appointment of Archbishop Errington whom he had removed from Westminster as coadjutor *cum juris successionis*'. However, Ullathorne also thought that the 'grave rebuke' issued to the bishops was as much to do with the college question as the Westminster succession, and did not take it too seriously.[14] No other names were asked for, and Manning, who had received one vote in the chapter was appointed.[15]

Manning's appointment was, as Newman recognised, 'a stunning compliment to the converts'[16] and Ullathorne reported a

[14.] AAW Ullathorne Correspondence, Ullathorne to Manning, 23 April 1865.

[15.] Ampleforth, Copy of letter Ullathorne to Brown, 21 July 1879.

[16.] Sheridan Gilley, *Newman and His Age* (1990), p. 338.

distinct lifting of his own spirits. The government reaction was less light-hearted; the Prime Minister, Palmerston, did not like Manning's appointment, although it was recognised that he was at least 'preferable to Dr Ullathorne in every respect'. The government drew comfort from the likelihood that 'Dr Manning will give the Roman Catholics far more trouble and annoyance than he can ever give to HM Government'.[17]

With huge delight at the beginning of May, Ullathorne began a letter to Manning with the words, 'My dear Archbishop Elect'. He gave a strong impression that Manning's appointment had come as a surprise to him, and mildly rebuked him for letting him read it in the press, while insisting that the Pope 'could not have done much better'. Ullathorne had a fierce determination throughout his life to stand apart from the ecclesiastical gossip machine, but he could not always ignore it. He knew that his own name was being whispered, and told Manning quite openly of his huge relief at escaping the task.

> I was descending on the station platform at Coventry yesterday morning when Mr Hansom [his architect friend] came up and put the *Star* newspaper into my hand. When I read the announcement I broke into a little laugh, and suddenly found a sort of lightening and expansion of the breast which proved to me that I had been for some days under an unconscious pressure of care.[18]

The new Archbishop took graciously both Ullathorne's some-what blundering self-absorption in responding to Manning's appointment, and his inability to resist acting the elder states-man and offering advice. Manning's reply set the tone for the next twenty years of close amity and co-operation; determined to ignore the tactlessness and keep Ullathorne on his side, he wrote the next day to 'My dear Lord and dear Friend, for so you have always been, and I trust always will be, for I could

[17.] Blakiston, *The Roman Question*, pp. 314–5.
[18.] AAW Ullathorne Correspondence, Ullathorne to Manning, 10 May 1865.

only lose your friendship by being unworthy of it.' He had been convinced that Ullathorne himself would be appointed, having pressed his case personally with Wiseman and in Rome.[19] For days, therefore, he had believed his own letter of appointment to be an error, and, when it became clear that it was not, wrote warmly of his reliance on their mutual confidence and friendship.[20]

Ullathorne's relationship with Manning was a complex one, often marked by disagreements, but equally characterised by respect and affection. It was not, as one Manning biographer has suggested, 'born in conflict'.[21] Their paths must have crossed soon after Manning became a Catholic in 1852, and by 1862, Manning was writing with great tact and modesty to compliment Ullathorne on his letter to the Birmingham clergy on *The Rambler*, in which he had dealt strongly with the 'highly mischievous' liberal school of thought. This letter already reflected a degree of confidence between the two men and is signed (as every letter between them over the next four decades) 'yours affectionately'.[22] They developed a friendship which grew out of shared views on a number of issues and an appreciation of each other's published writings on public affairs. In particular, they shared a common approach to the proponents of corporate reunion between Rome and Canterbury under the Association for Promoting the Unity of Christendom, and shared concern about the threat of Fenianism to English and Irish Catholic life.

Ullathorne built on Manning's confidence in urging him to have his episcopal consecration in London rather than Rome, and to take action to repair the coldness between himself and Newman, though advised against offering him an episcopal honour at this point.[23] Manning's invitation to Ullathorne to be the chief celebrant at his episcopal ordination sealed their confi-

---

[19.] Robert Gray, *Cardinal Manning: a biography* (1985), pp. 189–90.
[20.] AAW Ullathorne Correspondence, Manning to Ullathorne, 11 May 1865.
[21.] Gray, p. 185.
[22.] AAW Ullathorne Correspondence, Manning to Ullathorne, 28 October 1862.
[23.] AAW Ullathorne Correspondence, Ullathorne to Manning, 12–18 May 1865.

dence and gave public expression to it.[24] Theirs was not necessarily a smooth or easy relationship, though one of great warmth and respect. Manning often invited him to stay at Archbishop's House during the bishops' Low Week meeting, but perpetually sensitive to the possible misinterpretation of his closeness to Manning, and aware that the other bishops might suspect private plotting, he just as frequently declined the invitation to share Manning's table.[25] Ullathorne always stayed with his cousin, Owen Longstaff.[26] He often accepted Manning's invitation on other occasions and their conversations bore rich fruit in both Westminster and Birmingham. Years later, Ullathorne commented of Manning to a mutual friend, that he 'is one of those whose brain never rests, and who is always driving at one object or another with a certain vehemence'.[27] One of the objects at which he drove, and on which they differed in approach, was a solution to the Irish problem.

Following the collapse of the Irish popular rising in the 'year of revolutions' (1848) the hopes of building on Catholic Emancipation to create a united Irish voice at Westminster came to nought. During the 1850s the failure to create a cross party Irish block vote in Parliament played into the hands of the Irish bishops, who thought that alliance with one or other of the parties was the way to stability and the advancement of Irish Catholic interests. This policy was dominated by Paul Cullen, Archbishop of Dublin from 1851 and rector of the Irish College in Rome during the revolutionary period of 1848–9, who was prepared to work with any party to get what he wanted for the Church. He was rabidly anti-revolutionary, and his Roman experience sealed in him a fierce distaste for radical politics and its accompanying secularism. 'If the overthrow of the Pope and the murder of priests was where secular nationalism led, then Cullen wanted no part of it.'[28] This applied to all

24. AAW Ullathorne Correspondence, Manning to Ullathorne, 22 May 1865.
25. AAW Ullathorne Correspondence, Ullathorne to Manning, 18 April 1868. This was reiterated in 1869 (27 March 1869).
26. BAA B8215, Ullathorne to his sister, 25 June 1883.
27. College Irlandais Paris, Ullathorne to Kathleen O'Meara, 9 January 1878.
28. Colin Barr, *Paul Cullen, John Henry Newman, and the Catholic University of Ireland 1845–65* (2003), p. 137.

such movements, but especially to Fenianism. Cullen was a
fierce nationalist himself and passionately anti-British, believing colonial rule without doubt to be the source of Ireland's
misery. He was shaped in his politics by O'Connell, but would
have no truck with the secular, revolutionary nationalism of
Young Ireland and the Fenians. Newman's friendship with
Frederick Lucas, who supported Irish nationalism, especially
after he moved *The Tablet* to Dublin, was a major factor in
Newman's failure in Cullen's Catholic University project in the
1850s.[29] Whig government support for Italian revolutionaries
and the idealisation of Garibaldi was so offensive to Irish and
English Catholics that it even drove Cullen and Wiseman to
support the Tories in 1859. However, this alliance was short
lived, as Cullen distrusted English Catholics, believing them
unreliable on Irish affairs, especially those who threw their lot
in with the Tories.[30]

The main Fenian organisation, the Irish Republican
Brotherhood was founded in 1858 in Dublin, adopting the
republican ideas of Wolfe Tone and aimed at national independence. By 1860, at least one MP was calling for a return to an
Irish parliament,[31] and the Brotherhood was prepared to use
force if necessary.[32] Fenianism in the 1860s presented a political and religious threat to the Irish Church, competing with it
for influence over the mass of rural and urban working class
people, challenging the Church's political voice and calling for
separation of church and state.[33] This suggestion threatened
the very heart of the relationship between the Church and the
Irish people, by weakening religious influence in politics. To
the bishops, it was vital to keep the link in order to temper the
largely Protestant government of Catholic Ireland, and they
opposed Fenianism as much as the political leadership did, for
their own reasons. The inherent anticlericalism in the revolutionary movement, its attempt to be non-denominational and
its secrecy also fuelled the Church's antagonism.

---

[29] Ibid., pp. 139–42.
[30] Oliver Rafferty, *The Church, the State and the Fenian Threat 1861–5* (1999), p. 20.
[31] Ibid.
[32] J. Hickey, *Urban Catholics* (1967), p. 145.
[33] Rafferty, p. 21.

During the early 1860s, Ullathorne corresponded with Cullen about secret societies and their dangers. Catholic based associations for mutual support and the common good were commonplace in England, especially within the Irish diaspora. 'From the 1860s, Church-inspired organisations increasingly became a mainstay of the community's social life, organising teas, balls and dances; putting on lectures, readings and theatre; building reading rooms and libraries; organising day trips and excursions.'[34] Ullathorne was not worried about this sort of thing, or about the Oddfellows or Society of Foresters, but had some concerns about the Brothers of St Patrick, who at least were 'not numerous here' and even more about the Hibernian Society, which had about a dozen members in the Potteries.[35] He still seemed fairly relaxed about the presence of Fenians who were few in number, while complimenting Cullen on his anti-Fenian pastoral letter,[36] but he did not think that Cullen was the best judge of what was expedient in England regarding Fenians.[37]

Fenianism certainly became a political, religious and social issue in England in the later 1860s, as Irish Catholicism became a hot political potato again. Public opinion and foreign policy was sympathetic to the nationalist struggles in Italy, which had become profoundly anti Catholic and anti-papal. However, support for revolutionary nationalism did not extend to the Irish situation, and neither politicians nor onlookers (including Catholic Tories) were greatly concerned about economic and political conditions in Ireland, until Fenianism broke onto the English scene. Groups affiliated to the Irish Republican Brotherhood were formed in London, and it spread rapidly in the UK, until by 1865 it was estimated to have 80,000 members, and was publishing *The Irish Liberator*.[38] By 1865 there was talk of an armed rising in

[34.] Donald M. MacRaild, *Irish Migrants in Modern Britain 1750–1922* (1999), p. 96.

[35.] Dublin Archdiocesan Archives, Ullathorne to Archbishop Cullen, 16 October 1862.

[36.] Dublin Archdiocesan Archives, Ullathorne to Archbishop Cullen, 28 March 1864.

[37.] AAS Ullathorne Papers, Ullathorne to Grant, 7 April 1866.

[38.] Lynn Hollen Lees, *Exiles of Erin: Irish Migrants in Victorian London* (1979), p. 232.

Ireland and England, which finally materialised in 1867, resulting in the capture and imprisonment of many Fenian leaders. In February, a thousand Fenians descended on Chester, proclaiming a provisional government and an Irish republic, signalling an attempted co-ordinated rising in Ireland. The plan collapsed, as did the associated rising in Kerry,[39] but there were Fenian sympathisers in many of the Irish communities in the industrial towns of Britain and a number were prepared to take action, despite a clear statement from the English bishops that no Fenian could receive sacramental absolution unless he left the Brotherhood.[40] An attempt to blow a hole in Clerkenwell prison to free Fenian prisoners led to fifteen deaths and a hundred injuries, and the execution of the 'Manchester martyrs' – three men who had tried to free the Fenian prisoners – led to the shooting of a policeman and further executions. In other English towns there were symptoms of unrest and disturbance among the Irish population, especially at the time of the 1867 rising in Ireland, when the Catholic clergy were called upon by the civil authorities to exercise influence to prevent violence. The government recruited fifty thousand special constables in London alone, and feared a mass outbreak of revolutionary violence in England as well as Ireland.

The towns and cities of Ullathorne's diocese were full of Irish migrants and their descendants, so Fenianism inevitably found support there. Blood was stirred in the Midland towns by the anti-Catholic rabble rousing of William Murphy, which provoked the notorious 'Murphy Riots'. Wherever Murphy lectured, often accusing the Catholic clergy of conniving at Fenianism, he left a trail of riot, destruction of property, even loss of life. Appeals were made in Parliament to silence him. Clearly, many Irish were provoked into retaliation, raising the temperature.[41] Throughout 1866 and 1867 Murphy was lecturing around Birmingham and the nearby Black Country and sufficient trouble had occurred in his wake to persuade the Birmingham city council to refuse him the use of the Town

---

39. Rafferty, pp. 89–94.
40. Ibid., p. 95.
41. J Arnstein, *Mr Newdegate and the Nuns: Protestant versus Catholic in Mid-Victorian England* (1982), p. 101.

Hall in June 1867. Tensions ran high, the Irish turned up in large numbers, stones began to fly and windows were broken. Four hundred soldiers and six hundred special constables were drafted in and the Riot Act was read. A band of Murphy supporters attacked the Irish area, sacked houses and damaged St Peter's Catholic chapel; rumours of an attack on the cathedral and the nearby gun factories were only diverted by large shows of military force.[42]

Ullathorne was, perhaps fortunately, absent from home during these events, being in Rome for the celebrations marking the eighteenth centenary of SS Peter and Paul. This defiant and hugely symbolic celebration of papal authority and continuity in the face of persecution was also used by Pius IX to proclaim the calling of the Vatican Council. By 1867, the Italian secular state had been instituted, and nationalist troops were closing in on Rome, in order to capture it as the new capital. There was talk of the 'Third Rome': the Rome of the emperors and of the popes had both gone, and the Rome of the people was about to be inaugurated. The Pope was desperate and defiant. Ullathorne was also absent from a more domestic event, which he was much sorrier to miss, the death of one of Birmingham's greatest Catholic benefactors and a longtime friend, John Hardman junior. His death, in May 1867, was long expected and before leaving for Rome the kind-hearted bishop had urged his sister (Mother Juliana Hardman, superior of the Sister of Mercy at Handsworth) to stay with him as long as necessary, sending his 'kindest and most affectionate regards to your brother and best sympathy to Mrs Hardman'.[43]

Returning full of the excitement of the much talked of, but now officially announced Ecumenical Council, he was plunged straight back into the minutiae of local affairs. Further trouble arose in Wolverhampton and in Walsall, where Ullathorne was driven to speak publicly and to publish, in order to counter the anti-Catholic speeches and publications of Murphy. One of the most notorious and popular Victorian anti-Catholic pamphlets was *The Confessional Unmasked*; it had everything the public

---

[42.] Arnstein, pp. 90–94.
[43.] Handsworth, Ullathorne to M Juliana Hardman, 23 March 1867.

could want – secrecy, conspiracy, abuse of power and hints of sexual corruption. Ullathorne went into battle on this ground, lashing the 'designing men' whose 'demoralising conceits' were brought before 'a world that is entirely ignorant of the facts'.[44] Confessionals were as popular as convents in the prurient canon of anti-Catholic vitriol, and Ullathorne's pre-emptive strike, warning Catholics to stay away if Murphy should set up his stall in Walsall, proved equally popular: *The Confessional: a discourse delivered in the Catholic Churches of Walsall*, went through twelve editions in a year.

Ullathorne was anxious about the impact of anti-Catholic violence in the community, but also about the effects of Fenianism among the Irish Catholics under his care. He shared with Manning a distaste for nationalist and republican movements and for any revolutionary activities stemming from a secret society. Nevertheless, both men had great sympathy for the conditions of Catholics in Ireland, and knew what they were talking about from the evidence of the diaspora under their care in Birmingham and London.[45] In 1868 Manning published his *Letter to Lord Grey* on the state of Ireland, which contained an outspoken denunciation of government policy on Ireland, and a call for reform of the land laws and the removal of religious and educational inequalities. Ullathorne complimented him warmly on his 'exposition of the sentiments which animate the Irish bishops and clergy, and the rebuke to the cold and stolid tone of English depreciation of the Irish mind'.[46]

By the end of the year, however, despite his sympathy for the Irish, Ullathorne himself was contemplating the need for a public condemnation of Fenianism, which was driving a wedge between himself and the Irish Catholic population of the diocese.

We have a nest of Fenians here who are giving us some trouble. They have used the pretext of my last Pastoral to try to alienate the people from me, and to put me in the

---

44. *The Confessional: an Address delivered in the Catholic Churches of Walsall* (1867), p. 8.
45. Butler, *Life*, II, p. 139.
46. Ibid., II, p. 140.

same box with you in the *Universal News,* and in the minds of certain Irish members, G Moore[47] for example, so at last we are all fellows in misfortune. I hope to go without publicly noticing these men whose pretensions and movements I know pretty well, as I do not want to feed their importance. But if I see the need arise I shall come out sharply and mark them off.[48]

The reference was to his Advent pastoral letter of 1868 in which he had asserted the duty of obedience to civil authority and mentioned Fenians as among groups undermining it.

> Rebellion has become a craft and a science; it has its sects, its schools, its secret societies and its recognised authorities. And, mark the result, the whole of that Europe of which we form a part and which once constituted the greater part of the Christendom over which the Pope and Divine law presided, is now undermined by the plots and machinations of unprincipled adventurers, heading numbers of dupes, and banded together with them in secret societies – freemasonry, carbonarism, Fenianism, and under other denominations, aiming with anti Christian fury, at the destruction of the Church, as the one great representative of all divine, as of all human authority and obedience.[49]

This gave deep offence to Fenian sympathisers in England and the *Universal News* took up the matter, week after week attacking the bishop for having said that 'the Irish people' were the enemies of religion and the Church.[50] The press, especially the

47. George Moore came from a landed Irish Catholic family and was briefly educated at Oscott. He became a Liberal MP and from 1868 until his sudden death in 1870 supported the campaign for an amnesty for Fenian prisoners and secretly discussed co-operation with the Fenian leadership. R. V. Comerford, 'Moore, George Henry (1810–1870)', *Oxford Dictionary of National Biography,* Oxford University Press, 2004 [http://www.oxforddnb.com /view/article/19114, accessed 26 Sept 2005].

48. AAW Molloy Collection, Ullathorne to Manning, 30 December 1868.

49. Pastoral Letter, 16 November 1868.

50. Butler, *Life,* II, p. 142.

Irish People and the *Irish Liberator* was an effective and powerful machine for spreading Fenian ideas and sentiment beyond the ranks of a quasi secret society.[51] Public readings of newspapers would reach a far wider audience of semi-literate Irish folk than the actual circulation would suggest, and Ullathorne's fear of its influence was well-founded. The *Universal News*, founded in 1860 by Frederick Oakley, passed into the hands of Clinton Hoey and became linked with Irish nationalism, giving space to Fenian poets and demanding that Ireland receive the same liberation as Italy.[52] Among the English bishops Ullathorne bore the brunt of Irish journalistic opposition, especially in the *Free Press*, which in 1868 was condemned by ecclesiastical authorities and ceased publication. Ullathorne's most spectacular victory was the collapse of the *Universal News* as a result of its public conflict with him. He denounced the paper and was threatened with libel in turn, but the distributors, seeing the risks, refused to take the paper, and it was forced to close.[53]

Ullathorne's follow-up was a special pastoral letter on Fenianism in January 1869, in which he declared Fenianism, as it existed in Birmingham, to be a secret society of the kind condemned by the Church and its members were, therefore, debarred from the Sacraments. Appealing to the great mass of Irish Catholics against Fenianism, he reversed a famous phrase coined by Manning in the previous year, 'Show me an Irish Catholic who has lost the Faith and I will show you a Fenian' into the more ferocious, 'Show me a Fenian and I will show you a bad Catholic'.[54] His righteous anger roused a fierce mood in him and provoked the shepherd to take his staff in his hand and the watchman to lift his voice in warning (as he put it), 'lest the blood of his people be laid at his door, or their souls be required at his hand'.[55] He condemned in strong language the work of all secret societies, but especially the Fenians, whose

---

51. Owen Dudley Edwards and Patricia Storey, 'The Irish Press in Victorian Britain', in R. Swift and S. Gilley, *The Irish in the Victorian City* (1985), pp. 161–9.
52. Dudley Edwards and Storey, p. 161.
53. Ibid., p. 162.
54. *Pastoral Letter on Fenianism* (1869), p. 8.
55. Ibid., p. 6.

crimes were compounded by their current attempts to drive a wedge between the Irish people of his diocese and their bishop. He was furious at the accusations that he was ignorant of Irish history and its problems and the sufferings of the Irish people, reminding his hearers that in Australia and in Birmingham forty years of his life had been largely given to the welfare of Irish people. He had given his health and the best years of his life, 'in labouring to mitigate the evils, redress the wrongs, and soften the sorrows of twenty thousand Irishmen, the most of which had been brought about through the misgovernment of their country'. He insisted that Daniel O'Connell ('one of those colossal men who appear but rarely') was right in insisting that nothing was achieved by breaking the laws of either Church or State.[56]

The pastoral letter did little to cool the situation, if anything provoking further public antagonism towards him. He and Manning disagreed on the extent to which Catholic infidelity and Fenianism were linked, but Manning complimented him on the pastoral. 'We owe you thanks for speaking out. I wish both in Ireland and England we had all done so together some time ago.'[57] Ullathorne continued to speak out loudly and publicly against militant Irish nationalism, claiming to have lectured in every church in Birmingham against it, which the Birmingham police force probably appreciated more than the local Irish population.[58] He relished the fight, describing himself as engaged in

> a sharp conflict with the Fenians, and have the satisfaction of seeing myself abused in about a score of columns of their newspapers weekly. I hope that many of the poor people here are getting to understand the case better, but the Irish people are half mad through the notions put into their head by certain of their leaders. One of their points now is that in a conflict between the Church and Fenianism the first must give way.[59]

---

56. Ibid., p. 11.
57. Butler, *Life*, II, p. 144.
58. Rafferty, p. 108.
59. Colwich, Ullathorne to Prioress, 12 March 1869.

By the end of March he was able to tell Manning that, although the Fenian affair was not yet cooled down, opposition on St Patrick's Day had been reduced by the clergy to about 130 people.

A papal condemnation of Fenianism, obtained by the Irish bishops travelling to Rome for the Vatican Council, quelled a good deal of Catholic support as well as pleasing the government. By the mid-1870s, Fenianism as such was a spent force, in terms of its attempt to draw Catholicism and political action apart, and the renewed Home Rule campaign of later decades became much more closely associated with Catholicism.[60] As a revolutionary movement, Fenianism was a 'colossal disaster'[61] but it forced politicians from the 1860s onwards to re-evaluate their attitude towards Ireland. The political landscape and ecclesiastical opinion were transformed by Fenianism, and it was, 'a greater force in the social and political realities of Britain, Ireland and North America than is allowed for in much current Irish historiography'.[62]

Not only was Ullathorne preoccupied with protecting the faith of the poorer sections of the Catholic population, largely found among the Irish, but also with that of the burgeoning middle class and the increasingly vocal English gentry and aristocracy. Catholic Emancipation, the restoration of the hierarchy and the raised public profile of Catholicism (especially through highly publicised Anglican conversions) had all served to change the expectations of Catholics over a generation. Schools such as Oscott were also raising the level of educational provision, and once Gladstone's government had lifted the ban on non members of the Church of England taking degrees in 1871, the demand for university level education grew. The goal for many Catholics was access to the ancient universities on an equal footing, but this remained impossible while the Catholic bishops continued to forbid it. However, the debate over the possibility of Catholics attending the universities in some capacity (which was already happening *de facto*) arose long before 1871.

60. Letters, pp. 206–9 [16 January 1869].
61. Rafferty, p. 14.
62. Ibid., p. 15.

The 'university question' was the subject of correspondence with *Propaganda Fide* in 1864, leaving Ullathorne in no doubt that a Catholic could not be head of a hall in Oxford as he would have to be a member of the university's convocation and subject to the vice chancellor. Some notion was afloat that Patterson, one of the *Essays and Reviews* contributors had agreed to be nominal head of a Catholic hall, but this had fallen through, having caused something of a sensation in Oxford.[63] That would not have gone down well with Ullathorne, who had made his opinion of the liberal Protestant theology espoused in *Essays and Reviews* very clear in earlier years. The agitation continued, especially among Catholics resident in Rome, anxious that the bishops do something to meet their wishes for access to higher education. Ullathorne realised that the subject would not go away and that the bishops would be 'driven to the necessity of thinking out the subject, hinting to the Scotsman, Robert Monteith, one of his Roman correspondents, that if the laity agree and the bishops choose to "put shoulders together" something could be achieved'.[64] This suggests that initially he was not averse to finding some accommodation to allow Catholics to attend Oxford, and (despite his later denials) this was surely in the back of his mind when he approached Newman later that year. A conversation recorded by Newman in May 1865 even seemed to suggest that Ullathorne saw Oxford as the natural next stage for lay students from Oscott.[65]

Ullathorne had been anxious for years about the state of the Catholic mission in and around Oxford. The Jesuit missioner Fr Cobb had complained in 1850 about the unproductive mission and ungrateful congregation, and that (significantly in the light of later debates) young men were punished by the university authorities for contact with the Catholic mission.[66] As early as 1854 Ullathorne negotiated with the Jesuits to form

[63] Ampleforth, Copy of letter Ullathorne to Brown, 13 February 1864.

[64] Ampleforth, Copy of letter Ullathorne to Brown, 12 March 1864.

[65] L&D XXI, p. 457 Record of a visit by Bishop Ullathorne and Canon Walker, May 1865.

[66] Farm St (Residence of St Mary) William Cobb SJ to Ullathorne, 26 December 1850.

a mission within the city,[67] and was anxious about clerical appointments there, given the 'important influence of the Oxford mission'.[68] He raised the matter again with them in 1858, wanting to see a mission in the city and a church built. The Jesuits were enthusiastic about the idea, but fearful of a lack of resources to build a church.[69] The toing and froing dragged on into the autumn of that year, when Ullathorne finally offered the mission to the Institute of Charity instead.[70] In fact, the mission was handed to the diocese and served by two secular priests until 1871.

In August 1864 Ullathorne proposed that a Catholic mission, run by the Birmingham Oratory, should be established on land which Newman had bought in Oxford, on the site of the old workhouse behind St Giles. The bishop's proposal took Newman by surprise, and there seems to have been the usual difficulty in interpretation between them. This hinged on the question (which would become crucial) of whether Newman himself had any thought of going to live in Oxford.[71] Newman had previously been opposed to any suggestion of a Catholic house in Oxford, although it was obvious that Catholic lay students were frequenting the university in growing numbers. He was not averse to Ullathorne's proposal, but if an Oratory were to be established in Oxford, Newman was clear about his own personal intention to remain in Birmingham.[72] This was significant, as Newman's residence in Oxford would have been a definite attraction to educated Catholics. Nevertheless, he set about raising funds from wealthy friends, but Ullathorne became uneasy at Newman's fund-raising pamphlet which spoke of ministering to the Catholic youth in Oxford. Any hint

---

[67] Farm St (Residence of St Mary) Ullathorne to Provincial of SJ, 9 March 1854.

[68] Farm St (Residence of St Mary) Ullathorne to Provincial of SJ, 8 March 1859.

[69] Farm St (Residence of St Mary) Ullathorne to Provincial of SJ, 24 January 1858; SJ, Provincial to Ullathorne October 1858; Ullathorne to Provincial, 1 November 1858.

[70] Farm St (Residence of St Mary) Ullathorne to Provincial of SJ, 23 October 1858.

[71] L&D XXI, p. 206, 24 August 1864.

[72] The thought of going to Oxford was 'a step which I simply disliked and shrank from'. L&D XXI, p. 206, note.

of mixed Catholic/Protestant education still raised episcopal hackles; even if Newman had no immediate intention of founding a Catholic hall in the university, there were those among his supporters who did.[73] This may have been disingenuous on Newman's part, or even 'a trick to start with an Oratory and develop a Catholic hall once established'.[74] However, he insisted to Ullathorne that the only point of an Oxford Oratory was to meet the immediate need of protecting the faith of Catholics already at the university. If that need could be met either by a clear and definite ecclesiastical ban on Catholics attending the university or by the foundation of a Catholic university, then it was not worth his while to invest in a mission there.[75]

The issue was whether or not Newman could found a mission to offer pastoral care to Catholics already attending university lectures, without seeming to offer an invitation to more Catholics to sample the dreaming spires. For Ullathorne, the issue was how to achieve a decent Catholic mission in the only large city in the diocese still without one, which seemed to be solved by involving Newman. Newman made it clear to Ullathorne that his only interest was in a possible mission, and that he had 'no intention in any way to co-operate with the university or with the colleges of Oxford, whether by taking lodgers or private pupils or in any other way'.[76] Ullathorne was hugely encouraging and supportive, telling Newman that he wished to give the Oratory project 'all the approval and encouragement that I can' for two reasons: firstly the desperate need for a church in Oxford to replace the 'mean room' in which the Catholics presently met, and secondly that Newman's association with the project would assure its success. He also slipped in a third reason, that it would be a 'monument of gratitude to God for the conversions of the last thirty years'.[77] This suggests a slightly more 'political' view than his protestations would suggest, but he was forced to retract this

[73.] Sheridan Gilley, *Newman and His Age* (1990), p. 336.
[74.] V. A. McClelland, *English Roman Catholics and Higher Education 1830–1903* (1973), p. 199.
[75.] L&D XXI, p. 234, 23 September 1864.
[76.] L&D XXI, p. 239, 26 September 1864.
[77.] L&D XXI, pp. 277–8, 27 October 1864.

phrase by the distaste which it created among some of the old Catholics.[78]

The gathered bishops (despite a 'sharp debate' between Wiseman and Ullathorne) condemned the Oratory idea in December 1864, hoping to discourage Catholics from attending Oxford.[79] This view was confirmed by *Propaganda Fide* in January 1865 in a letter which discouraged Catholics from sending their sons to Oxford or Cambridge. No mention was made of Newman and the Oratory proposal, and Ullathorne took Newman's word and insisted that the Oratory scheme had nothing to do with Catholic youths attending colleges of the university. He argued that the two ideas were separate, and the Roman ruling did not affect any plans for an Oxford Oratory. In March, the bishops made clear their position:

> The bishops are unanimous in their disapproval of the establishing of a Catholic college at any of the Protestant universities. And they are further of the opinion that parents ought to be in every way dissuaded from sending their children to pursue their studies at such universities.[80]

Newman abandoned the idea of an Oxford mission, feeling a strong sense of grievance against Wiseman and Manning, who he believed had not clarified the distinction sufficiently, and sold the land to the university.[81]

Ullathorne, still anxious about pastoral care in the growing city of Oxford, revived the Oratory idea in August 1865, knowing that Newman had purchased another piece of land in Oxford. He was uneasy about the chosen site, right opposite Christ Church, an aristocrat among Oxford colleges which houses the Cathedral of the Diocese of Oxford, and therefore in the very heart of both university Oxford and Anglican Oxford. He still remained firmly opposed to the idea of a Catholic hall or college which had been pressed on Rome by a 'considerable party'. In Ullathorne's view, all they were after

---

[78.] L&D XXI, p. 284, 2 November 1864.
[79.] L&D XXI, pp. 346–8, memorandum, 19 December 1864.
[80.] AAW Ullathorne Correspondence, Copy of Circular letter from the bishops to clergy, 24 March 1865.
[81.] McClelland (1973), p. 216.

was 'a warrant for sending their sons to Christ Church or Balliol'. He was critical of the Catholic laity who pushed for access to Oxford for not using to the fullest extent the educational facilities already available to them.[82] He wanted to see a Catholic higher education programme for England, and approved links with London University, including through Oscott.[83]

His vague approach to Newman was followed up by something more definite in March 1866, when Ullathorne asked Newman outright if he was interested in taking on the establishment of an Oratory in Oxford. Newman was understandably cautious, recalling his last experience, but accepted after receiving assurances from Ullathorne about finance. Manning, by now Archbishop of Westminster, was hostile to the idea, and reported to Rome that the widely accepted view was that an Oratorian mission in Oxford would eventually lead to a college being set up,[84] but Ullathorne petitioned *Propaganda Fide* in June for approval of the plan for an Oxford Oratory to be formed under his episcopal authority in the Diocese of Birmingham.[85] Newman was uneasy about the Oratory's relationship with both the Oxford mission and the university, and came to the conclusion the the Oratory's presence in Oxford should only be temporary, until a mission, based in the burgeoning new estates housing railway and press workers, could be established. This view, he feared, 'may have frightened the bishop'.[86] Doubts soon set in and misunderstandings and misadventures followed thick and fast.

Ullathorne may have been unwittingly responsible for some of them, and has certainly been blamed by historians.[87] They arose over his apparent failure to invite Newman to Oscott to meet Cardinal Reisach, Prefect of the Congregation of Studies (in England on a private visit); Newman took it as a snub, although Ullathorne was under the impression that Newman

[82]. Ushaw UL17, Ullathorne to Walker, 7 December 1864.
[83]. McClelland (1973), p. 232.
[84]. Gilley, p. 336.
[85]. L&D XXII, pp. 244–5, 4 June 1866.
[86]. L&D XXII, pp. 236–8, Memorandum on interview with bishop, 17 May 1866.
[87]. David Newsome, *The Convert Cardinals* (1993), p. 259.

was away from home at the time.[88] This was, as so often
between Newman and Ullathorne, a storm in a teacup.
Ullathorne can hardly be judged guilty of keeping Newman
out of the picture, as Reisach was only at Oscott for a brief
overnight stay, and mentioned nothing to Ullathorne about the
possible Oxford Oratory.[89] In fact, Ullathorne later told
Reisach off for not visiting Newman at the Oratory when in
England.[90]

More problematic was Ullathorne's response to concerns
expressed by *Propaganda Fide* over the question of Catholics
being attracted to Oxford by a mission run by the Oratory. He
had to admit to Rome that a mission in Oxford would be attractive to Catholic parents inclined to send their sons to the
university, especially if Newman's name was associated with
it.[91] There still remained a certain ambiguity on the part of
both Newman and Ullathorne in wanting to offer pastoral care
for those Catholic youths who chose to go to Oxford, while not
wishing to encourage others to do so. Newman tried to insist
that 'In my [fund raising] Circular I did but recognise the fact
that Catholics were at the university, and I made that recognition, because I felt that in the fact of there being Catholics at
the university lay my call for undertaking the mission.'[92]
Newman still insisted that he had no intention of living in
Oxford, though both he and Ullathorne knew that his association with the project would help raise funds.

Ullathorne's prime concern was still to get a vigorous mission
and a church in Oxford, preferably based on an Oratory.
When, on Christmas Day 1866, he received agreement to the
scheme from *Propaganda Fide* with a secret condition attached,
that Newman should not reside in Oxford, he was not unduly
alarmed. Given that this was Newman's stated intention all
along, Ullathorne saw little difficulty in this proviso.[93] By not
revealing it to Newman, he sought to spare his feelings (and

[88.] Gilley, p. 343.
[89.] L&D XXII, pp. 237–8 n 3.
[90.] L&D XXII, p. 280 memorandum of conversation with bishop, 1
August 1867.
[91.] Butler, *Life*, II, pp. 15–16.
[92.] L&D XXII, p. 325, to Ullathorne, 9 December 1866.
[93.] L&D XXII, p. 331, from Ullathorne, 25 December 1866.

assumed that he could get his old friend Barnabo to lift the condition when he was in Rome on a scheduled visit in summer 1867). Ullathorne was also evidently irritated at Rome's involvement in the matter anyway, although he had raised it with *Propaganda Fide* himself. In a conversation with Newman on New Year's Day, he insisted that, as diocesan bishop, he had every right to permit an Oratory to be set up in Oxford or anywhere else. The only reason for *Propaganda Fide's* involvement was to do with the Oratorian rule, to gain Newman the 'privilege' of being based temporarily at an Oratory in Oxford without formally leaving Birmingham. *Propaganda Fide* had 'availed itself of the opportunity of reviewing the whole matter, and had given a decision fuller and broader than was imperative'.[94] The only reason for this was the pressure which Manning on the one side, and powerful lay Catholics on the other, were bringing to bear in Rome. In January 1867 Manning (who had also been in ignorance of the 'secret condition') tried to arrange a meeting with Newman and Ullathorne to sort out the whole matter, but Newman declined, mistrusting Manning's part in what had been said in Rome.

As Newman's bishop and friend, Ullathorne felt it incumbent upon him to defend Newman's position, but was placed in difficulty acting as mediator between him and Manning.[95] He also went into print to try and set the record straight and defuse the growing row fuelled by letters in the *Weekly Register*, which Manning thought unwise.[96] In March 1867, *Propaganda Fide* suggested to Manning that the matter be brought before a full meeting of the bishops, and Ullathorne insisted that, if such a discussion were to take place, Newman should be invited to be a party to it.[97] Manning agreed to this, being saddened that Newman saw him as an opponent in the matter, but was fearful that it would put a strain on his own friendship with Ullathorne.[98]

[94] L&D XXII, p. 7, memorandum of conversation with bishop, 2 January 1867.
[95] AAW Ullathorne Correspondence, Ullathorne to Manning, 5 August 1867.
[96] Butler *Life*, II, p. 28.
[97] AAW Ullathorne Correspondence, Ullathorne to Manning, 18 March 1867.
[98] AAW Ullathorne Correspondence, Manning to Ullathorne, 9 April 1867.

By April, Ullathorne had thought it best to put Newman in the picture about the 'secret condition', and received a chilly response and a refusal to take on the Oratory on the Roman basis: 'If I am missioner at Oxford, I claim to be there as much or as little as I please.'[99] Newman was initially furious and sarcastic about Ullathorne's reputation in Rome for 'keeping a wild beast like me in order'.[100] He did, however, accept that Ullathorne had not been at liberty to tell him the particulars of the 'secret instruction' and had tried to slow matters down until he was in Rome in June and could sort it out personally.[101] Newman assured one of his friends in April 1867 that 'no sort of blame attaches to our bishop, who is my good friend'.[102] The whole matter had become personal for Newman, with regard to the Roman view of him, still overshadowed by the *Rambler*, and Ullathorne had a good deal of sympathy for Newman's position. He was aware that 'his feelings have been sorely tried and deeply wounded', and was himself irritated at what he saw as mischief making by 'unauthorised zealots' in Rome.[103]

The rescript from Rome on the University question came through from Rome in August, spelling out the impossibility of Newman's residence in Oxford and revealing publicly Ullathorne's lack of disclosure to Newman. This provoked Newman to withdraw from the Oxford scheme entirely. Ullathorne was sympathetic to Newman's decision, and would have done the same himself in his position, but felt the root problem was that Newman had been 'shamefully misrepresented at Rome, and that by countrymen of our own'.[104] Newman decided that it was unwise to make an enemy of Ullathorne and refused to blame him publicly, while condemning both Manning and the chatter in Rome.[105] His private view, expressed in a letter to James Hope Scott, was sharper;

99. L&D XXII, p. 131, 6 April 1867.
100. L&D XXII, p. 135, 8 April 1867 to Ambrose St John.
101. L&D XXII, p. 157, memorandum of conversation with bishop, 15 April 1867.
102. L&D XXII, p. 164, 16 April 1867 to Henry Wilberforce, and n. 2.
103. Farm Street OR/5, Ullathorne to T. Harper SJ, 17 April 1867.
104. L&D XXII, p. 312, n. 2.
105. Gilley, pp. 347–9.

accusing Ullathorne of publishing his *Facts and Documents relating to the Mission and contemplated Oratory at Oxford*, in order to put Newman right with the other bishops and with Rome, he concluded savagely, 'He sincerely wishes to be kind to me, but to stand well with people at Rome supersedes in his mind every other wish. So he is a coward.'[106]

The question of Catholics attending the universities continued to rumble on for many years. Ullathorne continued to be fiercely opposed to the idea, going as far as to talk of the 'sinfulness' of sending youths to the universities.[107] However, Ullathorne had come to understand and appreciate Newman's way of thought and action and the frustrating and embarrassing position in which he found himself. He sharply told Grant that 'if the authorities at Rome think there is something to be corrected in Dr Newman or his proceedings', then the best course of action would be, 'writing to him plainly, and without any unnecessary circumlocution beyond that courtesy and consideration which they always exercise'. This might put an end to 'misgivings' and 'misconceptions'.[108] He was clearly fed up of being the go-between. Ten years later, copying a letter in which he had refused to blame Ullathorne, Newman commented that he would not say the same thing now, knowing Ullathorne better. 'I quite believe him well disposed to me, but justice, truth, kindness, paternity, generosity would have no chance with him, if Pope or *Propaganda* spoke otherwise.'[109] Is this an accurate view of Ullathorne, that he would allow Rome to override his own judgement on anything? His comments to Grant suggest otherwise, and his own dealings with Rome do not bear this out. It probably says more about the rawness of Newman's wounded pride than a serious judgement on Ullathorne, but it indicated the continued strains between them. It also suggests, along with his earlier description of Ullathorne as a coward, that Newman did not understand Ullathorne's character or position as well as Ullathorne was coming to understand him. The one thing of

---

[106.] L&D XXII, p. 296 To James Hope Scott, 13 August 1867.
[107.] AAS Ullathorne Papers, Ullathorne to Grant, 25 September 1867.
[108.] AAS Ullathorne Papers, Ullathorne to Grant, 24 February 1869.
[109.] L&D XXII, p. 164, To Henry Wilberforce, 16 April 1867 and n. 2.

which Ullathorne could never stand accused was cowardice, but his belief that he could sort things out singlehandedly clearly made difficulties for others.

Relations with Manning remained cool for a time, while Ullathorne took out his irritation on a hapless secretary charged with compiling returns for the forthcoming *ad limina* reports to Rome. Declining Manning's request to draft a joint pastoral letter on the subject, he insisted that this was out of deference to the opinions of other bishops rather than 'any feeling towards any individual'.[110] Manning did his best to mollify, but Ullathorne seemed determined to be irritated and resentful at being given the 'odious office of acting as the common mouthpiece'.[111] Manning sent more soothing words in response and there appears to be a gap of over a month in their correspondence, after which Ullathorne decided to stop sulking and deliberately shifted the focus onto more common ground between them. The scuffles in the playground were over, for they both knew that there was more that united them than divided them, and important tasks lay ahead.

His attitude on the university question was not, as Butler suggested, unclear,[112] and he issued a crystal clear pastoral letter in which he virtually forbade Catholic parents from sending their children to the universities.

To send them to these universities is to place them within an atmosphere and beneath a combination of influences so completely and exclusively Protestant, that it cannot be otherwise than perilous to the faith and conscience of Catholic youth … At this unsettled time above all others, does the Catholic youth need the firm but gentle guidance of his Catholic preceptors, and yet it is at this period that some persons would throw him into the vortex of anti-Catholic sentiment and thought, without pilot, rudder or compass. Protestant influences and courtesy will overwhelm, and the presence of Catholic tendencies

---

110. AAW Ullathorne Correspondence, Ullathorne to Manning, 15 September 1867.
111. AAW Ullathorne Correspondence, Ullathorne to Manning, 29 September 1867.
112. Butler, *Life*, II, p. 31.

in Oxford is no help, because it is merely accidental . . .[113]

The question of higher education for Catholics was certainly not going to disappear, and in late 1867 a subcommission was set up by the bishops to look into the whole matter. The highly respected and experienced president of Oscott, James Spencer Northcote (himself an Oxford man and convert) was nominated to represent the secular colleges. The subcommission was forbidden to reopen the Oxford question, but the survey of opinion conducted by it carefully excluded opponents of the idea, and the final, 'superficial and loaded'[114] report favoured reopening the Oxford question. Northcote himself favoured the extension of the existing Jesuit mission to allow for Catholic students to be resident in the university.[115] The subcommission report was inconclusive, and the university question was again shelved until 1872 when it would become even more contentious.

Manning presented a draft paper on higher education for submission to *Propaganda Fide*, based on the subcommission report, with which Ullathorne took issue on a number of points. He felt it was unfair to the subcommission members who had understood that their report would go in to Rome as it stood, instead of which, Manning was offering a critical gloss which contradicted what had been said previously. Northcote, when asked for his opinion on the draft report, replied to Ullathorne:

> I never read a document which so much disgusted me from its palpable injustice and even occasional falsehood; and that it goes very far in my mind towards justifying the hardest things that Newman has ever said of its author. I suppose it arises from sheer inability to take in any view of a subject which differs from his own – but if this is a sample of the way in which a case is laid before Rome for decision between two opposing views, one cannot be surprised at the decision not being much respected by

---

[113.] Pastoral Letter, 13 October 1867.
[114.] McClelland (1973), pp. 247–50.
[115.] Ibid., p. 264.

those whose views are at variance with those of the ruling power ... unless some counter statement is sent in by somebody, I fear the whole of this agitation of the question will do an immense amount of harm, and breed very serious disaffection in well-disposed minds ... I cannot believe that the five bishops who considered that the whole question might and ought to be reopened for examination by *Propaganda*, will allow such a document as this to go to Rome as the means of reopening it.

His view was that Manning had misused the subcommittee report, and had not taken account of the views of the colleges. He was irritated that contrary voices were entirely ignored in Manning's document, and asked Ullathorne to ensure that it was not the only document which went forward.[116]

Manning was giving the impression of a united episcopate on this issue, which Ullathorne denied, insisting that the subcommission report was unsatisfactory because the bishops themselves had not given the members sufficient guidance as to what was wanted.

> You know well that I have no sympathy with the proposals to unite higher education with residence at Oxford, but it appears to me that this report scarcely meets the whole intention contemplated by the bishops at our meeting ... that therefore it would be expedient to appoint a committee to consider [the points] and then draw up a report to the Holy See to be submitted previously to the [ad limina] visit of the bishops.[117]

In the early 1870s the Jesuits took over the Oxford mission again and the long hoped for church was built and dedicated to St Aloysius, with the same caveat as had applied to the Oratorians: no school or college was to be attached to it without express authority from Rome.[118] Ullathorne, delighted

116. AAW Ullathorne Correspondence, Northcote to Ullathorne, Whitsunday 1872.
117. AAW Molloy Collection, Ullathorne to Manning (unfinished), 16 May 1872.
118. Farm Street (Residence of St Mary, Ullathorne to SJ Provincial, 3 February 1871.

at last to fulfil his original purpose of a proper mission church to serve the city, laid the foundation stone of the new church in spring 1873, brushing aside rumours of opposition to it. 'I have heard nothing whatever of this nonsense ... If I do [they] will hear something in return.'[119] Some years later, sending faculties for the Jesuit priest and poet Gerard Manley Hopkins to minister within the diocese in Oxford, Ullathorne spoke warmly of the success of the Oxford mission under the Jesuits, insisting that for years he had argued that 'it only required an able and large minded man to make the Oxford mission one of importance'.[120]

The long dispute over the possible formation of an Oxford Oratory, which involved complex crosscurrents in Birmingham, Rome and London, finally destroyed Newman's confidence in Manning, and to some extent in all religious superiors. He remained on the warmest personal terms with Ullathorne, but was left feeling that he could not trust his superiors, only obey them. Ullathorne had taken on the might of Manning and *Propaganda Fide* for Newman, but on his own terms, and Newman was dismayed to find that Ullathorne had kept things from him in doing so. He was dismayed, having, as he thought, acted in good faith and with the express permission of his bishop and of Rome.[121] Newman was left feeling like a pawn between the episcopal players, but what was at stake for them was far different from his priorities.

Setting aside the particular and complex question of higher education for the articulate and wealthy Catholics, the educational issue which preoccupied the bishops during much of the nineteenth century was the provision of mass education for the poorest and simplest of their flock. This, the greatest social and religious campaign in which the Church became involved with civil government, came to a climax in the late 1860s. Ullathorne had long given priority to the provision of schools for the poor, and this was one of the great achievements of the women religious, whose apostolic work he so encouraged in

[119.] Farm Street (Residence of St Mary, Ullathorne to SJ Provincial, 17 April 1873.

[120.] Farm Street (Residence of St Mary, Ullathorne to SJ Provincial, 29 November 1878.

[121.] L&D XXVI, p. 8, 8 January 1872.

Birmingham. On the question of popular education, Ullathorne was in a minority of one among the bishops, and disagreed vehemently with Manning over the Church's relationship with the state in educational provision. This was the crucial battle for the future of Catholic education, and the success of the Catholic schools system over the ensuing century suggests that Ullathorne may have got it wrong on this occasion. However, his implacable resistance to government control over Catholic schools and his personal pressure on Manning also played a significant part in retaining the crucial independence for Church schools under central government funding.

State involvement in education was one of the great social and political developments of the mid-nineteenth century, as the lack of provision for basic education became a major issue in the country. Basic education was regarded as an economic necessity and a moral requirement for the stability and progress of Victorian England. Traditionally, the churches had been the providers and controllers of education, which therefore had a significant religious component, but massive population growth now meant that they could not cope. Catholic schools funded by charitable provision had existed in towns and cities since the start of the century, in addition to the more established practice of the recusant period of schools run by local clergy and laywomen, and institutions such as Sedgley Park and Old Hall Green. The first Catholic Sunday Poor School in Birmingham had been opened in 1807 adjoining the chapel of St Austin (on the site of the later cathedral) and a separate girls' school followed in 1815. In 1823, the Catholic community opened one of Birmingham's first day schools for poor children. Local charitable activity struggled to meet the growing demand for places, and a second school was launched in the early 1830s, but was dogged by internecine disputes.[122]

From 1833 treasury grants had been made available by the government to aid the provision made by Church organisations, and from 1839 the Catholic Church had been in receipt of grants. Uniquely among European nations, Britain was content to leave education to church-sponsored charity schools, attended on a voluntary basis. By the mid-nineteenth

122. Champ thesis, pp. 229–34.

century, religious bodies of one kind or another were educating 1,049,000 out of 2,109,000 children in day schools, mainly those run by the Evangelical supported National Society, founded in 1811.[123] Attendance was poor until social legislation began to remove children from mines, workshops and heavy industry, but even so, few stayed at school beyond the age of ten. State funding and compulsory attendance only gradually came into being, largely because of disputes with the existing religious providers, of which the Catholic Church was one of growing influence. Education was a major priority for Ullathorne and all the bishops; resources were stretched to breaking point and although the number of schools was increasing (Birmingham had five by the late 1840s) less than half the estimated Catholic children received any formal education.[124]

In 1850, a government proposal for state provision of secular based education for all children struck horror into Ullathorne's soul, and he saw it as nothing short of the secularising of the nation. This was not true education, which sought to raise the human mind and spirit, but a degradation, he believed. It was also a gross social injustice, in that it treated rich and poor differently and took away the religious independence of the poor. A sort of 'vague natural religion pervades the atmosphere' of such schools, which could hardly be compensated for by the provision of religious catechetics outside school. Drawing on his own childhood memories of education at non-Catholic hands, he described it as an ordeal which he was lucky to survive. Such a system of 'so-called education' was in conflict with 'the Catholic formation of the soul'. It was not only inimical to Catholic faith but to social order.

> Train men for earth only; give them new objects of desire, with increased powers, and this world for a motive; put pagan maxims in the place of the Christian's moral sense; hold it up that virtue consists in power not in patience, in winning human applause and not in loving and serving

---

[123.] David Bebbington, *Evangelicalism in Modern Britain* (1989), p. 70.
[124.] For an overview of Birmingham Catholic schools up to this point, see Champ thesis, pp. 216–45.

God; and you form a race of men discontented with their lot, whatever that may be, envious of their fellows, despisers of the parental home, ambitious of new things, contemners of the drudgery of labour, and of the humility of subordination … Establish over the land a net of schools without religion as a preservative to their teaching, and you make all England one great school of deism and sow the germs of perpetual revolutions.[125]

This trenchant exposition of Ullathorne's views on state sponsored education set the tone for his position over the coming decades when education would be one of the most contentious and important social, political and religious issues of the age.

The Catholic Poor Schools Committee was set up in 1851 to receive the government grants through the Committee of the Privy Council on Education, but the chief problem was ensuring a fair division of the available resources and establishing an adequate succession of Catholic teachers to staff the schools. Thomas Allies, a convert Anglican clergyman influenced by the Oxford Movement, and a disciple of Newman, became secretary of the Catholic Poor Schools Committee in August 1853. He held this post until retirement in 1890, so was a determining influence on the policy of the Catholic community in the rise of mass education. As secretary of the Education Crisis Fund in 1870–3 he raised about £50,000 to enable Catholics to meet the demands of the 1870 Education Act.[126] Ullathorne, though not an admirer of Allies, was a great supporter of the committee and its chairman, Charles Langdale, 'whom may God long preserve to us'. The committee's work 'is eminently a Catholic work and pre-eminently the work of our day. It is the only work in which all the Catholics of England are joined together in united action'.[127]

Ullathorne's views on education were closely linked with his attitude towards convents. The work of the active convents,

---

125. *Remarks on the Proposed Education Bill* (1850), pp. 16–17.
126. W. B. Owen, 'Allies, Thomas William (1813–1903)', rev G. Martin Murphy, *Oxford Dictionary of National Biography*, Oxford University Press, 2004 [http://www.oxforddnb.com/view/article/30393, accessed 14 Sept 2005].
127. Pastoral Letter, 16 June 1854.

especially in education, gave Ullathorne enormous pride; he admired what they could achieve particularly in the girls' schools, and he wished that he had male religious in the diocese who could achieve as much in the boys' schools. Ullathorne was already conscious of what, to many, has seemed a very modern problem in all Christian Churches, that of keeping boys interested in the practice of their religion.

> For they at once enter into a most corrupt state of society and very many of them fall away from every religious practice. This is the source of the greatest part of the perversions which have to be deplored. The girls remain pious, many boys become corrupted, and not a few fall away from religion altogether.[128]

The Sisters of Charity of St Paul became the most numerous and influential religious order involved in education in the diocese, having, by the time of the foundress's death in 1903, fifty-two houses, four hundred fully professed sisters and thirty-five novices and postulants, and a mother house established at Selly Park in the growing suburbs of Birmingham.[129] The Sisters of Charity of St Paul grew from the arrival of two French sisters from a convent in Chartres who settled in Banbury in 1847 at the invitation of the resident missioner Fr William Tandy.[130] One of these two was Genevieve Dupuis, who became the foundress of the English congregation, which expanded from Banbury all over the country and eventually internationally. Ullathorne was enthusiastic about the foundation as soon as he arrived in Birmingham, and at once saw the value of moving their mother house from Banbury to Birmingham, writing prophetically at the time, 'I feel confident in the spirit of the Institute from my observations at Banbury, that it is precisely what I want and what I could, with God's grace, in time enlarge and expand to great usefulness.'[131]

[128.] Stone G/ULL/V/2.1, Status Animarum of the Diocese of Birmingham, 1856.
[129.] Anne E. Cunningham, *Genevieve Dupuis (1813–1903)* (1984), p. 57.
[130.] Mgr Hudson, *Mother Genevieve Dupuis, foundress of the English Congregation of the Sisters of Charity of St Paul*, (1929), pp. 57–9.
[131.] Selly Park, Ullathorne to Genevieve Dupuis, 8 February 1849.

Within the Birmingham Diocese Ullathorne placed considerable reliance on the Sisters of St Paul, to support local schools and missions. Ullathorne's active support and encouragement led to many applications from priests in the diocese for sisters to work in their schools and missions. The unique advantage of the Sisters of Charity of St Paul, in the bishop's eyes, was that they were the only institute in England which would place as few as two sisters in a mission, so that they could operate in poorer missions where there were not resources to support a convent.[132] There was a realism in this on the part of bishop and foundress, which enabled much more practical good than more grandiose schemes might have done. Convents were opened in Radford, Walsall, Erdington, Spetchley, Dudley, West Bromwich, Brewood, Atherstone, Stourbridge, Worcester, Avon Dassett, Studley, Coleshill and Kidderminster and the influence of the Sisters of Charity of St Paul on the life and work of the diocese was immense and long lived.[133] Genevieve Dupuis became another of Ullathorne's close female friends and collaborators among the religious superiors of the diocese and his letters to her were full of support, sympathy and understanding, urging her in times of suffering to cling to the darkness, for God was to be found there and reassuring her that, despite her trials, 'all will be well'.[134]

Ullathorne was a significant guide and encouragement in her development of the community. 'To the nuns of his diocese Bishop Ullathorne was a rock of sense and a deep well of spiritual wisdom. He did not offer them scented bouquets of spirituality; he led them down the narrow path of detachment, patience, humility and obedience.'[135] He and Mother Dupuis had a close and affectionate friendship, and he took an active interest in the formation of her novices. 'There can be no doubt that he exercised a profound influence on the formation and development of the community in England.'[136] The sisters'

---

[132]. Selly Park, Ullathorne to Bp of Chartres, 15 September 1857. The favoured arrangement was to have four sisters, and it became common Selly Park parlance to talk of 'making up a four' so that a house could be made viable.
[133]. Hudson, p. 151.
[134]. Selly Park, Ullathorne to Genevieve Dupuis, 15 June 1860.
[135]. Hudson, p. 109.
[136]. Ibid.

involvement in education in Birmingham was immense, beginning in 1853 when they took over from the Sisters of Mercy at
St Chad's school. There they worked not only in the schools
but in the parish too, and throughout the second half of the
nineteenth century the sisters of St Paul expanded all over the
city area, especially in the poorer, predominantly Irish quarters. Genevieve Dupuis had put a scheme to Ullathorne for a
'training convent' which delighted him, and he hoped that
some of the teachers, already working in schools run by the
sisters in Birmingham, might be inclined to enter religious life
and form the core of a new institution, possibly to be placed in
the old Oratory premises in the city centre.[137]

The Catholic Poor Schools Committee strongly expressed a
wish to see a religious institute set up a training college for religious to be trained as teachers. Ullathorne's immediate
response was to suggest the Sisters of St Paul. 'The only institute that I am acquainted with in England of standing and
experience and that has such a plan for the basis of their rule.'
They were quite prepared for such work, he said, and to
submit their teachers and schools to inspection. The sisters
were prepared to co-operate with the Poor Schools Committee
in establishing a model house – probably in Birmingham, and a
plan was to go before the Committee within days.[138]

So evident was Ullathorne's enthusiasm for the cause of
Catholic education and the prospects offered by the work of
the Sisters of Mercy and Sisters of Charity of St Paul, that an
idea was floated at one point of him leaving the diocese in
order to run a projected national teaching institute. He was
taken with the idea, but could not envisage one bishop having
oversight without impinging on the jurisdiction of another.[139]
He came to the conclusion, attractive though the idea was to
him, that it 'would never work. Nor would the bishops entertain such a proposition, or the Holy See approve it ... What I
said was that I would joyfully leave my see to form a teaching
institute, but that the very fact of being a bishop would render
the working of it out impracticable however I might be

[137.] Selly Park, Ullathorne to Genevieve Dupuis, 12 February 1853.
[138.] AAW 130/1, Ullathorne to Wiseman, 30 March 1853.
[139.] Ushaw UL10, Ullathorne to Walker, 6 February 1857.

disposed to be the humble servant of some other bishop'.[140]

Ullathorne's policy on schools was based on a determined independence. He insisted that government inspection of religion in Catholic schools was 'unsound in principle', and was scathing about the 'fanatical spirit of trust in the government' which he perceived in Thomas Allies, the secretary of the Poor Schools Committee. He certainly did not allow the propagation of such ideas in the Diocese of Birmingham.[141] Ullathorne felt so strongly on the issue of government grants for the building and maintenance of elementary schools, that he published a seventy-two-page pamphlet in 1857, *Notes on the Education Question*, in which he sought to 'investigate certain leading details of the present system of education, and to suggest due care and forethought to such Catholics, and especially to the clergy, as may be bringing themselves under its influence'.[142] Wary of giving up 'our greatest earthly blessing', the freedom of action which the Catholics had enjoyed in respect of education, he was in the minority among the bishops in rejecting the view that accepting government grants meant that they had to accept a measure of government supervision or inspection.[143]

The extent of government supervision was to be determined by the Kemerton Trust, which defined the terms under which schools building grants should be held and administered. Ullathorne urged caution, for fear that religious freedom would be threatened by such a system.[144] What, he argued, if new conditions should be added to the existing contract between Parliament and the Church? Or a government in the future take on a 'no popery' hue? Then the Church schools would become vulnerable.[145] He was determined that the clergy had to be put in the picture so that 'they might understand what they were doing and that it was better the cat was out of the bag at once, and before we were further committed'.[146] He was insis-

140. Ushaw UL11, Ullathorne to Walker, 15 February 1857.
141. AAS Ullathorne Papers, Ullathorne to Grant, 8 October 1856.
142. *Notes on the Education Question* (1857), Preface.
143. Ibid., p. 8.
144. Richard J Schiefen, *Nicholas Wiseman and the Transformation of English Catholicism* (1984), p. 265.
145. *Notes on the Education Question* (1857), pp. 13–14.
146. Ushaw UL10, Ullathorne to Walker, 6 February 1857.

tent on dealing very carefully with government over questions
such as building grants for schools, always preferring to sup
with a long spoon where politicians were concerned. Something
like the matter of school building grants, committing all the
bishops and their successors permanently and irrevocably to a
'specific policy with a Protestant government' should be drawn
up with all the care of a synodical decree.[147] In private, to an old
friend, he made even clearer his mistrust of the government.

> Cowper's appointment to Committee of Council for
> Education, Art and Science makes him in effect Minister
> of Public Instruction and he is much influenced by
> Shaftesbury [the leading Evangelical reformer] …
> Depend upon it we shall lose nothing by keeping our eyes
> open, and that government will be all the more cautious
> with us if they see we are on the watch, and that we fear
> not our own people so far as to hide things from them.[148]

Although much of his pamphlet was devoted to political and
financial questions relating to inspection, grants etc., in the
longest single chapter, on teachers and training schools, he
took the opportunity to reiterate publicly his admiration for
the work of women religious in schools and in teacher training.
Fears were being expressed that, in the new educational
system, the secular element would dominate at the expense of
the religious. There was one certain remedy for this: 'It cannot
take place in schools conducted by Religious persons'.[149] His
one regret, as he had expressed it a year earlier in his *ad limina*
report, was the shortage of male religious to look after the
education of boys, but he was insistent that it was not appropriate for the female religious to teach in boys' schools. It was
'unnatural' and would force them either to neglect the boys'
moral education or become involved in 'very coarse matter, not
befitting religious'.[150] He could see clearly that education, and
a national system of schools could play a crucial part in halting
the disintegration of society, but insisted that the vital element

---

[147.] AAS Ullathorne Papers, Ullathorne to Grant, 30 May 1857.
[148.] Ushaw UL 10, Ullathorne to Walker, 6 February 1857.
[149.] *Notes on the Education Question* (1857), p. 36.
[150.] Selly Park, Ullathorne to Genevieve Dupuis, 6 August 1864.

was for Catholic schools to remain as independent as possible in order to inculcate the religious and social values which created stable families.[151]

The effects of industrialisation on social and family life, especially in the towns and cities of the diocese, had quickly become obvious to Ullathorne. He had soon concluded from his travels around his huge diocese, that the destruction of traditional society and family life had been brought about savagely by the spread of mining, manufacturing and railway building. What they had given the working man 'is summed up in one word, they have ceased to have a home'.[152] The lives of the poor, and especially, 'our poor, dear, Catholic Irish', and relations with employers were bitter and abusive, and led to a 'general coarseness of mind and deadness to moral feeling'.[153] He had quickly recognised the pointlessness of worrying about matters like school attendance, without a real understanding and empathy for the reality of the lives of the poor. His understanding of poverty and his deep and genuine sympathy for the poor rivalled that of Henry Mayhew and even Dickens, but his perspective was a profoundly Christian one, which placed the emphasis on the family. He considered it 'miraculous' that so many of the poor were virtuous, considering their circumstances, but believed that 'the fundamental cause of all this misery' was the lack of a home in the traditional sense, stemming from 'the absence of mothers from their homes'.[154]

The trust deed establishing the Kemerton Trust was accepted by the bishops at the Low Week meeting in April 1857 in the teeth of opposition from Ullathorne, who took Wiseman's statement published in *The Tablet* as a personal rebuke for his publication and another assertion of the archbishop's high-handed independence of the rest of the hierarchy.[155] Ullathorne wrote to the Birmingham clergy insisting that he had been no party to any agreement, and asserted that the matter had never been agreed at Low Week but rather at later, informal meetings between Wiseman and a

---

[151.] *Notes on the Education Question* (1857), p. 70.
[152.] Ibid., p. 52.
[153.] Ibid., pp. 52–4.
[154.] Ibid., p. 58.
[155.] Butler, *Life*, I, p. 181.

group of bishops. Wiseman hastily wrote round to all the bishops to try and secure agreement to his statement that the Kemerton Trust deed could be accepted as the basis for building grants. Ullathorne pressed for a matter of such gravity being subject to a synodal decree,[156] but nothing was forthcoming at the third provincial synod which took place at Oscott in 1859.

Ullathorne's insistence on pursuing the education issue resulted in a trenchant pastoral letter in early 1859, in which he raised the stakes, arguing that (in the light of the debacle over the previous Low Week meeting) the unity of the bishops had been weakened and therefore that of the Church itself.[157] He also addressed the vexed question of inspection of schools, which touched on the same issue of Catholic independence. A Royal Commission of 1858 had instituted state inspection of schools. When the Poor Schools Committee requested Catholic input before inspections took place in their schools, this was declined, and matters came to a head when it became clear that the commissioners intended to inspect religious as well as secular education. It also appeared that Protestant inspection had been happening in reformatories for juvenile delinquents, which could be classed as prisons rather than schools. The Royal Commission, in Ullathorne's view, set a dangerous precedent. The bishops met jointly in November to consider the two matters, resulting in a joint letter to all clergy cautioning them against permitting the proposed inspection, based on the principle of keeping Catholic education entirely in Catholic hands.

Mass educational provision, and the continued claims of the Churches to have some control over that provision, was one of the most complex and intractable social and political issues of the mid-nineteenth century. Massive population growth and economic expansion made large-scale provision urgent. The Churches could not offer sufficient schools without government aid, but the relationship between money and freedom of action was tricky, and for the Churches to walk away from education would have been a grave risk in the growing secular

[156.] Schiefen, pp. 265–7.
[157.] Pastoral Letter, 28 February 1859.

atmosphere. All the Christian denominations, but especially the Catholics, kept up the pressure to retain denominational control over education, but by the late 1860s it was becoming clear that the scale of the educational task among the poor meant that the state would have to intervene directly. The 1867 Reform Act enfranchised a million new voters and political fear of the long term effects of widespread illiteracy was considerable.

William Forster's name became permanently associated with the partial solution of the 1870 Education Act. He came from the radical social reform tradition characteristic of Victorian Quakerism. Entering Parliament in the 1860s, he became increasingly involved in the education question and was keen to find a legislative framework for elementary education. He wanted a mandatory and comprehensive system of basic schooling, publicly funded from local rates, which incorporated religious education of a non-denominational kind, and sponsored the first Education Bill in 1868 which contemplated giving the government powers of compulsion.[158]

This was to be the flashpoint of opposition, and the Catholic Church was inevitably in the front line. The greatest opponent of direct government action in education among the bishops was, not surprisingly, Ullathorne, and he called a public meeting in Birmingham in 1869, before he left for Rome, at which he spoke against Forster's proposed measure.[159] He was particularly critical of the proposed school boards, and was furiously opposed to Manning's suggestion of co-operation with them, describing it as the 'virtual surrender' of Catholic education.[160] Manning agreed with him on the need for joint episcopal action, but argued forcefully that Catholic membership of boards would be the only way to save certain Catholic schools from closure. Non co-operation (which Ullathorne

---

[158.] Allen Warren, 'Forster, William Edward (1818–1886)', *Oxford Dictionary of National Biography*, Oxford University Press, 2004 [http://www.oxforddnb.com/view/article/9926, accessed 14 Sept 2005].

[159.] V. A. McClelland, *Cardinal Manning: his public career and influence 1865–92* (1962), p. 65.

[160.] AAW Ullathorne Correspondence, Ullathorne to Manning, 7 October 1870.

advocated) would leave the Catholic Church exposed to the hostility and opposition of the School Boards.[161]

Gladstone himself opposed non-denominational religious education, which then opened the way for others, including the Catholics. McClelland makes clear Manning's active involvement and influence over Gladstone in the planning and passage of the Bill.[162] The key issue was whether or not religiously based education should continue alongside state provision and receive funding to do so. The original Bill, which included the proposal of a state examining body was roundly condemned by the Catholic bishops, and was ultimately dropped. Ullathorne was, as ever, wary of dealings with government, believing that if a point was yielded, this was likely to be regarded as yielding the principle. He would have clearly preferred Catholic education to be wholly independent of government interference and funding, and was sceptical about the policy of the Catholic Poor Schools Committee which appeared to make it 'almost a crime' to run a Catholic school independently.[163]

As soon as the English bishops returned from Rome in the late summer of 1870 after the suspension of the Vatican Council, they were faced with the huge political issue of the impending Education Bill debate. The Bill was introduced to the House of Commons in February 1870, while the bishops were still away, but Manning stayed in contact with Gladstone from Rome. Their unavoidable absence in Rome had left the bishops with little time to influence the legislation as it proceeded through Parliament, and individual bishops were feeling their way without any coherent policy to guide them.[164] By contrast, the Protestant Nonconformists were well organised and active in lobbying Gladstone for a 'conscience clause'.[165] Manning was keen to co-operate, 'to the utmost of

161. Ibid.
162. V. A. McClelland, *Manning*, pp. 62–76.
163. AAW Ullathorne Correspondence, Ullathorne to Manning, 27 March 1869.
164. AAW Ullathorne Correspondence, Ullathorne to Manning, 7 October 1870.
165. John T. Smith, 'The Wesleyans, the "Romanists" and the Education Act of 1870' in *Recusant History* vol. 23 (1996), pp. 127–43.

our power' by means of accepting any invitation to put clergy on the new school boards, in order to influence matters to the advantage of the Catholic community.[166] Ullathorne, however, was sceptical, and unimpressed at Manning's actions. He was scathing when Manning did not appear to know what was on offer, and had not fully explored it with the government, and dubious about the newly proposed school boards. He favoured staying independent of them, even if it meant loss of resources.[167] He remained opposed to Manning's attempt to gather the English bishops together to consider giving up Catholic inspection in schools in return for other advantages envisaged in the Bill before Parliament. McClelland is certain that such a meeting never took place, which may well be true if Ullathorne dug his heels in, but the other bishops were also equally reluctant.[168] In the event, Manning wrote to Gladstone: 'We will forego the School Rate to be still under the Privy Council.'[169]

Manning kept up political pressure on Gladstone to achieve a 'dual system' of state schools and denominational schools with government funding, with Catholic participation in the School Boards. Ullathorne was unconvinced, and continued to resist Manning's policy of co-operation with School Boards.[170] The final scheme set out a national system based on supporting the existing schools run by the Established Church, and making provision for religious education in the new state schools subject to a conscience clause. The 'Cowper-Temple' clause, amending the Act, eventually construed a formula which prohibited any denominational catechesis in Board Schools, on the condition that voluntary schools were funded directly from the treasury and not from local rates. This kept the Church Schools separate and independent of the School Boards and secured continued state funding.

[166.] AAW Ullathorne Correspondence, Manning to Ullathorne, 17 September 1870.
[167.] BAA B4796, Ullathorne to Vicar General O'Sullivan, 23 February 1870.
[168.] McClelland, p. 80; AAW Ullathorne Correspondence, Manning to Ullathorne, 21 October 1870.
[169.] Quoted in McClelland, *Manning*, p. 67.
[170.] Ibid., pp. 70–2.

The Forster Act sealed the separation between the state schools and voluntary schools and created the dual system which continues to this day, and continued government funding for voluntary (church) schools.[171] This Act, which was so fundamental to the creation of the modern education system, has been described as Forster's 'greatest political and legislative achievement'.[172] It was also a triumph for the Church Schools, which arguably would not have been achieved without the pressure Ullathorne brought to bear on Manning. Ullathorne's mistrust of government control and insistence on independence for Catholics was more effective in this instance than Manning's attempt at conciliation.

However, Ullathorne was clear about the implications of the education crisis for the Catholic community. The money had to be found to keep Catholic children out of the Board Schools.

We are left then to make the choice, whether we will establish and support sufficient schools and teaching of our own for our own Catholic children, or whether, through our neglect, we are to leave our children under the compulsion of having to attend schools in which they will either learn no religion, or a teaching that is in opposition to the Catholic religion ... If we have sufficient schools, with proper accommodation and effective teaching of our own, we shall save the Catholic children from these rate schools, and secure their being trained in the Catholic faith.[173]

This was a persuasive argument, which carried weight, and became the predominant Catholic viewpoint. As a result, the greatest achievement of the ensuing century was the creation of the Catholic schools system in England.

Most of the social and political issues in which the English Catholic leadership became involved, like the education ques-

---

[171.] Allen Warren, 'Forster, William Edward (1818–1886)', *Oxford Dictionary of National Biography*, Oxford University Press, 2004 [http://www.oxforddnb.com/view/article/9926, accessed 14 Sept 2005].

[172.] Ibid.

[173.] Pastoral Letter, 27 October 1870.

tion, concerned independence from government interference and freedom of action. Catholic Emancipation in 1829 had gained Catholics the right of Parliamentary representation, and the restored hierarchy of 1850 had created a formally constituted and recognised leadership which had both the authority of Canon Law behind it and a measure of respect from the civil powers. This was only the beginning. In every sphere of life, the Catholic Church had to fight for rights and freedoms: the liberty of women to live in convents unmolested by inspection; the right to train teachers and teach the Catholic faith alongside the growing state education system; the acceptance of Catholic chaplains to serve the armed forces of the British Empire; the acknowledgement of the right of Catholic prisoners to receive pastoral care from their own clergy – all of these were hard-won battles.

From the time of the Crimean War in 1853, Bishop Thomas Grant of Southwark had responsibility for negotiating with the government to get Catholic chaplains permission to minister to the troops. The first chaplains (alongside the nuns who nursed with Florence Nightingale) volunteered for the Crimea, and in some cases gave their lives. England's first war memorial in honour of a Catholic chaplain is a window commemorating John Wheble at Oscott College. Wheble was one of the first group of priests to volunteer for service as chaplain, and died of dysentery in November 1854. He was Master of Ceremonies and Wiseman's 'right hand man' at the first Synod of Westminster held at Oscott in 1852; at the second Synod in 1855, Wiseman unveiled his memorial.

Involvement in military chaplaincy also gave Grant a way into opening discussions about prison chaplains through the question of military prisons. From 1854 he was responsible for prison chaplaincy, working with Bishop Robert Willson over conditions in the remaining convict colonies in Hobart, and it was Willson who gave Grant his agenda for government negotiations.[174] In 1858 a committee of lay and clerical Catholics was established to lobby the government for better access for Catholic prisoners in the UK to chaplaincy care. The

---

[174.] Michael Clifton, *The Quiet Negotiator: Bishop Grant of Southwark* (1993), p. 131.

fundamental problem was that all civilian prisoners were placed under the care of the Church of England chaplain, who was paid on a per capita basis and had considerable influence over release and punishment decisions, and it was difficult for Catholic clergy to obtain entry to prisons. Change was a long time in coming, and not until 1863 did the Prison Ministers Act allow for full-time paid Catholic chaplains in larger prisons and officiating chaplains in others.[175] This had only limited effect in certain parts of the country and much was left to the discretion of prison governors, leading to a renaissance of the Catholic committee in 1865, lobbying for further concessions. In particular, the committee demanded free access to prisoners, provision for Catholic instruction and worship and the weeding out of anti-Catholic tracts from prison libraries.[176]

Ullathorne's interest in, and commitment to penal reform had not disappeared after his involvement in the immediate question of transportation in the late 1830s, and he continued to keep up with contemporary debates about prison reform in England. One of his concerns expressed in his first *ad limina* report in 1856 had been the difficulty of getting proper provision for Catholics in prisons and reformatories, and he commented on the 'bitter anti-Catholic spirit' he found in the penal system.[177] He also identified the need for Catholic run reformatories to deal with juvenile delinquents – the products of an educational system which, in his view, was failing boys.

The question of prison reform re-entered parliament in the mid-1860s, and revived Ullathorne's active interest. 'At present I am bringing my Australian experience to bear on the prison question, preparatory to next session in Parliament.'[178] The pending parliamentary bill provoked him to go into print again on a subject he had not touched since Australia. 'I have sent you by the President General of the Benedictines a copy of my paper read to the Academia, *On the Management of Criminals*, in which I hope you will find both curious and interesting

[175.] Ibid., p. 133.
[176.] Ibid., p. 135.
[177.] Stone G/ULL/V/2.1, Status Animarum of the Diocese of Birmingham, 1856.
[178.] VEC Talbot Papers, Ullathorne to Talbot, 17 December 1865.

matter.'[179] The 'curious and interesting matter' was a detailed history of the old, unreformed penal system, including a good deal of repeated material from his published accounts of transportation to Australia and the conditions there. His knowledge of the history of penal reform and of recent writings on the theme is evidence of a deep and abiding interest. What was fresh was a lengthy exposition of the reformed penal system in England under the four headings of the Solitary, the Separate, the Silent and Aggregate and the Mark systems.

This last system, based on the principle of earning release by 'marks' awarded for good behaviour, was originated by Alexander Maconochie, the reforming superintendent of Norfolk Island between 1840 and 1844. He was, in Ullathorne's opinion, 'destined to be a future celebrity' alongside the great penal reformer, John Howard.[180] Ullathorne was clearly an enthusiastic supporter of what Maconochie had tried to achieve on Norfolk Island, but pessimistic that he would be able to imbue all his gaolers with the same spirit, in order to make it work. He was convinced that the mark system was of 'inestimable value' when used in conjunction with the other existing penal systems.[181]

Maconochie was already well known as a radical writer on penal reform before he left England in the 1830s, and a critical report on Van Diemen's Land resulted in him being sacked from there; ironically, Governor John Franklin of Van Diemen's Land, who sacked Maconochie, was a cousin and childhood friend of Ullathorne's mother.[182] He attempted to put his ideas into practice on Norfolk Island, and reformed it into a peaceful and ordered prison, and those who left the island ('Maconochie's Gentlemen') were noted for their good behaviour.[183] In 1844, however, after a critical report, he was sacked, and returned to England, 'a disappointed though not disheartened man'.[184]

179. VEC Talbot Papers, Ullathorne to Talbot, 19 March 1866.
180. *Management of Criminals*, p. 30.
181. Ibid., p. 37.
182. *Autobiography*, p. 3.
183. Norval Morris, *Maconochie's Gentlemen: the story of Norfolk Island* (2002), p. 164.
184. Morris, p. 163.

He returned to active campaigning, and was appointed governor of the new prison in Birmingham in 1849.[185] Matthew Davenport Hill, the first native of Birmingham to be called to the bar, was recorder of Birmingham from 1839 until 1866, and as a leading advocate of penal reform played a major part in Maconochie's appointment in Birmingham. Within two years Maconochie was dismissed after a Royal Commission of inquiry implicated him in its criticisms of the management of the prison.[186] After Maconochie's dismissal, Hill became the main advocate of the mark system, so he and Ullathorne obviously crossed paths in Birmingham.[187] The new prison, something of a showplace in its day, supplemented a forty-year-old building which could only take pre- and post-trial prisoners; all Birmingham's criminals until then served their sentences in Warwick Gaol.[188] The most recent study of Maconochie suggests that Ullathorne was also part of the campaign to get Maconochie appointed to Birmingham, but does not give a source for Ullathorne's involvement.[189] It is certainly likely that he did press his case. Ullathorne clearly knew Maconochie well, and they had corresponded and met in Australia, where Moconochie had tested out his ideas for Norfolk Island on him.[190]

Ullathorne was convinced that any worthwhile penal system must be geared towards the possibility of penitence and reform in the individual, and Maconochie's mark system had a part to play. Maconochie described the mark system as putting the

185. M. F. G. Selby, 'Maconochie , Sir Alexander (1787–1860)', rev. Felix Driver, *Oxford Dictionary of National Biography*, Oxford University Press, 2004 [http://www.oxforddnb.com/view/article/37725, accessed 14 Sept 2005].

186. Ibid.

187. P. W. J. Bartrip, 'Hill, Matthew Davenport (1792–1872)', *Oxford Dictionary of National Biography*, Oxford University Press, 2004 [http://www.oxforddnb.com/view/article/13286, accessed 14 Sept 2005].

188. Victoria County History, *A History of the County of Warwickshire: Volume 7: The City of Birmingham* (1964), 'Political and Administrative History: Local Government and Public Services', pp. 318–53.

189. Morris, p. 166.

190. *Management of Criminals*, p. 32.

keys of the prison into the prisoner's hand. Penitence, reform of life and consequent amended behaviour earned privileges and remissions. Savage treatment only made behaviour worse. For this reason Ullathorne abhorred flogging, particularly when inflicted as a casual punishment for minor misdemeanours. Even its controlled use in English prisons, he insisted, had a brutalising and hardening effect both on the criminal and the officials responsible for it. Ullathorne understood human nature, and could appreciate the provocation endured by prison warders and their preference for 'a sharp and decisive instrument of repression', but insisted that the stress of the situation would lead to restraint and discretion being abandoned. 'The very threat is enough to conjure up all the bad blood that has hitherto slept in a man's veins.'[191] His solution for hardened and brutalised criminals was separate incarceration, and the use of the lash only rarely and subject to a sentence given in open court.

His other abhorrence was for the practice of public execution, which he had witnessed at close quarters in New South Wales. This tradition was centuries old and the grisly spectacles of the burning of heretics, gibbeting of murderers' corpses and hangings on the scaffold were part of the public life of English society. Even after burnings were consigned to history, beheading ended in 1824 and gibbeting ended in 1832, only gradually did attitudes turn against public execution. A Royal Commission of 1866 recommended its abolition, but it was not until 1868 that public executions were stopped. The last man to be hung in public being Michael Barrett, one of the Fenians involved in blowing up a wall of Clerkenwell prison.[192]

By then, public execution was widely regarded as uncivilised by an increasingly squeamish public, who nonetheless wished capital punishment to continue. The behaviour of the watching crowd was also a source of embarrassment to political and social leaders.[193] Ullathorne brought another dimension to the debate. While many Christian penal reformers had wished to

---

[191.] Ibid., p. 17.
[192.] V. A. C. Gattrell, *The Hanging Tree: execution and the English People 1770–1868* (1994), p. 589.
[193.] Gattrell, pp. 590–1.

place greater emphasis on inducing repentance in the convicted criminal and an awareness of sin in the watching crowd, few took it as seriously as Ullathorne, or wrote of it as perceptively. The criminal life and the risk of the gallows had a 'morbid charm', and execution offered the criminal 'one great moment of excitement'. The conduct of executions in public and the 'irresistible propensity to display himself in a dying speech' glamorised the criminal and the occasion. Its effect on spectators was quite the opposite of the 'awful warning' which was intended, and it did nothing to deter other hardened criminals; rather, it made them blasé about the quick death meted out on a man whose time had come. The end result was a drunken wake celebrated by those left, and speculation about whose turn it might be next.

Ullathorne was a man of his time, and did not contemplate the abolition of the death penalty. Few, if any, of the Victorian penal reformers advocated abolition and, 'acceptance of capital punishment was also doctrinally rooted ... since within the Divine order pain was an ordained consequence of sin, pain must be inflicted within a righteous human order too'.[194] Ullathorne, however, suggested that a hanging be carried out behind the walls of the prison, where 'the very mystery of that lonely death would strike the imagination with some degree of awe, and men would think more about the criminal's soul than of his suspended body'.[195] It would concentrate the mind of the condemned person and of the waiting crowd on judgement and penitence. Mostly the reasoning behind the abolition of public hanging was to do with its effect on the watching crowd or the delicate sensibilities of the wider public. The Home Secretary, Gathorne Hardy, felt rather that the 'mystery and indefiniteness' of private hangings would be a greater deterrent to the criminal classes.[196] To Ullathorne it was much more about the individual concerned and concentrating his attention on eternal life. What he wanted to achieve in the mind and heart of the condemned, was what he had been able to bring about on Norfolk Island, a state of peaceful, humble and fervent penitence.[197]

[194.] Gattrell, p. 373.
[195.] *Management of Criminals*, p. 47.
[196.] Gattrell, p. 592.
[197.] *Autobiography*, pp. 120–1.

Whatever the conditions of imprisonment under the various programmes of reform, Ullathorne, not unlike the Evangelical penal reformers, traced their origins back to the penitential regimes of Christianity. The penitential system had borrowed from the eremitical and monastic life, but had created 'husks and shells of those modes of Christian discipline, stripped of their fruits and recast into rigid and relentless rules, enforced upon unwilling natures, and so deprived of their chastening and healing qualities'.[198] This analysis related to his long running concerns about the absence of Catholic religious influence in prisons. The only thing which would make a penal system work as a means of reformation was the presence of 'ministers of God and of the soul', who would 'hold up the Divine suffering and draw those unhappy hearts towards the Almighty patience exhibited on the Cross, and lead them thence into themselves'.[199] Only the presence of a priest and the sacrament of confession could elicit a response of conscience from the prisoner, which was the only route to penitence and reform.

However, as well as a theological and spiritual point about sin and penitence, Ullathorne was also making a political point. His concern was particularly with Catholic prisoners (as it had been in Australia), and his aim was to achieve equal status for Catholic clergy in the prison system alongside those of the Established Church. This could only be expressed in a way 'intelligible to everyone concerned', which meant public clarification of the chaplain's official position and stipend, and he called on the government to do for the clergy of the home country what it had done in Australia in 1836, and give Catholic clergy equal standing with others. Ullathorne took the unusual step when his public lecture was published as a tract of fifty pages of affixing a dedication: the dedicatee was Thomas Grant of Southwark, much of whose career had been devoted to obtaining better treatment for Catholic prisoners.

Ullathorne's support of and devotion to the convents under his care was never more tested than during the second half of the 1860s, when he once again went into battle on their behalf

198. *Management of Criminals*, p. 47.
199. Ibid., p. 48.

on several occasions. The attempts in the early 1850s to introduce government inspection of convents had fizzled out from lack of parliamentary enthusiasm, but there was a body of public opinion sustained by hard-line Protestants which continued to be highly suspicious of Catholic convents and of the small number of Anglican sisterhoods springing out of the High Church wing of the Church of England. One of the leading exponents of this view was Charles Newdegate MP, whose ancestral home, Arbury Hall, lay within Ullathorne's diocese, less than thirty miles from Birmingham. In April 1864, having been involved in the cause of an aggrieved individual who felt cheated of a legacy which had gone to the London Oratory, Newdegate brought the matter of monasteries and convents back to Parliament, pressing for a select committee of enquiry.[200] His own Tory party was unenthusiastic, indeed Disraeli was busy courting the Catholic vote. In 1864 and again the following year, government pressure ensured that Newdegate's Parliamentary motion was lost. Newdegate dragged up again the 'Colwich Nunnery Case' from 1856, and Ullathorne publicly refuted Newdegate's allegations about the secrecy and imprisonment, and invited him to visit Colwich and find out for himself.[201] Newdegate's refusal of Ullathorne's invitation, after a decade of pressing for convent inspection, rather gave the bishop the moral high ground, and the vigorous attack on Newdegate mounted by leading and well respected Catholics Charles Langdale and Sir Charles Clifford, both of whom both had sisters at Colwich, put paid to that aspect of the campaign.[202]

Newdegate however was not cowed and got himself re-elected to the 1865 Parliament on an anti-Catholic ticket and continued to lobby against any concession to Catholics, including the proposed amendment to the Parliamentary oath and the attempted repeal of the Ecclesiastical Titles Act.[203] He was also a staunch supporter of William Murphy whose anti-Catholic lectures were an irritant which Ullathorne found hard

[200] Arnstein, pp. 63–4.
[201] Ibid., pp. 69–70.
[202] Ibid., pp. 72–3.
[203] Ibid., pp. 78–82.

to ignore. For the bishop, the whole anti-Catholic campaign and the damage it did to the Catholics under his care became enmeshed with the danger from Fenianism. He treated it as a serious threat to the peace and safety of Catholics, particularly those of Irish descent:

> Nuns are insulted in the streets and the little sisters have been pelted with stones ... And now we have these miscreant deeds attributed to the Fenians, and our countrymen are in a panic, which, if we have more of their cruel and violent displays, will end in a terrible insurrection of feeling against the Irish people in this country. I am glad to say that the present tone of the newspapers is to separate the body of the Irish people from the acts of these miscreants, but there is no knowing what a repetition of their acts would bring about. You must all pray that God may avert such a calamity.[204]

He was not exaggerating: troops had been called in to quell riots when Murphy lectured in Wolverhampton, furious Irishmen rioted in Walsall and Murphy provoked the most serious outbreak of violence in Birmingham since the Church and King riots of 1792.[205] When he attempted to return two years later to speak about the proposed disestablishment of the Irish Church, Murphy was prevented from entering Birmingham under pain of arrest.[206] Although Newdegate distanced himself somewhat from Murphy's rabble rousing, he leapt to his defence on the issue of free speech.

Birmingham had its own 'Nunnery Scandal', provoked by a local anti-Catholic doctor, Thomas Gutteridge, who, in the course of a public lecture on 'Ritualism' launched an attack on convents. His tale was of the daughter of a 'gentleman of good commercial position', who had been placed in a convent by her family to prevent her contracting an unsuitable marriage. When the father tried to retrieve his daughter, he was initially prevented by the convent superior, and only the force of law

---

[204.] Colwich, Ullathorne to Prioress, 19 December 1867.
[205.] Arnstein, pp. 92–3.
[206.] Ibid., p. 101.

enabled him to extract the young woman from her 'imprison-ment'. The culmination of the story was the unexpected and sudden birth of a child – in the carriage on the way home – the result of rape by the convent confessor. Ullathorne and the local Catholic laity were up in arms, and a long and convoluted correspondence ensued between various respected laymen in the city and Dr Gutteridge. Eventually, after three months, a form of committee of enquiry was convened, and the source of the story, who turned out to be a nineteen-year-old seamstress in the Gutteridge household, admitted that the whole thing was a pack of lies.[207] Ullathorne ensured that the whole story became public.

Ullathorne's *Three Lectures on the Conventual Life* (1868), while repeating some material from his earlier publications of the 1850s, were his most developed exposition of the history, purpose and true significance of religious life. Provoked yet again into defending the honour of the women in religious life who were the objects of scurrilous and hostile tales of imprison-ment and sinister goings-on, Ullathorne leapt to his pen. Much of what he wrote covered relatively familiar ground, castigating the attackers of convent life, patiently explaining to the igno-rant, and carefully tracing the role of women religious in the history of the Church. The most interesting of the lectures is the last, in which he described aspects of the life and work of female religious, but which began with a reflection on freedom. 'Freedom is no stranger to convents. A nun is not a slave, nor is her obedience an act of slavery; on the contrary, it is intelli-gent, dignified and free.'[208] In this section, Ullathorne discussed with real insight and passion, the freedom inherent in serving God, and in particular the profound freedom of reli-gious life. This was not the freedom of action and personal liberty which liberal Victorian society understood the word to mean, but, 'an inward power, a spontaneous motion, a great moral quality, a vital force originating action from within us, the source and first principle of all responsibility, acting in the light of intelligence, from a motive of good, and for a worthy

---

[207.] *The Alleged 'Nunnery Scandal' at Birmingham: correspondence relating thereto and refutation of the slander* (1868), passim.
[208.] *Three Lectures on Conventual Life* (1868), Lecture 3, p. 3.

end'.[209] These words flowed confidently from a man who had come to understand freedom and responsibility in his mature years, and who also understood the driving force in conventual life. His own experience and spiritual struggles had taught him that 'freedom of soul as a habit is won through the way of the voluntary cross'.[210]

Speaking from his own experience as much as of that of the nuns, he insisted that 'deeper than all other obstacles to this liberating spirit works within us that pride of life, that rooted, all absorbing egotism, which nothing will loosen save our subjecting ourselves from our very centre to God'.[211] That surrender required obedience to the will of God, but Ullathorne was remarkably modern in insisting that obedience was not blind and submissive but should be practised, 'intelligently, heartily and of good conscience'. Then it became the most effective way of developing a vigorous and responsive will and a cheerful and happy spirit.[212] Whether Mr Newdegate and his like ever understood that 'without obedience to something higher than ourselves, nothing is ennobled in this world', is unlikely, but to the nuns' great defender, they were ennobled by striving for the 'art and science of spiritual perfection'.[213]

Once again, in the spring of 1870 Newdegate brought the matter of convent inspection back to Parliament. He managed to get a debate, which he won by a narrow margin. This reflected popular attitudes and culture to a growing extent, as Walter Arnstein suggested. 'The nun as a symbol of spiritual docility or of repressed sexuality or as a victim of disappointed love or physical cruelty constituted a subject of perennial fascination for Victorian artists'.[214] The bishops were in Rome at the Vatican Council when the Parliamentary vote was taken, but a campaign was soon launched to rebutt Newdegate's efforts and a massive Catholic petition containing nearly 285,000 signatures was generated within weeks.[215] Gladstone

[209.] Ibid., p. 4.
[210.] Ibid., p. 6.
[211.] Ibid., p. 8.
[212.] Ibid., p. 9.
[213.] Ibid., p. 9.
[214.] Arnstein, pp. 129–30.
[215.] Ibid., p140.

engineered an amendment which changed the focus of the committee of enquiry to property and finance, which assuaged some unease and pacified the vocal Parliamentary support for some action in relation to convents.

The committee met during the summer months of 1870, while the Catholic bishops continued their work at the Vatican Council in Rome. The main purpose, under Gladstone's amended terms, was to enquire into the legality of charitable trusts designed to support Catholic activities.[216] The technical question of trusts had troubled the Catholic leadership for twenty years, but in their case more as to whether trusts registered under the British legal system conflicted with the Canon Law of the Church. Ullathorne had been deputed to Rome in 1862 to get a definitive ruling on this question. An act of 1860 had required all charities to be enrolled with the Charity Commissioners established in 1853. In fact the committee of enquiry of 1870 revealed a basic injustice, that most convents had no protection under charity law as they depended on secret trusts held by de facto owners. This left them vulnerable to the basic laws of succession and inheritance.

The tide changed in the direction of ensuring proper legal standing for the convents and Newdegate retired from the committee in disgust. The report did not lead to legislation but encouraged the courts to lay down appropriate case law in the future. In 1872, Ullathorne, realising the continued vulnerability of the convents to legal and canonical misunderstanding, issued a document on these matters. It supplemented his 1869 *Instruction for the Superioresses and Communities of Religious Women*. Both of these are technical documents covering the canonical position of religious women in simple and perpetual vows, aimed at securing legal standing and protection to guarantee the future of women religious without interference from laity or clergy. In the light of the outcome of the Vatican Council, the creation of the new Kingdom of Italy and defeat of papal temporal power, and the emergence of Fenianism as a major political force, the government and political establishment had bigger fish to fry with the Catholic leadership than lurid tales of convent life. Convent tales continued to appear at

---

[216.] Ibid., p. 149.

intervals in the press and popular journals, but they generally attracted less public attention, as the social and educational work of the nuns became more familiar in society.

Much of the public furore over nuns in the late 1860s took place for Ullathorne against a backdrop of personal anguish, marked by the declining health and eventual death of his greatest friend and ally, Margaret Hallahan, in May 1868. They had forged a remarkable and close partnership since their days together in Coventry and she had been his confidante during the years when he had nurtured and encouraged the formation and growth of her congregation of Dominican sisters. The mother house at Stone had become his second home, and was his choice of burial place for his own mother and eventually for himself. For a bishop to be buried in a parish church attached to a convent, close to his mother and the woman he called 'my dear friend and sister', and not in his cathedral, was a mark of extraordinary human devotion and loyalty as well as personal humility. Although he formed friendships among his fellow Benedictines and other bishops, such as Manning, Grant and Brown these were inevitably focused on business and ecclesiastical matters on which opinions were shared and policy thrashed out. His friendships with women, particularly nuns, was of a different order.

Part of his sense of himself as a bishop and the isolated dignity and responsibility of the position which weighed heavily on him, was that he rarely wrote in intimate terms to his friends. In his early years in Australia and Coventry, he wrote confidential and revealing letters to his old mentor and friend Thomas Brown, but there was a distinct change of tone and content in his letters once Ullathorne joined the episcopal ranks. The letters became more formal, and their content less personal. It was only to his women friends, and particularly the nuns for whom he felt such affection, that he ever let down his guard. During all the aggravation of ecclesiastical politics and public affairs, the one thing which kept the private Ullathorne on an even keel was the peace and affectionate simplicity which he found in the religious houses of the diocese, especially those of the enclosed Benedictines where, of course, he felt a particular affinity. It was with the nuns that he could be light-hearted and even teasing. Even as a sixty-year-old bishop with a public reputation for standing on his dignity, he wrote (tongue in cheek) to one of the nuns at Colwich, where morale was low, following the adverse public attention.

> When you said that our holy Father [ie himself] had a large heart, I think you ought to have demonstrated its connexion with your petition. But whoever yet heard of a logical nun? Two immediate points demand proof:
> 1 Did our holy Father exhibit the large or the strict side of his heart on visitation?
> 2 Did he expect greater exactness or greater laxness of observance to follow on immediately after his visitation?
> But as my heart is not so large as it is weak, I must in justice, even though against myself, confess that even in the sanctuary itself I had formed the intention of asking for, or rather granting as part of the visitation, a day of recreation, to be given as soon as I left the choir. And now I must confess to another weakness by which my memory let my intention drop so soon as I again breathed the dissipating atmosphere of the parlour. But if you will consent to be my vicar for this one occasion, just to enable me to make restitution of that weak intention, I authorise you, in the most appropriate and religious way in which you can accomplish the act, to present this letter to mother prioress and leave the letter to say, *mea culpa*, I forgot to grant a recreation day, and as an act of penance for my dropped intention, I now ask for it to be given.[217]

On the other side, the women themselves, and in particular Margaret Hallahan, placed total trust in his guidance, not only in the practicalities of the building of convents and missionary work, but in the salvation of their own souls. Margaret Hallahan's trust in him was total: 'No person knows my nature so well and no other person will or does work for my perfection but yourself.'[218] She shared with him all her fears and doubts and all her impetuous impulses, and even in the last years of her life of continual service to God, with her religious founda-

---

[217.] Colwich, Ullathorne to Miss Bateman, 15 September 1867.
[218.] Stone G/ULL/IV/2, M. Hallahan to Ullathorne, 14 August 1859.

tion secure, it was only to her old friend that she revealed her, 'depression of the soul' born of the terrible 'fear of not being saved at the last'.[219]

Ullathorne himself was not in the best of health during the winter of 1867-8, but was preoccupied with the progress of Mother Margaret's final illness. His great friend was in continual agony, unable to rise from her bed, with spinal tumours. Five doctors had confessed themselves perplexed, but in view of her debilitating pain, Ullathorne had intervened and insisted on the use of available drugs rather than relying on traditional homeopathic remedies which the convent favoured.[220] Margaret Hallahan died after six months of painful illness on 11 May 1868. His grief at her death tore his heart. Her death was 'a loss unspeakable', and her sufferings in the last months, 'the most awful I ever knew'. Ullathorne was bereft at the loss of her: 'The greatest privilege of my life has been the twenty-five years of her friendship and confidence, of which I always felt myself unworthy.' Yet his loss was tempered with a strong sense that he and the Dominican sisters now had a powerful friend in heaven.

> The consolations which have followed the departure of my dear friend and sister are unspeakable. Periods of light and grace have flowed into the hearts of all her children. They seem all without exception to have been lifted into a higher and more supernatural sphere, and this is even the most conspicuous among those few who caused her most solicitude.[221]

Sr Imelda Poole, who succeeded Hallahan as superior told him,

> I am feeling poverty stricken and empty, missing that great and loyal mind that used to fill and engage and elevate mine. She was a grand reservoir of God's graces and gifts, but I know that the fountain that filled that

[219.] Stone G/ULL/IV/216, M. Hallahan to Ullathorne, January 1867.
[220.] AAW Ullathorne Correspondence, Ullathorne to Manning, 20 March 1868.
[221.] Ushaw UL 18, Ullathorne to Walker, 19 May 1868.

reservoir is open to my small heart and can and will fill it.[222]

Ullathorne's first choice of preacher for Mother Margaret's funeral was Newman, but he begged not to and suggested Northcote. Ullathorne dismissed this idea, as Northcote was 'like her own son, and would break down'.[223] The Dominican Congregation and Ullathorne finally judged it appropriate to ask Manning to preach at her funeral, in order to properly honour 'the foundress of a great religious work'.[224] In the event, Manning could not extricate himself from prior engagements to get to Stone for the funeral, so Ullathorne (not receiving Manning's letter until the morning of the funeral) had to 'screw himself up' to preach. This he managed to do for an hour and three quarters![225]

Ullathorne told his friend, Canon Walker in Scarborough, that

her life will be written, and then she will be known outside her communities. There are large collections of her letters, which are full of religious genius. We have traced her life from infancy, partly from those who know her, and who at my request wrote notes of her then remarkable vigour of character, developed from her seventh year, partly from her own nature. Her personal austerities were very great, and were renewed the year before she died to an extent which, had I known, I never could have permitted, yet they were known to her confessor. She told special sisters to whom she gave directions of her approaching death months before she was laid up. I firmly believe that from a child of nine years, she never lost the presence of God. Her humility during her sufferings I can only call intense, as her patience was strong, her head clear and judgement decisive to the last.[226]

222. Stanbrook 16, Ullathorne to Abbess Gregson, 22 May 1868.
223. L&D XXIV, to Ullathorne, p. 66, 24 April 1868 and n. 2.
224. AAW Ullathorne Correspondence, Ullathorne to Manning, 11 May 1868.
225. AAW Ullathorne correspondence, Ullathorne to Manning, 15 May 1868.
226. Ushaw UL18, Ullathorne to Walker, 19 May 1868.

The life of Margaret Hallahan was quickly compiled, as Ullathorne directed, and edited by one of her closest collaborators, who eventually became her second successor as superior.[227] It is clear from the number of references to it in his letters, that the biography was a source of great consolation to Ullathorne during his long absence from home at the Vatican Council.

There are very few copies of the *Life* in Rome, and these are being passed on from hand to hand. I presented my last copy to the American College yesterday. Bishop Grant has read the half dozen chapters on her spiritual life, the copy of which you sent me ... When I mentioned to him the analogy with St [Teresa],[228] he said he thought I should find a saint who bore a stronger general resemblance than either St Teresa or St Catherine, and instanced St Gertrude, her dominant devotion to the Blessed Sacrament, as well as her love of the Divine Office. Still I think her nature, style of mind and her humour savours more of St Teresa, and her interior heart of St Catherine, although there are such striking points of resemblance in her spiritual cast of work to St Gertrude. Father Hecker, the American, told me that her life had strongly taken hold in America before he left, and Mrs Monteith[229] said the Presbyterians were reading it in Scotland.[230]

227. Sr Francis Raphael Drane, *Life of Mother Margaret Hallahan: foundress of the English Congregation of St Catherine of Siena* (1869).
228. The text has Gertrude, but he seems to have meant Teresa.
229. Ullathorne often mentioned Robert and Wilhelmina Monteith. They were among the leading Scottish Catholic converts, received by Newman in 1846. His campaign for the reassertion of the law of nations at the Vatican Council of 1870–71 was a logical development of his view that conscription encouraged war as a regular arm of policy. Using a variety of influences – the *Diplomatic Review*, Bishop Mermillod of Geneva, the French sociologist Frédéric Le Play, a visit to Turkey to win over the Armenian bishops, and, not least, lavish Roman hospitality – he won the attention of the pope, and the issue reached the council'. Bernard Aspinwall, 'Monteith, Robert (1811–1884)', *Oxford Dictionary of National Biography*, Oxford University Press, 2004 [http://www.oxforddnb.com/view/article/51951, accessed 14 Sept 2005].
230. Stone G/ULL/III63, To Mother Prioress (Imelda Poole), 1 January 1870.

Ullathorne's extraordinary sympathy and understanding for nuns went far beyond defending them against humiliation and embarrassment and even beyond ensuring their proper status and security in the eyes of the Church. It was a deep inner sense of the spiritual life of women who wanted to commit themselves freely to lives ordered to the service of God. He admired them enormously, never patronised them and occasionally envied them their seclusion from the world. It was also often marked by them in little acts of kindness such as the refurbishment of his private chapel in Bishop's House to mark the feast of St Bernard and his twentieth year in Birmingham in 1868. His response was typically teasing, in accusing them of pirate-like rebellion in going behind his back, but also typically humble and tender in reminding them that his role as the 'servant of Christ's spouses' was a 'singular privilege' which brought him 'small pain and much content'.[231] The affectionate prayers and support of all the convents meant a great deal to Ullathorne, as he reminded the Abbess of Stanbrook in thanking her for tributes paid on the twentieth anniversary of his appointment to Birmingham.

> I thank God, who has given me so much veneration for his true daughters and has blessed me in the service of so large a number of them. If 1 am able to do them some service, it is much owing to their belief that I have that veneration for them, and that I account the serving of them to be a singular privilege which God has given to me.[232]

[231.] Selly Park, To Genevieve Dupuis, 20 August 1868.
[232.] Stanbrook 17, To Abbess Gregson, 20 August 1868.

Chapter 8

The Council 1870–1875

'I could tell you much that is very curious, and if ever the history of this part of the Council is fairly and honestly written, it will be a very instructive, but not in all respects an edifying history.'[1] The history of the first Vatican Council was written in 1930 by Ullathorne's biographer Cuthbert Butler, who made extensive use of Ullathorne's letters from the Council written to colleagues in Birmingham and to his friends, including Newman and Mother Imelda Poole, Margaret Hallahan's successor as superior at Stone. Butler's assessment of Ullathorne's position on the crucial issues of the Council was that he held 'a sober Ultramontanism of the theological Bellarmine type' and moreover was 'a representative of that great central body of opinion among the bishops that carried the definition as it is'.[2] Butler was careful to portray Ullathorne as holding thoroughly orthodox views while rejecting what Butler viewed as the extremism of Manning on the question of papal infallibility. This assertion of Ullathorne's moderate mainstream view has been perpetuated as the received wisdom on him ever since. Butler successfully portrayed both the man and the event of the Council as models of moderation and good order.

Newman's private view, expressed before the Council convened, was rather different. When Bishop Dupanloup of

[1.] Ushaw UL 24, Ullathorne to Walker, 20 December 1870.
[2.] Butler, *Vatican Council*, p. 119.

Orleans (who was well known for his liberal views before and during the Council) was seeking an English bishop to whom he might express his worries about a possible definition of papal infallibility, Newman believed that Ullathorne was 'in his own heart opposed to any doctrinal definition – he has good clear views – very angry with Ward – not at all partial to Manning'. However he could not be put forward as a reliable correspondent for Dupanloup, according to Newman (who knew him better than most) because his monastic instincts meant that he would not go against the Pope's private views; also, Newman said, he could not keep a secret![3] This last comment was to prove prescient.

The large gatherings of bishops in Rome in 1862 and 1867 had been a way of orchestrating the willing protective instincts of the Catholic Church and of demonstrating the independence of the Church's life from the political world around. The 1862 canonisation of Japanese martyrs, which took place with no Italian bishops present, (refused passports by the civil power in Turin), was a worldwide spiritual but also political event. Catholicism was showing its power and freedom. The 1867 gathering to celebrate the eighteenth centenary of SS Peter and Paul was equally political, an assertion of the Church's centuries-old international standing, with which no one, least of all Italy, could tamper. Ullathorne preceded his visit to Rome for that event with a pastoral letter which spelt this out in language his Midland hearers would understand.

> Staffordshire has not been more undermined in search of coal, than has the society of Italy for the extirpation of religion. And above ground we see the disastrous results in the unblushing confidence of those public men who imprison and exile the bishops and clergy, leave the flocks without shepherds, confiscate the Church's revenues, suppress the monasteries and convents, incorporate the ecclesiastics and religious in the army, plunder the churches and monastic libraries, and expose religion herself stripped and bleeding in every limb.[4]

[3.] L&D XXIV, pp. 325–6, to William Monsell, 3 September 1869.
[4.] Pastoral Letter, 26 September 1866.

The third and most powerful display of Roman freedom and independence was the calling of the Council, with the definition of papal infallibility almost certainly on the agenda. Owen Chadwick asserted that 'summoning the Council made a definition of the infallibility of the pope necessary'.[5] As he put it succinctly, to say nothing was impossible, to say anything risked ferocious debate. From the point of view of the historical situation, once the council was summoned, infallibility had to be discussed and once discussed, defined. If it was not defined the Pope would be 'shatteringly troubled in ecclesiastical influence at just the time when he was shatteringly troubled in politics'.[6]

The Council took place against a backdrop of hostility and high political tension. Napoleon III wanted to get his French garrison out of Rome, but could not unless the Piedmontese would guarantee not to move in. Cavour, Prime Minister of Piedmont, was determined that Italy must have Rome, and the inevitable agreement was reached without a word to the Pope. By the end of 1866 the French withdrawal was completed, and in autumn 1867 Garibaldi invaded the Papal States. Instantly the French army was back in Rome and Garibaldi was beaten at Mentana, a famous victory for the papal side, but which did not turn the tide as hoped. It was only a matter of time before Italy took Rome. The long struggle by Pius IX to hold onto the Papal States and the independence they gave him could not last much longer, but that same struggle had helped to build a close personal devotion among Catholics for the embattled Pope. As his depleted troops faced Garibaldi, Pius IX was almost a living martyr to most Catholics.

The bishops travelled to Rome for the opening of the Council in the early winter of 1869: not the ideal time for a sea crossing. Ullathorne went via Marseilles, Leghorn (Livorno) and Civita Vecchia rather than overland through France and across the Alps; the old sailor presumably relished winter storms in the Bay of Biscay rather than snow storms through Alpine passes. The Italian peninsula was also, of course, war torn between the Italian nationalists and papal forces, so was hardly a safe prospect. Ullathorne left England in high spirits

[5] Owen Chadwick, *A History of the Popes 1830–1914* (1998), p. 186.
[6] Ibid., p. 200.

in mid-November, meeting up with Bishop Roskell of Nottingham and his nephew in Marseilles, and they decided to make their own way rather than taking the boat chartered from Marseilles for twenty-five bishops and one cardinal. Brown of Newport (Ullathorne's oldest episcopal friend) was left in England as *locum tenens*, perhaps because he was known to be 'an inopportunist of the most militant kind'. At the age of seventy-two he was still vigorous and competent, with thirty years' experience behind him, but seems to have remained in Wales throughout, and out of touch with public events, including the controversial 1870 Education Act.[7]

The journey was far from uneventful, even for such a hardened sailor as Ullathorne. The section from Marseilles to Genoa was stormy, 'Neptune receiving his tribute from many of the passengers'.[8] Genoa to Leghorn was calmer, and from Leghorn the little party went sightseeing in Pisa but missed their train back to the port. According to Ullathorne this was due to the deliberate obstruction of Italian officialdom (he obviously shared the archetypal Victorian English combination of delight in all things Italian except its bureaucracy). Things then descended into farce: a carriage was found from somewhere, but the horse collapsed halfway to Leghorn and the party were forced to resort to their feet in the falling darkness, reaching the city gate just as dusk fell. They were scrambled into a boat and rowed out to the anchorage – only to find that their steamer had left a quarter of an hour earlier – with their luggage.

Forced to stay the night in Leghorn without any luggage but the photographs of Pisa he had bought for the nuns at home, Ullathorne and his companions continued their journey next day. They took 'the one and only train to Civita' arriving in the evening in torrential storms and hoping to be reunited with their luggage. Due to the storms no ships arrived for two days, but eventually they reclaimed their bags and set off post haste for Rome. The charter boat full of bishops had been forced to put in to Elba and had still not arrived at Civita when

---

[7.] McClelland, *Manning*, pp. 77–8.
[8.] Stone G/ULL/III/57, to Mother Provincial (Imelda Poole) from Rome, 26 November 1869.

Ullathorne and his two companions departed, after having done their best with a dinner laid on by the governor for the expected thirty honoured guests. The storm prevented the fishermen going out again next day, so when the shipload of bishops finally arrived, instead of the planned banquet, they were faced with salt cod and macaroni.[9]

Once in Rome, most of the English bishops were accommodated for the Council in the Venerable English College, in Via Monserrato. By early December, Rome was filling up with bishops from all over the world, although northerners travelling overland, including Clifford and Amherst from England, were delayed by winter weather over the Alps.[10] Ullathorne's high spirits were quickly dampened, despite the excitement of the opening of the Council. The weather in Rome was extremely wet, making the streets unwalkable and he was suffering from his 'old malady' (a stomach complaint).[11] He was pained to see so many of the bishops (mainly Spanish and Italian) forced by lack of resources to walk through the pouring rain to St Peter's, while 'a thousand carriages are in movement around them'.[12] Ullathorne's letters from the Council, mostly to his beloved sisters at Stone (the 'dear white circle'[13]) have frequently been quoted in parts and formed the basis of Cuthbert Butler's history of the Council, but what Butler often edited out were the Roman experiences outside the Council debates and the details of life for the bishop in the city. Ullathorne took great pains to bring this unique experience to life in the detailed letters to Stone, so as well as forming an invaluable record of the vital debates, they have left an account of Rome as it was on the brink of invasion by Italian nationalist troops. Rome ceased, after fifteen hundred years, to be the papal capital and became the capital of the new secular state of Italy within days of the departure of the bishops, so

9. Ibid.
10. Stone G/ULL/III/58, to Mother Provincial (Imelda Poole) from Rome, 2 December 1869.
11. Stone G/ULL/III/59, to Mother Provincial (Imelda Poole) from Rome, 9 December 1869.
12. Handsworth, 29 December 1869.
13. Stone G/ULL/III/60, to Mother Provincial (Imelda Poole) from Rome, 18 December 1869.

what Ullathorne has left in his letters was unwittingly valedictory.

The Council was opened formally on 8 December (the feast of the Immaculate Conception) in pouring rain, as Ullathorne described from his vantage point, seated

> in the third row from the top, having the Primates and Archbishops at his back, being among the few nominations by Gregory XVI, his number on the seat is 275, the numbers going from 1 to about 900, including Primates, Archbishops and Bishops, and he has one of the snuggest places as it is in the division nearest the Pope, and just the outside corner seat, from which he can step out without having to tread on anyone's toes.[14]

The procession of bishops began to enter St Peter's at 9 o'clock in the morning to the chanting of *Veni Creator Spiritus*, making its way slowly up the great nave to where the Blessed Sacrament was exposed on the high altar beneath Bernini's massive baldacchino. The procession then swung right into the transept which had been set out as the *Aula Conciliaris*, a sketch of which he thoughtfully provided in one of his letters to the nuns at Colwich.[15] At length the six hundred bishops, ten patriarchs and superiors of all the religious orders were seated in their variety of formal robes, looking for all the world 'like an acre of tulips, only there is a good deal of life in these episcopal flowers'.[16] Following on were 'Royal persons including the King of Naples, ex-Dukes of Tuscany and Parma, Empress of Austria etc., and the Ambassadors had tribunes on each side for the theologians of the Council, amongst whom I saw several Dominican fathers. Outside was the dense mass of the faithful and the sound of their voices and feet was as the sound of many murmuring waters on a seashore.'[17]

[14.] Stone G/ULL/III/59, to Mother Provincial (Imelda Poole) from Rome, 9 December 1869.

[15.] Colwich, 9 January 1870.

[16.] Handsworth, 29 December 1869.

[17.] Stone G/ULL/III/59, to Mother Provincial (Imelda Poole) from Rome, 9 December 1869.

After a series of prayers, pontifical Mass was celebrated and the book of the Gospels enthroned on the synod altar as the spiritual and symbolic focus of the Council. The Gospel read at the Mass was from St Matthew, recounting the sending out of the seventy-two disciples. The formal decrees opening the Council were read and voted on, and after a *Te Deum* of thanksgiving, the Pope retired and the bishops processed out at 3 o'clock in the afternoon. It was eight hours since they had begun to gather in the Vatican palace in the early morning but were still delighting in 'meeting their old school companions come from remote and strange countries, and all sorts of joys, tendernesses and congratulations'.[18]

The picture of the Council itself portrayed by Butler is clearly incomplete, even false, in its smoothing over of disputes and acrimony, and has been shown to be unjust in its portrayal of Bishop William Clifford of Clifton.[19] Butler suggested, rather naively, that Ullathorne, by his own intellectual efforts, drew off the Gallican influences current in his training and background and 'read himself out of Gallicanism into a solid but sober Ultramontanism'.[20] It must be remembered that for a churchman writing in the 1920s such a description was a high compliment and sign of esteem. The naivety in Butler's view lay in suggesting that Ullathorne's experiences in the Church in Australia and England, and his insights into the workings of Rome from an early age had not had rather more complex and nuanced influence on him by 1869. Ullathorne's view of the papacy and its role in the Church was shaped by the richness and variety of his experience – certainly broader than any other English bishop of his generation. He was devoted to the person and office of the Pope, but his devotion was tempered by his preoccupation with the proper role of the diocesan bishop in the Church. He could never be accused of any lack of loyalty or personal devotion to Pius IX, in return for which he was appointed an Assistant at the Papal Throne in 1859, and wrote in gratitude

---

18. Stone G/ULL/III/59, to Mother Provincial (Imelda Poole) from Rome, 9 December 1869.
19. Harding thesis, pp. 230–65.
20. Butler, *Life*, II, p. 48.

To His Holiness, for this addition to all his paternal and affectionate kindnesses to myself I feel more grateful than I can express, and the less I am worthy of his attention the more grateful I must feel. The grave afflictions to which so good a Pontiff has been and is subject is a constant source of affliction and distress to the good Catholics of this country, and the conduct of the miserable press and its instigators is to us a great misery and one for which we can see no remedy but silence and prayer.[21]

However, the fact that he wrote warmly and openly of his 'devotedness to the Holy Father, both in his sacred office and in his person'[22] did not make it any the less likely that the current of extreme Ultramontanism sweeping towards an unlimited definition of papal infallibility should cause him unease at the Council. Ullathorne had not struggled to bring order and good ecclesiastical government into the Church in Australia and England, only to have that order disrupted and unbalanced. In reality, his attitude to the matter of papal infallibility had more to do with ensuring order and, above all, unity in the Church than with his personal loyalty to the papacy and the person of Pius IX.

What Ullathorne detested above all was extremism and he feared the damage to the Church which might be done by open schism at the Council between opposing radical views. He was more aware than most of the perceptions which non-Catholics had of the Catholic Church in England and the use to which extreme infallibilist views might be put. In 1850 he had advised the Congregation of *Propaganda Fide* that it was his 'most firm conviction that it was not the establishment of the hierarchy that at all raised this disturbance but a combination of accidents among the chief of which was the unfortunate publication of a pastoral written in Rome.'[23] His experience of that and other incidents warned him that moderation and avoidance of ecclesiastical party politics was the surest way to a

---

[21.] VEC Talbot Papers, Ullathorne to Talbot, 26 September 1859.
[22.] VEC Talbot Papers, Ullathorne to Talbot, 16 August 1860.
[23.] *Propaganda Fide*, Ullathorne to Fransoni, 29 March 1851.

calm acceptance and understanding of Catholic teaching. Newman had sulkily complained that, 'to stand well with people at Rome'[24] was Ullathorne's priority. The Council would prove otherwise.

Ullathorne and his earlier biographer both asserted on numerous occasions that he was a 'moderate' at the Council, but in what was this moderation expressed? The issue for the majority of bishops was how any dogmatic definition of papal infallibility would affect the life and work of the Church. Few, except the outright Gallicans, who by the 1860s had been squeezed to the margins, really opposed the theological principle of infallibility. However, most of the rest held a variation of ideas as to what it meant, how it was to be understood, and how it would work in practice. It is perhaps not surprising that Ullathorne was accused of falling in with the inopportunists at the Council, as he was far more fearful of the negative effects of extreme infallibilists in the Church than he was of the liberals.

Yet Butler was at pains to emphasise Ullathorne's moderation and to minimise his opposition to the the position associated with Manning and W. G. Ward. He made use of a number of Ullathorne's letters in portraying what he apprehended to be Ullathorne's position, but an unpublished one from 1867, only months after the announcement of the Council, was more revealing of Ullathorne's true viewpoint. He could see, even before the Council had convened, that the Church was tending towards tacit acceptance and acknowledgement of the infallibility of the Church expressed by the Pope. 'The question of infallibility is still open, I apprehend, as it affects minor censures. But if we grant infallibility to the whole Church respecting them, I apprehend we must grant it to the Pope – if we allow him infallibility at all.' However, the tone of the letter suggests that he is unhappy about extending the notion of papal infallibility to cover 'minor censures'. He could see the rationale for making infallibility all embracing, in that 'minor censures involve moral perils as a rule and that their subjects involve the logical peril of leading the intellect into formal errors'. However he was anxious that a clear distinction should be made between the 'infallible pronounce-

24. L&D XXII, p. 296, To James Hope Scott, 13 August 1867.

ment of error and the equally infallible pronouncement of peril'. Revealingly, he went on to express unease about dogmatic definition: 'It is a question however that is rather settled by the action of the Church than defined by her decrees.' In other words the infallibility of the Pope was part of the lifeblood of the Church and flowed easily throughout the whole Church. It existed because of the infallibility of the Church and acceptance by the Church and was therefore vital to its existence. For Ullathorne the real issue was a quite separate one, 'the real question between Ward and Ryder' was 'when and in what documents he [the Pope] speaks infallibly to the Church'.[25]

It is possible to see in this letter the evolution of Ullathorne's personal stance on papal infallibility. For him, reception by the Church was a part of the picture – something which was specifically excluded by the final Council decree. He had no doubt about the reality of papal infallibility in the Church, but saw a problem in defining certain occasions as infallible pronouncements, as, 'for my part part I believe the Holy See sometimes attaches greater weight to certain documents after it has seen how the Church takes them and that this is the case with some documents quoted in the Syllabus'. The implication was that reception by the Church can give the weight of infallibility to certain teachings. In this Ullathorne was very much at odds with Manning and Ward and more in sympathy with the line to be taken at the Council by the inopportunists. The expression of these views dates from two years before the Council convened, but Ullathorne was not a man given to the careless or incomplete expression of views, even in private letters.

He was also aware of problems arising from the perception and interpretation of the Council in England. He was dismissive of the reporting of the Council in the English papers, whose accounts he described as 'so false, so ridiculous, so opposite to the truth that it seems here as if they were trying to show how wildly they could go from the truth'.[26] During the Council Ullathorne had cause to take issue with *The Times* (the source of the Papal Aggression furore in 1850) which had proclaimed

[25.] Ushaw UL 21, Ullathorne to Walker, 2 November 1867.
[26.] Handsworth, 29 December 1869.

him an anti-infallibilist. This provoked him to reply in print contradicting the assertion, and to seek an audience of Pius IX in order to reassure him.[27] He was well aware of the use made by the press of the machinations surrounding the Council, and was impressed at the American bishops, 'at immense cost' ensuring that their own translations of the documents (with which he helped) were telegraphed directly to the American papers.[28] He was unsurprised at the inevitable speculation surrounding the sessions from which the press and public were excluded, and was determined to steer a middle course. As he wrote to Northcote, 'Of course, outside the Council is an arena of policy and intrigue, and moderate men are disliked by the extreme of both parties. Still, I am quite satisfied with the position, and I know from most authentic sources that moderation will prevail.'[29]

Ullathorne's awareness and experience of the English scene, and of the way in which anything might be seized upon to the disadvantage of the Church, provoked his intervention in the general session on the constitution *De Fide*. His concern stemmed from the fear that Anglo-Catholics in the Church of England would pounce on any official document of the Church which appeared to support the branch theory of the universal Church. In his view, to begin the constitution with the words, 'Holy Roman Catholic Church' left it open to that interpretation. Clifford supported Ullathorne in wanting an alteration or elimination of 'Roman'. It was a tiny but serious point, with particular implications for the Church in England and resulted in an amendment of the words to 'Holy Catholic Apostolic Roman Church'. Yet Ullathorne could not help but see the funny side of such nit-picking. He wrote to his close friend, Canon Walker, after the Council closed:

> I shall have some day to tell you what a curious fight I had in the Council about a transposition of words in the first line of the first decree. After having the majority on their legs for it, I was foiled by the special congregation

[27.] Butler, *Life*, II, p. 57.
[28.] College Irlandais Paris, Ullathorne to Kathleen O'Meara, 21 July 1887.
[29.] Butler, *Life*, II, pp. 57–8.

and returned to the fight again, and at last with American help got the congregation round and a unanimous vote. It was one of the most curious incidents in the Council and involved, amongst other things, that discussion about a comma which has been so often referred to as a proof of minute care taken.[30]

As the Council got down to business, Ullathorne quickly became aware of the politicking which would go on throughout and the need, therefore for 'open ears and a guarded mouth'. William Barry, a seminarian from Birmingham studying at the English College, recalled that Ullathorne's attitude was, on the whole, 'that of reserve' and that he 'would never join private coteries'.[31] In the election for the first of the special congregations which would do the detailed work, the majority of the English bishops found themselves 'outwitted by what everybody considers an intrigue', which resulted in Manning rather than Grant being elected.[32] It is clear that during the Council, as in his 1867 letter, Ullathorne expressed more anxiety over 'the extremes on the orthodox side'.[33] He seemed to bow to the inevitability of a definition, without any great enthusiasm himself. In a famous and oft-quoted letter to his old friend Brown he gave a far from ringing endorsement of the *schema*,

I do believe that moderation will prevail and that the bulk of the bishops will feel the pressure of the times and control the enthusiasts. As [the bishop of] Grenoble said to me, coming to me in a fury against our friend in the consistory [Manning] 'C'e ne pas temps de casser les vitraux'. (This is not the time to be breaking windows) The Pope, I believe, is bent on the definition as the crowning glory of his reign. And I think it will in some shape probably pass.[34]

[30.] Ushaw UL 24, Ullathorne to Walker, 20 December 1870.
[31.] William Barry, *Memories and Opinions* (1926), p. 86.
[32.] Stone G/ULL/III/60, to Mother Provincial (Imelda Poole), 18 December 1869.
[33.] Butler, *Life*, II, p. 50.
[34.] Ampleforth, Copy of letter, Ullathorne to Brown, 28 October 1869.

The Council was not due to reconvene after a Christmas break until the Feast of the Epiphany (6 January) so, as well as the jockeying for position and influence, there was also time for some relaxation. Bishop William Vaughan of Plymouth was Ullathorne's next-door neighbour in the English College and they often shared expeditions together. Just before Christmas they joined the throngs in the Borghese Gardens for the review of the papal troops. It was a crowded, vivid and colourful affair, as described by Ullathorne, but with nagging and melancholy undertones of defeat also in the air.

> Bishop Vaughan and myself having one carriage in common started an hour after the time, and found the Porta del Popolo still chocked with the ruck of carriages. Some ten lines were all pushing in a close cram for the gate, and it was a curious scene, the carriages close to one another, the horses a complete crowd of heads and necks, now a few inches forward. Lots of nobby carriages turning off one after another in disgust, and taking the Pincian Hill instead of the gate. All quite good humoured. Our coacher (sic) tried this gate in three converging lines, one after another, at last he got close to the steps of S Maria, crowded with spectators, and so inclining on and back, at last, we could not say how, he shot in and through the gate and up the hill. What crowds! All Rome out on holiday. We got by ticket into the privileged garden on the height. There on the midst of a lake, under the columns of a temple, a large orchestra of music and singers of the first class are entertaining the elite, including sundry Royalties ... The trumpeters of the Zouaves trumpet with the right hand, carrying their rifles on the left shoulder. The band of the corps, Colonels Alette and Charette immense cheered, and brigade after brigade, by their bare necks, French grey uniform and white ankles, they step cleanly along, file after file, brigade after brigade, many of them very young, many others bearded and carrying their Mentana medals on their breasts, heartily cheered by all classes, whilst old bishops are dropping tears from their eyes. Then come the Antibes legion, a strong body all from France but in the papal

service. Next come the trumpets of the Papal Dragoons
and that fine corps itself on fine horses that cantered to
the music and seemed to fancy themselves more important than their high-helmed and red plumed riders ...
The rearguard, and then this little army of 15,000 men
have past the saluting point, and all that remains is to
cheer General Hausler as he salutes with bare head and
rides with his gaily gilded and feathered staff from the
ground. There are 10,000 more on duty elsewhere. And
now for the remarks, what a difference from the old papal
army! How spirited they are and how well they marched!
They are as well equipped as any army one may see! And
there the greybeards form in. They are too many, they
are too many and too few, too many for Garibaldi and his
crew, too few for the Italian army. This can't last always,
says a bishop. We can keep the Pope as well as any sovereign is provided, but we can't always keep an army of
25,000 men in this condition. And then another says –
Irish of course – drops of tears came to my eyes, for if
they have a chance they will care nothing for their lives,
the dear boys.[35]

Ullathorne at times was clearly stirred by the sights which illustrated the disintegration of the old Europe, and in his letters to
'the dear white circle' often fell to musing, in ways which he
presumably did when in the company of the sisters. After
describing the splendours of the papal Mass in St Peter's on
Christmas Day, he reported a tiny incident which obviously
moved him very much:

as the great function closed, the Empress of Austria, the
venerable old Grand Duke of Tuscany, who is always at
his prayers and a dozen more all representing fallen
royalty, fathers and mothers and children, stole down
from their place of honour and stood in all simplicity, like
any other persons, just within the line of Zouaves, to get
the Pope's blessing, and see the Pope, cardinals and

[35.] Stone G/ULL/III/60, to Mother Provincial (Imelda Poole), 18
December 1869.

bishops pass down the nave. Few, if any, seemed conscious who they were, although their appearance ought to have explained the fact. Just as I was coming down amidst the mass of mitres, two young French bishops, to get in a little sooner, slipped behind the troops and then came pushing and diving to get into the line again, amongst the soldiers, who stood as firm as they could to protect the fallen royalties standing in front of them. But the mitred and coped bishops shoved and pushed and scolded, and brushed their way indignantly, unconscious no doubt that they were shoving rudely upon and through the line of fallen sovereigns and their children, nephews and nieces. Uprose the fire and the bile within me, for these princes were so gentle, but I was in the crowd, those near me did not understand the case, and the offenders were gone before I could get at them, still pushing and ploughing their hasty way. There, thought I, is a lesson not to be forgotten. One never knows what refined spirits get wounded by one's hastiness.[36]

The constant rain continued throughout the winter and parts of Rome flooded as usual, including the Pantheon, leading to fears of fever.[37] The machinating outside the Council was well under way even before the first proper session began on 6 January, but Ullathorne declined most social gatherings and 'formally declined uniting with any party representing extreme views'.[38] The groups agitating for various viewpoints at least had the virtue in his eyes of making people think about the real issues more carefully; he was already in no doubt that 'the subject about which the whole world is talking' would provoke a long and serious discussion and that the great powers would do their best to stop it.[39]

[36.] Stone G/ULL/III/62, to Mother Provincial Imelda Poole, Christmas Day 1869.
[37.] Stone G/ULL/III/63, to Mother Provincial Imelda Poole, 1 January 1870.
[38.] Stone G/ULL/III/65, to Mother Provincial Imelda Poole, 6 January 1870.
[39.] Ibid.

By February his anxiety was tempered by the course of events. 'The *zealates* are cooling down considerably and the spirit of moderation prevails and will prevail.'[40] There was no doubt that for Ullathorne, and indeed for the whole Council, the real battle was not between inopportunists and the rest, but between extreme enthusiasts for a wide definition and the rest. For Ullathorne the danger lay in neglect of the proper role of the bishops and in the lack of safeguards around the scope and status of infallible statements. Without some protection on both counts he feared

> a wild enthusiasm especially on the part of converts and a disposition among the clergy and even the laity to lower the powers of the episcopate, and a stronger centralisation leading ultimately to reaction, and a narrow door presented to those who are seeking the Church, and a fanatical extending of the papal prerogatives beyond the fact, after the style of Ward.[41]

His hopes for the outcome of the Council rested on his belief in the good sense and authority of the bishops and his fear was that an open definition would lead to the diminution of episcopal authority. This again related (as did his comment about converts) to the specific conditions of England, although his knowledge of the colonial Church in Australia suggests that it also had wider application. He had laboured to bring about the restored hierarchy and to establish proper episcopal authority in relation to clergy and people. He had clashed with Wiseman when the Cardinal tried to assert undue authority by placing himself between the Pope and the other English bishops. For twenty years Ullathorne had tried to secure what he saw as the rightful position of the episcopate in the Church in the peculiarly difficult conditions which England presented. He was not about to have this undermined by extremists influencing the Council, and he was confident that the discussions were doing much good, 'as each portion of the church is teaching the rest.

[40.] BAA B4796, Ullathorne to O'Sullivan, 23 February 1870.
[41.] Ampleforth, Copy of letter, Ullathorne to Brown, 28 October 1869.

Even the party warfare outside the Council is doing its valuable office of grinding things by its diagonal action into the ways of caution and moderation. All will come right, and begins to look like coming right. No extreme party will prevail. *Virtus in media'*.[42]

His determined and public refusal to be a member of any party or faction at the Council was well calculated to add weight and credibility to what he was saying. He relied on the natural assumption that none of the bishops present would wish to see their office diminished, and his assertion of independence won support for his public statements on the importance of the episcopate. However, he professed himself 'quite calm and at peace on the whole subject', being satisfied that the *schema* on infallibility would not pass without huge changes.[43] Manning however, 'keeps his isolation from us and is endlessly active with everybody else that he can take by the button'.[44] Ullathorne's own first speech, he felt to have been a success, negotiating 'delicate prejudices'.[45]

The prolonged absence of the bishops in Rome was problematic at times; communications with the diocese were obviously slow and minor irritations could become big issues while the bishop's response was awaited. Ullathorne was perhaps uniquely conscious of this, knowing from his Australian experience the difficulties which could arise from long distance government. Dealing with domestic issues from a distance called for judgement and delicacy and he found himself having to tread carefully with affairs which arose in the diocese; he was also conscious of the mood of heightened expectation and excitement as the whole church awaited the outcome of the Council. In the absence of the bishop, tensions arose and he had to pour oil on a number of patches of troubled water, not least a falling out between his vicar general and secretary, who were running the diocese in his absence, as well as misunderstandings with the influential Northcote at Oscott. Perhaps ironically, given his own tendency to outspokenness,

---

[42.] Stone G/ULL/iii/70/, to Mother Provincial (Imelda Poole), 24 January 1870.
[43.] BAA B4802, Ullathorne to Estcourt, 8 March 1870.
[44.] Ibid.
[45.] BAA B4807, Ullathorne to O'Sullivan, 28 March 1870.

Ullathorne counselled silence rather than the expression of disagreement in the present circumstances.[46]

Other public issues also raised their heads, including renewed Protestant interest in the lives and practices of convents. He was not best pleased when the question of convent inspection, this time more concerned with finance, was raised again, nor was he happy with the way in which matters were being handled, fearing that the financial reports being sought would breach the privacy of the convents. Once again, his tact and sensitivity towards the privacy and freedom of action of the convents is remarkable and his insistence that they should be able to expect protection from the bishops, 'lest the printed papers they have drawn up should get either into the papers, or in the hands of the parliamentary committee'.[47] He was adamant that 'only the legal gentlemen engaged, beyond the vicar general of their particular diocese [in the absence of the bishops] should know in detail how any particular convent stands as to its pecuniary and property affairs'.[48]

The long running sore of Newman's alleged lack of orthodoxy and his relationship with Manning became tangled up with the issue of papal infallibility. In 1869, just before leaving for the Vatican Council, Manning got wind of an allegation that he had (during Wiseman's lifetime) suppressed a letter from Newman which would have cleared him of the allegations relating to the *Rambler* article in respect of the infallibility of the Church. Manning denied all knowledge, but asked Ullathorne to investigate with Newman, clearly anxious to clear the ground before the expected debates on infallibility at the forthcoming Council.[49] This was odd, because as Ullathorne assured him, there was never any criticism of Newman on the grounds of statements about infallibility, only about consulting the laity. Newman insisted that he had no suspicion that Manning had suppressed a letter written by him to Wiseman as long ago as 7 May 1860, in which he offered to explain the offending passages. He had never received a reply from

---

46. BAA B4818, Ullathorne to O'Sullivan, 16 May 1870.
47. Ibid.
48. Ibid.
49. AAW Ullathorne Correspondence, Manning to Ullathorne 31 October 1869.

Wiseman.[50] Ullathorne reiterated, with some bitterness, Wiseman's failure to fulfil his office in relation to Newman's difficulty with *Propaganda Fide* by acting on that letter. However, to soothe Manning's anxiety, he enclosed a bald statement written by Newman that he 'never have had, nor have, nor can have' the slightest suspicion of Manning suppressing any letter between him and Wiseman.[51] A series of letters over the ensuing few days make it clear that this was a matter of some anxiety to Manning, though not to Ullathorne or Newman. This storm in a teacup is indicative of the way in which Newman's position and his relationship with Manning continued to dog the Church in England, and Ullathorne was often the mediator. It also illustrates the way in which, on the eve of the Council, infallibility was like a spark in a woodpile, capable of inflaming arguments. Tensions were running high in Rome and in the local Church.

Newman, having declined several invitations to attend the Council as a theological advisor, nevertheless took an active interest in proceedings, and wrote to Ullathorne in Rome, 'one of the most confidential letters that I ever wrote in my life'.[52] In it he set out his real opinion and feeling about the papal infallibility issue under debate at the Council.

> When we are all at rest, and have no doubts, and at least practically, not to say doctrinally, hold the Holy Father to be infallible, suddenly there is thunder in the clear sky, and we are told to prepare for something, we know not what, to try our faith we know not how. No impending danger is to be averted, but a great difficulty is to be created. Is this the proper work for an Ecumenical Council?

He described the supporters of the definition as 'an aggressive, insolent faction' who were causing distress and difficulty for others (including himself) who were confused and anxious

[50.] L&D XXIV, pp. 369–70, 10 November 1869.
[51.] AAW Ullathorne Correspondence, Ullathorne to Manning, 1 November 1869.
[52.] L&D XXV, pp. 18–20, 28 January 1870.

about being placed in the position of having to defend the indefensible, such as papal scandals of earlier times.

He wondered whether or not he should go public with his views, but Ullathorne tried to reassure him that his letter 'repeats what many here are feeling', and that 'the zealots are doomed to future confusion'. Many of the bishops were acting with the 'sole view of enforcing moderation'. Ullathorne's own view was clearly expressed to Newman, when he wrote:

> For my part, I have quietly, and in private maintained that I should not oppose a calm and moderate definition, provided it was duly balanced by strengthening the authority of the Episcopate, provided also it was duly limited so as to save us from enthusiastic and fanatical interpretations.

He had been active in denouncing false accusations about his own position and that of the other English bishops, and was now confident that 'calmer and more prudential views are taking the ascendancy'.[53]

In the event, Newman's views did, unintentionally, become public. Ullathorne showed Newman's confidential letter to Clifford, who took a copy, which Errington and Moriarty also copied. Inevitably, one of these copies fell into press hands in England, and the letter was quoted in *The Standard*. Ullathorne was deeply embarrassed at Clifford's 'indiscretion' which caused him 'very great annoyance'.[54] He wrote a letter of explanation and apology to Newman for his part in the debacle:

> I am much distressed at your letter to me having got out into other hands, though without my concurrence, and proceed by return of post to explain all that I know about it. I showed your letter to some four of the English Bishops, all your friends, and all having strong feelings of difficulty, greater indeed than I have, about the definition. One of these was Bishop Clifford, the only one to

[53.] L&D XXV, p. 25, 4 February 1870.
[54.] BAA B4807, Ullathorne to O'Sullivan, 28 March 1870.

whom I parted with it out of my sight, he living in another part of Rome, promising he would let no-one see it, and that he would return it to me next morning, after reading it. We were at the moment leaving the Council in opposite directions. To my surprise on returning it next morning he told me he had taken a copy of it. On expressing my annoyance at this, he solemnly promised that no-one should see it without my express permission, and I was satisfied, though not altogether so.[55]

Ullathorne blamed Clifford for the leak, but was squirming about his own part in it, and must have been surprised at Newman's reaction. 'Don't mind for me, my dear Lord – I have had too many knocks to care for this.'[56]

As more and more people applauded his expression of misgivings, Newman began to be glad that the decision whether or not to publish had been taken out of his hands. Having at first denied that he had used the phrase, 'an insolent and aggressive faction', Newman was forced to acknowledge that he had indeed been so outspoken, and apologised to Ullathorne for contradicting him, clearing him publicly of any part in the unfortunate circulation of his letter.[57] Newman came to regard the publication as God's will and declared that he could not 'unsay a word of what I did say'.[58] Given Newman's tendency to oversensitivity and to suspect plots and machinations, it was remarkable that he insisted so often and so publicly that Ullathorne was not to blame for the publicising of his 'most confidential' letter. There can be little doubt that Clifford, who took a copy of the letter without Ullathorne's knowledge, was the culprit[59] and he later admitted to Ullathorne that Errington had taken a copy from his copy.[60]

Nevertheless, it is difficult to exonerate Ullathorne entirely

---

[55] Birmingham Oratory Archives, Vatican Council Box 1, 18 March 1870.

[56] L&D XXV, pp. 62–3, 22 March 1870.

[57] L&D XXV, p. 61, To the Editor of *The Standard*, 22 March 1870.

[58] L&D XXV, p. 80. To Thomas Kiernan, 6 April 1870.

[59] Harding thesis, p. 200, n. 5.

[60] BAA B4814, Ullathorne to O'Sullivan, 25 April 1870.

from blame in showing it to three or four of his fellow bishops, even if it did reflect some of his and their misgivings.

> With respect to the allusion made in the meeting to Dr Newman's letter, I think it well to remark that that letter was private and intended to be private; and that neither Dr Newman nor myself had the slightest intention of making it public. That publication was occasioned through the unguardedness of another Bishop, a friend of Dr Newman's to whom it was shown by me under specific conditions, and I very much regret it. In that letter Dr Newman communicates to me his personal conviction of the infallibility, whilst he is driven through the difficulties of other persons to put his ideas on the policy of the question of opportuneness before me. This, in the private way in which it was done, was a legitimate proceeding, but I think, and very prudent Bishops on what I may call both sides of the question unite with me in thinking, that it would be unfair and ungenerous to treat that private letter, addressed by a priest to his Bishop, as if it had been a formal and intended publication.[61]

Yet why had Newman sent such a clear and uncompromising expression of his views if he did not hope somehow to influence the debates in Rome, at least among his fellow countrymen?[62] In the event, Newman seemed (to Ullathorne's immense relief) not prepared to make an issue of it between himself and the bishop. A couple of months later, replying to Ullathorne's news of Bishop Grant's death, Newman was gracious, witty and concerned about how the bishop was coping with the summer heat in Rome.[63] The matter was closed.

By May the wet Roman winter had finally released its grip, but the political and military tension continued. In

---

[61.] Birmingham Oratory Archives Ullathorne Correspondence 1869–76 124, Ullathorne to Provost Bagnall, 19 May 1870.

[62.] L&D XXV, pp. 98–9. To Henry James Coleridge, 13 April 1870. 'Can anything I say move a single bishop? And if not, what is the good of writing?'

[63.] L&D XXV, pp. 138–9. To Ullathorne, 6 June 1870.

Ullathorne's view 'the' question would soon be settled now.

> But the clergy little understand the nature of the contest going on. It is no contest against the definition, unless it be on the part of a very small number. It is a contest that the Catholic Church shall not be excluded from the Rule of Faith, so that there shall be nothing left as witness, judge or arbiter, subjectively or objectively, but the Pope. Of course I write in confidence to you. Do not you conceive the gravity of the case. It is a new definition, the substance of which was originally developed by Franzelin but was long before respected by Bellarmine. After months of debate, many are only now beginning to understand it. As it begins at last to be understood it has split the *deputatio* and the majority. The Pope has at last taken alarm, and sent for a grave, learned bishop who opened his eyes, and he has this day declared to a bishop, a friend of mine, that he is having another drawn up to meet the crisis. We have been in an excruciating crisis. Light is beaming out at last, thanks to the perseverance and energy of the ablest men. I have for twenty years been an infallibilist of the old definition. This I was prepared to say. I could not have accepted the new unmodified. I don't know any able man who was prepared to accept it without modification. It would have put the Church in a most critical state. The whole Council has been split in all directions as its real sense dawned upon them. A day will, I hope come, when I can tell you all, meanwhile be assured that what has been going on cannot be understood at a distance. At this very time that the sounder policy is revealing itself on all sides, Dr M[anning] is trying to get up a petition to close the debate, and so leave it where it stands. But this will not go, and many who once stood by him are shrinking away. Some plainly telling me so. There will be a turn of the tide, but in another and wiser way. In short *the Church* will be saved, as it always is, by the Providence of God. The Jesuits are harking off from their extreme men, to save themselves in this turn of tide.[64]

64. BAA B4830, Ullathorne to O'Sullivan, 30 June 1870.

In respect of papal infallibility, Ullathorne was from an older school of thought and detested the hotheads, but he had great confidence in the process of the Council itself, and its capacity to bring moderation and good sense to bear on the agitation caused by the hotheads. 'Of this you may be quite assured, that the most active and political agitation of strong measures is going down on all sides, and is beginning to be found inconvenient. The weather-wise, even among the *Praelati*, are beginning to say – I don't sail in —'s track, he overdoes it.' He cited as another example of common sense prevailing, the abandonment of an attempt to get a dogmatic definition of the bodily assumption of the Virgin Mary into heaven. Enthusiasm was tempered in the end by 'the tradition of doubt', ie, no satisfactory theology justified a definition: that would wait until the only clear exercise of papal infallibility as defined by the Council, in 1950. The arch-infallibilists in 1870 would not get it all their own way and would be contained by the moderate majority.

> Be assured, my dear friend, that, whatever mischief is doing outside by our own newspapers, to which many of us are alive, moderation will be the upshot in the Council. If you could but see, as I see, *schemata* brought in, only to be pulled to pieces, and sent out again, bleeding in every limb, to be reconstructed by the special committees, by the light given in the Council, you would realise how the general sense of the fathers prevails over all party views and idiosyncrasies.[65]

Ullathorne was determined that, if infallibility was to be dogmatically defined, it should be done in a form 'rendered theologically precise',[66] fearing that anything vague and ill-defined would leave the way open for fanaticism. With this precision in mind he urged the inclusion of the phrase '*ex cathedra*' in the definition.[67] It was a phrase in familiar ecclesiastical

[65] L&D XXV, pp. 25–7, 4 February 1870 [except PS omitted, transcribed from Oratory VC Box (1) 44].
[66] Butler, *Life*, II, p. 74.
[67] Butler, *Vatican Council*, II, p. 350.

usage and clearly understood as having a definite meaning and limitation, and was taken up by others in the consideration of the final text. Its purpose was to ensure that only formal teaching statements by the pope, speaking from the seat of authority, could be regarded as infallible. Vagueness about infallibility was rendered impossible. Its inclusion in the agreed text was something of a victory for Ullathorne's theological understanding of infallibility, that it required careful, deliberate and rigorous definition.

He had further plans to influence the final text, but was prevented from speaking in open session by a sudden bout of illness which confined him to bed and caused him to miss his turn to speak. His health had not been of the best during the whole Council and periodic bouts of stomach trouble and diarrhoea (as on this occasion) had frequently curtailed his activities. His proposed amendment was to include the words, '*ex magisterio ecclesiae*' (from the teaching of the Church) in the definition, to make clear that the Pope's infallibility was that of the entire Church and that the Pope, in speaking infallibly, acted within the tradition of the Church.[68] Due to his indisposition, Ullathorne's amendment was lost. He later claimed to be happy with the final constitution as voted on by the Council, but the interpretation of the teaching of the Council in the following century and a half would have been greatly elucidated by his amendment.[69] It would have done something to prevent the emergence of 'an ecclesiology "from above" [which] took shape that viewed all ecclesial power flowing from the Pope'.[70]

His position on the question of the definition reflected his preoccupation with the role and character of the episcopate. This was an issue addressed at length in the debates of the Council, in relation to papal primacy, and the decree on primacy was subject to radical revision.[71] Ullathorne was insistent that the wording of any definition was 'one of the most difficult and delicate that was ever mooted in a council'[72] and

[68.] Butler, *Vatican Council*, II, p. 366.

[69.] Butler, *Life*, II, p. 78.

[70.] Patrick Granfield, *The Limits of the Papacy; authority and autonomy in the Church* (1987), p. 42.

[71.] Butler, *Vatican Council*, I, pp. 344–5.

[72.] BAA B4818, Ullathorne to O'Sullivan, 16 May 1870.

he was keen to get clarity into the definition of infallibility in order to curb excesses afterwards. It must be clear that the Pope, when speaking infallibly, expressed the mind of the Church, under the influence of the Church's Magisterium and infallibility. Hence his pressing for the inclusion of the phrase '*ex cathedra*'. The amendment which illness prevented him from proposing in the Council, of the inclusion of the words '*ex magisterio ecclesiae*' also clearly had the intention of rooting papal infallibility in the infallibility of the whole Church. His amendment was suitably anti-Gallican, as were the majority of Council Fathers, but also, in Butler's words, 'avoided the suggestion of isolation or separation of Pope from Church' (particularly in Ullathorne's mind, separation from the bishops.[73] He wrote to Newman, 'I have quietly and in private maintained that I should not oppose a calm and moderate definition *provided* it was duly balanced by strengthening the authority of the episcopate.'[74] Ullathorne's sensitivity about the place of bishops in the Church proved to be prescient. It has been acknowledged that the first Vatican Council was unsatisfactory in its treatment of the relationship between papal and episcopal authority, and the question of the role of the episcopate in relation to primacy and infallibility was to dog the Church until it re-emerged at Vatican II. '*Pastor Aeternus* did not give a precise and satisfactory answer to the relationship between respective competencies of pope and the bishops. The debates are helpful but they are somewhat ambiguous.'[75]

There was never the opportunity to resolve any ambiguities, or, indeed, to complete the Council's other business. The vote on the crucial question of papal infallibility took place on 18 July in dramatic circumstances: 'the *placets* of the fathers struggled through the storm, while the thunder pealed above and the lightning flashed in at every window and down through the dome and every smaller cupola, dividing, if not absorbing the attention of the crowd'. In virtual darkness, although it was

---

[73.] Butler, *Life*, II, p. 71.
[74.] Butler, *Vatican Council*, I, p. 185.
[75.] Granfield, p. 40.

midday, the Pope read the final proclamation by the light of a taper.[76] The definition of papal infallibility was secured, and the bishops began to leave for home as war broke out between France and Prussia. The French Empire collapsed, the Roman garrison was withdrawn and on 20 September, the walls of Rome were breached by nationalist forces. The bishops, due to reconvene in November, stayed away from the new secular Italy, with its Roman capital city and a pope in self-imposed exile within the walls of the Vatican palace. The task which remained for the bishops, as they waited in vain for the Council to reopen, was to elucidate the definitions already promulgated, on papal primacy and infallibility in particular, for the clergy and people of their dioceses.

Ullathorne produced a lucid and thorough pastoral letter explaining the decree to his diocese and laying particular emphasis on his own phrase, '*ex cathedra*'. He made clear the limitations which this placed on the actions of the pope, and emphasised his own loyal assent to the definition.[77] However, his private view was less sanguine. 'I have not heard about the talk of reassembling the Council in Belgium. It could only be after the war terminates. The sooner it can be reassembled the better. The chapters *De Ecclesia* are much needed to balance the definition *De Romano Pontifice*, and they are more than half discussed ...'[78]

He followed up his pastoral letter with a more detailed discussion of the significant issues surrounding the relationship between papal infallibility and the Church. He was crystal clear in his assertion that,

> there is but one infallibility in the Church of God. But this infallibility is either active or passive. It is active in the Church teaching as appointed by Christ; it is passive, but equally secure, in the obedience of the Church taught ... The teaching authority of the Church is in Christ's Vicar and in the bishops ... The bishops are the witnesses of doctrine; they are the judges of faith; they deliver what they have received from their predecessors; their voice is

---

76. Butler, *Vatican Council*, II, p. 163.
77. Pastoral Letter, 27 October 1870.
78. Ushaw UL 24, Ullathorne to Walker, 20 December 1870.

infallible, but only when they teach in union with Christ's vicar, only when his teaching is the confirmation of theirs.[79]

He was at pains to demonstrate that the pontiff and the bishops, as head and body of the teaching Church

cannot be considered as separate from each other, but as one vital organisation, so that the members, at one with the head, share the infallibility of the head. When they sit in Council with the Pontiff and judge and define a doctrine with him, they share this infallibility actively. But when dispersed they receive his definitions *ex cathedra* and promulgate them, they share it passively.[80]

Equally clear, in the light of his experience at the Vatican Council, was the reason why bishops were there at all, and their function when gathered in a Council.

In a Council the bishops are not the representatives of the clergy or of the people, but they witness to the faith of the clergy and the people; for the faithful flock share in their degree the supernatural life of the Church of which the Holy Ghost is the principle. In a Council the pope and the bishops, before defining a doctrine, have to certify these two points – that the doctrine is revealed in God's Word, and that the sense of it pervades the Church.[81]

In other words, an infallible pontiff did not render the bishops gathered in council redundant. This was both a fear at the time and a view expressed later.

After more than twenty years as a bishop, he had reflected long and hard on the practical tasks involved and the qualities required of an individual bishop, and also on the theological role and purpose of the episcopate in the Church. His position at the Council flowed from this, and he returned to the topic

---

[79.] *The Accord of the Infallible Church with the Infallible Pontiff* (1870), p. 13.

[80.] Ibid., p. 14.

[81.] Ibid., p. 15.

two years later, speaking at the consecration of Herbert
Vaughan, the new Bishop of Salford. He appealed to Scripture
and the Fathers and to the history of the ancient English
Church, demonstrating that a bishop's power came from the
Holy Spirit, and his authority from the successor of the
Apostles, the Pope. The call to office came through the Vicar of
Christ but the Holy Spirit is the 'interior consecrator'.[82] Again
Ullathorne spoke out of his own experience, of the burden, the
paternal responsibility for the souls of his flock and the extent
of episcopal duties. There is no doubt that his was a paternal
view of episcopacy, enhanced by his advancing years and experience.

> Once clothed with his jurisdiction and invested with his
> mission, the bishop is the ruler of the churches, the
> guardian of the revealed truth, the witness and the judge
> of faith, the custodian of God's law, the enforcer of the
> Church's canons, the father of his clergy and their judge,
> the pastor of his people, the chief preacher of the Word of
> God to the flock and the guide of souls. All other
> ministries are exercised in dependence on him. Whoever
> are gathered into the flock are gathered into him. For the
> Church is in the bishop.[83]

If anything, his concept of the central role of the bishop, of his
apostolic character in relation to the local church had become
greater with the years. There was no question of minimising
the office of bishop in the light either of developing diocesan
organisation or of the increasing centralisation on Rome. The
autonomy of the local church under the bishop was vital and
he acknowledged the duty of the bishop to heed the counsel or
even obtain the consent of the chapter before he took action.

The protection for the Church against overweening episcopal power lay in the law of the Church. 'No man has such a
laborious life of subjection and obedience to law and rule as a
Catholic bishop.'[84] After sketching the history of episcopal rule

---

82. *Discourse* (1872), p. 90.
83. Ibid., p. 103.
84. Ibid., p. 103.

in the Church and the loss of the Catholic episcopate to England he posed the question, 'What is a Catholic bishop in this nineteenth century? His character and spiritual power are ever the same, but he is called on to display different characteristics of his Divine Master in different ages.' The contemporary threat was more than intellectual. 'The age is striving to do without God; in science, in government, in the education of the people, man is held up to himself as all sufficient for himself.'[85] Thus the bishop had to be the mouthpiece of God and 'represents the prophetic character of Christ'.[86] This is a newer development in Ullathorne's thinking on the episcopate, one born of his experience over twenty years and an aspect not mentioned in 1850. It indicated a more outward looking sense of the Church, in so far as he saw a need, not just to rule, guide and protect his flock from the dangers around, but to challenge the values of the world, to stand as a prophetic symbol of other values and teaching. There was, after twenty years, scope for him to place less emphasis on the need for administrative and ecclesiastical structure and financial management. Those were all more or less in place, and it was time to reflect more on the sacramental nature of the episcopate. The bishop expresses 'the prophetic character of Christ' in three ways – he preaches, he rules and he consecrates and in all of these reaches out to the world with a freedom which Ullathorne had come to recognise.

> Never were the bishops of the Church placed in a better position for the exercise of their prophetic office. Stripped of earthly splendour, disencumbered of the world, set free from the odium that fell upon them from alliance with the State and standing on no other ground than that of apostolic authority, the bishop of the nineteenth century is all the stronger for the change ... If ever a Catholic bishop was strong, he is strong at this hour of the world's history. He is strong because he is free. He is strong because he lives a simple and frugal life. He is strong because he is a bishop and nothing but a bishop;

85. Ibid., p. 111.
86. Ibid., p. 112.

strong, therefore, in the vivid consciousness of his high office.[87]

This was a powerful and liberating insight which only gradually came to bear on Ullathorne's mind. His constant reference to the history of the Church had previously made him bemoan the contemporary situation in England, and to see it mainly in terms of regularising order and good canonical government. He now began to see, and to pass on to the next generation, the way in which the history of the Church in England freed it in a particular way. He described it in terms of the prophetic freedom of the bishops, but in truth it was a freedom for the whole Catholic community, only gradually realised. Ullathorne was becoming aware of this on a larger scale himself, as he expressed it in a pastoral letter of 1868.

> It is true that in various places the powers of the world are withdrawing temporal aids and sanctions they gave to to the Church's laws; it is true that these powers are stripping her even to her primitive poverty, and threatening other of her institutions; but the Church is thereby only driven back to her own spiritual powers bequeathed to her by Our Lord, and to that position of a missionary Church in which she had her glorious beginning. Being in the world she is not of the world; and certainly the less she is mixed up with those who hold the high places of this world, however great the loss to them, the more she will show forth to all men the inherent force of her spirit and her independence of human support.[88]

To hear Ullathorne use the language of freedom and prophetic character seems extraordinary in the period of rigid Ultramontane government in the Church, yet it points forward to the insights of a later generation. Eventually it came to be seen on the universal scale that the loss of temporal power on the papal, as well as episcopal level, was the source of great moral, political and prophetic freedom for the Church – but it

[87.] Ibid., pp. 112–3.
[88.] Pastoral Letter, 16 November 1868.

was an unexpected view from an old fashioned Ultramontane bishop shaped and formed by English recusancy.

When Ullathorne returned home after the premature closure of the Council, it was the end of his tenth and (as it turned out) his final visit to the Eternal City. During the 1870s, Rome was not an easy place to visit after it became the capital of the new Italy, and the Pope became the 'prisoner of the Vatican'. Perhaps Ullathorne was happy not to experience the new Rome under its secular government. Even so, by the time the next major Anglo-Papal crisis arose over the question of relations between the bishops and the religious orders in the early 1880s, although he was much involved, his health would have prevented another visit to the Vatican. In fact, he returned to England in poor health in the summer of 1870, and was forced to take a prolonged period of convalescence in Broadstairs.[89] Newman described it as 'delirium'[90] and the bishop did not make his way back to Birmingham until autumn. Newman did not see him until October.[91] Whatever this chronic illness was, it afflicted him until the end of his days, and he regarded himself as an invalid after 1870. Although he took up active leadership of the diocese and involvement in crucial social and political affairs, his health never fully recovered from this point. 'I am myself an invalid, and have been more or less since the Council of the Vatican, and shall be for the rest of my life.'[92] Until the creation of the Tiber embankments in the last decades of the century, Rome continued to have endemic malaria; Ullathorne had also explored the Campagna, where marshy ground favoured by mosquitos was common, so it is possible that his stomach and bowel problems and the 'delirium' denoted malaria, which was chronic and liable to return at any time.

However, he was soon back in action, addressing the Catholic Reunion at the Birmingham Town Hall in December on the subject of papal temporal power and crossing swords

---

[89.] AAW Ullathorne Correspondence, Ullathorne to Manning, 14 September 1870.

[90.] L&D XXV, p. 177. To Ambrose St John, 11 August 1870.

[91.] L&D XXV, p. 214, Diary 9 October 1870.

[92.] SCA H412/19, Ullathorne to Sr M Xavier Williams, 15 November 1880.

with the local *Birmingham Post* which objected to his language.[93] It is not surprising, therefore, to hear him in spring 1871, wishing that he had tried a bit harder to avoid episcopal office a quarter of a century earlier. 'Had we known the weight and complication of difficulties with which the temporal administration of the diocese was to be loaded, our struggles to be saved from so heavy a responsibility would have been even greater than they were'.[94] At the celebrations for his episcopal silver jubilee on 21 June 1871 (the actual date was 26 July), Newman was delegated to write the address on behalf of the clergy – his willlingness being a sign, perhaps, that all was forgiven over the letter to Rome. Despite the formality of the occasion and the public nature of the text, there is a genuine warmth of appreciation in Newman's words.

My Lord, we come before you with this address, young and old, but whatever be our age, according to the years that we have experienced of your governance, we gratefully recognise in you a vigilant, unwearied pastor; a tender father; a friend in need; an upright, wise and equitable ruler; a superior who inspires confidence by bestowing it; the zealous teacher of his people; the champion by word and pen, of Catholic interests, religious and social; the defender of the defenceless; the vindicator of the sacred ordinances, amid the conflicts of political parties and the violence of theological hostility; a faithful servant of his Lord, who by life and conduct claims that cheerful obedience which we hereby with a full heart offer to you.[95]

However, the 1870s offered little in the way of opportunity to rest on his laurels and take life a little easier. Bishop William Clifford of Clifton had expressed unease during the Vatican Council about the impact of defining papal infallibility on countries like his own, where Catholicism was in the minor-

---

[93.] L&D XXV, p. 271 To Ambrose St John, 19 January 1871.
[94.] Pastoral Letter, 14 March 1871.
[95.] L&D XXV Appendix I, p. 458. Address to Bishop Ullathorne on his Episcopal Silver Jubilee.

ity.[96] The political impact of the definition, he argued, could be damaging, and so it proved. Gladstone, often described as 'a Tractarian in a blue coat' had taken a lively interest in all matters ecclesiastical while climbing the political ladder, and was, of course, an old friend of Manning. However, he looked on with unease in the 1860s as the growing influence of Ultramontanism meant that 'it was becoming axiomatic that whatever the Pope promulgated was to be accepted without question' and liberal Catholicism championed by the likes of Acton and Dollinger had been dealt a mortal blow.[97]

Dollinger, the leading voice in European liberal Catholic circles, believed the Syllabus of Errors, issued by Pius IX in 1864, to be a calamity and the thought of consecrating it by a dogmatic definition of papal infallibility even worse. Ullathorne, like most of the bishops, did his best to dampen the fire surrounding the Syllabus, which had stated that it was impossible for the Pope to be reconciled to modern civilisation and political developments. Ullathorne tried to set this most contentious article of the Syllabus in the context of contemporary Italian politics and the attacks on the Church, and explain that, as the preserver of civilisation, the papacy can never be reconciled with those who attack and destroy it.[98] Despite such efforts, the state governments of Europe reacted nervously at the prospect of an infallible definition of the articles of the Syllabus, especially Austria and Bavaria among the Catholic states and Prussia, which had a large Catholic minority. Gladstone was not only apprehensive about the broad European question, but fearful of how the planned Council would affect his attempts to do his best for Ireland. 'No Pope ever embarked on a course of action which so many leaders of European states regretted so ruefully.'[99]

Vatican support for Liberal party policy in Ireland would have been desirable in selling it to the Irish Church, but the rise of Ultramontanism seemed to make that increasingly

---

96. Harding thesis, p. 204.
97. David Bebbington, *The Mind of Gladstone: Religion, Homer and Politics* (2004), p. 223.
98. Pastoral Letter, 23 March 1865.
99. Chadwick, *Popes 1830–1914*, p. 192.

unlikely. This was a misreading by English Liberal politicians of the political priorities in Rome, and the Vatican Council exposed 'the ambivalence of a policy which relied on clerical influence in Ireland as a means of social control and excoriated it elsewhere as a cause of social delay'.[100] Gladstone was left with the vain hope that the old Pope would die quickly and leave the Council as a bit of elaborate, meaningless Roman ceremonial, quickly forgotten. Ironically, as Gladstone was trying to prevent the proclamation of infallibility, his government was also busy repealing the Ecclesiastical Titles Act of 1851, the knee-jerk reaction of Lord John Russell's administration to the 'Papal Aggression', and a dead letter from the beginning.[101]

The repeal of the 1851 Act was welcomed by Catholics, but it did little to retain political support for Gladstone among Catholic voters, who disliked his attitude to Rome and Ireland, and his education policy.[102] By the 1874 General Election, Catholic votes had moved decisively away from Gladstone and played a part in the defeat of the Liberal government. He was viewed as an opportunist, and his policy on education and opposition to Irish Home Rule were decisive.[103] Gladstone became convinced the Catholic politics was priest-ridden, and went on the attack, firstly in the *Contemporary Review*, and then in a pamphlet, *The Vatican Decrees in their bearing on Civil Allegiance: a Political Expostulation*, published, appropriately enough, on 5 November 1874.

Ullathorne wasted no time in publishing a response, which took the form of a Pastoral Letter, issued in the diocese on 17 November. In a hard-hitting text, reprinted as a pamphlet under the title, *The Dollingerites, Mr Gladstone and Apostates from the Faith*. Ullathorne classed the Dollingerites or Old Catholics, who had ended up as the tiny minority opposed to infallibility in principle, alongside the heretical groups of the Early Church such as Arians and Pelagians. There had already been a public exchange of arguments between Ullathorne and

---

[100.] Dermot Quinn, *Patronage and Piety: the Politics of English Roman Catholicism 1850–1900* (1993), p. 20.
[101.] Ibid., p. 25.
[102.] Ibid., p. 28.
[103.] Ibid., pp. 29–30.

Gladstone during the Council, and the bishop was incredulous that Gladstone should return to the fight when he had been assured, on the authority of the Vatican as well as Ullathorne himself, that 'there was no intention in any act or decree of the Council to invade the civil sphere'.[104]

Encouraged by the Old Catholics, Gladstone had reasserted his fear of Catholic disloyalty, only to receive a trenchant response from Ullathorne.

> But let Mr Gladstone and all men know, that we Catholics – your brethren, your priests and your bishops – besides the motives common to other men, have a motive for obedience to the civil power that is peculiar to ourselves; and that is the fixed and unchangeable doctrine and enforcement of the Catholic Church; that, not merely for man's sake, but much more for God's sake, and as part of our religion, we should be loyal and obedient to whatever civil government is constituted and established over the society in which we live.[105]

Manning was very complimentary about Ullathorne's pamphlet challenging Gladstone and his 'insolent and arrogant' publication. He urged Ullathorne to go on speaking out, as he feared Gladstone was being used by others who pushed for 'an atheistic doctrinaire' school of thought.[106]

A year later, Ullathorne did return to the fray in more detail, in *Mr Gladstone's Expostulation Unravelled* (1875) in which he entered on a more detailed rebuttal of Gladstone's *The Vatican Decrees in their Bearing on Civil Allegiance*. The nub of his attack on Gladstone was in impugning to him the motive of encouraging Catholics to inconsistency. 'Few are perfectly consistent in practice, but Mr Gladstone invites us to be inconsistent with principle; and there with Catholics he must utterly fail.'[107] The text ends with a personal message to Gladstone, in which

---

[104.] *The Dollingerites, Mr Gladstone and Apostates from the Faith* (1874), p. 16.

[105.] Ibid., p. 13.

[106.] AAW Ullathorne Correspondence, Manning to Ullathorne, 27 November 1874.

[107.] *Mr Gladstone's Expostulation Unravelled* (1875), p. 19.

Ullathorne accused him of fanning the flames of centuries of anti-Catholic prejudice, just at a time in history when, 'every Christian force is needed to check the advance of unchristian, infidel and atheistic invasions upon the peace and happiness of mankind'.[108] Not only had his attack revived anti-Catholic prejudice in England, but in its undermining of the Pope at a time when he was encircled by enemies, Gladstone had committed the unforgivable and unEnglish crime of kicking a man when he is down. Inevitably, of course, as Ullathorne gleefully concluded, this had drawn Catholics even closer in support of the embattled pontiff.[109]

Manning also joined the attack on Gladstone, and Newman's salvo in his *Letter to the Duke of Norfolk* was a resounding triumph in England, although it caused unease in Rome.[110] Newman had held off from writing, knowing that Ullathorne was going into print, and not wanting to crowd him, but was finally provoked into action.[111] His mention in the *Letter* of the unintended publication of Newman's letter to Ullathorne at the Council again raised hackles and gossip that the bishop had betrayed Newman's confidence.[112] Once again, Ullathorne leapt to Newman's defence in the *Dublin Review*, and the matter was quietly shelved.[113] The Pope let it be known to Ullathorne that, although there were certain passages in the pamphlet with which he was unhappy, he had no intention of censuring Newman.[114] Newman's mind and heart were soon overshadowed by the sudden death of his beloved friend and confrère, Ambrose St John, in May. A touching instance of Ullathorne's attempts at sensitivity where Newman was concerned was his offer to attend the funeral or not, as Newman wished, and to accept with perfect grace that the Oratory's wish for a private family funeral would be compromised by the public presence of the bishop.[115]

[108.] Ibid., p. 78.
[109.] Ibid., p. 80.
[110.] Butler, *Life*, II, pp. 100–6.
[111.] L&D XXVII, pp. 188–9, 14 January 1874.
[112.] L&D XXVII, p. 207, 28 January 1875.
[113.] L&D XXVII, p. 209, 1 February 1875.
[114.] L&D XXVII, p. 223, 16 February 1875.
[115.] L&D XXVII, p. 303, 26 May 1875.

It was evidently a great relief to Ullathorne after the strenuous events in Rome and his prolonged illness, to get back into
the round of domestic visits. He became enmeshed in the question of monastic reform at Stanbrook (although it was an
exempt house), and carried out two visitations at Colwich
(which was under his direct supervision). The year 1874
marked the fiftieth anniversary of his clothing as a monk of
Downside, and in thanking Colwich for their greetings, he was
as generous as ever.

> You are always too good to me and all the communities
> treat me much better than I deserve. It would be
> hypocrisy not to admit that I have tried to serve you all
> and them all, but my little services are incommensurate
> with the great kindness I constantly receive.[116]

To Handsworth he wrote that, 'it would be affectation for me
to deny that I have always had a tender care of the religious
communities entrusted to me; but this has always been the
most agreeable and satisfactory part of my duty, so I deserve
nothing for it.'[117] However, he was not uncritical about the
nuns and his criticisms could be unsparing. He lashed Colwich
for gossiping, especially about matters which did not concern
them. He advised them to go before the Lord and pray for
humility, patience, charity and submission, and, 'don't leave off
begging until you have been heard ... Let no one say such a
one is a great contemplative if she is not patient ... My sisters if
you wish to be contemplatives, carry your troubles and trials in
your heart and bear them up before God in silence'.[118]

Stanbrook was in difficulties in the early 1870s, and
Ullathorne agreed with the Benedictine President General that
two nuns should visit Solesmes and absorb something of the
great restoration of French monasticism of Dom Prosper
Guéranger.[119] This was only partly successful, as the reforms

[116.] Colwich, Ullathorne to Prioress, 16 March 1874.

[117.] Handsworth 19, 12 March 1874.

[118.] Colwich, Notes in another hand on Episcopal visitations. Dates
later added – 25 April 1872, 7 July 1874.

[119.] Ampleforth, Ullathorne Correspondence 246/13, Ullathorne to
Burchall, 30 September 1871.

based on Solesmes were rendered 'futile' by the inability of Abbess Gregson to govern the community.[120] However, things began to move in the right direction, and Ullathorne was pleased to see 'religious order, discipline and observance refreshed and restored' and reflected on the blessings showered upon the refugee English convents now restored to native soil.

> Everywhere God is moving them through his spirit to strict rule and observance, and it is impossible not to think that God has new designs upon them; and that as they kept the faith and piety of the Catholic women of this country in life and vigour in disastrous times, so are they now intended to be among the vigorous centres where the sound traditions of religious life, shaken everywhere by the powers of evil on the continent, are to be continued and preserved.[121]

It was no coincidence that, addressing the diocesan clergy on the subject of preaching at the Diocesan Synod in 1875, he insisted on the duty of catechesis and preaching for all priests, but made special mention of the importance of preaching to nuns. Some convent confessors or chaplains, he said, never spoke to the nuns outside the confines of the confessional. His view of this was characteristically clear. 'This is not just a disadvantage, it is a disqualification for the task.'[122]

The tasks of the priesthood and the proper formation and pattern of life for priests were preoccupations of Ullathorne, and ever since his days in the Western District, he had been conscious (particularly as he was not one himself) of the need to support the diocesan clergy in a particular way. Many of Ullathorne's pastoral letters as bishop were devoted to the needs of seminary formation and priestly life, but these were only one part of a long stream of public and private disquisitions on the same theme. Seminaries, as places for the

---

[120.] BAA B5170, Laurence Shepherd to Ullathorne, 28 September 1872.
[121.] Stanbrook 31, Ullathorne to Abbess Gregson, 7 May 1875.
[122.] *Synodal Discourse* (1875), p. 7.

formation of priests, (literally 'seedbeds') emerged from the Council of Trent in its last session in 1563, but took a long time to take root in the European Counter-Reformation. The English refugee colleges on the Continent, on which the recusant Church relied, were not seminaries in the full Tridentine sense, having no relationship with a particular diocesan bishop. The same can be said of the newer native colleges like Oscott, which emerged out of the chaos of the French Revolution. It was only in the nineteenth century, and particularly after 1850, that the English hierarchy was able to begin to reorder the colleges or found them anew as Tridentine seminaries. Ullathorne's active and direct interest in the management of Oscott reflected this, and his insistence on proper financial control was not only to ensure solvency but to move the college towards a more Tridentine identity. It is very obvious that he saw the provision, training and guidance of priests to be a primary function of the episcopate, and in his very first pastoral letter as Vicar Apostolic of the Central District in 1848 he set this out clearly. 'Our first care, dearly beloved brethren, has been directed to our episcopal seminary; that nursery, or shall we call it, the very fountain of the future prosperity of the District'.[123] His priorities had not altered forty years later, when on the brink of retirement, he wrote,

> The whole work of a diocese depends upon the number and character of its clergy, which again, depends upon their long and effective training. To look to this is one of the first duties of a bishop, to help him in this, where help is needed, is one of the first duties of the laity.[124]

What underpinned Ullathorne's determination to institute proper seminary education was his developed understanding of the nature and purpose of priesthood and the qualities and tasks required of the individual priest. Ullathorne's thinking on priesthood clearly emerged from his own missionary experience in Australia and in Coventry before his episcopal ordination, but of course, he had never experienced seminary

---

[123.] Pastoral Letter, 16 November 1848.
[124.] Pastoral Letter, 4 May 1888.

formation at first hand. His Benedictine formation and education at Downside had been somewhat sketchy, and in the emergence of his theology of priesthood the evidence of his self-education is clear. Australia taught him a great deal about the need for order and authority in the organisation of clergy as missioners, but also about the strain of solitary missionary life on the spirit and energy of a priest, and the need for deep inner spiritual and psychological resources in situations which bred isolation and depression.

After the period of what John Bossy christened 'trusteeism' or congregationalism from roughly 1780 to 1840,[125] when newly wealthy industrial laity usurped the quietist gentry leadership of the eighteenth century, the clergy gradually took over the driving seat in the English Catholic community. The transition to clerical training in England, the fading of private chaplaincies and gradual abandonment of riding missions, the influence of growing Ultramontanism in Europe and the restored hierarchy of bishops set a new pattern of Catholic life. Emergent parochial life (although parishes were not canonically erected until 1918) centred around the sacramental authority and temporal control of the resident priest, ordained and appointed by the local bishop as missionary rector. Clerical life became increasingly perceived as a separate (and higher) order of life than that of the laity, as the Tridentine values of separation of life and education were gradually taking root.

Ullathorne's role in this was immense, given his insistence on the need for separate clerical education and the spiritual and material resources he poured into it. He saw the priesthood in his own time and situation as essentially missionary, and exhorted his priests to take the same view.

> We are missioners. O name, rich with the most noble and generous associations! Our work is that of the apostles ...
> Unless he make himself into a sacrifice, as an apostle would, for the souls of his brethren, he may be a priest, but he is unworthy to call himself a missioner. A missioner

---

125. John Bossy, *The English Catholic Community 1570–1850* (1975), pp. 295–322.

is a priest, laborious, patient, not easily discouraged, ingenious by the force of that ardour which the spirit of his position enkindles to meet wants as they arise.[126]

Thus, while he saw his clergy as an intrinsic part of the new order which was to advance the Church in England, they were never to regard themselves as settled freeholders. The organisation of dioceses, seminaries and quasi-parishes was only a means to enable the exercise of missionary zeal. Nineteenth-century England was unquestionably missionary territory, and the care of the small Catholic flock was only one aspect of the priestly and episcopal task.

Despite his own monastic origins, Ullathorne had a special respect and devotion for the diocesan clergy, but a lifelong abhorrence for the term 'secular' when commonly applied to the clergy. On many occasions, publicly and privately, he advocated the adoption of the term 'pastoral clergy' to denote the men he described as 'Our Lord's own Pastoral Order'.

> I have thought more and more that the designation as 'seculars' is a calamity for them; that it misleads the mind as to their true character as a sacred order, to which Our Lord said: 'You are not of this world, as I am not of this world'. I have thought that if they had been designated as the sacred Pastoral Order and if the theory of their sacred vocation had been drawn out and kept before them with its spiritual laws and rules, as the regular bodies have had their position and sacred obligations drawn out and epitomised in the formulary of their rules, it would have exercised a vast influence upon their sanctity as well as upon their spiritual influence.[127]

He objected strongly to the implication that 'secular' clergy were somehow less religious in their way of life or less dedicated than the men of the religious orders, and also to the idea that they lived a more secular way of life. Speaking to his clergy

---

[126.] *Discourse delivered at the conclusion of the first Diocesan Synod of Birmingham* (1853).
[127.] *Autobiography*, p. 264.

at the diocesan synod in 1864, he had encouraged his priests to be 'wellsprings of light and grace' in the Church, and 'authoritative witnesses' to God's brightness and purity, remembering that the word secular denoted not their spirit, but the field of their labours.[128] In a letter to his friend Bishop Grant of Southwark, he even hoped, before the Vatican Council, that something might be done about it there:

> I think the term 'secular' appended to the pastoral clergy a most unfortunate one, and that it is like giving a dog a bad name, even though it be consecrated by long usage and incorporated in the law, and that a better term to distinguish them might be introduced in any new Council. I do think that whilst the regulars have worked out a system of perfection for their state, the pastoral clergy need a system drawn out and constantly kept before them as to a perfection belonging to their state at which they should aim ... I think this is a question deserving the utmost consideration and that the best traditions of the Church regarding the sanctity attached to the pastoral life and the care of that frankly should be drawn out.[129]

Ullathorne's emphasis on the diocesan clergy and their central role in building up Catholicism in England reflected his determination to regularise ecclesiastical life, and to move away from the ad hoc arrangements of the recusant period. It was more than the natural desire to have enough clergy to maintain and enhance the availability of Catholic sacramental life; it derived from his understanding of the proper ordering of the Church, and the priest, in his person as *alter Christus* fulfilling Christ's promise to be with His Church to the end of time. Withdrawal from the world was as significant to the spiritual life of the pastoral clergy as to the monk, and indeed Ullathorne regarded a non-monastic vocation as in some ways the more difficult one. This conviction came from his own experience, particularly in the unusually difficult setting of the

---

[128.] *Discourse delivered to the Clergy in the Diocesan Synod* (1864), pp. 6–7.
[129.] AAS Ullathorne Papers, Ullathorne to Grant, 19 August 1868.

Australian mission. It was also related to his conviction that Benedictine missioners should live in missionary priories, to avoid isolation and enhance their monastic life while on the mission. Neither was he happy about secular clergy living in isolation on the mission.

Ullathorne's passionate and long held desire for full seminary formation, without the worldly distractions of the lay school at Oscott, eventually nurtured in his mind a plan to establish a separate institution which could grow into a full scale Tridentine seminary. Ullathorne's dream of a seminary separate from Oscott was not only born of the desire to distinguish between lay education and that of Church students, but to form the clergy in a house specifically owned and run by Birmingham, without influence or interference from other dioceses, as at Oscott. Further reform after his own ideal at Oscott, while other bishops had a permanent interest in it, was impossible, and a new Birmingham seminary was the only answer.[130]

The vision of a separate, and fully Tridentine seminary away from Oscott was in Ullathorne's mind at least from the mid-1860s, and was obviously well known in the diocese. While he was in Rome for the centenary celebrations of SS Peter and Paul in the summer of 1867, the clergy of the diocese decided to do something about advancing his dream. They set up a fundraising committee of clergy and laity and drafted an address to the bishop to accompany whatever sum of money they could raise towards starting the project.[131] This was clearly as much a sign of personal affection and support for the bishop who had been nearly twenty years in their midst, as it was a practical move towards the longed for seminary. The initial sum raised and presented to Ullathorne on his return from Rome was £2,700 offered as 'proof of the interest felt in so important an object' and as a 'pledge of the zeal with which we are prepared to cooperate for its accomplishment'.

Ullathorne's response to the presentation was heartfelt and

[130.] AAW Ullathorne Correspondence, Ullathorne to Manning, 7 July 1865.
[131.] BAA B4545, Printed circular and subscription list for diocesan seminary.

sincere in acknowledging 'those spiritual bonds of grace, of faith in each other and of mutual charity'. He went on to reiterate his three great hopes expressed at his episcopal ordination in 1846: the restoration of the hierarchy, the institution of cathedrals and chapters and the establishment of seminaries. He recalled the history of the idea of seminaries at the Council of Trent and the part played in the prelude to it by the English Cardinal Reginald Pole, and suggested that 'it remains for us to restore the work that Pole began'. His practical good sense meant that he insisted on modest beginnings, like the mustard seed, in order to put down firm and permanent roots, proposing to begin with a few men in a rented house near the cathedral, as set down by the Council of Trent. This would be the chrysalis of a larger and more suitable establishment in time.[132]

His vision of the direction which a seminary would follow had already taken concrete shape in his mind.

My plan is a *grande seminaire* for higher studies. I would begin in Rhetoric and so on to Logic, Metaphysics and Theology. They shall begin in tonsure and soutane and a good deal of attention shall be paid to sacred Rhetoric and the model of the Fathers and saintly preachers. I prefer the bent of Bartholomew Holzhauser's rules and spirit to any other I know. His rules were approved by Innocent XI and flourished in Germany about the time St. Sulpice began. He also contemplates common life for the secular clergy, without any vows, and has an admirable view, once followed in Staffordshire, but not well followed. If I can get this common life in the seminary, it will act on the missions having more than one priest ... I do not lose sight of the importance of not having youths shut up from childhood away from all other commerce, therefore, for the present at least I prefer my students mixing with other lads up to a certain age. Then I propose to bring them into the seminary to get the Church stamp on them, and that firstly. I wish

[132]. BAA B4553, Printed address to Ullathorne and his reply, 18 July 1867.

them to mix at certain times with their superiors, which
was the great advantage of monastic training, that they
may not come out mere raw youths as they go into the
seminary. This is more than half the battle in their formation. I shall myself give instruction from time to time and
mix with them in conversation, to open their minds. I will
have no Oscott men to begin with, for I must cut off the
old traditions.[133]

The friend with whom he shared these aspirations was Canon
John Walker, who had been a close confidante since an acci-
dental meeting in Durham, when Ullathorne was en route to
Ushaw College for his ordination to the priesthood in
September 1831. Walking the four miles from Durham to
Ushaw, the two young men became acquainted, talking of
philosophy and theology. His new friend expressed shock at
Ullathorne's knowledge of Protestant writers such as Richard
Hooker and Jeremy Taylor, but as Ullathorne wryly recalled,
he himself 'obviously knew something of these selfsame
writers'.[134] Walker was, at the time, on the professorial staff at
Ushaw, but left in 1835, having become embroiled in a theological row between the vice-president Charles Newsham and
Richard Gillow, professor of dogmatic theology. Walker allied
himself with Gillow in humiliating Newsham in front of his
students, and this led directly to his dismissal from Ushaw and
appointment to the mission of Scarborough, where, nursing his
resentment, he lived out the rest of his days.[135] Newsham
equally never relinquished his bitterness, warning Newman in
1857 against using Walker in a Bible translation project,
because of his tendency to 'cavil'.[136]

In Scarborough, of course, he was parish priest to
Ullathorne's widowed mother, and the main reason why she
stayed there.[137] He was a close friend and correspondent from
1837 of the eminent historian John Lingard, who wrote of him:

[133.] Ushaw UL 20, Ullathorne to Walker, 28 August 1867.
[134.] *Autobiography*, p. 53.
[135.] David Milburn, *A History of Ushaw College* (1964), p. 160.
[136.] M. Haile and E. Bonney, *Life and Letters of John Lingard 1771–1851*
(1911), p. 261.
[137.] Ushaw UL 25, Ullathorne to Walker, 9 July 1873.

'He can write and write well, if he please, but though he may begin, he never goes through with anything.'[138] Walker has been described as one of finest literary critics of his time, but was 'a man of whims, working by fits and starts, and as likely – after burning the midnight oil for a week over a treatise or pamphlet – to throw it in the fire, as to send it to the publisher'.[139] Lingard likened him to Milner as being 'too ardent', but they were such close friends that Walker went to Lingard at once when the aged historian was gravely ill, and was with him when he died in September 1851.[140] As a consequence, Ullathorne wrote to Walker:

> I suppose Lingard has left remains of some kind. His letters must be valuable. Who is to be his editor and biographer – you? I suspect you ought to be. Our Catholic history will slip away for want of histories of our leading men. I can get no-one at work on a life of Milner.[141]

Walker was also friends with both Newman and Wiseman, visiting the Great Exhibition with Wiseman in the spring of 1851.[142] He was an annual visitor to the Birmingham Oratory, being welcomed warmly every Easter,[143] which presumably meant that he also paid a visit to Ullathorne at the same time. The appeal of Walker's friendship to Ullathorne was obvious: a north countryman with a strong interest in theological and philosophical writings, and one of the last personal links with his home and family and the traditions of Lingard's generation which warmed Ullathorne's heart.

Newman's record of a conversation between the three friends shows the seeds of Ullathorne's thinking about the seminary being nurtured long before the diocesan collection was launched. The seminary idea was already in Ullathorne's

138. Haile and Bonney, p. 261.
139. Ibid., pp. 261–2.
140. Ibid., p. 367.
141. Ushaw UI.1, Ullathorne to Walker, 7 September 1851. He did eventually get Frederick Husenbeth to write a life of Milner, published in 1862.
142. Haile and Bonney, p. 366.
143. L&D XXVI to William Walker (nephew), 27 June 1873.

head, but money was the inevitable problem, and thinking aloud, and looking very hard at Newman as he spoke, he wondered if someone could be persuaded to buy Oscott as a lay school. Newman mused that it could become 'a first rate college', but never pursued the notion. The real issue concerned the care and nurture of the church students at Oscott, which was at the time 'deplorable', largely because they were so outnumbered – twenty of them to a hundred and fifty schoolboys. The parents of the schoolboys exercised huge influence (through the pursestrings) and the recent 'miserable affair of Fitzgerald v Northcote' was only the worst example of the 'evil'.[144]

Henry Weedall, it seemed, had been pressured by the parents of lay boys into favouring the schoolboys and dismissing three church students in six years. Ullathorne had felt reluctantly obliged to back him, believing the students to be blameless, and after transfer to another seminary, the three had turned out excellent priests. This had created huge ill feeling among the priests of the diocese towards Oscott. Northcote, despite the reforms he and Ullathorne had put in place, was only too eager to 'wash his hands of the lay boys and become the head of a pure seminary'.[145] The desperate state of things at Oscott, even after five years of Northcote's government, and Ullathorne's continued insistence that the formation of priests was the most important task in hand, makes sense of his determination to build afresh away from Oscott, despite the cost.

Bartholomew Holzhauser, whose ideas Ullathorne enthused about and wanted to adopt, was a seventeenth-century Bavarian secular priest, who had met the future Charles II during the king's exile. He was only prevented from embarking on the

---

144. In 1865, James Spencer Northcote was taken to court by an aggrieved parent for unlawful imprisonment, after he had briefly locked a troublemaker in his room, prior to expulsion. The facts were undeniable; Northcote lost the case, but the court awarded derisory damages, indicating its view of the proceedings. See Judith Champ, *Oscott* (Archdiocese of Birmingham Historical Commission 1987), p. 16

145. L&D XXI, p. 457. Record of a visit by Ullathorne and Walker, May 1865.

English mission himself by a total ignorance of England and the English language. As a priest in his native Bavaria, he evolved a plan to foster a pattern of life for secular clergy by the formation of an 'Institute of Clerics Living in Common'. As part of this Institute, the parish clergy should live in small groups, with no female housekeepers, at the disposal of the local bishop, but also subject to the superior of the Institute. The purpose of the Institute was to develop individual spirituality through mutual support and a firmly structured daily routine. Its emphasis was on a common life for priests and the use of the Rosary, litanies, popular prayers and at least one hour a day of communal meditation.[146] He was initially told by Rome that his ideal was so obvious as to need no official sanction, but under Innocent XI the Institute was canonically erected by two papal bulls of 1680 and 1684, years after Holzhauser's death – the first only weeks after the English Dominican Cardinal, Philip Howard, arrived in Rome as Cardinal Protector of England.

Howard was a great advocate of the virtues of Holzhauser's Institute, and contemplated imposing its rule of life on the English College in Rome. Cardinal Howard's only pastoral letter to the English clergy, issued in 1684, was wholly devoted to advocating Holzhauser's Institute. Several London clergy joined the Institute and John Morgan (a protégé of Howard's) recruited several priests in Staffordshire. However, opposition took root, mainly orchestrated by John Sergeant, the secretary of the English Chapter. The main objection was the danger it posed to the authority of the Chapter, and eventually Sergeant secured the suppression of the Institute in 1703.[147] The ideal of a common life for secular clergy with some sort of 'rule of life' did not completely disappear from England, and re-emerged in Ullathorne's vision for his seminary.

Two leading figures of the nineteenth-century European Catholic revival were responsible for Holzhauser's re-emergence, Wilhelm Ketteler (1811–77) a leading proponent of Social Catholicism in Germany and Bishop of Mainz, and Felix

---

[146.] T. A. Birrell, 'Holzhauser and England: three episodes' in *Grenzgange Litertatur und Kultur in Kontext* (Amsterdam 1990), pp. 453–63.

[147.] Ibid., p. 458.

Dupanloup (1806–78), a powerful voice in Catholic education, Bishop of Orleans and 'one of the most outstanding figures of the period and of the Council'.[148] Both men were leading inopportunists at the Vatican Council, but this evidently did not prevent Ullathorne sharing their enthusiasm for Holzhauser. Dupanloup absorbed Holzhauser's ideas from Jean Gaduel, a leading educationalist from St Sulpice in Paris. Gaduel published a treatise on Holzhauser's Institute in 1853, quoting Cardinal Howard with approval, and a life of Holzhauser in 1861. These were presumably Ullathorne's source.[149]

In 1871, having purchased forty acres of land in Olton near Birmingham, Ullathorne began planning his seminary buildings with the architect Edward Joseph Hansom. He moved cautiously, anxious to avoid debt, and only proposed to build half the architect's plan. In the end, his caution limited the seminary's development and its practical usefulness.[150] It is interesting to compare this careful, cheese-paring approach with the almost reckless ambition shown by Walsh at Oscott forty years earlier. The debts Ullathorne inherited, particularly in relation to Oscott and his brief experience of a debtors' gaol bred in him extreme financial caution. It is perhaps true that 'the heroic church building of the days of Pugin and Shrewsbury had been firmly curtailed by the new hierarchy',[151] but this was realism. Shrewsbury was long dead and the reality was that it was the pennies of parishioners which paid for church building in the second half of the century. Ullathorne was not interested in spectacular and eye-catching projects, but in solid and modest building schemes which enabled the mission of the Church to be fulfilled without burdening the people of the diocese with further crippling debts. The money raised from his frequent and impassioned appeals for church building was not to be lavished in extravagance, nor was the generous collection raised by the clergy themselves for the new seminary to be spent rashly.

[148.] Butler, *Vatican Council*, I, p. 65.
[149.] Birrell, p. 459.
[150.] Mary McInally, *Edward Ilsley, Archbishop of Birmingham* (2002), p. 42.
[151.] Roderick O'Donnell, *The Pugins and the Catholic Midlands* (2002), p. 31.

Charles Hansom had been the first architect with whom Ullathorne ever worked, at St Osburg's, Coventry, which was also Hansom's first major church building.[152] It was not surprising that his son Edward, Ullathorne's godson, (previously in partnership with his father, but by 1871 in partnership with A. M. Dunn) was the choice for Olton. Hansom and Dunn were also responsible for the new monastic buildings and church at Downside, of which Ullathorne wholeheartedly approved.

> Week before last I gave a *triduo* to the fathers at Downside before entering their new monastery, and blessed it on the Sunday, when they took possession. The buildings are equal to the best medieval monastic structures, and the cloister of the monastery proper is simply perfect'.[153]

Several other Hansom churches followed in the Diocese of Birmingham.

During the summer of 1871 there was constant stream of correspondence between Ullathorne and Hansom over the details of the building and its fittings.[154] Olton, although very much Ullathorne's personal project, was only one instance of the detailed attention he paid to building projects. He commented closely on the building of Stone convent in 1853 (also by Charles Hansom) and, in the 1870s, on work by E. W. Pugin at Stanbrook. His enormous practical good sense is very clear – even to reminding the nuns to ensure that the plans were deposited in the archives for future reference![155] His disinclination to use E. W. Pugin caused several rows, including over work at Oscott, the building of the church at Hanley in the Potteries and Pugin's accusation that Ullathorne had

---

152. Denis Evinson, 'Hansom, Charles Francis (1817–1888)', *Oxford Dictionary of National Biography*, Oxford University Press, 2004 [http://www.oxforddnb.com/view/article/48460, accessed 14 Sept 2005].
153. Stanbrook 37, Ullathorne to Abbess, 13 September 1876.
154. BAA B4956ff.
155. Stanbrook 37, Ullathorne to Abbess, 13 September 1876.

favoured his godson, Edward Hansom, not only at Olton, but in giving him the prestigious contract for the third city centre church in Birmingham, St Catherine's.[156] The younger Pugin was even more difficult and irascible than his father had been.

In spring 1874 the Bishop was dragged into a pointless and vicious row between Pugin and Ullathorne's old friend, the artist, J. R. Herbert, who had engaged Edward Pugin (whom he had known since Pugin's infancy) as architect for his own London house. Relations between client and architect deteriorated, leading to a stream of vitriol from Pugin to Herbert, which also included poisonous attacks on Ullathorne. Herbert eventually took Pugin to court for libel and defamation. He begged Ullathorne to attend the Old Bailey, which he did, although he was not called to give evidence.[157] The whole case was bizarre, with no less a figure than Gladstone summoned by both sides! Having been a friend of Herbert's for twenty or thirty years, he gave evidence on his behalf, but to no avail. The court took the view that Pugin's letters had been scurrilous but not libellous and threw the case out.[158]

The foundation stone of St Bernard's Seminary, Olton (named after Ullathorne's own monastic patron, St Bernard of Clairvaux) was laid in 1872 and Edward Ilsley was appointed rector. This was regarded as a 'surprise' appointment, as Ilsley had been labouring in a mission in the Staffordshire Potteries for twelve years and was not a public figure in the diocese. He was only thirty-five, and perhaps Ullathorne saw echoes of his own younger self in Ilsley's proven capacity for organisation and order.[159] The two senior professors, Victor Schobel and William Barry, also vice rector, were twenty-five and twenty-four respectively, but his own experience told Ullathorne that young men could grow into difficult posts in new situations. Holzhauser's scheme was duly adopted and Ullathorne was delighted in what he described as, 'one of the most important

---

156. BAA B5359–5412, Correspondence between Pugin, Ullathorne and Fr Molloy at Hanley.
157. BAA B4932 Telegram from Herbert to Ullathorne, 13 July 1874.
158. BAA B5433 *The Times* Law Report, 12 July 1874.
159. McInally, p. 43.

germs that can be planted in England'.[160] He insisted so strongly on a complete separation from Oscott and a new beginning, that the first Olton students were the small group studying in Douai, which included Henry Parkinson, who would go on to be rector of Olton and of Oscott. They were to stay in Douai until Olton was ready, and not to go 'anywhere else' (i.e. Oscott). He assured them excitedly that Olton would be, 'as the Church intends, the family of the bishop, in which he will take a singular interest, and over which he will exercise a singular care; to which his whole heart will be given'. Its purpose would be to produce 'fervent and pure hearted missionaries'.[161]

Ullathorne took a very close interest in the planning of Olton and of all that went on there, including the personal conduct of the students, 'I insist much on manners, even the manner of doing the commonest things ...'[162] He had long been planning what his ideal of a seminary would be like, and quickly involved himself in setting rules and regulations. The seminary began with eleven students and in October 1873 the formal opening took place. The contrast with life at Oscott, which Ullathorne had long wanted to see, was marked in his prohibition of plays and farces at Olton, which were a regular part of life at Oscott, even among the Church students.[163] He was also very clear that priests should not only shun play acting, but politics too:

> I should only be inclined to interfere with the clergy if they habitually threw themselves into public politics, and then on a general principle rather than on the ground of the special case ... it is not good for the clergy to take an open lead on these burning political questions. It would confirm the notion, which the press is quite willing to work, that the Church is going in for democratic politics.[164]

[160.] Quoted in McInally, p. 46.
[161.] BAA B4965 Ullathorne to students at Douai, 15 June 1871.
[162.] Quoted in McInally, p. 45.
[163.] McInally, p. 56.
[164.] AAW Ullathorne Correspondence, Ullathorne to Manning, 2 March 1873.

Another major change took place in the diocese in 1873, which shaped education and preparation for the priesthood for the next century, which was the transfer of Sedgley Park School (founded in 1763 by Challoner on a site near Wolverhampton) to Cotton College in North Staffordshire. The school was founded for the sons of the Catholic 'middling sort' who needed their sons to go into business rather than scholarship, but many of Sedgley Park's alumni had gone on to Oscott as seminarians. During the 1860s, Ullathorne had set up a diocesan commission to look at the state of Sedgley Park, which recommended that it was inadequate. Cotton Hall had been part of the Shrewsbury estate and leased firstly by Faber for his short-lived and problematic venture, and later by the Passionists. By chance it came on the market in 1865, and became the property of the diocese. The preparatory school moved there in 1868, and in 1873, after the death of the long serving president of Sedgley Park, James Moore, the main school moved to its new home.[165]

Provided with more spacious premises and land for expansion, Cotton College became the nursery of generations of priests in the Diocese of Birmingham until its final closure in the 1980s. It was closely linked to Oscott, and its first two presidents, Joseph Souter and John Hawkesford, both went on to serve as rectors of Oscott. Ullathorne was an enthusiastic supporter of Sedgley Park and Cotton, and the character of the clergy he shaped was largely that of Cotton and Oscott or Cotton and Olton, which had an influence in the diocese for generations to come.

There was no doubt that the world of Thomas McDonnell and his ilk was passing away. Ullathorne was aware that the Church was operating in a new world, and was keen for the bishops to undertake a detailed discussion of pastoral life and the role of the clergy in contemporary society.[166] He and Manning obviously exchanged ideas about the pastoral clergy in the early 1870s, leading to Manning's suggestion that it be the main subject of discussion at the Provincial Synod of

[165.] W. Buscot, *The History of Cotton College* (1940), pp. 205–9.
[166.] AAW Ullathorne Correspondence, Manning to Ullathorne, 6 January 1873.

1873.[167] His influence on the shape and content of Manning's *Eternal Priesthood* (published in 1883) was substantial.[168]

Few bishops in the history of the Church live to take part in an Ecumenical Council, still less one in such dramatic historical times as those of 1870. Ullathorne was well aware of the significance of what he had been a part of and a witness to. The rigours of the Vatican Council and its aftermath had taken their toll on Ullathorne's energies.The achievement of Olton redressed the balance, and gave him huge satisfaction, representing, as it did, one of the most cherished of his hopes. After close on a quarter of a century of the new English hierarchy, Ullathorne could begin to see some of the fruits of its achievement in the growth of English Catholicism, its people, its churches, convents, schools and charitable associations. He was far from being finished with matters of organisation and structures, but in the latter part of his life, it is possible to discern more of the inner man, through his friendships and his writings.

[167.] AAW Ullathorne Correspondence, Manning to Ullathorne, 15 April 1872.
[168.] See Chapter 9.

Chapter 9

Friends Depart 1875–1885

By the end of 1875, Ullathorne had fallen a little in love, with a literary widow who had remarried to Edward Heneage Dering, a retired army officer, and become a Catholic. Lady Georgiana Chatterton was the daughter of Lascelles Iremonger, Prebendary of Winchester Cathedral and was therefore thoroughly steeped in the traditions of the Church of England. She was a deeply religious woman, and her second husband regarded her influence as the means of his becoming a Catholic, although he says that she herself expressed no evident inclination at that point.[1] He was received into the Catholic Church in 1865, but oddly, he records in his memoir of his wife that she did not immediately follow him.[2] In fact, it is clear from Newman's diaries that he received both husband and wife and her niece Miss Orpen in September 1865.[3] However, she clearly had considerable trials of conscience, and for a time gave up the practice of Catholicism, so her husband's recollection was perhaps tactful rather than totally accurate.[4] What followed for Lady Georgiana (recorded and shared by her husband) was ten years of anguish and agony of conscience, during which time Ullathorne became her guide and confidante. His letters to Lady Georgiana reveal a tender,

[1] Edward Heneage Dering, *Memoir of Georgiana, Lady Chatterton* (1878), p. 149.
[2] Ibid., pp. 152–3.
[3] L&D XXII, p. 57. Diary, 20 September 1865.
[4] L&D XXII, p. 57, note.

patient and warm side to Ullathorne, rarely if ever visible in the public dealings which gained him such harsh nicknames as, 'the Right Reverend Agitator General' or 'Monsignor Ego Solus'.

In 1867 Lady Georgiana's niece, Rebecca Orpen married Edward Marmion Ferrers of Baddesley Clinton in Warwickshire. Ferrers was the son of an ancient Catholic family, whose moated manor house at Baddesley Clinton had been a vital link in the network of Catholic houses which maintained and protected the Franciscan mission in that area in the seventeenth century. One of the family, Randolph Ferrers, was himself a Franciscan missioner. Edward Marmion was educated at the Franciscan school near the manor house and at Oscott College in the 1830s. He died childless, aged seventy, in 1884.[5] In 1868, Ullathorne visited Baddesley Clinton and met Edward Dering and Lady Georgiana for the first time (initially at nearby Wootton Hall which they rented for a time).[6] By then, Lady Georgiana was struggling with her Catholic faith.

Ullathorne was obviously charmed as quickly as anyone else who met Lady Georgiana: she had moved easily all her life in London fashionable and literary society but although she continued to write novels and verse, her inner life was now preoccupied with matters of religious faith. Her now largely unread writings, a mix of poetry, fiction, devotional and travel writing have been dismissed as 'uniformly unmemorable'.[7] She became one of a number of women who Ullathorne throughout his life regarded as friends and treated with the utmost seriousness, responding carefully and thoughtfully to their religious questions. His letters to Lady Georgiana are long and full in replying to her difficulties, and by no means patronising. They reveal his innate respect for a woman who was struggling with matters of faith with intelligence and courage. It would have been very easy for him to give ready answers and to iron

[5.] Gillow, II, pp. 253–4.
[6.] *Memoir*, p. 172.
[7.] G. C. Boase, 'Chatterton , Henrietta Georgiana Marcia Lascelles, Lady Chatterton (1806–1876)', rev Elizabeth Baigent, *Oxford Dictionary of National Biography*, Oxford University Press, 2004 [http://www.oxforddnb.com/view/article/5187, accessed 14 Sept 2005].

out the concerns which inhibited her full participation in Catholic life. Instead, he counselled her husband constantly: 'Don't hurry her'.[8]

In a series of letters between 1868 and 1875, Ullathorne explained carefully to Lady Georgiana some of the elements of Catholic faith and doctrine, not in the form of a detailed catechesis, but rather as a friend enjoying a conversation on matters close to his heart with a genuine seeker after truth. The letters are not heavy-handed and packed with scholarly references, but employ a gentler, lighter touch than Ullathorne used in his published works. 'My dear friend, the way to faith is through prayer. Get as near to God as you can.' The letters were never intended for publication, of course, but were printed in her husband's memoir and later in a pocket edition.[9] Although he presumably never realised it, this more intimate style which Ullathorne adopted with friends and confidantes was more effective than the public discourses packed with references to the Church Fathers and the theologians of which he was fond.

He addressed her concerns firstly about the Immaculate Conception (on which he had published a book after the definition in 1854), on the Eucharist (two letters in one day), on Faith, the Church, celibacy and the clergy, the rosary, Catholic ceremonial, feeling and will, and the love of God. Each of them were direct responses to points raised by Lady Georgiana and all, apart from the first, were written in the course of a few months in 1875, during which time she gradually became reconciled to Catholicism. By August of that year, she was so tormented that she placed herself under Ullathorne's immediate direction: 'Tell him that he knows me thoroughly. It is for him to command, and I will obey.'[10]

Ullathorne's reaction to her distress was an unusually sympathetic one which revealed his capacity for pastoral sensitivity. He instructed her to make a simple act of faith in the Catholic Church and 'cling with all her heart and will, in spite of all her imagination might suggest'.[11] This he believed would begin to

[8.] *Memoir*, p. 185.
[9.] *Doctrinal Letters of Archbishop Ullathorne* (CTS 1911).
[10.] *Memoir*, p. 243.
[11.] Ibid.

bring her peace of mind and enable her to make her confession to a local priest and be guided by him as regards receiving Holy Communion. She did so, and by the end of August had begun to practise as a Catholic and had found that peace of mind. Although she placed herself under direction from the local Catholic priest, Ullathorne continued to reply readily to the questions she raised with him about aspects of Catholic life. Theirs was not merely an intellectual dialogue, or the polite exchanges of a society hostess and the local bishop, but a tender and close friendship.

Ullathorne was a frequent visitor to Baddesley Clinton, and when he was there at Christmas 1875 she discussed with him a fear that her love for human beings was stronger than her love for God, and revealed to him alone her premonition that she would be dead within the year. The little scene which took place when he left Baddesley to catch the train back to Birmingham reveals a tenderness remarkable between a Victorian bishop and a married woman. When he was ready to go, she drove him to the railway station as usual and after they had parted and he had gone into the station, she called him back and asked him to give her his blessing. 'The bishop took her little fingers in his own, and with them made the sign of the Cross on her forehead.'[12]

Within a couple of days he had written another letter to her in response to her anxiety, which began: 'How many feelings do we have that we wish we had not! In such cases the feelings go one way and the will another.' He went on to write movingly, even passionately, about love, and supremely about the love of God which 'above all things and in all things brings us peace, because it brings us to the object of our soul, to the end of the soul's desires: to that Divine Good for which the soul is created'. However, that ultimate love would only be consummated in Heaven, and he told her that it was only by faith that human beings could strive towards that love while on earth. 'It is the action of grace which works in the human heart to perfect love and to quell pride which is the source of self love.' Yet, while speaking of Divine love, Ullathorne revealed a depth of understanding of human love, which could only have grown from his own experience.

[12.] Ibid., p. 265.

The love of a most dear friend, or of one yet more closely united to us, is a love in which not only the will, but all the senses, inward and outward, are engaged: there all the sensibilities flow together with the will. Here, if anywhere, is joy in loving. And where the love is pure and holy, still nature and grace move in one and the same direction ... When the love of God is supreme in us, then every other love partakes in this Divine love, becomes exalted, purified and sanctified. For this is the grandeur of divine charity, that it draws all loves into the divine love, and regulates them all ... for this is the grand double law of Catholic charity, that whilst we love God, and are subject to God, we likewise love God in our neighbour and are subject to God in being humble to our neighbour. We love in them what is of God, and are subject to them in what is of God; and all this is referred to God, and not merely to the creature as such. Thus we learn to see God's side, which is the beautiful side in all persons.

These are surely the words of a man who, if he was not at least a little in love with his correspondent, had surely known what it was to love another human being. His letter concludes with a suggestion of the struggle which is involved for the person who desires to love God wholly. '... there may be many failures, destroying many conceits ...' The true test of love is not feeling but desire. 'What we desire, that we love; what we desire intensely, that we intensely love. What we willingly obey, and to what we willingly subject ourselves, to that we give all proofs of love. Not what we feel, but what we do, is the manifestation of our love.'[13]

In a further letter dated 6 January 1876, Ullathorne took up the same theme, in response to fresh problems raised by Lady Georgiana about the love of God, so the focus shifted away from human love after one final coda which summed up his understanding of the relationship between human and Divine love.

The love which our fellow mortals give to us, and we to them, is either a human love, which goes not beyond the

[13.] Ibid., pp. 266–275.

powers of nature, and then it is the love of benevolence; or it is taken up into the love of God, so that we are loved, not merely for our own sake, but also for God's sake, whose children we are, and then it is the love of charity which sanctifies and pervades the entire human love, and raises it to a supernatural order, having present reward and reward to come.[14]

The language of intense desire and love was not commonplace in the writings of Victorian bishops, and in Ullathorne's words it contradicts many of the commonplaces about his arrogant and blunt manner. That may have been his way in public discourse, but there was still within him the romantic whose very being was stirred by the grandeur of God, whether manifested in the natural world, in the ideal of St Benedict or in the human heart.

On 5 February 1876, her premonition came true and Lady Georgiana died quite suddenly, aged seventy, the same age as Ullathorne himself. The blessing at the railway station had been the two friends' final parting. The bishop preached at her funeral, but no record of his words survived, for he told her bereaved husband that he had no definite recollection of what he had said: 'I never thought of what I was going to say till I stood up to say it. I poured it out from my heart.'[15] This was a rare extempore homily from a man who was never less than carefully prepared and armed with Scriptural and Patristic references before he spoke or wrote in public, and is further evidence of the unusual depth of his friendship for Lady Georgiana. She obviously also knew what lay close to Ullathorne's heart, as she left £1,000 in her will for the apple of his eye, the new seminary at Olton.[16] A valuable sapphire and diamond ring (worth £200 when bought) was given to him at the funeral by her widowed husband, who insisted that no one henceforth should wear it but the bishop of the diocese.[17]

In 1876, Ullathorne sat for a portrait by the eminent Scottish

[14.] Ibid., p. 277.
[15.] Ibid., p. 300.
[16.] Colwich, Ullathorne to Prioress asking for prayers for the repose of Lady Georgiana's soul, 21 February 1886.
[17.] BAA B5716, Ullathorne to Estcourt, 16 February 1876.

painter, John Pettie. Apart from the youthful drawings of him as part of his own family, Ullathorne was painted several times as bishop. An undated portrait of him in monastic habit and episcopal robes hangs in Archbishop's House in Birmingham, and a late undated portrait is at the Convent of Mercy, Handsworth. The earliest, by Richard Burchett in 1852 hangs at Downside Abbey; a second by Herr Barthelme of Munich was painted in 1859 for Oscott; and Pettie's was a more unusual commission, being a personal one by an otherwise unknown Birmingham convert businessman called Thomas Richards. It was owned by Mr Richards and his intention was that it would go to the diocesan seminary at Olton on his death.[18] It is not clear how the Pettie commission came about, as, although he did some portrait work, he was better known as a 'genre' painter of historical scenes of the English Civil War and Jacobite Risings. Many of his portrait sitters (not including Ullathorne) were also painted in historical costume.[19] By the time Ullathorne sat for him, Pettie had become a Royal Academician, and the painting was exhibited at the Academy in 1876 and at the Paris International Exhibition of 1878. Ullathorne himself was rather taken with the portrait, telling Estcourt that Pettie had 'made the picture so good that [he] warned him not to touch the face again'.[20] He wrote to his friend Kathleen O'Meara, who lived in Paris, telling her that the painting was to go to the International Exhibition there, and that it had been valued at £1,000. In the following year, she reported having seen the portrait, and told him the comments of an eminent American painter, George Healy, who was much struck with it, saying, 'it is a noble picture; the attitude is full of power, and there is a bold originality in it that is very striking'.[21] Its present whereabouts are unknown.

While Ullathorne was pursuing his dream of a Tridentine

[18.] College Irlandais Paris, Ullathorne to Kathleen O'Meara, 9 January 1878.

[19.] Ray McKenzie, 'Pettie, John (1839–1893)', *Oxford Dictionary of National Biography*, Oxford University Press, 2004 [http://www.oxforddnb.com/view/article/22062, accessed 14 Sept 2005].

[20.] BAA B5724, Ullathorne to Estcourt, 27 February 1876.

[21.] BAA B6458, Ullathorne to Mr Richards (quoting O'Meara), 11 February 1879.

seminary to provide for the formation of priests for Birmingham in the future, Manning was also following a dream of English Catholic university education for the laity. In the light of the insistence from Rome that Catholics should not attend the secular universities, Manning developed a scheme for a Catholic university college to meet the growing needs of the educated laity. It had not worked well in Dublin in the early 1850s and was doomed to failure in London in the 1870s. It also proved to be one of the great conflicts between Ullathorne and Manning. The clash with Ullathorne centred on whether the university college founded by Manning in Kensington was a Westminster project or a national one, and lack of co-operation between the bishops was a major factor in the ultimate failure of Kensington.[22]

As in so many of the new Catholic ventures of the second half of the nineteenth century, finding the right personnel was vital but often well nigh impossible. Thomas Capel's appointment by Manning to head the Catholic University College in Kensington in 1874 was a mistake: he was unenthusiastic about the project and did not share Manning's policies and ideals. It proved disastrous and the bishops unanimously asked him to resign in 1878, to which he responded with a threat to sue for damages.

After Capel's departure, Ullathorne refused sharply any involvement in Kensington, insisting that he was not able to offer names for a possible successor.

> I can offer no names from this diocese, where, instead of having anyone to spare, we are strained for want of priests; and of course I could not recommend the subjects of other bishops. To prevent possible mistakes, I think I ought to add that I have never pledged myself to any responsibility with respect to the college in question ... Mgr Capel always insisted with me, that as he was appointed by all the bishops, he was entitled to secure priests from all their dioceses whenever he stood in need of their services. In this I could never agree ... I should

22. V. A. McClelland, *Cardinal Manning: his public life and influence 1865–92* (1962), pp. 119–23.

have great and conscientious difficulties in taking the
responsibility of again giving an opinion on the appointment of a future rector, if that involves any responsibility,
whether as to the financial, the scholastic, or the spiritual
management of the college. Temporal administration
must be the responsibility of individual dioceses and
Birmingham is still burdened with debt inherited from
my predecessors.[23]

McClelland was critical of Ullathorne for reneging on a joint
hierarchy responsibility in Capel's appointment and in the
project as a whole. 'Panic seized certain members of the hierarchy, and in particular Ullathorne of Birmingham.'[24] In
declining to give names for a possible successor when asked by
Manning, Ullathorne 'tried to wriggle out of the responsibility
for the venture'.[25]

However, there was a background to Ullathorne's refusal to
be drawn into financial responsibility for Capel's claims or the
appointment of his successor. He had made it clear, in his dealings with Capel at the outset, over the choice of a Birmingham
priest as vice rector, that he did not regard himself as having a
share in responsibility for the University College. Ullathorne
was furious that Capel had approached Walter Croke Robinson
to teach Church History and be vice-rector of the college
without his permission. Ullathorne accused him of trying to
'turn Mr Robinson from ecclesiastical allegiance'. Capel
protested that he was doing no such thing and had only asked
Robinson to consider the appointment on condition that
Ullathorne agreed, and apologised profusely for any offence.[26]

Ullathorne refused to be pacified and, standing on his
dignity as diocesan bishop, was unwilling to accept Capel's
protestations. He replied, '... Mr Robinson is an ecclesiastical
subject of this diocese, and without a word of communication
to me, you have, it appears, done your best to influence his

[23.] AAW Molloy Collection, Ullathorne to Manning, 11 July 1878.
[24.] McClelland, *Manning*, pp. 119–23. p. 119.
[25.] Ibid.
[26.] AAW Molloy Collection, Capel to Ullathorne, 3 August 1875. His
temper was not improved by the fact that Croke Robinson not only
took up the post, but transferred to Westminster Archdiocese.

mind to leave his diocese for your college'. He had his own plans for the newly ordained Robinson, and for another priest, Clement Moore, and was annoyed that Capel had offered alternative attractions to both men without a word. 'I will give no assent or encouragement to this invidious transaction. If you are encouraged to play upon the susceptibilities of priests after this fashion, what bishop or diocese will be safe from interference.' Capel, he said, was mistaken in thinking in terms of the concrete support of other bishops for Kensington – it had no call on personnel or finances, but even if the reverse were true, it would not authorise Capel to act as he did. It would simply be the 'unhinging of the diocese, the demoralising of the spirit of the clergy, and the rendering of episcopal government impractical'.[27]

Ullathorne rarely saw disputes as individual episodes to be dealt with as they arose, but, as in the Croke Robinson affair, was inclined to see matters of principle at every turn. He was able to see, rightly or wrongly, that almost every decision made by his generation of bishops was setting a precedent for the future, and therefore needed to be viewed with great care. No decision which touched on the authority of a bishop was ever simple, whether taken by an Ecumenical Council or a college rector.

It could hardly have come as a surprise, then, to Capel or Manning in 1878 that Ullathorne did not regard himself as having any responsibility for the past or future of Kensington and did not consider himself under any liability. It was not true, as McClelland suggested, that 'the bishop knew he was as responsible as Manning for the University College, but he was unwilling to give any financial help'.[28] Rather this was clear proof of the position he had taken from the start, that the project was Manning's rather than a joint national project of the hierarchy. Ullathorne had made it clear to Manning, before the University College had opened, that he believed that joint action by the hierarchy on higher education was fraught with difficulty. He argued that it would be premature to issue a joint pastoral in the light of the unsettled

27. AAW Molloy Collection, Ullathorne to Capel, 7 August 1875.
28. McClelland, *Manning*, p. 122.

circumstances of the scheme for colleges of higher education. A joint pastoral letter would need to be clear and to inspire confidence, and at present the undertaking was 'crude and undigested'.

Offering critical comment on Manning's draft scheme in 1874, including remarks from two Birmingham chapter canons, he strongly rejected the idea of bringing the existing colleges into some sort of national scheme. 'As representative of Oscott I could not subscribe to the proposition'. He wanted nothing to do with the university college or with any national projects.

> In conclusion I would repeat that I think from all I have heard since we met, that the organisation both of the college and control are too immature for us yet to come forth with a formal and authoritative statement subscribed by the whole hierarchy. We ought to have everything clear, definite and reliable before taking so grave a step.[29]

This could hardly have left Manning or Capel in any doubt about Ullathorne's position, so to express surprise and hurt four years later was a little disingenuous on their part. One thing about dealing with Ullathorne on ecclesiastical affairs, was that his position was never unclear or ambiguous!

The Kensington university college was the sharpest flash-point of disagreement on policy between Ullathorne and Manning, and the antagonism lasted through the summer of 1878. Writing with some effort, and contrary to the express orders of his doctor, his mood not improved by a bout of ill health, he reminded Manning that despite numerous requests he had never produced an alleged letter of authority from Rome to found the university college. He rejected the whole scheme and certainly refused to go back on the agreed statement in the joint pastoral letter of 1874 that existing colleges (including Oscott) should be included in any national scheme.[30] Even at the beginning of 1879, Ullathorne was still

[29.] AAW Molloy Collection, Ullathorne to Manning, 23 June 1874.
[30.] AAW Molloy Collection, Ullathorne to Manning (copy), 19 August 1878.

grumbling furiously to Estcourt (the repository of all unpublishable views), even contemplating whether he should engage a lawyer over the Kensington row. He was firmly convinced that no bishop who founded a college could expect any more than moral support from the others. Despite regular invitations, he had not been near Kensington, nor had any intention of doing so. 'I have never been on a committee, or have signed any paper, or authorised my name to be used in any matter concerning the college.'[31]

The ruffled feathers over Kensington had scarcely been smoothed, when a further conflict arose between Ullathorne and Manning, this time involving Newman. These three ecclesiastical giants of their generation had sparred and scrapped with each other since the early 1850s, but the row in 1879 was the most deeply wounding for all three of the old battlers. The most complex and fruitful friendship and collaboration of Ullathorne's life was that with Newman. The final triumph of this great, if uneasy partnership was the decision to appoint Newman a cardinal by Leo XIII in 1879. Newman's own summing up was that 'the cloud is lifted from me for ever'.[32] However, it was also the most unpleasant culmination of Manning's difficult relationship with Newman, and the most telling instance of Ullathorne's loyalty and devotion to Newman. It also illustrated Newman's inability to cope with the machinery of the Church and the machinations of its princes, and his dependence on Ullathorne's support and determination.

Ullathorne had heard a rumour 'on the highest authority' that Newman was to be made a cardinal in the late autumn of 1878, but dismissed it.[33] When the first clear suggestion of a cardinal's red hat for Newman was made at the end of January 1879, through Manning, Ullathorne was almost more delighted than Newman himself. He urged him to accept, setting out in a letter no fewer than seven reasons why he should do so. Newman, while deeply moved at the honour proposed, feared that it would automatically mean that he

[31]. BAA B6527, Ullathorne to Estcourt, 17 January 1879.
[32]. L&D XXIX, p. 58, 1 March 1879.
[33]. BAA B6433, Ullathorne to Estcourt, 19 November 1878.

would be expected to live in Rome. At the age of seventy-eight, Newman was frail and lonely, and dreaded the thought of leaving his beloved Oratory.

Ullathorne was confident that 'the one intention of the Holy Father was to confer upon him this signal proof of his confidence and to give him an exalted position in the Church in token of the great services he has rendered to her cause'.[34] He was certain that no move to Rome was intended and he wrote a covering letter via Manning intimating as much, to accompany a brief reply of Newman's. His reply made it clear that 'nothing stands in the way of his most grateful acceptance except what he tells me greatly distresses him, namely the having to leave the Oratory at a critical period of its existence'.[35] Ullathorne also wrote privately to Manning of Newman's great age, loss of vigour, loneliness without his old companions St John and Caswall, and his humility at the prospect of the intended honour, and he reinforced the request that Newman be allowed to remain at the Oratory in Birmingham.[36]

Manning seemed to have misconstrued the whole thing as a refusal by Newman, and for some reason forwarded Newman's brief letter of reply to Rome, without attaching Ullathorne's fuller explanatory text as intended.[37] Manning chose to take Ullathorne's letter in his pocket with him to Rome. From Paris, Manning wrote to the Duke of Norfolk that Newman had declined the honour, and rumours began to circulate in London to this effect.[38] Within a couple of weeks it was in the columns of *The Times*.[39] Newman's embarrassment was acute and Ullathorne was furious. The news of Newman's 'refusal' provoked an avalanche of letters to the Oratory, adding to Newman's discomfiture. The Catholic Union, led by the Duke of Norfolk, went into action on Newman's behalf, busily dispelling misunderstanding in Rome

---

[34.] AAW Ullathorne Correspondence, Ullathorne to Manning, 3 February 1879.

[35.] Quoted in Sheridan Gilley, *Newman and His Age* (1990), p. 394.

[36.] The relevant letters are in L&D XXIX (1879–1881), pp. 16–20.

[37.] AAW Ullathorne Correspondence, Manning to Ullathorne, 4 February 1879.

[38.] Gilley, p. 395.

[39.] Ibid.

with vague diplomatic allusions to inaccurate press reports.

Ullathorne in the meantime, hearing the rumours and fearing Manning's actions, sent a copy of his covering letter, which was still in Manning's hands, with a fresh letter of his own, directly to Rome. He was insistent that Newman's 'disposition of mind should not be misapprehended'.[40] The combined actions had the desired effect and Manning informed Ullathorne that Leo XIII had agreed that Newman should remain as cardinal in his Birmingham home. Ullathorne was delighted and told Manning that he would ensure that the growing popular supposition that Newman had declined was quashed, regarding it as 'prudent' now that everything was public, to deny that Newman ever had declined.[41] Rumours persisted nevertheless, in *The Tablet* among others, forcing Ullathorne and Manning to deny strenuously any hint of refusal on Newman's part. Ullathorne, however, never forgave Manning for his part in it, accusing him of 'great weakness of character', and they argued over it, even on the last time they met in 1888.[42] The arrival of the letter of appointment in March 1879 was the crowning glory of Newman and Ullathorne's long and intimate friendship. Newman had proved his Catholicity, humility and his true intent. Ullathorne had proved his loyalty, his straightforward honesty and his true admiration.

By 1879 they were both old and weak in health, but as a powerful partnership had carried English Catholicism, especially in the Midlands, into a new era. The *ecclesia*, at the hands of which Newman had suffered, and which he defended to the hilt, finally made its reparation. Ullathorne, his ecclesiastical superior for thirty years, was the first to greet Newman on his return from Rome and to express his joy and that of the diocese and the nation. Though both were elderly and increasingly infirm, they had not finished with life or with each other yet, and Newman was a regular visitor to Ullathorne at his winter retreat at Oscott, a place full of memories (some bitter, some triumphant) for both of them. Each of them continued to

[40.] L&D XXIX, pp. 24–5, 11 February 1879.
[41.] AAW Ullathorne Correspondence, Ullathorne to Manning, 4 March 1879.
[42.] Butler, *Life*, II, pp. 158–60.

address each other in terms of affection, almost tenderness, as the old irritations and snipings fell into the distant past. In 1881 when Ullathorne reached the landmark of fifty years of priesthood, Newman along with many others, sent generous good wishes. In reply to Newman's fond greeting, Ullathorne spoke of their friendship as 'one of the sweet consolations of my episcopal life, as the Oratory has been one of the great works of the diocese'.[43] He reportedly told Manning during their last fierce argument about Newman that,

> there was no honester man on earth; that his only aim on this earth was to advance the cause of religion; that his deep humility forced him to come to the surface to show his sincerity; that he was an avowed hater of duplicity and intrigue, and much more to the purpose.[44]

Despite, or perhaps because of, all the ups and downs of their parallel careers, Ullathorne and Newman had finally come to revere and to love each other and to respect each other's achievements.

During the late 1870s Ullathorne increasingly began to feel his age and the mixture of ailments which had afflicted him off and on over the years became more of a burden. The death of Pius IX in 1878 (the longest serving successor of Peter) was, for Ullathorne, a sign of his own mortality as well as the loss of a much loved Pontiff who presented 'a magnificent spectacle to angels and to men'.[45] They had been consecrated as bishop on the same day in 1846, which had always given Ullathorne a very personal sense of affinity with the Pope. Ullathorne's many visits to Rome had nurtured a devotion and a mutual respect between them. His admiration and affection were unbounded: 'Pius IX has done his work, and has found his rest where none can ever trouble or afflict him more; but he will never leave this world. His life, his acts, his teachings, his sufferings, are an inheritance that cannot

---

[43.] L&D XXIX, pp. 418–9, 23/25 September 1881.
[44.] Butler, *Life*, II p. 160.
[45.] *A Discourse delivered at the Solemn Requiem for Pope Pius IX* (1878), p. 17.

die.'[46] He was also aware of the way in which Pius IX, for the first time in papal history, had become a familiar human figure to ordinary Catholics. In the huge explosion of pilgrimage to Rome in the nineteenth century, Pius IX himself had become one of the main attractions, and the process of issuing tickets for large scale papal audiences became firmly established during his papacy.[47] It was also true, though, that millions of people did not get the chance to go to Rome, and for them, cheaply reproduced prints and newspapers meant that 'they were familiar with his features, multiplied in every shape, they had heard many of his words, had read or listened to many anecdotes of his kindness, of his charity, of his firmness and constancy, and knew how much he had suffered for the cause of God and his Church'.[48]

Ullathorne's own health was poor over the winter of 1878–9 and on medical advice he spent several months 'reinvigorating an old constitution' at Oscott in the hope of a complete recovery and return to work.[49] He began to be treated by Dr George Vernon Blunt, of Portland House, Hagley Road, recommended by Estcourt and Newman, and placed great confidence in his 'kind and attentive' medical expertise for the rest of his life. By November he was up and about, and 'I think I may venture to say that the worst is over, and that I am verging on convalescence.' In fact, his death had even been prematurely rumoured.[50] That winter, however, set the pattern for the next few years, of spending the winter months in the healthier climes of Oscott's still rural hilltop location, where his rooms were kept heated and ventilated, and where the wind creaking in the trees reminded him of his long distant boyhood days on board ship.

> The music of the wind is like the old notes of a tempestuous sea which always plucks up the spirits, except that it wants the rattle of the braces against the

46. Pastoral Letter, 27 February 1878.
47. Judith Champ, *The English Pilgrimage to Rome* (2000), pp. 201–4.
48. Pastoral Letter, 27 February 1878.
49. Farm St (Letters of Bishops and Cardinals 1840–91) Ullathorne to Fr Waterworth, 2 January 1879.
50. BAA B6433, Ullathorne to Estcourt, 19 November 1878.

shrouds, which is not unlike bone music only on a grander scale, a weird and suggestive kind of music.[51]

Having always had something of the hermit about him, he relished the deserted college in the winter when the schoolboys departed for Christmas holidays,

> I am almost alone in this big house; and the winds wailed and sang mournfully through it last night, as if in pain at the expiring year, conscious of having witnessed more evil than good. It is a grand thing nevertheless to sit at a great organ like this and hearken to the pipings of nature, to which you have only to listen to hear many things superior to an orchestra of human instruments and voices. Give me God's music, and let men make their own, which in comparison is but the straining of a tempest through a colander.[52]

The set of rooms on the first floor of the college gave him a view through the beech woods across the farmland to the sprawling industrial city which had been his home for thirty years. He had always been a frequent visitor to Oscott and the Pugin furnished rooms were as familiar to him as those he had left in Bishop's House. He settled contentedly into his winter retreat, where, 'the superiors are as attentive as good sons can be, and as to the college, it never went on better or was better looked after. The rector has an eye to everything, and especially to economy'.[53]

While Manning was still in Rome handling the matters concerning religious orders and Newman's red hat, Ullathorne gave him the first inkling that he would consult the diocesan chapter about petitioning the Pope for an assistant bishop.[54] Anxious to get things moving quickly, lest the diocese become 'unhinged', he confided in Estcourt even before writing to

[51.] *Letters*, p. 460 [24 December 1884].
[52.] *Letters*, p. 420 [1 January 1882].
[53.] BAA 6433, Ullathorne to Estcourt, 19 November 1878.
[54.] AAW Ullathorne Correspondence, Ullathorne to Manning, 29 March 1879.

Manning. He clearly mistrusted Manning in this matter and was keen to get things sown up before he could intervene. 'If Manning can get in a man of his own he will, and he will if he dare, unless he is afraid of meddling with me.'[55] The day after the Chapter meeting on 4 April he wrote formally to Cardinal Simeoni; at that stage he appeared to have no names in his mind as a possible aide and likely successor.[56] He was seventy-three and had been a bishop for over thirty years. By the summer of 1879 he had not celebrated a High Mass for over a year, being unable to stand for that length of time. Although he had preached for an hour and a half at Olton, he had done so sitting down.[57] He began to reduce his travelling and really hoped that Rome would allow him to retire fully. As in 1862, his petition was rejected, but with rather more understanding and gentleness. He was asked to remain in office as his 'counsel may be of great use in the meetings of the bishops and may bring great light'.[58] Instead, Rome offered him the prospect of an auxiliary bishop and, unusually, invited him to put forward one name. There was no suggestion of the choice of a coadjutor bishop with right of succession, perhaps because of the long Roman memory of the bitterness surrounding George Errington's disastrous appointment to Wiseman. Ullathorne in any case was not an advocate of coadjutors, but preferred to make good use of a vicar general – a coadjutor, after all, he argued, was only a vicar general with episcopal dignity. The main problem was that he would either be left idle, or would gradually supersede the ordinary, because he 'has no defined position but what you give him, and this was what Archbishop Errington found to be his chief difficulty'. This was far from the only example where a bishop and coadjutor failed to work smoothly together.[59]

Despite Rome's request for a single name (a particular compliment and sign of confidence in Ullathorne's judge-

[55.] BAA B6597, Ullathorne to Estcourt, 24 March 1879.
[56.] AAW Ullathorne Correspondence, Ullathorne to Manning, 5 April 1879.
[57.] Colwich, Ullathorne to Prioress, 25 June 1879.
[58.] Butler, *Life*, II, p. 190.
[59.] Ampleforth, Copy of letter Ullathorne to Brown, 28 December 1868.

ment), in August he recommended consideration of three names: Edward Ilsley, John Hawkesford and Thomas Longman. Ilsley was rector of the seminary at Olton, Hawkesford president of Oscott and Longman was the cathedral administrator.[60] Longman's nomination smacked of desperation, when the bishop knew that he was exhausted and had asked to be relieved of the cathedral and given lighter duties.[61] Within a month he was advising Edward Ilsley which convents to contact to get vestments made for his episcopal consecration.[62] In his usual ghoulish language about the episcopate, he told Estcourt that Ilsley had 'submitted to the yoke',[63] but was clearly immensely relieved that within a few months, Bishop Ilsley had 'left a great impression at the four convents he has been to'.[64] The care of the nuns was, as ever, vital, so their opinion of the new auxiliary bishop was an important and reassuring one.

It is revealing to consider the names he rejected, or did not put forward. Two possible candidates were dismissed brutally (in private). 'I did not mention Hedley. I consider him fixed. He is stiff minded. Knight has everything except backbone, but that he wants deplorably. It is a sad pity, for otherwise he is just the man.'[65] It is puzzling that, among the three (not particularly strong) Birmingham diocesan candidates he put forward, Ullathorne did not mention either Estcourt himself, in whom he had such personal confidence, or James Spencer Northcote, another man whom he admired unstintingly. The only possible explanation is the same difficulty he himself was facing, of age and ill health. Estcourt had not enjoyed good health for years, and in the end, Ullathorne outlived him. Northcote had

60. BAA B6762, Ullathorne to *Propaganda Fide*, 18 August 1879.
61. AAW Ullathorne Correspondence, Ullathorne to Manning, 5 April 1879.
62. BAA B6774, Ullathorne to Ilsley, 15 September 1879.
63. BAA B6773, Ullathorne to Estcourt, 13 September 1879.
64. BAA B6892, Ullathorne to Estcourt, 19 January 1880. Cuthbert Hedley, an Ampleforth monk and head of the common noviciate for the EBC at Belmont, became Bishop of Newport in 1881 and preached at Ullathorne's funeral. Edmund Knight was the newly appointed auxiliary to Bishop James Brown of Shrewsbury, and his successor.
65. BAA B6597, Ullathorne to Estcourt, 24 March 1879.

retired from Oscott on health grounds in 1877, and although he recovered his energies and lived on to build a church and minister for thirty years in Stoke-on-Trent, this would not have been obvious in early 1879.

The winter of 1879–80 had been a long and bitter one, which had cost many lives, and Ullathorne suffered a bout of illness brought on by travelling in Staffordshire in the frost, which left him weakened.[66] His real frustration was that it delayed the publication of his long-planned book entitled *The Endowments of Man*. There is a popular legend attached to Ullathorne that he described his own book on humility as 'the best book on the subject'; this is not recorded anywhere, but rings true of a man not afflicted with false modesty, and who assured the Abbess of Stanbrook that his new book would just suit her and was 'quite original in its mode of treatment'.[67] When it was finally published, *The Endowments of Man* was well received and reviewed, even by 'female writers [of whom] I take no account'.[68] The book took the form of a series of lectures, developed from ones delivered at Olton, and was intended as a prelude to a consideration of Christian virtues. The fourteen substantial tracts consider the nature of mankind and Divine creation in a way intended to challenge contemporary thinking. Where quotations are used, they are invariably from Scripture or the Fathers, especially St Augustine. The essays are densely written, and any attempt at précis is futile, but the nub of his argument is to be found in the final chapter. Of all the endowments of man, reason is vital, and subject only to the 'incomparably greater' endowment which is 'the light of faith'. By this, 'man is brought into the higher sphere of light, in which God is more nearly seen, and his eternal mysteries are revealed to us'.[69] In this instance, as in all others, he accepted no money from publishers, believing it 'a most degrading thing to accept money for mental work, and that the venality of the products of the mind is one of the great causes of corrupt literature, if not the chief cause'.[70]

---

[66] Selly Park, Ullathorne to Genevieve Dupuis, 12 March 1860.
[67] Stanbrook 52, Ullathorne to Abbess, 25 February 1880.
[68] BAA B7109, Ullathorne to Estcourt, 10 October 1880.
[69] *The Endowments of Man* (1880), p. 379.
[70] Stanbrook 53, Ullathorne to Abbess, 26 March 1880.

'Corrupt literature' was among the *bête noires* of his latter years, and he was even provoked a couple of years later to issue a pastoral letter on the subject, attacking books, lectures, sermons, songs, poetry and all manner of 'insidious productions', which were as dangerous to the weak minded as drink.

> The literature of the world is the reflection of the world, and a great part of the world of letters has sunk so low, and has become so aggressive on the Christian mind, that one scarcely knows which of its books or periodicals to open in which there is not some open or covered assault upon the truths of faith, some attack upon the purity of morals.[71]

This was not his first broadside against the world of letters, in which journals such as the *Contemporary Review* or the *Nineteenth Century* invited all classes of writers, 'Atheists, Positivists, Deists, Protestants and Catholics', to publish in the same periodicals.[72] He viewed this as a dangerous way of spreading 'the subtle sophistries of unbelief', and as a result of his diatribe, Newman chose to stop writing for non-Catholic journals.[73] This did not stop Ullathorne from reading journals like *The Freethinker*.[74]

His own reading remained extraordinarily broad, across a range of religious and related topics. He was familiar with Johnson, Gibbons, Addison and other major writers of the previous century, and came late in life to a reading of one of the classics of eighteenth-century devotional writing, William Law's, *Serious Call to a Devout and Holy Life*.[75] Although clever, it

---

[71.] Pastoral Letter, 27 January 1883.

[72.] Pastoral Letter, 25 November 1877.

[73.] L&D XXVIII, p. 280, to Samuel William Wayte, 15 December 1877.

[74.] BAA B8110, Ullathorne to Estcourt, 9 February 1883.

[75.] William Law (1686–1761) was a well known nonjuror and spiritual writer. His most famous work, *A Serious Call*, published in 1728, drew on medieval mystics including Thomas a Kempis and was one of the most influential spiritual works in the Anglican tradition.

was 'essentially unsound', being based on a Pelagian moral principle. 'Anyone, according to him, can do anything in the way of an habitually devout life by the simple process of deciding to do so.'[76] Despite his apparently old-fashioned taste for the works of an earlier century, he also kept up with new publications, even those of an unusual turn of mind. As soon as it became available, he read Alfred Sinnett's *Occult World* (1881), an exposition of Theosophy, based in his contact with the wildly eccentric Madame Blavatsky who founded the movement.[77] Ullathorne had sufficient knowledge of spiritualism and Hindu and Buddhist doctrine (of which Sinnett's book was a mishmash) to be able to read it critically. His conclusion was that, 'though worth reading, it is a contemptible book'.[78]

By this stage in life, Ullathorne was beginning to take on something of the persona of the grumpy old man, resistant to new ideas and the directions the world was taking. Two of his pastoral letters from this time betray the way in which he was increasingly ill at ease in a world which he no longer fully understood. He was critical of the effects of British Imperial expansion and the consequent national hubris and jingoism, at its height by the 1870s. Prosperity and pride were all very well, but, 'Can we say that in the vast extension of the British Empire which modern times have witnessed, there has been no injustice or oppression to be thought over?' He was more modern than he thought, in questioning the accepted view that the British Empire was an unmitigated good for the world.[79] A few months later, he took up a related theme, in bemoaning the loss of the old simplicities of life in the rush to make

---

[76.] BAA B7157, Ullathorne to Estcourt, 28 November 1880.
[77.] Janet Oppenheim, 'Sinnett, Alfred Percy (1840–1921)', *Oxford Dictionary of National Biography*, Oxford University Press, 2004 [http://www.oxforddnb.com/view/article/38637, accessed 14 Sept 2005].
Richard Davenport-Hines, 'Blavatsky, Helena Petrovna (1831–1891)', *Oxford Dictionary of National Biography*, Oxford University Press, 2004 [http://www.oxforddnb.com/view/article /40930, accessed 14 Sept 2005].
[78.] BAA B7812, Ullathorne to Estcourt, 20 June 1882.
[79.] Pastoral Letter, 12 November 1879.

money. Economic success had been bought at a high price in the lives of the people.

> This has crowded populations together in a most unwholesome and unhealthy manner, both for body and soul. It has compelled men to a life of wearying anxiety and unceasing toil. It has made the interests of life to be highly complicated and very artificial.

The world he saw around him had become Godless in many respects, and he warned 'the children of faith' that, 'the pressure of the world will carry you off from the ways of God into its own way of living, thinking and dreaming'.[80]

Ilsley continued nominally as rector at Olton as well as auxiliary bishop for another four years, as Ullathorne slipped into a role as elder statesman. His interest in Olton was constant, and in 1876 he had been provoked by an attack in print on the seminary which was the apple of his eye. In a pastoral letter he staunchly defended the form of priestly training at Olton, which was, of course, very different in tone and style from that at Oscott. Withdrawal from the world in order to form the priestly identity was the key to what he was trying to achieve there.

> What is manliness? It consists in strength, elevation and magnanimity of soul. But strength of soul comes of patience, fortitude and the force to endure. And all these are spiritual qualities, that come of meditating on high truths and living up to them ... This strength and elevation of soul is not to be learnt of the world, for the world acts like a destructive acid or poison, dissolving or drying up those generous qualities that constitute real manliness.[81]

A student at Olton later recalled how, at Christmas dinner in 1879, Ullathorne with his, 'slow, deep-toned utterance delivered

---

[80.] Pastoral Letter, 3 February 1880.
[81.] Pastoral Letter, 19 March 1876.

to us his words on Christian patience and humility without an H, and spoke of St 'Ilary, the 'oly 'ermit', but also how, by the fire in the common room, he later held them spellbound with his tales of Australia.[82]

However, he continued as far as possible to keep a hand on the tiller and was involved in a remarkable number of routine decisions about missions and finance, and probably to a greater extent than was needed, carefully directed his new auxiliary bishop in some of his tasks. Ilsley's biographer made the apt point that Ullathorne was not necessarily thinking about succession at this point and had recommended to Rome a man after his own mind, 'who would simply obey and follow, rather than presume to act on his own initiative'.[83] Thus, Ullathorne's comment about Ilsley, which sounds like damning with faint praise: 'He does not shine either in the breadth or brilliance of his learning since his mind is less swift than firm in judgement; he has an unassuming manner and a capacity for hard work',[84] was really Ullathorne indicating to Rome that this was exactly what he wanted – someone who would take over the bulk of the work but not overshadow his superior.

Ilsley's appointment was a source of huge relief to Ullathorne, and enabled him to rally his spirits and energy. Despite his advancing years and infirmities, he did not appear to fall prey to depression, but continued to believe that 'the secret of happiness is to rejoice in God and fear oneself,'[85] and to exhort his correspondents to joy in the Lord, which 'lifts us above all our follies and cheers us under all our burdens.'[86] Although his body failed, his mind was as focused as ever, as he showed in 1883 when Manning asked for his comments on the draft of his book, *The Eternal Priesthood*, the content of which already owed much to conversations with Ullathorne. His comments were not brief, courteous and complimentary, but ran to four closely-written pages of detailed suggestions and references to specific points – and that only on the two

[82] Quoted in McInally, pp. 57–8.
[83] McInally, p. 83.
[84] Ibid.
[85] Handsworth, 31 December 1883.
[86] Selly Park, Ullathorne to Genevieve Dupuis, 31 December 1883.

final chapters.[87] Manning accepted them in every detail.[88]

Ilsley's episcopal work had increased so much by 1883 that he withdrew from responsibility for Olton and was replaced by James McCave. Over the next few years McCave impressed on Ilsley his clear view that Olton was inadequate for the number of possible candidates seeking entry and was definitely the poor relation to Oscott. In his view, the only solution was to get rid of the lay school at Oscott and move the seminary in there, lock, stock and barrel.[89] There is no evidence of this proposal ever being discussed with Ullathorne, but it must have been the common currency of clerical gossip in the diocese. Tact prevailed where the old bishop was concerned, but the decision was eventually taken by Ilsley within weeks of Ullathorne's death in 1889.

Thomas Brown of Newport, one of Ullathorne's oldest friends, dating back to his time at Downside where Brown was his theology tutor for a time, died in April 1880, but Ullathorne's health prevented him from keeping his promise to preach at the funeral.[90] When Cuthbert Hedley, another Benedictine, was appointed to succeed Brown in 1881, he congratulated him in lugubrious tones.

> I may as well say that I have never felt grateful to those who made me a bishop. I refused three sees in succession and was, as it were, forced into the fourth by pressure, and because of the then peculiar condition of the Western District. But I have never thought episcopacy a subject for congratulations.[91]

He did rally sufficiently to get to Stone, which always raised his spirits, for the 'very magnificent but very devout' celebrations of the fifth centenary of St Catherine of Siena on 29 April. His

---

87. AAW Ullathorne Correspondence, Ullathorne to Manning, 8 March 1883.
88. AAW Ullathorne Correspondence, Manning to Ullathorne, 9 March 1883.
89. McInally, pp. 99–100.
90. BAA B6997, Ullathorne to Estcourt, 14 April 1880.
91. Ampleforth, Copy of letter Ullathorne to Hedley, 16 February 1881.

great friend Sr Francis Raphael Drane, the most learned member of the Stone community, had written a new biography of the saint (the first in English).[92] The following year she succeeded Imelda Poole as the third superior of Margaret Hallahan's congregation of sisters and went on to edit the publication of Ullathorne's letters. It was she who urged him in the last months of his life to revise and complete his autobiography, but only the revision was ever carried out. Imelda Poole's death came suddenly in October 1881 when she was visiting another convent at Marychurch in Somerset, and took away another of the old friends who had worked alongside him and Mother Margaret.

Brown's death left Ullathorne as the last survivor of the hierarchy of 1850, and the last bishop who had also been one of the Vicars Apostolic. Despite his infirmity, Ullathorne continued to deal not only with routine business about missions, clergy moves and finance, but with more significant problems like the sudden breakdown in health of John Hawkesford, the president of Oscott, in the autumn of 1880.[93] Having the bishop under the roof could not have been easy for the president and staff at Oscott, and there were clearly clashes with Hawkesford's successor, Edward Acton, who Ullathorne believed, 'means well, but is of a shy disposition' and he feared that Acton was under the thumb of others. Relations in the college were clearly so unhappy, that Ullathorne contemplated moving out after the winter of 1880–1.[94]

The Tridentine model of a seminary had commended the proximity of the diocesan bishop, but at no point did Ullathorne appear to have contemplated moving to Olton, even when life at Oscott was problematic. It can only be assumed that the limited size and lack of resources at Olton made this impractical. Also, although he had built Olton, he was very fond of Oscott and had known it, off an on, ever since he attended the opening ceremony in 1838. The other puzzle is perhaps why he never, in later years, spoke of retirement to Downside, having craved a return to the cloister for so many

---

92. Selly Park, Ullathorne to Genevieve Dupuis, 8 May 1880.
93. BAA B7104, Ullathorne to Estcourt, 6 October 1880.
94. BAA B7182, Ullathorne to Estcourt, 21 December 1880.

years. There were practical reasons. Being asked to remain in office with Ilsley as auxiliary bishop meant that he was obliged to stay in Birmingham, and by the time of his final retirement he was far too frail to make the move. Nevertheless, he continued in the last decade of his life to take an active interest in all things Benedictine, particularly in the troubles and difficulties which dogged the English Benedictine Congregation (EBC). Downside was at the centre of them, and was a fractious place.

The powerful blend of monastic stability and freedom inherent in the Rule of St Benedict was a lifelong inspiration and source of strength to Ullathorne. His devotion to his religious order was absolute and did not diminish with the passage of years. It came up time and time again in his correspondence and that of fellow monks. Writing in 1849, Abbot Prosper Guéranger, the influential restorer of French Benedictine life at Solesmes had spoken of the love which he knew Ullathorne to hold for the Benedictine Order. In expressing confidence that he would continue to serve and protect 'the children of St Benedict' as he had in the past, he warmly assured Ullathorne of the prayers of all Benedictines in his work.[95] Ullathorne did prove to be a loyal friend to the English Benedictines during his episcopate, and fulfilled the hopes of Luke Barber, the President General, who, writing to him on his appointment to Birmingham, contrasted the English Benedictine Congregation's relations with Ullathorne with those of the other Benedictine bishop, Thomas Brown of Wales. One was the 'disinterested friend and brother', the other, 'the captious and querulous friend to ego'. Wondering if he has gone too far (Brown was one of Ullathorne's closest friends), Barber concluded, 'This is a very cosy way of talking to a bishop, but please remember that we are brothers.'[96] Clearly Ullathorne felt the same, as he recorded on Barber's death soon after, 'in no man's judgement did I ever put so much fraternal confidence. He is a particular loss to me, and I think that with others who he formed an especial link with the order.'[97] Throughout his long and busy career Ullathorne was a regular

---

[95.] BAA B1607, Guéranger to Ullathorne, 21 June 1849.

[96.] Ampleforth 253/14, McSweeney to Ullathorne, 22 March 1882.

[97.] Stanbrook 1, Ullathorne to Abbess Gregson, 31 December 1850.

advisor, guide and influence among the monks of the English Benedictine Congregation, and was regularly asked for opinions on a range of issues, but particularly those pertaining to jurisdiction. His warmth and interest were not always appreciated, nor his reserve in interfering in matters concerning the English Benedictine Congregation. Not all his confrères were as warm as Barber had been. He became aware that, 'there was an impression amongst some members [of the EBC] that I had not much zeal for the interests of the Congregation', but he asserted that he had 'never been silent before third parties where my evidence could be of use in vindication of what is good and meritorious in the body'.[98]

Looking back from his jubilee of monastic profession in 1874 he was sentimental about the past but hopeful for the future.

> It is a hopeful thing to look from past mercies upon the future. It is a joyful thing to instruct our younger brethren in our older experiences and to contribute to the tradition of our Congregation. It is a pleasant thing to see the zeal that prevails among the young for greater discipline than their fathers in religion knew.[99]

A few years later, he was touched by the dedication of a new edition of Benet Weldon's seventeenth-century *Chronological Notes* to him, and delighted that the Benedictines were at last doing something to raise awareness of their post-Reformation history, as 'one that may stand by the side of other histories of the like nature'.[100]

Over half a century had passed since his own first adventures in monastic life when one of his nieces, Philomena, decided to try her vocation as a Benedictine nun. In the Rule of St Benedict, he told her,

> you will have the most spiritual and profound rules united with great prudence and knowledge of the human heart ... There is no other rule so large and comprehen-

---

[98.] Ampleforth 246/46, Ullathorne to the President General, 20 July 1874.

[99.] Ampleforth 250/75, Ullathorne to Prior, 17 March 1874.

[100.] DA (unnumbered), Ullathorne to Prior, 30 October 1879.

sive, and yet so full and complete in whatever the soul requires.

He impressed upon her two words, which in his long experience, conveyed all the advice necessary to a beginner in religious life – openness and generosity.[101] Eventually, four of his nieces entered religious life, and it impossible to think that they were not in some way influenced by their eminent uncle's warm encouragement of female religious communities.

In 1875, the year after his golden jubilee of monastic life, Ullathorne gave an address on the festival of all Benedictine saints, which Butler described as the clearest and truest short exposition of the spirit of Benedictinism, and he reproduced the entire text in his biography.[102] Even after fifty years of activity outside the monastic walls, the spirit of Benedict was still alive in him. Ullathorne was never one to flatter or curb his tongue, so it can be taken from this that his love for and admiration of the monastic ideal was full and genuine. Perhaps because he had spent over forty years away from his conventual community, and had not had to live with its irritations, he emphasised strongly the binding creative power of community life and stability. Without it the spirit of largeness and freedom, which characterised the Rule of St Benedict, was apt to degenerate. The force with which he emphasised this suggested a longing in his soul for a return to a life of monastic stability.

> To prevent all such evils, and save the strength of the monk from being broken, St. Benedict binds his monks by the vow of stability to an irrevocable life in community, and in the community that has witnessed his training and profession.[103]

Yet he was in no doubt, from his own long experience, that the vow of stability was not incompatible with the missionary life of the Church.

[101.] BAA B6130, Ullathorne to his niece Philomena, 2 December 1877.
[102.] Butler, *Life*, II, pp. 213–21.
[103.] Ibid., II, p. 218.

To form saints, and to civilise mankind, have been the two great vocations of the Benedictine Order. Its stability accomplished the first of these vocations; its free spirit and largeheartedness achieved the second. With these two arms it was fitted to embrace the changeable conditions of the world of man.[104]

Those two arms were often to be found pulling in opposite directions in late nineteenth-century England, and the tension between mission and monastery created a long running and bloody battlefield in the English Benedictine Congregation. Ultimately, in terms of what he had hoped for, the EBC was something of a disappointment to Ullathorne. The real problem lay in his view of the conduct of missions. He believed that the solitary Benedictine missionary was a temporary arrangement, only acceptable during the recusant period as an emergency solution, and should be brought to an end. This had inspired his determination in Coventry to develop missionary priories in large towns, but which had never really taken root. However, his firm view, and his ambition for the EBC throughout his life was to move away from the 'provisional' state of things to a more settled monastic observance, which he believed 'in my whole intellect and conscience ... would secure the prosperity of the congregation to a far greater degree than has hitherto been realised'.[105]

His long life and broad experience had enabled Ullathorne to discern the changes under way in English Catholic life and to see that God's work was often done at a slower pace than people might like and would only succeed if built upon secure foundations.

I hope that the reform initiated in the recent Chapter respecting common life of the fathers on the mission will be the first step leading on to the institution of missionary monasteries in the great towns. Where courage arises to take this step the Benedictine order will spread, flourish

---

[104.] Ibid.
[105.] Ampleforth 246/46, Ullathorne to President General, 20 July 1874.

and strengthen. Without faith in the intrinsic force of the veritable rule, nothing great can be accomplished. How often have I had to vindicate the observances of the monasteries to persons who judged the congregation by its almost secular missions. This is a matter to be prayed for. But I think the start is so far right.[106]

Ullathorne was in no doubt as to the missionary value of Benedictine life, but having experienced it in a more extreme form than most other monks, he was convinced that the kind of life he had lived in Australia and Coventry had served its purpose, and by 1875 he was confident that 'the change for which the Order has toiled is come'.[107] Yet in the following year, he was appalled that the EBC superiors still did not seem to appreciate what the Holy See was urging on them in insisting on a greater emphasis on *vita communis*. Still, Ullathorne wrote in frustration, 'there is this tendency to take up missions where the monk is isolated'.[108] His ideal for the monastic missions was the priory of Beuronese monks at Erdington, on the edge of Birmingham and under his own episcopal care, a couple of miles from Oscott.

The church of SS Thomas and Edmund of Canterbury at Erdington had been built in 1850 by Daniel Haigh, a wealthy convert from Anglicanism, and as his health failed in the 1870s, he hoped for a religious order to succeed him there.[109] The monks of Beuron were in need of a refuge from the persecution of the German Kulturkampf, and in the summer of 1876, Haigh, along with two Beuronese monks visited Ullathorne at Oscott. He was sympathetic to their plight, having issued a pastoral letter that year, attacking the persecution of the Church in Prussia. The plan was quickly formulated and in October, the monks moved into Erdington. The presence of a monk bishop helped to overcome their misgivings and give Erdington the vote over other possible sites in Leicestershire

---

[106.] Stanbrook 27, Ullathorne to Abbess, 28 July 1874.

[107.] *Address* (1875).

[108.] DA (unnumbered), Ullathorne to Provincial Smith, 10 October 1876.

[109.] The following details come from Michael Hodgetts, *Erdington Abbey 1850–1876–2001* (EBC History Symposium 2001).

and Herefordshire. Ullathorne was delighted to have monastic neighbours, and the growing priory was exactly what he had dreamed of long ago in Coventry. The monks looked after the parish, ran a school and gave retreats, as well as maintaining the monastic Office.

> The fathers are much respected in the diocese, and are giving great edification through their religious spirit. The school taught by the fathers is prospering. The mission is in a good state. A number of priests from the missions and from Oscott are glad to go to the fathers as their confessors. Their services to religious communities as extraordinary confessors exercise a valuable influence. In short, all that I had anticipated in accepting the foundation is becoming more and more realised.[110]

He was sensitive to their exempt status as monks in the diocese, and aware of the endless rumbling arguments between EBC monks and bishops over jurisdiction. Anxious to set the right example, he advised his auxiliary Ilsley to 'avoid a collision' by drawing up a special *pro forma* for his visitation and by being sure only to inspect matters related to the missionary duties of the monks in the parish.[111]

Ullathorne's sensitivity to matters affecting episcopal visitation of exempt houses reflected the tensions which had long been present between bishops and the religious orders. This had been a running sore during the recusant times and had not been properly resolved since 1850. There were a number of causes célèbres, including, most famously, Vaughan's battle in Salford with the Jesuits.[112] Ullathorne was fiercely critical of the Jesuits in their dispute with the bishop and articles in the Jesuit journal, *The Month*.

> The Jesuits are certainly damaging their case at Rome, where all this will be read, and if they continue in this line of writing, will bring out from their respondents still

---

110. BAA B8507, Ullathorne to unnamed Abbot, 23 August 1884.
111. BAA B7571, Ullathorne to Ilsley, nd *c*.1881.
112. Robert O'Neill, *Cardinal Herbert Vaughan* (1995), pp. 211–36.

clearer proofs of their imprudence. It will teach the clergy and people how much power the bishop has over them, notwithstanding their exemption ... What a thing this corporate pride is, blinding even humble men to their own discomfort.[113]

Ullathorne himself had reservations about certain religious orders operating missions, and was not a fan of mendicancy, as practised by the Franciscans, preferring the stability of monasticism in religious life. The mendicant life, where religious depended on the personal charity of individuals for their livelihood was, 'attended with serious evils', including extravagance and bad management,

> but the worst thing is their getting into habits of intimacy with the females of families and also getting so spoilt by their style and comforts of living when on their tours of mendicancy, that on returning home, they are apt to find conventual poverty and restraint hard and difficult to submit to.[114]

Monasticism offered a much safer and more responsible option, but tensions had long existed between the Benedictines and the hierarchy over the limits which episcopal authority might place on the freedom of action of the EBC.

He was convinced that the good qualities in every religious order (including his own) were undermined by the opposite defects.

> Thus the temper of the Benedictine Order is largeness of spirit, or freedom, apt to degenerate into laxity. That of St Francis is poverty, apt to degenerate into sordidness. That of St Dominic is rigid law and science, apt to degenerate into the stiffness of the letter and pride of intellectual culture. That of St Francis de Sales is spiritual sweetness, apt to degenerate into spiritual softness. That of the Carmelites is contemplation, apt to degenerate into

---

113. BAA B6433, Ullathorne to Estcourt, 19 November 1878.
114. Ampleforth, Copy of letter Ullathorne to Brown, 3 May 1866.

leaving Our Lord's life and passion into abeyance. That of the Society of Jesus is the practical, apt to discard the contemplative spirit, and to degenerate into policy.

The danger he saw as inherent in all orders was the tendency to drift from the original spirit and purpose of the founder and get into work not envisaged. Then, 'its spirit evaporates in proportion, and it acquires some new spirit that is not in accordance with that of its founder'.[115] This was clearly what he believed had happened within the English missions, schools and colleges run by regular clergy.

Ullathorne did his best to stand back from the fray and offer objective advice as best he could; he had even expressed a hope that Rome would not ask him again for an opinion.[116] This would explain why some monks thought his support for the EBC lukewarm at best.

At the bishops' Low Week meeting of 1877, they finally decided to grasp this particular nettle, and Ullathorne was deputed to draw together evidence from the other bishops and produce a text to go to Rome.[117] Ullathorne was, despite his reluctance, deeply involved. He had endured difficulties himself as bishop with religious orders, and was well aware of the disputes which arose concerning his own order, so was unlikely to be left on the sidelines. When Manning proposed that the English bishops should attempt to get a new Apostolic Constitution to govern relations between bishops and regulars, Ullathorne was, however, lukewarm. He feared that Rome did not sufficiently understand the English situation, and the Bishop of Salford (Vaughan) had warned him that 'there is a strong feeling in Rome about Cardinal Manning's anti-regular feelings'. Certain that a fight would ensue and Manning's ignorance and 'extremism' on the issue would not help, he was insistent that for he himself to go to Rome was 'out of the question'.[118] His health was not good and his days of foreign travel were over, but even had his constitution been up to it, he was

---

[115.] *Autobiography*, p. 264.

[116.] DA (unnumbered), Ullathorne to Provincial Smith, 10 October 1876.

[117.] Butler, *Life*, II, p. 187.

[118.] BAA B5956, Ullathorne to Estcourt, 27 March 1877.

reluctant to get too closely involved. However, Ullathorne regarded the question of episcopal relations with religious orders as crucial for the future, and not only of England, but of all missionary countries, and insisted that, 'in conscience' Manning must go to Rome himself. Manning accepted his reason for declining to go to Rome and went himself, but still sought Ullathorne's advice.[119]

In Ullathorne's opinion, this was a turning point, at which providence was shaping a new future where the Church would be free in a way never known before. In the present environment, bishops and clergy were free to care for souls without secular responsibilities, religious women 'have become a great working element in the Church under the bishops' and while the religious orders were largely free to operate, they needed the protection of local bishops to resist any repetition of the suppression endured by the Jesuits in the previous century at the hands of secular powers.[120] He drew deeply on his own experience in Australia of taking religious missionaries into colonies without episcopal supervision. The continued growth of the British Empire made similar situations more frequent occurrences. His fear was ultimately that 'a certain tone and spirit' among the religious orders led to a diminution of episcopal authority.[121] The right solution was vital: this had to be one which allowed full episcopal authority over the staffing of missions, but respected the autonomy of the religious orders. A long and bloody battle ensued, with pamphleteering and appeals to Rome, as well as personal slanging matches. Butler's monastic sensibilities led him to avoid telling the story of the bitter controversies in Rome, referring his readers to Snead-Cox's *Life of Cardinal Vaughan*.[122]

Not surprisingly, Ullathorne and Clifford of Clifton (a skilled canon lawyer) were deputed by the other bishops to draw up a text for Rome. This was done quickly, and in view of

---

[119.] AAW Ullathorne Correspondence, Manning to Ullathorne, 21 May 1877.

[120.] AAW Ullathorne Correspondence, Ullathorne to Manning, 1 January 1879.

[121.] Ibid.

[122.] Butler, *Life*, II, p. 188.

Ullathorne's reluctance, Clifford set out for Rome alone, being joined later by Manning and Bagshawe of Nottingham, and the negotiations dragged on for months. Clifford later produced a manuscript history of the whole sequence of events, in which he described the first draft of the document to emerge from *Propaganda Fide* as 'voluminous and confused'.[123] It seemed that the Roman cardinals did not fully grasp the problem in England, but had decided to take the opportunity of clarifying matters in this area for the whole Church. This inevitably complicated matters. Clifford was obviously a major player in the achievement of the final version of the papal bull *Romanos Pontifices*, issued in May 1881, and probably wrote parts of it.[124] The thrust of the document was to reinforce the authority claimed by the bishops, and Ullathorne was happy with the result. One of the key defenders of monastic independence was Thomas Brown, Ullathorne's old Downside master, long time friend, and the first nineteenth-century Benedictine to be named as a vicar apostolic. He was a reluctant party to the restored hierarchy, fearing a loss of control by the missionary monks, and even tried to make his entire diocesan chapter comprised of monks.[125] Brown, who might have been less happy with the outcome, died a month before its promulgation.

As regards the life and work of the EBC, *Romanos Pontifices* was a beginning rather than an end. The publication of the decree was followed up with a visitation of the EBC by a papal legate. This had long been sought, but had only come about through the dispute with the bishops, and in the event happened quite suddenly in June 1881. Ullathorne's views were again influential, certainly shaping the thoughts of Dom Laurence Shepherd (chaplain at Stanbrook), one of the key figures, described as a 'revisionist' rather than a reformer. He was an Ampleforth monk, and a devotee of Guéranger, whose influential *L'Année Liturgique* he translated into English.

[123.] Harding thesis, chapter 13, analyses this text in full, pp. 319–34.
[124.] Ibid., p. 330.
[125.] Alban Hood, 'Stirring up the pool: Thomas Joseph Brown OSB and the Dispute between the Hierarchy and the English Benedictines' in *Recusant History* vol. 25 (2000), pp. 318–9.

Shepherd exercised huge influence on the development of that house,[126] and compiled much of the material for the pontifical visitation of the EBC carried out in 1881 by Prior Krug of Monte Cassino. He also shared Ullathorne's devotion to Augustine Baker, 'the holiest man that ever belonged to our congregation', and his mixed feelings about Edward Anselm O'Gorman, President General (1883–8 and 1896–9) who was 'energetic, positive and precise', but 'ignorant' of the Rule.[127] Again, Butler glossed over the impact of the visitation and the consequences of it and *Romanos Pontifices* for the EBC, presumably because, a generation on, he was still embroiled personally in the arguments centred at Downside.

Ullathorne was happy with the decree produced from the visitation, which set out clearly the proper terms of Benedictine life, with government emanating from monastic centres and missionary life being regulated by sound constitutions drawn up by men of the right character, spirit and sense.[128] Interestingly, he seemed as much concerned with the current reputation for slovenliness in the conduct of Curial business as with conduct on the Benedictine side.[129] Ullathorne longed, in his last days, to see peace and harmony in the English Benedictines, that they 'may again become that solid, learned and influential body, which it has always been in its best times'.[130] He had no illusions about the current state of English monasticism.

> Unquestionably something is wanting to strengthen the Congregation, and the weak state in which such houses as St Gregory's and St Laurence's were left for years has done much to weaken the reputation of the body, and especially the neglected state of ecclesiastical studies. All this is known at Rome, and unless promise is held out of a thorough revision of your position you will have much to

[126.] Peter Athanasius Allanson, *Biographies of English Benedictines* (Ampleforth 1999).
[127.] Margaret Truran OSB, *Dom James Laurence Shepherd's Vision of the EBC*, EBC History Symposium, 1985 (passim).
[128.] DA (unnumbered), Ullathorne to Prior Gasquet, 13 October 1883.
[129.] DA (unnumbered), Ullathorne to Prior Gasquet, 12 November 1883.
[130.] DA (unnumbered), Ullathorne to Fr Ford, 18 December 1888.

contend with. The only way to get clear of false accusations is to admit what is true, and express the willingness to put it right. Then you will stand on clear ground and easily get rid of what is just and untrue.[131]

However, he visited Downside for the opening of the new church in 1882 and was impressed, not only with the 'magnificent' buildings but with the spirit of the place.[132]

While he approved the reforms proposed by Rome, which were the very things wanted to 'raise the body, and give to it learning, discipline and solid growth'.[133] he was often gloomy about the ability of Rome to help, regarding Manning and the English Curial Cardinal Edward Howard as antagonistic to the Benedictine cause.[134] However, the real problem was that the majority of the EBC could not see the benefit of the reforms.[135] The EBC made matters worse for itself, in his view, largely by not following his advice. 'Every step taken has been an imprudence, and each has been taken against my advice, asked for, and given from long experience and some knowledge of the modes and proceedings of the Roman congregations.' The EBC was divided upon itself over the emphasis which should be placed as between mission and monastery, and this became clear to Rome. He described as 'absurd' the notion which had been put to Rome, that individual monks might choose themselves whether to live in the monastery or on the mission.[136]

Ullathorne would probably have agreed that 'the last decades of the nineteenth century were a time of missed opportunities'.[137] The battles were only finally resolved in 1900 with the revision of the Constitutions which brought about a partial adaptation to normality, though Ullathorne's dreams of missionary priories was lost. The 1880s were turbulent years for the English Benedictines, with on the one hand a strong movement for monastic reform that sought greater emphasis

---

131. Ampleforth 253/14, McSweeney to Ullathorne, 22 March 1882.
132. BAA B7865, Ullathorne to Estcourt, 23 July 1882.
133. Stanbrook 69, Ullathorne to Abbess, 6 December 1883.
134. BAA B8124, Ullathorne to Estcourt, 22 February 1883.
135. Stanbrook 69, Ullathorne to Abbess, 6 December 1883.
136. Stanbrook 60, Ullathorne to Abbess, 14 May 1882.
137. Daniel Rees in D. H. Farmer, *Benedict's Disciples* (1980), p. 305.

on monastic life in the English houses, and on the other a desire for the continuation and consolidation of the missionary system, with monks continuing to live away from their monasteries in the Benedictine missions, many of which dated back to the seventeenth century. In 1890 the missions were placed under the control of the monasteries, which, through the 1899 bull *Diu quidem*, became autonomous abbeys.[138]

Monastic disputes were not the only ancient battleground on which Ullathorne found himself fighting afresh in his last years; the university question had also refused to go away. In 1883 a proposal came from William Clifford, Bishop of Clifton to get Rome to reopen the question of Catholics and universities, on the basis that in the sixteen years since the original proscription, the world had moved on, and lay demands for higher education were more insistent.[139] Ullathorne was strongly opposed to reopening the question, insisting that the Holy See remained firmly convinced that the perils to Catholic faith and morals inherent in Oxford or Cambridge were even greater now than when the original injunctions were given in the 1860s. Any petition from the bishops asking Rome to reconsider would inevitably become public and the laity might look for movement, which might not come, and thus leave the bishops in difficulty. He was scathing about the laity's demands, revealing not only a certain dismissive paternalism in his attitude, but an inherent distaste for the social and political ambitions of the Catholic laity.

> We cannot possibly promise what the laity want. Not one in ten in our colleges complete the course provided. Nor are the studies the first thing looked to in the university but the social manners, and polish, and a certain status in society and in political influence – which can be provided nowhere but in the universities. Hence I always knew and predicted that the Kensington college would be a failure.[140]

138. Alban Hood, 'Hedley, John Cuthbert (1837–1915)', *Oxford Dictionary of National Biography*, Oxford University Press, 2004 [http://www.oxforddnb.com/view/article/48462, accessed 14 Sept 2005].
139. Harding thesis, p. 316.
140. Ampleforth, Copy of letter Ullathorne to Brown, 5 September 1883.

His reference to Kensington indicates that some years after, he was still sore from the one really major policy clash he had faced with Manning.

The university question, to Ullathorne's irritation, was taken up by a new generation of lay activists. An eccentric Oxford layman rejoicing in the name of Hartwell de la Garde Grissell, who was a collector of books (now at Oscott) and of relics (now lost) and a Papal Chamberlain petitioned the pope directly on the matter. Grissell, 'a meddling mischief-making man with some zeal and little discretion',[141] was known to hold curious religious gatherings in his rooms in Oxford, and used his spurious Roman contacts to publish a pamphlet contradicting the decision of *Propaganda Fide* on university access.[142] He was beneath contempt as far as Ullathorne was concerned, and Manning agreed that he was 'an instance of what residing in Oxford can do to a man',[143] but he was part of a campaign by Catholic laity which eventually obtained permission in 1894 for Catholics to take university degrees at Oxford and Cambridge.

Ullathorne's views on the university question reflect his inability or reluctance always to 'read the signs of the times' and to understand the changing needs of Catholics in England. Social, economic and political change was all around him, and while he was often able to diagnose the ills consequent upon it, he was becoming less able to respond positively. His response to the outpouring of 'cheap but wicked literature' was ferocious, and he feared for the 'young men who in the first ardour and glow of life think themselves competent for anything'. Non-denominational education was not the answer, but it lay in a solid grounding in Catholic philosophy, which, alas, 'so few of the parents of the easy classes see the importance of'.[144]

He now lived in the midst of the offspring of the 'easy classes' at Oscott, although he had almost no dealings with the institution around him. Despite his failing health and the loss of many

141. AAW Ullathorne Correspondence, Ullathorne to Manning, 4 June 1884.
142. AAW Ullathorne Correspondence, Ullathorne to Manning, 23 March 1885.
143. AAW Ullathorne Correspondence, Manning to Ullathorne, 25 March 1885.
144. Pastoral Letter, 27 January 1883.

of his closest friends and supporters, the old bishop was not quite ready to relinquish the reins, and when Oscott deteriorated under Acton's management, Ullathorne did not hesitate to act, rallying from a bout of illness which he was not expected to survive.[145] At Christmas 1884, he was asking the nuns' prayers to aid him in the 'troubles of government', in particular, 'one grave one,' on which he did not elaborate, but it was certainly the question of the government of Oscott.[146] In early 1885, Acton was removed. According to Ullathorne, he 'had not the energy for the position, he was frequently absent from the college, was seldom to be found in his room, and did not enter into the work of the college'. Acton attempted to clear the staff out and remodel the college in his own fashion, but had little taste for facing the bishop, so he would send notes in with a servant – despite the fact that their rooms adjoined each other.

After Ullathorne pressured him into resigning, he hung around the college sulking, refusing to speak to Ullathorne and trying to raise support among friends, including by a letter to *The Tablet* which provoked Manning to stop reading it and to castigate Vaughan personally for the management of the journal.[147] Acton was finally eased out and back to his old appointment in the mission of Stafford, to be replaced by Joseph Souter with John Caswell (previously spiritual director in the school) as vice-president.[148] Though in failing health and rarely seen outside his room, the vigour and authority of the old bishop was not to be dismissed lightly. It was also clear that he was not completely cut off from outside affairs, and continued to express strong opinions on public affairs, including Catholic education.

Ullathorne issued one of his barnstorming pastoral letters in 1883 on the issue of Catholic schools and the workings of the 1870 Education Act, making it clear that the issue still remained one of conscience and principle.

[145.] L&D XXX, p. 409, 7 October 1884, 'We are sadly anticipating our bishop's death ...' Newman described his recovery as, 'a great grace, almost a miracle', p. 450, 29 December 1884.

[146.] Handsworth, 26 December 1884.

[147.] AAW Ullathorne Correspondence, Manning to Ullathorne, 22 January 1885.

[148.] AAW Ullathorne Correspondence, Ullathorne to Manning, 21 January 1885.

The very rivalry, and it may be said with truth, the conflict which the Boards have taken up against the Denominational Schools, fully admitted, openly proclaimed and acted upon, supplies grave reasons why the Christian schools should be protected, by having a fair and equal support with their adversaries, unless, what we cannot believe, it should become the policy of the State, to efface the Christianity of the country.[149]

Writing to an unnamed fellow bishop, he spelt out his position on the education question, which reflected his general principle towards government intervention in matters concerning religion and the role of the Church in society. Compulsory education which now existed in England, was an 'enormous invasion of that parental freedom within the household which is the natural basis of every other freedom'. Worse still, it had been carried out by enactments which 'violate two other principles of freedom, principles which are supposed to lie at the foundation of the British Constitution, and these principles are liberty of conscience and the equal rights of all men before the law. It places Christians in a position of 'great and flagrant inequality before the law'.[150]

The key issue at the 1885 general election for Catholics was education and the 'free schools', and the Catholic Voluntary Schools Association was pledged to push for the repeal of a clause in the 1870 Education Act which allowed the government scope to refuse grants to voluntary schools if they were not deemed 'necessary' on numerical grounds. In time for the election, Catholic opinion in England was being mobilised through the networks of (mainly Irish) Catholic clubs and societies around the country. 'These organisations were to play a major role in the inculcation of a forceful, united and "grassroots" Catholic opinion on a number of the major political issues of the day.'[151]

The threat to voluntary (i.e. denominational) schools was further enhanced by Joseph Chamberlain's 1885 election

---

149. Pastoral Letter, 26 February 1883.
150. BAA B8404, Ullathorne to unknown bishop, 12 February 1884.
151. V. A. McClelland, 'The "Free Schools" Issue and the General Election of 1885: a Denominational Response', *History of Education* vol. 5 (1976), p. 143.

campaign proposal of free schools for all, and veiled hints about the future of religious schools.[152] It became clear that the Tory party was the best bet for Catholics on education, and Manning campaigned vigorously for a policy based on developing the 1870 Act to bring about full equality between Church Schools and Board Schools. Many of the bishops, including Ullathorne, devoted their Advent pastoral letter to the subject during the campaign and the voting. He was, as usual, outspoken. Free schools 'cannot be', and the present dual system was an 'evil' which placed Christianity in 'perilous danger'. He urged Catholic voters to regard voting in this election for candidates pledged to re-examine the 'grievous injustice' of the present system as a 'sacred duty'.[153]

It is impossible to gauge the effectiveness of his exhortations, but the election result and the outcome in later years suggest that they were heeded. The Catholic campaign to protect Church Schools, supported by the Church of England and Methodism, hit the Liberal vote and left them with a tiny majority which could be cancelled out by an alliance of Tories and Nationalists. The increase in Catholic MPs from sixty to eighty-two was a bonus for the Catholics (although nearly all were Irish and not English) and obtained a Royal Commission on the 1870 Act, in which Manning took part. This ensured that, under the new Act of 1891, which Ullathorne did not live to see, increased funding was made available and the 'free schools' issue ceased to threaten the survival of Catholic education.[154]

The Irish question came to the forefront in the mid-1880s, though in the 1885 General Election, denominational education was more important than Home Rule, leading most Catholics to vote Conservative, in the hope that they would tackle both issues. In the end, the Liberals won 335 seats, Tories 249 with Home Rulers holding the balance of 86.[155] Gladstone recognised after 1868 that nationalist sentiment in Ireland represented a dangerous alienation from Britain, and

---

152. Mc Clelland, *History of Education*, pp. 145–6.
153. Pastoral Letter, 13 November 1885.
154. McClelland, *History of Education*, pp. 153–4.
155. G. I. T. Machin, *Politics and the Churches 1869–1921* (1987), p. 165.

sought conciliation through reform, pushing many reluctant Liberals along the Home Rule road. Early in 1886, Gladstone introduced a Home Rule measure into Parliament, and was forced to call a second election on the issue only eight months after the last. Home Rule dominated the contest, with Home Rule candidates supported by Catholic clergy and the Irish National League of Great Britain.[156] After 1875, the Irish Republican Brotherhood in London had largely vanished from public view, though it did not cease to exist. A provisional supreme council and hierarchical structure reached from parishes up to groups of counties, but it declined in size and militancy and by the mid-1880s its function was limited almost exclusively to collecting of money to send to Ireland for the purchase of arms. Its leaders functioned less as a conspiratorial elite than as proselytisers for militant nationalism, drawing adherents into a wide variety of nationalist groups. Irish nationalism in London by the 1880s became more about clubs and Irish culture,[157] although Irish nationalist leaders did their best to exploit the Irish nature of English Catholicism, and the Catholic vote was organised as never before in support of Home Rule.[158] This was not enough, and the Liberal vote collapsed, leaving Lord Salisbury to form the first of a long series of Tory governments in July.

The English Catholics were certainly divided and any statement from the bishops would weaken their position. Ullathorne argued that the Irish bishops were the proper judges of what was expedient for Ireland; recommending a particular line to English Catholics would mean taking up a party political position and would raise widespread opposition. His own view was clear: he regarded Gladstone's plan of a single chamber parliament for Ireland as an 'impracticable absurdity'. Yet to recommend the courses advocated by Lord Salisbury, Mr Chamberlain or Lord Hartington would bring them into collision with the Irish bishops and people.

[156.] Ibid., p. 173.
[157.] L. H. Lees, *Exiles of Erin: Irish Migrants in Victorian London* (1979), p. 233.
[158.] J. Hickey, *Urban Catholics* (1967), p 146.

I have been for many years convinced that the English
mind can never withstand the Irish mind, or provide suitable legislation for the Irish people and that they ought to
be allowed to legislate for themselves.

Any joint action of English bishops would do more harm than
good.[159] He repeated his objections a few days later: 'I have the
strongest conviction that more harm than good would come
out of such an action', insisting that his auxiliary bishop
Edward Ilsley and his vicar general agreed with him. In the
end, he refused to attend a joint meeting called by Manning.[160]
He did however begin to recognise the need for land reform in
Ireland as a means of securing social justice.

England is beginning to understand that something must
be done with the Irish Land Laws, if it is only to prevent
the security of English landed property being shaken. But
I believe that there is a real desire to do something in the
way of settlement for Ireland among many people.[161]

If there was one social issue guaranteed to rouse Ullathorne to
indignation and frustration more than any other, it was that of
alcohol and the effects of drunkenness. Since his early years in
Australia, Ullathorne had been a vigorous campaigner against
the evils of excessive drink, but he has been completely ignored
in all accounts of one of the greatest Victorian social
campaigns, the Temperance Movement. Only Manning, who
in 1868 publicly associated himself with the Temperance
Movement, is mentioned among the Catholic bishops in histories of the Christian based efforts to turn Victorian society away
from its love of alcohol. At the time when parliamentary and
public pressure was building up for serious licensing controls,
in 1871–2, Manning formed the League of the Cross.
Ullathorne does not appear to have involved himself in the
political campaign for licensing controls, presumably because

[159.] BAA, Copy Letter Book, Ullathorne to Manning, 18 June 1886.
[160.] BAA, Copy Letter Book Ullathorne to Manning, 22 June 1886.
[161.] SCA H412/19, Ullathorne to Sr M Xavier Williams, 18 November
1880.

of his distaste for state interference in matters which he regarded as moral questions related to religious liberties. This quasi-military organisation aimed at Catholics persuaded more than 58,000 to take the pledge by 1876, and a hundred and seventy Westminster priests petitioned parliament when the second licensing bill came forward in 1872.[162] The figure of 28,000 actual members of the League of the Cross is more representative.[163] By 1890, Westminster and Southwark had forty-two branches led by eighty priests, and drunkenness among priests had ceased to be a problem, but, 'the ethic of thrift, sobriety, and self-help had to compete against other styles of life, which were deeply embedded in the culture of working-class Irish'.[164] Strangely, perhaps, there is no evidence of correspondence between Manning and Ullathorne on this subject, although the Archbishop must have known of his long-standing teetotalism and abhorrence of drunkenness. His universally acclaimed sermon, *The Drunkard*, preached numerous times in Australia, Ireland and England, had been in print in England since 1842.

Ullathorne continued to believe in the power of persuasion, despite its acknowledged ineffectiveness by many national temperance leaders, and in 1866 his Advent pastoral was dedicated to the subject.

> Drunkenness is not only a widespread, but we grieve to say, a fast increasing crime, and what vice, after the most unnatural crime of child murder, and the filthy vice of impurity, can be more abominable in God's sight than to blur, or for the time blot out, or habitually to dull, besot and enfeeble that light of reason which is the prime gift of God and chief character of man.

He condemned the 'crying evil' of 'spirit sipping' among women of all classes, often frequenting gin houses and taking children with them, but linked these social evils with the 'rapid

---

[162.] Robert Gray, *Cardinal Manning: a biography* (1985), pp. 241–2.
[163.] Donald M MacRaild, *Irish Migrants in Modern Britain 1750–1922* (1999), p. 95.
[164.] Lees, pp. 210–1.

growth of irreligion amongst the uneducated and men of small selfculture'. This, in turn, was the fault of infidelity and 'reasoning unbelief' among the educated, especially in the universities, which was leading the whole of society astray.[165]

The 1872 Licensing Act introduced the magistrate controlled licensing system, established fixed licensing hours and instituted police inspection and legal penalties for drunkenness.[166] However, it seems to be the case that, although the hugely popular Temperance Movement pushed the question up the political agenda, this controversial legislation was not, in fact, helped by the campaigners. 'Either they adopted a quietist and moral suasionist stance, or their prohibitionist rigidity obstructed the compromises essential to successful legislation.'[167] Moral suasion was a position adopted by a variety of people from the radical liberal, John Stuart Mill, to the Conservative peer, Lord Salisbury, on the basis that the drink problem was a personal moral one, more a matter for the churches than Parliament.[168] Ullathorne clearly also fell into this category, and in 1877 returned to the fray in another pastoral letter. Urging on people the notion that the start of Lent was a good moment to reform and to shun the public house, he spelt out in no uncertain terms his conviction that drunkenness and Catholicism were incompatible.

> There is one vice which besets our time and country, the dismal consequences of which are everywhere visible. You will see at once that we speak of the vice of inordinate and excessive drinking. The degraded creature that gives itself to this filthy intemperance is unworthy of the name of man or woman ... Foul in body, blind in mind, defiled in heart, before God abominable, before men a scandal and disgrace, is it possible to call this refuse of human nature a man, or to greet him as a Christian? ... We have seen many things and have understood many things; but

---

[165.] Pastoral Letter, 20 November 1866.

[166.] Brian Harrison, *Drink and the Victorians: the Temperance question in England 1815–72* (1971), pp. 271–6.

[167.] Ibid., pp. 276–7.

[168.] John Greenaway, *Drink and British Politics since 1830: a study in policy making* (2003), p. 10.

this which we have so often seen shall we never understand: how a reasonable man, and a man having in him the light of the Catholic faith; a man who has a wife and family and a home to maintain; a man who knows he has a soul to save and the eye of God upon him; a man who has worked hard all the week to maintain himself and his family; yet no sooner has he got his hard earned wages, than, with his mind yet perfectly clear, and with complete consciousness of what will become of it, for it has always come about week after week, he flings home, wife and family to the winds, and goes with his money to a drinking house.[169]

Despite the legislation of 1872, the moral suasion case continued to be put with force, and there was a growing recognition in the 1870s of the problems of the habitual drinker or alcoholic, as a victim of his or her addiction.[170] Licensing addressed some of the social problems, but not the personal moral and psychological ones. Although legislation only had partial success, by the early 1880s there was considerable frustration in the Temperance Movement with government inaction on proposals, at a time when any number of major issues, including Ireland, were pressing for parliamentary time.[171] Few Catholic bishops besides Manning and Ullathorne seems to have given support to teetotalism, despite the evidence of social and moral damage among the poor Catholic population in the cities, although Hedley accompanied Manning on his preaching campaigns.[172] The retired Bishop Amherst of Northampton probably expressed a more general opinion when he refused to identify himself with teetotalism, on the basis that drink in moderation was 'a good, useful and lawful thing, given us by Almighty God for our benefit and delight'. He went so far as to decline to chair a public meeting for the famous Liverpool campaigner Fr Nugent on the basis that the Temperance Movement, though good in origin, 'had become

---

169. Pastoral Letter, 5 February 1877.
170. Greenaway, p. 36.
171. Ibid., pp. 40–2.
172. McClelland, *Manning*, p. 203.

almost a superstition'.[173] Manning engaged in the political campaign, and made himself unpopular by doing so.[174] Bagshawe of Nottingham attacked Manning in print on the temperance issue, and Vaughan of Salford was equivocal in his support.[175]

Moral suasion still found a powerful voice, not least from the aged Ullathorne, as a new edition of *The Drunkard* was published in 1884, fifty years after he had first preached it in Australia. When sending a copy of it to Newman, he told of its genesis, and how an old military pensioner, having read it, had told an Australian friend of his, 'The man who wrote this must have drunk very hard at some point in his life'.[176] Though scarcely recognised by historians, Ullathorne's place in the Temperance Movement was appreciated by those in the forefront of the campaign. After his death, the President of the Manchester, Salford and District Temperance Union paid warm tribute to him as a pioneer of the Temperance Movement. Referring to his 'famous sermon', he pointed out that it was first preached in 1834, when the Temperance Movement was scarcely a glimmer on the horizon. Not only that, but, 'in the strength and vigour of its denunciation it has never been surpassed by anything spoken from a teetotal platform'.[177]

Old friends and colleagues were beginning to quit the stage, and to leave Ullathorne more isolated. Mother Juliana Hardman, who had founded the Birmingham convent of the Sisters of Mercy even before his own arrival in the city, died in 1884.[178] She was one of the few survivors among the Catholic leadership in Birmingham to connect Ullathorne with the early days, and was the first convent superior in the city of Birmingham, spending thirty-five of her forty-two years of religious life as superior. Her funeral was conducted by Ilsley, owing to Ullathorne's poor health, when she was described as, 'a woman of few words though of great works'.[179] On this

---

173. Mary Francis Roskell, *Memoirs of Francis Kerrill Amherst* (nd), p. 345.
174. McClelland, *Manning*, p. 205.
175. McClelland, *Manning*, pp. 206–7.
176. L&D XXX, p. 397 to Ullathorne, 10 September 1884, note 1.
177. *The Tablet*, 30 March 1889, p. 513.
178. *Letters*, pp. 445–7.
179. *The Tablet*, 12 April 1884, pp. 591–2.

occasion, he wrote to the community at Handsworth, who had lost their foundress, a letter full of tender sympathy and wisdom. He understood the depth of their loss of her 'calm and gentle ways' and 'motherly affection', and added his own appreciation of her qualities, which reveals the mutuality of his relationship with the women religious superiors.

> In a moment of confidence I once said to her, 'You are doing a great deal of good and charity, you and your community, and what gives it value is, that it is done without any show or ostentation.' In her modest simplicity she replied, 'It has cost you twenty years to make us so.' Whatever was the fact, her words were golden in their simplicity and self renunciation.

Typically practical though, was his advice to the sisters to look to the future and seek a successor, whose mind 'should be large and free, whilst zealous for faithful observance, it should not be contracted and narrow about trifles'.[180]

In his later years, Ullathorne had come to depend more than ever on the wisdom and good sense of the trusted Estcourt. The letters are more frequent and confidential, given that Ullathorne was no longer living in Bishop's House with Estcourt at his side, and always signed with the rarely used 'yours affectionately'. He could confidently be outspoken to Estcourt: 'What a mess Gladstone is in. Where will it all end?'[181] It is, above all, in the letters to Estcourt that the real tone of Ullathorne's voice can be heard, and the outspokenness in conversation for which he was notorious can be picked up here as it rarely was in the written word. In April 1884, the bishop's trusted support for most of his episcopal life was taken by death after a long illness. Their last meeting was 'a great trial to both of us' and Ullathorne was bereft at the death of his 'dearest and most devoted friend'.[182] Estcourt had been Ullathorne's right-hand man through all his years as bishop and had played a major part in rescuing the diocese from its

---

[180.] Handsworth, 27 March 1884.
[181.] BAA B7798, Ullathorne to Estcourt, 25 May 1882.
[182.] *Letters*, p. 449 [16 April 1884].

financial tangles. Not only was he a skilled administrator and trusted support amidst the burdens of office, but Ullathorne relied on him as an honest critic of his writings in draft form. Although he only ever published one monograph on *Anglican Orders* (1873) Estcourt was no mean scholar himself and a prodigious collector of books, which are in the Oscott library. Ullathorne's letter to the clergy of the diocese on his death described Estcourt as his 'affectionate and devoted friend for eight and thirty years and the devoted servant of the diocese for six and thirty years'.[183] He spoke with real warmth of Estcourt's qualities, not only as an able administrator, but as a kind, generous and sympathetic friend, and there is no doubt of the gap which his passing left in Ullathorne's life.

With Estcourt gone from his side, Ullathorne relied more and more on the presence of his young secretary, Joseph Parker. Trained at the English College, Lisbon, Parker was ordained in 1875 and after a few weeks residence at St Chad's, Ullathorne asked him to become his secretary. Parker kept a careful but unrevealing diary during his years as secretary, recording visits, Masses celebrated, tasks completed, but nothing of his relationship with Ullathorne. Its rather strangely worded beginning does, however, reveal something of Parker:

> 16 Sept. Went for a walk with his lordship, who proposed the secretaryship to me. Opened to him – told all ins and outs. Told me to think the matter over – did so. 17th Sept. After Mass and b'fast went to his lordship and told him that after thinking and praying, I had come to the conclusion that I was bound to say that I thought the nature of the work would not be too great a struggle against my nature.[184]

Although bishop and secretary remained devoted to each other until Ullathorne's death, there were occasions on which Ullathorne and his closest advisors wondered if the 'nature of

---

183. *The Oscotian*, Ullathorne Number (1886) Letter on the death of Canon Estcourt, 18 April 1884, p. 82.
184. BAA B5632 Diary of Joseph Parker, September to December 1875.

the work' was 'too great a struggle' against Parker's nature.[185] Parker remained at his side until his death fourteen years later, and was, in Ullathorne's own words, 'more than a son'. His personal care and 'real skill as a nurse' pulled the old bishop through several bouts of illness.[186]

Parker's devotion to his master was remarkable, but so was the honesty and directness which the young and inexperienced priest was able to bring in his dealings with the venerable bishop. He was able to respond critically and honestly to the writings which Ullathorne asked him to read in draft, and was the cause of a complete rewriting of *The Endowments of Man*. He was invaluable to his brother priests as a go-between, and was able to approach the aged, and perhaps rather intimidating bishop directly on difficult or delicate matters concerning other priests.[187] Butler recounted a story, recorded by Parker himself, of an occasion when Ullathorne's rough treatment had deeply upset a young priest, and Parker went to the bishop and told him bluntly that he had been heavy handed and 'broken the poor fellow's heart'. The result next morning was a humble and consoling letter from the chastened bishop to the priest concerned.[188]

However, his interventions on behalf of other priests were not always welcome, and Ullathorne had difficulties with Parker, who at times appears to have acted unwisely. Ullathorne found him over-sensitive to criticism and to his own rough approach, asking Estcourt over one incident to have a quiet word: 'if I speak to him it will half kill him'. He was 'a good fellow but sometimes scarcely understands his position, and forgets that I know more than he about matters, and act with knowledge of the cause. There have only been two or three escapades, but he gets so excited and self-tortured, that it is not pleasant'.[189]

185. BAA B7058 Parker to Ullathorne relating in detail a clash between himself and Thomas Longman, the vicar general, 18 July 1880.
186. *Letters*, p. 458 [3 December 1884].
187. Butler, *Life*, II, pp. 261–3.
188. Butler, *Life*, II, p. 262 Butler mentions in his account of Parker a memoir which he asked him to compile of his years with Ullathorne, but this does not appear to have survived in manuscript form.
189. BAA B6965, Ullathorne to Estcourt, 11 March 1880.

Nevertheless, somehow, the aged and rough-tongued bishop and his rather intense secretary seemed to find a way of living with each other, and Ullathorne came to depend on Parker more and more.

Settled at Oscott, Ullathorne travelled less and less, only occasionally visiting Stone or the Oratory. Baddesley Clinton continued to be a place of refuge and relaxation for Ullathorne until the death of the squire, Marmion Ferrers in 1884 and the death of Edward Dering the following year. He conducted the funerals of both his old friends, and delighted in retelling to other friends a homely tale of 'the dear old squire'.

> Let me tell you one anecdote to represent a thousand. Walking in his woods, a hundred acres still left of the old forest of Arden, he comes upon a poor old woman. She was alarmed at seeing the squire, conscious of her intrusion. But he spoke to her as kindly as a father to a child, helped her to complete her bundle, took it on his own shoulders, and walked chatting by her side until he reached her cottage, where he left it and her, with her heart singing with comfort. Everybody's heart rose at the presence of the 'dear old squire'.[190]

The attraction of Ferrers' friendship for Ullathorne was obvious. Described by his *Tablet* obituarist as 'a perfectly beautiful type of what the English squire ought properly to be',[191] Ferrers, 'living in his quiet country home, and occupied in promoting the welfare and happiness of those around him'[192] belonged to an older, simpler world. This was a world to which Ullathorne himself belonged, and increasingly found more amenable than the one in which he had to live.

By the 1880s, with Ilsley effectively running matters in the diocese, Ullathorne's attention could be less enmeshed with the day-to-day administrative questions. He could give his attention to larger questions, and take his own advice not to be 'contracted and narrow about trifles'. At long last, he could

[190.] Stanbrook 76, Ullathorne to Abbess, 2 September 1884.
[191.] *The Tablet*, 30 August 1884, p. 342.
[192.] *The Oscotian*, 1885, p. 241.

settle to complete the three large religious treatises which had long been planned and partially written. In 1880 he published *The Endowments of Man*, in 1882 *The Groundwork of Christian Virtues*, and in 1886, *Christian Patience*. These represent the drawing together of his lifetime's reading and reflection, the sermons and retreats he had given, and his attempt to offer a coherent account of the Christian virtues and how they might shape human life. These books were evidently of great personal significance to him, yet oddly they reveal only glimpses of the man. At the end of *The Endowments of Man*, he began a discussion of the virtue of humility, 'the procreative foundation of all the virtues',[193] which he went on to develop in *The Groundwork of Christian Virtues*. The second book in his series was dedicated to the Dominican sisters at Stone, who had been the recipients of the lectures on which it was based. Its developed theme was the virtue of humility, which 'consists in the sense of our dependence on God, on the help of his grace and on the rulings of his providence'.[194] When he completed *The Groundwork of Christian Virtues*, he regarded it as his last book, completing all the works he had planned in his life. 'The first was the hierarchy, the second was the cathedral chapters, the third was the ecclesiastical seminary, the fourth was this book, all of which were long on my mind before they were realised.'[195] This is a more personal work, both because it was based on thoughts he had worked out with the Dominicans, and because it was rooted in the Rule of St Benedict. Following St Benedict, he traced twelve grounds of humility, and came to the conclusion that, 'Whoever has good hold of this virtue, or rather is held by this virtue of charity, quits the shadow of things, comes to the one true substance and leaves the smoke of the vices to vanish.'[196] Humility, he proposed, leads to Christian magnanimity, which is generous, hopeful, confident and tranquil: the lack of it leads to 'pusillanimity' or 'littleness of soul'.[197] Ullathorne's own courageous struggles to achieve humility are all drawn together towards the end of his personal

[193.] *The Endowments of Man*, p. 389.
[194.] *The Groundwork of Christian Virtues* (1882), p. 83.
[195.] Stanbrook 64, Ullathorne to Abbess, 3 January 1883.
[196.] *The Groundwork of Christian Virtues* (1882), p. 411.
[197.] Ibid., p. 244.

journey, and reflected in his deeply Benedictine meditations on the theme:

> Soft and pusillanimous souls are too weak to walk stead-fastly before God through the pilgrimage of life; but the great-souled are subject from their inmost heart to God, accounting that nothing can be greater for them than to be in the hands of God. To be great-souled is to be full of faith, of a faith that so lights up the eternal world to them, that the mortal things of this world fade before their eyes like dying flowers. The great-souled are magnanimous in sacrificing the love of self to the love of God, until all their strength flows into charity. Happy they who are released from bondage to themselves, that they may be large and free in the generous atmosphere of light and grace. All that we require is that the soul is open and generous. Humility opens the soul; charity makes her generous.[198]

[198.] Ibid., pp. 251–2.

Chapter 10

The Summons Home 1885–1889

The last few years of Ullathorne's life were spent in almost complete retirement at Oscott, where he found the elevated situation in the midst of woodland, farms and open country more beneficial to his health than the city centre of Birmingham, where Bishop's House was cheek by jowl with the canal wharves and gun factories. When the weather was fine, he would take a daily stroll along the college terrace, often accompanied by one of the college students, who would be regaled with tales of the high seas recalled from the old man's youthful days on board ship. Otherwise, the college residents saw little of him, or of the distinguished visitors who called to see him.[1] In the spring of 1885 he submitted what was to be his final report to *Propaganda Fide* on the state of the diocese which Newman presciently described as 'a lasting memorial to a great episcopate'.[2] In it he records, out of a total population in the four counties of the diocese of 2,248,514, a Catholic population of 76,474, with 3,617 baptisms and 1,879 adult converts in the preceding year.[3]

As he prepared this *ad limina* report, he sketched out for the people of the diocese the progress made since his arrival in 1848. In 1848 there were seventy-three missions, mostly with

---

B. F. McClymont, 'Recollections of Archbishop Ullathorne's Last Days', *The Oscotian* 1936 pp. 264–5.

2. L&D XXI, p. 48, 23 March 1885.

3. BAA B8724, Handwritten draft of *Status Diocesus Birminghamiensis*, 31 December 1884.

small churches or chapels. Since then, forty-four new missions had been founded and sixty-seven new churches built, making a total of a hundred public churches throughout the diocese. Instead of the eighty-six priests of 1848, there were now a hundred and ninety-eight, plus five communities of religious men. The convents had, of course, exploded with new life and energy. Instead of the seven in 1848, two of which were involved in active apostolic work, in 1884 there were thirty-six houses, of which thirty were dedicated to social and charitable work. The dozen or so Catholic schools had grown to a hundred and fifty-eight, educating over 26,000 children, including 5,600 non-Catholics. However, these figures were not offered in order to obtain applause, but to urge the people on to greater generosity, especially in the provision of funds to train priests for the future.[4] The passage of time had done nothing to make Ullathorne any more sanguine about the future of Catholicism in England. The effects of industrial life in the cities, including poor housing and coarse company in factories, combined with mixed marriages, which all the bishops by the 1880s saw as the scourge of Catholicism, were wholly negative. Of the eight hundred or so converts received into the Church in his diocese each year, many drifted away, and of the seventy-two mixed marriages in one part of the cathedral mission, only sixteen remained regular communicants.[5]

By the summer of 1885, Ullathorne was seriously ill, coughing blood, which the doctor described, somewhat bizarrely, as 'a readjustment of the fibres of the lungs to a change in constitution such as age is liable to'.[6] Ullathorne wasn't fooled, and was increasingly aware of his mortality, 'which binds me all the closer to the clock'.[7] This in itself was almost a liberation. 'It is quite true that when an old sack of bones like mine gets such a twist and a shaking, the spirit gets more free, and that the vision of eternity with all it embraces comes nearer the soul.'[8]

[4.] Pastoral Letter, 14 March 1884.
[5.] College Irlandais, Paris, Ullathorne to Kathleen O'Meara, 20 February 1887.
[6.] Stanbrook 88, Ullathorne to Abbess, 29 September 1885.
[7.] Stanbrook 74, Ullathorne to Abbess, July 1885.
[8.] *Letters*, p. 461 [26 December 1884].

Despite his advancing years and increasingly poor health, he still made a remarkable job of keeping his hand on the tiller, even in small things letting people know he was still in charge. Gently remonstrating with the Benedictine nuns of Stanbrook for burying their late beloved chaplain Laurence Shepherd within the enclosed monastic cemetery, his half-humorous reprimand reflected the mood of his later years: he was too humane to intervene in what he had foreseen would happen, but just wanted to let them know that it had not gone unnoticed![9]

Anniversaries came thick and fast, as they will towards the end of a long life. By 1885 he was the last survivor of the original hierarchy of 1850 left to celebrate thirty-five years of its existence; his view of the world by his seventy-ninth year was far from optimistic, and only revived monasticism seemed to him to offer any hope.

> The whole world is hastening into sand-like heaps of democracy, without authority or coherence to regulate this distracted and half maddened humanity; and nothing can heal it but the authority, stability and obedience which emanates from monastic centres. Hence I see in the revival of true monasticism a great providential mercy of God. Open such centres in many places, and the very unsettledness and turbulence of the world, will drive generous souls into them, and they will react upon the world.[10]

In 1886 he celebrated forty years of episcopal ordination, or rather others did on his behalf, for the passing of years had done no more to convince him either that he should have been a bishop or that there was anything to celebrate in holding the office of bishop. Newman wrote touchingly of the 'affectionate and grateful recollections, which so holy and kind a superior could not fail to impress upon me', and the two old men no doubt talked of such recollections as they walked arm in arm along the first floor gallery outside Ullathorne's rooms

[9.] Stanbrook 79, Ullathorne to Abbess, 11 February 1885.
[10.] Stanbrook 88, Ullathorne to Abbess, 29 September 1885.

at Oscott.[11] Thanking Stanbrook for greetings on the anniversary of his episcopate, he remarked: 'It is a long and heavy responsibility to look back on. As Mother Margaret said at the time, "When his head and hands were bound, he looked like a victim". A victim he ought to have been, whether he has been is another question.'[12] Among the celebratory dinners was one for the clergy of Birmingham, at which he reflected on the developments over forty years, and the role played in those developments by the religious women, whose prayers, he was certain, would get him to heaven, rather than his own efforts.[13]

Although *The Groundwork of Christian Virtues* was intended to be his last book, he could not resist taking up his pen again, perhaps in the light of his close brush with death. In 1886, he published his last substantial work, *Christian Patience*, a volume of essays which was written as a companion to *The Endowments of Man* (1880) and *The Groundwork of Christian Virtues* (1882). Patience was the Christian virtue which Ullathorne had found hardest to embrace in his own life, and his funeral preacher would make the point tactfully that 'no-one who knew him can doubt that self-mastery and silent patience grew upon him as his life went on'.[14] He knew that this was his last work, and it was no accident that the final words of the book come from one of the last verses of the Bible: 'Behold, I come quickly; and my reward is with me, to render to every man according to his works.'[15] *Christian Patience* was movingly dedicated to his old friend Newman '... you have honoured me with a friendship and a confidence that have enriched my life ...'[16] Newman was deeply touched by this gesture: 'God reward you my dear Lord for your tenderness towards me, very conscious as I am of my great failings. You have ever been indulgent towards me.'[17] On one of Ullathorne's last visits to the Oratory, in August 1887,

---

[11.] L&D XXXI, pp. 145–6, 2 June 1886.
[12.] Stanbrook 95, Ullathorne to Abbess, 20 June 1886.
[13.] Selly Park, Ullathorne to Genevieve Dupuis, 24 June 1886.
[14.] Bishop Cuthbert Hedley OSB, Funeral Oration, *A Spiritual Man*, preached in St Chad's Cathedral, 26 March 1889.
[15.] Revelation, 22.12.
[16.] W. B. Ullathorne, *Christian Patience* (1886), dedication page.
[17.] L&D XXXI pp. 159–60, 1 September 1886.

Newman suddenly asked the bishop to give him his blessing, and fell on his knees before Ullathorne.

> I could not refuse without giving him great embarrassment. so I laid my hands on his head and said, 'My dear Lord Cardinal, I pray God to bless you and that the Holy Spirit may be full in your heart'. As I walked to the door, refusing to put on his biretta as he went with me, he said, 'I have been indoors all my life, whilst you have battled for the Church in the world'. I felt annihilated in his presence: there is a saint in that man.[18]

That final and moving scene, in which the roles of bishop and cardinal were reversed, encapsulated the complexity of their relationship. There was deep affection and respect between the two men, but it often appeared over the long series of controversies in which they participated, that they came from irreconcilably different positions. Ironically, although Ullathorne had battled for the Church in the world all his life, there was a strong part of him which had always yearned for the 'indoor' life of the cloister and library. He had come to understand and appreciate Newman to a greater extent than Newman had him; from his limited perspective at the Oratory, Newman had rarely understood the range of issues with which Ullathorne had to deal. Newman made an effort to build and maintain a relationship because Ullathorne was his Bishop, but real trust and understanding was often lacking.

Theirs was a relationship of creative tension, not without its battles and misunderstandings, but which ultimately was fruitful for both men. Ullathorne, to the end, dominated and even manipulated Newman, but it was he, as an increasingly influential bishop, who had made Newman's achievement possible. In learning to understand and appreciate the problems of jurisdiction and personality presented by Newman, and the sensitivities inherent in Newman's relationship with the hierarchy, Ullathorne learnt a good deal about the capacities and duties of a diocesan bishop. Newman, in turn, played a vital part in helping Ullathorne to make the transition from an old

18. Butler, *Life*, II, pp. 283–4.

style vicar apostolic to a wise, modern diocesan bishop. Newman's last visit to Ullathorne at Oscott was at Easter 1888; their last meeting on earth was at Stone in July of that year, where both men had spent so many happy years and where Margaret Hallahan had played such a vital part in reconciling them to each other's differences.

In 1887 Ullathorne's poor health deteriorated further, and for the first time he was forced to miss the bishops' annual Low Week meeting, and the visit of Queen Victoria to Birmingham in an icy March had to take place without him.[19] By July, he had been unable to say Mass or even the Divine Office for a month.[20] He had met at Baddesley Clinton a man who was also a fellow native of Pocklington, visiting Warwickshire. They exchanged letters and Mr Hudson visited him at Oscott in the summer of 1887, and later published the Bishop's reminiscences of people and places in the Pocklington newspaper. His visits to Yorkshire had been inevitably rare throughout his life, especially after his mother's death in 1860, but in August 1863 he had visited Pocklington, probably for the first time in nearly fifty years, to preach at the opening of the new church of St Mary and St Joseph. 'I could remember almost every house in the town, and who used to live in it, though I left the place at about ten years old.' Some of the older residents remembered him, to his great delight.[21] The small Early English style church was designed by Matthew Ellison Hadfield, to take a hundred and fifty people, and the mission was evidently still supported by Catholic gentry families, including the Constable Maxwells, as well as the local residents remembered by Ullathorne. Ill health and age had done nothing to dim Ullathorne's detailed memories, twenty years later, of John Linwood, the saddler ('a most worthy man'), Mr Holmes, the solicitor who first introduced him to *The Arabian Nights* and Dr Dolman the local GP whose sons had gone on to school at Oscott. He recalled the sweetshop which had been a favourite haunt, fishing with the other boys in the local streams and the great outdoor party held by the villagers on Easter Sunday

19. SCA H412/21, Ullathorne to Sr M. Xavier Williams, 21 March 1887.
20. Colwich, Ullathorne to Prioress, 30 July 1887.
21. *Letters*, pp. 151–2 [5 September 1863].

afternoon in the ruins of the old chapel on Primrose Hill.[22]

Ullathorne had retained a sentimental attachment to the county of his birth, and he never lost the dropped 'h' of his native accent to the end of his days. Coming across a copy of the medieval Wakefield Mystery Play in local dialect, he was delighted to read the story of the shepherds of Bethlehem adapted to a tale of Yorkshire sheep stealing, redeemed by the appearance of the angels announcing Christ's birth. Thinking perhaps of the long dead Yorkshire village folk of his childhood, he imagined how 'the Wakefield people were in those simple days both amused and edified with it'.[23]

Of the family in which he had grown up, few now survived, and his brother Bernard, to whom he was closest, died in 1886. One of Bernard's daughters, who entered the Dominican convent at Stone, had, to her uncle's delight, been one of the first group of Dominicans to go to Australia, sent to establish a house in Adelaide.[24] No fewer than four of Ullathorne's nieces entered religious life as Dominicans or Benedictines, surely to some extent influenced by their uncle. Bernard also had a son, John, who became a priest of the Birmingham diocese. He trained at the English College in Rome, was ordained in 1872 and lived on until 1923. Family correspondence played a larger part in Ullathorne's life as the cares of business receded, and in 1886, when the first group of English martyrs of the Reformation (including Thomas More) were beatified, he took huge delight in reminding all the family members of their link with More.[25] The next generation of the family were growing up, and were producing their children.[26] The old sailor showed his softer side when a young nephew decided to go to sea. His family were poor, and Ullathorne only had £1 in his

22. *Letters*, pp. 493–7 [August–November 1887].
23. Selly Park, Ullathorne to Genevieve Dupuis, 27 December 1882.
24. BAA B8215, Ullathorne to his sister, 25 June 1883.
25. BAA B9309, Ullathorne to niece Sr Philomena, 27 December 1886; B9310 Ullathorne to niece Sr Dominica Catherine, 27 December 1886; B9313 Ullathorne to Owen Longstaff, 31 December 1886; B9314 Ullathorne to Leonard Longstaff, 31 December 1886.
26. BAA B 8256, Ullathorne to nephew, congratulating him on the birth of his first child, 21 September 1883.

pocket, so he got Estcourt to send the boy £2 on his account.[27]

Six years of semi-retirement had meant that the diocese was slipping more and more from his direct oversight and he was able to travel less and less. During the summer of 1887 he seems to have suffered a stroke, but also to have endured a worsening of other chronic conditions. He spent the whole of July at Stone being nursed, in considerable pain and discomfort. A note to Parker, almost illegible, conveys something of his suffering. The complete letter was as follows: 'No more relief. Stomach inactive, heated, flatulent, have eaten but little. Swelling heated, pain growing in right testicle this two days. Spasm when moving in lower region, more on left with flatulence, thirst.'[28] He was not exaggerating when he told Manning of the severe deterioration in his health which rendered in him a 'languid state of prostrate infirmity'.[29] Manning made a token attempt to persuade him to stay on in office, but knew the end was near, when he wrote movingly of the

> six and thirty years we have known each other. They have been years of friendship and of confidence: and both have been matured and confirmed as we have drawn towards the end. I have to thank you for many acts of kindness, and especially for those you showed me when I first came among you as 'a dead man out of mind' to my former life.[30]

In Ullathorne's own mind, the necessary decision was so obvious that it was virtually made for him.

> The moment the doctor pronounced the word paralysis, I said to him, 'then I must resign' ... The affection is not in the nerves of feeling but of motion on the right side. There is nothing visible but a halt in the right leg. But one is never secure from a new access ... I felt conscious

27. BAA B8249, Ullathorne to Estcourt, 3 September 1883.
28. BAA B9434, Ullathorne to Parker, 4 July 1887.
29. AAW Ullathorne Correspondence, Ullathorne to Manning, 23 June 1887.
30. AAW Ullathorne Correspondence, Manning to Ullathorne, 24 June 1887.

that, isolated as I must be from the flock, I could no longer perform the duties of a ruler. His Holiness has been exceedingly kind, and has intimated to me, I may tell it to a friend, that in consideration of long labours and services in the Church he designs to transfer me to a titular archbishopric.[31]

His health worsened over the summer as he was afflicted with kidney stones and became desperate to lay down his burden, begging Manning to expedite matters in Rome.[32]

Word began to get out as he wrote to his friends of the decision to retire. 'In short ... this new infirmity and the probability of its increase has entirely disabled me from bearing the responsibility of office.' Initially, matters moved swiftly and by early August of 1887 his retirement had been formally accepted by the Holy See. Before the end of the month Manning had invited the other bishops to gather for formal consultation about a successor. The Birmingham Chapter made a clear and obvious choice of the auxiliary bishop, Edward Ilsley, to succeed Ullathorne as Bishop of Birmingham.[33] Ullathorne was concerned about the need for more learned men in the episcopate by this stage in English Catholic life, but saw the difficulty in getting the right combination of learning, administrative skill and 'sound and solid orthodoxy'.[34] Ilsley had fitted the bill as auxiliary, but he could not be described as a learned man. Nevertheless, he was well known and respected among the clergy and had been effectively taking over more and more direct responsibility for several years.

The same year saw celebrations in Rome to mark the golden jubilee of Pope Leo XIII's ordination as priest, which was kept with festivities unseen since before 1870. Representatives were sent from the diocese, including the president of Oscott.

A letter from Canon Souter tells me Rome is crowded,

---

31. Stanbrook 103, Ullathorne to Abbess, 13 August 1887, from Stone.
32. AAW Ullathorne Correspondence, Ullathorne to Manning, 7 July 1887.
33. BAA B9494, Manning circular to bishops, 26 August 1887.
34. Ampleforth, Copy of letter Ullathorne to Brown, 15 August 1887.

and that good order is kept, and no ecclesiastic insulted.[35] The cardinals are too much engaged with the festivities and bishops at Rome to attend to ordinary business, but the general opinion is that Bishop Ilsley will be appointed my successor.[36]

Due to some 'strange blundering at *Propaganda*',[37] the paperwork appointing Ilsley as Bishop of Birmingham was long delayed, but it finally arrived in March 1888, as Ullathorne entered the last year of his life. He mustered his usual quip about episcopal appointments in writing graciously to Ilsley, 'I never yet congratulated any man on being raised to episcopal responsibility, but I congratulate myself on having you as my successor, and I congratulate the diocese.'[38] In the following month, the scant few personal possessions and bits of furniture in addition to his clothes were finally removed from Bishop's House to Oscott.[39] Few priests or lay people in the Diocese of Birmingham could remember a time when William Bernard Ullathorne had not been their father in God, and the sense of transition was palpable. The true extent of his weak health became public when he was too ill to leave his rooms and attend Ilsley's enthronement as Bishop of the Diocese. No one could recall a diocesan occasion without his presence.

In honour of Ullathorne's long service to the Church, Pope Leo XIII did, as intimated, award him a titular archbishopric as a personal mark of esteem, naming him as Archbishop of Cabasa. The nuns were very excited about it, but although it was obvious that he was delighted at the honour, Ullathorne played it down, telling Colwich that, 'As to title I have had private communication from *Propaganda* that it is settled, but it has not yet arrived. But as the gentleman so often repeats in *Dombey and Son* – it's of no consequence.'[40] In fact, he too became quite excited about it, and took delight in discovering

35. Anticlericalism was still rife in the new Italy.
36. Stanbrook 105, Ullathorne to Abbess, 29 December 1887.
37. Selly Park, Ullathorne to Genevieve Dupuis, 18 March 1888.
38. BAA B9651, Ullathorne to Ilsley, 19 March 1888.
39. BAA B9684, List of articles belonging to Ullathorne sent to Oscott from Bishop's House, 12 April 1888.
40. Colwich, Ullathorne to Prioress, 7 May 1888.

that Cabasa was 'the old metropolitan see of Lower Alexandria, subject to the Patriarchate of Alexandria, whose bishop was at the Councils of Ephesus and Chalcedon'.[41]

On the other side of the world, 1888 saw great celebrations to mark the centenary of the First Fleet and the foundation of the colony of New South Wales. For the Catholic community in the colony it was also the golden jubilee of the foundation of the first female religious order, the Sisters of Charity, who had been taken to Australia by Ullathorne, and to whom he had felt great reason to be grateful during his last dreadful two years there. One of the first group of nuns was still alive, aged eighty-six, and one of the priests whom he had also recruited, Fr Rigney, was still there at eighty-one. As he commented ruefully on hearing of the fiftieth anniversary celebrations, 'This looks as if I were growing old'.[42]

Ullathorne had kept up as far as possible with news of Australia and with those of his old friends who remained. Occasionally, he had heard news of Sir Roger and Lady Therry, retired from judicial office in Australia and resident in France until both died in 1874, but he was now only really in touch with Mrs Mereweather and Mrs Galton who were connected to his old life. Mrs Galton, wife of an eminent engineer and sanitary reformer, Sir Douglas Strutt Galton, lived in Hadzor near Worcester; she was the convert daughter of Sir George Arthur, a reforming Governor of Tasmania while Ullathorne was in Australia, and a benefactor to the local Catholic mission.[43] He mentioned Lady Weld whose father was also Governor of Tasmania; 'her father was, her mother is, my intimate friends',[44]

41. *Letters*, pp. 521–2 [17 May 1888].
42. Stanbrook 106, Ullathorne to Abbess, 29 January 1888.
43. SCA H412/19, Ullathorne to Sr M. Xavier Williams, 15 November 1880.
44. Weld, a member of the illustrious Dorset Catholic family, was Premier of New Zealand, Governor of Western Australia and finally of Tasmania, retiring to Dorset in 1887. His wife was Filomena, daughter of Ullathorne's old friends from his Coventry days, Ambrose and Laura Phillips de Lisle.
Jeanine Graham, 'Weld, Sir Frederick Aloysius (1823–1891)', *Oxford Dictionary of National Biography*, Oxford University Press, 2004 [http://www.oxforddnb.com/view/article/28983, accessed 26 Sept 2005].

but regretted that he rarely saw anyone from 'the old country', though there were usually two or three boys in the school from New South Wales – one was head boy. He corresponded jovially with, and occasionally visited his 'dear old friend',[45] Mrs Mereweather, who was the sister of John Herbert Plunkett, onetime lawyer and politician in Australia and one of Ullathorne's closest friends in the 1830s. Plunkett had been heavily involved in establishing the schools system in Australia, but his most significant piece of legislation to benefit his fellow Catholics was the Church Act of 1836 which effectively disestablished the Church of England in Australia, giving legal equality to other denominations. Described by Ullathorne as 'my old and dear friend,'[46] Plunkett had died in 1869 and been given a state funeral in Sydney.[47]

He recounted to Mrs Mereweather how he had been contacted by an Australian journalist, Heniker Heaton, who, in the 1880s, published a work entitled *Australian Dates and Men of the Times*, which 'recalled old times to me in many ways'.[48] Though not a Catholic, Heaton was a great friend of Archbishop Bede Vaughan and Ullathorne thought he might get a baronetcy for services in Australia.[49] He later became Tory MP for Canterbury. In Ullathorne's view, he had given Mrs Mereweather's late brother his due in his book, but had,

> scarcely said enough about Sir Richard Bourke, whose government was the transition to better things; and that he has entirely omitted Bishop Willson of Hobart Town, whose influence was so great in improving the convict system, and who got the home government to break up the penal system in Norfolk Island. I am in possession of all his papers and ought to write a memoir of him.[50]

45. Stanbrook, Ullathorne to Mrs Merewcather, 14 April 1887 (lent to Stanbrook and transcribed in 1908).
46. Stanbrook, Ullathorne to Mrs Mereweather, 1 May 1874.
47. F. J. West, 'Plunkett, John Hubert (1802–1869)', *Oxford Dictionary of National Biography*, Oxford University Press, 2004 [http://www.oxforddnb.com/view/article/22417, accessed 14 Sept 2005].
48. Stanbrook, Ullathorne to Mrs Mereweather, 24 December 1884.
49. Stanbrook, Ullathorne to Mrs Mereweather, 1 February 1886.
50. Stanbrook, Ullathorne to Mrs Mereweather, 24 December 1884.

In fact he did just that, publishing a series of articles firstly in the *Dublin Review* and his complete memoir in 1887.

In this memoir he described Robert Willson, the first diocesan bishop appointed in the Antipodes (Hobart, Tasmania) in the warmest tones. 'It was impossible not to be impressed with the eminent justness of his character.'[51] Willson, of course, had given evidence alongside Ullathorne to the Molesworth Committee on Transportation of Convicts in 1838, and had been as vigorous an opponent of the system as Ullathorne himself. Returning to Australia as bishop, he had been closely involved in pressing for the final destruction of the system and the barbarity associated with it. Norfolk Island, where Ullathorne had found the worst instances of violence and degradation of the human spirit, came under the jurisdiction of the Tasmanian government from 1840. Willson, therefore, found himself with pastoral responsibilities there as bishop. He returned to Norfolk Island, which had so horrified both of them as young priests, and, 'horrible as was the state of things that we found there in 1835, eleven years later Bishop Willson found it incredibly worse'.[52] A further House of Lords Committee was set up in 1847 to examine progress in the penal colonies, to which Willson gave evidence, including the dramatic introduction of a set of leg irons weighing forty-seven pounds, which the convicts were made to wear while working. As Ullathorne reports in the memoir, these irons are now in the Oscott Museum, but in 1847 they proved a powerful and effective witness to cruelty and barbarity.[53]

He also followed current events in Australia, in particular Cardinal Moran's plenary synod in early 1886, in the Sydney newspapers. To Moran himself he wrote most warmly on his achievements in Australia, where the Church was growing, while declining in Europe. 'Australia, from its position between America and India, and its great and yet undeveloped resources, must become a very great country, especially with such an energetic population. Among the finest boys we get in this college [Oscott], for manliness and vigour, are the

[51.] W. B. Ullathorne, *Memoir of Bishop Willson* (1887), p. 19.
[52.] Ibid., p. 52.
[53.] Ibid., p. 55.

Australians.'[54] Like most people in old age, Ullathorne felt strong emotional ties with people and places from the distant past, and recalled Australia and those he knew there through a rose-tinted prism, choosing to forget the distress and difficulty which caused him to leave and his adamant refusal to return as a bishop.

The support and friendship of the Sisters of Charity had made his last couple of years in Australia tolerable, and he took great delight in any correspondence from that direction. His letters are full of affection and gently teasing in tone. In 1872, his first real female friend, Sr Mary de Sales O'Brien died, and he wrote tenderly to Sr Xavier Williams, the last survivor of the group of six nuns whom he had recruited and accompanied to New South Wales in 1838, and at whose profession he had preached. She was the first religious sister of any order to make her solemn profession of vows in Australia.[55] He became quite sentimental, recalling her 'thin little figure and loyal, affectionate ways', and her illness on board ship, 'and how when you got well and began to knit, that poor stocking used to get unravelled'. He yearned for an opportunity to talk over old times with her. 'No-one ever had a more reverential and true spiritual affection than I had for you and your religious sisters, nor is that feeling extinguished at this day.'[56] The feelings aroused were not only those of a religious superior but of an 'affectionate old father' as he signed himself. It was to her that he wrote of the inevitable *ennui* which old age, physical weakness and loneliness brought. 'I am simply an old man of eighty-three, with three serious infirmities, laid on the shelf, and seldom able to quit my rooms, even for a walk in our beautiful grounds.' Newman, he reported gloomily, was unlikely to last much longer, Manning had reached eighty and was unwell and Cardinal Edward Howard (the senior Englishman in Rome) was ill in London, and was unlikely to recover.[57] In the end, all of them outlived him.

[54]. P. F. Moran, *History of the Catholic Church in Australasia*, pp. 172–3 (8 February 1886).

[55]. SCA H412/41, Ullathorne Sermon, 13 April 1839.

[56]. SCA H412/19, Ullathorne to Sister M. Xavier Williams, 15 November 1880.

[57]. SCA H412/39, Ullathorne to Xavier Williams, 18 November 1888.

His beloved nuns who were more local than the Australian Sisters of Charity, were more important than ever to him, and he relied even more now on their prayers and affection.

> I have much to thank God for, and much to reproach myself with; but God is merciful above all. It is no light think (sic) to be responsible for so many years for a diocese like this. But of one thing I feel more assured, that I have never neglected the spouses of Christ, my love and veneration for them has always kept me to the duty of cherishing them and protecting them. I would to God that every other part of my duty had been as carefully complied with. If I do get to heaven, as I hope, the prayers of my nuns will have carried me there, despite all my shortcomings.[58]

Stone remained his second home, and it was his one small regret that among all the Christmases he had celebrated in over eighty years – in Rome, among the prisoners of Norfolk Island, in the Blue Mountains of New South Wales, on board ship in Barcelona harbour and on the high seas – he had never spent one at Stone.[59]

Ullathorne's deep affection and profound respect for the female religious congregations which flourished under his care was remarkable and unusual. The early theoretical vision he imbibed from reading Marsollier's *Life of St Francis de Sales* and his experience of working closely with the Sisters of Charity in Australia gave him both a theological and a human basis for his life's work. His friendship with Margaret Hallahan was the most important of his life, but other foundresses and convents were also the recipients of his special care and protection. This care was paternal but never overbearing or patronising, and as he emphasised at the end of his life, was soundly based on the teaching and practice of the Church.

> When engaged in my ecclesiastical studies I examined the early customs of the Church in the Apostolic

---

[58.] Stanbrook 95, Ullathorne to Abbess, 20 June 1886.
[59.] *Letters*, p. 460 [24 December 1884].

Constitutions, and could not fail to observe the singular respect with which the spouses of Christ were treated in the assemblies of the faithful, where they were placed by themselves, before the rest of their sex, nearest the sanctuary, screened off from the public eye, and with symbols of their holy state depicted on the wall by which they stood. I found it to be almost a doctrine, that the virgins of Christ were the choice portion of the Church and the peculiar care of her bishops.[60]

As a youth on board ship, following his conversion of heart at Memel, he had read of St Francis de Sales being inspired by 'the first ages of the Church' when 'there never existed any description of religious persons who were not dependent on the bishops ... in particular the care of Christian virgins had always been confided to them'.[61] He recounted much of this in a letter which was written in thanks for the visit paid to him at Oscott by all the superiors of the Sisters of Mercy in the diocese on his retirement. It was full of tender affection, describing their prayers as 'of a value beyond price', and signing himself one last time as 'your old and devoted father in God'.[62]

This early reading of Marsollier sowed seeds which obviously bore fruit later in life for the nuns with whom he worked. A large amount of his time and energy was expended on supporting and developing female religious life and ensuring that rules and constitutions were properly drafted to secure good government and freedom from clerical interference in the future. Ullathorne was pragmatic and realistic and knew the problems which could arise from lack of clarity or ambiguity in religious rules. He was unsentimental and constantly guarded against sentimentality among religious. He was not a proto-feminist, but a man of his time who saw no place for democracy in the Church, especially among women where it was 'absurd'.[63] He was, however, a remarkable advocate and

---

60. Handsworth, To the Reverend mothers and sisters of the Sisters of Mercy, 18 April 1888.
61. Marsollier vol. II, p. 345.
62. Handsworth, To the Reverend mothers and sisters of the Sisters of Mercy, 18 April 1888.
63. *Letters*, p. 329, nd.

enabler of the real and active ministry of women in the English Catholic Church.

It is obvious that the single aspect of episcopal duty from which Ullathorne had taken joy and happiness had been the care of the women religious under his charge. His relationship with them was extraordinary in its mutual respect, freedom and openness and, as their champion in all situations, Ullathorne did more than any other English bishop since 1850 to encourage and support the ministry of women and to overcome prejudice and opposition. Generations of girls who benefited from education in the schools run by the sisters, and of women whose household poverty was relieved by their charitable outreach or whose health was restored by their nursing, have an unlikely and largely unknown hero in a Victorian bishop. Without Ullathorne's stalwart support and respect, women's ministry in English Catholic life would have struggled much longer for recognition.

His deep affection for the nuns led him to become entangled in one final monastic dispute involving the Abbess of Stanbrook and the President of the English Benedictine Congregation, Edward Anselm O'Gorman. The difficulty also involved Manning who had an invalid niece, Johanna, who was a close friend of the Stanbrook community. It was suggested by the President that she might live within the Stanbrook monastic enclosure without taking religious vows. Nervous and physical fragility made monastic vows impossible, and she expressed no interest in becoming an oblate. Manning had concerns about this unusual arrangement, particularly in view of any later change of heart on the part of his niece, not least being what would happen to her capital given over to the convent, if she should wish to leave.[64] Ullathorne was not impressed with the 'anomalous' proposal. 'I must say I do not admire the tone of this letter. Just think of a delicate person, whom the President describes as fretful, left in such a position.'[65]

Ullathorne knew well that this curious difficulty was taking

[64.] AAW Ullathorne Correspondence, Manning to Stanbrook, 16 October 1886.
[65.] AAW Ullathorne Correspondence, Ullathorne to Manning, 26 October 1886.

place against a backdrop of prolonged difficult relations between O'Gorman and the Abbess of Stanbrook, following an, 'imprudent and excessive' visitation. O'Gorman had been hostile to the reforms introduced by Stanbrook's late and much beloved chaplain, Fr Laurence Shepherd,[66] and had humiliated and deposed the Abbess, much to the consternation of the community. As Stanbrook was an exempt house, the bishop could do nothing but offer personal support and sympathy, but clearly he was unimpressed with O'Gorman's handling of Stanbrook, and over Miss Manning he sternly opposed the President's 'unsound' proposal, regarding it as having no basis in the rule of St Benedict or the Constitutions of either the English Benedictine Congregation or Stanbrook.[67] O'Gorman, in Ullathorne's blunt assessment was 'evidently floundering'.[68] In the end, Ullathorne's wisdom prevailed and by the end of 1886, Johanna Manning was safely back in the family home in Ennismore Gardens in London.[69] Ironically, a year later, Manning found himself dragged back into Stanbrook affairs, to preside at an abbatial election – on which, of course, he was carefully tutored by his old friend.[70]

However Ullathorne's spirits were lifted by retirement: 'I feel as light as a schoolboy turned out for his vacation.' Physical infirmities were a 'distraction' but he continued to read and discuss public affairs avidly, including the recent condemnation of Antonio Rosmini's works.[71] Even in the dark months of his last winter on earth, despite being confined to his rooms at Oscott, he continued to take an interest in political developments and was able to give Manning a detailed and

---

66. AAW Ullathorne Correspondence, Ullathorne to Manning, 31 October 1886.
67. AAW Ullathorne Correspondence, Ullathorne to Manning, 16 November 1886.
68. AAW Ullathorne Correspondence, Ullathorne to Manning, 24 November 1886.
69. AAW Ullathorne Correspondence, Abbess Gertrude to Miss Manning, 31 December 1886.
70. AAW Ullathorne Correspondence, Ullathorne to Manning, 22 December 1887.
71. AAW Ullathorne Correspondence, Ullathorne to Manning, Easter Sunday 1888.

authoritative account of the General Election as it had been fought in Birmingham.[72] He bemoaned the inexorable spread of popular democracy, while recognising (as in his remarks on the need for a new type of bishop) that, 'It is impossible to deny the rising tide.'[73]

Having more time at his disposal, Ullathorne kept up a wide range of critical reading until the last days of his life, and was anxious about the influence of popular literature, 'drawn from [the world's] vices, full of its temptations, and reflecting the concupiscence of the eyes and the pride of life, written for idle hours, and to make hours idle that should be industrious'.[74] The mood of the time was increasingly one of religious scepticism and the influence of natural science was growing. The Church of England had tacitly accepted the theory of evolution and its implications for biblical scholarship, in Frederick Temple's Bampton Lectures of 1884 on *The Relations between Religion and Science*.[75] It was probably true that 'science contributed to the unsettlement of the educated English mind',[76] and Ullathorne was anxious about its infiltration into Catholic writing.

St George Jackson Mivart was one of the danger men for Ullathorne. Mivart (a convert to Catholicism as a teenager) had been educated briefly at Oscott in 1845. Although professionally a lawyer, his passion was zoology and in the 1850s and 1860s he became embroiled in the Darwinian controversy. He became a disciple and friend of T. H. Huxley and entered the world of natural science. Quarrelling with Darwinianism gained him a public reputation and notoriety.

> Mivart, however, was not only a faithful practising scientist but also a faithful practising Roman Catholic. He was the only English natural scientist of any reputation within a renascent English Catholic community seeking to define

---

72. AAW Ullathorne Correspondence, Ullathorne to Manning, 20 November 1888, 20 December 1888.
73. College Irlandais, Paris, Ullathorne to Kathleen O'Meara, 21 July 1887.
74. Pastoral Letter, 15 November 1887.
75. Owen Chadwick, *The Victorian Church* (1970), II, p. 23.
76. Ibid., p. 34.

its role in a still hostile society, and fearful of the threats
of the new science to its fundamental beliefs.[77]

Darwin was only part of the story, argued Mivart, and he
strove in his later writings to reconcile Catholic doctrine with
responsible use of science. He wanted to bring together science
and theology in a 'revitalised church [which] would stand as
the rationally selected victorious survivor over its failed
competitors'.[78] He had drawn hostility in 1884 by his expressed
frustration in the *Dublin Review* with the progress made by
English Catholicism.[79] St Chad's and Downside were listed
among a handful of churches where the liturgy was confessed
to be beautiful, but this did not impress Ullathorne, who
regarded him as a troublemaker. He was not, in any case, an
uncritical supporter of the *Dublin Review*, and was greatly
relieved when his fellow Benedictine, Cuthbert Hedley, took
over the editorship in 1876. Hedley was credited with moving
the journal away from the narrow, Ultramontane concerns
espoused by W. G. Ward, and Ullathorne congratulated
Hedley, commenting that, 'it is high time it became a Catholic
rather than a party review'.[80]

The article by Mivart with which Ullathorne particularly
took issue, in *The Nineteenth Century*[81] spoke of the essential
harmony between between the truths of science and those of
religion.[82] Ullathorne feared that the influence of Darwinism,
which was by the 1880s widespread, represented 'a leap out of
the Church's teaching' which would 'open the door to all kinds

---

77. Jacob W. Gruber, 'Mivart, St George Jackson (1827–1900)', *Oxford
    Dictionary of National Biography*, Oxford University Press, 2004
    [http://www.oxforddnb.com/view/article/18861, accessed 14 Sept
    2005].
78. Ibid.
79. Chadwick, II, p. 410.
80. Alban Hood, 'Hedley, John Cuthbert (1837–1915)', *Oxford
    Dictionary of National Biography*, Oxford University Press, 2004
    [http://www.oxforddnb.com/view/article/48462, accessed 14 Sept
    2005].
81. Vol. 18 (1885), p. 47.
82. Although Ullathorne kept up with what was published in secular
    journals like the *Nineteenth Century*, he was well known to object
    strongly to Catholics writing in them. L&D vol. XXVIII, p. 430 n. 2.

of pseudophilosophic theories'. Samuel Lilly's book, *Ancient Religion and Modern Thought* was equally dangerous, treating alike Buddhism, Hinduism, Zoroastrianism and Confucianism. Ullathorne vehemently insisted that joint episcopal action was needed and even intervention from the Pope himself.[83] Mivart's work, and reviews in *The Weekly Register, The Tablet* and *The Dublin Review*, in his opinion reflected the dangerous effects of liberal Catholic writing on the Church and the lack of a challenge from authority.[84] Eventually, after Ullathorne's death, Mivart clashed openly with the Church hierarchy, finding his work on the Index of forbidden books. Bracketed with the Modernists whose path he had paved, he died excommunicated from the Church in 1900.

Ullathorne also continued to take a vigorous and critical interest in the Church of England, and his views had changed little since his conflict with the Association for Promoting the Unity of Christendom in the mid-1860s. He had little time for the Church of England, and even less for the aspirations of 'Anglo-Catholicism' within the established Church.

> That poor old lady, the English Church is very seedy. She has lingered on for three hundred years – and now seems to be sinking fast … What we are coming to we cannot see; but there are plenty of signs that the name of the Protestant establishment will in a few years time be a matter of past history. The serious and really good members of the old lady's family are tending unconsciously to the Faith, while the naughty children are rushing into rationalism and infidelity.[85]

Convert clergymen had continued to trickle into the Catholic Church, and far from spurning them, as has been suggested, Ullathorne welcomed them with open arms. Before his retirement, he reckoned to have received into the Church no fewer than seventy-five former Anglican clergymen in his own chapel

83. AAW Ullathorne Correspondence, Ullathorne to Manning, 3 July 1885.
84. Ampleforth, Copy of letter, Ullathorne to Brown, 15 August 1887.
85. Quoted in Mary Francis Roskell, *Memoirs of Francis Kerril Amherst* (nd), pp. 274–5.

at Bishop's House.[86] He was consistently outspoken about the state of the Church of England and its internal divisions which were causing such disruption. Ritualists or Anglo-Catholics and Evangelical Anglicans were at each other's throats, and the consequent loss of confidence in the Church of England among a lot of people was, in his view, a major cause of infidelity, as people took the state of the Church of England to reflect the whole of Christianity.[87] The Ritualists, who had brought together in the expression of their faith elements of the sacramentalism of the Oxford Movement and the Gothic splendour of the post-Pugin building craze in a form of 'Anglo-Catholicism', were, 'thorough shams'. 'They rest more on private judgement than others, borrow their fragments of doctrine from our books, abuse us to conceal the theft, profess to rest upon Episcopal authority beyond other men, disobey their bishops, and abuse them heartily.'[88]

Another contemporary author who gave him cause for concern, but whose writings clearly absorbed him, was George Eliot, whose early life had been spent in Warwickshire. She was, of course, the heroine of the agnostic intellectuals of late Victorian England, and Ullathorne claimed personal knowledge of the Brays and Hennells, her Coventry friends, 'who in her youth turned her from Christianity'.[89] Charles Bray was a wealthy ribbon manufacturer in Coventry, a progressive in politics, and a philanthropist who used his wealth to set up schools and to support hospitals, all with a view to improving the social conditions of the poor. He was a freethinker in religion, who did not care what his neighbours thought of him. His large house, Rosehill, was a mecca for radicals and

---

86. *The Tablet*, Letter from Edmund Dease, 20 April 1889. Dease was an Irish Catholic landowner, who became a prominent MP and home rule supporter. Alan O'Day, 'Dease, Edmund Gerald (1829–1904)', *Oxford Dictionary of National Biography*, Oxford University Press, 2004 [http://www.oxforddnb.com/view/article/41275, accessed 14 Sept 2005].

87. College Irlandais, Paris, Ullathorne Letters to Kathleen O'Meara, 20 February 1887.

88. College Irlandais, Paris, Ullathorne to Kathleen O'Meara, 9 February 1886.

89. *Letters*, p. 467 [6 July 1885].

intellectuals, which must have been a source of irritation to Ullathorne as the local Catholic priest. Along with his wife, Cara, and her sister and brother, Sara and Charles Hennell, Bray offered Mary Ann Evans an intellectually challenging milieu, where she met many liberal thinkers, including the social philosophers Herbert Spencer and Harriet Martineau, the social experimentalist Robert Owen, the radical publisher John Chapman, and Ralph Waldo Emerson on his visits from America.

During the time of Ullathorne's residence in Coventry, Evans was living there and working on one of the most significant challenges to Christianity of the nineteenth century, the translation of David Strauss's *Life of Jesus*, which was published in 1846, the year of Ullathorne's departure. In it Strauss painstakingly investigated the events of Christ's life as told in all four Gospels and decided that they were not historical, but mythological, offering the wished-for fulfilment of Old Testament prophecies.[90] Apart from his brief comment about the Brays and Hennells, Ullathorne gave no hint of having personal contact with George Eliot during her formative years in Coventry, but it remains an intriguing possibility. His analysis of Eliot was that her whole life was a conflict between the remnants of her Christian conscience and the Positivism she imbibed from George Lewis. The only one of Eliot's novels of which he approved was *Adam Bede*, 'full of the best of English life and of the writer's experience of the people of Staffordshire and Derbyshire'.[91] The tragic story of Hetty Sorrell, of course, also touched on the horrors of transportation, so close to Ullathorne's heart. He contrasted the 'keen sense of religion' in *Adam Bede* with the 'frightful desolation' of the curious medieval Florentine romance of *Romola*.[92]

During the second half of the century, interest had grown among English Catholics in the stories of their forebears during the Reformation and recusant period who had died as

[90]. Rosemary Ashton, 'Evans, Marian [George Eliot] (1819–1880)', Oxford Dictionary of National Biography, Oxford University Press, 2004 [http://www.oxforddnb.com/view/article/6794, accessed 14 Sept 2005].

[91]. *Letters*, p. 469 [16 July 1885].

[92]. Ibid.

martyrs at the hands of the Protestant state. Frances Taylor (foundress of the Poor Servants of the Mother of God) published the first systematic account of the martyrs in *Tyburn and Those Who Went Thither* in 1857.[93] Their stories became important symbols of Catholic culture and identity, and as early as 1860, Wiseman had (unsuccessfully) petitioned Pius IX to institute a feast in England to honour the martyrs of the Reformation. In 1867, Ullathorne himself had devoted a pastoral letter to the traditions and heroism of English recusancy. In it, he recalled 'a small and scattered remnant, thrown back upon themselves through the prejudices of their neighbours, and clinging to their persecuted faith, their religion was all in all to them'. This was the world in which he had grown up, in recusant Yorkshire. His family was one of those who 'cherished the memories of their martyrs, now so much forgotten; and kept before their eyes the examples of the saints. Indeed the names of those martyrs and those saints were as household words, and like the memories of dear friends.' In his household, the cherished memory was that of Thomas More, an ancestor of his mother's family, where at one time personal items owned by the martyr had been preserved.[94]

In 1874 Manning ensured that the cause for beatification and canonisation of the English Reformation martyrs was opened officially in Rome. During the last quarter of the century, once access to post-war Rome became possible again, archival material was collected towards the English Martyrs project.[95] Ullathorne was an enthusiastic supporter of the process towards beatification of the English and Welsh Martyrs of the Reformation, and took particular delight in the presence of Thomas More among the fifty-four beatified by Leo XIII in 1886, because of his family connections with More.[96] In April 1887 Ullathorne ordered the decree announcing the beatification of the English martyrs to be sent to all churches in the diocese and put on the doors, 'thinking the people would be

[93]. Judith Champ, *The English Pilgrimage to Rome: a Dwelling for the Soul* (2000), pp. 187–9.
[94]. Pastoral Letter, 27 February 1867.
[95]. Champ, *English Pilgrimage*, pp. 197–9.
[96]. *Letters*, pp. 489–90 [31 December 1886].

struck with the number of common English names of martyrs'.[97]

He lent enthusiastic personal and episcopal support to the work of Fr John Morris SJ,[98] who, as Postulator for the cause, was overseeing the production of evidence. Ullathorne confirmed from his own reading of Augustine Baker the story of penal times told in different guises, of English Benedictine monks being scorned and rejected by continental religious because they did not wear the habit. Baker's own version of the story, reputedly from his own experience, was that some Benedictines he met in Italy left the table and refused to associate with him, when 'he told them that in England he wore a coloured coat and waistcoat and a sword'.[99] This tickled Ullathorne himself, having been the first monk in post-Reformation England to wear the monastic habit in public, at the 1845 consecration of St Osburg's church in Coventry.

Augustine Baker played a significant part in Ullathorne's own monastic spirituality, although he does not specifically mention him in his account of his monastic noviciate at Downside. Baker was, however, among the authors he had with him in Australia, and brought back to England.[100] The Welsh-born lawyer and convert who became a monk, Augustine Baker (1575–1641) was a key figure in recusant Benedictine life, particularly as the spiritual guide of the exiled nuns at Cambrai (who later found a home at Stanbrook) and posthumously through his writings, of the nuns at Paris (founded from Cambrai and later relocated to Colwich). His best known work, *Sancta Sophia* (Holy Wisdom) was compiled at Cambrai, and its survival is largely due to the fact that, as the nuns fled the Continent during the French Revolution, they brought the Baker manuscripts with them. Colwich was deeply rooted in Bakerite spirituality, and it was here that Ullathorne became most aware of this strange, mystical seventeenth-century monk who had so shaped the English

---

97. Colwich, Ullathorne to Prioress, 4 April 1887.
98. This was the same Fr Morris, who as Secretary to the Westminster Chapter, had done his best to ensure that Ullathorne did not succeed Wiseman in 1865. See Chapter 7.
99. Farm St1127, Ullathorne to Morris, 27 January 1887.
100. *Autobiography*, p. 205.

Benedictine convents now in his own diocese.[101]

In the spring of 1850 Ullathorne made his own private retreat at Colwich, making use of Augustine Baker's exposition of St Benedict's twelve rules of humility, and in particular Baker's simple injunction, 'Consider your call, that's all in all.' It was clearly an important moment in Ullathorne's personal spiritual development, as he wrote confidentially to Mother Margaret.

> My dearest sister in Christ, If it were but in mere gratitude I ought to write to you before I leave this place. It is long since I have had such a time, and I may safely say never so much light as to what God requires of me. Six syllables have been my main exterior instrument, and I do not see how I can ever need more.

In his meditation on Baker's exposition of Benedict's twelve rules of humility, he 'found practically how much more light God gives through the will than through the intellect'.[102]

Ullathorne also in turn played a part in encouraging the nineteenth-century revival of interest in Baker, ensuring that Colwich and Stanbrook were on the right lines in reading and interpreting his writings.

> I was looking into Fr Baker's *Emblems* the other day, of which I have a copy. One of his maxims for contemplation he takes from the pagan classics with a profound monastical sense – If people only knew the good that God has given them. And I would add, if they would only rejoice in that good, how it would kill their sadness and self love.[103]

Baker had also compiled a life of the Cambrai mystic, Gertrude More, great-great granddaughter of Thomas More (so presumably in some distant and convoluted way, related to Ullathorne

---

101. For a full discussion of Baker, see M Woodward (ed.), *That Mysterious Man: essays on Augustine Baker* (Abergavenny, 2001).

102. Colwich, Ullathorne to Mother Margaret Hallahan, 31 May 1850.

103. Stanbrook 70, Ullathorne to Abbess, 30 December 1883.

himself). He intervened at Colwich and Stanbrook to suppress a manuscript version of Baker's life of Gertrude More based on an abridgement in which 'Father Baker's guarded sense is not fairly rendered'.[104] Following a visitation to Colwich, he was critical of their use of Baker, accusing them of misreading him: 'He is right enough; it is the way you make use of him.'[105]

In his last years of semi retirement and eventually full retirement, Ullathorne's correspondence naturally became less focused on business and revealed more of his interests, his reading and his friendships. Through her writing of the life of Bishop Thomas Grant of Southwark, one of Ullathorne's closest episcopal friends, who died in Rome during the Vatican Council, he began to correspond with a young woman half his age, Kathleen O'Meara.[106] She was a relative of Barry O'Meara, the Irish physician who nursed Napoleon in his last years, and in consequence the family lived in Paris on a pension from the Second Empire. She wrote several novels under the pen name of Grace Ramsey, as well as several religious biographies, and was Paris correspondent of *The Tablet* for many years.[107]

Initially he was cool in his response to her draft of the life of Grant, which suffered (in his view) from a limited range of sources and from her lack of theological education.[108] However, his later letters are more encouraging and he gradually came to respect her work, not only on Grant but on Frederic Ozanam, and he discussed his own writings with her, sending her a copy of his *Ecclesiastical Discourses* in exchange for

[104.] Stanbrook 19b, copy of letter to Prioress of Colwich, 4 September 1872. No full printed edition was produced until 1910.

[105.] Colwich, Notes in another hand on episcopal visitations, 25 April 1872, 7 July 1874.

[106.] The correspondence between Ullathorne and Kathleen O'Meara is in the College Irlandais in Paris and is not currently available. I am grateful to the Archivists of the EBC for transcriptions and notes made by them in situ in 1988.

[107.] Thompson Cooper, 'O'Meara, Kathleen (1839–1888)', rev. Maria Luddy, *Oxford Dictionary of National Biography*, Oxford University Press, 2004 [http://www.oxforddnb.com/view/article/20756, accessed 14 Sept 2005].

[108.] College Irlandais Paris, Ullathorne to Kathleen O'Meara, 14 February 1873.

her book on Ozanam.[109] Eventually they became regular correspondents and he was a great help to her work on Grant,
correcting matters of information and even typographical
errors, until in 1885 he told her with great delight that 'the
pages breathe the aroma of his character'.[110]

By 1887 she had become 'my dear child in Christ', to whom
he wrote on a range of literary and religious topics as well as
recalling some of his unfortunate experiences when meeting
women – including the tale of escorting Mrs Hutchinson across
Europe and that of the young woman in Australia who went into
the outback on her own. Both stories are told in the autobiography.[111] His friendship with Kathleen O'Meara lasted until her
premature death in November 1888, and was conducted almost
entirely through letters which were chatty and full of interest
and humour, including a gentle ticking off for using the term
'monks' in her biography of Lacordaire, to describe Dominican
friars. He set her right on the difference between monks and
friars, concluding with the self-deprecatory comment, 'If this is
wanting in pomposity, I am much mistaken!'[112] They met only
once, in September 1887, when she and her sister and their
mother visited him at Oscott. By the end of the year, Mrs
O'Meara was dead, and her daughter followed her less than a
year later. He exchanged a few letters with her sister on the
death of 'my dear friend Kathleen',[113] before illness clouded the
last weeks of his own life. Ullathorne's admiration was obviously
shared more widely, judging by her brief but glowing obituary,
which, as well as praising her literary and biographical insight
and delicacy of touch, spoke of her 'earnest and generous spirit
... broad and just view of men and things [and her] quick
sympathy with the wants of others'.[114]

Following his final retirement, Ullathorne's life became
almost monastic in its quiet and solitude – which suited him.

[109.] College Irlandais Paris, Ullathorne to Kathleen O'Meara, 4
November 1876.
[110.] College Irlandais Paris, Ullathorne to Kathleen O'Meara, 11
December 1885.
[111.] *Autobiography*, p. 99 and pp. 245–53.
[112.] *The Oscotian*, Ullathorne Number (1886); *Letters*, pp. 159–63.
[113.] *Letters*, p. 537 [26 December 1888].
[114.] *The Tablet*, 17 November 1888, p. 789.

He lived quietly at Oscott, revising his autobiography, which he only ever intended to be kept with his papers at Stone, but which was published long after his death. Curiously, perhaps, he showed no interest in taking the story beyond 1850, believing that people would only be interested in the more obviously adventurous parts of his life. The world was passing him by as he prepared for 'the great transition', and the diocese slipped from his grip, as he ruefully commented that he now got no diocesan news 'except by accident'.[115]

By the end of his life, like many old men in any age, he saw the world getting 'worse and worse' and governments forced to be guided by 'the popular voice, which does not mend matters'.[116] His valedictory pastoral letter had a tone of gloom about it, in which he described the present life as a probation for eternal life and warned against 'a material world full of seductions and dangers to the soul ... was it ever so full of evil, and of temptations to error and evil, as this day?'[117] He was apt to become grumpy about the state of the Church, and crossly complained to the Prioress of Colwich, who was in dire need of a new chaplain that, 'the clergy are so fond of independence. Since my younger days the whole tone of things is utterly changed, and one is obliged to think a great deal about their feelings to save a great deal of difficulty.'[118] This reflected more the passing mood of an old man in poor health, and his real attitude to his clergy is better reflected in Hedley's funeral homily, in which he spoke of his single aim, which was to

> spiritualize the hearts of his priests, rather than drilling their steps. He was not a man for many rules or many questions. If he could make a young heart realise its God – if he could touch a priest with the mission and the message of his Lord – if he could get a labourer in the vineyard to listen to the love which speaks from the Cross – he was satisfied. The rest would come.[119]

115. Selly Park, Ullathorne to Genevieve Dupuis, 26 September 1888.
116. Selly Park, Ullathorne to Genevieve Dupuis, 26 September 1888.
117. Pastoral Letter, 15 November 1887.
118. Colwich, Ullathorne to Prioress, 17 May 1887.
119. Bishop Cuthbert Hedley OSB, *A Spiritual Man: Funeral homily preached in St Chad's Cathedral*, 26 March 1889.

There is little evidence of correspondence emanating from the first floor rooms at Oscott after the end of 1888. One of his last letters was one of gratitude to Michael Glancey, previously on the staff at Oscott (later auxiliary bishop in Birmingham) who with John Caswell, the vice-president of Oscott, had compiled a volume of *Characteristics from the Writings of Archbishop Ullathorne*, listing all his published writings and drawing on them for quotations on topics as diverse as 'English warm-heartedness', 'Obstinacy', 'Mixed Marriages', and 'Spiritual Pilotage'. As Glancey pointed out in his introduction, Ullathorne had been writing and publishing for fifty-five years, and during all that time 'the archbishop was always to be seen at the post of danger, beating down the barricades erected by ignorance, prejudice and malice, and fencing round Catholic truth with new lines of strength by his clear and solid exposi-tions'.[120] Glancey's preface to this collection of characteristic quotations from Ullathorne's writings makes clear how he was perceived by his younger contemporaries at the end of his life, and it is a judgement largely followed by historians. Ullathorne was not an original thinker, but he was a battler for the Church and for Catholic truth in the public arena.

Glancey makes a case for the importance of the three major tracts, *The Endowments of Man*, *The Groundwork of Christian Virtues* and *Christian Patience*, but it is the trenchant public statements of the pamphlets and pastoral letters which retain an echo of the voice and stir the heart, rather than the some-what dense and turgid spiritual writings. The richness of his spiritual wisdom shines through in his more personal reflec-tions in letters to friends and colleagues, and particularly to his nuns. Not surprisingly, it is in the voluminous correspondence that a glimpse of the real man can be gained. A late example of this can be found in Ullathorne's last letter to Mother Genevieve Dupuis, superior of the Sister of Charity of St Paul, in December 1888. It was full of warmth and appreciation, not only of her work, but of their friendship.

We all have our shortcomings more or less; God knows

[120.] Michael Glancey, *Characteristics from the Writings of Archbishop Ullathorne* (1888), p. VI.

them, and allows for them, for we are what we are, the poor frail mortals in whom God works in the main His will and way. It is this contrast between what we are, and what God does in us, that fills us with hope and trust in His goodness. You have nothing, my dear Mother, to ask of me, but I have much for which to thank you of edification and co-operation in what regards my past responsibilities. We have been friends in God, and more than friends, which is another subject for gratitude.[121]

From early January 1889 his health deteriorated and he was confined to his rooms at Oscott. During his last weeks, his devoted young secretary Joseph Parker and the vice-president of Oscott, John Caswell, were in constant attendance. The last Mass he was well enough to celebrate himself was on the feast of the diocesan patron, St Chad (2 March). After that, he relied on Parker to celebrate Mass for him in his room. His last attempt at correspondence was a letter of gratitude to Aidan Gasquet at Downside (later cardinal and eminent in the field of pre-Reformation monastic history). Gasquet had sent him volume two of his *Henry VIII and the Monasteries*, which Ullathorne had evidently read keenly and began, characteristically, to comment on in some detail. The letter ended abruptly in mid sentence, and Parker sent it on 13 March, as bid, 'with a last loving blessing' from the dying bishop.[122]

His final decline set in over the weekend of 16/17 March, though he had been strong enough on Thursday 14 March to lecture the doctor on St Thomas, St Augustine, St Athanasius, Plato and his beloved St Catherine of Siena – whose life by Mother Raphael Drane he made the doctor take away to read.[123] By Sunday it was thought serious enough for Mgr Joseph Souter (the president of Oscott) to give him extreme unction. Catholic practice at the time was that this was the last sacrament, only given in danger of imminent death. When he was told it was thought well for him to receive it, he replied, 'Do as you like, I am here to obey orders!'[124] In the afternoon

[121.] Selly Park, Ullathorne to Genevieve Dupuis, 9 December 1888.
[122.] *Downside Review* vol. VIII (1889), Obituary, p. 80.
[123.] Stone G/ULL/VII/20, Caswell to Stone, Thursday 6.15 pm.
[124.] Colwich, extract of a letter from Maryvale, undated.

he received the Blessed Sacrament, but remained conscious, sending blessings to one or another, especially the convents, and joking cheerfully.

The convents were kept in close touch with the dying bishop's last days and hours, for as was natural, they were praying constantly for the protector to whom they owed so much. 'Our thoughts and prayers are with our dear old father all day long, for we feel it is only by our prayers we can now in any way make return for all his loving care of us.'[125] Caswell kept Stone informed of the progress of 'the noble old saint' as he went about 'the business of dying ... patiently awaiting the call of the bridegroom'.[126] The telegraph boy was a constant visitor bringing messages from all over the world, night and day. Even the little maid who cleaned his room was not forgotten. As she crept quietly in to make up the fire and sweep the grate, he called her over to his bedside and said, 'Alice, I have missed you.' She timidly asked his blessing, which he gave, murmuring, 'pray for your old bishop' and remarked: 'This is a funny old world – you will think so when I am gone.'

He told his doctor that his mind was 'perfectly tranquil', but by Tuesday he was declining, his mind wandering at times. It was some time during these last hours that the exchange took place which is (not surprisingly) not recorded anywhere and has been bowdlerised in all previous accounts of Ullathorne, but is deeply rooted in the oral tradition of the Archdiocese of Birmingham. Leo Madigan took the polite version as the title for his edition of Ullathorne's autobiography, *The Devil is a Jackass*, linking it to a reference Ullathorne made in the Australian passages to a local word for a kookaburra – a laughing jackass.[127] Butler vouches for the fact (based on eyewitness accounts) that what was actually said was, 'The devil's an ass!'[128] The Birmingham tradition is somewhat different. Drifting in and out of consciousness, he asked Parker and Caswell if he had made his last confession. 'Yes, Your Grace,' came the reply. 'And have I been anointed?' 'Yes, Your Grace.'

[125]. Ibid.
[126]. Stone G/ULL/VII/17, Caswell to Superior of Stone, 12 March 1889.
[127]. Leo Madigan, *The Devil is a Jackass* (1995).
[128]. Butler, *Life II*, p. 295 (*Downside Review* 1889, Obituary, p. 136).

'And have I received Viaticum?' 'Yes, Your Grace.' Dropping back onto the pillow, he breathed a sigh of relief and muttered, 'Good. In that case, the devil can kiss my a***!'

Between Friday 15 March and his death on Thursday 21 March, Caswell sent brief poignant reports to many people including the Benedictine nuns at Colwich and, of course, the Dominicans at Stone. The brief bulletin on Sunday 17 March at 6.30 pm read: 'Weaker in mind and body during last 48 hours; tho' no signs of immediate dissolution yet. Sends you all his blessing and begs your prayers.'[129] By Tuesday evening the end was near:

A sleepless night, accompanied with severe wracking pains, has produced great prostration so that the doctor found much worse this morning and said the end must be near. The pains have continued all day, and were excessively sharp at 2.15 pm when we thought he was dying – but doses of wine and eau de vie gave a new stimulus to life and His Grace has rallied. But I don't think he can last more than 36 hours: to the dawn of St Benedict's Day. Too ill and mind too feeble to understand all your messages but when a chance comes I will give them. All your good prayers have brought grace to preserve his patience and he is quite ready to meet his God. Excuse the card, so many to send.[130]

Caswell's brief notes tell their own story: 'Wednesday 20 March 6.30 pm: Agony seems to have begun about 3.30 pm. Conscious at intervals. Happy feast to all' [the next day was the Feast of St Benedict]. 'Thursday 21 March 1889: Archbishop Ullathorne died today at 1.17 pm.'[131] Caswell wrote a fuller account of the bishop's last hours a day or two later.

His Grace's agony began, as I told you, at 3.30 pm on Wednesday and lasted till his death at 1.17 pm Thursday afternoon. He was conscious all that time with the excep-

129. Colwich, Caswell to Prioress, 17 March 1889.
130. Colwich, Caswell to Prioress, 19 March 1889.
131. Colwich, Caswell to Prioress, 21 March 1889.

tion of a few intervals. From 3.30 pm Wednesday to 11.30 he was rather restless on account of difficulty breathing and from prostration brought on by the want of food. He had refused nourishment during the morning, owing to difficulty of swallowing. About 11.30 another change for the worse appeared and I said for him the Litany of the Dying, to which he answered as well as he could. He recognised with especial pleasure the names of SS. William, Bernard, Chad, Benedict and Scholastica and gave an unusually loud reply to their invocations. I told him St Benedict's Day was close at hand. He went to sleep just before 12, to awake about five minutes after midnight. He then said, 'St Peter, pray for me; St Paul, pray for me! St Benedict – angels – saints – see'. I said to him, 'St Benedict's Day has just begun: you must go to heaven today. St Benedict will receive you. Do you see him and the angels?' 'Yes, yes,' he quickly answered. We summoned the clergy who remained till 2.00 saying prayers. As the end seemed not very near, they then retired to rise early to say Mass for him.

Fr. Parker said the Mass of St Benedict in the Archbishop's room at 8.00, but His Grace could not receive Holy Communion as he could not swallow. The doctor paid his visit at 9.00 and finding a great change, said that he might die at any moment of suffocation. The clergy were again assembled, together with the professors and divines – and we remained with him till his death. The boys went to the chapel and said rosary. About 12.30 another change passed over him, the breathing became slower, but still he recognised my voice and responded to my questions, and tried to repeat the ejaculations suggested. A few sighs and two spasms showing suffocation and all was over.

When the body was laid out in full pontificals, his face had resumed the usual appearance it had in life. The coffin has just been closed up, though there was no necessity for so doing. I enclose some of his hair which I think you may treasure. He was particularly grateful to Colwich for all its prayers, for I told him what you were doing for him and in his last agony I asked him to send his very last blessing to you all, which he did. May our end be like his.[132]

The last surviving witness of the scene at Oscott on the feast of St Benedict 1889, F. B. McClymont, later became a Benedictine himself. As a young deacon at Oscott, he found himself serving the last Mass in the dying bishop's presence, celebrated by Parker. Recalling the events in 1936, he was conscious that as a young student he had been unaware of the historic moment, or of the greatness of the man he saw passing from life; but he was aware that 'he was dearly loved by those in closest touch with him ... Men with long missionary experience, who had seen much of the ups and downs of life, who had looked death in the face not once but over and over again, now wept like children'.[133] With the black humour which often intrudes in such occasions, he recalled one of the canons present waving goodbye to his dying bishop, as if he was seeing him off on a train at Snow Hill Station![134]

The deceased bishop was vested in episcopal purple and lay in his room until Monday when Mass was celebrated for him in the college chapel and the body removed to St Chad's Cathedral where it lay in state, attended by the black-clad brothers of St Vincent de Paul, holding candles, amidst a further two hundred lighted candles around the black-draped catafalque.[135] The Requiem Mass next day was attended by many of the Catholic gentry and aristocracy, as well as Alderman Barrow, the Mayor of Birmingham, several other aldermen and the Town Clerk and Chairman of the Board of Guardians and his assiduous physician Dr Blunt. About half of the hierarchy were there (though not Manning), the Priors of Downside, Ampleforth and Erdington and some two hundred clergy. The cathedral gallery was packed with nuns from many of the convents.[136] The celebrant at the Mass was Ullathorne's successor as Bishop of Birmingham, Edward Ilsley, but the

---

[132.] Colwich, Caswell to Prioress, 23 March 1889.

[133.] F. B. McClymont OSB, Recollections of Archbishop Ullathorne's Last Days, *The Oscotian*, 1936, p. 266.

[134.] Ibid., p. 267.

[135.] *The Tablet*, 30 March 1889, pp. 502–4.

[136.] Ibid.

preacher was, appropriately, a Benedictine bishop. Bishop John Cuthbert Hedley, who had succeeded Brown as Bishop of Newport, was an Ampleforth monk who had a reputation as a sought-after preacher at Benedictine and episcopal occasions.[137] Like Ullathorne, he was an advocate of the contemplative tradition developed by Augustine Baker, so it was not surprising that he entitled his funeral homily, 'A Spiritual Man'. Hedley, along with Ullathorne, was influential in reviving the practice of contemplative prayer, as taught by Augustine Baker, through an article entitled 'Prayer and Contemplation', published in the *Dublin Review* in October 1876, which combined Baker's English Benedictine monastic spirituality with the pastoral spirituality of St Francis of Sales.[138] The title given by Hedley to the deceased bishop is worth setting in contrast to the popular view of Ullathorne as the bluff, outspoken, busy little Yorkshireman.

Hedley took as his text a passage from Isaiah (11.1–3); 'And the spirit of the Lord shall rest upon him. He shall not judge according to the sight of the eyes nor reprove according to the hearing of the ears. He shall judge with justice, and shall reprove with equity; and faith shall be the girdle of his reins.' Sketching Ullathorne's biography, Hedley made the point strongly that he had probably learnt less from other men than from books, in particular his lifelong devotion to the Fathers, especially St Augustine. However, the key to his life was the spirit of God dwelling in him, 'a mighty spirit, for nothing on earth can quench it ... a sweet spirit, a kind and gentle spirit, for it recognises its creator's loving touch in every man and every created thing'. This 'true spirit, not knowing how to lie, without fiction and without guile, simple and straight', had shaped and directed Ullathorne's long life and ministry. Hedley referred back to the letter Ullathorne had written from Warwick Gaol in 1853, and described it as 'a programme of his life' in which he spoke of God as 'our true place'.[139] As a fellow

---

137. Alban Hood, 'Hedley, John Cuthbert (1837–1915)', *Oxford Dictionary of National Biography*, Oxford University Press, 2004 [http://www.oxforddnb.com/view/article/48462, accessed 14 Sept 2005].

138. Ibid.

139. See Chapter 5.

monk-bishop, Hedley was able to discern what can only be glimpsed by any biographer, the depth of Ullathorne's life of prayer. He had lived 'a retired and unworldly life' in which he had found (or made) ample time for 'ardent, deep and true and lengthened' prayer. As Ullathorne would have wanted, the monk took precedence over the bishop in Hedley's tribute.[140]

After the solemn Requiem Mass on Tuesday, Ullathorne began his final journey, one so familiar to him, to the convent at Stone, for burial. This journey was not by train, but by road. The splendid oak coffin (reputed to weigh three tons) bore a brass cross only, and was carried in a glass hearse drawn by four rather too lively black horses.[141] Leaving St Chad's at 1.30 pm, the hearse was due at Stone by 7.00 in the evening, but did not arrive until 8.45, as the horses had to be pulled up and calmed. It was accompanied in a following coach by the faithful Parker and the bishop's nephew, Fr John Ullathorne. A considerable crowd accompanied the hearse as far as Handsworth, some two or three miles from the cathedral and the local police and brothers of St Vincent de Paul escorted it to the city limits. A few people even ran alongside the hearse for several miles.[142] Despite the late hour and darkness, the procession grew ever more elaborate as it approached Stone, where people walked a mile or two out of the town to greet it, and a hundred and fifty of the young men of the town escorted the cortège through the streets, past houses with windows shuttered as a mark of respect. At the church, the Dominican sisters, who greeted their old father for the final time, escorted him from the door of the church, all fifty of them lining the nave of the church holding candles.

The body was placed on a catafalque before the altar. However, once there, an element of farce entered the proceedings, as the vault prepared for his body was too small and a new one had to be hastily excavated overnight – Bishop Ilsley had also insisted that the position was wrong. In addition to the chaos of workmen, so many wanted to attend what had

[140.] John Cuthbert Hedley OSB, *A Spiritual Man: Funeral homily preached at St Chad's Cathedral*, 25 MArch 1889.
[141.] Stone G/ULL/VII/22, Ilsley to Provincial, 21 March 1889.
[142.] *The Tablet*, 6 April 1889, p. 542.

been intended as a quiet, private ceremony, that catering, and even admission tickets to control numbers, had to be hastily arranged. The church was draped in black silk, and many of the laity who had not been able to get into the cathedral for the Requiem attended this occasion. After the solemn liturgy to receive the body, the clergy and people retired, and the Dominican sisters had their old father to themselves one last time, as they chanted the solemn Office for the Dead and watched in turn by his body overnight before the traditional three Masses were celebrated next morning. Joseph Souter, the president of Oscott, was the celebrant, assisted by Canon Bathurst and Parker and other members of the clergy. Bishop Hedley gave the coffin a final blessing, sprinkling it with holy water once it was placed in the vault.[143] Finally, on 28 March, Ullathorne's grave was sealed, supervised by the local priest and his devoted secretary Joseph Parker, 'crying like children'. At the bishop's own insistence, no flowers were placed on his grave, but only a photograph taken after his death, a crucifix, an image of the blessed Virgin Mary, and just above his head a photograph of his old friend who lay only a few feet away, Mother Margaret.[144]

His estate amounted to a few pieces of furniture and pictures, his books, clothes, gold pocket watch, snuff box, ring and very little else, to a total value of £55. 15s. 0d.[145] By the time his funeral expenses had been paid, along with Dr Blunt's bill, half a year's bed and board at Oscott and sundry smaller accounts, the bishop who had lived a simple and frugal life, with scarcely a pound in his pocket, died in debt to the tune of £27. 8s. 8d.[146]

Parker himself was bereft, and two months later was still catching up on correspondence.

Sad as I was, I had to rush back to work and arrears of

---

143. *The Tablet*, 6 April 1889, p. 542.
144. Stone G/ULL/VII/24i Letter (incomplete) to another sister from Superior, 25 March 1889.
145. BAA B9998ff, Various receipts related to funeral and valuation of personal effects March, April, May 1889.
146. BAA B10050, Parker's account of personal estate of Ullathorne, 30 May 1889.

work, just as though nothing had happened. The great void is not filled and never will be. Some are forgetting him fast enough – but then they never knew him. Even I did not know him as he really was, till the last sickness came. He was not usually credited with being very pious: but the simple fact is that he purposely concealed it. Yet it was actually there. It was quite by accident that I discovered it and then I marvelled. His piety was of a strength and depth that I had never imagined, and the revelation of it was as gratifying as it was surprising. The memory of his life is something for the mind to fall back on at all times for refreshment: his death was a vivid picture that encourages one each time one has need of encouragement. The *living* manner in which – after a long life of principle – he walked into the presence of his judge was his reward and an example for us all. Often have people been vexed with him for what seemed unnecessary delay in giving decisions in a matter of moment. He was merely waiting till he had seen all round and all through the subject, and was certain of the principle on which he ought to act. The grand consequence of this was, that when the end was near, he had not a single misgiving: nothing had to be reconsidered. Not that he had not made mistakes; but they were not his fault. Not a few saw him die and they were all much impressed. The feeling common to all was: may our end be like his! May he rest in peace.[147]

Slipping quietly from the scene, within the year Parker was installed as parish priest of the tiny, rural and historic mission of Woodlane, Yoxall in Staffordshire. Here he spent the remaining forty-six years of his life ministering to the farming folk of Staffordshire, content with his memories of the man he had served so faithfully and discreetly. He is buried outside the church at Yoxall, and still remembered by older parishioners, including two brothers, Edmund and Peter Stonier, the latter of whom is a retired priest of the Archdiocese of Birmingham.

It was those diocesan clergy who, as Hedley said at

---

147. Colwich, Parker to Prioress, 26 May 1889.

Ullathorne's Requiem in St Chad's, 'were nearest to his heart'. Ullathorne's original intention of placing all seminary formation under one roof at Olton and separating it from the unhelpful influences of the lay school at Oscott never came to pass. No further building was carried out at Olton, despite the shortage of space. Ullathorne had remained as anxious about diocesan finances as he had been in the 1850s, but there is considerable evidence that he regarded the seminary building as a 'work in progress' for which funds should be canvassed. He hoped for more legacies like that of Lady Chatterton's £1,000, confident after only a few years of operation that the seminary would need enlarging, 'before very long'.[148] A few years later, he urged on Estcourt that 'we much want an enlargement at St Bernard's, and it will be soon time to think about it'.[149] A gift received in 1880 for the seminary was to go to 'the building fund',[150] and by 1883 he was pressing the case. 'We shall have seriously to think of enlarging the seminary next year. A collection might be made for that object.'[151] The explanation for the lack of development at Olton was a combination of factors: Ullathorne's own declining strength, the loss of Estcourt's judicious financial acumen and Ilsley's growing preoccupation with wider diocesan demands. The matter hung fire throughout the 1880s, and McCave, who had succeeded Ilsley as rector of Olton, was of a mind that the only practical solution was to move the seminary into Oscott. Ullathorne may well have felt that great building projects were not the business of an old man. The next phase of development, he confidently hoped, was in Ilsley's hands. It is conceivable that others, more in touch with diocesan affairs, could see that it was not building which was the problem, but staffing and maintaining two institutions.

Rumours spread quickly, even as far afield as the Channel Islands, of 'great and sweeping changes at Oscott' within a few weeks of his death,[152] and within a month the announcement

---

[148.] BAA B5644, Ullathorne to Estcourt, 12 October 1875.
[149.] BAA B6451, Ullathorne to Estcourt, 1 December 1878.
[150.] BAA B7109, Ullathorne to Estcourt, 10 October 1880.
[151.] BAA B8198, Ullathorne to Estcourt, 3 May 1883.
[152.] BAA B10005, Robert Walker, Guernsey to Vincent Holcroft, 3 April 1889.

was made. Olton would close, the lay school at Oscott would come to an end and the seminary would take over the entire college. Parker was confident that Ullathorne had picked up no inkling of this before his death, but perhaps no other decision so clearly and swiftly spelt out the end of an era. Yet, in one sense, it was the success of Ullathorne's constant endeavours and fundraising towards providing the diocese with the clergy it so desperately needed that made this decision inevitable. Oscott could house the growing numbers of students for the priesthood which had resulted from his efforts and Olton could not. It was not accidental that his last pastoral letter as Bishop of the Diocese, issued in March 1888, took exactly the same subject and almost repeated the same words as that of April 1850 – the needs of the Ecclesiastical Education Fund.

> All charities are provided for in this charity; for it is the clergy who look after the poor in their necessities, who comfort the afflicted, who look after the education of children, who instruct the ignorant, administer the sacraments, visit the sick and strengthen and console the dying.[153]

John Caswell, who had been a student, professor and vice-rector at Oscott since 1862 (with only a short break at Cotton 1883–5) and who was present with Parker as Ullathorne died, keeping his beloved nuns informed of events, had long been the college annalist. His last act before leaving Oscott for good was to set down 'the saddest day in the college record' when the decision was taken to close the school, and he inscribed in the college record book on 30 July 1889, 'Here endeth the record of St Mary's College, Oscott. RIP'.[154] There is a strong sense in his own affectionate obituaries of 1917,[155] that Caswell had continued to keep alive the spirit of an older Oscott among the surviving alumni, but the death of Ullathorne truly meant dramatic and irrevocable change for Oscott and Olton.

[153.] Pastoral Letter, 4 March 1888.
[154.] OCA College Record Book.
[155.] *The Oscotian*, 1918, pp. 1–29.

It seemed that Ullathorne's great project had failed, yet the ideal of seminary formation he had tried to create at Olton was translated into Oscott as the fashionable aristocratic carriages pulled away from its gates for the last time. Staff were transferred from Olton, including Henry Parkinson, one of the first group of Olton-trained priests, who had imbibed much of Ullathorne's vision for the seminary, including the inspiration drawn from Bartholomew Holzhauser. As rector of Oscott in years to come, he organised a collaborative project among a group of students with linguistic ability to translate Gaduel's French life of Holzhauser into English. The manuscript was completed in 1895–6, and obviously used for reading in the refectory, but never published.[156] The spirit of Olton was grafted onto Oscott and Ullathorne's determination to create a Tridentine diocesan seminary bore fruit.

Ullathorne was the last of the old vicars apostolic to die, and thus the last link with an older, simpler world, and he was also by many years the last survivor of the original hierarchy of 1850. His *Tablet* obituary described him as 'almost the last link that bound the present vigorous, wealthy and powerful Catholic body to the few who had lingered on scattered throughout the land, keeping the light of faith undimmed, from the days of persecution and the penal laws'.[157] Within three years of his death, Newman and Manning went to their reward, so the era of the great and dominant ecclesiastical leaders of the English Catholic revival was over. The decade after his death saw the publication of *Lux Mundi* within the Church of England, which eventually reconciled many of the biblical conflicts aroused by Darwin and *Essays and Reviews*; the beginnings of Modernism; the condemnation of Anglican Orders by Leo XIII which set the tone of ecumenical relations for half a century; and the granting of permission to lay Catholics to take degrees at British universities, which revolutionised English Catholic social and intellectual life. Ironically, it was Hedley, Ullathorne's friend and fellow Benedictine, who had preached eloquently at his funeral, who was the moving spirit in the advancement towards university education. He

---

[156.] OCA, MS translation of Bartholomew Holzhauser.
[157.] *The Tablet*, 30 March 1889, pp. 502–4.

was one of the new type of bishop which Ullathorne had predicted would be needed, and he was determined to engage with the modern world. Closely involved in the higher education debate, he 'understood above all, the needs of education. He could grapple with the spirit of the age. Hence he was found the fittest to be chosen in 1896 as President of the Catholic University Board.'[158] Despite the opposition of Cardinal Manning, Hedley advocated that Catholics be permitted to attend the ancient universities of Oxford and Cambridge; his efforts led to the ban's being lifted by Pope Leo XIII in 1895.

Ullathorne had been right when he said that a new type of bishop would be needed for changed circumstances. Kester Aspden, in writing of the next generations of English bishops, reiterated the commonly-held view that with the exceptions of Manning and Bagshawe, 'interest among the [nineteenth-century] bishops in social and political questions was slight'.[159] He perpetuated the view that it was the bishops of the generation after Ullathorne and Manning who 'to varying degrees recognised the urgency of the social question'.[160] This assessment does Ullathorne, at least, less than justice. He was no politician, but he was committed to achieving change in some of the great areas of social concern, including education, prison reform and the effects of alcohol. Politically, Ullathorne kept government at arm's length, and like many Catholics of his generation is perhaps best described as an old-fashioned Tory. However, he was no less unreliable as a political ally than Dermot Quinn found the mass of Catholic voters to be.[161] Ullathorne fitted the model proposed by Jeffrey von Arx, of a Catholic leadership geared towards engaging 'Roman Catholics in British politics, but not as a group apart from or over against existing politics. Rather their object was to encourage Roman

[158.] Alban Hood, 'Hedley, John Cuthbert (1837–1915)', *Oxford Dictionary of National Biography*, Oxford University Press, 2004 [http://www.oxforddnb.com/view/article/48462, accessed 14 Sept 2005].

[159.] Kester Aspden, *Fortress Church: the English Roman Catholic Bishops and Politics 1903–63* (2002), p. 8.

[160.] Ibid., p. 9.

[161.] Dermot Quinn, *Patronage and Politics*, pp. 161–3.

Catholics to become directly involved in democratic political
life through the existing parties.'[162] Ullathorne's concerns were
for those suffering from poverty, drunkenness and imprisonment, and not only from a charitable perspective; he was
concerned to see moral change and to see Catholic values
inculcated. This was one of the great achievements of the active
women religious, especially through their schools. He saw the
need for a new style of bishop, and the generation of men
shaped and influenced by him such as Henry Parkinson[163] and
William Barry[164] (neither of whom became bishops) were the
leading lights in the emergent Catholic social movement.

It was suggested in Chapter 2 that 'three key themes emerge
from Ullathorne's career in the Antipodes which shaped his
future approach to life: the absolute certainty that true religious and social freedom could only be achieved within a
framework of order and authority; the capacity he developed
for understanding human nature and dealing with men and
women; the social conscience which was shaped by his dealings
with convicts and alcoholics'. Much has been made in the past
of his role as an ecclesiastical organiser, bringing order and
authority to bear in the English Church, and he has been type-
cast as the blunt, straight-talking Yorkshireman, all too ready
to put others right, including Newman, Wiseman and
Manning. That is certainly part of the picture, but a limited
one, which leaves out the sheer humanity of Ullathorne and his
deep concern for those in his care. Such a view also does scant
justice to the monk. What he described in 1875 as the
Benedictine spirit of largeness and freedom characterised his
approach to life, balanced by the need for stability and order.
Within a clear framework (i.e. within the life and teaching of
the Church) that spirit could breathe. His understanding of
human nature and his social conscience flowed from this spirit
and from his constant insistence on the presence of God in
each individual, an emphasis he had learnt, in part, from
Margaret Hallahan. 'The man that seemed to some so unap-

[162.] J. Von Arx, 'Catholics and Politics' in M. Hodgetts and V. A.
McClelland (eds), *Out of the Flaminian Gate* (2000), p. 249.

[163.] *The Oscotian*, 1924, pp. 159–202.

[164.] Sheridan Gilley, 'William Barry: Priest and Novelist' in *Recusant
History* vol. 24 (1999), pp. 523–51.

proachable, that some deemed stern and uncompromising, had in him a depth of sympathy that those who experienced it can speak of with eloquence.'[165]

His greatness went beyond the evident achievements in establishing order in Australia, shaping the English hierarchy, influencing the first Vatican Council and overseeing the growth of a huge diocese. His human, pastoral and spiritual wisdom went a long way in enabling other people to flourish. It was rooted in monasticism, in the freedom and largeness of heart which he absorbed from St Benedict, and which he shared with those around him. He was a great enabler of others: Polding, Newman, Margaret Hallahan, Genevieve Dupuis, Estcourt, Northcote, Ilsley and even, at times, Manning. This went beyond the practical common sense with which he has been credited, and reflects a greater sense of vision. Firstly his parents, and then his monastic superiors, and ultimately Pope Gregory XVI had taken a chance on him, and allowed him to take responsibility and leadership at a young age, and he was never afraid to place similar trust in others. Ullathorne had a reputation as a pompous, arrogant person (Mgr Ego Solus), who sought episcopal office and relished it. His manner must have conveyed some of this; the man behind the public persona was reluctant to hold office, but once given it, was prepared to exercise it. In this, he understood and lived out a kind of humility which does not gain recognition – that of the instrument of God's will. 'It is this contrast between what we are, and what God does in us, that fills us with hope and trust in His goodness', as he told Genevieve Dupuis at the end of his long life.

He was a prolific speaker and writer, often outspoken where he believed necessary, and determined to use his pen in support of his pastoral vision. He was no theologian, but well read in the teaching of the Church. The three great treatises into which he poured years of spare time and energy (*The Endowments of Man, The Groundwork of Christian Virtues* and *Christian Patience*) are not the things for which he should mainly be remembered, impressive though they are in weight of learning and authority. Even the otherwise admiring

165. *Downside Review* vol. VIII (1889), *Obituary*, p. 79.

reviewer of Butler's *Life* in the *Downside Review* was forced himself to admit that, 'It is, I am afraid, undeniable that these truly great books are not easy to read. The matter is too closely packed, and there is a certain unconsciously pedantic heaviness about the manner which increases their intrinsic difficulty.'[166] His Downside obituarist in 1889 was even more polite, describing them as 'works that need careful and patient reading', but he readily acknowledged, as is clear in the preceding pages of this biography, that it is the 'innumerable letters' which reveal the interior spirit.[167]

It is obvious that Ullathorne has been overshadowed by his contemporaries, in the recounting and interpreting of the history of nineteenth-century Catholicism. This does not do him justice. He was at the heart of English Catholic life for over half a century, and was a foundational figure in Australian Catholic history. Why has he been neglected? Ullathorne has been treated by historians (apart from Butler) through the prism of other men's lives, mainly Newman, Wiseman and Manning, all of whom have received far more biographical and historical attention. He has stood, historically, in their shadow and, while acknowledged as significant, has never received due attention. He was, of course, the cardinal who never was. On two occasions, in 1850 and in 1865, he was widely expected to be nominated to Westminster. In 1850 this would only have happened if Wiseman had been recalled to Rome, so was more speculative, but as the architect of the new hierarchy, it was recognised by many as an obvious move. In 1865 he had support in Rome and among some English Catholics and other bishops, but not in Westminster or Whitehall. The reasons for his historical back seat are related to the fact that he was, in his lifetime, seen as somewhat difficult and an awkward customer. The caricature of the blunt, outspoken, snuff-taking Yorkshireman, who dropped his h's and stood firmly on a rather rigid set of self-imposed principles was well established in his lifetime. Few, if any, of his contemporaries saw the rounded personality, and that was, in part, because he kept it

---

[166.] Algar Thorold, 'Ullathorne the Man' in *Downside Review* XLIV (1926), p. 143.
[167.] *Downside Review* VIII (1889), Obituary, p. 79.

carefully guarded. He was an intensely private man behind the persona of the public figure who believed that the episcopate was a duty placed on him by God, which he fulfilled reluctantly. Duty, and a strong sense of what a bishop should be, drove him into the field of public affairs, when his heart was more at home in the monastery, the seminary or the convent. He was by nature eremitical, and shunned company, which enabled his contemporaries to settle for the 'first impression' gained on brief acquaintance. The hermit was a part of his makeup – Robinson Crusoe was never too far away. When he died it was commented that 'though he was such a public man, few were less known to the world'.[168] Most people since have settled for the caricature.

The first post mortem impression conveyed in *The Tablet* obituary also offers a partial explanation. By the time of his death, Ullathorne was something of a relic; he was venerated as the grand old man of English Catholic life, and a remarkable link with its earlier history, but, however tactfully and delicately put, it was obvious that he was an irrelevance to the different world of the late nineteenth century. The obituarist had to acknowledge that to the rising generation of clergy and laity, Ullathorne's long years of retirement had rendered him 'hardly more, perhaps than a venerable name ... Not mixing in society and rarely seen in London, Dr Ullathorne took no pains to keep the world in mind of him. He lived a retired, and towards the end a somewhat lonely life. He was, before all things, a man of the cloister and the library.' While his massive achievements were acknowledged, it was clear that to a young (anonymous) writer of the last decade of the century, Ullathorne was a curiosity. The tone of the obituary, while unfailingly respectful, nevertheless spoke of his 'downright, abrupt manner' and even his 'frank eccentricity' as well as his learning and his personal kindness. This was a description of a revered dinosaur.

He was a link between the days of declining persecution and the age of School Boards. It was this, indeed, that lent a charm to the venerable figure and benignant,

[168.] Ibid.

thoughtful countenance of Bishop Ullathorne. He was a memory from the past in so many ways; his speech and bearing, his bent in devotions, his spirit of retirement, his love of books, his quaint unworldly fashions might all, or nearly all, be traced to the influence of a world which knew nothing of steamboats or telegraphs ... The Archbishop was a picturesque figure with a history of his own, as various as it was curious; and now its parts fall into a whole, not unromantic to look upon. By turns a sailor, a monk and a missionary; then a bishop and an ecclesiastical writer; a great traveller and a recluse; remarkable once for exceeding youthfulness of mien, but for long years the very embodiment of age; and throughout the most pronounced individuality, full of odd and striking traits, William Bernard Ullathorne, whatever else he was, had little in him of the average or the commonplace.[169]

This first impression has been perpetuated in all historical discussion of him. Butler's *Life*, augmented by the same author's Vatican Council book, is very much that of the public ecclesiastical figure; although written from a monastic perspective, it is bland in its discussion of his relationship with the EBC and his understanding of monasticism. It ignores virtually entirely (with the exception of some passages on Margaret Hallahan) his work with the women religious, and inevitably relies heavily on Ullathorne's own account of the first half of his life. Ullathorne's real concerns do not emerge clearly – his love of people and care for their needs, counterbalanced by a natural solitariness and his struggle to achieve in himself as much as others, humility and patience. Hedley suggested, in his funeral homily, that Ullathorne had learned more from books than from other men, and this is certainly true. He kept others at arm's length and worked out problems for himself, rather than in consultation, and this has shaped the way in which he has been perceived before and after death. His self-contained manner gave an impression of arrogance and self sufficiency, and there are glimpses throughout life that he was

169. *The Tablet*, 23 March 1889, p. 442.

aware of this and struggled to overcome his 'damnable pride'. What is also true is that it was more likely to be his close female collaborators who broke through the carapace and drew out of him human and spiritual depths. Without an appreciation of this, only half of Ullathorne is visible.

Collins called Ullathorne 'the pivotal figure of the period of foundation' [of the Catholic Church in Australia], but he has been equally neglected by historians of Australian Catholicism.[170] Collins mentions the works of T. L. Suttor, *Hierarchy and Democracy in Australia 1788–1870* (1965) and James Waldersee, *Catholic Society in New South Wales 1788–1860* (1974) as beginning to give more credit to Ullathorne for what he achieved in Australia, but Collins' own work is the solitary attempt to give Ullathorne his true place in Australian Catholic historiography. He suggested that part of the problem lay in the Australian historiographical debate between those who emphasise the role of the Benedictines and those who stress the pioneering work of Irish missioners. Irish writers have dismissed him as opposed to Therry, Benedictine apologists as opposed to Polding, and so he has appeared as a peripheral figure. The emphasis on missionary heroes, as opposed to necessary organisation and structures, and Ullathorne's unfortunate manner as a young man, have perhaps made him unattractive to other Australian writers.[171]

Ullathorne's own autobiography is a unique and invaluable source, but one to be treated with care. An uncritical reading of it can perpetuate the image of a man inordinately proud of his achievements, and determined to let people know of his role in great events. In fact, of course, Ullathorne never intended the text for publication. It is a memoir rather than an autobiography, setting down for the nuns at Stone his own recollections of events, and coloured by stories and anecdotes. Even when persuaded to revise and correct it late in life, he resisted the suggestion that he should continue the story beyond 1850, and two thirds of it is devoted to his early life and Australia. The first manuscript was compiled just before Margaret Hallahan's death in 1868, and at her instigation. Francis Raphael Drane

---

[170.] Collins thesis, p. 6.
[171.] Collins thesis, pp. 402–4.

urged the revision and continuation in the 1880s, perhaps with a view to publication, as she later did, alongside a volume of edited letters. Too many people were still alive in the 1880s, including Newman and Manning, for Ullathorne to complete the story, or was it rather that the years spent in Birmingham were not the stuff of memoirs? In his view, were they simply years of striving to do the job he had been called to, against his own desires and inclinations? These years, therefore, were years of duty and responsibility, which weighed heavily, years of complex cross-currents between ecclesiastical and political affairs which he found difficult to unravel. Instead, he wrote and published as occasion demanded, on religious matters and public affairs, to meet pastoral needs.

Throughout his long and unusual life, the sea and the natural world were enormously influential in shaping Ullathorne's view of the world. He saw and experienced at close quarters the splendour, beauty and power of God's creation on a scale far beyond that of most of his contemporaries. The language of the sea constantly punctuated his writing, and he was deeply conscious of the smallness of humanity in the face of the greatness and power of God, 'the one great metaphysician, who creates and illuminates all spirits ... the sublime architect of the universe, and the artist of all the beauty that is seen in the world, drawing all its colours from the one simple element of His created light'.[172] This had been revealed to him in the balmy Mediterranean, the Baltic lands of midnight sun, and the towering seas of the south Atlantic and Pacific. On the title page of this book is a quotation from Daniel Defoe's *Robinson Crusoe*, a favourite book of Ullathorne's, which first stirred his passion for the sea and his romantic sensibilities. While marooned on his island, Crusoe undergoes a religious conversion which inspires him to a regular life of prayer and devotion and frequent reading of the Bible. The narrative indicates that this was a major factor in Crusoe retaining a measure of psychological stability, and directed his life after his rescue and return home. He hoped that anyone reading his story would be drawn to recognise that '... whenever they come to a true sense of things, they will find

---

[172.] *The Endowments of Man*, p. 87.

deliverance from sin a much greater blessing than deliverance from affliction ...'[173] Ullathorne's youthful romantic religious conversion of heart to a 'true sense of things' was not unlike Crusoe's, which mellowed into a deep and abiding faith in God and the driving power in his life.

As he entered his old age and infirmity, he commented to a friend planning a new biography of St Charles Borromeo, that 'Guissano's life of St Charles must always be the basis of any other life. When I received the mitre, I learned more from it of a bishop's work than from any other book.'[174] The biography to which he refers, by Giovanni Pietro Giussano, was written in 1610, and not translated into English until 1884. That edition, to mark the third centenary of Borromeo's death, carried a preface by Manning. What he said of the great Tridentine bishop could equally be applied to Ullathorne.

> The character of St Charles will be best understood by reading his life. He was not a great theologian, or a great orator, or a great statesman. But he was a great pastor, a ruler, a lawgiver, a guide and a judge in the church of God. No man was more in the world, and less of the world.[175]

Perhaps, though, the final word on this different kind of monk should go to a fellow Benedictine:

> He was never small, nor mean, nor selfish. Those who came into contact with him felt that they had met a real man, rooted and founded in unmistakable solid earth – a man who might rebuff you, but would never pass you false coin ... Whatever monument we build to his memory, his soul lives on for ever, and his name will be cherished by his children's children for many a generation yet to come.[176]

[173.] Daniel Defoe, *Robinson Crusoe*, Penguin paperback, p. 111.
[174.] College Irlandais Paris, Ullathorne to Kathleen O'Meara, 9 January 1878.
[175.] G. P. Giussano, *Life of St Charles Borromeo* (English edition 1884). Preface by H. E. Manning, pp. xxii–xxiii.
[176.] John Cuthbert Hedley OSB, *A Spiritual Man: Funeral homily preached at St Chad's Cathedral*, 26 March 1889.

Bibliography

Ullathorne's Published Writings

§ indicates citation or quotation within text of book.

Autobiography: Various editions exist of Ullathorne's autobiography. For ease of reference, the edition used here is Leo Madigan, *The Devil is a Jackass* (Gracewing, Herefordshire, 1995).§

1833
A few words to the Rev H. Fulton and his readers, with a glance at the Archdeacon.

1834
Observations on the Use and Abuse of Sacred Scriptures as exhibited in the Discipline and Practice of the Protestant and Catholic Communions.§

1834
Sermon against drunkenness, preached to the Catholics of diverse parts of New South Wales, (Sydney).§

1835
A Reply to Judge Barton, on the State of Religion in the Colony.

1836
The ceremony of blessing and laying the foundation stone of a new church, (Sydney).

1837
The Catholic Mission in Australasia.§

1837
The Horrors of Transportation briefly unfolded to the people, (Dublin).§

1837
Report to the Holy See on the Mission to Australia, (Rome).

1842
Sermons with Prefaces (dedicated to Polding).§
1 *The Penitent.*
2 *The Love of God.*
3 *The Drunkard.*
4 *The Evil Tongue.*
5 *The Sinner's Delay.*
6 *A Christmas Sermon.*
7 *The Profession of a Sister of Charity.*
8 *The Ceremony of blessing and Laying the Foundation Stone of a new church.*

1843
The Blessing of the Calvary on the Grace Dieu Rocks.§

1848
Funeral Oration for the Rev William Richmond at Brewood.§

1850
Remarks on the Proposed Education Bill.§

1850
The Office of Bishop, delivered at the thanksgiving for the Restoration of the Hierarchy.§

1851
A Plea for the Rights and Liberties of Religious Women, with reference to the Bill proposed by Mr Lacy.§

1853
A Discourse delivered to the clergy at the conclusion of the diocesan synod.§

1854
The Holy Mountain of La Salette: a pilgrimage of the year 1854.§

1854
A letter to Lord Edward Howard on the proposed Committee of Enquiry into Religious Communities.§

1855
The Immaculate Conception; an exposition§ (Art and Book Co., London).

1855
Discourse delivered at the opening session of the Second Provincial Synod.§

1856
A Pilgrimage to the proto-monastery of Subiaco and the Grotto of St Benedict.§

1857
Notes on the Education Question.§

1858
Letters on La Salette.§

1860
Discourse delivered at St Mary's Priory, Princethorpe.

1860
Speech on the question of the Pontifical States.§

1862
A Letter on the Rambler and Home and Foreign Review: to the clergy of Birmingham.§

1862
Discourse preached at the funeral of Councillor Maher.§

1863

*On Certain Methods of The Rambler and Home and Foreign Review:
a second letter to the clergy of Birmingham.*§

1864

A discourse delivered to the clergy at the diocesan synod.§

1864

*A letter on the Association for Promoting the Unity of Christendom,
addressed to the clergy of Birmingham.*§

1865

A Sermon delivered at the Requiem of the Very Rev T. Flanagan.§

1865

*The Anglican Theory of Union, as maintained in the 'Appeal to Rome'
and Dr Pusey's 'Eirenicon'. A second letter to the clergy of
Birmingham.*§

1866

On the Management of Criminals.§

1866

*The Rock of the Church: a discourse delivered at the dedication of St
Peter's Church, Belfast.*§

1867

*The Confessional: a discourse delivered in the Catholic Churches of
Walsall.*§

1867

Address presented to Bishop Ullathorne and His Lordship's reply.§

1867

*Sermon preached at St Mary's Abbey, Oulton at the Jubilee of the
Abbess.*

1868

Three Lectures on Conventual Life.§

1869
A Pastoral Letter on Fenianism.§

1869
An Instruction for the Superioresses and Communities of Religious Women.§

1869
Catholic Education: an address in Birmingham Town Hall.§

1871
The Restoration of the Hierarchy.§

1874
A memorial of gratitude from four Benedictine Jubilarians.§

1874
The Dollingerites, Mr Gladstone and the Apostates from the Faith: a letter to the Catholics of the diocese.§

1875
Discourse delivered at the Diocesan Synod.§

1875
Mr Gladstone's Expostulation Unravelled.§

1875
Discourse delivered at the Diocesan Synod.

1875
Sermon on All Monks.§

1876
The Prussian Persecution: a pastoral letter.

1876
Ecclesiastical Discourses delivered on Special Occasions (collected sermons).

1878
Discourse delivered at the Requiem for Pius IX at St Chad's.§

1880
The Endowments of Man§ (Burns Oates, London).

1880
Church Music: a discourse given in St Chad's Cathedral on the half jubilee of its choir.§

1881
A Circular Letter of thanks for Masses and Prayers on Golden Jubilee of Priesthood.

1882
Groundwork of Christian Virtues§ (Burns Oates, London).

1884
Circular Letter to clergy on the death of Canon Estcourt.§

1886
Christian Patience§ (Burns Oates, London).

1887
Memoir of Bishop Willson§ (Burns Oates, London).

1888
Reply to the address of the clergy on his retirement.§

Archive Collections

Abbreviations as in text:
AAW: Archives of the Archbishop of Westminster
AAS: Archives of the Archdiocese of Southwark
Ampleforth: Ampleforth Abbey Archives (OSB) Ullathorne Papers and Copies of Letters to Thomas Brown
BAA: Birmingham Archdiocesan Archives (B Series)
Birmingham Oratory
Cardiff: Archives of the Archdiocese of Cardiff: papers of Bishop Thomas Brown, held at the National Library of Wales

CDA: Clifton Diocesan Archives

College Irlandais, Paris: Letters of Ullathorne to Kathleen O'Meara, partially transcribed by EBC archivists

Colwich: Archives of St Mary's Abbey, Colwich (OSB) Ullathorne Papers

DA: Downside Abbey Archives Morris Papers and Birt Collection

Dublin Archdiocesan Archives

Farm St: Archives of the British Province of the Society of Jesus (Letters of Bishops and Cardinals 1840–91)

Handsworth: Archives of the Sisters of Mercy at St Mary's Convent, Handsworth, Letters to the Community 1842–88

Leeds Diocesan Archives Briggs Correspondence

NSWSA: New South Wales State Archives (Copies provided by Paul Collins)

OCA: Oscott College Archives (at BAA)

Propaganda Fide: Archives of the Congregation of Propaganda Fide, Rome, Scritture Riferite dei Congressi Anglia 12, (T6 Oceania 1858–60, 602–805 Copies provided by Paul Collins)

SAA: Sydney Archdiocesan Archives (Copies provided by Paul Collins)

SCA: Sisters of Charity Archives, Australia

Selly Park: Archives of the Sisters of Charity of St Paul Letters from Bishop Ullathorne to Genevieve Dupuis 1849–88 Box 4 68/B400

Stanbrook: Archives of Stanbrook Abbey Ullathorne Papers Box 8

Stone: Third Order Dominican Provincial Archives, Ullathorne Papers G/ULL/I-VII

Ushaw: Archives of Ushaw College, Durham

VEC: Archives of the Venerable English College, Rome Talbot Papers

Books

Peter Athanasius Allanson, *Biographies of English Benedictines* (Ampleforth Abbey, 1999).

Peter Athanasius Allanson, *A History of the English Benedictine Congregation* 1619–1856 (Ampleforth Abbey, 1999).

J. Altholz, *The Liberal Catholic Movement in England* (Burns Oates, London, 1962).

Anstruther: Godfrey Anstruther OP, *The Seminary Priests* vol. IV (Mayhew McCrimmon, Great Wakering, 1977).

Walter L. Arnstein, *Protestant versus Catholic in mid-Victorian England: Mr Newdegate and the Nuns* (University of Minnesota Press, Columbia and London, 1982).

Kester Aspden, *Fortress Church: the English Roman Catholic Bishops and Politics 1903–63* (Gracewing, Herefordshire, 2002).

Colin Barr, *Paul Cullen, John Henry Newman, and the Catholic University of Ireland 1845–65* (University of Notre Dame Press, Notre Dame Indiana, 2003).

William Barry, *Memories and Opinions* (Putnams, London and New York, 1926).

David Bebbington, *Evangelicalism in Modern Britain* (Unwin Hyman, London, 1989).

David Bebbington, *The Mind of Gladstone: Religion, Homer and Politics* (Oxford University Press, Oxford and London, 2004).

Margaret Belcher, *The Collected Letters of A. W. N. Pugin vol. II* (Oxford University Press, Oxford and London, 2003).

D. A. Bellenger, *The French Exiled Clergy in the British Isles after 1789* (Downside Abbey, 1986).

D. A. Bellenger, *William Bernard Ullathorne* (Archdiocese of Birmingham Historical Commission 2001).

Mark Bence-Jones, *The Catholic Families* (Constable, London, 1992).

Geoffrey Best, *Mid-Victorian Britain 1851–75* (Schoken, New York, 1972).

Birt, Pioneers: Henry Norbert Birt, *Benedictine Pioneers in Australia* 2 vols (Herbert and Daniel, London, 1911).

Noel Blakiston (ed.) *The Roman Question: extracts from the despatches of Odo Russell from Rome 1858–70* (Chapman and Hall, London, 1962).

Evelyn Bolster, *The Sisters of Mercy in the Crimean War* (Mercer Press, Cork, 1964).

John Bossy, *The English Catholic Community 1570–1850* (Darton Longman and Todd, London, 1975).

Michael Bourdeaux, *Land of Crosses: the struggle for religious freedom in Lithuania 1939–78* (Augustine Publishing company, Devon, 1979).

H. R. T. Brandreth, *Dr Lee of Lambeth* (SPCK, London, 1951).

W. Buscot, *The History of Cotton College* (Burns Oates, London, 1940).

Butler, *Life:* Cuthbert Butler, *Life and Times of Bishop Ullathorne 1806–1889* 2 vols (Burns Oates, London, 1926).

Butler, *Vatican Council:* Cuthbert Butler, *The Vatican Council 1869–70* 2 vols (Longmans, London, 1930).

Owen Chadwick, *The Victorian Church,* 2 vols (A&C Black, London, 1966/1970).

Owen Chadwick, *A History of the Popes 1830–1914* (Oxford University Press, Oxford and London, 1998).

Judith Champ, *Oscott* (Archdiocese of Birmingham Historical Commission, 1987).

Judith Champ (ed.), *Oscott College 1838–1988: a volume of commemorative essays* (Oscott College, 1988).

Judith Champ, *The English Pilgrimage to Rome: a dwelling for the soul* (Gracewing, Herefordshire, 2000).

Judith Champ, *A Temple of Living Stones: the Chapel of St Mary's College, Oscott* (Oscott College, 2002).

C. M. H. Clark, *A History of Australia* vol. II (Melbourne University Press and Cambridge University Press, 1968).

Michael Clifton, *The Quiet Negotiator: Bishop Grant of Southwark* (Archdiocese of Southwark, 1993).

Paul Collins, *Hell's Gates: The Terrible Journey of Alexander Pierce* (Hardie Grant Books, Victoria, 2002).

Anne E. Cunningham, *Genevieve Dupuis (1813–1903)* (Selly Park, 1984).

Daniel Defoe, *Robinson Crusoe* (1719), Penguin paperback.

Edward Heneage Dering, *Memoir of Georgiana, Lady Chatterton* (Hurst and Blackett, London, 1878).

Brian Doolan, *The Pugins and the Hardmans* (Archdiocese of Birmingham Historical Commission, 2004).

Drane, *Life*: Francis Raphael Drane, *Life of Mother Margaret Hallahan: foundress of the English Congregation of St Catherine of Siena* (1869) (Longmans, London, 1929 ed.).

Letters: Francis Raphael Drane (ed.), *Letters of Archbishop Ullathorne* (Burns Oates, London, 1892).

Ian Duffield and James Bradley (eds), *Representing Convicts: new perspectives on convict forced labour migration* (Leicester University Press, 1997).

Robert Eaton, *The Benedictines of Colwich 1829–1929* (Sands and Co., London and Edinburgh, 1929).

David Edwards, *Christian England* (vol. III) *from the eighteenth century to the first world war* (Collins, London 1984).

Francis Edwards, *The Jesuits in England from 1580 to the present day* (Burns Oates, London, 1985).

Barbara English, *The Great Landowners of East Yorkshire 1530–1910* (Harvester Wheatsheaf, Hemel Hempstead, 1990).

D. H. Farmer, *Benedict's Disciples* (Fowler Wright, Leominster 1980).

C. Fitzgerald Lombard, *English and Welsh Clergy 1801–1914* (Downside Abbey, 1993).

Radegund Flaxman, *A Woman Styled Bold; the life of Cornelia Connolly 1809–1879* (Darton Longman and Todd, London, 1991).

V. A. C. Gattrell, *The Hanging Tree: execution and the English People 1770–1868* (Oxford University Press, Oxford and London, 1994).

Sheridan Gilley, *Newman and his Age* (Darton Longman and Todd, London, 1990).

Ruth Gilpin Wells, *A Woman of her Time and Ours: Mary Magdalen Taylor SMG* (Laney Smith, Charlotte N Carolina, 1988).

G. P. Giussano, *Life of St Charles Borromeo* (English edition Burns Oates, London, 1884), Preface by H. E. Manning.

M. Glancey, *Characteristics of the Writings of Archbishop Ullathorne* (Burns Oates, London, 1888).

C. Gobinet, *The Instruction of Christian Youth in Christian Piety* (Edward Walker, Newcastle upon Tyne, seventh edition, 1809).

Patrick Granfield, *The Limits of the Papacy; authority and autonomy in the Church* (Darton Longman and Todd, London, 1987).

Robert Gray, *Cardinal Manning: a biography* (Weidenfeld, London, 1985).

John Greenaway, *Drink and British Politics since 1830: a study in policy making* (Palgrave Macmillan, Basingstoke, 2003).

A. Haig, *The Victorian Clergy* (Croom Helm, London and Sydney, 1984).

M. Haile and E. Bonney, *Life and Letters of John Lingard*

1771–1851 (Simpkin and Marshall, London, 1911).

Ruth Harris, *Lourdes: Body and Spirit in the Secular Age* (Allen Lane, London, 1999).

Brian Harrison, *Drink and the Victorians: the temperance question in England 1815–72* (Faber & Faber, London, 1971).

J. Hickey, *Urban Catholics* (Catholic Book Club, London, 1967).

M. Hodgetts and V. A. McClelland (eds), *Out of the Flaminian Gate* (Darton Longman and Todd, London, 2000).

Eric Hopkins, *The Rise of the Manufacturing Town: Birmingham and the Industrial Revolution* (Sutton, Stroud, 1989).

R. W. Hoyle, *The Pilgrimage of Grace and the Politics of the 1530s* (Oxford University Press, Oxford and London, 2001).

Mgr Hudson, *Mother Genevieve Dupuis, foundress of the English congregation of the Sisters of Charity of St Paul the Apostle* (Sheed and Ward, London, 1929).

Robert Hughes, *The Fatal Shore: a history of the Transportation of Convicts to Australia 1787–1868* (Collins, London, 1988 pb. edn.).

F. C. Husenbeth, *Life of Bishop John Milner* (James Duffy, Dublin and London, 1852).

H. Jedin, *History of the Church* vol. VIII, *the Church in the Age of Liberalism* (Burns & Oates, London, 1981).

B. L. Kentish, *The Chronicles of an Ancient Yorkshire Family* (private publication, 1963).

L. H. Lees, *Exiles of Erin: Irish Migrants in Victorian London* (Manchester University Press, Manchester and London, 1979).

K. T. Livingstone, *The Emergence of an Australian Catholic Priesthood 1835–1915* (Australia, 1977).

Donald M. MacRaild, *Irish Migrants in Modern Britain 1750–1922* (Macmillan, Basingstoke, 1999).

V. A. McClelland, *English Roman Catholics and Higher Education 1830–1903* (Oxford University Press, Oxford and London, 1973).

V. A. McClelland, *Cardinal Manning: his public life and influence 1865–92* (Oxford University Press, Oxford and London, 1962).

Mary McInally, *Edward Ilsley, Archbishop of Birmingham* (Burns Oates, London, 2002).

G. I. T. Machin, *Politics and the Churches 1869–1921* (Clarendon

Press, Oxford, 1987).

M. de Marsollier, *St Francis of Sales, Bishop and Prince of Geneva*, W. H. Coombes (tr.), (Keating and Brown, Shepton Mallett, 1812).

David Milburn, *A History of Ushaw College* (Ushaw College, 1964).

Norval Morris, *Maconochie's Gentlemen: the story of Norfolk Island* (Oxford University Press, Oxford and London, 2002).

J. H. Newman, *On Consulting the Faithful in Matters of Doctrine* (Geoffrey Chapman, London, 1961 edn.).

David Newsome, *The Convert Cardinals* (John Murray, London, 1993).

Peter Nockles, *The Oxford Movement in Context* (Cambridge University Press, Cambridge and London, 1994).

Edward Norman, *The English Catholic Church in the Nineteenth Century* (Oxford University Press, Oxford and London, 1984).

J. S. Northcote, *Celebrated Sanctuaries of the Madonna* (Longman, London, 1868).

John O'Brien, T. J. Linane and F. A. Mecham (eds), *The Men of '38 and other pioneer priests* (Kilmore, Victoria, 1975).

Roderick O'Donnell, *The Pugins and the Catholic Midlands* (Gracewing, Herefordshire, 2002).

Frances O'Donoghue, *The Bishop of Botany Bay: the Life of John Bede Polding* (Angus and Robertson, London and Sydney, 1982).

Mary O'Driscoll OP, *Catherine of Siena* (Strasbourg, 1994).

K. O'Meara, *Thomas Grant* (W. H. Allen, London, 1874).

Robert O'Neill, *Cardinal Herbert Vaughan* (Burns Oates, London, 1995).

M. & B. Pawley, *Rome and Canterbury Through Four Centuries* (Mowbray, Oxford, 1975).

Margaret Pawley, *Faith and Family: the life and circle of Ambrose Phillips de Lisle* (Canterbury Press, Norwich, 1993).

John Pemble, *The Mediterranean Passion: Victorians and Edwardians in the South* (Clarendon Press, Oxford, 1987).

Nicholas Perry and Loreto Echeverria, *Under the Heel of Mary* (Routledge, London, 1988).

Henriette Peters, *Mary Ward: a World in Contemplation*, (Gracewing, Herefordshire, 1991) (trans. Helen

Butterworth, 1994).

E. S. Purcell, *Life and Letters of Ambrose Phillips de Lisle* (Macmillan, London, 1900).

Dermot Quinn, *Patronage and Piety: the Politics of English Roman Catholicism 1850–1900* (Stanford University Press, Stanford, California, 1993).

Oliver Rafferty, *The Church, the State and the Fenian Threat 1861–5* (Macmillan, London, 1999).

Mary Francis Roskell, *Memoirs of Francis Kerril Amherst* (Art and Book Club, London, nd.).

R. Rouse and S. C. Neill, *A History of the Ecumenical Movement 1517–1948* (SPCK, London, 1954).

R. J. Schiefen, *Nicholas Wiseman and the Transformation of English Catholicism* (Patmos Press, Shepherdown, 1984).

Victor Skipp, *The Making of Victorian Birmingham* (private publication, 1983).

K. D. M. Snell and P. S. Ell, *Rival Jerusalems: the Geography of Victorian Religion* (Cambridge University Press, Cambridge and London, 2000).

Alberic Stacpoole (ed.), *Mary's Place in Christian Dialogue* (St Pauls Publications, Slough, 1982).

Roger Swift and Sheridan Gilley, *The Irish in the Victorian City* (Croom Helm, London, 1985).

Mother Marie Therese, *Cornelia Connolly, a study in fidelity* (Burns Oates, London, 1963).

Wilfred Ward, *Life and Times of Cardinal Wiseman* 2 vols (Longman, London, 1897).

Nicholas Wiseman, *Recollections of the Last Four Popes and of Rome in their times* (Hurst and Blackett, London, 1858).

John Wolffe, *The Protestant Crusade in Great Britain 1829–60* (Oxford University Press, Oxford and London, 1991).

John Wolffe, *Religion in Victorian Britain* vol. V, *Culture and Empire* (Manchester University Press and Open University, 1997).

John Wolffe (ed.), *Borthwick Texts and Calendars No 25, Yorkshire Returns of the 1851 Religious Census*, vol. 1, *Introduction, City of York and East Riding* (University of York, York, 1998).

M. Woodward (ed.), *That Mysterious Man: essays on Augustine Baker* (Three Peaks Press, Abergavenny, 2001).

Periodicals

Australian Catholic History
Australasian Catholic Record
Clergy Review
Downside Review
History of Education
Historical Studies
Journal of the Australian Catholic History Society
Journal of Ecclesiastical History
Journal of Religious History
The Oscotian
Recusant History
Studies in Church History

Reference Works

Oxford Dictionary of National Biography (2004) online edition
Gillow: Joseph Gillow, *A Bibliographical Dictionary of English Catholics* (5 vols) (1885)
Catholic Directory
Catholic Record Society, Records Volumes 1904 to present
Historical Records of Australia, Series 2, vol. XVII
House of Commons Parliamentary Papers 1837–8 vol. 22
L&D: John Henry Newman, *The Letters and Diaries of John Henry Newman*, Edited at the Birmingham Oratory, 29 vols (1978ff)
Victoria County History, *A History of the County of Warwickshire*: vol. 7: *The City of Birmingham* (1964)

Theses

Champ thesis: Judith Champ, *Assimilation and Separation: the Catholic Revival in Birmingham 1650–1850*, Ph.D. University of Birmingham (1985).
Collins thesis: *Paul Collins, William Bernard Ullathorne and the Foundation of Australian Catholicism 1815–1840*, Ph.D. Australian National University (1989).

Harding thesis: J. A. Harding, *Dr William Clifford, Third Bishop of Clifton* (1857–1893) Ph.D., University of London (1991).
J. N. Moloney, *John Hubert Plunkett in New South Wales 1832–69* Ph.D. Australian National University (1971).

Websites

www.list.jaunay.com/ausnzpassengers
www.pitcairns.org (Norfolk Island)
http://setis.library.usyd.edu.au

Misellaneous

Typescript, J. H. Cullen, *The Catholic Story of Norfolk Island* (copy provided by Paul Collins).
English Benedictine Congregation History Symposium Papers.
Dominic Minskip, *A History of St Peter's Mission, Scarborough* (1783 to the present).
'Scarborough Records': notes and records compilied by Sydney Foord (unpublished 1970).

Index